Why Do You Need This New Edition?

Six good reasons why you should use this new edition of *Connections: A World History*

1. This edition is tied more closely than ever to the innovative website, MyHistoryLab, which helps students save time and improve their performance. MyHistoryLab icons appear in the textbook, highlighting important connections between the textbook and MyHistoryLab resources. At the end of each chapter, a *MyHistoryLab Connections* table provides a checklist of the most important *MyHistoryLab* resources—including specific documents, audio, video, maps, and images—related to the chapter, helping students integrate their study of the textbook and the website.

2. A new introductory section, "Making Sense of World History," provides a framework on how to use the book by explaining its organizational structure.

3. The treatment of gender and social-cultural history receives greater emphasis throughout the text.

4. The coverage of India, Persia, Byzantium, Africa, Latin America, and the post-World War II period has been enhanced.

5. Focus questions have been added to each document. These questions help identify important themes and issues raised within the documents and can also be used to facilitate classroom discussion.

6. Chapters have been updated and condensed, the overall narrative has been streamlined, and coverage has been strengthened by emphasizing key themes and important topics.

PEARSON

VOLUME 2: SINCE 1400

Second Edition

Connections
A World History

Edward H. Judge

Le Moyne College

John W. Langdon

Le Moyne College

PEARSON

Boston   Columbus   Indianapolis   New York   San Francisco   Upper Saddle River
Amsterdam   Cape Town   Dubai   London   Madrid   Milan   Munich   Paris   Montréal   Toronto
Delhi   Mexico City   São Paulo   Sydney   Hong Kong   Seoul   Singapore   Taipei   Tokyo

Editorial Director: Craig Campanella
Editor-in-Chief: Dickson Musslewhite
Executive Editor: Jeff Lasser
Editorial Assistant: Julia Feltus
Editorial Project Manager: Rob DeGeorge
**Senior Manufacturing and Operations Manager
  for Arts & Sciences:** Mary Fischer
Operations Specialist: Christina Amato
Director of Marketing: Brandy Dawson
Senior Marketing Manager: Maureen E. Prado Roberts
Marketing Assistant: Samantha Bennett
Senior Managing Editor: Ann Marie McCarthy

Senior Project Manager: Denise Forlow
Director of Media and Assessment: Brian Hyland
Media Project Manager: Tina Rudowski
Digital Media Editors: Andrea Messineo and Alison Lorber
Senior Art Director: Maria Lange
Cover Design: T-9 Design
AV Project Manager: Mirella Signoretto
Cartographer: Maps.com
**Full-Service Production, Interior Design, and
  Composition:** PreMediaGlobal
Printer/Binder: R.R. Donnelley/Willard
Cover Printer: Lehigh-Phoenix Color/Hagerstown

Cover images: Left, *Sequoyah and His Cherokee Alphabet*, Library of Congress; center, *Japanese View American Steamship in Harbor, 19th century*, Library of Congress; right, *The Chinese Empress Wu Zetian*, Photolibrary.

Credits and acknowledgments borrowed from other sources and reproduced, with permission, in this textbook appear on appropriate page within text and on page C-1.

Library of Congress Cataloging-in-Publication Data
Judge, Edward H.
    Connections : a world history / Edward H. Judge, John W. Langdon.—2nd ed.
        p. cm.
    Includes bibliographical references and index.
    ISBN 978-0-205-83550-8 (combined vol. : alk. paper)
    ISBN 978-0-205-83544-7 (volume 1 : alk. paper)
    ISBN 978-0-205-83545-4 (volume 2 : alk. paper)
 1. world history.   I. Langdon, John W.   II. Title.
    D21.J73 2012
    909—dc23

                                                    2011019803

10 9 8 7 6 5 4 3 2 1

Combined Volume:	Books a la carte Volume 1:
ISBN 10: 0-205-83550-3	ISBN 10: 0-205-09435-X
ISBN 13: 978-0-205-83550-8	ISBN 13: 978-0-205-09435-6
Examination Copy:	Volume 2:
ISBN 10: 0-205-09433-3	ISBN 10: 0-205-83545-7
ISBN 13: 978-0-205-09433-2	ISBN 13: 978-0-205-83545-4
Volume 1:	Books a la carte Volume 2:
ISBN 10: 0-205-83544-9	ISBN 10: 0-205-09437-6
ISBN 13: 978-0-205-83544-7	ISBN 13: 978-0-205-09437-0

PEARSON

Brief Contents

Contents

Making Sense of World History: An Introductory Overview for Students

ERA SIX Global Upheavals and Global Integration, 1900–Present

CHAPTER 31

The Great War and the Russian Revolutions, 1890–1918 **718**

Documents

Maps

Connecting with World History Students: Why We Wrote This Book

We are two professors who love teaching world history. For the past two decades, at our middle-sized college, we have team-taught a two-semester world history course that first-year students take to fulfill a college-wide requirement. Our students have very diverse backgrounds and interests. Most take world history only because it is required, and many find it very challenging. Helping them to understand it and infecting them with our enthusiasm for it are our main purposes and passions.

This is an exciting time to be teaching world history. In an age of growing global interconnectedness, an understanding of diverse world cultures and their histories has never been more essential. Indeed, it is increasingly apparent that students who lack this understanding will be poorly prepared to function in modern society or even to comprehend the daily news.

At the same time, the teaching of world history has never seemed more challenging. As the amount of material and its complexity increase, students can get bogged down in details and inundated with information, losing sight of the overall scope and significance of the human experience. Conveying world history to college students in a comprehensible and appealing way, without leaving them confused and overwhelmed, is one of the toughest challenges we face.

To help meet this challenge and better connect with our students, we have written a compact, affordable world history text that is tailored to meet their needs. In developing this text, we pursued several main goals:

First, because students often find it difficult to read and process lengthy, detailed chapters, we sought to write a text that is *concise and engaging*, with short, interesting chapters that focus on major trends and developments.

Second, since students often see history as a bewildering array of details, dates, and events, we chose a unifying theme—connections among world societies—and grouped our chapters to reflect the growth of such connections from regional to global.

Third, having seen many students struggle because they lack a good sense of geography, we included more than 200 maps—far more than most other texts—and provided a number of other features designed to help readers better understand and process the material.

A Concise and Readable Text

Since even the best text does little good if students do not read it, we endeavored above all to produce one that is concise and readable. We addressed ourselves to first-year college students, using a simple, straightforward narrative that tells the compelling story of the peoples and societies that preceded us and how they shaped the world. To avoid drowning our readers in a welter of details, we chose to take an introductory approach rather than an encyclopedic one. With this text, students will become familiar with the most important trends, developments, and issues in world history, and they will gain an appreciation for the vast diversity of human societies and endeavors.

To make our book less overwhelming and more accessible to students, we have limited most chapters to about 10,000 words and divided each chapter into short topical subsections. By writing concise chapters, we have enabled average students to read them in an hour or so. By keeping subsections short, we have partitioned the text into manageable segments, so that readers can process material before they move on. By furnishing focus questions at the start of each chapter, marginal notes that highlight our main theme, and a perspective section at the end, we have kept in sight the overall trends and developments, without interrupting the narrative's basic flow.

Connections in World History

In our teaching we have found that many students find world history confusing and overwhelming, in part because they have no overall framework for understanding it. To help them sort things out, we have focused our text on a central theme of connections among world societies. By stressing this theme, we have sought to maintain a sense of coherence and purpose, and to give our readers a framework that will help them to make sense of history.

Rather than divide our text into ancient, medieval, and modern eras, an arrangement that works for Europe but has limited value elsewhere, we have instead grouped our chapters into two overlapping ages: an Age of Regional Connections, lasting until about 1650 C.E., and an Age of Global Connections, dating from roughly 1500 to the present. Each age is then subdivided into three eras, reflecting the expansion of connections from regional to global levels. This framework, summarized in our Introductory Overview ("Making Sense of World History") and in our table of contents, is designed to give students the "big picture" of world history that they often lack.

Within each era are chapters that provide both regional and global perspectives, stressing not only each culture's distinct features but also its connections with other regions and cultures. Readers thus can readily appreciate both the diversity and the interconnectedness of human societies.

Within each chapter, on almost every page, are **marginal notations** that summarize material and highlight our connections theme. Readers thus can easily keep sight of the overall context.

An Extensive and Consistent Map Program

Many students approach world history with only a rudimentary understanding of world geography, and maps are a crucial tool in understanding world history. Our text contains an abundance of carefully crafted maps, designed within each chapter to build one upon another. With more than 200 maps throughout the book, *Connections* offers one of the most extensive map programs of any world history survey textbook.

Most chapters begin with a **foundation map**, positioning chapter events in a global context or highlighting a key part of the world under discussion.

We have worked very hard to make the maps clear and to place them where readers can refer to them without turning pages. As much as possible, the maps use colors, fonts, labels, and other markers consistently, so that students will find these features familiar from one map to the next.

Finally, the map captions were carefully written to clarify the maps, to connect them with surrounding text, and to guide the students' attention to the most important elements in that map. Each map caption includes a question to help students consider critical issues.

Features

We have incorporated in our text a carefully selected set of features, each chosen with this basic guideline in mind: Will it help students to better envision, understand, and process the material they are reading?

VISUALS   We provide an ample array of photos and other visuals, selected to illustrate developments explicitly discussed in the text. To ensure that students will connect the text with the images, we have placed them in the margins near the passages that they illustrate.

PRONUNCIATION GUIDES   Since students often struggle to pronounce unfamiliar names and places, we have placed parenthetical pronunciation guides immediately following first use of such names and places in the text.

CHAPTER-OPENING VIGNETTES   Each chapter opens with a vignette designed to capture the reader's interest and introduce the chapter's main themes.

PRIMARY SOURCE DOCUMENT EXCERPTS   To acquaint students with primary sources and illuminate materials covered in our text, we have provided concise excerpts from selected historical sources, in feature boxes placed where the document is discussed in the text, and marginal links to numerous additional documents online at MyHistoryLab.

CHAPTER REVIEW SECTIONS   Each chapter has a comprehensive end-of-chapter review section that incorporates the following features:

- **Putting It in Perspective.** This feature provides a concise overview of the chapter's main themes, highlights key connections, and puts them in historical perspective.
- **Key Concepts.** Key concepts are highlighted in boldface in the text, defined in the text when first discussed and also in an alphabetic glossary, and listed at the end of each chapter with page references to facilitate review.
- **Key People.** Important individuals mentioned in the text are also listed at the end of each chapter, followed by page references to facilitate review.
- **Ask Yourself.** A set of questions at the end of every chapter encourages further reflection and analysis of topics, issues, and connections considered in the chapter.
- **Going Further.** A list of books at the end of each chapter provides resources for teachers and students interested in delving more deeply into topics covered.
- **Key Dates and Developments.** Each chapter contains a comprehensive chronology that lists the key dates and developments, helping students to see at a glance the sequence of important events.

A Student-Centered Textbook

For several years, we and our colleagues have used our text, with highly encouraging results. Since the book is affordable and portable, we find that most students buy it and bring it to class. Since chapters are concise and engaging, we find that students actually read them before coming to class and thus are better prepared to understand and discuss key issues. Students who completed questionnaires or wrote reviews of our chapters said they found them clear and compelling. By pointing out passages they found dry or confusing, these students also helped make the book more readable. We went to great lengths to create a text that is useful, accessible, and attractive to our students. For they, after all, are the reasons we wrote this book.

Ed Judge
judge@lemoyne.edu
John Langdon
langdon@lemoyne.ed

New to This Edition

- A new introductory section, "Making Sense of World History," provides students with a framework on how to use the book by explaining its organizational structure.
- The emphasis on the *connections* theme has been strengthened throughout the text.
- The treatment of gender and social-cultural history receives greater emphasis throughout the text.
- Many photos and illustrations have been enlarged, making them more useful as historical documents.
- The coverage of India, Persia, Byzantium, Africa, Latin America, and the post-World War II period has been enhanced.
- Focus questions have been added to each document. These questions will help students identify important themes and issues raised within the documents and can also be used to facilitate classroom discussion.
- Chapters have been updated and condensed, with main themes highlighted even more effectively than in the first edition.
- Numerous maps have been revised to make them easier for students to read.
- The end-of-chapter review material has been revised to emphasize key topics and themes.
- The overall narrative has been streamlined, while coverage has been strengthened by emphasizing key themes and important topics.

About the Authors
Edward H. Judge
John W. Langdon

Edward H. Judge and John W. Langdon are professors of history at Le Moyne College, where they team-teach a two-semester world history course for first-year students and courses on modern global history for upper-level students. Ed earned his doctorate at the University of Michigan and spent a year in the USSR as an IREX scholar. John earned his doctorate at Syracuse University's Maxwell School of Public Affairs, where he was a National Defense Fellow. Ed has taught at Le Moyne since 1978, was the College's Scholar of the Year in 1994, and was awarded the J. C. Georg Endowed Professorship in 1997. John has taught at Le Moyne since 1971, directed its Honors Program, and was awarded the O'Connell Distinguished Teaching Professorship in 1996. Each has been named the College's Teacher of the Year and has chaired its Department of History. They have written or edited eight books: three in collaboration with each other, three as individuals, and two in collaboration with other scholars. They love teaching world history, especially to students of diverse backgrounds and interests, and they derive great joy from infecting their students with a passion and enthusiasm for the study of the human past.

Supplements for Qualified College Adopters	Supplements for Students
MyHistoryLab	**My**HistoryLab
MyHistoryLab (www.myhistorylab.com) *Save Time. Improve Results.* MyHistoryLab is a dynamic website that provides a wealth of resources geared to meet the diverse teaching and learning needs of today's instructors and students. (See page xxxvii for a description of the MyHistoryLab features.)	**MyHistoryLab (www.myhistorylab.com)** *Save Time. Improve Results.* MyHistoryLab's many accessible tools will encourage you to read your text and help you improve your grade in your course. (See page xxxvii for a description of the MyHistoryLab features.)
The Instructor's Resource Manual Available at the Instructor's Resource Center, at www. pearsonhighered.com/irc, the Instructor's Resource Manual provides lecture outlines, chapter summaries, learning objectives, discussion questions, Connection Questions, and suggestions for audiovisual materials for each chapter in this book.	**CourseSmart (www.coursesmart.com)** CourseSmart is an exciting new choice for students looking to save money. As an alternative to purchasing the printed textbook, students can purchase an electronic version of the same content. With a CourseSmart eTextbook, students can search the text, make notes online, print out reading assignments that incorporate lecture notes, and bookmark important passages for later review. For more information, or to purchase access to the CourseSmart eTextbook, visit www.coursesmart.com
The Test Item File The Test-Item File includes over 3,000 questions (multiple choice, essay, short answer, true/false, and map questions). The Test Item File is available at the Instructor's Resource Center, at www. pearsonhighered.com/irc.	***Books à la Carte*** Books à la Carte editions feature the exact same content as the traditional printed text in a convenient, three-hole-punched, loose-leaf version at a discounted price—allowing you to take only what you need to class. You'll **save 35% over the net price** of the traditional book.
The Instructor's Resource Center (www.pearsonhighered.com/irc) Text-specific materials, such as the Instructor's Resource Manual, Test Item File, map files, and PowerPoint™ presentations, are available for downloading by adopters.	***Primary Source: Documents in Global History DVD, 2/e,*** is an immense collection of textual and visual documents in world history and an indispensable tool for working with sources. Extensively developed with the guidance of historians and teachers, the DVD includes over 800 sources in world history—from cave art to satellite images of the earth from space. More sources from Africa, Latin America, and Southeast Asia have been added to the latest version of the DVD. All sources are accompanied by head notes and focus questions and are searchable by topic, region, or time period. The DVD can be bundled with *Connections: A World History*, Second Edition, at no charge. Please contact your Pearson representative for ordering information. (ISBN 0-13-178938-4)
MyTest Available at www.pearsonmytest.com, MyTest is a powerful assessment generation program that helps instructors easily create and print quizzes and exams. Questions and tests can be authored online, allowing instructors ultimate flexibility and the ability to efficiently manage assessment anytime, anywhere! Instructors can easily access existing questions and edit, create, and store using simple drag-and-drop and Word-like controls.	Titles from the renowned **Penguin Classics** series can be bundled with *Connections: A World History*, Second Edition, for a nominal charge. Please contact your Pearson sales representative for details.

Supplements for Qualified College Adopters	Supplements for Students
PowerPoint Presentations Available at the Instructor's Resource Center, at www.pearsonhighered.com/irc. All maps in the book are included in the PowerPoints, along with many photos from the text and lecture outlines.	*Library of World Biography Series* www.pearsonhighered.com/educator/series/Library-of-World-Biography/10492.page Each interpretive biography in the Library of World Biography Series focuses on a person whose actions and ideas either significantly influenced world events or whose life reflects important themes and developments in global history. Titles from the series can be bundled with *Connections: A World History*, Second Edition, for a nominal charge. Please contact your Pearson sales representative for details.
	The Prentice Hall Atlas of World History, **Second Edition** Produced in collaboration with Dorling Kindersley, the leader in cartographic publishing, the updated second edition of *The Prentice Hall Atlas of World History* applies the most innovative cartographic techniques to present world history in all of its complexity and diversity. Copies of the atlas can be bundled with *Connections: A World History*, Second Edition, for a nominal charge. Contact your Pearson sales representative for details. (ISBN 0-13-604247-3)
	Longman Atlas of World History This atlas features carefully selected historical maps that provide comprehensive coverage of the major historical periods. Contact your Pearson sales representative for details. (ISBN 0-321-20998-2)
	A Guide to Your History Course: What Every Student Needs to Know Written by Vincent A. Clark, this concise, spiral-bound guidebook orients students to the issues and problems they will face in the history classroom. Available at a discount when bundled with *Connections: A World History*, Second Edition. (ISBN 0-13-185087-3)
	A Short Guide to Writing about History, **Seventh Edition** Written by Richard Marius, late of Harvard University, and Melvin E. Page, Eastern Tennessee State University, this engaging and practical text helps students get beyond merely compiling dates and facts. Covering both brief essays and the documented resource paper, the text explores the writing and researching processes, identifies different modes of historical writing, including argument, and concludes with guidelines for improving style. (ISBN 0-205-67370-8)

MyHistoryLab (www.myhistorylab.com)

For Instructors and Students

Save TIME. Improve Results.

MyHistoryLab is a dynamic website that provides a wealth of resources geared to meet the diverse teaching and learning needs of today's instructors and students. MyHistoryLab's many accessible tools will encourage students to read their text and help them improve their grade in their course.

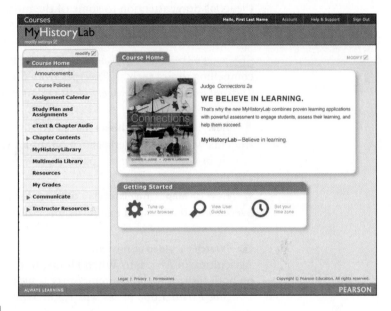

Features of MyHistoryLab

- **Pearson eText**—An e-book version of *Connections: A World History* is included in MyHistoryLab. As with the printed text, students can highlight and add their own notes as they read the book online.
- **Audio Files**—Full audio of the entire text is included to suit the varied learning styles of today's students. In addition there are audio clips of speeches, readings, and music that provide another engaging way to experience history.
- **Pre-tests, Post-tests, and Chapter Reviews**—Students can take quizzes to test their knowledge of chapter content and to review for exams.
- **Text and Visual Documents**—A wealth of primary source documents, images, and maps are available, organized by chapter in the text. Primary source documents are also available in the MyHistoryLibrary and can be searched by author, title, theme, and topic. Many of these documents include critical thinking questions.
- **History Bookshelf**—Students may read, download, or print 100 of the most commonly assigned history works, such as Homer's *Iliad* or Machiavelli's *The Prince*.
- **Lecture and Archival Videos**—Lectures by leading scholars on provocative topics give students a critical look at key points in history. Videos of speeches, news footage, key historical events, and other archival videos take students back to the moment in history.
- **MySearchLab**—This website provides students access to a number of reliable sources for online research, as well as clear guidance on the research and writing process.
- **Gradebook**—Students can follow their own progress, and instructors can monitor the work of the entire class. Automated grading of quizzes and assignments helps both instructors and students save time and monitor their results throughout the course.

NEW In-text References to MyHistoryLab Resources

Read, View, Watch, Listen, and **Study and Review Icons** integrated in the text connect resources on MyHistoryLab to specific topics within the chapters. The icons are not exhaustive; many more resources are available than those highlighted in the book, but the icons draw attention to some of the most useful resources available on MyHistoryLab.

▐●▌Read the **Document** on **myhistorylab.com** Primary and secondary source documents on compelling topics such as *Excerpts from Sundiata: An Epic of Old Mali, 1235* and *Tang Taizong on the Art of Government* enhance topics discussed in each chapter.

⦿▐View the **Image** on **myhistorylab.com** Photographs, fine art, and artifacts provide students with a visual perspective on topics within the chapters, underscoring the role of visuals in understanding the past.

⦿▐View the **Map** on **myhistorylab.com** Atlas and interactive maps present both a broad overview and a detailed examination of historical developments.

👁▐Watch the **Video** on **myhistorylab.com** Video lectures highlight topics ranging from Agriculture in Africa, to Witch Hunts, to the Columbian Exchange, engaging students on both historical and contemporary topics. Also included are archival videos, such as *The Silk Road: 5,000 Miles and 1,500 Years of Cultural Interchange* and *Teotihuacán Ruins in Mexico.*

((•▐Listen to the **Audio** on **myhistorylab.com** For each chapter there are audio files of the text, speeches, readings, and other audio material that will enrich students' experience of social and cultural history.

✓●▐Study and **Review** on **myhistorylab.com** MyHistoryLab provides a wealth of practice quizzes, tests, flashcards, and other study resources available to students online.

NEW MyHistoryLab Connections

At the end of each chapter, a new section, MyHistoryLab Connections, provides a list of the references within the chapter and additional documents, maps, videos, or additional resources that relate to the content of the chapter.

Acknowledgments

In conceiving, composing, and bringing out this book, we are deeply grateful to the many people who helped us along the way. Our senior colleagues Bill Telesca and Fr. Bill Bosch, with whom we first taught world history, shared with us their many decades of experience as teachers and scholars. Our current colleagues, Doug Egerton, Bruce Erickson, Godriver Odhiambo, Holly Rine, Yamin Xu, and Bob Zens have class-tested our book and provided us with feedback from their students and insights from their expertise in Atlantic World, Latin American, African, Amerind, East Asian, and Islamic history. Yamin Xu has also been particularly helpful with the spelling and pronunciation of East Asian names. Connie Brand and her colleagues at Meridian Community College have likewise class-tested our book with their students.

We also thank the many scholars and teachers whose thoughtful and often detailed comments helped improve our book. Whatever errors remain are, of course, our own.

Reviewers of the First Edition

Sanjam Ahluwalia, Northern Arizona University
Patricia Ali, Morris College
Stanley Arnold, Northern Illinois University
Robert Becker, Gainesville State College
Brett Berliner, Morgan State University
Rebecca Berry, Wake Technical Community College
David Blaylock, Eastern Kentucky University
Connie Brand, Meridian Community College
Beau Browers, Central Piedmont Community College
Ras Michael Brown, Southern Illinois University
Robert W. Brown, University of North Carolina, Pembroke
Brian Bunk, University of Massachusetts—Amherst
Fred Burkhard, University of Maryland, University College
Robert J. Caputi, Erie Community College
Harry E. Carpenter III, Western Piedmont Community College
Abdin Chande, Adelphi University
Nupur Chandhuri, Texas Southern University
Ken Chauvin, Appalachian State University
Yinghong Cheng, Delaware State University
David Christian, San Diego State University
Charles Crouch, Georgia Southern University
Lisa M. Edwards, University of Massachusetts—Lowell
Charles H. Ford, Norfolk State University
John H. Frederick, South Louisiana Community College
Patricia A. Gajda, The University of Texas at Tyler
Karl Galinsky, University of Texas
Leonard Gordon, Columbia University
Megan Greene, The University of Kansas
Donald A. Grinde, Jr., SUNY, Buffalo
Mary Gross, Marian College of Fond du Lac
Anthony Gulig, University of Washington, Whitewater

Mark Gunn, Meridian Community College
Brian Gurian, Harrisburg Area Community College
Edward M. Hanlon, John Jay College
Anne Hardgrove, University of Texas at San Antonio
Donald J. Harreld, Brigham Young University
Paul Hatley, Rogers State University
Randolph Head, University of California, Riverside
Padhraig Higgins, Mercer County Community College
Marie Hooper, Oklahoma City University
Michael Houf, Texas A&M University—Kingsville
Clark Hultquist, University of Montevallo
Michael Jacobs, University of Wisconsin—Baraboo
Ellen J. Jenkins, Arkansas Tech University
Timothy Jenks, East Carolina University
Rhea S. Klenovich, Lakeland College
Robert Kunath, Illinois College
Joseph Tse-Hei Lee, Pace University
Lester Lee, Salem State College
Yi Li, Tacoma Community College
Benjamin Lieberman, Fitchburg State College
Valdis Lumans, University of South Carolina, Aiken
Farid Mahdavi, San Diego State University
Susan Maneck, Jackson State University
Cathlyn Mariscotti, Holy Family University
David John Marley, Vanguard University
Joel McMahon, Georgia Perimeter College
David K. McQuilkin, Bridgewater College
Cristina Mehrtens, University of Massachusetts—Dartmouth
David Meier, Dickinson State University
Greg Miller, Hillsborough Community College
Laura Mitchell, University of California, Irvine
Robert Scott Moore, Indiana University of Pennsylvania
Luke A. Nichter, Bowling Green State University

William Ochsenwalk, Virginia Polytechnic Institute and State University
Chris Padgett, American River College
Robert Parkinson, Shepherd University
Jeffrey Pilcher, University of Minnesota
Van Plexico, Georgia Perimeter College
Tracie Provost, Middle Georgia College
David Rayson, Normandale Community College
Sean Redding, Amherst College
Scott S. Reese, Northern Arizona University
Maria Theresa Romero, Saddleback College
Steven J. Salm, Xavier University of Louisiana
Pamela Sayre, Henry Ford Community College
Linda Scherr, Mercer County Community College
David Simonelli, Youngstown State University
Govind P. Sreenivasan, Brandeis University

Anthony J. Steinhoff, University of Tennessee, Chattanooga
Elizabeth Stice, University of Hawaii, Hilo
Rachel Stocking, Southern Illinois University, Carbondale
Michael Swope, Schoolcraft College
Gordon Thomasson, Broome Community College (SUNY)
William Van Norman, James Madison University
John Van Sant, University of Alabama, Birmingham
Charles Weber, Wheaton College
Theodore Yoo, University of Hawaii at Manoa
Khodr Zaarour, Shaw University
Qiang Zhai, Auburn University
Alex Zukas, National University

Reviewers of the Second Edition

Robert Bond, San Diego Mesa College
Gregory S. Crider, Winthrop University
Peter Dykema, Arkansas Tech University
Kirk W. Larsen, Brigham Young University
David Longfellow, Baylor University
Mary Lyons-Barrett, University of Nebraska at Omaha/Metro Community College

Robert A. Saunders, Farmingdale State College
John R. Stanley, Kutztown University
Robin Underhill, University of Delaware
Karl E. Westhauser, Alabama State University
William Zogby, Mohawk Valley Community College

Numerous others have contributed immensely to this work. Kathryn Buturla, Greg Croft, Gwen Morgan, Dan Nieciecki, Adam Zaremba, and the late Marc Ball assisted us with various aspects of our research and writing. Jaime Wadowiec, Vicky Green, and Jenna Finne each read our work at various stages and supplied us with a student's perspective on its clarity, structure, coherence, and appeal to readers. James Kellaher helped us with our maps. Erika Gutierrez, Lisa Pinto, and Janet Lanphier challenged us, believed in us, supported us, and pushed us to expand our vision and our goals. Our various editors and collaborators, including Phil Herbst, David Kear, Charles Cavaliere and Rob DeGeorge, poured their hearts into editing our work, correcting our mistakes, improving our style, sharpening our insights, enlivening our narrative, clarifying our explanations, enhancing our maps and images, and pressing us to excel.

Our biggest debt of gratitude is the one that we owe to our wives. Sue Judge and Jan Langdon sustained, encouraged, and supported us, especially when the going got tough, enduring numerous sacrifices as they shared both our burdens and our joys. We owe them far more than words can express or than we can ever repay. This book is rightfully theirs as much as it is ours.

A Note on Dates and Spellings

In labeling dates, like many other world history teachers, we use the initials B.C.E. (Before the Common Era) and C.E. (Common Era), which correspond respectively to the labels B.C. (Before Christ) and A.D. (*Anno Domini*, "The Year of the Lord"), long used in Western societies. In spelling Chinese names, we use the Pinyin system, internationally adopted in 1979, but we sometimes also give other spellings that were widely used before then. (In Chapters 32 and 35, for example, Chinese Nationalist leader Jiang Jieshi is also identified as Chiang Kaishek.) Our spelling of names and terms from other languages follows standard usage, with alternative versions given where appropriate. (Chapter 17, for example, notes that Central Asian warrior Timur Lenk was also called Tamerlane in Europe.)

Making Sense of World History: An Introductory Overview for Students

The study of world history is exciting, filled with fascinating insights, exploits, ventures, tragedies, and triumphs. But it can also be daunting. Faced with countless details, dates, and events, how can we possibly make sense of it all?

One way is to organize the past around a theme that applies the world over. Our central theme in this book is *connections*: the ways that people and societies interact with each other over time. We focus not only on actions and achievements of people in diverse societies, but also on how they learned from, traded with, and conflicted with each other.

To put these connections in global context and illustrate the "big picture," we divide the past into two main *ages* and six overlapping *eras*, reflecting the expansion of connections from regional to global levels, with the six main parts in our table of contents each covering an era. This structure is artificial, imposed by us on the past, but it furnishes a useful framework for making sense of world history.

I. An Age of Regional Connections, to 1650 C.E. (Chapters 1–20)

In our first age, connections were regional, and people survived mainly by finding or raising food. After foraging for food in small nomadic bands for tens of thousands of years, people increasingly took up farming and lived in more permanent settlements, typically villages surrounded by fields on which they grew crops or grazed animals. In regions unsuited for farming, people hunted and/or herded animals, moving periodically to find fresh grazing grounds. In regions where farming supplied surplus food, some people came to live in towns and cities, specializing in such pursuits as governance, warfare, religion, crafting goods, and trading with other regions. As populations grew, some societies formed states, territories run by a central government, often headed by a powerful ruler. Eventually some states conquered others to create large empires, expanding regional and transregional connections.

ERA ONE. EMERGENCE AND EXPANSION OF REGIONAL SOCIETIES, TO 300 C.E. (CHAPTERS 1–8)
During this lengthy era, as foraging gave way to farming in some regions, food production and population increased. People formed regional states—groups of villages, towns, and cities ruled by a single government—first in northeastern Africa and West Asia, and later in India, China, the Americas, and elsewhere. States connected and conflicted with each other, eventually creating transregional empires—large expanses with various lands and cultures under a single government—such as those established by Persians, Macedonians and Greeks, Indians, Chinese, and Romans. By the era's end, many regions were also connected by land and sea trade routes and by belief systems such as Buddhism, Hinduism, Zoroastrianism, Confucianism, Daoism, Judaism, and Christianity.

Meeting of Cambyses, King of Persia (r. 530–521 B.C.E.) and Psammetichus III (Late Period Egyptian pharaoh, r. 526–525 B.C.E.), along with their attendants. This encounter took place in Egypt after it fell to Cambyses and his forces in 525 B.C.E.

ERA TWO. TRANSREGIONAL CONFLICTS AND RELIGIOUS CONNECTIONS, 200–1200 C.E. (CHAPTERS 9–14)   During this thousand-year era, connections among diverse regions were often created by expansive religions offering hope of salvation, and by states that espoused and spread these religions. Christianity, originating in Palestine in the first century C.E., spread across West Asia, Europe, and North Africa, until challenged by Islam, a new faith that soon linked much of Africa and Eurasia religiously, culturally, and commercially. Buddhism, after taking hold in India by the first century C.E., divided into branches and spread through much of Asia, until challenged by resurgent Hinduism and Confucianism.

ERA THREE. CROSS-CULTURAL CONFLICTS AND COMMERCIAL CONNECTIONS, 1000–1650 (CHAPTERS 15–20)   Our third era was marked by the formation of vast new political and commercial empires. Some were land based, created by Central Eurasian Turks and Mongols and by Aztecs and Inca in the Americas. Others were sea based, forged by Portuguese and Spanish sailors and soldiers. Their conquests brought mass devastation but also fostered new connections among distant and diverse cultures, laying foundations for the emergence of a global economy.

II. An Age of Global Connections, 1500–Present (Chapters 21–37)

Our second age has been marked by the growth of global connections and commerce. Instead of raising their own food, people increasingly worked in commercial pursuits, selling goods and services for money to buy food and goods. More and more people came to live in urban areas, engaged in enterprises using technologies to provide goods and services, and connected by global networks supplying resources, products, fuels, and information. Conflicts, too, became global, as nations vied for resources and markets as well as for lands and beliefs, and revolutionary ideals fueled upheavals the world over.

ERA FOUR. THE SHIFT FROM REGIONAL TO GLOBAL CONNECTIONS, 1500–1800 (CHAPTERS 21–25) In this era, wealth and power shifted from East to West. Seeking direct commercial access to India, China, and Indonesia, Europeans wrested Indian Ocean trade from the Muslims (who connected much of Eurasia and Africa) and also developed American colonies sustained by an Atlantic slave trade. As global commerce expanded, Western nations such as Spain, France, and Britain grew to rival in power and wealth the Chinese and Islamic empires. Russia, too, became a world power, expanding to the east, west, and south to create a Eurasian empire.

ERA FIVE. REVOLUTION, INDUSTRY, IDEOLOGY, AND EMPIRE, 1750–1914 (CHAPTERS 26–30) During our fifth era, revolutionary forces reshaped the West and eventually much of the world. Political revolutions in North America, Europe, and Latin America spread ideas of liberty and equality. An industrial revolution, beginning in Britain, spread across Europe and North America, radically altering societies. These upheavals bred new ideologies, including liberalism, socialism, and nationalism, fueling new revolts. As

This busy street in Hong Kong contains a dizzying array of advertising that illustrates the extent to which a global culture has taken hold in the early 21st century.

European nations industrialized, they forged new connections through imperialism, using new weapons and technologies to dominate Africa and Asia. Africans and Asians, their cultures threatened by Western domination, began adapting the new ideas and technologies to fit their own cultures and needs.

ERA SIX. GLOBAL UPHEAVALS AND GLOBAL INTEGRATION, 1900–PRESENT (CHAPTERS 31–37) By the 20th century, Western nations had connected much of the world under their economic and political sway, while competing among themselves for resources and power. Their competition spawned two world wars, destroying much of Europe and millions of people, followed by a long cold war, dividing Europe and encompassing the globe. Africans and Asians, capitalizing on these conflicts while selectively adapting Western ways, freed themselves from Western domination and sought to modernize their economies. By the 21st century, the world was divided politically into numerous nations, but connected commercially by an increasingly integrated global economy.

Ask Yourself

1. Why and how did humans transition from foraging to farming and organize themselves into settlements and states?
2. What roles did empires, religions, commerce, and technologies play in expanding connections among cultures?
3. What were the advantages and disadvantages of increased connections among cultures? Why and how were such connections often accompanied by conflict, exploitation, and suffering?
4. Why and how did societies transition from economies based on subsistence farming to economies based on commerce and technology? What impacts did these transitions have on the lives of ordinary people?
5. Why is it important for modern people to learn and understand world history?

Global Exploration and Global Empires, 1400–1700

((•—Listen to the **Chapter Audio** for Chapter 19 on **myhistorylab.com**

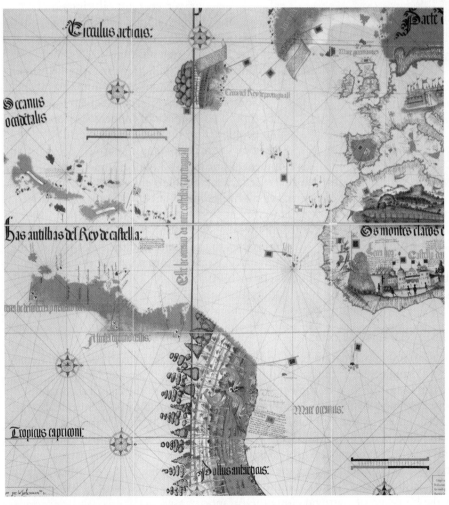

Portuguese Claims in Africa and Brazil

A 16th-century map shows Portuguese claims in Africa and Brazil. Few would have predicted that tiny Portugal would lead the way in European exploration of the globe (see page 418).

- Why were the Iberians the first Europeans to carry out overseas exploration?

- What were the main features and impacts of the Portuguese seaborne empire?

- What similarities and differences existed between the empires in the Western Hemisphere?

- How did the European settlements in North America affect Amerind peoples?

- What were the advantages and disadvantages of the Columbian Exchange?

Morning dawned foggy and damp, but by 8 AM the Portuguese sun was burning off the mist. Already merchants, artisans, vendors, and shoppers were moving toward the docks in Lisbon. It was a typical day in early September 1600, and a fleet had arrived the previous evening from the Indian Ocean. Now its ships were being unloaded and the docks stacked with exotic plants, animals, minerals, and manufactures. Those who arrived early would have first pick from the cargoes.

The
Portuguese
Empire

The Spanish
Empire

Cramming the docks of Lisbon was a staggering variety of commodities from four continents. From Europe itself came wheat, wool, brassware, glass, weapons, tapestries, and clocks. North Africa provided dates, honey, barley, and indigo, as well as ornate metalwork. West Africa contributed gold, ivory, musk, parrots, and slaves. East Africa sent ebony, coral, salt, and hemp. Arriving from India were calico, pepper, ginger, coconut oil, cinnamon, cloves, and nutmeg. Southeast Asia furnished sandalwood, resins, camphor, and saffron. From Macao came porcelains, silks, and medicinal herbs. Finally, Brazil supplied sugar, brazilwood, and monkeys from the Amazon. Lisbon in 1600 was the commercial focus of Europe, a cosmopolitan connector of products and peoples from throughout the world.

Lisbon's prosperity was a relatively recent development. Prior to 1453, world trade focused on the Mediterranean, where Italian city-states like Venice and Genoa competed with Muslim merchants for cargoes and profits. But Mehmed the Conqueror's dramatic victory at Constantinople, which at first appeared to expand Islamic power, actually weakened existing Muslim trade networks. By stimulating Europeans to seek overseas routes to the Indies and the Spice Islands, the fall of Constantinople reoriented European trade, to the eventual benefit of the eager buyers who swarmed over the Lisbon docks in 1600.

The Iberian Impulse

Portugal was an unlikely location for a commercial nexus. The Iberian Peninsula, home to Spain and Portugal, sits at the far southwestern edge of the Eurasian landmass, separated from the rest of Europe by the Pyrenees mountains. From the eighth through twelfth centuries, most of Iberia was linked to the Islamic world by Muslim rule. By the mid-1200s, however, fired by the *Reconquista* (Chapter 16), the Christian kingdoms of the North had retaken most of the region. In 1479 the two main Spanish kingdoms, Aragon and Castile, were linked by the marriage and joint rule of their respective monarchs, Ferdinand and Isabella, laying the base for a united Spain. By 1492, when they expelled the Muslims from Granada in the South, this couple ruled most of Iberia—except for the kingdom of Portugal along the Atlantic coast.

The Iberian interest in
sea voyages is largely
anti-Muslim

By this time Spain and Portugal, far from Europe's centers of commerce and wealth, were embarking on great sea voyages that would soon enlarge European ideas about the geography of the globe. Determined to bypass the Muslims, who controlled the land links and profitable trade with East Asia, both Iberians and Italian city-states searched for an all-water route to India, the Spice Islands, and China, regions that Europeans called collectively the East Indies. The Portuguese, who had been exploring southward along the Atlantic coast of Africa since the early 1400s, finally found a sea route in

1498, arriving in India by way of the Indian Ocean after sailing around Africa. Six years earlier the Spanish had funded an ill-conceived effort to reach East Asia by sailing west across the Atlantic. In the process, and by accident, they discovered what seemed to them a "New World," and they went on to create a western hemispheric empire that rivaled even that of the Mongols in size and significance.

Like Mongols, Iberians had a warrior culture, bred by centuries of *Reconquista*. Like Mongols, they used technologies adopted from other civilizations, such as gunpowder weapons and navigational tools from Asia. Like Mongols, they killed untold thousands through combat, slaughter, and the spread of infectious diseases, gaining wealth and power by exploiting and enslaving millions. And like Mongols, they connected cultures.

Unlike Mongols, however, Iberians zealously imposed their faith on the people they ruled. And unlike Mongols they created new societies that would endure even after their empires were gone.

Portuguese Overseas Exploration

Given the small size and relative poverty of Portugal, it is surprising that this kingdom started the European drive for overseas exploration. But the forces it set in motion had an immense impact.

Like other European nations, Portugal suffered a drastic 14th-century population decline from the Black Death and the famines and epidemics associated with it. Depopulation of villages and poorly producing farmland left much of the landed nobility impoverished. Some tried to compensate for their losses by turning to plunder. In 1415 Portuguese raiders captured the Moroccan seaport of Ceuta (*THĀ-oo-tah*), but Portugal's small population and limited resources prevented it from conquering all Morocco in a land war.

The sea offered an alternative route to plunder. Portugal was a nation of farmers and fishermen with a lengthy Atlantic seacoast. Following the conquest of Ceuta, Prince Enrique (*awn-RĒ-kā*), the third son of the king of Portugal and therefore unlikely to inherit the throne, decided to pursue his own interests by organizing maritime expeditions to chart the western coast of Africa. Starting in 1418, these expeditions sought to determine how far south Muslim rule prevailed in Africa and where the Christian faith could be advanced at the expense of Islam (Map 19.1).

The Portuguese also wanted to develop trade relations with African Christians, including the mythical Christian kingdom of Prester John, sought by Europeans since the Crusades. Slowly, Portuguese explorers and traders moved south along Africa's west coast. They covered fifteen hundred miles, reaching as far as present-day Sierra Leone by the time Enrique died in 1460. Later generations called him Prince Henry the Navigator.

The Ottoman seizure of Constantinople had stunned Christian Europe and disrupted its merchants. Muslims were now in control of the eastern Mediterranean, the meeting point of three continents and the focus of world trade for centuries. They took over the traditional land–sea trade routes and raised the fees for safe passage to levels that enriched the Ottoman Sultan and cut deeply into European profits. Their middlemen squeezed European merchants even more by marking up the prices of spices and luxury items as much as 1,000 percent. These burdens were enough to convince several Western nations to search for alternative routes to the East Indies.

Henry's expeditions gave Portugal a sizable lead in this search. Its ships reached the equator in 1471 and discovered that, contrary to legend, the ocean there did not boil. They also found that the heat decreased as they sailed farther south. In 1487, Portugal's King João (*ZHWOW*) II dispatched a land expedition across Africa to search for Prester

View the **Map**

Spanish and Portuguese Exploration, 1400–1600, on **myhistorylab.com**

Iberians and Mongols share more similarities than differences

Henry the Navigator initiates Portuguese expansion

Constantinople's fall intensifies Portugal's maritime quest

Note the principal voyages of European exploration, all undertaken for differing reasons. Vasco da Gama's journey to India built on several decades of Portuguese exploration of the western coast of Africa. Columbus's westward expedition was designed to reach first Japan and then the Spice Islands by a route that Columbus believed to be shorter than sailing around Africa. Magellan's circumnavigation of the globe was intended to demonstrate that Columbus could have established a commercially viable connection to Asia had America not been in his way. Why did that conclusion prove incorrect?

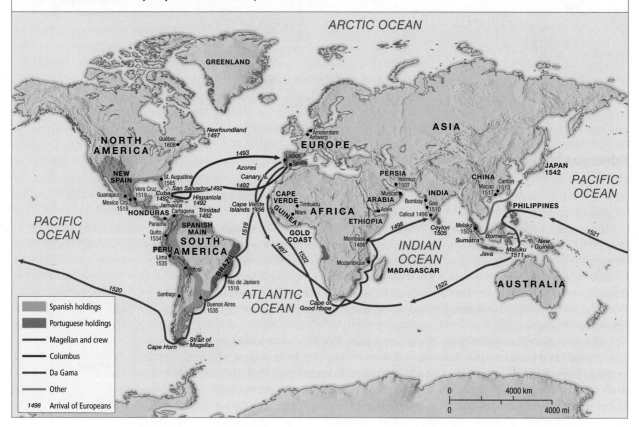

John and for a connection to the Indian Ocean and a sea expedition to search for a route around Africa. The land expedition failed to find Prester John but did reach India. The sea voyage, commanded by Bartholomeu Días (*DĒ-ahz*), rounded the Cape of Good Hope at Africa's southern tip and could have gone on to India had not the sailors insisted on returning home. When Días sailed into Lisbon in 1489, he reported that Portugal had found a way to undercut Muslim traders, since cargoes could be shipped by sea for a fraction of the cost by land. Present in Lisbon when Días arrived was a Genoese navigator named Cristóbal Colón, whose proposal for a voyage to find a route to the Indies by sailing westward across the Atlantic had been previously rejected by João II. The Latinized version of this navigator's name was Christopher Columbus.

Columbus's Enterprise of the Indies

Columbus's errors lead to unwarranted optimism

An experienced mariner and cartographer, Columbus knew that the earth was round, and he calculated the distance from Portugal to China at fewer than five thousand miles. He was right about the shape of the earth but wrong about its size. His calculations of one degree of longitude at the equator were off by 15 miles, a mistake that caused him to think that the circumference of the earth was 18,750 miles rather than 25,000. His sources for the size and locations of Asian lands were also inaccurate. But he was able to make a plausible argument that Europeans could reach East Asia by sailing west, across the Atlantic, on voyages that would be shorter and less expensive than going around Africa to the Indies. Moreover, since the journey would be east to west instead of north to south, the winds, currents, and climatic changes encountered along the way would be less troublesome. In 1484 Columbus presented his **Enterprise of the Indies,** a detailed plan for a westward maritime expedition, to João II, and asked for Portuguese financial support.

João referred this request to a committee of experts, who agreed with Columbus that the world is round—a well-known fact by 1484—but considered his estimate of the earth's circumference ridiculously small. This committee, relying in part on the 11th-century calculations of al-Biruni of Khwarazm, who estimated the radius of the earth at 3,930 miles, projected the distance from Portugal to Japan at 13,100 miles, a highly accurate prediction that placed East Asia well beyond the range of any expedition that expected its sailors to carry their own food and drink. Rather than reconsider his estimate, Columbus tried his luck with King Isabella of Castile (although female, Isabella was officially a *king*, and she insisted on being called by that title). She established a similar committee that reported similar findings. Columbus was about to try the Portuguese court again when Días returned to Lisbon in 1489 with good news about the route around Africa. Recognizing that Portugal would pursue that route for trade, Columbus sought support from Venice and Genoa. But these city-states, with established interests in existing routes through the eastern Mediterranean, turned him away.

Still convinced that his calculations were right, Columbus went back to Isabella in 1492 and was rejected again. However, as he was preparing to leave for Paris to try to interest the French, he was called back to Isabella's court. Her finance minister, Luís de Santander (*loo-ESS-dā sahn-tahn-DARE*), had scolded his sovereign for lack of imagination and offered to finance the Enterprise himself by loaning funds to Isabella. If Columbus were mistaken, Santander argued, he would die on the voyage and a small investment would be lost; but if, against the odds, he turned out to be right, Castile would have a more direct route to the Indies than either Portuguese or Islamic merchants.

Isabella now gave the Enterprise more careful thought. She and her husband Ferdinand, kings of Castile and Aragon, respectively, hoped to instill a militant, crusading Catholicism in all the Spanish kingdoms and unite them under the rule of their daughter Juana. A new route to the Indies would not only make this unified Spain rich, they reasoned, but also make it possible to convert hundreds of millions of Asians to their faith. Isabella accepted Santander's offer, gave Columbus letters of introduction to the emperor of China, and sent him on his way with three ships, the *Niña*, the *Pinta*, and the *Santa Maria*. Columbus sailed from Palos (*PAH-lōs*), Spain, on August 3, 1492, and made landfall on an island, most likely in the Bahamas, in what is today the Caribbean Sea on October 12 (see "Columbus Describes His First Encounter with People in the Western Hemisphere, 1492"). It was a voyage of fewer than three thousand miles.

Watch the **Video**

Christopher Columbus and the Round World

on **myhistorylab.com**

Isabella finances Columbus's gamble

Columbus's first encounter with Indians.

DOCUMENT 19.1 Columbus Describes His First Encounter with People in the Western Hemisphere, 1492

The Enterprise of the Indies sighted land before dawn on October 12, 1492, and Columbus went ashore after dawn broke. He recorded the events in his own words, including his assumption that his expedition was then very close to Asia.

As I saw that [the native people] were very friendly to us. . . I presented them with some red caps, and strings of beads to wear upon the neck, and many other trifles of small value, wherewith they were much delighted, and became wonderfully attached to us. Afterwards they came swimming to the boats, bringing parrots, balls of cotton thread, javelins and many other things which they exchanged for articles we gave them, such as glass beads, and hawk's bells; which trade was carried on with the utmost good will. But they seemed on the whole to me, to be a very poor people. They all go completely naked, even the women, though I saw but one girl. All whom I saw were young, not above thirty years of age, well made, with fine shapes and faces; their hair short, and coarse like that of a horse's tail, combed toward the forehead, except a small portion which they suffer to hang down behind, and never cut . . . Weapons they have none, nor are acquainted with them, for I showed them swords which they grasped by the blades, and cut themselves through ignorance. They have no iron, their javelins being without it, and nothing more than sticks, though some have fish-bones or other things at the ends. They are all of a good size and stature, and handsomely formed. I saw some with scars of wounds upon their bodies, and demanded by signs the cause of them; they answered me in the same way, that there came people from the other islands in the neighborhood who intended to make them prisoners, and they defended themselves. I thought then, and still believe, that these were from the continent [of Asia]. It appears to me, that the people are ingenious, and would be good servants; and I am of opinion that they would very readily become Christians, as they appear to have no religion . . . If it please our Lord, I intend at my return to carry home six of them to your Highnesses, that they may learn our language.

SOURCE: Christopher Columbus, *Journal of the First Voyage to America* (New York: A. and C. Boni, 1924), 24–26.

Columbus assumed that he had reached islands off the eastern coast of Japan, but the inhabitants did not wear Japanese clothing (indeed, they wore no clothing at all), did not speak Japanese, and did not seem to know anything about Japan. The plant and animal life was unlike anything Asian, and when Columbus returned to Spain in 1493 with samples of what he had found, the general conclusion was that he had landed in an unknown part of the world. Columbus, however, did not agree. He mounted three more expeditions in search of Japan, dying in Spain in 1506 without ever knowing what part of the world he had reached.

Columbus may have been mistaken concerning the nature of the lands he encountered, but Isabella was not. She repaid Santander handsomely and made the discoveries her personal property. Then she appealed to Pope Alexander VI for recognition of Castile's claims to the Indies and its exclusive right to the westward passage. In Christian Europe at that time, such matters were routinely referred to the Vatican. Alexander, a Spaniard, divided the entire world known to Europeans between the two Iberian nations, drawing an imaginary line from pole to pole 450 miles west of the Azores and the Cape Verde Islands (though they are not at the same longitude). Ignoring the rights of the inhabitants whose lands he gave away, he granted everything east of the line to Portugal and everything west to Castile. The Portuguese, who had not yet actually sailed all the way to India, were outraged and threatened war.

Subsequent negotiations between the Portuguese and the Spanish in 1494 resulted in the **Treaty of Tordesillas** (*taur-dɑ̄-SĒ-yahss*), an agreement that drew the Line of Demarcation 1,675 miles west of the Cape Verde Islands (Map 19.2). Both sides were

▶ Read the Document

Christopher Columbus "The Letters of Columbus to Ferdinand and Isabel" on **myhistorylab.com**

Portugal and Spain claim the entire world

reasonably dissatisfied but proceeded to claim their halves of the world. The other European powers, not having been consulted, saw no need to comply; nor did Muslims, who paid no attention to the pope. Still, although Europeans did not yet know about South America, the treaty's main effect would be to give most of it to Spain, while leaving to Portugal the large eastern section later known as Brazil.

The Voyage of Magellan

The Spanish followed up on the voyages of Columbus by creating an American empire, first colonizing several Caribbean islands and later conquering the Aztecs in Mexico and the

| MAP **19.2** | The Treaty of Tordesillas and the Line of Demarcation, 1494 |

Observe that the line drawn by the Treaty of Tordesillas not only divided the Western Hemisphere between Portugal and Spain; it went around the world and bisected the Eastern Hemisphere as well. One can only imagine the reactions of the Japanese and Chinese emperors and the various rulers of India, had they known that their lands had been assigned to two European nations by a treaty of whose very existence they knew nothing. Europe had progressed from exploring the world (Map 19.1) to dividing it. Why did Europeans believe they had a right to divide the world in this way?

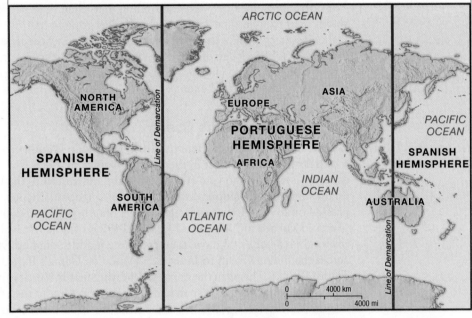

Inca in Peru (Chapter 18). Some, however, continued to believe that profitable trade routes to Asia could be found by sailing westward from Spain.

Thus, while Cortés was conquering Mexico, Ferdinand Magellan (*mah-JEL-lin*), a Portuguese mariner sailing for Spain, was finally accomplishing what Columbus had set out to do. By now it was obvious that the Americas were not part of Asia: in 1497 and 1498 English expeditions had explored the coast of North America, and in 1513 a Spaniard named Balboa saw another great ocean on the western side of the American continents. But although ancient Polynesians knew the width of the Pacific, no European yet knew this, and the dream of sailing westward from Europe to reach the riches of Asia lived on.

In pursuit of this dream, Magellan set out from Spain in 1519 with five ships and about 280 men. They headed

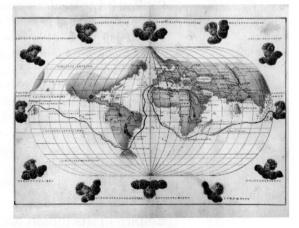

Magellan's circumnavigation of the globe.

Magellan proves it impractical to sail west from Europe to the Spice Islands

for South America, where for a year they probed the coast for a passage, finally sailing through what is now called the Straits of Magellan in November 1520. For the next four months, with only three ships left, they crossed the seemingly endless Pacific, eating leather and ship rats once supplies ran out. In March 1521, the near-starving survivors reached the Philippines. They claimed the islands for Spain, but the next month Magellan and many of his men were killed in a conflict with Filipino peoples.

Eventually, in September 1522, one ship with 18 men made it back to Spain, having sailed around the globe. Their voyage had proven that it was indeed possible to reach Asia by sailing west from Europe. But it had also revealed that the trip was three times the distance Columbus had calculated, and that given the distance and dangers involved it was not really worth the trouble.

The Portuguese Seaborne Empire

The Portuguese, meanwhile, were finding that using their new sea routes was very much worth *their* trouble. The Treaty of Tordesillas granted half the world to Portugal, and Lisbon set out to make the most of it. Portugal's new oceanic empire rested on firm foundations: knowledge of currents, winds, and coastlines; superb sailing vessels; and first-rate seamanship. The curiosity of Prince Henry the Navigator turned out to have tremendous commercial benefits.

Empire in the Atlantic Ocean

Vasco da Gama connects Portugal to India

A generation after Prince Henry's death, King João II authorized the establishment of a fortress and trading post in the Gulf of Guinea in 1482. The next year a Portuguese explorer named Diogo Cão (*COWM*) found the mouth of the Congo River, eventually establishing good relations with the Kongo Kingdom (Chapter 23). Other Portuguese pressed on toward India, as King Manoel (*mahn-WELL*) I commissioned Vasco da Gama to sail around Africa to India. In 1497 da Gama left Lisbon, reaching the Cape of Good Hope after 93 days, then rounding it and sailing up Africa's east coast and across the Indian Ocean to India (see "Vasco da Gama's Expedition Observes the Spice Trade, 1498"). This was the greatest seafaring feat in European history to date. As a follow-up, King Manoel dispatched a 12-ship fleet under the command of Pedro Alvares Cabral (*PĀ-drō AHL-vah-rez kah-BRAHL*) in 1500. Blown off course by a violent storm, Cabral made landfall on an "island" in the western Atlantic, claiming it for Portugal before continuing on to India. It was not an island at all—it was Brazil.

Portuguese sailors bump into Brazil

Manoel decided to assess the value of Brazil as an intermediate base for future voyages to India. In 1501 he sent a three-ship expedition to the new land, with Amerigo Vespucci (*ah-MARE-ih-gō vess-POO-chē*) aboard as cartographer and chronicler. In this capacity on a future trip, Amerigo named the entire hemisphere after himself: America. The expedition explored two thousand miles of coastline, leading Manoel to suspect that this was not an island after all. It also brought back samples of a type of brazilwood, a tree whose wood could be used to produce red dye for textiles. This wood gave Brazil its name and Portugal a reason to explore the area further, since it lay too far west to be useful as a way station en route to India. Later, the Portuguese learned that they could make a fortune growing sugar in Brazil, provided they settled it with colonists and African slaves. But for the moment, the Eastern Hemisphere seemed more attractive.

Empire in the Indian and Pacific Oceans

Portugal builds an empire based on commerce

The Treaty of Tordesillas, amplified by a papal edict of 1514 forbidding other European powers to interfere with Portuguese possessions, enabled Portugal to avoid European competition in the Eastern Hemisphere for most of the 16th century. Its superior gunnery, vessels, and seamanship held off its occasional Asian enemies. But the Portuguese seaborne realm was less an empire than a network of commercial ports and fortifications, designed not for settlement but for trade.

DOCUMENT 19.2 Vasco da Gama's Expedition Observes the Spice Trade, 1498

Vasco da Gama's first voyage to India enabled the Portuguese to observe the nature and extent of the spice trade. This excerpt from the journal of one of the sailors charts the course of that commerce. Notice the emphasis placed on the dangers of overland travel, the frequent payment of customs duties, and the enormous income the sultan of the Ottoman Empire derived from those duties. All of these facts led the Portuguese to seek a sea route to the Indies in the first place.

From this country of Calecut, or Alta India, come the spices which are consumed in the East and the West, in Portugal, as in all other countries of the world, as also precious stones of every description. The following spices are to be found in this city of Calecut, being its own produce: much ginger and pepper and cinnamon, although the last is not of so fine a quality as that brought from an island called Ceylon, which is eight days journey from Calecut . . . Cloves are brought to this city from an island called Malacca. The Mecca vessels carry these spices from there to a city in [Arabia] called Jiddah, and from the said island to Jiddah is a voyage of

fifty days sailing before the wind, for the vessels of this country cannot tack. At Jiddah they discharge their cargoes, paying customs duties to the Grand Sultan. The merchandise is then transshipped to smaller vessels, which carry it through the Red Sea to a place . . . called Tuuz, where customs duties are paid once more. From that place the merchants carry the spices on the back of camels . . . to Cairo, a journey occupying ten days. At Cairo duties are paid again. On this road to Cairo they are frequently robbed by thieves, who live in that country, such as the Bedouins and others.

At Cairo, the spices are embarked on the river Nile . . . and descending that river for two days they reach a place called Rosetta, where duties have to be paid once more. There they are placed on camels, and are conveyed in one day to a city called Alexandria, which is a seaport. This city is visited by the galleys of Venice and Genoa, in search of these spices, which yield the Grand Sultan a revenue of 600,000 cruzados in customs duties . . . [about $15 million in 2006 dollars].

SOURCE: *A Journal of the First Voyage of Vasco da Gama, 1497–1499,* translated by Eric Axelson (Cape Town: Stephan Phillips Ltd., 1998), 77–78.

Vasco da Gama's voyage to India opened the Indian Ocean to Portuguese traffic. In 1500, after Cabral bumped into Brazil, one of his ships located Madagascar. The Portuguese established trading posts in India and connected them with their newly founded station at Kilwa in East Africa.

In 1505 the first Portuguese **viceroy**, or vice-king, arrived in India, and beginning in 1510 the second viceroy, Afonso de Albuquerque, began developing the system of fortified posts at strategic locations that guaranteed Portuguese domination of Indian Ocean trade. This entire region already enjoyed dense commercial networks managed by Arab, Chinese, and Indian merchants. Portugal's contribution was to connect these networks to each other.

Albuquerque conquered Goa in 1510 and made it Portugal's headquarters in Asia. During the next five years, his forces took Melaka, Maluku, and Hormuz. Portuguese seamen reached China shortly thereafter, and in 1557 they established a trading post at Macao. The Portuguese controlled the Persian Gulf from Hormuz, and their installation at Melaka dominated the passageway from the Indian Ocean to the South China Sea. Fortified Portuguese trading posts were located all along the East African coastline and the seacoasts of India and Ceylon.

Albuquerque's strategy helps Portugal dominate the Indian Ocean

Portugal's Commercial Empire in 1600

The Portuguese created their far-flung empire skillfully, employing their navigational expertise to master the seas and sail them at will. They guarded their knowledge jealously, refusing to share it with competitors. They carefully selected important strategic locations that would help them dominate Indian Ocean trade, occupying those locations through a combination of diplomacy and intimidation. Once installed, they protected their positions by negotiating trading rights in contracts that benefited local merchants as well as themselves, giving those merchants a stake in Portuguese success. This strategy enabled a nation with a tiny population of fewer than two million people to develop a commercial network spanning the globe.

Portuguese ships carry goods across enormous distances

The Portuguese were responsible for establishing regular oceanic trade across vast spaces: between the Atlantic and Indian oceans, between West Africa and Brazil, between southwest Europe and West Africa, and between the North and South Atlantic (Map 19.3). These sea routes regularized connections between these regions and enhanced commercial and cultural contacts between societies.

Portuguese vessels carried spices from the Indian Ocean to Europe, and while this was a valuable trade route, Portuguese shipping lanes from one part of Asia to another were even more profitable. The Portuguese sold Chinese silk not only in Europe but also in India, the Maluku Islands, Borneo, Timor, and Hormuz. Cloth from India, spices from the Malukus, minerals from Borneo, and sandalwood from Timor were distributed throughout the Portuguese empire, as Portuguese ships connected these sites not only to Lisbon but to one another.

In addition to goods, Portuguese sailors and merchants carried diseases from one region of the world to another. Malaria spread rapidly across the tropics as mosquitoes

---

MAP **19.3** The Flow of Commerce in the Portuguese World, ca. 1600

The Portuguese impulse to expand overseas created commercial connections linking four continents. Note that a bewildering variety of goods, some of which are depicted in the chapter opener, flowed into Lisbon from across the globe. Customs, rituals, languages, clothing, and ideas moved not only to and from Lisbon, but between each of the ports depicted on the map. The result was a vast increase in cosmopolitanism and knowledge from one end of the Portuguese world to the other. Why did this Portuguese challenge worry the Islamic world?

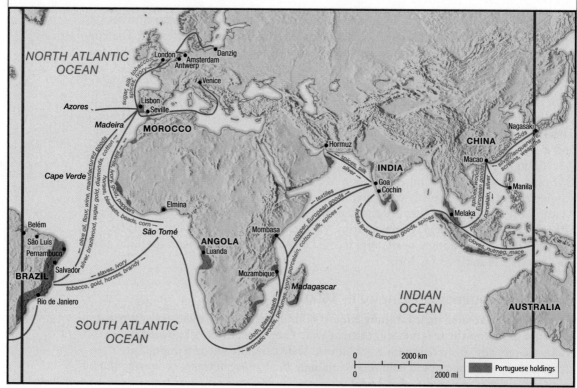

bred prolifically in the water carried on Portuguese ships. Asians and Africans were generally immune to the most drastic effects of Eurasian diseases, but Brazilian Amerinds were devastated by smallpox, influenza, and measles. More than a century after Cabral reached Brazil, smallpox remained lethal enough to wipe out the entire Amerind population of Sao Luís in northern Brazil in 1621.

In addition to the transmission of germs, goods, and people, the Portuguese spread European culture and practices throughout their empire and scattered bits of information about Asian, African, Amerind, and Brazilian cultures everywhere they went. Building and artistic materials such as rare woods, gems, dyes, and metals were shipped from Asia, Africa, and Brazil to Europe, where they were used in churches, libraries, jewelry, paintings, and furniture. The Portuguese built European-style churches in India and churches with Asian motifs in Brazil. Amerind art was widely sold in Brazil, Angolans purchased colorful Amerind textiles, and Brazilian-inspired furniture graced parlors in Portuguese homes. The Portuguese seaborne empire facilitated widespread transmission of styles and tastes.

A modern-day replica of a Portuguese caravel.

Portuguese commerce connects Asia to Europe

This transmission operated in several directions simultaneously. European clothing was introduced in Angola and Brazil, with sometimes comical results: top hats were widely worn by foremen of labor gangs in Rio de Janeiro, and for a brief period, Portuguese-style baggy pants were all the rage in Nagasaki. Brazilian tobacco was smoked in Portugal and coveted in Angola, where *arrobas*, bundles of tobacco twisted into ropes and soaked in molasses, became so popular that they were used as currency. West African foods and words entered the culture of eastern Brazil, and African slaves transported to Brazil by the Portuguese became devoted converts to Portuguese Catholicism while retaining rituals and songs from their African religions. The cross-fertilization of cultures produced by the Portuguese seaborne empire was as stimulating, and penetrating, as the connections generated by conflict and conquest among the many great land-based empires of previous centuries.

The Spanish and Portuguese Empires in America

Once the great Amerind empires had fallen to the Spaniards, Spain began consolidating what had become the largest territorial possession in human history. From California to Cape Horn, Spain controlled everything except Portuguese Brazil (Map 19.4). Subduing Mexico proved relatively easy after the conquest of Tenochtitlán. In Peru, however, the Inca found ways to neutralize Spain's mounted cavalry, and although they were unable to expel the invaders, they created an independent Inca kingdom high in the Andes that lasted until 1572. Elsewhere the weaker, less centralized Amerind cultures, including the vestiges of the once-imposing Maya civilization, offered only occasional resistance to their new masters.

At the same time, the Portuguese began recognizing the economic potential of Brazil. Their eastern seaborne empire involved profit-sharing with Muslim traders, but Brazil was entirely theirs, and they used it to profit from the growing European taste for sugar. Unlike Spanish America, with its centralized Amerind societies, Brazil was home to native cultures that lived in the inaccessible interior and had not developed central institutions. These cultures fled from the Portuguese rather than resist them but could not provide the labor required for sugar cultivation. Nor, given their small population, could the Portuguese.

MAP **19.4** The Iberian Empires in the Western Hemisphere, 1750

Spain and Portugal, two small countries on the Iberian Peninsula on the southwestern fringe of Europe, constructed enormous empires in the Western Hemisphere. European languages, customs, and products spread throughout these empires, while American, African, and Asian resources, customs, and cultures moved through Iberia into Europe. But notice that large portions of South America—the Amazon Basin, the interior of Brazil, and Patagonia—remained untouched by Europeans. Why?

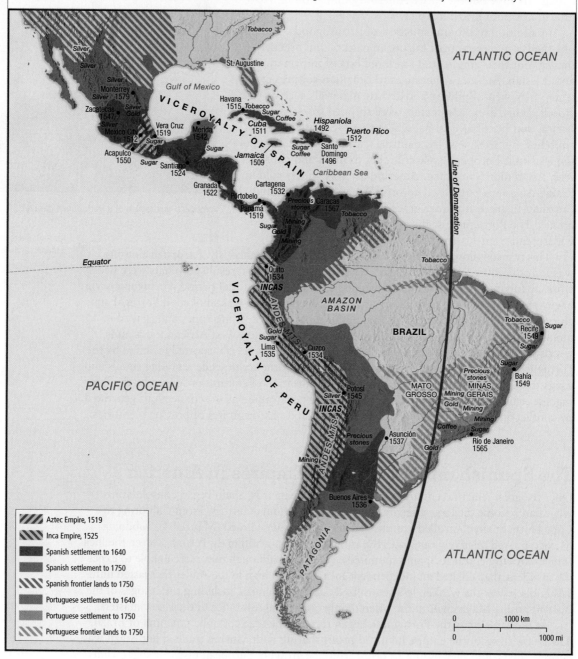

Legend:
- Aztec Empire, 1519
- Inca Empire, 1525
- Spanish settlement to 1640
- Spanish settlement to 1750
- Spanish frontier lands to 1750
- Portuguese settlement to 1640
- Portuguese settlement to 1750
- Portuguese frontier lands to 1750

The Amerind Foundation

Spain, in contrast, could construct its empire on the foundations of Amerind societies. Particularly helpful to the Spanish effort was the hierarchical structure of the Aztec and Inca empires. It proved relatively easy for the Spaniards to substitute the king of Spain for the Aztec or Inca emperor at the top of the hierarchy and to expect that the king's orders would be obeyed without hesitation.

Aztec and Inca polytheism also contributed to this submission. Accustomed to a large array of gods, the conquered peoples interpreted their defeat as indicating that their own gods were weaker than those of the Spaniards. It seemed logical to worship the gods who were stronger. The Spaniards, noting this tendency, did nothing to discourage Inca and Aztecs from considering Catholic saints and angels as powerful gods. Mary, the mother of Jesus, actually had a parallel in Aztec religion, in which one female goddess was the mother of all the gods. Through this blending of Christian and Amerind traditions, the defeated societies were encouraged to accept their fate and embrace the new European faith.

Iberians build empires on existing Amerind societies

Slave Labor

Once Mexico and Peru were pacified, Spaniards began arriving steadily from the mother country, drawn to the Americas by the prospect of wealth in gold and silver or in sugar production. For labor in the mines and fields they expected to use Amerinds, but Amerinds were not easily enslaved for these purposes. First, smallpox and other European diseases to which Amerinds had no acquired immunity killed large numbers of them. Moreover, those who survived had greatly reduced life expectancies, either owing to Spanish cruelty or because they simply found unrelenting labor unendurable in the absence of the religious significance it had had under the Aztec and Inca Empires. Third, many Catholic missionaries to the Americas protested strongly against the enslavement of Amerinds. They argued to the king that Amerinds were people with souls, not draft animals.

The missionaries' genuine concern for the well-being of the Amerinds, however, did not extend to Africans, many of whom were soon imported as slaves. With Amerind workers unavailable, the American colonies needed a labor force accustomed to tropical conditions. There were not enough men in all Iberia to supply this labor force, and if there had been, few could have survived manual labor in tropical climates for very long.

Here the Portuguese took the lead. Having experienced serious labor shortages in Brazil, they imported slaves from trading posts that they had established along the west coast of Africa. Spain followed, and before long Portuguese and Spanish ships carried human cargoes from West Africa, thousands upon thousands of slaves to be sold at auction in the port cities of Central and South America. Iberian America quickly became a mixed society of people of Amerind, European, and African descent who produced a physical and cultural blending unlike anything in the Eastern Hemisphere.

Read the **Document**

Bartolemé de las Casas, from Brief Account of the Devastation of the Indies

on **myhistorylab.com**

Iberians replace Amerind labor with African slaves

Government and Administration

Governing such diverse and distant empires required new strategies. At first Isabella of Castile, who owned Spanish America outright by virtue of Santander's financing and the Treaty of Tordesillas, simply appointed her chaplain to administer the entire area. When this overworked priest died in 1503, one year after Isabella herself, her husband Ferdinand established a Board of Trade to oversee the increasingly profitable transatlantic commerce. After the final unification of Spain in 1516 under Carlos I (who three years later also became Holy Roman Emperor Charles V), the Americas were governed through councils. Rather than delegate responsibility to a number of ministries or departments (as was done in France and England), authority was assigned in 1524 to a single board, the **Council of the Indies**.

The Council of the Indies supervised every aspect of governance in Spanish America, including legislative, judicial, commercial, financial, military, and religious matters. Meeting in Seville between three and five hours daily, it approved all significant expenditures, decided which Spanish laws should apply unchanged in the New World, drafted revisions for those that required adjustment, and advised the king on everything pertaining to colonial affairs. Formal votes were not unheard of, but usually the Council reached agreement on important matters before submitting its unanimous recommendations to the king for review.

But distance proved to be the most significant difficulty facing those who tried to govern the Western Hemisphere. Sailing from Portugal to Brazil took an average of seventy to one hundred days; from Spain to Panama, about seventy-five. Troublesome winds and currents made the return trip even longer. Atlantic crossings were always unpleasant, often dangerous, and occasionally fatal. Ships from the Americas, laden with treasure and exotic goods, were frequently set upon by pirates, although convoys protected by warships eventually reduced this danger. Royal orders and colonial reports took months to cross the Atlantic and were often lost altogether.

The empires thus could not be run from Iberia. Kings and councils might issue laws and edicts, but who would enforce them in America? Clearly agents of unquestionable loyalty were required, men who knew the royal will instinctively, without having to ask questions at every turn. The rulers found such agents in their viceroys, or "vice-kings."

Viceroys were responsible for the execution of the king's orders on virtually every aspect of colonial administration. Until 1717 there were two viceroyalties in Spanish America: New Spain (from California south to Panama, including the Caribbean), and Peru (from Panama south to Cape Horn). In the 18th century, Peru was subdivided into two additional viceroyalties because of its overwhelming size.

Spain and Portugal find different ways to administer their empires

Portuguese America developed in a less centralized fashion. King João III in 1534 divided the eastern seaboard into 12 hereditary captaincies, varying in width between 100 and 270 miles and extending indefinitely into the uncharted interior. The proprietors were responsible for the recruitment of settlers and the economic development of their captaincies. The system never worked effectively, and in 1549 João III placed Brazil under the direct administration of a governor-general, whose duties were similar to those of a Spanish-American viceroy. This action accelerated development and attracted thousands of Portuguese settlers to Brazil.

Viceroys and governors-general administer in the king's name

Whether Spanish or Portuguese, these vice-kings were men of talent and expertise, but the principal qualification for the post was loyalty to the king. They had to make decisions in the king's best interests even when the king's orders might be impractical, or irrelevant to conditions in the New World. Under such circumstances, the Spanish viceroy could delay implementation or initiate a reassessment of the situation by invoking the Spanish legal maxim, "I obey but I do not enforce." Portuguese governors-general acted similarly, but without the maxim. A wise monarch would consider such an opinion carefully before overruling his representative.

But the kings of Spain and Portugal were customarily suspicious, and viceroys, like the officials who served under them, were always subject to the *residencia* (*rez-ih-DEHN-sē-ah*). This was a thorough audit of all the appointee's actions during his term of office. It was conducted by a royal bureaucrat sent from the mother country, and it restrained those who might otherwise have been tempted to engage in illegal activity or abuse of power.

All authority came from the king. Neither Spanish nor Portuguese America contained any institution providing representation within the government for ordinary people. Spain itself had such a body, called a *cortés*, but because it was a representative institution that restricted royal power, Spanish kings refused to introduce it into the empire. The only truly representative body in the Spanish Empire was the town council, which maintained roads, policed the streets and markets, and regulated local affairs. But the authority of town councils was limited to the towns themselves. The extensive centralized powers exercised by the Iberian kings over their American empires helped them hold those distant territories for more than three centuries.

The Colonial Church

Iberian expansion was driven not only by a quest for gold and glory, but also by the desire to save the souls of Amerinds, who had never before heard the message of Jesus Christ. That ambitious goal was pursued by the Spanish and Portuguese branches of the Roman Catholic Church.

The Plaza de Armas in Cuzco, Peru, displays 16th-century Spanish colonial architectural style.

Iberian empires are shaped by Catholicism

Ferdinand and Isabella, calling themselves "the Catholic kings," had completed the *Reconquista* by 1492 and had made Catholicism an element of Spanish nationality that helped bring unity to their diverse kingdoms. In America Catholicism would help assimilate conquered peoples into either Spain's or Portugal's colonial order. The pope supported this effort, granting the Iberian monarchs extensive rights over the appointment of bishops, the activities of religious orders, and the organization of all Catholic undertakings in the Western Hemisphere. In return, the kings assumed responsibility for supervising the Church in its evangelical, educational, and charitable efforts overseas.

At first these efforts were directed by the Franciscan, Dominican, and Augustinian religious orders. They concentrated on converting Amerind chiefs, who then saw to it that their people would be baptized. To preach to the newly converted and teach them the elements of the faith, the friars learned dominant Amerind languages and promoted their widening use as a means of centralization.

The Amerinds reacted to conversion in a variety of ways. Some were enthusiastic, eager to worship the new gods who had proven themselves stronger than the old. Others converted for practical reasons, considering it both wise and useful to adopt the belief system of the conquerors. Still others rebelled, like the Inca of the central Andes, who objected to the destruction of their mummies and idols. Considering this destruction to be sacrilegious, bringing natural disasters and diseases, these Inca rebels returned to their ancient beliefs in the 1560s. Their action provoked a stern response from the viceroyalty of Peru, which worked vigorously over the next decade to eliminate the movement.

By 1549 in Brazil and 1572 in Spanish America, priests from the Jesuit order arrived and quickly became influential. Emphasizing similarities between native belief systems and Catholicism, as they did in China (see Chapter 21), they defended their Amerind followers against many who wished to enslave them. As did the other orders, the Jesuits grew prosperous through their access to native labor. The Church thus became wealthy and earned the resentment of colonial elites. In a land without a banking system, the Church became the principal source of funds for agricultural or commercial investment. It also became the largest property owner in the Western Hemisphere and a powerful manufacturer of pottery, fabrics, and leather goods.

The Catholic Church dominates commerce and education

Education in the colonies was handled exclusively by the Church. It operated all primary and secondary schools, educated Amerinds as part of the conversion process, and founded institutions of higher education such as the Universities of Mexico (Mexico City) and San Marcos (Lima), both established in 1551. In Brazil, however, the Portuguese Church did not establish a university until the 19th century. Before that, Brazilians seeking a university degree had to pursue it in Europe.

Religious orders for women expanded during the colonial period and played a major role in social and economic life. Convents attracted Spanish women who wanted to manage their own affairs, obtain a good education, and live lives of piety and service.

Some women entered convents in order to escape the burdens imposed by husbands and children, or to lead well-protected lives. Most, however, took their vows seriously and contributed greatly to colonial life. Much more important in Spanish than in Portuguese America, convents owned substantial properties, provided funds for investment, and cultivated literary and artistic pursuits. Through its male and female orders, its strong belief in the importance of its work, and its active involvement with Amerinds, the colonial Church exercised a powerful influence over Iberian America.

Society in the Iberian Empires

The people of Spain and Portugal were predominantly white, although a few Iberians were of African descent. But Spanish and Portuguese America contained a great many racial and ethnic groups, and in the Iberian empires a new social order emerged.

Race mixing shapes Iberian colonial societies

THE IBERIAN-AMERICAN SOCIAL HIERARCHY. At the top of the social ladder were white Spaniards and Portuguese, who tended to consider free people of other races as undesirable **mestizos** (*mes-TĒ-zōs*). Mestizos were people of mixed descent, often the result of unions between the invading Iberians—almost all of whom were male—and Amerinds. Children born from Iberian-African unions were termed **mulatto**. Only 5 percent of these unions were marriages, and children born outside of marriage were discriminated against. In Spanish America, whites excluded such people from artisan guilds in the 1540s, from the priesthood in 1555, and from any position carrying with it the possibility of social advancement. Children of mixed race were not, of course, exclusively the product of Iberian-Amerind or Iberian-African unions; Amerinds and Africans interacted as well. The result has been a racial mixture found nowhere else on earth.

As time went on, increasing numbers of Africans were imported to make up for the high death rate among slaves. The Spanish and Portuguese did not encourage slave family formation, as it proved far less expensive to buy and transport Africans than to raise African children to adulthood. Male and female slaves were customarily housed separately. Slaves performed all sorts of physical labor and menial services, ranging from domestic chores and handicrafts to the difficult and life-shortening occupations of miner and field hand.

Iberia had long had slaves, both from Islamic areas and from sub-Saharan Africa, and neither Spaniards nor Portuguese considered black Africans a slave race. For Iberians, enslavement was a matter of social class or wartime misfortune, and it was possible for slaves to purchase their freedom. Still, slavery was a brutal, degrading institution, and even those able to buy their way out of it found their lives severely restricted. Many officials and most Iberians treated all Africans as slaves, even if they were legally free.

Africans and Amerinds occupy inferior social positions

Africans, free or unfree, lived on the margins of society in the Iberian empires, as did Amerinds. Africans were subjected to a superficial assimilation, and they hid their culture and customs away from the view of whites. Amerinds converted to Catholicism in large numbers, but most proved less adaptable than Africans to the Iberian colonial way of life. Thus, many Spaniards and Portuguese valued Africans over native peoples as workers.

In their own villages, however, Amerinds maintained independent, largely self-sufficient lifestyles based on their traditional social structures. Spaniards and Portuguese forced Amerinds to work through labor exchanges, in which Amerind villages were compelled to provide a specified number of adults for forced labor for a specified number of days each year. Amerinds adapted themselves to market structures and unwillingly interacted with the Iberian agricultural world. But they played little or no role in colonial town or city life, leaving skilled labor to mestizos and free Africans.

A Spanish-American family of mixed races. The man is European, the wife is African, and the child is mulatto.

Social class in Iberian America was not based primarily upon skin color, although race was certainly an important factor. Portuguese and Spanish societies were organized according to a European structure of three estates: clergy, nobility, and commoners. The upper levels were reserved for high-ranking bishops and nobles, although Spanish colonial nobles tended to be lower-ranking dignitaries who had earned their ennoblement through military service during or after the Spanish conquests in America. The highest-ranking Spanish nobles had no motivation to go to America, except occasionally as a viceroy or general.

Iberian colonial societies are organized according to European structures

Colonial nobles distinguished themselves from commoners largely by their ownership of great estates. On those lands the nobles built lavish manor houses and presided over large numbers of laborers, servants, and slaves. Most Spaniards in America, of course, were commoners, and they earned their livings as shopkeepers, clerks, overseers, doctors, lawyers, notaries, accountants, merchants, craftsmen, or manual laborers. Some were wealthy, others were poor, but all were European in origin.

Mestizos, excluded from many lines of work, often had to make their living by their wits and skills. By the early 1600s, many had found niches as silversmiths, wheelwrights, tailors, and carpenters, but most worked as servants or unskilled laborers. Free Africans and Amerinds were even less fortunate. Constrained by descent and skin color, they could never move into the commoner class.

Among whites of Iberian descent, one additional distinction was made—between peninsulares (*pehn-ihn-soo-LAH-rāz*) and criollos (crē-YŌ-yōs). **Peninsulares** were white people born in the Iberian Peninsula (hence their name). They monopolized the highest offices in church and state and looked down on **criollos**, white people born in the Western Hemisphere. The names of these groups varied in Portuguese America, but the principle remained the same. The distinction arose with the efforts of Iberian kings to fill the most important positions in their empires with men of social stature whom they knew well. But over time, peninsular status came to be required even for midlevel colonial positions, and eventually the poorest Iberian-born newcomer considered himself the social superior of people whose families had been born and prospered in America for generations. This unfair treatment angered criollos, alienating many who might otherwise have remained loyal to their king but who later gladly joined independence movements.

Iberian whites dominate colonial societies

THE ROLE OF GENDER. Gender distinctions were particularly evident in the Iberian colonial economy. Elite white women usually married, raised large families, and as widows administered the estates of their late husbands. But they could not engage in professional or commercial activity, and those who were frustrated by patriarchal restrictions frequently entered convents in order to gain limited autonomy. Middle- and lower-class white women worked at a wide variety of occupations, including spinning thread, taking in laundry, sewing, peddling goods, selling food, and serving as free domestics in the homes of the elite. Amerind women dominated the town marketplaces as food vendors. Free African women were restricted to domestic service and cooking in inns and marketplaces. Most free women performed some type of paid labor during much of their lives. Survival in Iberian America below the level of the elites was not easy, and women's incomes, however meager, were badly needed.

Women play significant economic roles in the Iberian empires

Amerinds and Europeans in North America

Before the 16th century, the peoples of North America were largely isolated from the rest of the world. Influenced only by occasional trade with Mesoamerican cultures that flourished to their south, the numerous tribes and nations of North American Amerinds developed distinctive cultures, values, beliefs, and institutions, without having to deal with outside interference.

View the **Map**
Civilizations in North America
on **myhistorylab.com**

Then, in the 16th century, European explorers began to map the continent's coastlines and rivers, looking for gold and a passageway to Asia. In the 17th century, having found neither, Europeans started settling in North America, exploiting its resources and farming its lands. In the process, the intruders displaced the Amerinds, whose numbers were already diminished by European diseases.

Coalitions and Contacts

North of Mexico there were no great settled empires like those that existed in the Eastern Hemisphere. Most North Americans lived in village-based societies that rarely included more than a few thousand people, and even the larger nations probably numbered only in the hundreds of thousands. Usually these societies were ruled by powerful kings or chiefs who exercised religious and political authority. They presided over rituals aiming to establish harmony with the spirits of nature, and over councils made up of prominent warriors and advisors.

The Haudenosaunee create an alliance of Amerind nations

Occasionally some societies combined for protection but rarely surrendered their autonomy. In the 1500s, for example, the Haudenosaunee (*HOW-din-ō-SAW-nā*) people of what is now upstate New York organized themselves into a League of Five Nations, later called the Iroquois (*EAR-uh-kwoy*) Confederacy. According to oral tradition, a legendary figure called the Peacemaker, along with a mighty chief known as Hiawatha, persuaded regional leaders to end their constant warfare and join together for the common good. But the League, despite an intricate governance system, was more an alliance than a union: each of its five members (Seneca, Cayuga, Onondaga, Oneida, and Mohawk) remained a sovereign nation.

North American Amerinds preserve their autonomy

North American Amerinds were politically divided and culturally diverse, but they were not isolated from each other. Using the continent's extensive river systems, they could attack their enemies, travel to distant hunting and fishing grounds, conduct long-distance trade, and maintain a network of contacts with other societies.

Through contacts with Mexico, some North Americans knew that there was a powerful, wealthy empire to their south. They could not know, however, that there existed across the ocean mightier and wealthier empires, whose warriors carried weapons against which the Amerinds had no defense and diseases against which they had no immunity. Unlike Asians, Africans, and Europeans, who constantly feared conquest by more powerful neighbors, North Americans did not anticipate the catastrophe to come.

The Coming of the Europeans

Not long after the first voyage of Columbus, Europeans looking for a new route to Asia began arriving in North America. In 1497 Italian mariner Giovanni Caboto explored the northeast coast, staking a claim for his English employers, who called him John Cabot. In 1500 Portuguese explorers reached Newfoundland; soon fishermen from Portugal, England, and France were fishing the cod-rich waters off the northeastern banks. They also made contact with coastal Amerinds, who proved willing to trade food and furs for European trinkets and tools.

A 1607 map of the northeast coast of North America, drawn by the French explorer Samuel de Champlain.

In the following decades, while the Spanish conquered the Aztecs and built an empire in Mexico, French and English explorers farther north found neither gold nor a climate in which sugar would grow. Lacking such financial incentives, Europeans in the 16th century made little effort to colonize the north.

After 1600, however, as the French, Dutch, and English challenged the dominance of Spain, Europeans began to establish permanent settlements in North America. Enchanted by a voyage up

MAP **19.5**   European Exploration and Colonies in North America, 1607–1763

European intrusion into North America caused competition for territory, both among European nations and with Amerind peoples. The French, Dutch, and English maneuvered for advantage in what is today the northeastern United States, while the Spaniards amassed massive holdings with minimal opposition from other Europeans. Note that the English colonies of New Hampshire, Massachusetts, Connecticut, Pennsylvania, Virginia, and North Carolina had no western borders; theoretically, each of them claimed land running all the way to the Pacific Ocean. Amerinds adopted a variety of strategies to counter the intrusions, including collaboration, alliance-building, and outright opposition. How did these conflicting European claims and Amerind strategies shape the development of North America?

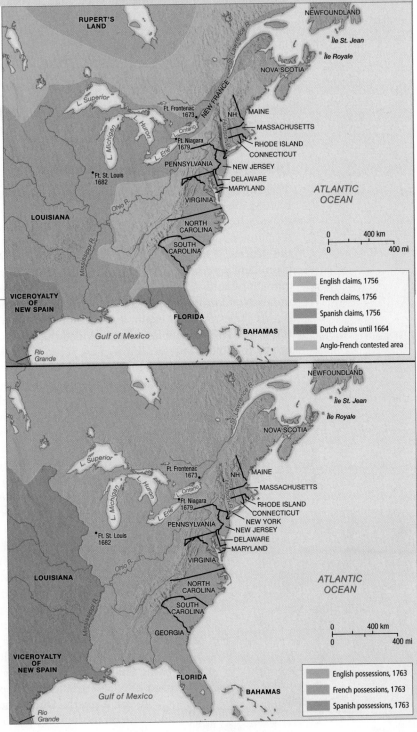

the Saint Lawrence River in 1603, French explorer Samuel de Champlain helped start a small colony in Acadia (now Nova Scotia) the next year and founded a settlement at Quebec in 1608. Eventually he established good relations with the region's Huron Amerinds, using French forces and firearms to help them defeat their Iroquois foes. He also helped the Hurons develop a profitable trade in furs. French fur traders followed, as did soldiers who fought the Iroquois, Jesuits who spread Christianity, and explorers who traveled the Great Lakes and the Mississippi River. By century's end the French had claimed these regions as a colony called New France (Map 19.5), based mainly on the fur trade with the Amerinds, most of whom were unaware that their lands were now supposedly subject to someone called the king of France.

Meanwhile other Europeans were arriving. In 1607 about a hundred hearty Englishmen, searching for gold and adventure, founded an outpost called Jamestown (named for King James I) in a region they knew as Virginia (named for Elizabeth I, the "Virgin

Europeans establish colonies in North America

((••— Listen to the Audio
Exploitations
on **myhistorylab.com**

Queen"). In 1609 Henry Hudson, sailing for the Dutch, traveled up the great river that now bears his name, seeking a new passage to Asia. He found no such route but did discover a region rich in furs. In the 1620s the Dutch founded the colony of New Netherland, which four decades later was seized by the English and renamed New York. In 1620 about 50 self-styled "Pilgrims" and 50 other English voyagers arrived at a place they named Plymouth, in a region soon called New England. Within a few decades, thousands of other English Puritans, seeking religious freedom, had joined them in forming a Massachusetts Bay Colony. Other English religious groups followed: Catholics created a Maryland colony in the 1630s, and Quakers founded Pennsylvania in the 1680s. By 1700 there was a string of English colonies along the Atlantic coast.

Disease and Demographic Decline

The coming of the Europeans brought disaster to the North American Amerinds. Like their Spanish rivals to the South, the French, Dutch, and English brought deadly diseases to which the Amerinds had no immunity. Europeans also brought agricultural techniques involving large farm animals, metal tools and plows, and crops that required the clearing of huge tracts of forest. With a concept of possession that let individuals claim land parcels as their property and exclude all others, they constantly expanded the amount of land under cultivation. Over time these practices, combined with growing numbers of European immigrants, destroyed the Amerinds' way of life.

📖•— Read the Document

*William Bradford, excerpt
from Of Plymouth
Plantation*

on **myhistorylab.com**

At Jamestown, for example, the colonists at first related well to the local Powhatan (*POW-uh-TAHN*) peoples, who provided the newcomers with corn, meat, and fish that helped the colony survive. But as more settlers arrived from England and the Powhatans were ravaged by European diseases, the relationship changed. The peoples clashed, the Amerinds attacked, and the English responded by seizing Powhatan lands. Then, rather than planting food, the colonists grew tobacco, which Amerinds had taught them how to cultivate, and shipped it for sale to England, where smoking became the rage. Within decades the whole region was covered by tobacco plantations, and surviving Amerinds were forced off their lands.

At Plymouth the colony initially survived with the aid of Massasoit (*mass-uh-SŌ-it*), chief of the Wampanoag (*wahm-puh-NŌ-ug*) nation, who in 1621 agreed to help the Pilgrims if they would support his people in battles against tribal foes. Soon, however, clashes occurred between the disease-ravaged Amerinds and growing English communities, which rapidly claimed increasing amounts of land for farms and used firearms when necessary to enforce their claims. In 1675, desperate to save the Wampanoag way of life, Massasoit's son Metacom (*MEH-tuh-kahm*), whom the colonists called King Philip, attacked the Europeans. A brutal war followed, during which the English slaughtered thousands of Amerinds and sold the survivors into slavery. After Metacom was captured and beheaded in 1676, the Plymouth colonists displayed his head on a pole for 25 years. "King Philip's War" effectively ended Amerind resistance, leaving most of New England in European hands.

The English Captain John Smith is condemned by a Powhatan chief.

To the West, the Dutch and English settlers brought tragedy and triumph to the Iroquois Confederacy. On one hand, as elsewhere, the colonists brought disease, such as a smallpox epidemic that killed perhaps half the Iroquois population in the 1630s. On the other hand, the Dutch and English gave the Iroquois firearms to help them fight Hurons and French, enabling the Confederacy to carve out an empire extending from the Hudson River to the Great Lakes.

Similar events occurred elsewhere along the coast. Sometimes Europeans allied with Amerinds to fight common foes, and sometimes Europeans slaughtered Amerinds or drove them off their lands. Sometimes the Amerinds held off the Europeans for awhile, but in the long run their way of life collapsed in the face of European diseases, European weapons, and the spread of European settlement.

In contacts between Europeans and Amerinds, the Amerinds are at a disadvantage

The Columbian Exchange

The initial contact between European and American civilizations involved not only conflict and conquest but connection. Since the two hemispheres had been separated from each other since the submersion of the Bering land bridge more than ten thousand years earlier, many varieties of living things had developed in each hemisphere that were totally unknown in the other. The Eastern Hemisphere had wheat, grapes, horses, cows, sheep, goats, and pigs; the Western Hemisphere had potatoes, tomatoes, maize, cacao, and tobacco. When people from the two hemispheres encountered one another, their connections involved an interchange of crops and animals. In reference to Christopher Columbus, scholars call this process the Columbian Exchange.

Some exchanges of crops improved the quality of life in both hemispheres. The impact was immediately obvious in the Western Hemisphere. Before long wheat and grapes were being grown for the first time in the New World, to make the bread and wine that were central to the European diet and religion. Farm animals brought in by the Iberians provided transport, labor, and food, and they flourished in the Americas.

For the Eastern Hemisphere, corn (maize), potatoes, tomatoes, peanuts, and manioc (*MAN-ē-ok*)—a starchy root plant, now grown widely in Africa and Brazil, also called *cassava* or *tapioca*—proved hardy and rich in nutrients. Eventually becoming staples in Europe, Africa, and Asia, they later helped foster a global population explosion. Other American plants, like cacao (the basis for chocolate) and tobacco, were also sought by people around the world.

Microorganisms were also part of the Columbian Exchange. Syphilis, for example, a debilitating venereal disease that first showed up in southern Europe in the 1490s, was probably introduced by sailors who returned from the Western Hemisphere. But the exchange of diseases proved far more devastating for the Amerinds. Smallpox, measles, and chicken pox, to which most Europeans had been subjected as children and thus developed immunities, ran rampant through unprotected Amerind populations. About 30 percent of children and 90 percent of adults who came down with smallpox died. As a result, Amerind farming was interrupted, social structures shattered, villages depopulated, and entire regions abandoned. Smallpox weakened Aztec and Inca resistance to the Spaniards. Throughout the Spanish possessions in the Western Hemisphere, smallpox and measles ravaged Amerind communities off and on throughout the 16th century.

There are no reliable statistics on pre-1492 Amerind populations, but scholars estimate that the Americas contained between 15 million and 125 million people. In 1600, Spanish estimates indicated a population of one million Amerinds in the viceroyalty of New Spain (Mexico, Central America, and the Caribbean islands). It is clear that European diseases destroyed the overwhelming majority of the Amerind peoples in the greatest demographic catastrophe in history.

Watch the **Video**
The Columbian Exchange
on **myhistorylab.com**

The Columbian Exchange brings benefits as well as devastation

European diseases devastate Amerind societies

African women preparing manioc.

CHAPTER
REVIEW

Putting It in Perspective

Tremendous consequences flowed from the Iberian overseas expansion of the 15th century. Under different circumstances, China might have discovered a sea route around Africa, or Japanese mariners might have sailed east and found the Pacific coastline of North America. But it was the Europeans whose curiosity and seamanship broadened human geographic knowledge and extended the horizons of the entire world. When they found previously unknown lands, they conquered and exploited them, motivated by a combination of greed and religious faith.

The clash of civilizations in the New World changed forever societies previously isolated from outside influences. Amerind societies largely collapsed in the face of conquest and disease. In their place the Iberians imposed new governance systems, religious beliefs, and social structures. They created a new economy, based on the cultivation of cash crops by imported slave labor. Finally, they transplanted their whole way of life, bringing plants, animals, foods, and diseases common in Europe but hitherto unknown in the Americas.

The political and economic impacts were immense. The Spanish and Portuguese, and later the French, Dutch, and English, were set on a course to become world powers, surpassing the great Asian and Islamic empires. The Atlantic Ocean soon replaced the Indian Ocean and the Mediterranean Sea as the center of world commerce. Eventually, Europe led the world in power and prosperity, in large part due to its exploitation of Africa and the New World.

But the most direct Iberian legacy was the new culture created in the conquered lands. The Spanish and Portuguese empires ended in the early 1800s, but their legacy lives on today. Though modern Latin American societies remain intensely hierarchical, the peoples of these societies, displaying a broad variety of outlooks and customs, celebrate this cultural synthesis as their unique contribution to the human experience.

Reviewing Key Material

KEY CONCEPTS

Enterprise of the Indies, 421
Treaty of Tordesillas, 422
viceroy, 425
Council of the Indies, 429
mulatto, 432

residencia, 430
mestizos, 432
peninsulares, 433
criollos, 433

KEY PEOPLE

Prince Henry the
   Navigator, 419
João II, 420
Bartholomeu Días, 420
Christopher
   Columbus, 420
Isabella of Castile, 421
Luís de Santander, 421
Ferdinand of Aragon, 421
Pope Alexander VI, 422
Ferdinand Magellan, 423
Vasco da Gama, 424

Manoel I, 424
Pedro Alvares Cabral, 424
Amerigo Vespucci, 424
Afonso de Albuquerque, 425
João III, 430
John Cabot, 434
Samuel de Champlain, 435
Henry Hudson, 436
Massasoit, 436
Metacom, 436

ASK YOURSELF

1. Why did Portugal take the lead among European nations in promoting overseas expansion?
2. Why did the Iberian nations enslave Africans and transport them to their empires in the Western Hemisphere?
3. In what ways did the Spanish and Portuguese empires differ from each other? In what ways were they similar?
4. How did the conflicts between Iberian and American civilizations forge connections that changed them all?

GOING FURTHER

Boorstin, Daniel. *The Discoverers.* 1985.
Boxer, C. R. *The Portuguese Seaborne Empire.* 1971.
Burkholder, Mark, and Lyman Johnson. *Colonial Latin America.* 2000.
Burns, E. Bradford. *A History of Brazil.* 1998.
Callaway, Colin. *New Worlds for All: Indians, Europeans, and the Remaking of Early America.* 1997.
Crosby, Alfred. *The Columbian Exchange: Biological and Cultural Consequences of 1492.* 1972.

Diffie, W., and G. Winius. *Foundations of the Portuguese Empire, 1415–1580*. 1979.

Liss, Peggy. *Mexico Under Spain*. 1984.

Lockhart, James, and Stuart Schwartz. *Early Latin America*. 1982.

Parry, J. H. *The Discovery of South America*. 1979.

Pearson, M. *The Portuguese in India*. 1987.

Pescatello, Ann. *Power and Pawn: The Female in Iberian Families*. 1976.

Ramírez, Susan. *The World Upside Down: Cross-Cultural Contact and Conflict in Sixteenth-Century Peru*. 1996.

Russell-Wood, A. J. R. *The Portuguese Empire, 1415–1808*. 1998.

Scammell, Geoffrey. *The First Imperial Age: European Overseas Expansion, 1400–1700*. 1989.

Schaeffer, Dagmar. *Portuguese Exploration in the West and the Formation of Brazil, 1450–1800*. 1988.

Schnaubelt, Joseph, and Frederick van Fleteren. *Columbus and the New World*. 1998.

Smith, Roger. *Vanguard of Empire: Ships of Exploration in the Age of Columbus*. 1993.

Stern, Steve. *Peru's Indian Peoples and the Challenge of Spanish Conquest*. 1993.

Tracy, J. *The Rise of Merchant Empires: Long-Distance Trade in the Early Modern World, 1350–1750*. 1990.

Key Dates and Developments

1415	Portugal captures Ceuta from the Muslims		**1516**	Carlos I becomes king of Spain
1415–1460	Expeditions financed by Prince Henry the Navigator		**1519–1521**	The Cortés expedition overthrows the Aztec Empire
1489	Bartholomeu Días rounds the Cape of Good Hope		**1519–1522**	The Magellan expedition circumnavigates the globe
1492	Christopher Columbus reaches the Caribbean islands		**1524**	Establishment of the Council of the Indies
1494	Treaty of Tordesillas divides the world between Portugal and Spain		**1524–1532**	Pizarro's three expeditions to Peru
			1532	Capture of Atahuallpa at Cajamarca, Peru
1498	Vasco da Gama reaches India		**1549–1572**	The Jesuits arrive in the New World
1500	Pedro Alvares Cabral lands in Brazil			

PEARSON myhist**o**rylab Connections

Reinforce what you learned in this chapter by studying the many documents, images, maps, review tools, and videos available at www.myhistorylab.com.

Read and Review

✓●⎯Study and Review Chapter 19

▭●⎯Read the Document

Christopher Columbus "The Letters of Columbus to Ferdinand and Isabel," p. 422

Bartolemé de las Casas, from *Brief Account of the Devastation of the Indies*, p. 429

William Bradford, excerpt from *Of Plymouth Plantation*, p. 436

🔍⎯View the Map

Interactive Map: Spanish and Portuguese Exploration, 1400–1600, p. 419

Map Discovery: Civilizations in North America, p. 434

((●⎯Listen to the Audio

Exploitations, p. 436

👁⎯Watch the Video

Christopher Columbus and the Round World, p. 421

Research and Explore

👁⎯Watch the Video

The Columbian Exchange, p. 437

⎯⎯ ((●⎯Listen to the Chapter Audio for Chapter 19 on myhistorylab.com ⎯⎯

The West in an Age of Religious Conflict and Global Expansion, 1500–1650

(((•──Listen to the **Chapter Audio** for Chapter 20 on **myhistorylab.com**

Luther Confronts the Emperor.

In the 1500s, as Martin Luther and the Protestants defied the Holy Roman Emperor and Catholic Church, engulfing the West in an age of religious conflict, European officials, merchants, and missionaries—many of them serving the emperor and Church—were forging global connections. Here Luther is shown confronting the emperor in 1521 at the Diet of Worms.

- What were the main causes and effects of the Protestant Reformation?

- How did the Catholic Church respond to the Protestant challenge?

- What were the main results of Europe's religious and political strife?

- What factors led to the globalization of Western Christianity and commerce?

- How was Western society affected by religious and economic change?

On April 18, 1521, the Imperial Diet, an assembly of the Holy Roman Empire's leading princes and nobles, met in the German town of Worms (*VOHRMSS*). The previous day, the Diet had ordered a monk named Martin Luther to retract his writings, which defied the authority of the Roman Catholic Church. Now, in the emperor's presence, Luther delivered a bold reply that would echo throughout Europe for decades: "Unless I am convicted by . . . Scripture or by evident reason . . . I cannot and will not recant . . ."

Angered by this defiance, Holy Roman Emperor Charles V, then barely 21 years old, issued a stinging rebuke. A single monk must not be allowed to deny what Christianity had held for more than a thousand years. To defend the Catholic faith, Charles declared, he was prepared to use "all my possessions, my friends, my body, my blood, my life, and my soul." Thus were drawn the battle lines of religious conflict.

At first it was mainly a conflict among European Christians. Backed by Germans who feared imperial power and resented Church corruption, Luther defied both emperor and pope. His success led others to do likewise, creating new religions that fragmented Western Christendom.

Soon, however, the conflict was connected with worldwide developments. In 1521, as Charles vowed at Worms to defend the Catholic cause, his subjects were conquering distant lands such as Mexico and the Philippines, building a global Spanish empire. In ensuing decades, as officials and religious orders spread Catholicism throughout that empire, Charles and his heirs exploited its wealth to fight their European foes.

The result was a century of religious strife, accompanied by zealotry and witch hunts. But it was also accompanied by increased global trade, new kinds of commerce and production, expansion of learning and literacy, and changes in family life. While Europe was torn by religious and political strife, its monarchs, missionaries, and merchants were forging global connections.

European Colonies and Claims

The Christian West

The Protestant Reformation

In 1500 almost all Western Christians still belonged to the Catholic Church. Headed by the pope and run by a hierarchy of bishops and priests, it had long been a source of authority and unity in the West. But soon this authority and unity were shattered by religious revolts, collectively known as the Protestant Reformation.

Roots of the Reformation

Church corruption and political unrest help spark Reformation

The Reformation was rooted in two key concerns. One was corruption in the Roman Catholic Church, which most Europeans looked to for salvation. The other was political unrest in the Holy Roman Empire, an assortment of Central European states, loosely united by their recognition of its emperor as overlord (Map 20.1).

Renaissance Europe had sophisticated culture, but death and disease still surrounded its people, whose main concern was thus eternal salvation: When they died would their souls go to heaven or hell? Most believed that the Catholic Church held the keys to salvation, providing the rules and rituals needed to reach heaven. Chief among the rituals were **sacraments,** sacred rites believed to bestow the graces needed for salvation.

FOUNDATION MAP **20.1**   Europe in the 16th Century

Holy Roman Emperor Charles V (1519–1556) inherited the Habsburg possessions, including Spain, Austria, the Netherlands, much of Central Europe and Italy, and a growing Spanish-American empire. Why did the Protestant Reformation pose a threat to his power?

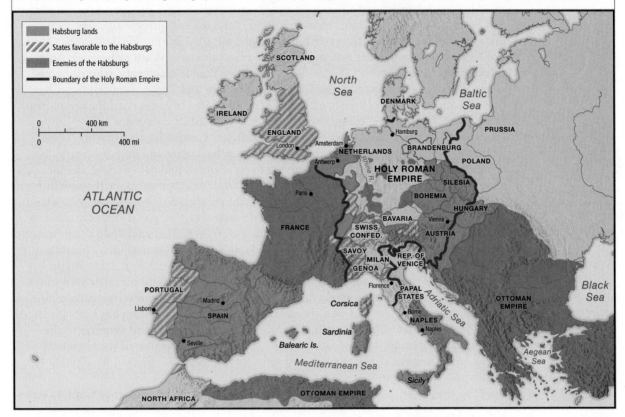

The main sacraments were baptism, the Eucharist, and penance. To make it to heaven, one first had to undergo baptism, the ritual use of water that brings membership in the Church. Then one had to lead a virtuous life, doing good works and avoiding serious sins. Those who committed such sins and died with them unforgiven were damned to eternity in hell. But through the Eucharist (or Communion), the consumption of consecrated bread and wine believed to be Christ's body and blood, Christians could gain grace to avoid sin. And through penance, the confession of one's sins with sincere repentance to a priest, Christians could have their sins forgiven.

After that, however, they still had to atone for their sins. If they died without doing so, the Church taught, they had to endure **purgatory**, a place of suffering that purified the soul so it could enter heaven. But people could also atone for sins while still alive. Through certain prayers and sacrifices—such as fasts, pilgrimages, and charitable works—they could earn an **indulgence**, a remission of the punishment still due for sins that had been forgiven through penance, to reduce or eliminate suffering in purgatory. As popes started granting indulgences for *financial* sacrifices, such as donations to the Church, it began to look as if people could purchase salvation.

This sale of indulgences was one of the abuses that added to Church wealth and corruption. Others included simony (*SIH-muh-nē*), the sale of Church offices and benefits, and pluralism, a practice by which some clerics held multiple church offices, thereby

Indulgence sales and other abuses increase Church corruption enhancing their incomes. Furthermore, while popes and bishops lived lavishly in sumptuous palaces, poorly educated parish priests were often neither sober nor chaste.

Over the years, several individuals had condemned such abuses. John Wyclif (*WICK-liff*) (1330–1384), theology professor at England's Oxford University, denounced the sale of indulgences and Church offices. Asserting that the Church must practice piety and poverty, he called on civil rulers to reform it and seize its possessions. He also declared that divine authority rested in the Bible, not the Church. His followers, called Lollards, were harshly suppressed, with some even burned to death as heretics. Another Church critic was John Hus (1369–1415), rector of Prague University, who promoted similar ideas in Bohemia (now the Czech Republic). In 1415 he was invited to a Church council with a promise of safe conduct but then convicted of heresy and burned to death at the stake. For the time being, the Church thus silenced its dissidents.

Scandalous Renaissance popes discredit papacy

Read the Document

Desiderius Erasmus, "Pope Julius Excluded from Heaven," 1513–1514

on **myhistorylab.com**

In time, however, Renaissance popes supplied new reasons for resentment. Pope Sixtus IV (1471–1484) sold Church offices to enrich his family and imposed heavy taxes on the Papal States. He also proclaimed that living people could gain indulgences for souls already in purgatory. Pope Alexander VI (1492–1503), who became pope through bribery, used Church wealth to indulge his illegitimate children, including a daughter with whom he was alleged to have had sexual relations and a son who used papal armies in a bid to create his own kingdom. The next pope, Julius II (1503–1513), a vain and violent man, led wars to enlarge the papal domains and sold indulgences to finance lavish projects—including the construction of a grandiose new church, Saint Peter's Basilica in Rome.

Meanwhile, political unrest in Central Europe, the Reformation's other root cause, spread among the German people. Irked by Italians, who saw themselves as culturally superior, many Germans resented the use of money collected in Germany, through indulgence sales and other Church payments, to fund the costly wars and ventures of the Renaissance popes. Devout Germans, such as those in the Brethren of the Common Life, a lay movement stressing piety and simplicity, were also dismayed by Church wealth and worldliness.

Sketch of Friar John Tetzel selling indulgences.

Furthermore, the heads of the numerous German states were anxious to protect their autonomy against the ambitions of the Holy Roman emperor. Austrian Archduke Maximilian of Habsburg, elected emperor in 1493, seemed intent on ending this autonomy by transforming the empire into a centralized monarchy. By arranging favorable marriages for himself and his son, he also assured that his grandson, the future Emperor Charles V (1519–1556), would inherit not only Austria, the Netherlands, Sicily, Sardinia, and much of Central Europe and Italy (Map 20.1), but also Spain (where he was King Carlos I) and its American empire. Alarmed, many German princes and nobles resolved to resist any further Habsburg ambitions.

The Lutheran Revolt

Into these troubled waters waded Martin Luther (1483–1546), a devout German monk obsessed with fears of death and eternal damnation. As a young man he planned to study law but, when caught in a severe storm, vowed to enter a monastery if God let him survive. He lived to join the Augustinian order and became an exemplary monk, repeatedly fasting, praying, and confessing his sins. But he still felt unworthy of salvation and feared he was doomed to hell. A 1510 trip to Pope Julius II's Rome only intensified his fears: how could a Church so worldly and corrupt help save his soul? In confronting this question, Luther plunged Western Christendom into turmoil.

At the University of Wittenberg (*VIT-in-bārg*), in the central German state of Saxony, Luther studied scripture and became a doctor of theology, finally developing a doctrine that eased his torment. No one, he concluded, is worthy of salvation. It is not something one can *earn* by doing good works. It is rather a *gift* from God, who freely bestows his saving grace on those who have faith in him. We do not gain grace by doing good, reasoned Luther; we do good because we have grace. We are "justified" not by our deeds but by God's grace, which we receive through faith.

The doctrine of "justification by faith alone," which Luther grounded on the writings of Saint Paul, implicitly threatened the Catholic Church. For if faith alone brought salvation, who needed sacraments and indulgences? Indeed, who needed the Church?

Trouble arose in 1517 when a friar named John Tetzel traveled through German lands selling indulgences to build the new Saint Peter's and pay the debts of a corrupt archbishop who had purchased his post. Assuring donors that coins put in his coffer would earn indulgences to free departed loved ones from purgatory, Tetzel allegedly used slogans like "As soon as the coin in the coffer rings, the soul from purgatory springs!" Appalled, on October 31 Luther responded by issuing **Ninety-Five Theses**, propositions challenging the Church's power to forgive sins and grant indulgences. Legend says he posted his theses on the Wittenberg Castle Church door.

The theses circulated widely, winning Luther broad support among Germans and religious reformers, while evoking Rome's anger. In a 1519 debate, he defended the views of John Hus and denounced the Church for Hus's execution. In 1520 Luther published an *Address to the Christian Nobility of the German Nation*, urging German nobles to cast off Rome's control and seize Church property, artfully appealing to both their German pride and their zest for wealth and power. The pope responded with a papal *bull* (edict) condemning Luther's views as heresy.

Luther burned the papal bull and continued his assault. God's truth was found, he said, not in Church teachings but only in the Bible, which people must read and interpret themselves. He denied all sacraments except baptism and Communion, finding no biblical basis for the rest. He renounced not just indulgences but also belief in purgatory, pilgrimages, fasts, papal authority, and even monastic life. Proclaiming a "priesthood of all believers," he rejected priestly celibacy and encouraged clergy to marry.

In truth, then, Luther was not just a reformer who attacked *abuses* the Church could correct, but a rebel who denounced *doctrines* the Church saw as inspired by God. Luther essentially denied the Church's authority and divine mission. And this no pope could accept.

Statue of Martin Luther in Wittenberg, Germany.

Luther asserts that faith alone, not the Church, brings salvation

[ ]•[Read the **Document**

Martin Luther, "Ninety-Five Theses" (Holy Roman Empire), 1517

on **myhistorylab.com**

Luther urges German nobles to reform the Church and seize its property

The Rising Tide of Rebellion

In 1521, alarmed at the danger Luther posed to both Church and empire, Holy Roman Emperor Charles V summoned Luther to face the Imperial Diet. Ordered to repudiate his views, the religious rebel held firm (see "Excerpts from Luther's Reply at Worms"). Then, denounced by the emperor as a heretic, he was secretly taken to the castle of Saxony's ruler, Frederick the Wise, a German prince dismayed by Church corruption

DOCUMENT 20.1 Excerpts from Luther's Reply at Worms

In 1521, when asked at the Diet of Worms to retract his writings, Luther responded with a bold refusal, excerpted below. How did his writings and teachings pose a threat to the Catholic Church? How did he justify his refusal to retract them?

. . . I humbly pray your Imperial Majesty and lords, to consider carefully that my books are not all of the same kind. There are some in which I dealt with faith and life in such an evangelical and simple manner that even my opponents must admit that they are useful . . .

The second group of books is written against the papacy and papal scheming and action, that is against those who through evil teaching and example have ruined Christendom laying it waste with the evils of the spirit and the soul. No one can deny or obscure this fact, since experience and complaint of all men testify that the conscience of Christian believers is sneered at, harassed and tormented by the laws of the Pope and the doctrines of men. Likewise the goods and wealth of this most famous German nation were and are devoured through unbelievable tyranny . . . Were I, therefore, to revoke these books I would only strengthen this tyranny . . .

Since your Imperial Majesty and Lordships demand a simple answer I will do so . . . as follows: Unless I am convicted by the testimony of Scripture or by evident reason—for I trust neither in popes nor in councils alone, since it is obvious that they have often erred and contradicted themselves . . . my conscience is captive by the Word of God. Therefore I cannot and will not recant, since it is . . . dangerous indeed to do anything against one's conscience. God help me. Amen.

SOURCE: The California Institute for Ancient Studies – Reformation History. Luther's Appearance at the Diet of Worms. http://www.specialityinterests.net/lutherwords.html

---

and the emperor's growing power. There Luther hid for a year and began translating the Bible into German.

The printing press and German nobles help spread Luther's ideas

Aided by the new printing press, developed by German inventor Gutenberg in the 1400s (Chapter 16), and by German nobles eager to expand their wealth and power at Church expense, Luther's ideas spread quickly. Central Europe was soon divided between Lutherans, who adopted these new ideas, and Catholics, who stayed loyal to emperor and pope.

The situation soon grew more complex. By denying Church authority and urging people to interpret the Bible on their own, Luther freed others to dissent, fragmenting Christendom into additional sects. In 1522, a dissident priest named Huldrych Zwingli (*TSVING-le*) began his own movement in Switzerland. More extreme than Luther, he rejected anything not literally in the Bible, including the belief that Christ is present in Communion bread and wine. Soon zealots called *Anabaptists* (or Rebaptizers), who baptized adults (rather than infants) as a sign of conscious faith commitment, split with Zwingli and started communities throughout Central Europe. Believing that the Church should be separate from the state, they opposed war, refused to take oaths, and suffered persecution as radical nonconformists.

Other religious rebels backed radical social reforms, inspiring a violent Peasants' Revolt against German nobles in 1524–1525. Zwingli supported it, but Luther did not. Reliant on noble support, and anxious to keep his religious movement from becoming a social rebellion, Luther urged authorities to "smash, strangle, and stab" the rebels, who were killed by the thousands.

Diverted by other conflicts, emperor and pope cannot stop "Protestants"

Meanwhile, neither emperor nor popes could stem the Lutheran tide. The emperor was resisted by an alliance of German Lutheran princes, called "Protestants" after 1529, when they formally protested his efforts to curb their religion. He was also diverted by wars against the Ottoman Turks, who conquered much of Hungary in 1526 and besieged Vienna in 1529 (Chapter 17), and even the Catholic French, who so greatly feared his power that they sided against him with Protestant German princes and Islamic Turks. Several successive popes rejected calls for a Church council to confront the issues, fearing it might also reduce papal powers. And a growing conflict with England's king further impeded the papacy.

Henry VIII and the English Reformation

England's Reformation, unlike Luther's, was rooted in royal affairs, not doctrinal disputes. Luther's ideas did attract interest there, but English humanist Thomas More, though critical of Church corruption, condemned the Lutheran creed. And King Henry VIII (1509–1547) was a staunch Catholic who in 1521 issued a *Defense of the Seven Sacraments*, for which the pope proclaimed him "Defender of the Faith." England seemed safely in the Roman Catholic fold.

Anne Boleyn.

But things began to change in 1527, when Henry aspired to end his marriage to Catherine of Aragon, a Spanish princess by birth. She had borne him six children, but only one, their daughter Mary, survived. As he and his wife got older, Henry feared he would have no male heir, leaving the realm in crisis after he died. Besides, he was in love with youthful Anne Boleyn (*boo-LIHN*), one of his wife's attendants.

The Church did not permit divorce, but it could grant an annulment, a ruling that the marriage was never valid. Since Catherine had first wed Henry's older brother and then, when he died, had married Henry, and since the Bible said a man who took his brother's wife would die childless (Leviticus 20:21), Henry saw his lack of a son as a sign that God disapproved of his marriage to Catherine. He thus asked Rome to annul it.

The request put Pope Clement VII (1523–1534) in a difficult bind. He did not want to anger Henry and risk losing England from the Church. But Catherine was the aunt of Emperor Charles V, whose soldiers occupied Rome, and whose help the Church needed against Luther and the Turks. And Charles opposed the annulment: Catherine's marriage was his family's link to England, which he hoped to strengthen by wedding his son Philip to Henry's daughter Mary, who would one day be queen if there were no male heir. Besides, since a prior pope (Julius II) had permitted Henry to wed his brother's widow, an annulment would admit that popes erred, as Lutherans asserted. So Clement delayed his decision.

As Henry's case moved slowly through the papal courts, he grew increasingly impatient. By 1533, his mistress Anne was pregnant, so Henry could wait no longer. To legitimize his expected heir, he married Anne and got the Archbishop of Canterbury (England's highest cleric), a Lutheran sympathizer named Thomas Cranmer, to annul Henry's marriage to Catherine without waiting for Rome. Anne was crowned queen, and a few months later gave birth—not to the desired son, but to a girl who was named Elizabeth.

Having acted on his own, in defiance of the pope, in 1534 Henry persuaded Parliament to pass an Act of Supremacy, naming him "supreme head of the Church of England" and formally breaking with Rome. Then, over the next five years, he closed the English monasteries and seized their property, selling much of it to local nobles. Henry thus ensured their support, since to keep their new lands the nobles would have

The English ruler becomes head of the "Church of England"

to back him against the pope. But he also disbanded distinguished institutions that had been centers of learning and charity for centuries.

Henry also tarnished his legacy in other ways. In 1535, humanist Thomas More was beheaded for refusing to support the Act of Supremacy. In 1536, Anne Boleyn, having failed to produce a son, was accused of adultery and likewise beheaded. A third wife finally bore Henry a boy but perished while giving birth. The king went on to wed three more times before dying in 1547.

Despite his break with the Roman Church, however, Henry VIII was no religious rebel. He stayed true to most Catholic teachings and resisted Protestant practices promoted by Luther and others. Only after Henry's death did the Church of England adopt serious doctrinal changes.

Calvin and the Elect

Meanwhile, a new religious rebel widened the Reformation. John Calvin (1509–1564), raised in France and trained as a lawyer and theologian, was initially attracted by Lutheran ideas. But in 1533 he reportedly had a conversion that crystallized his views in a flash of light. He concluded that faith, for Luther the key to salvation, was a gift God gave only certain people, and that the Roman Church was an evil institution that should not be reformed but destroyed.

After fleeing to Switzerland to escape a crackdown on Protestants by French authorities, in 1536 Calvin published the *Institutes of the Christian Religion*, soon the central work of Protestant theology. That same year he settled in Geneva, which under his influence soon became the center of the Protestant world.

Calvin preached **predestination**, the notion that God long ago decided each person's eternal fate. Some are destined for heaven and others for hell, no matter what they do. Earlier Church thinkers had promoted predestination but had not gone as far as Calvin in dismissing free will and personal choice. Like Luther, Calvin felt no one could earn salvation, but unlike Luther he believed God saved only **the elect**—those God had chosen beforehand for salvation.

Although God alone knew who the elect were, Calvin's followers felt people like themselves, who led lives of faith and virtue, were among the elect. But for them faith and virtue were *results* of their salvation, not causes. Unlike Catholics, who led good lives in order to gain salvation, Calvinists did so as a sign that they were already saved. For Catholics salvation came *after* one's life and was based on how one had lived; for Calvinists salvation came *before* one's life and determined how one would live.

Calvinists were **puritanical**, promoting a strict moral code and "pure" religious practices. They held simple worship services, centered on sermons and Bible readings rather than elaborate rituals, in unadorned buildings rather than grandiose churches. Calvinists abhorred the ornate altars, vessels, statues, and stained-glass windows that adorned Catholic churches.

The Calvinist model Christian community was Geneva, widely seen as the Protestant answer to Rome. Reformers came from all over Europe to experience Geneva's religious life and learn from Calvin himself. A religious commission, under Calvin's influence, supervised moral behavior, prohibiting offenses such as gambling, dancing, and drinking. Graver crimes, such as blasphemy, adultery, and witchcraft, were punished by secular leaders, who sometimes used torture and executions. Geneva thus was a sober and austere community.

Calvin settles in Geneva, which becomes key Protestant center

Read the **Document**

Calvin on Predestination (16th Century)

on **myhistorylab.com**

Calvin's Geneva becomes model of Protestant Christian community

Read the **Document**

John Calvin, "Ecclesiastical Ordinances" (Geneva, Switzerland), 1533

on **myhistorylab.com**

John Calvin.

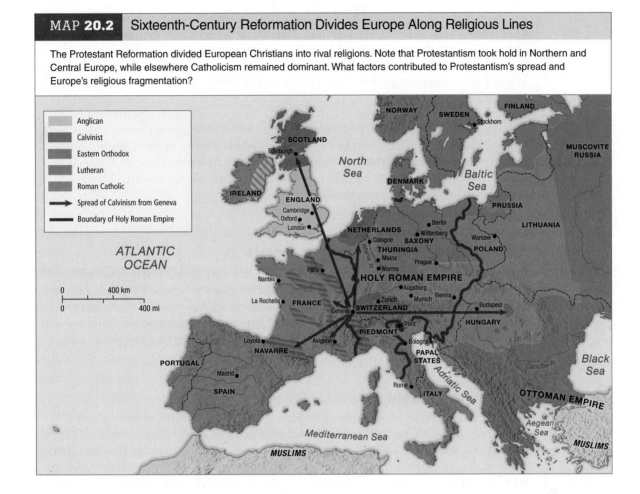

MAP 20.2   Sixteenth-Century Reformation Divides Europe Along Religious Lines

The Protestant Reformation divided European Christians into rival religions. Note that Protestantism took hold in Northern and Central Europe, while elsewhere Catholicism remained dominant. What factors contributed to Protestantism's spread and Europe's religious fragmentation?

The Spread of Protestantism

Geneva sent disciples far and near to spread Calvinist beliefs, which took hold in parts of Northern and Central Europe, while Lutheranism spread from Germany to Scandinavia, and the Church of England embraced many Protestant beliefs (Map 20.2).

John Knox, one of Calvin's followers, took the faith from Geneva home to Scotland, where it later became Presbyterianism. Calvinist communities also emerged in Bohemia, Hungary, and Poland; in the Netherlands, where they constituted the Dutch Reformed Church; in France, where they were called Huguenots (*HYOO-guh-notz*); and in England, where they were known as Puritans. Calvinist churches were largely independent of each other: rejecting the authoritarianism of popes and bishops, they formed no centralized international institution like the Catholic Church.

> Lutherans and Calvinists form smaller churches, not a large centralized church

Nor did the Lutherans develop one centralized church; instead, they relied on secular rulers to adopt the new faith for their domains. Many rulers did so, not only because they liked Luther's ideas but also as a way to confiscate Catholic Church property and control religion in their realms. Aided by such rulers, Lutheranism spread across northern Germany and Scandinavia, becoming the main faith of the Baltic region.

The Church of England, too, was controlled by the rulers, who after Henry VIII's death began making it more Protestant. Under Henry's sickly son Edward VI (1547–1553), Archbishop Cranmer brought in Protestant theologians, simplified liturgies, allowed priests to marry, and imposed his own *Book of Common Prayer* for church services. Queen Mary (1553–1558), the Catholic offspring of Henry's first marriage, tried to restore full Catholicism, executing Cranmer and several hundred Protestants. But her efforts were undone by Queen Elizabeth I (1558–1603), the Protestant daughter of Henry's second marriage. Determined to secure her throne by avoiding religious strife, Elizabeth pursued a middle path intended to satisfy most subjects. The English (or Anglican) Church thus combined Catholic-style liturgies and rituals, performed by bishops and priests, with the Protestant theology introduced under Cranmer.

By the 1560s Protestantism had spread throughout Northern and Central Europe and into parts of France and Eastern Europe (Map 20.2). But by then, the Catholic Church, still prevailing in the south, had launched a vigorous counterattack and extended its connections far beyond Europe.

The Catholic Counterreformation

In the 1540s, after failing for years to stop the Protestants, Rome finally mounted an effective response. Pope Paul III (1534–1549) called a general council to initiate Church reforms, authorized tribunals to prosecute Protestants for heresy, and approved new religious orders that reinvigorated the Roman Church. He thus began the Catholic Reformation, also called the Counterreformation, since it involved a counterattack against Protestants.

The Council of Trent

Council of Trent reaffirms Catholic teachings and sacraments

In 1545, after years of pressure from Emperor Charles V, Paul III convened a great council of Catholic Church leaders. The Council of Trent, which met in 1545–1547, 1551–1552, and 1562–1563, shaped Catholic doctrine and worship for four hundred years. Although Charles V wanted it to compromise with Lutherans, and some bishops wanted it to limit papal power, the council went the other direction. It affirmed many things that Protestants denied, including indulgences, papal supremacy, priestly celibacy, the Latin Mass, and the Church's power to forgive sins. It insisted that salvation required *both* faith *and* good works, not faith alone. It declared that divine revelation came from *both* Bible *and* Church tradition, not Bible alone. It reasserted Church teaching that there were seven sacraments, not just the two (baptism and Communion) that Luther recognized. And to reinforce Church unity, the council reaffirmed the pope's preeminence.

Read the Document

The Council of Trent, 1545–1563

on **myhistorylab.com**

The Council of Trent also enacted reforms. Although it affirmed indulgences for pious deeds and prayers, the council forbade their *sale*, the practice that had triggered Luther's revolt. To eliminate pluralism, the council allowed each bishop only one diocese in which he must reside. To improve the education of clergy, which Luther had derided as deficient, it ruled that each diocese must have a *seminary*, a training school for priests. These reforms did not win back the Protestants, but that was not their intent. They were designed to purify and strengthen Catholicism for battle against Protestantism, which lasted far longer than anyone at Trent could foresee.

The Roman and Spanish Inquisitions

The Counterreformation's tactics were sometimes extreme. In central Italy and Spain, where Catholics were in control, they employed Inquisitions, Church tribunals to investigate, arrest, and prosecute people suspected of heretical beliefs. In Rome the Inquisition operated under the Holy Office, a council of six cardinals formed in 1542 by Pope Paul III. It fined, imprisoned, and sometimes executed people it convicted of false teachings. Starting in 1559, it also published an *Index of Forbidden Books*, works Catholics were forbidden to read without special permission. Officially designed to protect the faithful from heresy, the *Index* in time banned numerous works, including even novels such as *Les Miserables* and *The Hunchback of Notre Dame* (Chapter 27), perceived as offensive by the Church.

The Spanish Inquisition, which functioned under Spain's rulers, had been set up in 1478 to investigate Jews and Muslims who had outwardly converted to Catholicism. Now it also targeted people suspected of Protestant views. To extract confessions, inquisitors sometimes used tortures such as the rack, which stretched the victim's body, and the thumbscrew, which crushed the victim's thumbs. Those found guilty of heresy were often burned to death.

Spanish Inquisition persecutes Muslims, Jews, and Protestants

Using closed trials, secret informers, tortures, and executions, the Inquisitions enforced Catholicism and virtually eradicated Protestantism in Italy and Spain. But elsewhere their main effect was to increase anti-Catholic hostility among Protestants, who sometimes employed similar methods against their religious foes.

New Religious Orders

Amid this tumult, Catholicism had a spiritual revival, led by dynamic individuals and new religious orders. Even before the Reformation, the Brethren of the Common Life, an association of laypersons and clergy who led simple lives imitating Christ, had spread through Northern Europe. In Italy a similar group, the Oratory of Divine Love, stressed works of charity and devotion as antidotes to worldly corruption. In the 1530s an Italian woman, Angela Merici (*muh-RĒ-chē*) founded the Ursuline (*UR-suh-lĭn*) order, a community of nuns who educated Catholic girls in Italy, France, and the Americas. But the most influential new order was begun by a Spanish nobleman.

Ignatius Loyola (1491–1556), an heir to Spain's crusading tradition, was a soldier until 1521, when he was crippled in battle by a cannonball. During a long, painful recovery, he read books about Christ and Christian saints and then embarked on a spiritual crusade. He withdrew to a cave, where he prayed and lived in great austerity. There he developed the Spiritual Exercises, a four-week regimen of prayer and meditation designed to prepare one for selfless discipline in service to God and Church.

After a trip to the Holy Land and brushes with the Spanish Inquisition, Ignatius enrolled at the University of Paris, where he attracted a group of like-minded men. In 1537 they formed a "Company of Jesus," and in 1540 Pope Paul III formally approved them as the Society of Jesus.

Soon known as the Jesuits, they became Catholicism's most zealous champions. Highly selective, they accepted only men of talent and discipline. Organized on military lines, they vowed strict obedience to their superiors and the pope. Refusing to withdraw and live as monks or beggars, they served in the world as educators, missionaries, preachers, and political advisors.

Ignatius of Loyola.

As educators, Jesuits combined Renaissance humanism (Chapter 16) with Catholic ideals, promoting both secular learning and religious faith, while creating a global network of schools and universities. As missionaries, they worked tirelessly to convert Amerinds, Africans, and Asians to Catholicism, helping to transform that European faith into a worldwide religion. As preachers to European Christians and advisors to Catholic rulers, they led an intensive anti-Protestant campaign, helping to stem the Protestant tide

Jesuits work to globalize and strengthen Catholicism

Watch the **Video**
The Global Mission of the Jesuits
on **myhistorylab.com**

and even restoring parts of Central Europe to the Catholic fold. Known for both eloquence and political intrigue, they made many enemies, adding to Europe's religious and political strife.

Religious and Political Strife in Europe

The Reformation sparked a century of religious and political conflict. Bolstered by the riches of their Spanish overseas empire, the Catholic Habsburgs strove to impose their power and faith by force on Protestant regions. But the Protestants mounted an effective defense, perpetuating the fragmentation of Western Christianity.

The Spanish Catholic Crusade

In 1556 Emperor Charles V, longtime Catholic champion and ruler of the Habsburg realms, retired to a monastery. Deeming his domains too vast for one ruler, he split them between his brother and his son. His brother Ferdinand received the Habsburg lands in Austria, Bohemia, and Hungary, and succeeded Charles as Holy Roman emperor. His son Philip got the rest, including Spain and its American empire, the Netherlands, Sardinia, Sicily, and parts of Italy. As King Philip II, he ruled these lands from 1556 to 1598.

> The wealth of its American empire makes Spain a global power

By this time Spain was Europe's mightiest country, owing largely to its American empire. The conquest of the Aztecs and Inca, with their enormous riches (Chapter 18), was followed in 1545 by discovery of vast silver deposits near Potosí (*pō-tō-SE*) in what is now Bolivia. These immense resources, exploited by Spaniards using Amerind and African slaves, soon supplied Spain with tremendous wealth, which Philip used to further the Catholic cause.

A zealous Catholic, he launched a crusade to reinforce his religion in his realms and restore to his Church the lands it had lost. In Spain, he used the Inquisition to suppress Protestantism. In America, missionaries fostered his faith and his officials enforced it, so successfully that Spanish America became a Catholic stronghold. In the Mediterranean he joined forces with Venice and the pope to defeat the Turkish fleet at the Battle of Lepanto (near Greece) in 1571. Elsewhere, however, Philip ran into problems.

Philip's first setback came in England, which he hoped to restore to Catholicism with the help of its Catholic Queen Mary (1553–1558), who was also his wife. But in 1558 she died in a cholera epidemic, and her Protestant successor Elizabeth, spurning his marriage proposals, became a formidable foe.

> English and Dutch combat Spain's anti-Protestant campaign

His next setback was the Dutch Revolt, a rebellion in the Netherlands against his rule. In 1566, alarmed that he might impose the Inquisition there, Dutch Calvinists rebelled, attacking Catholic churches and smashing sacred vessels, statues, stained-glass windows, and artwork. Enraged by this "Calvinist fury," Philip tried to reassert control by executing rebels and confiscating lands of Calvinist nobles. By 1579 he subdued the Netherlands' southern Catholic provinces, soon called the Spanish Netherlands (now Belgium). But the northern Protestant provinces then declared independence as the United Provinces of the Netherlands. This new nation, often called Holland (after its main province), fought Spain for three more decades.

View the **Map**
Map Discovery: The Netherlands During the Dutch Revolt, ca. 1580
on **myhistorylab.com**

In 1585, fearing Spain might prevail and then use the Netherlands as a base to attack her country, England's Queen Elizabeth sent money and troops to aid the Dutch. Philip, in turn, prepared to invade England. Tension increased in 1587, when Elizabeth approved the execution of her cousin Mary Stuart (Mary Queen of Scots), the Catholic claimant to the English throne. The next year Philip dispatched the "Invincible Catholic

Armada," a fleet of 130 huge ships, to land in the Netherlands and take the Spanish army to England.

Its ships emblazoned with crosses and Catholic banners, the Armada set sail in May 1588. In July it met the English fleet in the English Channel. England's smaller and faster ships harassed the Armada's huge vessels and kept them from landing. A fierce gale, which the English dubbed the "Protestant Wind," blew the Spanish off course, and further storms did even more damage as the Armada's remnants, trying to return to Spain, sailed around Scotland and Ireland.

The Spanish Armada's defeat did not end the fighting, which continued until 1604. But it did help the English and Dutch to foil Philip's Catholic crusade, to continue their Protestant course, to challenge Spain for control of the seas, and to found their own American colonies.

English ships confront Spanish Armada.

The Wars of Religion in France

From 1562 to 1594, as Catholic Spain battled Dutch and English Protestants, France was torn by internal conflicts called the Wars of Religion. Although France remained mostly Catholic, about 7 percent of its people—and 40 percent of its nobles—were Calvinists. Known as Huguenots and led by the Bourbon family, they fought Catholic factions in a complex struggle for religious and political power. Catherine de Medicis (*MED-ih-chē*), the influential mother of three Catholic kings who reigned from 1559 to 1589, tried to preserve her family's power by reconciling hostile factions. In 1572, however, fearful of growing Protestant strength, she helped plot the massacre of several thousand Huguenots gathered in Paris for a wedding. But even this atrocity could not save Catherine's clan. In 1589, following her death and the murder of her last royal son, the head of the Huguenot Bourbons inherited the throne as King Henri IV.

French Catholics, however, refusing to accept a Protestant king, blocked Henri's efforts to enter Paris and assume the throne. So Henri, pragmatically concluding that "Paris is worth a Mass," formally became a Catholic in 1593, thereby gaining acceptance in Paris as king in 1594. Seemingly betrayed by their champion, the Huguenots resisted Henri's rule until 1598, when he won them over with religious toleration, issuing the Edict of Nantes (*NAHNT*). This historic document gave French Protestants full civil rights, the freedom to hold worship services in their own manors and towns, and the right to fortify these towns with their own troops. It also helped to make Henri IV one of France's most popular kings. But Henri's tolerant edict did not please everyone: in 1610 he was murdered by a fanatical Catholic. Religious animosities did not die easily in France.

Calvinist King Henri IV becomes Catholic and enforces toleration

Read the Document

The Edict of Nantes, 1598

on **myhistorylab.com**

The Thirty Years War

Nor did they die easily in Germany, where Lutherans and Catholics for decades had observed an uneasy truce. In 1608, the Calvinists, prevalent in parts of the Holy Roman Empire, joined with Lutherans in an alliance called the Protestant Union. The next year, the Austrian Habsburgs, backed by their Spanish cousins' wealth, created a rival coalition called the Catholic League, setting the stage for a calamitous conflict known as the Thirty Years War (1618–1648).

It began in 1618 with the "Defenestration of Prague" (*dē-FEN-ih-STRĀ -shun*: throwing someone out a window). Protestant nobles in Bohemia, irked by Habsburg efforts to restrict their rights, threw two imperial agents out of a high palace window. Despite their survival—credited by Catholics to divine intervention and by Protestants

Catholic Habsburg rulers battle Central Europe's Protestant nobles

to the fact that they landed in a dung heap—the fragile peace was shattered. Emperor Ferdinand II (1619–1637), aided by the Catholic League and his Spanish relatives, crushed the Bohemians and other Protestant forces, moving steadily to bring all Germany under Catholic control. By 1629 the Protestant cause seemed lost.

Then, however, two powerful outside forces intervened on the Protestant side. One was Gustavus Adolphus (*gus-TAH-vus ah-DOLL-fus*), Sweden's Lutheran king, who feared for his realm should northern Germany come under Catholic rule. A gifted warrior, he defeated the Habsburgs in several key battles before dying in combat in 1632. The other force was Cardinal Richelieu (*RISH-lih-YOO*), France's chief minister, who first supplied aid to the Protestants and then had France join the war on their side in 1635.

As a cardinal in the Catholic Church, Richelieu seemed an unlikely supporter of Protestants. But his main loyalty was to France, which already faced Habsburg Spain to its south and the Spanish Netherlands to its north. Bent on blocking Habsburg unification of Germany to the east, he aided Protestants as a way to keep Germany divided and weak.

The war's last phase, from 1635 to 1648, was disastrous. France and Spain, both involved in the German conflict, battled each other as well. As warring armies crisscrossed Central Europe, disease and famine stalked the land. The German population was devastated, and wolves roamed the streets in desolate towns and villages.

Although France and Spain fought on until 1659, the German nightmare ended in 1648 with the Peace of Westphalia (Map 20.3). Each German state remained autonomous,

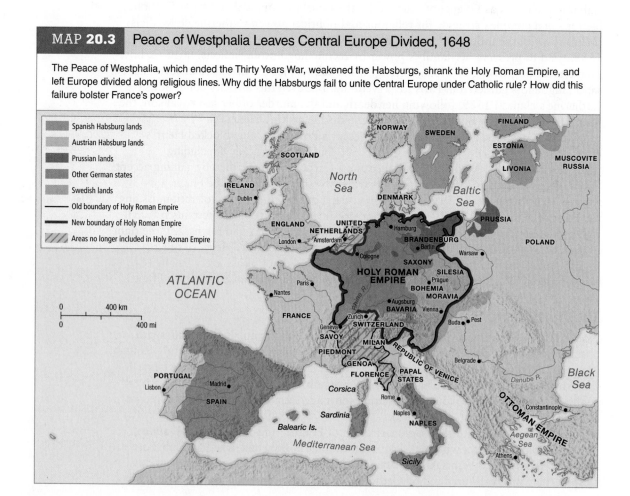

MAP 20.3 Peace of Westphalia Leaves Central Europe Divided, 1648

The Peace of Westphalia, which ended the Thirty Years War, weakened the Habsburgs, shrank the Holy Roman Empire, and left Europe divided along religious lines. Why did the Habsburgs fail to unite Central Europe under Catholic rule? How did this failure bolster France's power?

Spanish Habsburg lands
Austrian Habsburg lands
Prussian lands
Other German states
Swedish lands
—— Old boundary of Holy Roman Empire
—— New boundary of Holy Roman Empire
//// Areas no longer included in Holy Roman Empire

with rulers free to run their own affairs and decide if their realms should be Catholic, Lutheran, or Calvinist. The Holy Roman Empire retained only nominal authority and lost its Dutch, Swiss, and Italian states. The Habsburgs remained emperors, but their efforts to unify Germany and make it fully Catholic had failed. Europe remained divided along religious lines.

The Globalization of Western Christianity and Commerce

Europe's fragmentation was, paradoxically, accompanied by global expansion. In the 16th and 17th centuries, as Europe was torn by religious and political strife, European Christianity and commerce were spread across the globe by officials, missionaries, and merchants.

Catholicism's Global Expansion

Catholic empire builders and religious orders took the lead. The Spanish and Portuguese, who justified imperial expansion by claiming to carry Christianity to distant lands, systematically imposed their faith on those they conquered (Chapter 19). In their American colonies, where Iberian Catholics controlled governance and commerce, and where Catholic priests and nuns ran missions and schools, most people became Catholics through coercion, convenience, or conviction.

Jesuits, joined and often rivaled by other Catholic orders, also strove to implant Catholicism in Asia. In the 1540s Francis Xavier (*ZĀ-vē-ur*), one of the first Jesuits, worked among India's poor pearl fishers and founded missions in Malaya and the Spice Islands. From 1549 to 1551, he lived in Japan, whose culture he greatly admired, and converted thousands to his faith. In 1552 he set out to proselytize China but died on an island off its coast.

Xavier's deep respect for Asians, and tireless efforts to learn their languages and cultures, set an example for Jesuits who followed in his footsteps. They learned local languages, adapted local customs, and blended Catholic teachings into local cultures, rather than seeking to impose European ways. Their success in Asia was limited by resistance from Asian religions and rulers, and by Asian and Muslim perceptions of Westerners as culturally inferior. Still, spread by Jesuits and others, Catholicism became a global faith, with missions, parishes, schools, and followers around the world (Map 20.4).

Jesuits and other orders work to convert Asians to Catholicism

Read the **Document**

Jesuit in India (1530s–1550s), St. Francis Xavier

on **myhistorylab.com**

Jesuits gain some success by adapting to Asian cultures

Merchant Capitalism and Global Trade

As some Europeans globalized their faith, others transformed and globalized the economy. Western merchants, eager to enhance their incomes, worked to gain control over goods production and create global trading networks. European governments, seeking to increase state wealth, encouraged overseas commerce and exploitation of colonies.

For centuries merchants East and West had conducted interregional trade, engaging in practices—such as credit, banking, and marketing goods—later associated with **capitalism**, an economic system based on competition among private enterprises. But merchants usually did not manufacture the goods they sold. Goods were typically produced by artisans, who owned their tools and workshops, purchased raw materials such as metals, leather, wool, wood, and wax, and used their labor and skill to make them into finished products. The artisans then sold the goods to customers or merchants,

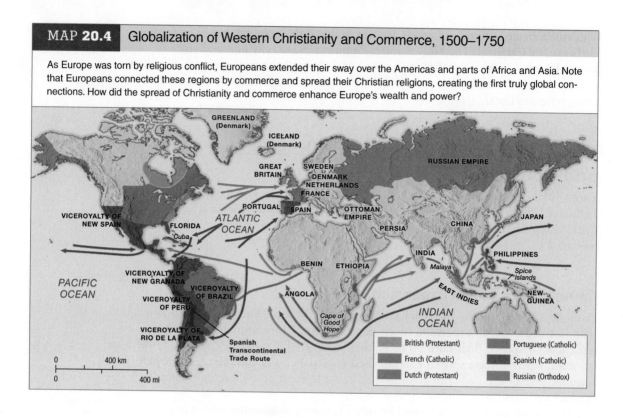

MAP 20.4   Globalization of Western Christianity and Commerce, 1500–1750

As Europe was torn by religious conflict, Europeans extended their sway over the Americas and parts of Africa and Asia. Note that Europeans connected these regions by commerce and spread their Christian religions, creating the first truly global connections. How did the spread of Christianity and commerce enhance Europe's wealth and power?

often at prices fixed by artisans' guilds. Merchants were mostly middlemen: traders who bought goods in one place, took them elsewhere, and sold them at a profit.

From the 15th century onward, however, European merchants increasingly sought to enhance their profits by gaining control of production. They bought mines, woodlands, and herds of sheep and cattle, acquiring their own raw materials. They also bought tools and equipment and hired their own workers, reducing their dependence on artisans and guilds, many of whom in turn organized their own enterprises. Thus arose a dynamic new class of capitalists: entrepreneurs who created and ran enterprises that both made and sold goods.

European capitalists increasingly control both production and commerce

In this system, later called merchant capitalism, the merchant entrepreneur owned the means of production—tools, machines, and raw materials—and decided how much to produce and to charge for finished goods. The producer worked for the merchant and was paid a fixed wage or a prearranged price for each piece made. Finished products were thus owned by the entrepreneur, who arranged their transport and sale, setting prices to compete in a free market based on supply and demand. Over time, independent artisans were largely replaced by wage laborers, employed and paid by merchant capitalists.

In expanding production and trade, merchant capitalists often found allies in their national monarchs. Rulers increasingly realized that, as commerce grew, so did their tax and tariff revenues, which they could use to hire armies and officials to expand their power. Rulers hence instituted policies, later known as **mercantilism**, that aimed to create a favorable balance of trade—one in which a country's exports exceeded its imports in value. Since the nation as a whole would thus sell more than it bought, fortune supposedly would flow into the realm, and into its royal treasury.

Mercantilist policies therefore included government support of overseas trade. In the 1400s and 1500s, Portuguese voyagers backed by the government set up trading posts on African and Asian coasts, creating a commercial empire that made one of Europe's smallest kingdoms one of its richest (Chapter 19). In the 1600s, England, the Netherlands, and France supported overseas trade through **charter companies**, trading associations protected by royal monopoly. Since overseas trade involved risks and expenses beyond what one investor could bear, merchants in these countries pooled their resources to form a large company in which many owned shares. To support the company and protect it from competition, the country's ruler then issued a charter giving the company a monopoly of trade between that country and a specified region.

Especially notable were the English East India Company, which monopolized commerce between England and India starting in 1600, and the Dutch United East India Company, founded two years later, which dominated trade between the Netherlands and the East Indies. For the next two centuries, these companies and others, with large fleets of merchant vessels, ran profitable trading posts in many parts of the world, gaining riches for themselves and their rulers. Global trading networks supplied European consumers with products from distant lands, such as silks, spices, sugar, coffee, tea, and tobacco, while revenues from this trade helped European monarchs centralize their governments and increase their power.

English and Dutch East India Companies dominate East–West trade

View the **Map**

Map Discovery: Dutch Trade Routes, ca. 1650

on **myhistorylab.com**

Colonies, Commerce, and Religion

Overseas colonies also enhanced a country's commerce and power. The foremost example was Spain, which used silver from its American colonies to buy luxury goods in Asia for resale elsewhere, and to finance its powerful armies and navies, making it 16th-century Europe's richest and mightiest realm. Another example was Portugal, which gained wealth in that century through the sale of sugar, grown in Brazil and other colonies using African slaves.

Other Europeans, seeing these successes, imitated the Iberians by founding American colonies. The French set up trading posts in eastern Canada and the Mississippi Valley, bartering with Amerinds for animal furs that sold for fortunes in Europe. The Dutch did likewise in the Hudson Valley of what is now New York State. The English established a Virginia colony that prospered in time from tobacco, a crop Amerinds taught them to grow, which sold in Europe for big profits. The French, Dutch, and English also set up colonies on Caribbean islands that, like the Spanish West Indies and Portuguese Brazil, profited immensely from slave-grown sugar. By the late 1600s, bolstered by wealth from their commerce and colonies, England, France, and the Netherlands had replaced Spain and Portugal as Europe's dominant political and economic powers.

These developments also had religious implications. France, like Spain and Portugal, promoted Catholicism in its colonies, aided by Jesuits and other French priests who worked among French settlers and Amerinds. Dutch Calvinists established settlements in the Hudson Valley, while English Calvinists called Puritans, fleeing persecution in their homeland, moved in large numbers to what became New England starting in the 1620s. English Catholics colonized Maryland in succeeding decades, while Anglicans and other English Protestants formed new North American colonies. By the mid-1600s, like Europe itself, North America had a variety of Christian denominations (Map 20.4).

French Jesuit baptizing Amerind convert.

The French, Dutch, and English impose their religions in their colonies

Western Society in an Age of Religious and Economic Change

As Europeans spread their creeds and commerce to diverse lands and peoples, religious divisions and global expansion transformed Europe's society. Religious strife fostered suffering and fear, while global expansion fostered growing prosperity.

Warfare, Disease, and Witch Hunts

Religious upheaval brought hardship to many Europeans. Religious leaders and warriors, fueled by righteous fury, conducted wars and persecutions, claiming to be doing God's will. Bands of armed fighters, feeding on the chaos, roamed the countryside looting, pillaging, and raping. Dislocation and devastation followed in their footsteps.

War and global connections help produce syphilis pandemic

Adding to 16th-century anxieties was a pandemic of syphilis, a sexually transmitted disease whose victims suffered sores and rashes, and later often blindness, insanity, and death. Some experts think syphilis was a virulent form of an earlier European ailment; others think European sailors brought it from the Americas after contracting it from Amerinds. Either way, it spread fear in Europe, where it was called the great pox (as distinguished from smallpox) or the "French disease" (as often blamed on French soldiers).

Watch the **Video** *Hunting Witches* on **myhistorylab.com**

Even more unsettling were the witch hunts of the 16th and 17th centuries. At least a hundred thousand people, mostly women, were put on trial for witchcraft, supposedly for using supernatural powers to make evil things happen. Perhaps fifty thousand were executed for this alleged crime.

Dissent, devastation, disease, and disasters help to promote witch hunts

Various factors fueled the witch hunts. One was the Reformation, which led Catholics and Protestants alike to persecute heretics and to accuse dissenters of the devil's work. Luther, Calvin, and the Catholic Church all favored burning witches.

Another factor was the misery bred by religious war, leading many to seek scapegoats for the suffering. A third factor was the syphilis pandemic, causing miscarriages, stillbirths, blindness, and insanity, easily ascribed to the occult. A fourth may have been a cooling climate, marked by long cold winters and harsh weather, causing crop failures and other disasters widely blamed on witchcraft.

A fifth factor was *Malleus Maleficarum* (*MAH-lā-oos MAH-lā-f ē-CAH-room*), "The Hammer of the Wicked," a pamphlet published by two Dominicans in 1486. Circulated widely in the next two centuries, it sought to supply an explanation of witchcraft. It said witches made pacts with the devil, sealed by sex with him, which empowered them to make evil things happen. It portrayed witches mainly as women, whom it considered weaker than men and more easily won over to evil (see "Excerpts from *Malleus Maleficarum*"). Witches were said to meet devils at assemblies called synagogues or sabbaths, indirectly linking witchcraft to Jewish worship.

Women accused of witchcraft being hanged.

Those accused of witchcraft were usually women, typically single or widowed, aging, and poor, who often had no family to protect them and thus were easy targets. Older women, beyond childbearing age, were sometimes seen as burdens on society and accused of erratic behavior. Aging might bring deeper voices and haggard appearance, leading fearful neighbors to label them "hags." Women's customary roles as midwives and healers also left them open to blame when infants or sick people died. Such circumstances, and depictions of women as tools of the devil going back to the biblical Eve, reinforced the tendency to link witchcraft with women.

Women depicted as witches were blamed for varied misfortunes, such as accidents, illness, sudden death, bad weather, infertility, and sexual impotence. Charges were typically brought by someone who had suffered a loss or by professional witch hunters who made careers of targeting witches. Many of the accused were tortured, often until they confessed or implicated others to save themselves. The convicted might be burned to death, hanged (in England), banished, or imprisoned. Some may actually have tried witchcraft, but most were no doubt innocent victims of fear, superstition, and witch hunts.

Watch the **Video** *Witch Hunts* on **myhistorylab.com**

DOCUMENT 20.2 Excerpts from *Malleus Maleficarum*

This widely circulated pamphlet, purportedly a "study" of witchcraft, asserted that women were by nature more likely than men to be witches. What attitudes, stereotypes, and prejudices do the excerpts below reflect?

Let us now . . . consider women; and . . . why this kind of perfidy is found more in so fragile a sex than in men . . . And the first [reason] is that they are more credulous; and since the chief aim of the devil is to corrupt faith, therefore he rather attacks them . . . The second reason is that women are naturally more impressionable, and more ready to receive the influence of a disembodied spirit . . . The third reason is that they have slippery tongues, and are unable to conceal from the fellow-women those things which by evil arts they know; and . . . they find an easy and secret manner of vindicating themselves by witchcraft . . . since they are feebler both in mind and body . . .

But the natural reason is that she is more carnal than a man . . . Therefore a wicked woman is by her nature quicker to waver in her faith, and consequently quicker to abjure the faith, which is the root of witchcraft. And as to her other mental quality, that is, her natural will; when she hates someone whom she formerly loved, then she seethes with anger and impatience in her whole soul . . . Women also have weak memories; and it is a natural vice in them not to be disciplined, but to follow their own impulses . . . Let us consider another property of hers, the voice. For as she is a liar by nature, so in her speech she stings while she delights us . . . Let us consider also her gait, posture, and habit . . . There is no man in the world who studies so hard to please the good God as even an ordinary woman studies by her vanities to please men . . . .

To conclude. All witchcraft comes from carnal lust, which is in women insatiable . . . Wherefore for the sake of fulfilling their lusts they consort even with devils . . . , it is no . . . wonder that there are more women than men found infected with the heresy of witchcraft . . . .

SOURCE: Heinrich Kramer and James Sprenger, *Malleus Maleficarum* (Wicasta: Online Edition, 2008) Part I, Question VI. First published in Germany in 1487.

Social Effects of Economic Expansion

Less dramatic, but more enduring, were changes wrought in Western society by capitalism and global trade. The main beneficiaries were the growing middle classes who lived in towns (burgs) and cities, and hence were called *burghers* or *bourgeoisie* (*boorzh-wah-ZE*). They included merchants and bankers who profited from trade; doctors, lawyers, and others who prospered by serving wealthy people's needs; and artisans and manufacturers who raised prices on their products as more wealth became available.

Urban middle classes benefit from global commerce

Global trade helped prosperous townsfolk live well, enjoying cottons, furs, tea, coffee, sugar, spices, and later tobacco and chocolate, imported from the Americas and Asia. Towns and cities sported markets, plazas, taverns, inns, banks, shops, and rows of tidy townhouses. Wealthy bourgeois even challenged the nobles for social and political preeminence. But many wage laborers were hurt as prices rose faster than their incomes. And the urban poor, roughly half the townsfolk, lived in squalid slums full of vermin, beggars, criminals, prostitutes, drunks, and gangs.

The changing economy also affected the nobles, descendants of medieval lords and owners of rural estates. Many came to live in cities, dwelling in elegant townhouses and enjoying luxuries supplied by global trade, while hired stewards ran their rural estates. To enhance their incomes, some nobles invested in commerce or married their young to children of wealthy bourgeoisie. In Western Europe, where access to sea trade enhanced the size and wealth of the bourgeoisie, the nobles' power declined as monarchs and merchants shaped strong political and economic institutions. But in Central and Eastern

Europe, where lack of access to such commerce kept urban middle classes small and weak, nobles retained their political and economic dominance.

Initially, the peasants, who lived in rural villages with little access to the wonders of the wider world, were little affected by the economic changes. Occasionally they might travel to a town to visit its markets or attend an annual fair. Usually, however, they rose with the sun, worked the fields by day, and retired to their village by night. In Eastern Europe most peasants were still serfs, bound in service to their landlords; in the West, most were legally free but subject to burdensome taxes and dues.

New "cottage industries" tie rural villagers into global economy

By the 1600s, however, capitalist commerce was affecting many peasants. To bypass town artisans and guilds, merchants started lending, or "putting out," equipment and raw materials (such as weaving looms and wool) to peasant families, who used them to make products (such as clothing) in their own huts and cottages. The merchant capitalist paid a fixed price for items thus produced and then sold them at lower cost than goods made by guild artisans. This "putting out" system, later called **cottage industry** or the "domestic system," lowered merchants' costs and the price of goods, while raising peasant incomes and making them less beholden to the landlords.

Peasant couple at market (engraving by Albrecht Dürer).

Family, Gender, Education, and Diet

Religious and economic change also affected family patterns, gender roles, education, and diet. Arising in the 1500s, these effects became increasingly visible in the following century.

In the 1500s, as in eras past, the basic units of Western society were patriarchal families headed by men. Noblemen were lords of the family estate and often also military officers or government officials. Middle-class men ran the family business or practiced the family trade, while peasant men farmed the strips of land allotted to their family in fields around their village. As household heads and providers, men expected to be served by their wives and to make key decisions for their children, including assignment of family duties and selection of spouses.

Although seen as subservient to men, women played central roles in family life. They raised children, baked bread, prepared meals, and made clothes, using social circles to support and learn from other women. Women also were midwives and caregivers, delivering babies and treating illnesses with folk remedies passed on from previous generations. Lower-class mothers nursed their own infants, while wealthy women hired wet nurses to breast-feed theirs. Peasant women sustained their families mainly on dark bread and soups made from peas, beans, cabbages, and carrots, supplemented sometimes by eggs, butter, and cheese. Meat meals, white bread, and sweet pastries, standard fare for upper classes, were rare among common people.

Women typically have little freedom or choice

Yet women had little control over their own lives. Parents arranged their marriages, often caring more for enhancing family status than for their daughters' happiness. Women who wound up with drunken, abusive, or unfaithful husbands had little choice but to endure their plight—and women who tried to run away could be tracked down and returned. Since childhood diseases killed 20–30 percent of all children, women commonly bore at least six or seven children to ensure that some would survive to adulthood.

👁 **Watch** the **Video**

Contact and Encounters in the Early Modern Mediterranean

on **myhistorylab.com**

By the 1600s, despite much continuity, basic family patterns were changing. Increased income from commerce and cottage industry helped many married couples maintain separate households, rather than live with their extended families. **Nuclear families,** made up of only parents and children, increasingly became the norm. And, although their parents still had to approve their marriages, young people increasingly chose their own spouses, often after years of courtship, waiting to wed until their mid-twenties when they could support themselves. Divorce and remarriage, banned by the Catholic Church, were typically allowed among Protestants, especially in cases of adultery or abuse.

Learning and literacy likewise became more common. Increasing numbers of books produced by printing presses, combined with Protestant emphasis on individual reading of the Bible, accelerated the spread of education. Protestant pastors and Catholic orders set up schools to teach reading and writing, not only to offspring of merchants and nobles but also to growing numbers of lower-class children. Although mainly boys attended schools, prosperous parents increasingly educated their daughters too, enabling them to play larger roles in social and cultural life.

European diets also evolved as new foods from the Americas were added. In the 17th century, European farmers began growing crops developed by Amerinds, such as corn (maize), which originated in Mexico, and potatoes, which came from Peru. Potatoes proved especially useful, since they took less space to cultivate than grains, were easier to preserve, and could feed more people. Global connections thus enhanced Europe's food supply as well as its prosperity.

Printing press and religious schools boost literacy and learning

 **View** the **Image**
Early Print Shop
on **myhistorylab.com**

Diets are enhanced by new foods such as potatoes from the Americas

Changes in the Role of Religion

Religion's role was likewise altered in the age of religious conflict. Before the Reformation, most Europeans sought salvation through the Church, so religion was central to society. The Church provided sacraments and religious education, collected and distributed donations for the poor, and kept records of births, deaths, baptisms, and marriages. It also offered festival occasions, including baptisms, weddings, and holy days such as Christmas and Easter. It even condoned midwinter Carnival festivities—also called Shrovetide, Mardi Gras (*MAR-dē GRAH*), or Fasching (*FAH-shing*)—during which people donned costumes and ate and drank excessively in preparation for Lent, a 40-day period of fasting and sacrifice preceding Easter.

After the Reformation, changing outlooks started altering religion's role. Protestants needed no Church for salvation, so their faith was often private and plain, marked by Bible reading at home and simple Sunday services. Their sober moral code also disfavored excessive pre-Lenten festivities, while their certainty of salvation removed the need for Lenten fasts and sacrifices.

Religious wars and witch hunts also bred disenchantment with religion, while growing prosperity left Europeans less focused on death and salvation. In Protestant areas, and even Catholic lands, the saints, shrines, monasteries, pilgrimages, and fasts that earlier meant so much grew less important. Freed by Luther and Calvin from the need to earn salvation, many Protestants focused on material success—and ambitious Catholics did too.

Most people still worshipped and prayed, but their lives were less centered on religion than before and they were less inclined to look to religious leaders for guidance. Europe's age of religious conflict, begun by efforts to enhance religion and diminish the wealth and worldliness of the Roman Church, instead diminished the role of religion and enhanced the wealth and worldliness of European society.

Religious wars, witch hunts, and economic change diminish religion's role

CHAPTER

REVIEW

Putting It in Perspective

In the early 1500s, hoping to reform the Catholic Church, reduce Church corruption, improve public morals, and increase people's piety, religious reformers started a rebellion known as the Protestant Reformation. They were supported by many political leaders, alarmed at the growing power of the Habsburg rulers, and by numerous people who resented Church extravagance, financed by donations of the faithful.

But the Reformation's outcome was not what its originators intended. It shattered Europe's religious unity, generating numerous new beliefs and competing Christian churches, as religious strife and zeal fueled wars, inquisitions, persecutions, and witch hunts. Central Europe was left divided and weak,

thwarting Habsburg efforts to transform the Holy Roman Empire into a centralized state. And Europe was left divided among diverse states, each with its own religious institutions and issues.

Despite this destruction and division, however, Europe's wealth and influence expanded. The worldwide spread of Western Christianity, the growth of global commerce and capitalism, the exploitation of the Americas, the flourishing of the bourgeoisie, and advances in literacy and learning all enriched European countries, especially those that bordered the Atlantic. By the late 1600s, profiting from connections created by global expansion, the West was emerging from religious strife more prosperous and powerful than ever.

Reviewing Key Material

KEY CONCEPTS

sacraments, 442
purgatory, 443
indulgence, 443
Ninety-Five Theses, 445
predestination, 448
the elect, 448

puritanical, 448
capitalism, 455
mercantilism, 456
charter companies, 457
cottage industry, 460
nuclear families, 461

KEY PEOPLE

Martin Luther, 442
Emperor Charles V, 442
John Wyclif, 444
John Hus, 444
Pope Sixtus IV, 444
Pope Alexander VI, 444
Pope Julius II, 444
Maximilian of
   Habsburg, 444
Friar John Tetzel, 445
Frederick the Wise, 445
Huldrych Zwingli, 446
King Henry VIII, 447
Catherine of Aragon, 447
Anne Boleyn, 447
Pope Clement VII, 447
John Calvin, 448

John Knox, 449
King Edward VI, 449
Queen Mary, 450
Queen Elizabeth I, 450
Pope Paul III, 450
Angela Merici, 451
Ignatius Loyola, 451
King Philip II, 452
Mary Stuart (Queen of
   Scots), 452
Catherine de Medicis, 453
King Henri IV, 453
Emperor Ferdinand II, 454
King Gustavus
   Adolphus, 454
Cardinal Richelieu, 454
Francis Xavier, 455

ASK YOURSELF

1. Why did Luther challenge the Catholic Church's authority? Why did his challenge become a revolt against the Church, rather than a reform movement within the Church?

2. Why did Luther's challenge result in formation of many new Christian sects? How did the Calvinist and English reformations differ from Luther's?

3. How did the Catholic Church respond to the Protestant challenge? Why were popes and Habsburg rulers unable to crush the Protestants?

4. What circumstances led to the globalization of Western Christianity and commerce? What roles did missionaries, merchants, and monarchs play?

5. What factors account for Europe's economic and social changes in this era? Why were women so often the targets of witch hunts?

GOING FURTHER

Asch, Ronald. *The Thirty Years' War.* 1997.
Bainton, Roland. *The Reformation of the Sixteenth Century.* Rev. ed. 1985.
Barstow, A. *Witchcraft: A New History of European Witch Hunts.* 1994.
Benedict, Philip. *Christ's Churches Purely Reformed: A Social History of Calvinism.* 2002.

Bonney, Richard. *The Thirty Years War, 1618–1648.* 2002.

Braudel, Fernand. *Capitalism and Material Life, 1400–1800.* 1973.

Briggs, Robin. *Witches and Neighbours.* 2nd ed. 2002.

Brodrick, James. *The Origin of the Jesuits.* 1971.

Cameron, E., ed. *Early Modern Europe: An Oxford History.* 1999.

Collison, Patrick. *The Reformation: A History.* 2006.

Davidson, Nicholas S. *The Counter-Reformation.* 1987.

Duplessis, R. *Transitions to Capitalism in Early Modern Europe.* 1997.

Holt, M. P. *The French Wars of Religion, 1562–1629.* 1995.

Kamen, Henry. *Empire: How Spain Became a World Power.* 2004.

Kittelson, J. M. *Luther the Reformer.* 1986.

Levack, Brian. *The Witch-Hunt in Early Modern Europe,* 3rd ed. 2007.

Lindberg, Carter. *The European Reformations.* 1996.

MacCulloch, Diarmaid. *The Reformation: A History.* 2005.

Maltby, William. *The Reign of Charles V.* 2002.

Marty, Martin. *Martin Luther.* 2004.

Mattingly, Garrett. *The Armada.* 1959, 1988.

McGrath, A. *A Life of John Calvin.* 1990.

Oberman, Heiko A. *Luther: Between God and the Devil.* 1989.

Olin, J. C. *The Catholic Reformation: From Savonarola to Loyola.* 1993.

O'Malley, J. W. *The First Jesuits,* 1993.

Ozment, Steven. *Protestants: The Birth of a Revolution.* 1992.

Parker, Geoffrey. *The Thirty Years War.* 2nd ed. 1997.

Parker, T. H. L. *Calvin: An Introduction to His Thought.* 1995.

Rublack, Ulinka. *Reformation Europe.* 2005.

Thomas, Keith. *Religion and the Decline of Magic.* 1971, 1982.

Warnicke, R. *Women of the English Renaissance and Reformation.* 1983.

Weir, Allison. *The Life of Elizabeth I.* 1999.

Wiesner, Merry E. *Women and Gender in Early Modern Europe.* 3rd ed. 2008.

Key Dates and Developments

1517	Luther's Ninety-Five Theses initiate Reformation
1519	Charles V becomes Holy Roman emperor
1521	Luther appears before Diet of Worms
1525	German nobles crush Peasants' Revolt
1527	King Henry VIII begins to seek annulment
1529	Ottoman Turks besiege Vienna
1533	Henry VIII defies Rome and marries Anne Boleyn
1534	Parliament makes Henry VIII head of English Church
1536	Calvin publishes *Institutes of the Christian Religion*
1540	Pope Paul III approves Society of Jesus (Jesuits)
1545	Pope Paul III convenes Council of Trent
1556	Charles V retires; Philip II becomes king of Spain
1562–1594	Wars of Religion in France
1566	Dutch Revolt begins
1588	Spanish Armada defeated
1598	Edict of Nantes in France
1600	English East India Company founded
1602	Dutch United East India Company founded
1618	Defenestration of Prague begins Thirty Years War
1648	Peace of Westphalia ends Thirty Years War

myhistorylab Connections

Reinforce what you learned in this chapter by studying the many documents, images, maps, review tools, and videos available at www.myhistorylab.com.

Read and Review

✓• Study and Review Chapter 20

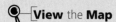 Read the Document

Desiderius Erasmus, "Pope Julius Excluded from Heaven," 1513–1514, p. 444

Martin Luther, "Ninety-Five Theses" (Holy Roman Empire), 1517, p. 445

Calvin on Predestination (16th Century), p. 448

John Calvin, "Ecclesiastical Ordinances" (Geneva, Switzerland), 1533, p. 448

The Council of Trent, 1545–1563, p. 450

The Edict of Nantes, 1598, p. 453

Jesuit in India (1530s–1550s), St. Francis Xavier, p. 455

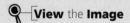 View the Map

Map Discovery: The Netherlands During the Dutch Revolt, ca. 1580, p. 452

Map Discovery: Dutch Trade Routes, ca. 1650, p. 457

View the Image

Early Print Shop, p. 461

Watch the Video

The Global Mission of the Jesuits, p. 452

Hunting Witches, p. 458

Research and Explore

Watch the Video

Witch Hunts, p. 458

Watch the Video

Contact and Encounters in the Early Modern Mediterranean, p. 460

((•• Listen to the Chapter Audio for Chapter 20 on myhistorylab.com

The Search for Stability in East Asia, 1300–1800

((•—Listen to the **Chapter Audio** for Chapter 21 on **myhistorylab.com**

Imperial Lion in the Forbidden City

This splendid bronze lion in Beijing's Forbidden City, a magnificent complex of palaces and courtyards built for Chinese emperors, is a powerful symbol of China's quest for strength and stability.

- Why and how did Japan seek stability in the 16th and 17th centuries?

- What were the main features and achievements of Japan in the Tokugawa era?

- Why and how did China seek stability in the Ming and Qing eras?

- What were the main features and achievements of China in the Ming and Qing eras?

- How did connections with other countries influence Korea and Vietnam?

In 1587, Japan's leading general, Toyotomi Hideyoshi (*TŌ-yo-TŌ-mē hē-dā-YŌ-shē*), took several steps to restore stability and reinforce traditional values. In July, fearful that the spread of Christianity by foreigners from the West was undermining age-old Japanese beliefs, he ordered Christian missionaries evicted. In August, concerned that widespread possession of weapons promoted internal unrest, he conducted a Great Sword Hunt, aiming to confiscate the arms of all nonsoldiers. In November, exalting a time-honored custom, he staged a Grand Tea Ceremony, personally serving tea in exquisite porcelain vessels to hundreds of people. The art of serving tea, long used in Japan to foster discipline and respect, blended elegance with order, tradition, and tranquility.

East Asia

After decades of conflict and foreign meddling in Japan, Hideyoshi was eager to restore unity and order. His anti-Christian edict was not strictly enforced, his Great Sword Hunt did not end violence, and his Grand Tea Ceremony lasted only a day, yet together they showed his resolve to stabilize Japan and secure its traditions. Following his lead, Hideyoshi's successors developed a stable regime, persecuted Christians, and cut most contacts with the West.

Meanwhile, seared by the Mongol-induced upheavals of the 13th and 14th centuries, China, too, sought to reinforce stability. In China, as in Japan, internal warfare and outside meddling created instability. In China, as in Japan, Western missionaries and ideas intruded. In China, as in Japan, rulers responded by strengthening control and resisting foreign influence, until forced by outsiders to do otherwise.

From the 14th through 18th centuries, East Asia's leading states thus sought stability, a condition combining security from foreign and domestic threats with consistency and structure. Rulers and regimes sought to centralize power and enhance internal connections, while also seeking to control and limit contacts with outside cultures. But contacts nonetheless continued, as regional and global connections affected Asian cultures and commerce.

The Search for Stability in Japan and Korea

Japan's official ruler was its emperor, a hereditary monarch revered as a god, reigning in Kyoto, the capital (Map 21.1). But in 1192, the shogun, as main military commander, had become the real ruler, exercising power in the emperor's name (Chapter 14). And in the 1200s, the Hojo family leaders ruled as regents for the shoguns.

Then came the Mongol invasions of 1274 and 1281 (Chapter 15). After bravely and successfully resisting them, Japanese samurai warriors expected grants of land in reward, as was the usual custom. But no land had been conquered, so there was none to distribute. Furthermore, as samurai divided their estates among their heirs, individual landholdings grew smaller, leaving many warriors impoverished and embittered. Blaming their plight on the Hojo regents, resentful samurai supported various **daimyo** (*DĪ-myō*), hereditary regional warlords who dominated parts of Japan. By the 1330s, Japan was ripe for rebellion.

Rebellions, Warring States, and Intruders

When young Emperor Go-Daigo (*gō-DĪ-gō*) came of age to rule in 1331, the Hojo regents tried to force him to retire, as was their usual practice, so they could continue to rule in the name of a new child emperor. But instead, Go-Daigo, supported by resentful

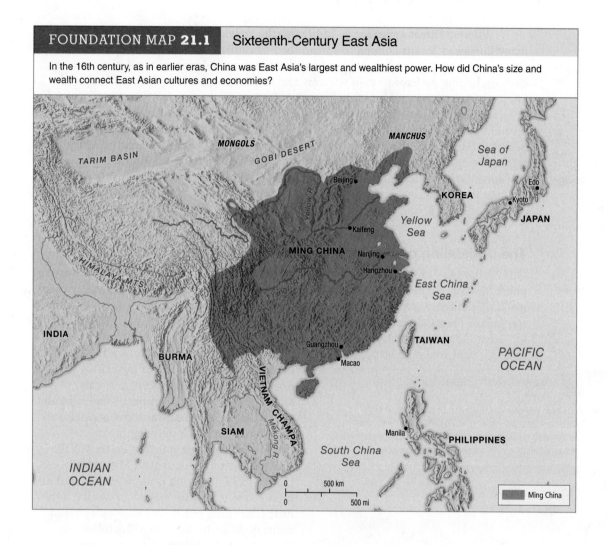

FOUNDATION MAP **21.1**   Sixteenth-Century East Asia

In the 16th century, as in earlier eras, China was East Asia's largest and wealthiest power. How did China's size and wealth connect East Asian cultures and economies?

samurai, rebelled. In 1333, General Ashikaga Takauji (*AH-shē-KAH-gah tah-kah-OO-jē*), sent by the Hojo to crush the revolt, switched sides and helped it succeed, ending Hojo rule. But when Go-Daigo refused to make him shogun, Ashikaga Takauji seized Kyoto and installed a new emperor who did, thus initiating the Ashikaga Shogunate (1336–1573). Go-Daigo fled south and began a new revolt but died in 1339. His successors fought on until 1392, when Ashikaga forces compelled Go-Daigo's grandson to return to Kyoto as a puppet emperor.

Eventually, however, as regional daimyo increased their power at Kyoto's expense, a new civil war in the Ashikaga family began an era called the Age of Warring States (1467–1568), similar to China's Warring States Era (Chapter 4) and Europe's Thirty Years War (Chapter 20). In a century of almost constant conflict, many Japanese daimyo, acting as independent warlords, battled each other with their own samurai armies. Some also functioned as sea lords, forming pirate companies to raid the Chinese coast.

In 1543, as wars still raged among daimyo, a new source of instability threatened Japan. In the south appeared strange foreigners, equipped with deadly weapons the Japanese called "lightning sticks," as Portuguese sailors with firearms arrived by sea. Before long, Japanese were trading with Westerners for firearms and making large numbers of their own.

⊙ **Watch** the **Video**
Japan, Age of the Warring States
on **myhistorylab.com**

Rebellions and warring states destabilize Japan

Foreign intrusions add to Japan's instability

A different threat appeared in 1549 with the arrival of Francis Xavier, the first of many European Jesuits coming to spread their Catholic faith (Chapter 20). Although at first coolly received, the Jesuits won favor by adapting to Japanese ways. Soon several daimyo, hoping perhaps to gain firearms and fortune from trade with the Europeans, adopted Christianity and imposed it on their people. In the ensuing decades, as Spanish Franciscans and other Western missionaries came to compete with the Jesuits for converts, several hundred thousand Japanese became Christians. The new faith was professedly peaceful, but some in Japan saw its growth as a threat to their Shinto and Buddhist traditions, and its loyalty to a distant pope as a menace to their autonomy.

View the **Image**
A Japanese View of European Missionaries
on **myhistorylab.com**

Some Japanese warlords, meanwhile, equipped their armies with firearms, hoping to conquer their rivals and unify Japan. Two tenacious warriors, Oda Nobunaga (*Ō-dah nō-boo-NAH-gah*) and Hideyoshi, ultimately proved successful.

The Unification of Japan

Oda Nobunaga and Hideyoshi work to unify Japan

Oda Nobunaga (1534–1582), son of a minor daimyo, set out in the 1560s to unite Japan under his rule. He built a powerful army, equipped it with firearms, placed it under command of a military genius named Hideyoshi, and used it to conquer rival daimyo in central Japan. Then Oda moved on Kyoto, capturing the capital in 1568 (Map 21.2).

Next Oda's forces moved westward, using the new weapons to defeat other daimyo. In 1573 he deposed the last Ashikaga shogun and ended the shogunate. By 1582, Oda Nobunaga controlled 32 of Japan's 68 provinces. That year, however, he was ambushed by one of his generals and committed suicide to avoid capture. Someone else would have to finish unifying Japan.

The person best suited to do so was the commander of Oda's armies. Hideyoshi (1536–1598), son of a peasant soldier, had no class status, no family name, no wealth, and little education, but he did have exceptional military skills. In the eight years following Oda's death, Hideyoshi defeated or gained allegiance from all the remaining warlords, completing Japan's unification. The emperor made him chief minister and gave him a family name, Toyotomi.

Moving to consolidate control, Hideyoshi gathered data on the size and yield of all farmlands, to improve collection of taxes. He let defeated daimyo keep substantial lands, turning former foes into allies. And, as noted above, he ordered Christian missionaries expelled and Japanese people disarmed, to secure stability. By 1590, though officially still serving the emperor, Toyotomi Hideyoshi was master of Japan.

Hideyoshi's ambitions, however, were far from fulfilled. According to legend, in 1592 he visited the shrine of Minamoto Yoritomo, the warrior who four centuries earlier had unified

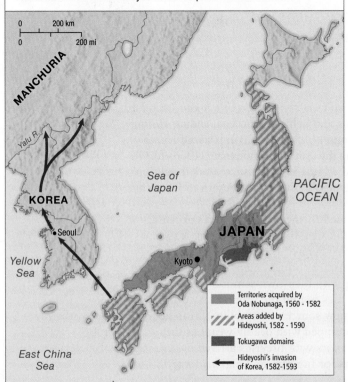

MAP **21.2** Japan's Unification, 1560–1590

In the late 1500s, two key warriors unified Japan. Note that Oda Nobunaga united central Japan from 1560 to 1582, and Hideyoshi finished the job by 1590. What factors contributed to Japan's unification? What factors thwarted Hideyoshi's subsequent invasion of Korea?

MANCHURIA

Yalu R.

KOREA

Seoul

Yellow Sea

Sea of Japan

PACIFIC OCEAN

JAPAN

Kyoto

East China Sea

Territories acquired by Oda Nobunaga, 1560 - 1582

Areas added by Hideyoshi, 1582 - 1590

Tokugawa domains

Hideyoshi's invasion of Korea, 1582-1593

Japan, and revealed some astonishing plans. "You and I are the only ones who have been able to unite all Japan," he allegedly informed his predecessor's spirit. "Now I intend to go much further than you did—I intend to conquer China!" That same year he began his quest by invading Korea.

Hideyoshi resolves to conquer China

Korea and the Japanese Invasion

Korea had longstanding connections with China (Chapter 14). In the 13th century, when the Mongols overran China, they also conquered Korea, oppressing its people and forcing its rulers to marry Mongol women and adopt Mongol ways. Then, after China ousted the Mongols in 1368, Korean admirers of China's new Ming dynasty fought Korea's Mongolized monarchy. In 1388, when the Ming sent in forces, the Korean general ordered to repel them instead overthrew his own rulers. Later this general, Yi Song-gye (*YĒ sōng-gyeh*), formed a new regime called the Chosŏn (or Yi) dynasty (1392–1910). It restored Korea's connections with China, copying its Confucian institutions and paying it annual tribute.

In the 1590s, when Japan invaded, these connections benefited both Korea and China. First the Koreans rejected Hideyoshi's request to let his forces pass freely through Korea to China. Then, in 1592, when he sent to Korea a 160,000-man army equipped with firearms and samurai swords, the Koreans sought help from the Chinese, who eventually sent half a million soldiers. This force did not arrive in time to prevent Hideyoshi's armies from overrunning Korea, but it did manage, with Korean help, to push back the Japanese forces. Meanwhile Korea's navy, whose innovative **"turtle ships"** had decks that were protected with iron plating, dealt several stunning defeats to the Japanese fleet.

Hideyoshi.

Hideyoshi then tried to bargain, offering to divide Korea with China. In 1597, however, after several years of futile talks, he renewed the war. But it ended the next year when Hideyoshi fell ill and died, distressed that his dream of conquering China would never be fulfilled.

Korea thus survived and eventually recovered from the devastation done by Japan. The Chosŏn dynasty lasted three more centuries, retaining Korean autonomy, while maintaining strong connections with China and paying tribute to its rulers.

Japanese invasion reinforces Korean connections with China

Japan Under Tokugawa Rule

Castle in Himeji, Japan, built under Hideyoshi and Tokugawa Ieyasu.

After Hideyoshi's death, a regency council governed Japan for his 5-year-old son Hideyori (*hē-dā-YŌ-rē*). But one council member, Tokugawa Ieyasu (*TŌ-koo-GAH-wah Ē-ā-YAH-soo*), an astute old warlord with large estates in eastern Japan (Map 21.2), quickly became dominant. By 1603 he defeated all his rivals and compelled the emperor to appoint him shogun, thereby both restoring that office and making him Japan's real ruler.

As shogun, Tokugawa Ieyasu focused on consolidating Japan's unity and stability. Determined to start his own dynasty, in 1605 he formally retired and had his son, Tokugawa Hidetada (*hē-dā-TAH-dah*), named shogun. The aging Ieyasu nonetheless exercised great influence until his death in 1616. In 1614 and 1615, Tokugawa forces attacked Hideyori, seeing Hideyoshi's son, now an adult, as a potential threat. When Hideyori fled and committed suicide, the Tokugawa triumph was complete.

The Tokugawa Shogunate, begun by Ieyasu and continued by his heirs, lasted until 1868. It sought to maintain stability, partly by controlling the daimyo and their samurai, and partly by isolating Japan from the outside world. But the Tokugawa years brought significant changes to Japanese society, including the emergence of a new urban culture.

The Tokugawa Shoguns

In the Tokugawa era, though the emperor still reigned in Kyoto, the shoguns actually ruled Japan from the city of Edo ($\bar{A}$-$d\bar{o}$), today called Tokyo. They headed a regime that embraced the daimyo but centralized power in the shogun's hands.

The shogun directly ruled much of Japan, including its three main cities, Kyoto, Edo, and Osaka. He ruled the rest indirectly, through more than 250 daimyo vassals, who fell into three groups: *related daimyo* (Tokugawa relatives), *house daimyo* (loyal vassals raised to daimyo status by Ieyasu and his successors), and *outer daimyo* (heirs of former independent warlords). The lands of the outer daimyo, many of whom resented Tokugawa rule, were mostly on Japan's periphery, away from the centers of power (Map 21.3).

The shoguns used clever devices to keep their vassals in line. Daimyo were required to provide soldiers for the shogun's army, laborers for his projects, and officials for his regime. All were obliged to spend half their time at Edo, under the shogun's watchful eyes, and while they were gone their families had to live there—in effect serving as hostages to ensure against revolt. These obligations reduced the daimyo's powers by making them court aristocrats rather than warlords, and impoverished many by making them support more than one household.

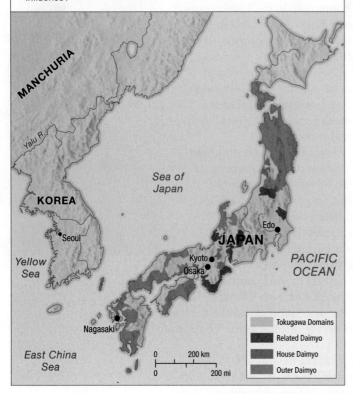

MAP 21.3 Tokugawa Japan, 1603–1868

Although Japanese emperors reigned in Kyoto as religious figures, the Tokugawa shoguns actually ruled Japan from Edo. Observe that they ruled much of Japan (Tokugawa domains) directly, and other parts indirectly through related daimyo, house daimyo, and outer daimyo. What steps did the shoguns take to reinforce their rule and minimize outside influence?

Tokugawa Domains
Related Daimyo
House Daimyo
Outer Daimyo

Shoguns strive to curtail Western connections

The Tokugawa regime, aware of Spanish rule in the Philippines to the south, also sought to end Western influence in Japan. In 1612–1614, fearful that Japan's growing number of Christians (by then about three hundred thousand in a population of perhaps twelve million) could facilitate foreign interference, the regime began enforcing Hideyoshi's edict expelling European missionaries. It forced Japanese Christians to renounce their faith, sometimes by stepping on a Christian cross or picture of Christ, and by 1660 executed more than three thousand who refused. In the 1630s it forbade Japanese people to travel abroad or contact outsiders. A Christian revolt in 1637–1638, sparked by oppression and taxation, reinforced the regime's hostility to the foreign faith. After crushing the revolt, in 1639 the regime evicted all Europeans except the Dutch, whose focus seemed to be commerce, not conversion, allowing them to trade at an island near the port of Nagasaki. Japan thus embarked on over two centuries of self-imposed isolation.

Japan's isolation was nonetheless incomplete. Connections continued with Korea and China, as many outer daimyo in coastal domains pursued both piracy and

Read the Document

"Closed Country Edict of 1635" and "Exclusion of the Portuguese, 1639"

on **myhistorylab.com**

commerce. The Dutch presence near Nagasaki also supplied some contact with the West, as Japanese who dealt with the Dutch learned their language and ways. The spread of this knowledge, which the Japanese called **Dutch learning**, acquainted some in Japan with Western approaches to art, science, shipbuilding, weaponry, music, and medicine, even in an age of isolation.

The Evolution of Japanese Society

Tokugawa rule brought unity and stability, but it did not prevent change. In the 1600s and 1700s, each of Japan's main classes—samurai, peasantry, and urban dwellers—was slowly transformed.

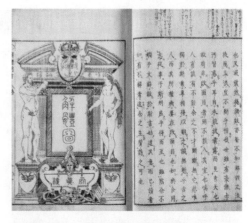

Anatomy text translated from Dutch in Tokugawa Japan.

The samurai by custom were loyal, self-disciplined, and proud, but two centuries of peace slowly dulled their fighting edge. With no one to fight, they became civil servants more than warriors. Required to live at their lords' castles, the samurai lost their rustic frugality, as castle towns grew into urban centers fostering pleasures such as sex and sake (*SAH-kā*), an alcoholic beverage made from fermented rice. They still brandished samurai swords and trained in martial arts, supplementing their bow and sword skills with **jujitsu** (*joo-JIT-soo*), a form of hand-to-hand combat using holds, blows, and throws to disable foes. But they focused no longer on warfare.

The peasants, in theory esteemed as food providers, in practice were often oppressed. In earlier times they had supported the samurai by serf labor; now they did so through high taxes, raised from 30 to 50 percent of their rice crop as samurai ways grew more lavish. Some farm families became destitute, sparking several peasant revolts in the 1700s. Others turned from growing rice to cash crops such as mulberry leaves (which fed the caterpillars that spun the thread for silk) and tobacco (introduced into Japan from the Americas by the Portuguese and Dutch). Rural Japan thus included both prosperous peasants owning large farms and landless families renting marginal farmlands and living in poverty.

Urban dwellers thrived as increasing commerce spurred the growth of towns and cities. Trade expanded from simple bartering of rice and tools to complex commerce that included housewares, textiles, brewing, banking, and lending. Banking houses and businesses gained great influence, as lavishly-living daimyo and samurai grew deeply indebted to bankers and merchants. The population of Osaka, Japan's commercial center, increased to more than four hundred thousand, while the shogun's city of Edo grew to almost a million.

View the Image

Eighteenth-Century Japanese Painting, *A Meeting of China, Japan, and the West*

on **myhistorylab.com**

Stability and urban culture modify samurai ways

Read the Document

Injunctions to Peasants, Tokugawa Shogunate, 1649

on **myhistorylab.com**

Urban Culture and the Roles of Women

As cities grew larger, Japan's urban culture became increasingly sophisticated. Merchants and other townsfolk, born without prestige, strove to secure it through education and promotion of literature and the arts. To sustain their superior social status, samurai often did the same.

Learning thus flourished, though mainly among men. Private schools were established in cities, towns, and Buddhist temples, as merchants, samurai, and wealthy peasants sought to educate their sons. By the 1800s Japan had more than ten thousand schools and almost 50 percent male literacy.

Along with emerging urban culture, rising literacy helped promote growth in literary and artistic works. Book publishing prospered, producing popular literature

Tokaido Highway, the main trade route connecting Edo with Kyoto and Osaka.

DOCUMENT 21.1   Examples of Haiku Poetry

Haiku, a form of Japanese poetry imitated in other languages, expresses a great deal in a few words. What aspects of Japanese society and culture does this art form reflect?

Beginning of spring—
the perfect simplicity
of a yellow sky

Chrysanthemums bloom
in a gap between the stones
of a stonecutter's yard

rain at the window—
how many more ants before
the end of summer?

the cat fluffs his fur
and tries to avoid the cold
of his own shadow

loving its whiteness
I walk around the birch tree
to the other side

when the tide goes out
all the minnows leave the pool
it's cloudy weather

SOURCE: Clark Strand, *Seeds from a Birch Tree: Writing Haiku and the Spiritual Journey* (New York: Hyperion, 1997), 13, 19, 27, 30, 40, 50.

ranging from religious to erotic. **Haiku** (*HĪ-koo*), concise 17-syllable poems, organized in three lines of five, seven, and five syllables, became a stylish rage (see "Examples of Haiku Poetry"). Arts and crafts flourished with realistic paintings of vibrant urban life and exquisite works of porcelain and lacquered wood. Multicolored prints, made by using dozens of intricately carved woodblocks that each imprinted one hue, helped reproduce masterpieces at reasonable cost.

Male culture was illusive. On the surface samurai exemplified discipline and Zen Buddhist virtue, while merchants were diligent, sober, and frugal family men. But urban amusement areas, often called the **floating world** (to reflect the fleetingness of earthly pleasures), offered them an indulgent nightlife in teahouses, restaurants, theaters, fashion shops, and brothels. Puppet shows and **kabuki** (*kah-BOO-kē*), a form of drama with elaborately made-up and costumed men performing both male and female roles with exaggerated and seductive gestures, were also in vogue.

Women had few such privileges and pleasures. In Japan, as elsewhere, parents arranged marriages to improve family status. Wives were subject to their husbands, expected to stay home, raise children, and handle household chores. Peasant women might also help the men in the fields or do the tedious work of producing silk.

Even wives of wealthy men were considered servants by their husbands. Largely required to stay hidden in the home, a woman was expected to discreetly wait on her husband and his guests. Sexual infidelity by women was forbidden and harshly punished. Men of means, however, were typically free to have mistresses or patronize the floating world's brothels. And many samurai, despite their strict moral code, engaged in various heterosexual and homosexual liaisons.

Not all women, however, were confined to the home. In cities and towns, some were employed making clothing; others waited on men in restaurants and teahouses. Some women, sold as children into servitude by destitute parents, became singers, dancers, musicians, and courtesans, later known as geisha (*GĀ-shuh*). In such roles they could live in comfort and gain some social status—but only as a consequence of serving the pleasures of men.

"Floating world" breeds indulgent urban nightlife

Women in traditional gowns play Japanese musical instruments.

The Search for Stability in China

China, like Japan, struggled to find stability in the 14th through 18th centuries. Battered by decades of Mongol rule, famine, and plague, the Chinese finally expelled the Mongols in 1368. A new dynasty, the Ming (1368–1644), revived China's pride and independence, restoring the strength and splendor of ages past, while focusing mainly on stability, security, and control.

((•—[Listen to the **Audio**
Growth in Asia
on **myhistorylab.com**

The Ming Ascendancy

In the early Ming era, China was probably the world's mightiest and wealthiest empire. With the Mongol rulers gone and stability restored, farming and commerce flourished, while China's million-man army, equipped with cannons and gunpowder grenades, was East Asia's dominant military force. Surrounding lands such as Korea and Vietnam, and even for a time Japan, were compelled to recognize Chinese supremacy and pay tribute for the right to trade with China.

Chinese domination connects East Asia

Zhu Yuanzhang, the peasant rebel leader who ousted the Mongols and began the Ming dynasty, devoted his reign (1368–1398) to enforcing China's security and his own power. Using his huge army, he pushed north into Mongolia, destroying the Mongols' fortresses and dividing their forces, but failing to fully subdue them. Ruling from Nanjing, he restored the civil service system of earlier eras, reviving the civil service exams and the role of Confucian scholar-bureaucrats. Determined to run his own regime, he abolished the post of chief minister and personally read hundreds of reports each day. Since he titled his reign Hongwu (HŌNG-WOO), meaning "vast military power," he is called the Hongwu Emperor.

For all his success, however, Hongwu was no innovator. Rather than create a new China, he sought to resurrect the China of the Tang and Song eras. Rather than maintain Mongol-forged connections with the Muslims and the West, he persecuted foreigners and all who had worked with the Mongols. Recalling his peasant roots, he tried to help the lower classes, abolishing slavery and taxing the rich to provide land and seed for the poor. But in the long run, he failed to narrow the gap between rich and poor. His huge army drained the economy, and the conservative Confucian bureaucracy became more powerful than ever. The emperor himself, after surviving an attempted coup, grew paranoid. Instituting a secret police that made heavy use of spies and torture, he executed thousands of alleged conspirators. Hongwu thus left a legacy of conservatism and cruelty, creating a regime almost as repressive as the Mongol one it replaced.

Hongwu's fourth son, who seized power in 1402 and ruled until 1424 as the Yongle (YŌNG-LUH) Emperor, shared his father's focus on military might. To fortify the north against the Mongols, he rebuilt China's Great Wall in its modern form: compacted earth enclosed by brick and stone, roughly 20 feet wide, 25 feet high, and 4,000 miles long. He led five campaigns against the Mongols in the north and extended his control into Vietnam in the south. He also moved the capital back north to Beijing, where he converted the old Mongol imperial compound into the magnificent Forbidden City, whose great red walls, gold-tiled roofs, marble courtyards, and lavish palaces have since symbolized China's mystery, majesty, and might (see page 465).

Unlike some later Ming rulers, Yongle cultivated connections. To ensure the flow of food and supplies from south to north, he dredged, repaired, and widened the Grand Canal. To increase China's trade and tribute, he built huge fleets of large sailing ships and sent expeditions to many foreign lands. The most extensive were led by

Aerial view of the Forbidden City.

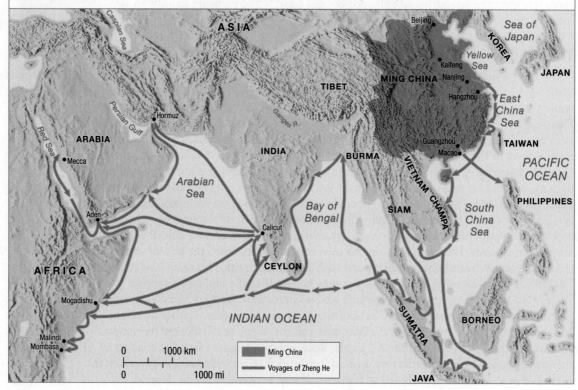

| MAP **21.4** | Zheng He Explores the Eastern World, 1405–1433 |

Decades before the great Portuguese and Spanish sea voyages, Zheng He, a Muslim mariner from China, led huge fleets on seven great sea expeditions. Note that his voyages took him to numerous lands, including Southeast Asia, India, and many parts of the Muslim world. What were the aims of his voyages, and what did they accomplish?

Zheng He sails to many Asian and East African lands

Zheng He (*JUNG-HUH*), a former court eunuch and gifted Muslim mariner, commissioned by Yongle to explore the whole known world. From 1405 to 1433, in seven great voyages with fleets of up to 70 ships and crews of up to thirty thousand men, Zheng He sailed to the Philippines, Southeast Asia, India, Persia, Arabia, and even down Africa's east coast (Map 21.4). His crews brought back exotic animals such as ostriches, zebras, and giraffes, as well as extensive knowledge of foreign countries (see "Excerpts: Zheng He's Inscription on His Voyages"). But the voyages found nothing to challenge the superiority of Chinese ways and goods.

Indeed, Zheng He's expeditions, undertaken decades before the Portuguese and Spanish voyages of exploration (Chapter 19), reaffirmed China's sense of superiority, especially in commerce, technology, and ocean travel. But unimpressed by contacts with cultures they considered inferior, subsequent Ming rulers launched no follow-up voyages. Ming China had the wealth and technology to explore and forge global connections, but its rulers chose not to do so. That path, instead, was pursued by Europeans.

**View** the **Map**

Interactive Map: Chinese Voyages of the Ming Dynasty

on **myhistorylab.com**

Challenges to Security and Stability

Ming rulers curtail overseas connections

Ming leaders thus ended the great sea expeditions, choosing instead to focus their resources on maintaining external security and internal stability. Supported by conservative advisors, emperors opted to preserve past traditions and sustain the status quo. Commerce, however, continued to grow, as Chinese merchants forged commercial connections throughout East Asia.

DOCUMENT 21.2 Excerpts: Zheng He's Inscription on His Voyages

On the seventh of his great voyages, while awaiting favorable winds at a port in southeast China, Zheng He summarized his exploits in an inscription that was carved in stone. How did his reports reinforce China's sense of superiority?

The Emperor . . . has ordered us . . . at the head of several tens of thousands of officers and flag-troops to ascend more than one hundred large ships . . . From the third year of Yongle [1405] till now we have seven times received the commission of ambassadors to countries of the western ocean . . . We have traversed more than one hundred thousand li [over 30,000 miles] of immense water spaces and have beheld in the ocean huge waves like mountains rising sky-high, and we have set eyes on barbarian regions far away hidden in a blue transparency of light vapours, while our sails loftily unfurled like clouds day and night . . . traversing those savage waves as if we were treading a public thoroughfare . . .

    I. In the third year of Yongle [1405] . . . we went to [Calicut] and other countries. At that time the pirate Chen Zuyi had gathered his followers in . . . [Palembang], where he plundered the native merchants. When he also advanced to resist our fleet, supernatural soldiers secretly came to the rescue so that after one beating of the drum he was annihilated . . .

    II. In the fifth year of Yongle [1407] . . . we went to [Java], [Calicut], [Cochin] and [Siam]. The kings of these countries all sent as tribute precious objects, precious birds and rare animals . . .

    III. In the seventh year of Yongle [1409] . . . we went to the countries [visited] before and took our route

by the country of [Ceylon]. Its king . . . was guilty of a gross lack of respect and plotted against the fleet . . . [The plot] was discovered and . . . that king was captured alive . . .

    IV. In the eleventh year of Yongle [1413] . . . we went to [Hormuz] and other countries. In the country of [Samudra] there was a false king . . . who was marauding and invading his country . . . We went thither with the official troops under our command and exterminated some and arrested [other rebels], and . . . captured the false king alive . . .

    V. In the fifteenth year of Yongle [1417] . . . we visited the western regions. The country of [Hormuz] presented lions, leopards with gold spots and large western horses. The country of [Aden] presented [giraffes], as well as the long-horned animal [oryx]. The country of [Mogadishu] presented [zebras] as well as lions. The country of [Brava] presented camels . . . as well as camel-birds [ostriches] . . .

    VI. In the nineteenth year of Yongle [1421] . . . we conducted the ambassadors from [Hormuz] and the other countries ... back to their countries . . .

    VII. In the sixth year of Xuande [1431] . . . we have left for the barbarian countries in order to read to them [an Imperial edict] and to confer presents. We have anchored in this port awaiting a north wind to take the sea, and . . . we have thus recorded an inscription in stone.

SOURCE: From *China and Africa in the Middle Ages*, by Teobaldo Filesi, translated by David Morison, Copyright © 1972 Frank Cass. Reproduced by permission of Taylor & Francis Books, UK.

    Various challenges complicated Ming efforts to secure stability. One was the drain of responding to the continued Mongol threat. The move to Beijing and rebuilding of the Great Wall fortified northern defenses but exhausted China's resources, and the new capital's northern location left the regime more vulnerable to Mongol attack. Regional rivalries intensified between the north, which had political and military power, and the south, which had prosperous commerce, fertile farmlands, and most of the population.

    A second challenge was the ongoing influence of eunuchs, castrated males who ran the imperial court. Although Hongwu had decreed that these men, emasculated to prevent sexual contact with the emperors' concubines, must not hold high posts or ranks, they were the ruler's constant companions and often his closest advisors. Some eunuchs used this status to gain power and wealth and intrigue against government officials. In 1449 influential eunuchs talked a rash young emperor into leading an ill-fated attack at Datong (*DAH-TŌNG*), where there was a pass in the Great Wall, against some Mongols who had refused to pay tribute. The result was a disaster: the Chinese army was routed and the emperor was captured.

Although the Mongols were later driven back (and returned the hapless emperor after China refused to pay ransom), the defeat at Datong began a long decline in Ming military power. The north was left exposed to periodic Mongol raids, while the south hated paying high taxes to secure and support Beijing. Fortunately for China, the Mongols were temporarily diverted by internal conflicts. But in 1550, the Mongols reunited, then penetrated the Great Wall, pillaged the outskirts of Beijing, and terrorized northern China for years thereafter.

A third challenge was the erratic character of several Ming rulers. Some, like Hongwu and Yongle, were talented and conscientious but capricious and cruel. Others, having little concern or capacity for governance, buried themselves in court pleasures. One ruler reportedly liked Korea's food and women so much that he sent officials to there to bring him cooks and maidens. Another allegedly got so engrossed in court pleasures that he failed to fill many vacant official positions, leaving much state business undone. A third supposedly never learned to write but focused his energies on woodworking, while his favored eunuch amassed enormous wealth and influence.

Confucians resist innovation and outside commerce

A fourth challenge was the traditionalism and anticommercialism of China's civil service. In the Ming era, as in the past, civil servants drawn largely from sons of landed gentry staffed the imperial administration. To pass the very rigorous civil service exams, these scholar-bureaucrats, known in the West as **mandarins** (a Portuguese version of a Southeast Asian term for government ministers), immersed themselves in the ancient Confucian classics. Steeped in the values of the past, and protective of a system that gave them power and prestige, Confucian officials resisted innovation and disparaged commerce. Certain that China's ways and goods were superior, many mandarins saw little value in connections with outsiders. With Confucian disdain for avarice and greed, they scorned merchants as parasites who profited from selling goods they had not made, ranking them below farmers and artisans who produced useful things. Since most of the gentry's incomes came from agriculture and most of the regime's revenues came from land taxes, many bureaucrats saw little to gain from commerce, either for themselves or the government.

Domestic and Foreign Trade

Farming advances produce surplus food, spurring commerce and urban growth

Yet commerce flourished during much of the Ming era. Until the disasters of the dynasty's last decades, the economy thrived, strengthened by expanding food production and extensive trade.

Farming, as always, was the backbone of China's economy. The growing cultivation of Champa rice, a fast-growing, drought-resistant crop adopted from Southeast Asia during the Song dynasty (Chapter 14), vastly increased food supplies. Aided by seed breeding and experimentation, Ming-era farmers in southern China could raise a rice crop in two months or less, enabling them to grow three or four crops a year. With ample food available, China's population, which may have fallen to 60 million in the Mongol era, rebounded to at least 100 million by 1500, and grew to around 150 million during the next century.

Surplus food also enabled more people to live in towns and cities, the main centers of commerce. By the late Ming era, China had at least a dozen cities with metropolitan populations of a million or more. Merchant and craft shops lined the streets, conducting brisk trade in items such as porcelain and stoneware, copper and iron tools, and silk and cotton cloth. The countryside, moreover, had numerous market towns, where peasants could exchange their produce for seeds, tools, and clothing. Commerce was so profitable that many court eunuchs, and

Ming porcelain vase.

even some mandarins, engaged in business ventures, despite the official Confucian disdain for mercantile activities.

Although officially discouraged, foreign trade expanded as well. Neighboring countries typically paid tribute to the Chinese emperor, partly for military protection and partly for the right to send trade missions to China. Ming regulations limited the size and number of such missions, restricting them to certain ports, but traders from Southeast Asia and Indonesia often ignored these restrictions, as did many Chinese merchants. The resulting commerce, featuring mainly silks and porcelains from China and spices from Indonesia, grew substantially in the 16th century, aided by aggressive intruders from Europe and Japan.

Foreign trade connections increase despite restrictions

Intruders from Europe and Japan

From the south came Europeans, whose great sea voyages (Chapter 19) were driven by dreams of lucrative trade with Asia (Map 21.5). First to arrive were mariners and merchants from Portugal, who reached southern China in 1514. Their disregard for Chinese laws, the

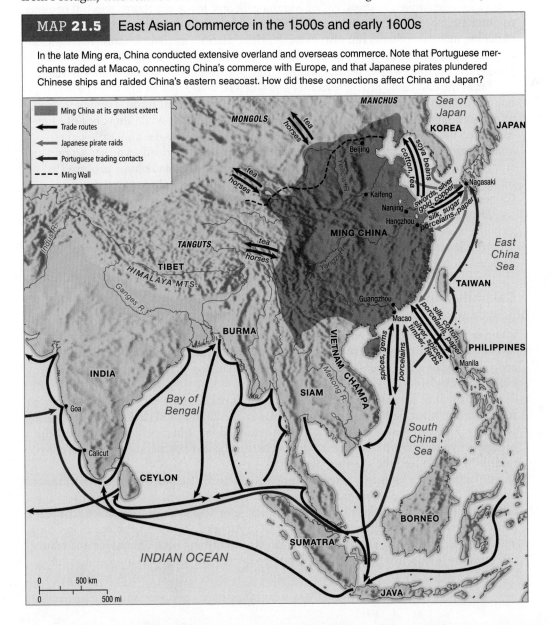

MAP 21.5   East Asian Commerce in the 1500s and early 1600s

In the late Ming era, China conducted extensive overland and overseas commerce. Note that Portuguese merchants traded at Macao, connecting China's commerce with Europe, and that Japanese pirates plundered Chinese ships and raided China's eastern seacoast. How did these connections affect China and Japan?

stench of their unwashed bodies, and their purchase of Chinese children as slaves led many in China to view them as crude "ocean devils." They enraged Ming officials by firing their ships' cannon near the great port city of Guangzhou (*GWAHNG-JŌ*), which the English later called Canton, and building an island fortress off the nearby coast. In 1522 Chinese forces drove them out, but the Portuguese persisted, and in 1557 they were allowed to set up a trading post at Macao (*mah-COW*), on a peninsula south of Guangzhou, in return for paying annual tribute. During the next few centuries, as Dutch and English merchants joined the Asia trade, Macao served as a center for commerce between China and the West.

So did the city of Manila in the Philippine Islands. Founded by the Spanish in 1571, six years after they opened a trans-Pacific route between Mexico and the Philippines, Manila became the focal point of trade between Asia and America. For more than two centuries, until 1815, ships filled with Chinese silks and porcelains made annual trips across the Pacific to Acapulco in Mexico, where their cargoes were sold for Spanish silver mined in the Americas. The goods were bought by Spanish colonists or sent to markets in Europe, while the ships, called Manila galleons, made the return trip full of silver to purchase more Chinese products (Map 21.6). Silver thus flowed into China, not only enriching many merchants but also causing price inflation: as silver became more plentiful, it became less valuable, with more and more silver needed to buy the same goods. As goods thus became more expensive, many Chinese consumers suffered serious hardships.

From the east came Japanese sailors and soldiers, also eager to tap China's wealth, but increasingly unwilling to pay the tribute required for official trade. Turning instead to plunder, Japanese pirates ravaged Chinese merchant vessels, while ships full of samurai landed in China to pillage and then quickly leave by sea. By the mid-1500s, these attacks were an organized industry, sponsored by Japanese warlords who set up raiding companies, hired many Chinese to participate as pirates, and made huge profits. The Ming fought back by banning trade with Japan, but this ban only prompted more Chinese to engage in smuggling or join the Japanese raiders.

Then, in the 1590s, came Japan's invasion of Korea, planned by Hideyoshi as stepping stone to conquest of China, as described above. A massive Ming army helped deter the Japanese in Korea, but its huge cost further drained China's treasury, already depleted by the extravagance of Ming rulers, relatives, and eunuchs.

Calamity and Rebellion

By the early 1600s, the Ming regime was in trouble. The war with Japan had exhausted it and drained its resources, but the emperors and their entourage continued to live lavishly and impose oppressive taxes. And a cooling of the climate, which shortened growing seasons and decreased harvests, seemed to suggest that the regime was losing Heaven's Mandate.

In 1628, as famine swept northern China, bands of starving peasants and unemployed soldiers began ravaging the region. Several years later, a fired postal clerk named Li Zicheng (*LĒ zuh-CHUNG*) joined his uncle's robber band and led it in rebellion. With the help of supportive scholars, he became a popular hero, a benevolent bandit who reportedly raided the rich to feed the starving poor.

Calamitous developments aided the rebellion. In 1639, lacking the resources to restore order, the Ming regime raised taxes even higher, prompting even more people to join the rebels. That same year, a clash between the Chinese and Spanish in Manila led to a suspension of trade, disrupting the flow of silver from America. As silver grew scarce in China, many people quit buying goods or paying taxes, diminishing both commerce and state revenues. As floods, droughts, and smallpox epidemics amplified the human disaster,

Westerners are permitted to trade at Macao

Manila galleons connect Asia with Spanish America

1628 famine leads to chaos and rebellion

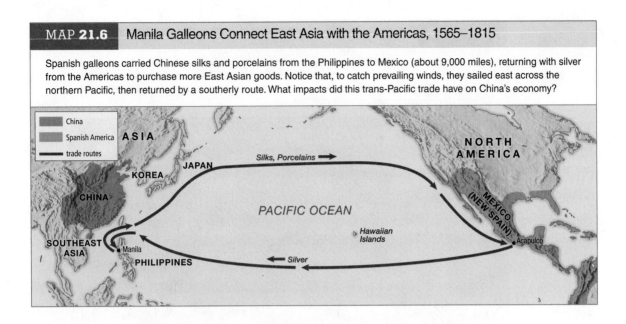

MAP 21.6   Manila Galleons Connect East Asia with the Americas, 1565–1815

Spanish galleons carried Chinese silks and porcelains from the Philippines to Mexico (about 9,000 miles), returning with silver from the Americas to purchase more East Asian goods. Notice that, to catch prevailing winds, they sailed east across the northern Pacific, then returned by a southerly route. What impacts did this trans-Pacific trade have on China's economy?

support grew for Li Zicheng. In 1644 he captured Beijing, while the Ming emperor hanged himself on a nearby hill. As with the origins of the Han and Ming dynasties (Chapters 4 and 15), it looked as if a man of the people had gained the Mandate of Heaven.

The Qing Empire

The events of 1644, however, resulted not in a new Chinese dynasty led by Li Zicheng, but in China's conquest by Manchus, nomadic people from the region of Manchuria northeast of China. Called in by Ming loyalists to help defeat the rebels, the Manchus proceeded to form their own dynasty, the Qing (*CHING*), adopting Chinese ways and ruling through China's bureaucracy. Creating an empire that included all of China and some neighboring lands, Qing rulers ushered in a new era of stability and prosperity, lasting until decline set in during the late 1700s.

The Manchu Conquest

In the early 1600s, the Manchus, descendants of the Jurchens who had ruled northern China before the Mongol conquests, created a powerful regime in Manchuria. Their brilliant leader Nurhachi (*NOOR-HAH-chē*), who started like Genghis Khan (Chapter 15) by avenging his father's murder, developed an imposing army, united most of Manchuria, and proclaimed himself khan in 1616. After Nurhachi died in 1626, his work was continued by his son Hong Taiji (*HŌNG TĪ-JĒ*), known in China as Huang Taiji, who before his own death in 1643 had started moving into northern China (Map 21.7).

Manchu expansion had only just begun. When Li Zicheng's forces took Beijing in 1644, an ambitious Ming general named Wu Sangui (*WOO sahn-GWĀ*), rather than surrender to the rebels, asked the Manchus for help. This invitation was all the Manchus needed. With the aid of Wu's forces, they attacked and overran Beijing, expelling and later destroying Li Zicheng's army. But instead of restoring the Ming, they named Hong Taiji's young son the new emperor of China.

Ming general calls in Manchus to help resist rebels

MAP **21.7**	Manchu Expansion Creates the Qing Empire, 1600–1800

Expanding from their homeland in Manchuria, the Manchus created a vast realm called the Qing Empire. Notice that, after early Manchus conquered most of China, later conquests added Taiwan, Mongolia, Xinjiang, and Tibet. What factors enabled them to conquer and rule such a vast and populous realm? Why did other countries pay tribute to the Qing regime?

Thus began a new dynasty called the Qing (meaning "Pure") that would reign from 1644 until 1912. At first, however, it ruled only the north, while an aspiring new Ming emperor sought to hold onto the south. But the former Ming general Wu Sangui, now a Manchu vassal, gradually defeated the Ming remnants, killing their last ruler in 1662. This left Wu and two other Chinese warlords in control of southern China, which they ruled as Manchu vassals until 1673. Then, turning against the Manchus, the three warlords joined forces in a massive revolt that lasted until 1682.

Kangxi and the Consolidation of Manchu Rule

By then, however, the Manchus had a gifted new ruler. Only 19 years old when the revolt began, the Kangxi (*KAHNG-SHĒ*) Emperor (1662–1722) possessed extraordinary talent and vigor. Not confined like some earlier emperors to the comforts of his court, Kangxi led his armies in battle, deftly planning strategy, dividing the rebel coalition, and proving a brilliant general. Wu Sangui persisted—and even made plans to claim Heaven's Mandate for himself—but the old warlord finally grew feeble and died in 1678. Kangxi then annihilated Wu's heirs while also crushing a Mongol revolt by 1682.

Yet one pressing problem remained. In the mid-1600s, as revolt and civil war gripped China, its southeast coast and the island of Taiwan were dominated by Ming loyalist Zheng Chenggong (*JUNG CHUN-GŌNG*), a pirate of Chinese and Japanese ancestry known by Western merchants as "Koxinga." After his death in 1662, his pirate empire, ruled from Taiwan by his son, continued to torment the Manchus. At one point, hoping to undermine this realm by depriving it of plunder, they tried depopulating China's southeast coast by forcing its people to move inland. Finally, in 1683, Kangxi sent forces to occupy Taiwan and end the pirate regime, completing the Manchu conquest. As in the Mongol era, foreigners from the north again ruled all of China.

But the foreigner Kangxi proved a splendid Chinese emperor. He forbade intermarriage between Manchus and Chinese and gave precedence to Manchu officials, but he also fostered harmony between Manchu and Chinese civil servants, demanding honesty and talent from both. A frugal and effective administrator, he lowered taxes and improved bureaucratic efficiency, while initiating numerous public works such as flood control and water conservation projects. A man of enormous energy, he rose daily before dawn and dealt with stacks of official reports. During his reign he led many military expeditions and made six grand tours of his realm to ensure that it was well governed. He gained renown as one of history's ablest and wisest rulers.

Kangxi's foreign ventures were equally effective. After sending forces north to confront unruly Russians infringing on his domain, in 1689 he negotiated a treaty with Russia that defined the borders between the two empires. Later he led armies into western Mongolia, mastering that region and vastly diminishing the Mongol menace. He also sent forces to subdue Tibet, bringing the Dalai Lama (*DAH-lī LAH-mah*), leader of Tibetan Buddhism, under Manchu protection.

Kangxi strengthens and expands China's borders

An admirer of China's culture, Kangxi generously patronized intellectual and cultural pursuits, including an official history of the Ming era and a comprehensive literary encyclopedia. In certain areas of study, such as mapmaking, mathematics, and astronomy, he even used foreign scholars, foremost among whom were Jesuits from Europe.

The Jesuits in China: Cultural Connections and Controversy

The Jesuit presence in Asia was part of a global effort to spread Catholic Christianity (Chapter 20), begun by Francis Xavier in the 1540s. In 1582 an Italian Jesuit named Matteo Ricci (*mah-TĀ-ō RĒ-chē*), a gifted intellectual, arrived in China, where he lived until his death in 1610. He and his successors learned the Chinese language, adopted Chinese dress, befriended Chinese scholars, translated Western books into Chinese, corrected Chinese maps and calendars, and even predicted an eclipse. They also studied Chinese literature and philosophy and observed Chinese medical practices, including the technique, later used in the Ottoman Empire and Europe, of infecting people with a mild form of smallpox to help them develop immunity. By the time of Kangxi, Jesuits were welcome at the emperor's court, serving as astronomers, architects, mapmakers, engineers, and interpreters. In 1689, they even helped negotiate China's treaty with Russia, possessing the background and linguistic skills to communicate with both sides.

Jesuits blend Chinese and Western learning

But Jesuit adaptation to Chinese ways ultimately caused problems. In seeking to spread their faith, the Jesuits connected Christian ideals with Confucian virtues (equating, for example, Christian compassion with Confucian humanity, or *ren*) and even took part in Chinese rites involving ancestor worship. This blending of traditions antagonized many Confucians, who saw it as corrupting their own beliefs and practices. It also upset other Christians, including Franciscans and Dominicans, who complained to the pope in Rome,

Blending of ideas upsets Confucians and Christians

Qianlong.

asserting that Jesuit participation in Chinese rites compromised Catholicism. Kangxi backed the Jesuits and gave them supportive documents to take to Rome. But in 1704 the pope denounced Catholic participation in Chinese rites, formally banning it in 1715. Kangxi's successors, influenced by disgruntled Confucians and by a later pope's extension of the ban in 1742, actively suppressed Christianity in China, thus undoing the work begun by the Jesuits.

The Height of the Qing Regime

After Kangxi died, his fourth son seized power in a coup against his brothers and reigned as the Yongzheng (YŌNG-JUNG) Emperor (1723–1735). Harsh and despotic, he repressed all signs of dissent and imposed strict censorship. But he also enforced efficiency and discipline, combating corruption and paving the way for his son, the Qianlong (ch'YEN-LŌNG) Emperor.

Like his grandfather Kangxi, Qianlong (1736–1795) was a champion of cultural pursuits and an effective warrior. A capable scholar, poet, and painter, Qianlong ordered the compilation and printing of a massive collection of classical Chinese writings. He also assembled in his palace a huge collection of artworks and lavishly supported the work of artists, architects, and scholars.

Qianlong likewise excelled at military expansion (Map 21.7). In the 1750s he subjugated the Mongols, completing Kangxi's effort to end the age-old threat from the northern nomads. He annexed the vast province of Xinjiang (SHIN-J'YAHNG), or Chinese Central Asia, extending China west to its current borders. He repressed revolts in Taiwan and southwestern China, and even sent armies to Nepal and Burma, forcing them to accept the Manchus as overlords.

For most of his reign, Qianlong was an excellent ruler. In his last years, however, as population growth taxed the realm's resources, the aging ruler came under the sway of Heshen (HUH-SHUN), a handsome court guard. Using his favored status to acquire vast wealth through corruption, Heshen allegedly amassed for himself almost two tons of silver. Combined with rising poverty and taxes, this corruption helped trigger the White Lotus Rebellion (1796–1804), a massive peasant uprising in western China led by the White Lotus Society, a religious cult promising the removal of the Manchus and return of the Buddha. It took the regime eight years to put down this revolt, in part because Heshen pocketed money earmarked to suppress the rebels.

In 1795, in a display of Confucian filial piety, Qianlong formally retired so his reign would not last longer than that of his grandfather Kangxi. But the retired ruler continued to influence affairs until his death in 1799, by which time the Qing dynasty, riddled with corruption and internal rebellion, clearly was in decline.

Vietnam Under Chinese Sway: Expansion and Foreign Influence

One repercussion of Manchu decline was increased foreign meddling in the lands on China's periphery. In the late 1700s, for example, exploiting China's weakness and Southeast Asian strife, the French intervened in Vietnam, a Chinese vassal state that long had blended Chinese institutions with its own native culture (Chapter 14).

The strife in Southeast Asia stemmed from several centuries of Vietnamese autonomy and territorial growth. After occupying Vietnam in the early 1400s, China had withdrawn its troops in the face of Vietnamese resistance, letting Vietnam run its own affairs in return for tribute payments. In the 1470s, responding to sea raids from their south, the Vietnamese had invaded Champa, beginning a southward expansion that lasted three centuries (Map 21.8). Led by the powerful Nguyen (*n'WEN*) family, they extended their control over Southeast Asia's entire eastern coast by 1757.

But Vietnamese rule was resented by Champa's people, mostly Buddhist peasants growing Champa rice. In 1771, three brothers called Tay-Son (the name of their native village) led a massive peasant revolt beginning in Champa. Fueled by resentment of Vietnam and its Chinese overlords, the Tay-Son Rebellion drove out the Nguyen and overran all Vietnam, proclaiming one of the brothers its new ruler in 1788. From China Qianlong sent forces to repress the revolt, but they, too, were driven out.

Nguyen Anh, of the ousted Nguyen family, appealed to the French for help. Competing with the British and Dutch for Asian influence, the French were quick to comply. With French assistance, Nguyen Anh eventually defeated the Tay-Son and proclaimed himself emperor of a united Vietnam. But the French, having gained a foothold, later expanded their influence, and the Nguyen dynasty (1802–1945) in time became a French puppet regime (Chapter 29), adding a French Catholic element to Vietnam's blend of Chinese and Southeast Asian cultures.

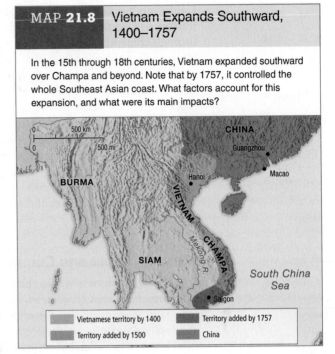

MAP **21.8** Vietnam Expands Southward, 1400–1757

In the 15th through 18th centuries, Vietnam expanded southward over Champa and beyond. Note that by 1757, it controlled the whole Southeast Asian coast. What factors account for this expansion, and what were its main impacts?

French aid in ending revolt In Vietnam creates new connections

Chinese Culture and Society in the Ming and Qing Eras

Chinese culture in the Ming and Qing eras was characterized by contrast. Elite education and scholarship, promoted by the government and embodied in its civil service, typically reflected the regime's focus on stability and tradition. But popular culture was often original and unorthodox, reflecting the aspirations and experiences of the Chinese people.

Chinese society likewise was marked by divergence. Urban life was sophisticated and complex, with a wide array of comforts, amusements, opportunities, and challenges. Rural life, by contrast, was often rough and routine, dominated by family and farming. Expanding commerce and food production brought prosperity to urban and rural areas alike, but increasing population in time created serious problems for both.

Civil Service, Scholarship, and the State

As in earlier eras, society and learning in Ming and Qing China were dominated by the government and its Confucian scholar-bureaucrats, functioning as an educated elite. In village or town schools, and often under private tutors, boys studied the Confucian classics to prepare for civil service exams on the county, province, and national levels. Since the multistage examination process removed all but the brightest and most orthodox candidates, it gave the civil service a very high level of learning and stability, but it also tended to discourage radical innovation.

Even those who challenged the dominant neo-Confucian philosophy, dating from the Song era, did so to refine and expand it rather than supplant it. While accepting the

Confucian civil service supplies stability and learning

Confucian moral code, for example, Wang Yangming, the Ming era's most influential thinker, argued that everyone possesses innate moral knowledge, which can be discovered through contemplation and experience, not just by prolonged study of Confucian classics. His assertions implied that even common people could comprehend Confucian virtue, inspiring efforts by scholars to interact and connect with the masses. They also inspired over a century of vigorous debate, as scholars sought to refine and expand, but not to replace, the Confucian heritage.

The emperors, who presided in Beijing over the highest civil service exams, also patronized scholarship. As noted above, Kangxi sponsored an extensive literary encyclopedia and an official history. Qianlong went even further, employing about three hundred scholars and four thousand scribes for more than ten years to assemble the 36,000-volume *Complete Collection of the Four Treasuries*, a compilation of China's great works of literature, art, history, philosophy, science, and medicine. Seven sets were initially published, with a library built to house each set.

Popular Culture and Commerce

Not all major Chinese works, however, were in the collection. Qianlong, like other emperors, had censors suppress and bureaucrats destroy any works deemed subversive, especially those critical of the regime. And Confucians officials often frowned on fiction as frivolous and subversive.

Despite this official disapproval, several novels gained great popularity, aided by the spread of printing and literacy in Ming and Qing times. *Romance of the Three Kingdoms*, compiled and published in various forms, was based on the age-old often-told saga of three third-century blood brothers (Chapter 14). *The Water Margin* (also translated as *All Men Are Brothers*) told of 108 honest outlaws, driven to crime by an unjust regime, who harmed the rich and powerful while helping the poor and oppressed. Although suppressed as seditious by imperial authorities, it was widely cherished among common folk (as well as by modern Chinese Communists). *The Dream of the Red Chamber*, written in the 1700s, is often regarded as China's greatest novel: with vivid psychological insight it recounts a prominent family's decline, interweaving many poignant and tragic subplots. These three works, and various others, attained the status of literary classics.

Commerce and culture thrive in China's cities

Market towns connect rural masses with wider world

Culture and commerce flourished in China's great cities, including Beijing, Hangzhou, Guangzhou, and Nanjing, which were home to millions. Wealthy urban families adorned their homes with majestic landscapes and vivid still-life paintings, colorful silk tapestries, exquisite blue and white Ming vases (see page 476), and multicolored Qing porcelains. Entertainment districts featured teahouses and theaters, bustling markets displayed vast arrays of goods, and streets were crowded with peddlers, artisans, and workers. Merchants and craftsmen who dealt in the same product often clustered in one district, combining in guilds to regulate prices and trade.

China's countless market towns, though less urbane and affluent than the cities, were also central to the country's economy. They linked the peasant masses with the outside world, providing farmers with a place to sell their surplus, buy household goods, and engage in such amusements as drinking, smoking (a habit derived from the Americas), and card playing (a practice that spread with printing from China to the West).

Guangzhou (Canton), one of China's great centers of culture and commerce.

Village Farming and Population Growth

Even peasant villages, much smaller and less sophisticated than the cities and towns, advanced China's prosperity by producing plentiful food. As fast-growing Champa rice expanded output in lush, moist regions, harvests in less fertile areas were enhanced by new crops such as sweet potatoes and corn, cultivated initially by Amerinds and brought to China by European traders via Macao and the Philippines. Improved irrigation using water pumps, the mechanized sowing of seeds, the planting of northern wheat as a winter crop in the south, and the massive use of fertilizers (including human waste, or "night soil," brought daily from the cities by bucket brigades) contributed to agricultural abundance.

New crops from abroad enhance China's food supply

As food supply increased, China's population, which had more than doubled in the Ming era, doubled again to more than 300 million by the late 1700s. At first this increase, associated with prosperity and growing agricultural output, was welcome: it enlarged both the market and the work force for China's expanding economy. Eventually, however, the growing population caused problems: urban crowding and high crime rates afflicted China's swelling cities, while in rural areas, as woodlands were relentlessly cleared to make room for new cultivation, deforestation led to soil erosion and flooding. By the end of the 18th century, the population increase was outpacing the food supply, reviving in China the poverty of the past.

The Functions of the Chinese Family

In cities, towns, and villages, in good times and in bad, the patriarchal family remained China's basic social unit: the main provider of training for the young, health care for the sick, and material support for the aging. Elder males formally headed the households—making decisions, enforcing discipline, leading the family in ancestor worship, and arranging marriages—while women typically managed the household in service to their husbands and families. Raising girls, who would one day leave home to serve their husband's family, was often deemed a burden: as in ages past, poor peasant families sometimes sold their daughters into servitude, while urban parents subjected their daughters to foot binding, since tiny feet were considered helpful in attracting wealthy husbands (Chapter 14). For the most part, China's families were sources of stability, reinforcing ancient traditions and resistant to change.

Patriarchal families reinforce tradition and stability

Still, in times of misfortune and turbulence, when long-suffering peasants were pushed beyond their limit, rural families and villages served as sources of rebellion and change. They had done so in the 1640s, as Li Zicheng's rebels helped to overthrow the Ming dynasty. They did so in the 1790s, as the White Lotus Rebellion challenged the Qing regime. And they would do so time and again in the 19th and 20th centuries.

In hard times rural masses become sources of change

CHAPTER

REVIEW

Putting It in Perspective

In the 16th through 18th centuries, despite occasional upheavals, the countries of East Asia ranked among the world's most prosperous and stable. Japan, united by ambitious warlords and then led by Tokugawa shoguns, achieved considerable stability and prosperity. China, despite internal rebellions and rule by outsiders from Manchuria, expanded its great power and wealth. Korea and Vietnam, having far less power and wealth, enjoyed substantial security as vassals and tributaries of China.

Both Japan and China, in seeking stability and security, tried to limit outside influence. Both traded with the Westerners who arrived in the 16th century, but Japan eventually restricted this trade to a single Japanese port, and China incorporated it into its tribute system, by which outside countries had long paid tribute for the right to do business with China. Both Japan and China for a time welcomed Jesuits and other Christian missionaries, but both eventually suppressed Christianity as disruptive of traditional beliefs.

These efforts to resist outside influence were not fully successful. Although their economies continued to be based on village farming, both Japan and China experienced increased foreign and domestic commerce,

significant urban growth, and the development of urban cultures. Japan was united by warlords using firearms, and its intellectual life was influenced by Dutch learning, both brought to Japan by people from the West. Crops from the Americas and Southeast Asia advanced China's farming, Spanish silver from the Americas added to China's wealth, and Jesuits from Europe contributed to China's scholarship and diplomacy. Thus, even as they sought external security and internal stability, East Asian societies were seriously affected by connections with other cultures.

Reviewing Key Material

KEY CONCEPTS

daimyo, 466
turtle ships, 469
Dutch learning, 471
jujitsu, 471

haiku, 472
floating world, 472
kabuki, 472
mandarins, 476

KEY PEOPLE

Go-Daigo, 466
Ashikaga Takauji, 467
Oda Nobunaga, 468
Hideyoshi, 468
Yi Song-gye, 469
Tokugawa Ieyasu, 469
Zhu Yuanzhang (Hongwu), 473
Yongle, 473
Zheng He, 474
Li Zicheng, 478
Nurhachi, 479
Hong Taiji, 479

Wu Sangui, 479
Kangxi, 480
Zheng Chenggong (Koxinga), 481
Dalai Lama, 481
Matteo Ricci, 481
Yongzheng, 482
Qianlong, 482
Heshen, 482
Tay-Son brothers, 483
Nguyen Anh, 483
Wang Yangming, 484

ASK YOURSELF

1. What factors disunited Japan in the 15th and 16th centuries? How was it reunified?
2. Why did the Tokugawa shoguns persecute Christians and try to isolate Japan from outsiders? What were the benefits and drawbacks of these policies?
3. What factors led to the fall of the Ming and establishment of Qing (Manchu) rule in China?
4. How did China's Ming and Qing rulers seek to achieve stability and limit foreign influence? Compare and contrast these efforts with those of Japan's Tokugawa shoguns.

5. Compare and contrast the culture of Qing China with that of Tokugawa Japan. How do you account for similarities and differences?

GOING FURTHER

Berry, Mary Elizabeth. *Hideyoshi*. 1982.
Brockley, Liam M. *Journey to the East: The Jesuit Mission to China, 1579–1724*. 2007.
Brook, Timothy. *The Chinese State in Ming Society*. 2005.
Brook, Timothy. *The Confusions of Pleasure: Commerce and Culture in Ming China*. 1998.
Chase, Kenneth. *Firearms: A Global History to 1700*. 2003.
Cohen, Warren. *East Asia at the Center*. 2000.
Crossley, Pamela K. *The Manchus*. 2002.
Ebrey, Patricia B., et al. *East Asia: A Cultural, Social, and Political History*. 2006.
Elliott, Mark C. *The Manchu Way*. 2001.
Elman, B. A. *A Cultural History of Civil Examinations in Late Imperial China*. 2000.
Elman, B. A. *On Their Own Terms: Science in China, 1550–1900*. 2005.
Gordon, Andrew. *A Modern History of Japan: From Tokugawa Times to the Present*. 2003.
Huang, Ray. *1587, A Year of No Significance*. 1981.
Ko, D., J. K. Haboush, and J. R. Piggott, eds. *Women and Confucian Cultures in Premodern China, Korea, and Japan*. 2003.
MacDonald, D. S. *The Koreans*. 1990.
Matsunosuke, N. *Edo Culture: Daily Life and Diversions in Urban Japan, 1600–1868*. 1997.
Mungello, David E. *The Great Encounter of China and the West, 1500–1800*. 2nd ed. 2005.

Nakane, Chie, and Shinzaburo Oishi, *Tokugawa Japan.* 1990.

Palis, J. B. *Politics in Traditional Korea.* 1991.

Pomeranz, Kenneth. *The Great Divergence: China, Europe, and the Making of the Modern World Economy.* 2001.

Reid, Anthony, ed. *Sojourners and Settlers: Histories of Southeast Asia and the Chinese.* 2001.

Spence, J. D. *Emperor of China: Self-Portrait of K'ang Hsi.* 1974.

Sullivan, M. *The Arts of China.* 4th ed. 1999.

Tong, James W. *Disorder Under Heaven: Collective Violence in the Ming Dynasty.* 1991.

Totman, Conrad. *Tokugawa Ieyasu.* 1983.

Varley, H. Paul. *Japanese Culture.* 4th ed. 2000.

Wakeman, Frederick. *The Great Enterprise: Manchu Reconstruction of Imperial Order in Seventeenth Century China.* 1985.

Warshaw, Steven. *Japan Emerges.* 1987.

Whitmore, J. *Vietnam.* 1985.

Woodside, A. *Vietnam and the Chinese Model.* 1988.

Key Dates and Developments

1331–1392	Go-Daigo's rebellion in Japan
1336–1573	Ashikaga Shogunate in Japan
1368–1644	Ming dynasty in China
1392–1910	Yi dynasty in Korea
1467–1568	Age of Warring States in Japan
1471–1757	Vietnamese expansion south to Mekong Delta
1514	Portuguese arrival in southern China
1543	Portuguese arrival in southern Japan
1562–1590	Unification of Japan by Oda Nobunaga and Hideyoshi
1582–1610	Work of Jesuit scholar Matteo Ricci in China
1592–1598	Japanese invasions of Korea
1603–1868	Tokugawa Shogunate in Japan
1639	Eviction of Westerners from Japan
1644	Fall of Beijing: first to rebels, then to Manchus
1644–1912	Manchu rule (Qing dynasty) in China
1661–1722	Reign of Kangxi in China
1704–1742	Papal banning of Jesuit participation in Chinese rites
1736–1795	Reign of Qianlong in China

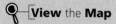 Connections

Reinforce what you learned in this chapter by studying the many documents, images, maps, review tools, and videos available at www.myhistorylab.com.

Read and Review

✓•⌐Study and Review Chapter 21

📖•⌐Read the Document

"Closed Country Edict of 1635" and "Exclusion of the Portuguese, 1639" p. 470

Injunctions to Peasants, Tokugawa Shogunate, 1649, p. 471

Guidelines for Tributary Missions, Qing Dynasty, 1764, p. 482

🔍•⌐View the Image

A Japanese View of European Missionaries, p. 468

Eighteenth-Century Japanese Painting, *A Meeting of China, Japan, and the West*, p. 471

Engravings Showing the Military Victories of the Emperor Qianlong I, p. 482

((•⌐Listen to the Audio

Growth in Asia, p. 473

👁•⌐Watch the Video

Japan, Age of the Warring States, p. 467

Research and Explore

🔍•⌐View the Map

Interactive Map: Chinese Voyages of the Ming Dynasty, p. 474

((•⌐Listen to the Chapter Audio for Chapter 21 on **myhistorylab.com**

Southern Asia and the Global Shift in Wealth and Power, 1500–1800

((•—[Listen to the **Chapter Audio** for Chapter 22 on **myhistorylab.com**

- Why did Europeans choose to confront Muslims in southern Asia?

- How was India transformed by the confrontation between Europeans and Muslims?

- What factors permitted Muslims and Hindus to cooperate peacefully in Southeast Asia?

- What caused the decline of Safavid Persia?

- How did the Ottoman Empire respond to Europe's challenge?

Batavia in the 18th Century

The commercial port of Batavia in the Dutch East Indies is shown in this 18th century drawing. The Dutch United East India Company helped transfer wealth and commercial domination from southern Asia to Europe (page 501).

In the stifling early morning heat of June 23, 1757, Siraj-ud-Daulah (*sir-AHJ ud-DOW-luh*), ruler of the East Indian region of Bengal, surveyed his fifty thousand soldiers as they prepared for battle on an open field near the village of Plassey. Looking across the field at the tiny forces of his British opponent, Siraj was confident of victory. The British possessed modern weapons, technologically superior to those manufactured in Asia, but Siraj had purchased some for his own men. The 2,800 troops commanded by the young British officer, Robert Clive, could hardly expect to defeat such a large Bengali host.

Across the field, Clive had long since reached the same conclusion. Weeks earlier, recognizing that he was unlikely to win on the battlefield, he had opened secret negotiations with local Hindu bankers interested in preferential trading agreements with Britain. These wealthy men helped Clive convince Siraj's commanding general to betray his master. So when this general approached Siraj on the morning of June 23, it was not to ask for instructions. Instead, he informed the Bengali ruler of his decision to support the British. Faced with this treachery, Siraj fought bravely but was forced to retreat. Clive would later be hailed in England as the "victor of Plassey."

Victory takes many forms, of which success in battle is only one. Economic influence and technological innovation can also prove decisive, as southern Asia's ruling Muslims discovered when challenged by Europeans in the 17th and 18th centuries. Europe's success in confrontations with these Islamic empires integrated the Indian Ocean into a global trading network and set in motion a tremendous transfer of wealth and power from Asia to Europe.

Southern Asia

Confrontation: Europe and Islam in Southern Asia

In 1600 nearly all of southern Asia, from Anatolia to Indonesia, was dominated by Islam. The three great Islamic empires—Mughal India, Safavid Persia, and the multinational empire of the Ottoman Turks—ruled huge and populous domains, while Muslim merchants exercised commanding influence on trade and culture in Malaya and Indonesia. Connected by Islamic culture and linked by flourishing overland and Indian Ocean trade, these regions together constituted one of history's mightiest and wealthiest civilizations (Map 22.1).

Europeans challenge Islamic dominance in southern Asia

By 1800, however, Islamic preeminence in southern Asia had yielded to the Europeans, whose economic and technological strength helped reorient the global balance of wealth and power. Indian Ocean trade had always been regional rather than global. It was more profitable than Mediterranean trade even before the Ottomans took Constantinople in 1453, and in the early 1500s it dwarfed the emerging Atlantic trade. But when the Europeans moved into the Indian Ocean with monopolistic trading companies, they connected Atlantic, Mediterranean, and Indian Ocean commercial networks into a global trading system. Commercial power thereupon became global rather than regional, and wealth flowed *out* of the Indian Ocean region through the trading companies and *into* Europe. Southern Asia's empires lost this struggle for economic power, gradually succumbing to a combination of external threats and internal decline.

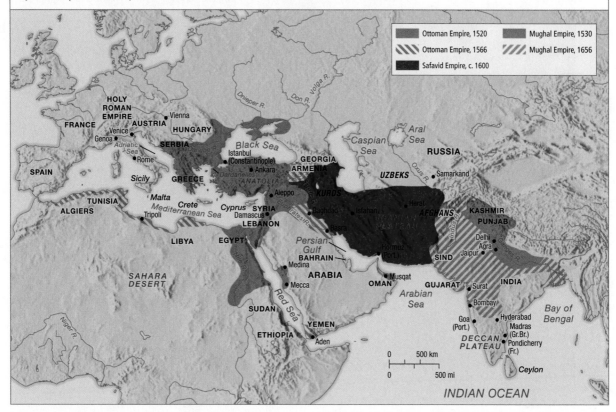

| FOUNDATION MAP **22.1** | Islamic Asian Empires in 1600 |

As the 17th century began, Islam's position in the world seemed unshakable. Notice that the great Islamic empires consolidated in the 16th century spread across southern Asia, southeastern Europe, and northeastern Africa. Using the Indian Ocean as a commercial highway, Muslims dominated oceangoing trade in the Eastern Hemisphere. The Arabic language, colored and enriched by Persian, united the Muslim faithful in a spiritual and cultural community spanning thousands of miles. What advantages and disadvantages can you identify for these empires?

The Indian Ocean Trade

During the 16th century, and in the centuries immediately preceding it, the Indian Ocean basin served as the world's main center of maritime trade. Riding seasonal monsoon winds, which generally blow to the south and west from November to March, and to the north and east from April to September, Arab and Persian sailors carried on a lively commerce connecting India, Persia, Arabia, the city-states of East Africa, and Europe. Farther east, Chinese and Southeast Asian ships carried merchandise back and forth from India to Southeast Asia and the East Indies, and through the Straits of Melaka to the South China Sea and southern China.

Indian Ocean commerce was highly specialized, with each region typically supplying products that were locally raised, manufactured, or mined (Map 22.2). East Africa supplied ebony, ivory, slaves, and especially gold, mined in southeastern Africa and shipped from the great port of Kilwa. Arabia and Persia provided horses, figs, dates, and incense, as well as fine woven tapestries and carpets. India was known for its superb cotton textiles as well as for various dyes (including indigo), leather goods, carpets, knives, and assorted spices, including especially cinnamon and pepper. Southeast Asia and the East Indies produced rubies, gold, tin, sandalwood, and spices such as cinnamon and ginger.

The Indian Ocean connects world trade networks

MAP **22.2**	Trade Routes Across the Indian Ocean, 1600

Hindu, Muslim, and Chinese traders crisscrossed the Indian Ocean using trade routes that had been established for centuries. Their familiarity with and systematic exploitation of these routes guaranteed their wealth and power. Note that the Indian Ocean's central position linked the Pacific Ocean with the Mediterranean/Red Sea trade. Why did the arrival of the Europeans in the 16th century challenge this established network?

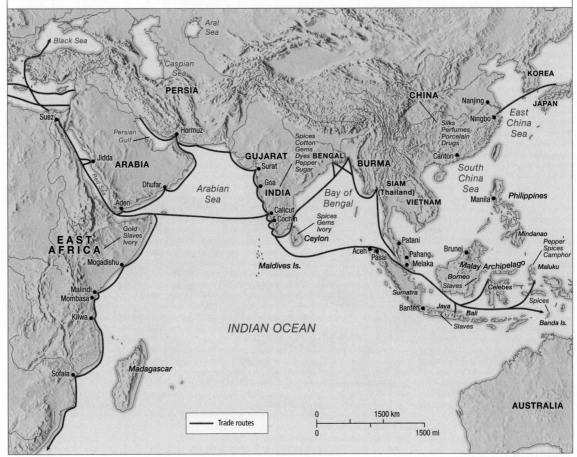

The Maluku islands in the eastern East Indies were famous for their nutmeg and cloves; Westerners called them the Spice Islands. And Chinese products, such as porcelains and silks, were valued throughout the Indian Ocean basin and in Europe.

To handle all this trade, thriving seaports grew up along Asia's southern coast. These commercial centers included Aden at the mouth of the Red Sea, Hormuz at the entrance to the Persian Gulf, and Calicut on India's southwestern seaboard, known as the **Malabar Coast**.

Farther east, Melaka, on the straits connecting the Indian Ocean with the South China Sea, served as the region's greatest commercial center. Although Muslim merchants and mariners conducted much of the commerce, many of these cities were religiously and culturally diverse, with Hindus, Buddhists, Jews, and others engaging in crafts and commerce.

Islamic empires rely on Indian Ocean trade

The empires of southern Asia derived substantial benefits from the Indian Ocean trade. It added immensely to the wealth of their realms and helped fill the treasuries of their rulers, who charged a variety of licensing fees, taxes, and customs duties on artisans, merchants, and shippers. To a certain extent, then, the wealth and power of the Muslim world derived from Islamic domination of the Indian Ocean trade.

Ironically, one of Islam's greatest triumphs—the conquest of Constantinople in 1453 by the Ottoman Turks—set in motion events that eventually undermined this domination and the fortunes of Islamic southern Asia. For in the late 15th century, Portuguese sailors had initiated the European voyages of discovery (Chapter 19) and challenged Muslim control of the Indian Ocean.

Shifting Balances of Power and Commerce

Europe's explorations produced conflict with the Islamic societies of southern Asia. The newcomers were interested mainly in trade but also used their warships to project their power in the Indian Ocean. Sixteenth-century European warships were engineered to include powerful cannons whose shot could penetrate the hulls of enemy ships. Mounted on wheeled carriages to make them quickly interchangeable with one another, so that if one failed another could easily be brought up, these weapons revolutionized naval warfare. European nations such as England and Holland developed iron-smelting industries to produce large numbers of naval cannons. The Islamic navies of southern Asia found themselves at a great disadvantage, one that the Europeans were quick to exploit.

European technology puts Muslims at a disadvantage

At first the European traders and merchants came mainly from Portugal, which established trading posts in Melaka, Macao, Timor, and elsewhere. But soon the Portuguese had to share the region with commercial enterprises from England and Holland (also called the Dutch Republic or United Provinces of the Netherlands). Channeling the talents of their ambitious middle classes, these countries constructed large maritime trading empires. Using advanced weaponry, improvements in navigational instruments, and superb organizational skills, they accumulated unprecedented wealth. Although these newly arrived entrepreneurs came mainly to seek riches and frequently fought one another, eventually they had a profound political and economic impact on India, Indonesia, and mainland Southeast Asia.

Portugal's Indian Ocean outposts survived into the 20th century, but by the middle of the 17th its hold on the Southeast Asian trade had been seized by the Dutch. During the next two centuries, the Dutch gradually established territorial sovereignty over Indonesia, which they called the Dutch (or Netherlands) East Indies. France and Britain competed for influence in the Indian subcontinent, and by 1763 the British emerged victorious. British domination of India gave London effective control of the Indian Ocean, with naval and military bases in East Africa, the Red Sea, the Persian Gulf, and the Malay archipelago. France, removed from the subcontinent, expanded elsewhere in the 19th century, eventually dominating much of North Africa and the Southeast Asian mainland.

The Dutch seize Asian trade routes from Portugal

At the same time, however, the focus of the global economy was shifting away from the Indian Ocean. As Europe's trade with the Americas became more profitable than its trade with the East, the busiest commercial routes shifted to the Atlantic. Traffic in Asian luxury goods, which had stimulated Europe's initial explorations in the 1400s, was now surpassed by exponential growth in the Atlantic trade, involving slaves from Africa and sugar, silver, tobacco, and coffee from the Americas. A modern mercantile system was in place, as Europe's colonies supplied their mother countries with the raw materials from which to fabricate finished goods. The mother countries then sold those goods on the open market, using the profits to increase their investment in their colonies and obtain more raw materials. Mercantilism enabled England and Holland to seize the dominant commercial status previously enjoyed by the Islamic world. Global networks, controlled by the English and Dutch, linked Indian Ocean trade with the Atlantic trade. The Indian Ocean commerce itself, however, was clearly in decline, and the Islamic trading centers were dominated, directly or indirectly, by Europeans.

▶ Read the **Document**

Jan van Linschoten on Dutch Business in the Indian Ocean

on **myhistorylab.com**

Atlantic commercial routes become more valuable

Islamic empires decline as their commercial networks are lost

From the 16th to the 18th century, as commerce and control of the global economy shifted to the land- and sea-based empires of Europe, the Islamic realms declined. Mughal India dissolved into several competing provincial states and gradually came under British control. The trading states of Indonesia became, for the most part, economic appendages of Holland. Safavid Iran, deserted by tribes that had once been its vassals, was plagued by Afghan, Russian, and Turkish invaders. The Ottoman Empire became politically decentralized, militarily weak, and vulnerable to attacks from Austria and Russia. For Islamic southern Asia, the transition to a global economy, and the consequent shift in the global balance of power, had a highly negative impact.

Transformation of the Indian Subcontinent

View the **Map**

Map Discovery: French, British, and Dutch Holdings, ca. 1700

on **myhistorylab.com**

India was the first southern Asian region affected by Europe's expansion. In 1497–1498, Portuguese explorer Vasco da Gama's voyage round the southern tip of Africa brought him to India's Malabar Coast, where he established commercial contacts in the port of Calicut. In the centuries that followed, increasing numbers of merchants and traders from Europe made their way to India, bringing Western wealth, products, weapons, and ways. By the end of the 18th century, as the Mughal Empire declined, much of the subcontinent came under European control.

Europeans Arrive in India

When da Gama's two ships entered Calicut harbor in 1498, their appearance perplexed virtually everyone in the port. The admiral explained that he had been sent to develop a southern trade route that would bypass the ancient land connection now dominated by Muslims and preyed on by Mongols. That explanation made a certain amount of sense in Calicut, and as the Portuguese had been instructed to pay any price for spices, Indian traders stopped asking questions and started counting their profits. Competing Arab and Chinese merchants, long established in the region and aware of actual values, thought the Portuguese were fools. But when da Gama returned to Portugal, he sold his cargo for 3,000 percent more than the entire cost of his expedition. Soon hundreds of Portuguese ships were sailing regularly to India, and other Europeans eagerly pushed their way into this highly profitable trade. They created a baffling new challenge for India's Muslim rulers.

Read the **Document**

Excerpt from the Travel Journal of Vasco da Gama

on **myhistorylab.com**

Portugal intrudes on Indian Ocean trade

PORTUGUESE AND MUSLIM RIVALRY. Portuguese seamen soon realized that, although their sea route cut out the land-based Ottoman middlemen, they were now competing for spices with seagoing Muslim merchants in the Indian Ocean. In 1501 Portuguese navigator Pedro Alvares Cabral brought six ships to Calicut after being blown off course along the way and landing accidentally on the coast of Brazil. He left 54 Portuguese merchants in India, directing them to buy spices at the lowest prices possible and store the goods until the next ships arrived. On his way back to Portugal, Cabral captured and looted an Arab merchant ship, provoking Muslims to kill all the Portuguese he had left behind in Calicut. In 1502 Vasco da Gama returned with a powerful fleet, pulverized the port of Calicut with his cannons, and sliced off the ears, noses, and hands of eight hundred Muslim seamen. Indian Muslims then left the Portuguese alone. But the Portuguese government in Lisbon realized

View of Goa in the middle of the 17th century.

that it would have to protect its traders, so in 1509 the Portuguese king appointed Dom Afonso d'Albuquerque as his viceroy in the East.

Albuquerque, a passionate Catholic who despised Islam, built bases on the Persian Gulf, the Red Sea, and the Straits of Melaka. At his suggestion, Portugal seized the island of Goa on India's Malabar Coast; it served as Lisbon's Indian headquarters from 1510 until 1961. By cutting in half the taxes of every Hindu on the island, the Portuguese won local support against the Muslims. Albuquerque devised a number of bizarre schemes to destroy Islam, most of which—such as stealing the remains of Muhammad or damming the Nile so Egypt would starve—were beyond the capacity or interest of the Portuguese Empire. But he did succeed in making his king fabulously wealthy, as Portuguese imports at bargain prices generated a huge increase in European demand for spices.

Portugal's power was brief, however. While the Hindus of South India welcomed the Portuguese as traders and as potential allies against Islamic rule, in the 1560s several Central Indian Muslim sultanates declared *jihad* against the Hindus. They defeated the South Indian Hindu kingdom of Vijayanagar, depriving Portugal of the South Indian trade and jeopardizing its Malabar Coast position.

Islamic states strike back against Portugal

Shortly thereafter, King Philip II of Spain inherited the Portuguese crown, creating a union between Spain and Portugal that lasted from 1580 until 1640. Philip, like Albuquerque a devoted Catholic, promptly closed the Portuguese port of Lisbon to Protestant shipping. Protestant nations such as Holland and England, previously content to buy their spices from Portugal, now sought their own sea routes around Africa to India. The Portuguese tried using their bases in Angola and Mozambique to blockade the relatively narrow passage around the Cape of Good Hope, but blockading was an inexact science and their efforts failed. Moreover, after England destroyed the Spanish Armada in 1588 (Chapter 20), the Iberian threat to Dutch and English shipping diminished substantially.

View the **Image**
Portuguese Church in Southern India
on **myhistorylab.com**

THE ENGLISH AND DUTCH EAST INDIA COMPANIES. In 1600 and 1602, the English and Dutch governments each created a large commercial enterprise and gave it a national monopoly over trade with India. Before long, these ventures, known respectively as the English (later British) East India Company and the Dutch United East India Company, were vigorously pursuing this trade. The problem was that India was not particularly interested in expanding commerce with Europe. The Portuguese were valued customers because they paid in gold, but the Dutch and English companies wanted to create a balance of trade in which they would pay for spices with money that the Indians would then return to them in exchange for manufactured goods. India neither wanted nor needed anything made in Northern Europe at that time and was already selling enough spices to Portugal to satisfy its need for gold. But after a demonstration of English naval power in 1612, when one English ship defeated four Portuguese galleons, India's Mughal emperor decided that dealing with London was worth his time.

The Mughal emperor also turned to England for protection from pirates, asking its navy to escort the annual pilgrim ship to and from Mecca. As one of the Five Pillars of Islam, the pilgrimage to Mecca played a vital role in unifying Muslims throughout the world, and the Mughal Empire sponsored an annual ship to transport the faithful. Previously the Portuguese navy had provided the escort, but now, in return for trading privileges, England took over.

England was willing to cooperate commercially with Holland against Portugal, but the Dutch shortsightedly shut the English out in Indonesia, eventually establishing a colony there known as the Dutch East Indies. England, in turn, excluded the Dutch from India, thereby laying the foundation of what would become by the 19th century a vast British Empire.

England and Holland contend for trade routes

Meanwhile the English were building further connections with India. Since Indians were unwilling to buy English goods, the English East India Company tried to reduce its

England creates connections with India

Monogram of the Dutch East India Company.

Europeans have differing motives for entering South and Southeast Asia

gold payments by establishing factories in the region. Recognizing that the Indian cotton cloth known as **calico** (since it came from Calicut), already fashionable in England, could also be used in the spice trade, the English built a textile factory on the east coast of India, paying Indian weavers in gold to make calico cloth. The cloth was then traded for spices in the Maluku Islands. Using calico, the English were able to get three hundred times the spices that the gold they paid the weavers could have bought. At the same time, the English, by using inexpensive local labor, reduced the cost of calico in the English home market and tied India more closely to England itself.

THE MUGHAL RESPONSE. By this time India's Great Mughal rulers were beginning to notice European activities. The Mughal Empire had earlier been able to control Arabian Sea traffic into Indian ports, but now the English dominated those waters. Also worrying the emperor was London's construction of Fort Saint George beside the East Indian seaside village of Madras (*MAH-drahs*), a sleepy town that would soon become, with Calcutta and Bombay, one of the three principal British ports in India. Obviously the English intended to protect their trade, but a fort constructed for protection could also be used for domination.

The Mughals were uncertain of the precise nature of the threat and didn't know how to handle it. India for centuries had been invaded by land (the Mughals themselves were simply the last in a long line of Central Asian conquerors), but Europeans had not come by land and did not seem to be invading. They apparently had no desire to move entire populations to India, as previous invaders had done; rather, they sought economic relations, to which the empire had no objection. What was worrisome, however, was the military and naval power of the Europeans and the English construction of Fort Saint George. For the moment the Mughals watched and waited. They did not realize that once the Europeans had gained a foothold on the coasts of the subcontinent, it would be nearly impossible to expel them.

DIFFERING EUROPEAN INTERESTS IN SOUTH AND SOUTHEAST ASIA. Regimes throughout South and Southeast Asia were similarly perplexed about European intentions. Their confusion was compounded by sharp differences in motivation among various European groups.

One difference concerned geographic focus. The Portuguese, who arrived first, were interested in the entire region, hoping to turn the Indian Ocean into a Portuguese-controlled commercial zone. Later arrivals focused more narrowly. The Dutch were primarily concerned with Southeast Asia, the English and French with India. It took nearly a century for local rulers to appreciate fully the implication of this difference: if Europeans were interested not only in commercial relations but also in political control, dividing up the region would make individual parts of it easier to conquer.

A second difference concerned religious attitudes. The Catholic Portuguese and French intended not only to make money but also to save souls. Catholics viewed Indians, both Hindus and Muslims, as highly civilized people who needed the Gospel preached to them by missionaries of the universal Roman Catholic Church. The Protestant English and Dutch, on the other hand, were principally interested in doing business. Protestantism rejected the concept of a universal Church structure, so establishing a Protestant Church of England in India made little sense, except to serve the spiritual needs of transplanted English subjects. The Dutch, as Calvinists, were even less interested in encouraging conversion: since Calvinism held that everyone on Earth was predestined either to heaven or to hell, there seemed to be no point in laboring strenuously in vain efforts to change what God had already decided.

These differences among Europeans were at first unclear to South and Southeast Asian rulers. When the differences became clear, the motivations behind them remained difficult to understand. And when those motivations became clear, it was too late to dislodge the Europeans.

The Mughals in Decline

As the English were establishing a foothold on the coasts of India, the Mughal Empire was weakening from within. The oppressive Aurangzeb, who reigned from 1658 to 1707, destroyed Akbar's legacy of tolerance. Aurangzeb's militant Muslim policies alienated Hindus and Sikhs who had previously supported the regime, and he drained the imperial treasury to put down rising opposition from these groups. After his death, central control of the empire deteriorated as separate groups competed for power. The chaos ended in 1719 when the Sayyid (*SĪA-yēd*) brothers, two influential and ruthless courtiers, became the powers behind the throne.

The Sayyids selected the weak but cultivated Muhammad Shah as emperor. His lengthy reign (1719–1748) was culturally beneficial: Hindus and Muslims drew closer to one another, primarily through their common use of the **Urdu** (*UR-doo*) language, a Hindu tongue written with the Persian alphabet and employing many Persian terms. Urdu poetry flourished at Delhi, and the Mughal court tolerated Hindu deities and myths as cultural curiosities, though not as gods deserving of worship.

But Muhammad Shah's rule further weakened the empire's political unity. He tried but failed to restore confidence in central authority, and some of his policies actually strengthened his adversaries. For example, he sought to gain the loyalty of the **Marathas** (*mah-ruh-TAHZ*), a staunchly Hindu people of Central India, by recognizing their autonomy and granting them taxation authority. In the short term, the Marathas ceased their opposition, but in the long term these concessions helped them become more powerful. To counterbalance the Marathas, Muhammad Shah then tried to win the loyalty of local princes, or **nawabs** (*NĀ-wabs*) by granting them taxation privileges in their own regions. The nawabs took the tax advantages but did not prove loyal. Gradually the Mughal Empire dissolved into independent states, owing nominal rather than real allegiance to the emperor in Delhi.

As Mughal power in India declined, the Afghans invaded Persia. Nadir (*NAH-dēr*) Shah, the Persian ruler, asked Muhammad Shah for help, but the Mughal emperor, who was fighting the Marathas, refused. Exasperated, the Persians moved against Afghanistan on their own and then continued across the Indus River to punish the Mughals. In 1739, they sacked Delhi and captured Akbar's legendary Peacock Throne. Carrying it back to their capital at Isfahan (*ISS-fah-hahn*), they made it the throne of all Iran's shahs until 1979.

The Persian sack of Delhi marked the end of Mughal centralized authority, although the empire officially continued into the 19th century. Afghans, Iranians, Sikhs, Marathas, and minor Muslim states fought over pieces of the empire, and petty rajahs and nawabs played roles well beyond their financial means and political capacities. For many Muslims, these startling developments called into question not only Islamic political power but also the future of Indian Islam.

Mughal power deteriorates

((•—Listen to the **Audio**
Mughals
on **myhistorylab.com**

The Marathas become an important force in India

View the **Map**
Map Discovery: The Maratha Kingdoms
on **myhistorylab.com**
Persians sack Delhi and end Mughal authority

The Crisis of Islamic India

Islam conquered India but never converted it. Hinduism remained the subcontinent's dominant faith, and India's caste system defied repeated Islamic efforts at social leveling. Muslims successfully installed their own political systems, but religiously and culturally India remained Hindu, a fact impossible to ignore when Mughal authority collapsed. This political crisis caused soul-searching among Indian Muslims.

Indian Islam faces a crisis

Ever since waves of Muslim cavalry poured forth from the Arabian Peninsula in the seventh century C.E., Islam had identified closely with Arab and Persian cultures. This connection had enabled most Muslims, from West Africa to Indonesia, to consider themselves part of a cosmopolitan cultural world centered in Southwest Asia. But the Indian subcontinent had always been different. There Islam was the religion of the ruling elites, not the common people. India's complex Hindu culture resisted Arab-Persian influences and offered a viable alternative to the faith and customs of its Muslim conquerors. Most of the Indian population retained pre-Islamic ways. Even where elements of Islam were assimilated into the local culture—such as in the Punjab, where Sikhism offered a popular synthesis of Hinduism and Islam (Chapter 17)—Muslims viewed the result as a corruption of the pure monotheism of the Prophet.

Europeans take advantage of Mughal decline

Elsewhere, in Afghanistan and Anatolia, for example, Muslim conquest had brought in large numbers of Islamic immigrants. But few Muslims immigrated to India, and those who did had to work hard to avoid being assimilated into the Hindu masses. They therefore isolated themselves in the top political structures of the Delhi Sultanate and the Mughal Empire, structures that remained closed to Hindus. Their only success in converting Hindus was among the lower castes, a development that made Indian Islam even less attractive to well-born Hindus.

Delhi's Golden Mosque, built by Muhammad Shah in 1722.

The collapse of Mughal authority brought Indian Muslims face to face with a disturbing possibility: no longer in power, they might be absorbed into Hindu culture, which they considered idolatrous. Many viewed emigration or political separation from Hindu India as their only practical alternative. This crisis of confidence troubled Indian Islam from 1739 until 1947, when India was divided into separate Hindu and Muslim states.

British and French Rivalry in India

Meanwhile, a new group of Europeans was making inroads in India, ready to take advantage of Mughal decline. In 1664 France founded the French East India Company, which from 1674 was headquartered at Pondichéry (*pawn-dih-share-RE*), 85 miles south of the English East India Company's base at Madras (Map 22.3). As the French began to challenge the English, Anglo-French trade became intensely competitive. By 1739 both Madras and Pondichéry had grown to cities of fifty thousand inhabitants as their respective companies jockeyed for position.

This Anglo-French rivalry took on a new dimension in 1740, when Britain and France went to war against each other in the War of the Austrian Succession (1740–1748). This war was fought not only in Europe but also in each nation's colonial possessions. In 1746, the French, led by Joseph-François Dupleix (*zhō-SEFF frahn-SWAH doo-PLAY*), governor of Pondichéry, captured the British fort at

Madras. Among those in the garrison who were expelled was a 21-year-old bookkeeper named Robert Clive.

Clive had become so bored in his job with the British East India Company that he allegedly attempted suicide, only to have the gun he was using misfire. The fall of Madras suggested to him that it might be more exciting to shoot French soldiers than to shoot himself, and the following year he enlisted in the British forces. In 1748 the English regained Madras, pushing the French back to Pondichéry as the war in Europe closed. Clive returned to Madras, watched Dupleix work at Pondichéry, learned from him, and became his rival.

Using a combination of military force, bribery, and behind-the-throne manipulation, Dupleix extended French civil authority throughout southern India by early 1751. But in 1751, Clive, now a captain, struck a deal with Maratha leaders and led a joint English-Maratha force that defeated the French. Thereupon the French East India Company recalled Dupleix, who had been appointed, the company contended, to make a profit, not to create a French empire in India.

Britain, by contrast, backed Clive and his ambitions for empire. War resumed in 1756

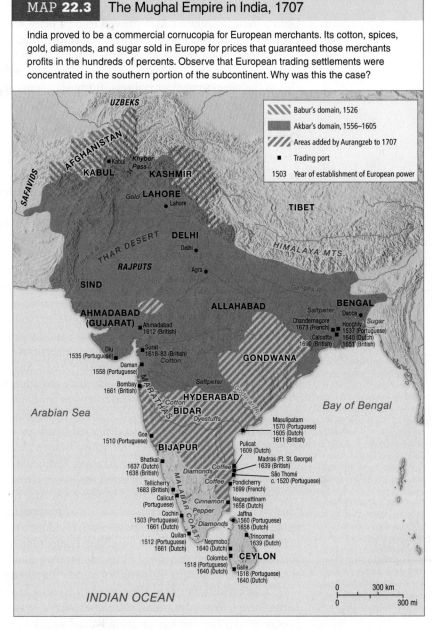

MAP 22.3   The Mughal Empire in India, 1707

India proved to be a commercial cornucopia for European merchants. Its cotton, spices, gold, diamonds, and sugar sold in Europe for prices that guaranteed those merchants profits in the hundreds of percents. Observe that European trading settlements were concentrated in the southern portion of the subcontinent. Why was this the case?

(the Seven Years War), and in 1757 Clive won the victory at Plassey described at the beginning of the chapter. By 1763 Britain had conquered nearly all of France's Indian possessions, establishing a foundation for British domination of the entire subcontinent. In 1765 Clive became governor of Bengal, with enough money to buy off the nawabs and enough soldiers to defend the company's assets.

Britain outmaneuvers France in India

The British thereafter expanded their influence in India, gradually transferring power from the company to the British government. Following Clive's policy, they sent out a few tough, competent Englishmen to oversee British rule through Indian leaders. During the next century, India became the "jewel in the crown" of the British monarchs—the cornerstone of England's worldwide empire and a principal element in its prosperity. Once again the Indian subcontinent was unified under foreign rule.

Muslims and Europeans in Southeast Asia

Unlike India, Southeast Asia proved to be a place where Islam could continue to expand. Located at a crossroads of international trade, it interested both Muslims and Europeans. But the large number of islands in the Indonesian and Malayan archipelagos and the imposing mountain ranges and rain forests of the Southeast Asian mainland all proved obstacles to the development of political unity across the region.

Coexistence Between Muslims and Hindus

The expansion of Islam into Southeast Asia was carried out by merchants rather than warriors. The Indonesian kingdom of Srivijaya controlled the Straits of Melaka (Chapter 12), and therefore also the flourishing seaborne trade between China and India. Srivijaya was a Hindu kingdom, unlike the Buddhist societies of the Southeast Asian mainland, and might have been expected to resist Islam with the same intensity demonstrated by Hindus in India. But Indonesia gradually accepted Islam as its dominant belief system. A number of factors made this outcome possible.

Muslims and Hindus prove compatible in Indonesia

First, while Muslims came to India as conquerors, they came to Southeast Asia as commercial partners. Islamic merchants settled in Indonesia and the Malay archipelago, established businesses that enriched the communities in which they lived, and married into the families of local elites. Several rulers converted to Islam in the expectation that it would improve their position with regard to rival Hindu states in central Java (Map 22.4). Conversion was also useful for trade, as Muslim connections could bring the India–China trade into Islamic trading networks across the Indian Ocean. Since there were no atrocities of the kind committed against Hindus in India, Muslims were not demonized in Southeast Asia.

Second, Islam appealed to the common people of the region by advocating the essential equality of all believers in the sight of Allah. Since Southeast Asian Hindus did not practice the caste system that so offended Muslims in India, they were not conditioned to lives of inequality and discrimination. Islam's radical leveling, derived from the horizontal social structure of the Arabian Peninsula and from the Prophet's message that all were slaves before God, attracted the lower classes without threatening elite interests.

Finally, Islam was transmitted to Southeast Asia by Sufi mystics who accompanied Muslim merchants. Sufis practiced a form of **pantheism**, the belief that God is present in all things, both animate and inanimate. Since Hinduism is both polytheistic and pantheistic, Indonesians and Malays found Sufi Islam compatible in this respect with their own beliefs. Sufis also worshiped saints and believed that they could heal the sick, doctrines and practices abhorred by mainstream Muslims but widely practiced in pre-Islamic Southeast Asia.

These conditions eased the spread of Islam across the region beginning in the 13th century. When Iskandar, ruler of Srivijaya, was overthrown by princes from central Java around 1400 and driven from Palembang, he converted to Islam and founded the trading state of Melaka. Soon it was a center of Islamic culture, and the prosperous connections it built with China, Java, and India helped disperse this culture across the region. By the time the Portuguese arrived in 1511, Islam was the most widely accepted belief system in Malaya and Indonesia.

Islam restricts Southeast Asian women

Information about Southeast Asian women prior to the arrival of Islam is difficult to come by, but it is clear that Islamization restricted female roles significantly. Southeast Asian women traditionally served as connectors between the world of the living and that of the spirits, but Islam insisted that all worship be focused on Allah and that only men could lead prayers. Politically, many women had ruled or acted as regents before Islamization, and as late as the 17th century, women had functioned as armed guards for kings and royal households. Such behavior was now prohibited.

MAP 22.4 Southeast Asia and Indonesia, 1500–1700

Southeast Asia's strategic location at the juncture of the Indian Ocean, the Pacific Ocean, and the South China Sea made it an indispensable thoroughfare for Eastern Hemispheric trade. The region produced spices in abundance and boasted several useful natural harbors. Notice the enormous number of islands in the Malayan, Indonesian, and Philippine archipelagos, making the development of centralized government extremely difficult. How would this geographic handicap leave the region vulnerable to European intrusion?

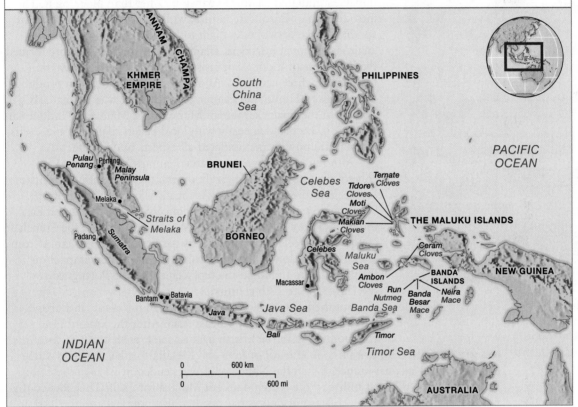

The European Intrusion

Portugal's conquest of Melaka in 1511 forced Muslims to move into the interior forests of Sumatra, Java, and Borneo, thus accelerating the geographic spread of the faith. Other Muslims traveled up the Malay Peninsula and established sultanates there. Once the ordinary people of those regions were introduced to Islam, significant numbers of conversions followed. The Malay sultanate of Johore (*jeh-HŌR*) and the Javanese kingdom of Mataram (*mah-TEHR-rum*)—both Muslim realms—developed into formidable rivals of the Europeans by 1650. By that time Portuguese commercial dominance had been supplanted by the Dutch.

Having gained independence from Spain through a prolonged and bitter revolt in the late 1500s (Chapter 20), the Calvinist Dutch found themselves denied access to Lisbon's pepper and spice markets by the Catholic kings of Spain, who also ruled Portugal from 1580 to 1640. Accepting this exclusion as the price of liberty, the Dutch promptly sailed for the East Indies and waged naval warfare against the Portuguese. Through their Dutch United East India Company, they founded Batavia in 1619 (see page 489); in 1949 it was renamed Djakarta (*juh-KAR-tuh*) and is now Indonesia's capital. In 1641 they joined with Johore to capture Melaka from the Portuguese, and in 1658 they took Palembang.

The Chronicles of Java.

The Dutch challenge Portuguese commercial supremacy

European domination changes from commercial to colonial

View the **Map**

Map Discovery: The Stages of Dutch Expansion in Java
on **myhistorylab.com**

By this time the Portuguese were in full retreat from Southeast Asia, pulling back to the Indian Ocean, where their struggles against the Ottomans and the British were also going badly. The Portuguese were expelled from the Persian Gulf in 1650, and from East Africa (with the exception of Mozambique) by 1696.

Dutch supremacy in Indonesia, like the earlier Portuguese impact, stimulated Islamic expansion rather than blocking it. The introduction of European culture, with values so alien to those of southern Asia, provoked a flight to Islam as a form of reaction against the Dutch intruders. Islamic institutions and culture formed the backbone of Indonesian resistance to European domination for the next three centuries. Additionally, Sufi pantheism produced a synthesis of Hindu and Islamic practices that was particularly notable in the Javanese state of Mataram. In Malay and Indonesian villages, Islam blended easily with local beliefs that demons, spirits, and natural powers manipulated all aspects of daily life.

Although European commercial empires continued to control trade and exclude rival powers, they had minimal impact on local culture and customs. At the close of the 18th century, Southeast Asian Muslims were unconcerned that the Dutch East India Company fell victim to British competition and the French conquest of Holland in 1795. They assumed that the change from Dutch domination to British would have no greater impact on their daily lives than had the replacement of the Portuguese by the Dutch in the 17th century.

But their assumptions were mistaken, for events in Europe had a direct impact on Southeast Asia. After the king of Holland collaborated with the British against the French occupation of his country (Chapter 26), Britain took control of Java and Melaka for their military value in a global war against France. When the Napoleonic Wars ended in 1815, a victorious Britain returned the East Indies to the Dutch but kept Malaya for itself. This new configuration of European influence was not only economic but also political and territorial. Southeast Asian Muslims, long accustomed to Dutch and British *commercial* exploitation, suddenly found themselves subjects of European *colonial* empires.

The End of Safavid Persia

Islam's conquest of Persia in the seventh century C.E. had enriched the new monotheistic faith with the splendor of Persian language and culture. That enrichment survived the rise and fall of dynasties and a series of invasions across the Iranian plateau. In the 16th century, the Safavids reconstituted a strong Persian state as a rival to the neighboring Ottoman Empire (Chapter 17). From their capital at Isfahan, the Safavids presided over a golden age of commerce, refinement, and reform. But by the mid-18th century, this Persian dynasty was gone.

Safavid Centralization and Decline

The successors of Abbas I centralize the Safavid Empire

The death of Abbas I began the empire's decline. His immediate successors, Safi (*SAH-fē*), who ruled from 1629 to 1642, and Abbas II, who ruled from 1642 to 1666, ended the decentralized provincial administration under which the empire had thrived and replaced

MAP **22.5**	Safavid Persia in 1736

Safavid Persia's pivotal location between the Ottoman and Mughal Empires prevented the creation of a unified Sunni Muslim state across southern Asia in the 16th, 17th, and 18th centuries. Note that the Ottoman Empire could never penetrate any further into Persia than the western edge of the Zagros Mountains. But also notice the presence of Russia on Persia's northern border. How might this fact call into question the survival of the Safavid dynasty?

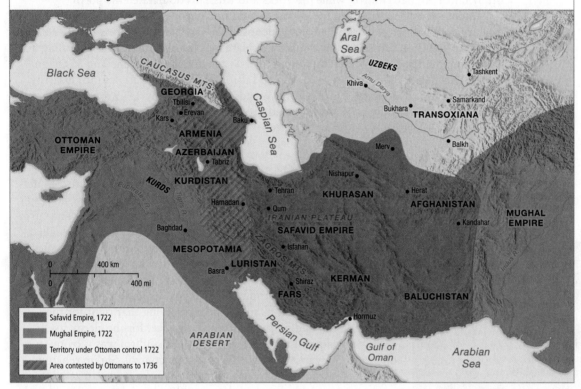

it with repressive centralization. This concentration of power at the center caused increasing corruption and inefficiency at the local level, as governors responsible directly to the shah neglected rural roads and defenses in order to please their royal master by maximizing imperial tax revenues. Surrounded by envious neighbors searching for any evidence of Safavid weakness, Persia grew increasingly vulnerable.

At the same time, Safi decided to confine all the royal princes within the harem, hoping thereby to minimize the possibility that the heir would be challenged by his brothers. But Safi thereby lost the opportunity to train his successor for rule. Traditionally, the heir to the throne served an apprenticeship as governor of the strategically and economically valuable province of Khurasan (Map 22.5). There he would learn the practical arts of governance from provincial chiefs and royal advisors, in a setting in which the errors typically made by an inexperienced young man would not prove serious. His brothers were traditionally appointed to lesser posts, providing them with valuable administrative experience and also with power bases from which they often challenged the heir upon their father's death.

These rebellions by younger brothers were what Safi hoped to prevent, but by ordering that all princes remain secluded he produced a succession of emperors after Abbas II who preferred the pleasures of the harem to the duties of statecraft. Authority passed to the court eunuchs and the mothers of competing princes, who intrigued constantly against one another and ignored the legitimate needs of the state.

Afghans, Turks, and Russians attack Persia

One of the most important of those needs was imperial defense. By 1700 the Safavid army was disintegrating into regiments led by officers jealous of competing authorities, and in response to this weakness various provinces of the empire rose in revolt. Taking advantage of this civil unrest, Afghan rebels captured Isfahan in 1722. Their success encouraged the Russian and Ottoman Empires to attack Persia. Two years later southern Iran was firmly under Afghan control, while the Turks and Russians dominated the north.

Under such circumstances, the dynasty could not survive. Nadir Shah, a Persian military commander of Turkish ancestry, deposed the last Safavid emperor in 1736 and drove the Turks and Russians off the Iranian plateau. Nadir, a Sunni Muslim ruling a Shi'ite empire, tried unsuccessfully to unify Persia religiously by reconciling Sunni and Shi'ite Muslims. In 1739 he sacked Delhi and threw the Mughal Empire into disarray. But after he was assassinated in 1747, his kingdom fell apart. By 1779 a new regime, the Qajar (*kah-JAR*) dynasty, consolidated its power in Isfahan. The Qajars ruled Persia until the 20th century.

Shi'ite Islam After the Safavids

Shi'ite Islam opposes centralized government in Persia

The end of Safavid rule carried with it sobering implications for Persia's future. Shi'ite Islam, despite Nadir Shah's efforts, refused to support the new regime. Under the Qajar dynasty, Shi'ism transformed itself into an inward-looking spiritual movement concentrating on the eventual reappearance of the **Twelfth Imam** (also called the Hidden Imam), a messianic leader whose return Shi'ites believed would create a religious kingdom and usher in a period of prosperity and peace enduring until the Last Judgment. The Shi'ite clergy, through its religious schools, became the principal adversary of any dynasty that claimed the right to rule Persia, reserving that right for the Twelfth Imam and, in his continued absence, for the clergy itself.

Cover of a Persian book, circa 1800.

At the close of the 18th century, then, Shi'ism was moving in a direction contrary to that of secular state control. Shi'ite religious reformers insisted that society and government be organized according to genuine Islamic principles, that the Shari`ah replace civil and royal legal codes, and that only religious scholars and teachers lead the *umma*. In the face of growing Russian and British interest in the strategically located Iranian plateau, Shi'ism reasserted itself as the best guarantee of spiritual and moral strength. If the state could no longer defend Persia, Islam itself must do so.

These events separated Persia from other modernizing Muslim cultures. In most such cultures, modernization began with Western economic contact that escalated into colonial and imperial control. But in Persia, the desertion of the dynasty by the religious establishment preceded the introduction of European influence. The spiritual authorities, never fully understood by the Europeans, considered themselves the only genuine caretakers of Persian Islamic culture. They stood in opposition to both internal and external political forces, hoping one day to seize the state for themselves.

The Ottoman Response to Europe's Challenge

The Ottomans had for centuries been a formidable power, but by 1700 they had lost the initiative. As the tide increasingly turned against them, they belatedly responded to Europe's challenge by adapting to European ways. In Arabia, however, Wahhabism, an

DOCUMENT 22.1 A European Visitor Describes Arabia

John Ovington, an English merchant and traveler, traversed the Indian Ocean in 1689. On his journey he stopped in many Islamic countries, including Arabia, which he describes here.

Muscatt is a city in Arabia the Happy, which lies to the eastward of that kingdom, situated upon the Persian Gulf . . . It abounds with many useful and beneficial commodities, with several kinds of drugs, with balsam and myrrh, incense, . . . dates, gold, frankincense and pearl, and maintains a constant trade of rare and valuable goods to Persia, Egypt, Syria, the Indies, etc. . . .

These Arabians are very courteous in their deportment, and extreme civil to all strangers; they offer neither violence nor affront to any; and though they are very tenacious of their own principles, and admirers of their own religion, yet do they never impose it upon any, nor are their morals leavened with such furious zeal, as to divest them of humanity, and a tender respect. A man may travel hundreds of miles in this country, and never meet with any abusive language, or any behavior that looks rude. And if you happen to be loaded with any money in your travels, you need no arms to defend your person, nor any guards to secure your purse; for you may sleep with it in your hands in the open fields, or lay it by you with safety as you repose yourself in the king's highway.

SOURCE: John Ovington, *A Voyage to Suratt in the Year 1689* (London: J. Tonson, 1689), 187, 192.

austere Muslim movement, blamed Islam's decline on lax devotion, condemned the Ottomans for modeling themselves after unbelievers, and warned that Muslims could triumph only by rigidly adhering to the Prophet's original message.

The Ottomans Lose the Initiative

In 1683, the Ottomans' last great invasion of Central Europe had taken their forces to the gates of Vienna, where they were stopped by a multinational coalition of Christian powers led by the king of Poland. Then, suddenly and unexpectedly, the Christian powers seized the offensive, setting out to reconquer Southeastern Europe from the Ottomans and push them back to Constantinople.

Although it was unable to expel the Ottomans from Europe, the coalition recaptured most of Hungary. In 1699, the Peace of Karlowitz transferred these lands from the Ottomans to the Austrian Habsburgs, sealing the failure of Islam's thousand-year quest to conquer Europe for the faith. The Habsburgs had stood for two centuries on the front lines opposing the Muslim advance, and their success in doing so accelerated the erosion of Ottoman power. But while the Safavid decline had led to collapse in only one century, the Ottoman slide took more than two, in part because of the Ottoman Empire's greater power and wealth, and in part because its multicultural, tolerant nature minimized internal dissatisfaction.

The Ottoman Empire begins to decline

The Ottoman position with respect to Europe had been deteriorating even before 1699. Within a half-century after the conquest of Constantinople in 1453, which consolidated Islamic control over the profitable trade routes connecting Asia with Europe by land, the sea voyages of da Gama and Cabral had opened the Indian Ocean to Portuguese vessels. As European traders increasingly bypassed the Muslim-dominated land routes, Ottoman income from trade and taxes declined. Unwilling to accept this loss of income, in the 16th century the Ottomans competed vigorously against Portugal for Indian Ocean trade. But by the beginning of the 17th century, England and Holland had pushed both the Portuguese and the Ottomans aside (see "A European Visitor Describes Arabia"). The efforts of the energetic British and Dutch East India Companies drew commerce to the European sea routes across the Atlantic and Indian Oceans, and trade on the Muslim land routes across Eurasia decreased further. As Ottoman commerce became increasingly marginalized, the Ottoman sultan's cash flow fell steeply. These commercial conditions contributed greatly to the empire's economic decline.

Ottoman central authority grows weaker

This decline also stemmed from a gradual weakening of Ottoman central authority. In the 17th century, the Ottomans, like the Safavids, had begun to seclude young princes within the harem, depriving them of the possibility of training in administration and politics. Sultans became less competent, while courtiers and provincial governors grew more powerful as greater authority was delegated to them.

Finally, the termination of Ottoman expansion with the Karlowitz treaty of 1699 accelerated the empire's decline. As there were no newly conquered lands for the Ottoman armies to loot, the absence of plunder produced riots in the army over pay and a breakdown of discipline in the sultan's elite corps of Janissaries. Individual generals who could satisfy their soldiers' desires for payment by diverting tax revenues gained power at the expense of Istanbul and undermined the empire's defenses at the same time.

Russia threatens Ottoman security

After 1699, Russia transformed itself from a potential area of Ottoman conquest into a grave threat to that empire's continued existence. Having taken Azov (*ah-ZOFF*) in the Crimea from the Turks in 1696, Russian Tsar Peter the Great modernized his forces and prepared for more extensive campaigns against them. While briefly fighting on Sweden's side in 1710–1711 in the Great Northern War, the Ottomans managed to trap Peter's army and force him to return Azov; in the next decades they reclaimed some of their earlier territorial losses. But Peter went on to defeat the Swedes in 1721, and Russia's emergence as Eastern Europe's dominant power eventually undercut the Ottoman position there.

In 1768 the Russians renewed their advance. After annihilating the Ottoman navy off the Turkish coast in 1770, they secured access to the Black Sea through the Treaty of Kuchuk Kainarji (*koo-CHOOK kā-NAR-jē*) in 1774. Two decades later Russia took the entire northern Black Sea coast. All these losses troubled the sultan greatly, not only in themselves but for what they meant. With Russia posing a serious threat, the Ottomans could no longer think of European powers as their inferiors. By 1800 the combination of commercial decline, decentralization, military losses, and Russian pressure had reduced the once-imposing Ottoman Empire to a condition that would later lead a Russian tsar to label it "the sick man of Europe."

Ottoman Reform and Cultural Synthesis

The entertainment room of Topkapi Palace in Constantinople (Istanbul), with a large throne on the left from which the sultan could observe the proceedings.

The Ottomans' difficulties in competing with Europeans commercially and militarily forced the rulers to recognize that the empire had to change to survive. But early in the 18th century, many highly placed officials believed that the empire had nothing to learn from unbelievers. Ottoman deterioration, they felt, could be reversed only by strengthening Ottoman practices and insights. Battlefield defeats, the sultan's advisors told him, were caused by the failure of Ottoman armies to follow the time-tested techniques of the past; they had nothing to do with the superiority of European weaponry. In the face of such obstinacy, serious reform seemed impossible. Centuries of hostility had isolated the Ottomans from the West and left them largely ignorant of the scientific, technological, commercial, and industrial advances that had transformed Europe since the boyhood of Suleiman the Magnificent.

The Ottomans innovate by turning westward

When Russia's naval victory in 1770 destroyed the entire Ottoman maritime high command, some saw a chance to reform the navy without entrenched resistance from admirals. In the 1780s, the Ottoman government imported Western experts to assist in creating modernized military units. Sultan Selim III (1789–1807), building on these beginnings and pressured by defeat in war with Austria and Russia in 1792, created a new European-style military force with modern weapons and training. But it never exceeded 10,000 soldiers at a time when the French were placing hundreds of thousands of men under arms. Once again the old army remained hostile to the new.

But Selim's military schools for his modernized forces introduced Western knowledge into the empire, and his European military experts ended Istanbul's isolation from the West. During the 19th century, extensive reforms based on Western models changed the empire significantly. Contempt for Western accomplishments gave way to grudging respect. European fashions in art, architecture, and clothing inspired Ottoman syntheses. Decentralization permitted healthy increases in local autonomy without compromising the Ottoman state as a whole. The empire once again appeared formidable and cohesive. It might be sick, but it was far from being dead.

Decentralization strengthens the Ottoman Empire

Wahhabism in Arabia

The Ottoman Empire controlled most but not all of southwestern Asia. Central Arabia lay outside its domain, but not outside the feelings of disgust and shame sweeping the Islamic world at the sight of Muslim weakness. In Arabia in the 1740s, a young religious scholar named Muhammad ibn abd-al Wahhab (*wah-HAHB*) concluded that all Islamic states, and especially the Ottoman Empire, had strayed from the path of strict observance of the teachings of the Prophet. In doing so they had incurred the wrath of Allah. Only by returning to this strict observance, al-Wahhab preached, could Islam triumph over unbelievers, whose ranks included (in his opinion) not only Jews, Christians, and polytheists, but also most Muslims.

Wahhabism transforms Arabia

Wahhabism, the austere, deeply puritanical brand of Islam preached by al-Wahhab and still practiced in Saudi Arabia today, contended that the sultan's authority derived neither from God nor from the *umma*; indeed, the sultan had no legitimate claim to power at all. Both the Ottoman religious elite and the entire state apparatus were un-Islamic by nature. Veneration of holy people, living or dead, was idolatry, as were pilgrimages to sacred shrines and gravesites. Sufi mysticism was reprehensible nonsense. The teachings of al-Wahhab, troubling to many Muslims, made him an outcast in Arabia until 1744, when he forged an alliance with the house of the Amir Ibn Saud (*sah-OOD*), who immediately established a small central Arabian state on Wahhabist principles.

Al-Wahhab died in 1791, but by the early 19th century Ibn Saud's grandson had taken Mecca and Medina and, following al-Wahhab's opposition to pilgrimages to gravesites, had desecrated sacred Muslim tombs located there—including, to the horror of most Muslims, the tomb of the Prophet himself. Wahhabist raids on Shi'ite holy sites in Iraq left faithful Shi'ites frantic and finally exhausted Ottoman patience. By 1818 Wahhabism was suppressed by force, but in the 20th century it seized control of the Arabian Peninsula and created Saudi Arabia.

Medina in the 18th century.

CHAPTER

REVIEW

Putting It in Perspective

By the end of the 18th century, the global balance of power and prosperity had clearly shifted away from the Muslim world. Islamic southern Asia, which had long drawn strength and wealth from its control of the land and sea routes connecting East and West, declined as European countries seized control of the Indian Ocean trade and then intruded, commercially and militarily, on southern Asia itself. Of southern Asia's three great Islamic empires, India's Mughal Empire was fragmented, Persia's Safavid Empire was gone, and the multicultural Ottoman Empire was clearly in decline.

As Muslims struggled to meet the Western challenge, two very different responses had emerged. One approach, pursued by the Ottoman Turks, was to adopt some Western ways, seeking to modernize

their economic and military structures along European lines. The other response, pursued by Wahhabists and Shi'ites, was to reject Western ways and restore traditional Islamic practices, seeking to preserve and purify their faith so as to draw strength from their seventh-century religious roots.

Neither approach proved effective in slowing the Islamic world's political and economic deterioration. By the 18th century, the center of the global trade network had shifted from the Indian Ocean to the Atlantic, where Europe was deriving vast power and wealth from its connections with Africa and the Americas. These connections were both immensely profitable and exploitative, for in the Atlantic world, prosperity was increasingly linked with slave labor transferred by ship from Africa to the Western Hemisphere.

Reviewing Key Material

KEY CONCEPTS

Malabar Coast, 492
calico, 496
Urdu, 497
Marathas, 497

nawabs, 497
pantheism, 500
Twelfth Imam, 504
Wahhabism, 507

KEY PEOPLE

Siraj-ud-Daulah, 490
Robert Clive, 490, 499
Vasco da Gama, 494
Pedro Alvares Cabral, 494
Afonso d'Albuquerque, 495
Philip II, 495
Aurangzeb, 497
Muhammad Shah, 497
Nadir Shah, 497

Joseph-François Dupleix, 498
Shah Abbas I, 502
Shah Safi, 502
Shah Abbas II, 502
Peter the Great, 506
Selim III, 507
Muhammad ibn abd-al Wahhab, 507
Ibn Saud, 507

ASK YOURSELF

1. How did control of the Indian Ocean trade benefit Islamic southern Asia? How were Europeans able to gain control of this trade?
2. Why were the Mughals unable to mount an effective resistance to Europeans in India?
3. Why were Muslims and Hindus able to coexist peacefully in Southeast Asia, but not in India?
4. How did Shi'ism shape the character of post-Safavid Persia?
5. How and why did Wahhabism develop as the dominant strain of Islam in Arabia?

GOING FURTHER

Bayly, C. A. *Indian Society and the Making of the British Empire*. 1988.
Bose, Sugata, and Ayeshia Jalal. *Modern South India*. 1998.
Boxer, Charles. *The Dutch Seaborne Empire*. 1989.
De Schweinitz, Karl. *The Rise and Fall of British India*. 1989.
Hintze, Andrea. *The Mughal Empire and Its Decline*. 1997.
Ikram, S. M. *History of Muslim Civilization in India and Pakistan*. 1989.
Inalcik, Halil, and Donald Quataert, eds. *An Economic and Social History of the Ottoman Empire, 1300–1914*. 1994.
Keay, John. *The Honourable Company: A History of the English East India Company*. 1991.
Keay, John. *India: A History*. 2000.
Legge, John D. *Indonesia*. 1965.
Morgan, David. *Medieval Persia, 1040–1797*. 1988.

Morris, Jan. *Pax Britannica*. 1980.

Palmer, A. *The Decline and Fall of the Ottoman Empire*. 1992.

Prakash, Om. *The Dutch East India Company and the Economy of Bengal, 1630–1720*. 1985.

Richards, John. *The Mughal Empire*. 1993.

Shaw, Stanford. *History of the Ottoman Empire and Modern Turkey*. 1976.

Spear, Percival. *Twilight of the Mughuls*. 1951.

Woodruff, Philip. *The Men Who Ruled India*. 1954.

Key Dates and Developments

ca. 1400	Iskandar founds the trading state of Malacca
1510	Portugal seizes Goa
1511	Portugal conquers Malacca
1600	Establishment of the British East India Company
1602	Establishment of the Dutch East India Company
ca. 1650	Mataram and Johore dominate Southeast Asian trade
1658	Dutch expel Portuguese from Indonesia
1664	Establishment of the French East India Company
1699	Peace of Karlowitz
1739	Nadir Shah sacks Delhi; the Mughals lose control
1740–1748	War of the Austrian Succession
1744	Alliance between al-Wahhab and Ibn Saud in Arabia
1747	Collapse of Safavid Iran
1756–1763	Seven Years War
1757	Clive's victory at Plassey
1774	Treaty of Kuchuk Kainarji
1779	Qajar rule in Iran
1792–1807	Sultan Selim III reforms the Ottoman Empire
1795	France conquers Holland; Britain moves into Southeast Asia
1818	Ottomans suppress Wahhabism in Arabia

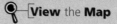

PEARSON
myhistorylab Connections

Reinforce what you learned in this chapter by studying the many documents, images, maps, review tools, and videos available at www.myhistorylab.com.

Read and Review

✔• Study and Review Chapter 22

📖• Read the Document

Jan van Linschoten on Dutch Business in the Indian Ocean, p. 493

Excerpt from the Travel Journal of Vasco da Gama, p. 494

🔍 View the Map

Map Discovery: The Maratha Kingdoms, p. 497

Map Discovery: The Stages of Dutch Expansion in Java, p. 502

🔍 View the Image

Portuguese Church in Southern India, p. 495

((•• Listen to the Audio

Mughals, p. 497

Research and Explore

🔍 View the Map

Map Discovery: French, British, and Dutch Holdings, ca. 1700, p. 494

((•• Listen to the Chapter Audio for Chapter 22 on myhistorylab.com

Africa and the Atlantic Slave Trade, 1400–1800

((•—Listen to the **Chapter Audio** for Chapter 23 on **myhistorylab.com**

Njinga of Ndongo

In the 15th through 19th centuries, African realms were ravaged and transformed by the Atlantic slave trade. In this famous image, Anna de Sousa Njinga, ruler of the realm of Ndongo, meets with Portuguese officials while using a servant as a throne to maintain her royal dignity.

- ■ What factors account for the diversity of African societies?

- ■ What were the roots and realities of African and Islamic slavery?

- ■ How did the Atlantic slave trade originate and operate?

- ■ How did the Atlantic slave trade affect African societies and families?

- ■ How did the Atlantic slave trade help reallocate global wealth and power?

In 1482, the Central African kingdom of Kongo had some unexpected visitors. Portuguese sailors, searching for a route from the Atlantic to the Indian Ocean, sailed up the Congo River, and later met Kongo's king, the manikongo ("lord of Kongo"). Intrigued by his visitors' guns and goods, the manikongo opened trade with the Portuguese. He even sent his royal prince to Lisbon to study their language and religion. These connections proved useful in 1491, when Portuguese forces, their banners emblazoned with Christian crosses, helped the manikongo crush a local revolt. Impressed by the apparent power of the Europeans' faith and firearms, both the king and the prince converted to Christianity.

The prince, later known as Manikongo Nzinga Mbemba ('*n-ZIHN-gah 'm-BEM-bah*), or by his Christian name, King Afonso I (1506–1543), eventually had reason to regret the Portuguese connection. Despite his Christian faith, his people resisted conversion, and profit-minded Portuguese began to carry off Kongolese men as slaves for sugar plantations overseas. In 1526 he wrote to the king of Portugal that slave traders "are taking every day our natives" and that "our country is being completely depopulated." But the slave trade continued, as Afonso could not even stop his own subjects from trading captured Africans for European guns and goods.

The Kongo story is but one example of the transformation that began in coastal Africa during the 15th century. As Europeans came by sea, Africans often welcomed them, creating commercial and cultural connections based on mutual interests. But as Europeans started sugar plantations—first on islands off the African coast and later in American colonies—these connections increasingly centered on slaves. For Europeans, the slave trade, and the sale of goods produced in the Americas by African slaves, brought growing global wealth and power. In Africa, however, the Atlantic slave trade fueled violence and greed, upset traditional economic patterns, disrupted family life, and transformed the political landscape. The sale of slaves enriched and empowered some Africans, but it condemned millions of others to brutal bondage.

Major Slave Destinations

Major Sources of Slaves

Africa's Diverse Societies

In the early 15th century, before the European intrusion, Africa's many cultures reflected its geographic diversity (Map 23.1). Most Africans, however, belonged either to urban cultures that centered on commerce and Islam, or to village societies that focused on farming and worshipped local gods and spirits.

Trade and Islam connect North Africa and West Africa

North Africa was fully Islamic, connected by land and sea with West Asia and by trans-Sahara camel caravan trade routes with West Africa. Egypt, where farming flourished in the Nile Valley, was North Africa's most populous and prosperous realm, linked commercially and culturally with both Islamic West Asia and sub-Saharan Africa.

West Africa was partially Islamic. Its thriving cities were typically Muslim commercial and cultural centers, but most of its people lived in farming villages and worshipped diverse local deities. Mali, West Africa's most powerful kingdom, had long prospered from its rich gold mines and its role in the trans-Sahara trade.

East African culture blends Arabic and African features

East Africa's coastal city-states were deeply influenced by Islamic faith, Indian Ocean commerce, and Swahili culture, which blended Arabic and African features. In the East

FOUNDATION MAP 23.1 | Fifteenth Century African Connections

In the 15th century, as in ages past, Muslim trade routes connected West Asia and North Africa by land across the Sahara with West Africa and by sea with East Africa's commercial city-states. Note that, in the mid-1400s, Portuguese voyages down Africa's west coast began creating new connections that later would link Africa with Europe and the Americas. How were Africa's connections shaped by its climate and geography?

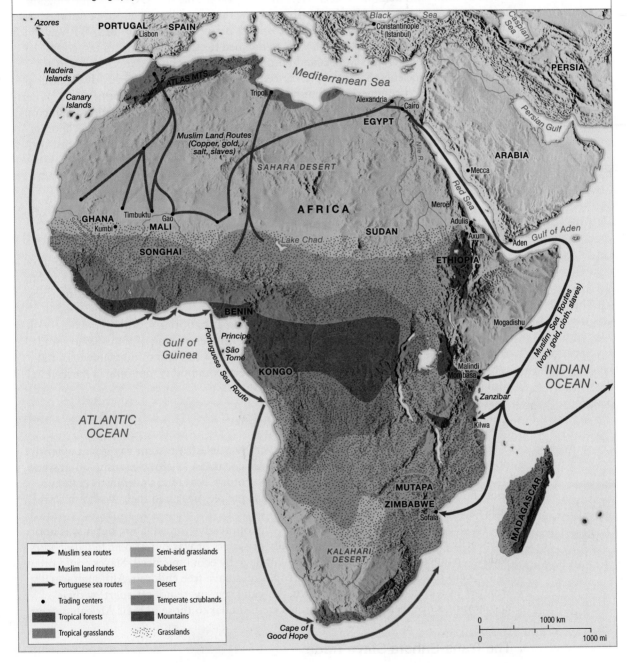

➤ Muslim sea routes	Semi-arid grasslands
— Muslim land routes	Subdesert
➤ Portuguese sea routes	Desert
• Trading centers	Temperate scrublands
Tropical forests	Mountains
Tropical grasslands	Grasslands

African interior, however, farmers and hunters retained their traditional worship of nature spirits, while to their north Ethiopians practiced an ancient form of Christianity.

Central and South Africa, not yet influenced by Muslims or Christians, were populated mostly by farmers and herders who worshipped various nature spirits and gods. These regions had numerous **stateless societies**—independent villages and federations of villages ruled by local patriarchs and chiefs—as well as several sizable states. One was the kingdom of Kongo, a prosperous agricultural realm near the mouth of the Congo River. Another was the kingdom of Zimbabwe (*zim-BAHB-wā*), south of the Zambezi (*zam-BĒ-zē*) River, which supplemented its cattle-based wealth with gold mined for sale along Africa's east coast.

Like their counterparts in Asia and Europe, then, 15th-century Africans lived in a broad range of societies. Some people were educated and cosmopolitan city-dwellers, connected by faith and commerce with distant lands. Most, however, were farmers and herders, unaware of the world beyond their clans and villages. In the following centuries, numerous African societies were disrupted and transformed by the emergence of a global economy based on overseas commerce. Central to that commerce was traffic in human beings.

Slavery and the Slave Trade in Africa

Since ancient times, many world societies practiced **slavery**, an institution in which some people owned other people and used them for their labor. Often slaves were prisoners of war or victims of raids who were forced to serve their captors. Some were criminals or debtors placed in bondage to pay off crimes or debts; others were children sold into servitude by destitute parents. Some slaves were household servants; others worked on farms, in mines, or on construction projects. But all were at the mercy of their masters, who ranged from benevolent to inhumanly harsh.

In Africa, as elsewhere, slavery had emerged in ancient times, both in the Nile Valley and in the vast grasslands south of the Sahara. With the opening of trans-Sahara trade routes by the second century C.E., and the formation of Muslim trading networks five centuries later, African slaves became a commercial commodity, not only in Africa but also in much of the Islamic world (Chapter 13).

African Slavery

Some African societies measure wealth in slaves

Scholars disagree as to how widespread slavery was in Africa: some say it was extensive, others relatively rare. Most likely slavery in Africa, as elsewhere, was common in some places and uncommon in others. By the tenth century, however, slavery was common enough in some parts of Africa that prosperous people measured their wealth in slaves, rather than in land or in livestock.

African slavery was often harsh, involving oppressive forced labor, but it was not necessarily permanent. Slaves were typically prisoners of war but also included debtors, widows, paupers, and others driven into bondage by economic need. Slaves could often buy or earn their freedom, marry free people, and have free children. Although usually enslaved by a clan other than their own, African slaves were not set apart by their appearance, since their color and features were similar to those of their African owners.

The Trans-Sahara Slave Trade

The opening of caravan routes across the Sahara by the second century C.E. added a new dimension to African slavery. Along with copper, gold, and salt, slaves became a key feature of the trans-Sahara trade. North African merchants traveled south to buy slaves in West Africa, then transported them back across the desert and sold them in North Africa.

The Islamic conquest of North Africa in the seventh century expanded the trans-Sahara slave trade, incorporating it into the Muslim world that extended from Spain to India. In time Muslim merchants transported up to ten thousand African slaves a year to destinations in Islamic lands. East African city-states, coming under Muslim control, also got involved in trading slaves.

Islamic connections expand the trans-Sahara slave trade

African Slaves in the Islamic World

In Islamic lands the most common form of slavery was domestic servitude, with slaves serving in the homes of wealthy families. Most such slaves were women, who typically did household chores and sometimes also served as concubines. Widely seen as exotic commodities from distant lands, African slaves were highly prized as symbols of their owner's wealth and prestige.

Wealthy Muslims prize African women as domestic slaves

The lot of these slaves was difficult, but their servitude was not necessarily perpetual or hereditary. When a slave woman had a child by a Muslim master, for example, by Islamic tradition she and her child typically became free. Furthermore, since Islam discouraged the enslavement of Muslims, slaves could sometimes secure their freedom, or at least that of their children, by converting to Islam.

Still, although Islam asserted the equality of all people before God, the presence in many Islamic lands of numerous black African slaves led some Muslims to link dark skin with servitude. One who did so was the writer and traveler Ibn Khaldun (*ib'n khahl-DOON*), who wrote in the 14th century that black Africans accepted servile status because they had a "low degree of humanity." Depicting slaves as less than human no doubt helped many Muslims—and later many Christians—to sidestep religious teachings about treating fellow humans well.

But slavery in the Muslim world was not based mainly on skin color. In addition to enslaving Africans, Muslims also enslaved large numbers of Southern Europeans and Slavic people from Russia and Eastern Europe. Indeed, so many Slavs were enslaved that the very word *slave* may derive from the ethnic term *Slav*.

Muslims import slaves from Europe and Russia

By the 15th century, commerce in African slaves was long established. Particularly in West Africa, rulers and traders often took captives from their own or neighboring lands, then sold them to Muslim merchants for transport to faraway places. So accustomed were West Africans to such commerce that their leaders and merchants did not hesitate to sell slaves to Europeans, who in that century began to appear in sailing ships along the coast.

The Atlantic Slave Trade

The Europeans who first came to West Africa did not come to buy slaves. The Atlantic slave trade, like the European conquest of the Americas (Chapter 19), was an unforeseen outgrowth of European efforts to discover an all-water trade route from Europe to Asia.

The Africans and the Portuguese

In the early 1400s, the Portuguese had started sailing south along the African coast in search of a sea route to Asia. Sailing farther with each successive voyage, they set up trading posts along the coast to do business with Africans. By mid-century, West African merchants were trading their gold, salt, ivory, and pepper for European firearms, cloth,

ironware, and copper goods. By the 1480s, African kingdoms along the Gulf of Guinea (*GIH-ne̅*) and farther south were likewise trading with the Portuguese. Thus, by 1497–1498, when Portugal's Vasco da Gama finally sailed all the way around Africa to India, various peoples along Africa's coast had established connections with Europeans.

At first, eager to bypass the Muslim merchants who controlled the trans-Sahara trade, West Africans gladly did business with the seafaring newcomers, who brought attractive new goods (including guns, textiles, and tools) and often offered better deals than the Muslims. Pleased to have a new outlet for their products—and to get European firearms—African leaders bartered with the Portuguese and welcomed their trading posts.

This commerce initially appears to have been based on mutual interest and respect, each side treating the other as a valued trading partner. But as coastal commerce came to center increasingly on African slaves, mutual interest and respect began to disappear.

Portuguese slave trading post at El Mina on the Gulf of Guinea.

Africans trade with Portuguese for new goods and guns

👁— **Watch** the **Video**
Atlantic Connections: Sugar, Smallpox, and Slavery
on **myhistorylab.com**

Slave plantations support growing sugar trade

Sugar and the Slave Trade

Almost from the outset the Portuguese trafficked in slaves, shipping their first human cargoes from West Africa in the 1440s. These newest victims of the ancient trade were used, not as household servants like slaves in Muslim lands, but as field laborers on sugar plantations.

By then demand for sugar was growing rapidly. Popularized in the Christian West through contacts with Muslims during the crusades and Spanish Reconquista (Chapter 16), sugar provided huge profits to its suppliers. In the 14th and 15th centuries, sugar cultivation was attempted in Spain and Portugal and on Mediterranean islands. But sugar cane, which requires vast amounts of sunshine and water, a 12-month growing season, and intensive labor, was not well suited to Europe. So later in the 15th century, profit-minded Portuguese set up sugar plantations off the African coast, on tropical islands such as Madeira (*mah-DA̅-rah*), São Tomé (*SOU'n too-MA̅*), and Principe (*PRE̅N-se̅-pe̅*) (Map 23.1). To work these plantations, they used African slaves, who were accustomed to the tropical climate.

Brazilian sugar plantations import African slaves

🔍 **View** the **Image**
West African Slave Market
on **myhistorylab.com**

In the 16th century, as Europeans colonized the Americas, they also expanded the slave trade. The Portuguese colony of Brazil, with abundant sunshine and rainfall, proved ideal for growing sugar, but countless workers were needed to cultivate, harvest, and process it. Portugal, with a small population and a labor shortage, could not supply enough workers to meet the need. Portuguese paupers and convicts sent to Brazilian sugar plantations often died quickly due to heat, humidity, and tropical disease. Efforts to use Amerinds as laborers likewise proved futile, as they died in vast numbers from diseases such as smallpox carried by Europeans (Chapter 19).

But Africans were accustomed to hot climates and resistant to tropical diseases, so the Portuguese soon began shipping them in large numbers to Brazil's sugar plantations. Before long, West Africa, the Gulf of Guinea coast, and the Congo River region had all become major sources of slaves. In the 1570s Portugal built a large trading port named Luanda (*loo-AHN-duh*) a few hundred miles south of the Congo River, establishing there a

Slaves processing harvested cane into sugar on Brazilian plantation.

MAP 23.2	The Atlantic Slave Trade in the 16th Through 18th Centuries

In the 16th through 18th centuries, the Atlantic trading system centered on African slaves. Notice that Europeans shipped guns and other goods to Africa, traded them there for slaves, and then shipped the slaves to the Americas to produce sugar, coffee, tobacco, and other goods, which were sold back to Europe. Why were slaves so central to this commerce? How did it contribute to Europe's wealth and power?

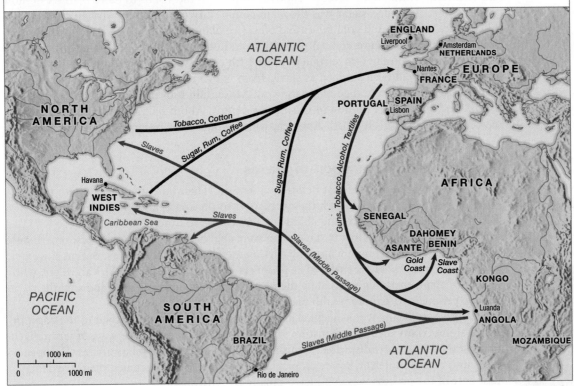

colony that came to be called Angola. By the 1600s Angola had become a major source of slaves, and the slave trade had become the main form of commerce on the West African coast.

The Atlantic System

Portugal's domination of the slave trade did not last. As other Europeans saw the huge profits supplied by slave-grown sugar, they, too, began to get involved. By the 17th century, the Spanish, French, English, and Dutch had set up sugar plantations on Caribbean islands, which, like Brazil, had abundant sunshine and rainfall. At first the Portuguese supplied these plantations with most of their African slaves. After 1650, however, the English and the Dutch, and later the French, also shipped numerous slaves.

The Atlantic slave trade was part of what has been called the Atlantic System (Map 23.2). From European ports such as Lisbon, Nantes, Amsterdam, and Liverpool, ships sailed to Africa bearing guns and textiles, and sometimes alcohol and tobacco products. There, at coastal trading posts, they exchanged these goods for slaves. Then the ships, callously laden with human cargo, crossed the Atlantic to slave centers in the Americas. There the captives were sold, and the ships were loaded with goods—such as sugar, coffee, tobacco, and rum (an alcoholic liquor distilled from sugar cane)—produced

Watch the **Video**

From Triangular Trade to an Atlantic System: Rethinking the Links That Created the Atlantic World

on **myhistorylab.com**

Atlantic slave trade links Europe, Africa, and the Americas

View the Map

Map Discovery: Atlantic Slave Trade

on **myhistorylab.com**

in the Americas by slaves. Finally the ships returned to Europe, where the traders sold these goods at huge profit, a portion of which could be used to buy goods for their next trading trip to Africa. This commerce was controlled mainly by Europeans, who supplied the ships and pocketed most of the profits, but many African slave traders profited, too.

In the 17th and 18th centuries, the slave trade exploded. Overall volume increased exponentially, from about 300,000 captives shipped in the 1500s to more than six million in the 1700s. Although sugar was the main commodity produced by African slaves, they also worked in silver and gold mines and on coffee plantations in Spain's American empire, and on tobacco (and later cotton) plantations in England's North American colonies. By the time the slave trade was curtailed in the 19th century, an estimated eleven to twelve million people had been shipped as slaves from Africa to the Americas, and perhaps another two million had died along the way. More than four million Africans went to Brazil, and another six million to Caribbean islands. About half a million (less than five percent) went to English North America, which would later become the United States.

The Capture and Transport of Slaves

The captives suffered a fate that defies imagination. Their hardships began with their capture in Africa, increased with their transport to the coast, and intensified further with their sale to Europeans and shipment across the Atlantic.

African rulers trade captives for wealth and guns

Some captives were already slaves who were sold by their African masters; others were people seized by slave hunters hired by African merchants or local rulers. But most were probably captured soldiers enslaved as prisoners during African wars. African rulers, who sought to avoid enslaving and selling their own people, instead enslaved and sold their captive prisoners to acquire wealth and guns.

Captives typically were shackled and chained together, then marched to the coast in processions. Many died of exhaustion or took their own lives on the way; others arrived at coastal trading posts dispirited, famished, and diseased. Since relatively few Europeans went into Africa's interior, where tropical heat and diseases threatened their lives, this first part of the process was conducted mostly by Africans.

Once the captives reached the coast, they were herded naked into cages, examined to see if they were fit for hard labor, and then sold to Europeans, who branded them with hot irons and crowded them on ships for transport overseas. As the middle part of their three-part journey—from Africa's interior to its coast, from there across the sea to the Americas, and from American ports to plantations or mines—this oceanic crossing was called the **Middle Passage** (Map 23.2).

Packed into ships in layers like freight, with scarce room to move, up to six hundred captives might be carried in a vessel barely 100 feet long. Their skin was rubbed raw by the planks on which they lay and the chains that bound them during the three- to six-week voyage. The air stank from sweat and the tubs of human waste where they relieved themselves. Typically 10 to 20 percent of them died on the trip, from malnutrition, suffocation, stifling heat, or diseases that spread unchecked among them. Ship captains, who routinely overcrowded their vessels to ensure a big profit despite the high death toll, callously disposed of corpses by casting them overboard. Some captives also jumped overboard, ending their lives to escape their unbearable fate.

African Slaves in the Americas

When survivors of the Middle Passage arrived in the New World, their situation scarcely improved. At slave markets in port towns such as Havana in the West Indies or Rio de Janeiro in Brazil, merchants and plantation owners poked and prodded the Africans,

Loading plan for a slave ship.

inspecting them as if they were farm animals for sale. Once purchased, the slaves were transported to plantations or mines, where they were subjected to relentless hard labor and often physical abuse.

Unlike the slaves in Islamic lands, many of whom were women, most Africans shipped to the Americas were men. Selected for their size and strength, the slaves who labored on sugar plantations were often simply worked to death. Most died within five or six years, usually from exhaustion or disease, but sometimes from beatings inflicted by their masters. Rebellions by slaves were typically put down with European firearms, and escape attempts by slaves also often proved futile, since runaways were recognizable as slaves by their dark skin.

Despite these hardships, Africans endured in the Americas. On plantations they formed their own communities, supporting each other and adapting their African cultures to the new surroundings. In some French and Spanish colonies, for example, where slaves were often convinced or compelled to adopt the Catholic faith, they integrated African spiritualism, music, and dance into their worship.

Slave market in Rio de Janeiro, Brazil.

Some created blended religions, such as Santeria (*san-tuh-RĒ-uh*) and Vodou (*vō-DOO*), which incorporated African rituals and assigned traits of African gods to Christian saints. Runaway slaves, sometimes called **maroons**, fled to the wilderness and established independent communities, where they lived by farming and hunting, maintained many African customs, and forcibly resisted recapture. Despite oppression and abuse, transplanted Africans and their descendants, later called the **African diaspora**, managed not only to adapt to their new homelands but also to create their own new cultures (Chapter 30).

Africans adapt their cultures to life in the Americas

Riches, Race, and Racism

Slavery and the slave trade brought substantial economic benefits to Europe. Slave labor helped exploit the abundant resources of Europe's American colonies, thereby contributing to Europe's wealth and power. Indeed, cheap raw cotton supplied by slave plantations later helped support an Industrial Revolution that catapulted Western Europe to world domination (Chapter 27).

African slavery in the Americas also enabled many Europeans to indulge in new pleasures and comforts. Thanks largely to the Atlantic slave trade, middle-class Europeans were increasingly able to enjoy such commodities as sugar, coffee, tobacco, and comfortable cotton clothing—undeterred by the fact that they were supplied through the suffering of African slaves.

To rationalize the inhumane treatment of millions of people, many Europeans and European Americans depicted Africans as inferior beings, or even as subhuman. Africans were portrayed as primitive pagans with little capacity for government, education, or advancement, who willingly accepted slavery because they lacked intellect and ambition. Some Europeans even asserted that the captives were no worse off as slaves than they had been as villagers in their native Africa.

In time, such attitudes, along with encounters among diverse cultures fostered by the opening of the Atlantic, nurtured the notion of **race**. This concept divided humans into categories called "races," based on external appearance, especially skin color. Like earlier notions of nobility and caste, race had little biological basis; it rested instead on arbitrary classifications used by some groups to assert superiority over others. The result was the rise of **racism**, the belief that race was the main determinant of human traits and abilities, with white Europeans often claiming a greater capacity than others for intellectual and cultural advancement. In the 19th century, racial thinkers codified these concepts into an elaborate system, later used by German Nazis and others to rationalize the suppression and destruction of people they deemed undesirable.

Race reinforces European suppression of Africans in America

Long before these developments, however, the Atlantic slave trade was based on race and rationalized by racism. Race reinforced the enduring suppression of Africans in the Americas, where the parents' slave status was almost always inherited by their children, dooming each new generation to live and die in bondage. And even when Africans in the Americas managed to gain their freedom, they were still often targets of racial discrimination. The racial slavery that emerged in the Americas was thus more harsh and dehumanizing than the traditional slavery long practiced in Africa and the Muslim world.

The Transformation of Africa

The Atlantic slave trade's impact on Africa varied from place to place. The coasts where commerce was conducted, and the nearby lands where slaves were captured, were the regions most directly affected. Because of their proximity to the Americas West Africa, the Guinea coast, and the Central African regions of Kongo and Angola, supplied the largest number of slaves. By the 19th century, as these areas were depleted of able-bodied men, even East Africa became a source of slaves bound for the Americas.

Guns and trade shift power from Africa's interior to its coast

In the 16th through 18th centuries, as Africa's coastal kingdoms gained weapons and riches from their commerce with Europe, power and wealth shifted from the continent's interior to its seaboard. This change was most apparent in West Africa, where the cities and states of the interior, whose wealth depended on trans-Sahara trade, declined as commerce moved from the Sahara to the Atlantic. But the impact was also felt elsewhere. New African powers emerged, their wealth enhanced by the sale of slaves and their might by guns acquired from Europeans in exchange. Europeans also formed colonies on the African coast. By the 19th century, when the slave trade was banned, much of Africa had been politically and economically transformed.

The Reorientation of West Africa

The West African interior, made up mostly of grasslands stretching south from the Sahara Desert, had long been one of Africa's wealthiest regions. From the 13th through

Timbuktu, a center of Islamic commercial and cultural connections.

15th centuries, the kingdom of Mali had dominated the grasslands of the western Sudan, along the Senegal (*SEN-ih-gahl*) and upper Niger (*NĪ-jur*) rivers (Map 23.1). Profiting from the trans-Sahara trade in gold, salt, ivory, and slaves, and from commercial and cultural connections with the rest of the Islamic world, Mali had amassed extensive power and prosperity (Chapter 13).

In the centuries that followed, however, West Africans increasingly sold such goods to European traders who arrived by sea, rather than to Muslims who came across the desert. The growth of the shore trade and decline of the Sahara trade reoriented West Africa's economy and shifted its political balance of power from the interior to the coast.

THE SONGHAI AND KANEM-BORNU EMPIRES. West Africa's transformation began with the rise and fall of Songhai (*SAWN-GĪ*), a regional power that conquered the declining Mali kingdom in the 1400s (Map 23.3). With a swift horse cavalry and a fleet of river boats, Songhai ruler Sonni Ali (*saw-NĒ ah-LĒ*), who reigned from 1464 to 1492, overran Mali and gained control of the whole upper Niger River region. His successor Askia Muhammad al-Turi (*ah-SKĒ-ah moo-HAH-muhd ahl-TOO-rē*), reigning from 1493 to 1528 as Muhammad I Askia, further expanded the Songhai Empire. Under him it became a vast, prosperous realm extending over a thousand miles east to west, controlling the region's gold and salt mines and its trans-Sahara trade. Intent on imposing his Islamic faith, Askia appointed Arab Muslims as judges and officials, imported Islamic scholars and lawyers, and used his immense treasury to build a multitude of mosques.

In the early 1500s, under Askia's capable leadership, the Songhai Empire was West Africa's largest, wealthiest, and mightiest state. It had strong armies, stable institutions, a cosmopolitan culture, and a flourishing trade in gold, salt, and slaves. To those who dwelt or did business in its thriving cities, it would have seemed unthinkable that Songhai's days were numbered.

But numbered they were. The empire's decline began in 1528, when Askia was murdered by one of his sons. It was weakened by further succession struggles, often involving intrigues and assassinations, and by the steady shift of trade from the Sahara to the coast. Stability was restored for a while mid-century, but in the 1580s a new succession crisis led to all-out civil war.

Meanwhile, Morocco, a Muslim realm in northwestern Africa fortified by connections with Portugal and Spain, sought to expand its share of the trans-Sahara trade. Armed with cannons and firearms, and aided by Spanish and Portuguese mercenary soldiers, Moroccans took advantage of Songhai's turmoil. In 1591 they crossed the desert with a vast camel caravan and battled the Songhai army at Tondibi (*tawn-DĒ-bē*), north of Gao, the Songhai capital. Although outnumbered ten to one, the Moroccans used their guns to great effect. They crushed the Songhai forces, then sacked the great cities of Gao and Timbuktu, reducing Songhai to a modest domain.

Although the Atlantic slave trade did not directly cause Songhai's fall, the shift in trade patterns benefited coastal countries such as Morocco, while undermining the once vibrant economy of West Africa's interior. In the next few centuries, as the interior's commerce further declined, its urban centers gradually became obscure backwaters. By the 1800s, when French explorers arrived in the dusty remnants of these once great cities, the tales they heard of bygone empires with fabulous wealth seemed too fantastic to believe.

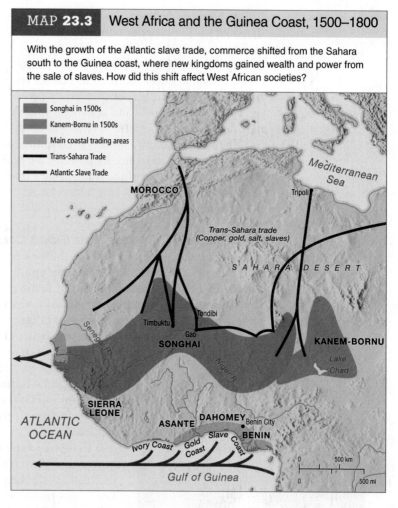

MAP 23.3   West Africa and the Guinea Coast, 1500–1800

With the growth of the Atlantic slave trade, commerce shifted from the Sahara south to the Guinea coast, where new kingdoms gained wealth and power from the sale of slaves. How did this shift affect West African societies?

- Songhai in 1500s
- Kanem-Bornu in 1500s
- Main coastal trading areas
- Trans-Sahara Trade
- Atlantic Slave Trade

MOROCCO
Tripoli
Mediterranean Sea
Trans-Sahara trade (Copper, gold, salt, slaves)
SAHARA DESERT
Timbuktu
Tondibi
Gao
SONGHAI
KANEM-BORNU
Lake Chad
Senegal R.
Niger R.
SIERRA LEONE
ATLANTIC OCEAN
ASANTE
DAHOMEY
Benin City
Slave Coast
BENIN
Ivory Coast
Gold Coast
Gulf of Guinea
0   500 km
0   500 mi

📖 **Read** the **Document**

Leo Africanus Describes Timbuktu

on **myhistorylab.com**

Songhai Empire connects much of West Africa

Morocco battles Songhai for trans-Sahara trade

Songhai declines as trading patterns shift

Idris Alawma unites
Kanem-Bornu and
expands Islam's role

As Songhai declined, new regional powers arose. To the east, around Lake Chad, a dynamic Muslim warrior named Idris Alawma (*id-RĒS ah-LAW-mah*), aided by firearms and a camel cavalry, united the kingdoms of Kanem (*KAH-nem*) and Bornu (*BOR-noo*) into a modest empire, which he ruled from around 1570 to the early 1600s. Taking advantage of Songhai's decline, he enhanced his realm's wealth by expanding its trans-Sahara trade. A devout Muslim, he also avidly promoted his faith, building numerous mosques, replacing local customs and laws with Islamic courts and judges, and vigorously combating adultery and obscenity.

The Kanem-Bornu Empire lasted until around 1700, when weak rulers and extended famine combined to reduce its power. Like Songhai before it, Kanem-Bornu also suffered from the decline of the trans-Sahara trade, as commerce shifted southward to the Gulf of Guinea coast, which increasingly became a source of goods and slaves for the Atlantic trade.

Benin rulers resist
European exploitation

New African powers
emerge from the Guinea
coast trade

THE SLAVE TRADE'S IMPACT ON THE GUINEA COAST. South of Songhai, near the Gulf of Guinea coast, the grasslands of the western Sudan give way to tropical forests. This region's dominant power, largely unaffected by outsiders until the Portuguese arrived in 1485, was the kingdom of Benin (*beh-NĒN*) at the mouth of the Niger River (Map 23.3). Its ample forests and mineral deposits supplied fuel and ore for its metalworkers, who produced abundant weapons, tools, and metal works of art. And its magnificent capital, known today as Benin City, had miles of walls and moats, a sumptuous palace, guilds of artisans and artists, and rows of splendid houses along wide clean streets largely free of clutter and crime.

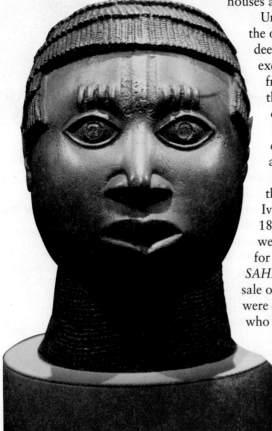

Unchallenged by Islam, which had not reached that far south, the oba (king) of Benin was also head of the local religion, deemed by his people to have supernatural powers. Using this exceptional authority, the obas sought to protect their realm from European exploitation, restricting but not fully banning the overseas slave trade. Although Benin subsequently declined, it left behind hundreds of exquisite iron, ivory, brass, and bronze sculptures and plaques, testifying to its cultural wealth and the remarkable skill of its artisans and artists.

West of Benin, along the Gulf of Guinea, were lands that Europeans dubbed the Slave Coast, Gold Coast, and Ivory Coast, based on their main exports. In the 17th and 18th centuries, some kingdoms in this region achieved great wealth and power, largely by trading slaves, gold, and ivory for European firearms. Especially prominent were Asante (*ah-SAHN-tā*), which derived vast riches from its goldfields and the sale of slaves, and Dahomey (*dah-HŌ-mē*), whose powerful armies were equipped with muskets and fortified by formidable women who served as palace guards and soldiers.

These riches and weapons helped the rulers expand their realms and acquire more slaves, establishing a ruthless but effective cycle. To hold their own, neighboring states were compelled to get their own guns by trafficking in slaves. Hence, although trade with Europe brought wealth and power to some Guinea coast kingdoms, they gained it through their willingness to sell other Africans as slaves.

Bronze sculpture from Benin.

The Depopulation of Central Africa

Central Africa, a hot, humid region embracing the Congo River basin's rain forests and the tropical grasslands to their south, had little contact with the larger world before the 1480s. Central Africans were mostly farmers, living in small states and stateless societies centered on villages and clans, but one large state, the Kongo Kingdom (Map 23.4), had emerged by the 14th century. The European intrusion, beginning with the Portuguese arrival in the last few decades of the 15th century, in time had a devastating impact on the region, especially its coastal areas.

CHRISTIANITY, SLAVERY, AND THE KONGO KINGDOM. Of all the Africa peoples, none received Europeans more warmly than those in the Kongo Kingdom, and none suffered more severely for their efforts. Prior to 1482, this Central African realm had no direct contacts with Europe. In that year, however, Portuguese navigator Diogo Cão (*dē-Ō-gō COW*), also called Diogo Cam, searching for a waterway connecting the Atlantic and Indian Oceans, sailed up the Congo River.

As noted at the start of this chapter, the Kongolese king, the manikongo, established good relations with the Portuguese, and the Kongo's crown prince even went to Lisbon to learn Portuguese ways. After returning to Kongo, he became a Christian and, as King Afonso I (1506–1543), he sought to convert his people to the Catholic faith. With firearms provided by his Portuguese friends, he also endeavored to increase his power and expand his kingdom.

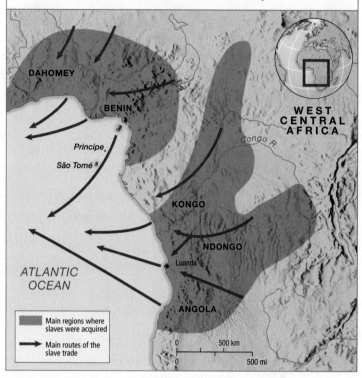

MAP 23.4 West-Central Africa and the Slave Trade in the 15th Through 18th Centuries

West-central Africa was a major source of slaves for sugar plantations, first on offshore islands such as Principe and São Tomé, and later on plantations in the Americas. Note that Africans captured in the interior were marched to the coast in chains to be sold and shipped across the Atlantic. Why did some Africans capture and sell other Africans into slavery?

Legend:
- Main regions where slaves were acquired
- → Main routes of the slave trade

Kongo king embraces Portuguese commerce and Christianity

His efforts ultimately failed. Some members of the Kongo elite embraced the new faith, but most Kongolese continued to worship their traditional gods. Furthermore, the Portuguese traders who came to Kongo were more interested in profits than in proselytizing. As Kongo lacked gold and other valuable trade goods, they turned mainly to procuring slaves.

At first Afonso provided the slaves, most of whom were prisoners captured in battles won with guns supplied by the Portuguese. But in time the Portuguese began bypassing him, buying slaves from Kongolese warlords and conducting slave raids that carried off Kongolese subjects. Turning against the slave trade, in 1526 the Christian manikongo wrote the king of Portugal, asking for help in stopping the enslavement of his people (see "Excerpts of Letters from the King of Kongo to the King of Portugal").

Portuguese buy slaves from warlords, bypassing manikongo

Read the Document

Letters from the King of Kongo to the Kings of Portugal

on **myhistorylab.com**

Disillusioned with the Portuguese, Afonso restricted the Christian missionaries, whom he had initially welcomed. But the slave trade continued, since neither Afonso nor his successors could prevent their people from dealing directly with the Europeans. By the century's end, as both their subordinates and their enemies openly defied them, the manikongos had lost much of their clout.

DOCUMENT 23.1 Excerpts of Letters from the King of Kongo to the King of Portugal

In 1526 the Kongo king Nzinga Mbemba, also called Afonso I, wrote to the king of Portugal asking for help in suppressing the slave trade. What were Afonso's main frustrations and concerns? How did he seek to win the sympathy of the Portuguese king?

Sir, Your Highness should know how our Kingdom is being lost in so many ways . . ., since this is caused by the excessive freedom given by your agents and officials to the men and merchants who are allowed to come to this Kingdom . . ., doing a great harm not only to the service of God, but the security and peace of our Kingdoms and State as well.

And we cannot reckon how great the damage is, since the . . . merchants are taking every day our natives, sons of the land and the sons of our noblemen and vassals and our relatives, because the thieves and men of bad conscience grab them wishing to have the things and wares of this Kingdom which they are ambitious of; they grab them and get them to be sold; and so great, Sir, is the corruption and licentiousness that our country is being completely depopulated . . . . That is why we beg of Your Highness to help and assist us in this matter . . ., because it is our will that in these

Kingdoms there should not be any trade of slaves nor outlet for them . . . .

Moreover, Sir, in our Kingdoms there is another great inconvenience which is of little service to God, and this is that many of our people, keenly desirous . . . of the wares and things of your Kingdoms . . ., in order to satisfy their voracious appetite, seize many of our people . . ., and take them to be sold to the white men who are in our Kingdoms . . . .

And as soon as they are taken by the white men they are immediately ironed and branded with fire, and when they are carried to be embarked, if they are caught by our guards' men the whites allege that they have bought them but they cannot say from whom, so that it is our duty to do justice and to restore to the freemen their freedom, but it cannot be done if your subjects feel offended, as they claim to be. . . .

SOURCE: "Letters from the Kings of Kongo to the King of Portugal," *Monumenta Missionaria Africana*, ed. Antonio Brasio, (Lisboa: Agencia Geral do Ultramar, 1952), vol. 1: 262–63, 294–95, 335, 404, 470, 488, trans. Linda Wimmer; reprinted in *The Global Experience: Readings in World History*, ed. Stuart B. Schwartz, et al. (New York: Addison Welsey Longman, Inc., 1997) 240–42.

Portuguese start a slave colony called Angola

King of Kongo receives Dutch ambassadors.

In the next century, desperate to be of free Portuguese domination, the manikongos allied with the Dutch, who were moving in on the African trade. In 1665, however, the Portuguese defeated the Kongo forces and beheaded the manikongo. Thereafter, the once powerful Kongo Kingdom disintegrated into smaller domains, mostly controlled by African warlords who were willing to cooperate with the Portuguese. By then, however, the bulk of the slave trade had shifted south to a Portuguese colony called Angola.

THE ANGOLA SLAVE COLONY. South of the Kongo Kingdom, among a people called the Mbundu (*'m-BOON-doo*), a centralized state called Ndongo (*'n-DAWN-gō*) emerged in the late 1400s. As its ruler was called the *ngola* (*'n-GAW-lah*), the Portuguese arriving in the region referred to it as Angola.

In the 1500s this realm was raided regularly by intruders from Kongo, who carried off the Mbundu as slaves and sold them to Portuguese traders. In time, however, as the demand for laborers in Brazil's sugar fields grew, the Portuguese sought new sources of slaves. In 1571 they made Angola their colony, and four years later, on its coast, they founded the port of Luanda.

But Portuguese efforts to exploit the interior met fierce opposition. In the 1620s, Anna de Sousa Njinga (*AH-na duh SOO-suh 'n-JIHN-gah*) emerged as Ndongo's ruler, succeeding her father and brother. Since the realm had no experience with female monarchs,

Njinga of Ndongo, as she is commonly called, took on the attributes of a king (see page 511). She dressed as a man, commanded armies in combat, and reportedly even had male concubines, clothed as women to stress her kingly status. She also engaged in the slave trade, used it to arm her troops with European guns, and stubbornly fought Portuguese colonial expansion. In these struggles she allied for a time with the Dutch, who temporarily gained control of Luanda from 1641 until 1648.

Njinga of Ndongo resists European domination

Despite Njinga's resistance, however, the Portuguese ultimately prevailed. First they drove out the Dutch, and then, in the 1650s, they forced Njinga to sign a treaty granting Christian missionaries access to her lands. After her death in 1663, the Portuguese extended their control over the interior, finally conquering Ndongo in 1683.

The result was catastrophic for the Mbundu peoples. Angola became Portugal's main source of slaves, supplying as many as three million, or about a quarter of all the captives shipped in the Atlantic slave trade. Countless villages were pillaged of young males, and not until the 1800s did the region's population recover. Angola remained under Portuguese rule until 1975.

Angola's population depleted by slave trade

The Contest for East Africa

Africa's eastern coast was dominated by Swahili city-states such as Mogadishu (*mo-gah-DĒ-shoo*), Mombasa (*mōm-BAH-sah*), and Kilwa (Map 23.5). Built on coastal islands and peninsulas, these thriving ports controlled the nearby mainland and conducted Indian Ocean commerce with Arabia, Persia, and India. Although the city-states had not united into a political empire, each exercised considerable commercial power, trading local products such as ivory, ebony, leopard skins, and cotton for porcelains, glassware, pottery, and cloth from the East. The coastal cities also dealt in slaves, brought to them from the interior, and gold, mined in southern Africa and transported up the coast to Kilwa, which by the 1400s had emerged as the wealthiest and grandest of the Swahili states.

East African cities thrive on Indian Ocean commerce

Commerce, Christianity, Conflicts, and Colonies. At first East Africa was little affected by the Atlantic trade. Although Vasco da Gama had stopped there on his way to India in 1498, the Portuguese who followed him had little interest in using this region as a source of slaves for the Americas. The Americas, after all, were a long way from East Africa, which already had a thriving Indian Ocean trade the Portuguese were eager to exploit. Not until the 1800s, when the slave trade was banned and curtailed by ships that patrolled the West African coast, would captives from East Africa be shipped in large numbers to the Western Hemisphere (Chapter 30).

The European impact on East Africa was nonetheless profound. In the early 1500s, aiming both to expand Christianity and to gain control of the Indian Ocean trade, the Portuguese bombarded the Swahili ports, subjected some to tribute, and eventually erected imposing fortresses at places such as Kilwa and Mombasa. A substantial part of the coastal trade thus temporarily fell under Portuguese domination.

Portuguese domination, however, did little to advance either Christianity or commerce in East Africa. The Swahili cities, managed by Muslims for centuries, steadfastly refused to adopt the Christian faith. Offended, no doubt, by the Christian militancy and domineering trade policies of the Portuguese, many Africans in the interior refused to do business with them. Shipping and

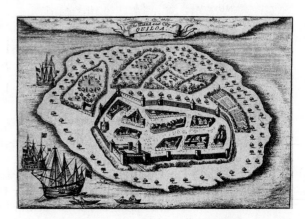

View of Kilwa.

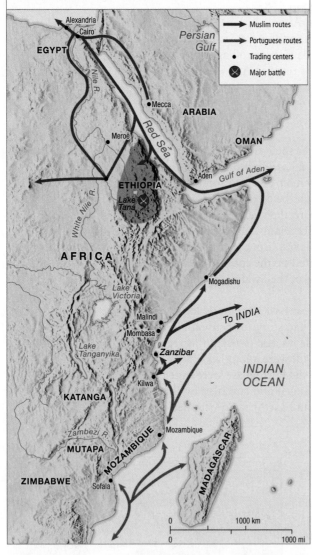

MAP 23.5 East African Commerce and Connections, 1500–1800

East Africa's coastal city-states were culturally and commercially connected with Asia by Muslim sea routes. Note, however, that in the 1500s the Portuguese intruded, subjecting some city-states to tribute, establishing connections with Christian Ethiopia, and eventually creating in the southeast a colony called Mozambique. How did the Portuguese intrusion affect East African commerce? How did East Africans respond?

commerce steadily dwindled until 1698, when Arab raiders from Oman in Arabia combined with local Africans to oust the Portuguese. The Omani Arabs later established a thriving commercial center on the island of Zanzibar, which dominated East African trade until the mid-1800s, eventually furnishing numerous captives for the overseas slave trade.

In southeastern Africa, the main attraction for the outsiders was the gold that had long been mined in the kingdom of Zimbabwe, south of the Zambezi River (Map 23.5). In the 1400s that kingdom had split apart, with much of it eventually controlled by a series of rulers who took the title Mwene Mutapa (*'m-WĀ-nā muh-TAH-pah*), meaning "master conqueror." In time they formed a federation called the Mutapa kingdom, whose wealth, like Zimbabwe's, was based on the gold trade.

In the 1500s, lured by this gold, profiteers from Portugal moved inland, rather than simply conduct coastal trade as they did elsewhere in Africa. After setting up a naval base in 1505 at a place called Mozambique (*mō-zahm-BĒK*) on the coast, they soon established settlements along the Zambezi River. These efforts brought connections and conflict with the Mutapa kingdom, whose people for decades resisted all efforts to conquer and Christianize them.

In 1575, however, in a bid to get European weapons, the reigning Mwene Mutapa signed an agreement allowing the Portuguese to mine his gold in return for providing him with firearms. Eventually, as its rulers made further concessions, the Mutapa realm was reduced to the status of a Portuguese vassal. In the 1630s, when a revolt arose against the foreign overlords, Portugal crushed the rebels and extended control over the whole region.

A Portuguese colony called Mozambique thus emerged in southeastern Africa. Eventually, in addition to its gold, it also became a significant source of slaves. Like Angola in the west, it remained under Portugal's rule until 1975, long after both the Atlantic slave trade and Portuguese prowess were gone.

Mozambique becomes a large Portuguese colony

THE BATTLES FOR ETHIOPIA. No African domain was more distinctive—or fascinating to European Christians—than Ethiopia (Map 23.5). In the fourth century, Ethiopians had adopted Coptic Christianity, a Monophysite (*muh-NOFF-ih-sīt*) or "single-nature" creed holding that Jesus Christ was only divine, not both human and divine as other Christians believed (Chapter 10). Since then they had clung resolutely to their faith, even after being cut off for centuries from the rest of Christendom by Islamic expansion. Although they were mostly farmers, Ethiopians did conduct commerce, including some traffic in slaves, with the Muslim world.

In the 12th century, European crusaders were enthralled by rumors of a wealthy Christian kingdom in the East, allegedly led by a powerful king-priest known as Prester John, said to command a sizable army capable of crushing the Muslims. Three centuries later, despite the obvious improbability that he could still be alive, Portugal sent expeditions to East Africa to search for this mythical Christian monarch. So intoxicating was the legend that, when a Portuguese mission arrived in Ethiopia in 1520, its connection with that ancient Christian kingdom evoked as much excitement in Europe as Columbus's voyages to the Americas had elicited in the 1490s.

At first the new connection proved fortunate for Ethiopia. In 1529 and 1531, a neighboring Muslim warlord attacked the realm, forcing many Christians to adopt Islam. But the Ethiopians appealed for help to the Portuguese, who in time sent an expedition headed by Vasco da Gama's son. He was captured and beheaded by Islamic forces, but a joint Ethiopian-Portuguese force finally vanquished the Muslims east of Lake Tana in 1543 (Map 23.5).

Christian Ethiopians defeat Muslims with Portuguese help

Later, however, the European ties proved troublesome, especially when Jesuits came to Ethiopia seeking to replace its Coptic Christian faith with the "dual-nature" Roman Catholic version, holding that Christ was both human and divine. In the 1620s, the Jesuits converted Ethiopia's emperor, who then tried to impose his new faith on his subjects. But the Coptic Christians rebelled, ousting this ruler in 1632, and soon his successor expelled the Jesuits and most other outsiders. Henceforth, through centuries of regional conflict, Ethiopians retained their independence and their Coptic creed, resisting the intrusions of both Muslims and European Christians.

South Africa and the Dutch

Southernmost Africa, remote from both Europe and Asia, was initially spared from outside intrusion. Its indigenous peoples spoke unique languages, now called **Khoisan** (*KOY-sahn*), distinguished by clicking sounds. The Khoisan-speakers were mostly farmers and herders, although some still lived in hunter-gatherer societies. Their lives remained undisturbed, even when the Portuguese began sailing around South Africa in the late 1400s, because at first the Europeans did not colonize the region.

South African colony helps Dutch connect with the East Indies

In 1652, however, on the southwest coast, the Dutch East India Company set up a way station for Dutch ships traveling between Europe and the East Indies. That settlement, later called Cape Town (Map 23.6), grew into a small colony, as the mild climate and rich soil attracted settlers from the Netherlands.

Dutch settlement proved disastrous for South Africans, especially when settlers called Boers (*boorz*), a Dutch term meaning "farmers," moved north into the interior. Using

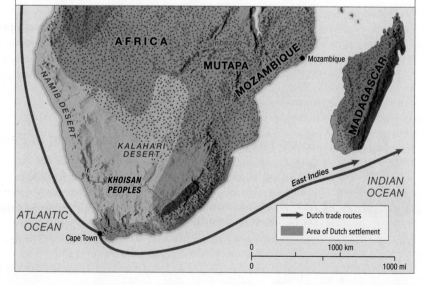

| MAP **23.6** | South Africa and the Dutch Incursions, 1652–1806 |

Due to its great distance from Europe and Asia, South Africa was spared from outside incursions until the mid-1600s. Observe that in 1652 the Dutch set up a station, later called Cape Town, for ships traveling to and from the East Indies, and that Dutch farmers from Europe eventually settled on surrounding lands. What impact did these settlers have on Africans in this region?

Dutch trade routes
Area of Dutch settlement

Dutch fort at Cape Town.

their guns to drive the local Africans off their lands, the Boers enslaved or exterminated most of the Khoisan-speakers. By 1806, when the colony passed from Dutch into British hands, it had become a racially stratified society, dominated by Dutch South Africans who called themselves Afrikaners.

The Impact on Africa of the Atlantic Slave Trade

Although each part of Africa reacted differently to the European intrusions, the overall impacts were extensive and profound. Traditional trade patterns were disrupted, replaced by exploitative systems that typically favored those who trafficked in slaves. Historic states and kingdoms were weakened or destroyed, while rulers who seized slaves and sold them for guns grew in power and wealth. Wars, rebellions, and slave hunts abounded, as ruthless and ambitious Europeans and Africans sought to fill the insatiable demand for slave labor in the Americas.

Demographic Dislocation

The demographic dislocation caused by these events was monumental. During the Atlantic slave trade, from the 16th through 19th centuries, sub-Saharan Africa lost at least 15 million people. Eleven or twelve million were shipped as slaves to the Americas, perhaps two million more died along the way, and several million others were transported to North Africa and Asia by Muslim merchants.

New crops from the Americas help offset population loss

Historians differ in assessing the impact of these losses. Some think they were catastrophic, leading to Africa's destitution and destroying its traditional cultures. Others contend that in time the decline was offset by nutritious new crops from the Americas, such as sweet potatoes, peanuts, and maize. Especially important was **cassava** (*kuh-SAH-vuh*), also called manioc (*MAN-ē-ock*), a large hardy plant whose edible part grows below the ground, like a carrot or potato. Cassava can be cooked or eaten raw, ground into flour for bread, processed into tapioca and starch, and even used to make an alcoholic drink. Brought to Africa from Brazil, probably by Portuguese traders, it was widely adopted by African farmers because of its hardiness and its ability to feed more people per acre than most other major crops. Such new crops, according to some historians, helped increase Africa's food supply and thus over time its population, offsetting its vast loss of people to the Atlantic slave trade.

Notice announcing a shipment of African slaves.

Disruption of Family Life

Thus, unlike the Amerinds, whose population never fully recovered from the demographic disaster of the 16th century (Chapter 19), many African societies in time regained the population lost due to European intrusions. Nothing, however, could offset the suffering of the slaves or the disruption of families losing their loved ones.

In Africa, as elsewhere, most people's lives centered on their families and clans. Although some Africans dwelt in cities with specialized professions, most lived with their kinfolk in rural villages, raising crops or livestock on surrounding lands. Men did most of the field work, but women and children often helped with sowing and tilling. A man's prestige was typically based on his physical prowess, while a woman's status was based on her bearing of children.

As in most premodern societies, African marriages were arranged by the parents of the bride and groom. Some African societies were **matrilineal**, with children tracing their heritage through their mothers, and even **matrilocal**, with married couples living in or near the wife's family. In general, however, African wives were subject to their husband's authority. **Polygyny**, the practice by which a man has more than one wife at a time, was relatively common in some parts of Africa, even before the Atlantic slave trade. In Africa, as elsewhere, the bride's family often gave the groom a dowry, but in some African cultures the husband's kin were expected to provide a **bridewealth**—a payment from the groom to the parents of the bride to make up for the loss of their daughter and assure them he would treat her well.

The slave trade ravaged millions of African families. During the centuries of its operation, families were robbed of the labor and talents of many of their most productive members. Since American plantations demanded mostly men, the population remaining in West and Central Africa was predominantly female, disrupting the traditional gender balance, and requiring women to take on duties (such as field work and cattle herding) traditionally done by men. In these regions polygyny persisted, since the number of available brides far exceeded the supply of potential grooms. In East Africa, conversely, polygyny was less pronounced, since much of the slave trade there was with the Muslim world, where female slaves were frequently preferred.

Africans typically connected in families and clans

Atlantic slave trade ravages African families

African Slaves and the Global Shift in Wealth and Power

In the 15th and 16th centuries, when Portuguese sailors were laying the foundations for the Atlantic slave trade, the Muslim world and China were the main centers of connections, wealth, and power. Indian Ocean trade, conducted mainly in Muslim ships, connected East Africa, Arabia, Persia, India, Southeast Asia, and the East Indies, while other land and sea routes connected this commerce to China, North Africa, West Africa, and Europe. The Chinese dominated trade in East and Southeast Asia, with other countries paying tribute to China for the privilege of partaking in its commerce.

In the 16th through 18th centuries, however, Europeans not only intruded into Indian Ocean commerce but also opened sea routes across the Atlantic and Pacific Oceans, creating history's first truly global connections (Map 23.7). The Atlantic Ocean, hitherto the western edge of international commerce, gradually became its center. And the nations of Western Europe, hitherto small states on the periphery of international trade, now became the main carriers of oceanic commerce, rulers of great world empires, and centers of a global economy. As trade shifted westward from the Indian Ocean to the Atlantic, wealth and power shifted to the Europeans, who controlled and profited from this trade.

Commerce expands from regional to global connections

Central to this process were African slaves, who produced the sugar, rum, and coffee, mined much of the silver, and later grew the tobacco and cotton that fueled Europe's growing global commerce. This commerce in turn helped produce the wealth

View the **Map**

Map Discovery: European Empires, ca. 1660

on **myhistorylab.com**

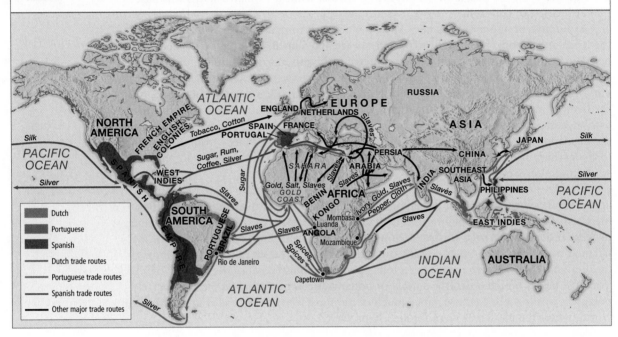

MAP 23.7   Seventeenth- and Eighteenth-Century Commercial Connections

By the 1600s the Atlantic slave trade was part of a growing global commercial network. Notice that the Portuguese, Spanish, and Dutch dominated global trade routes, but that others also took part in this trade. Which key routes and commodities involved African slaves?

African slaves enhance Europe's commercial wealth

that sustained the armies, navies, weapons, and bases that projected European global power and paid the officials who ran Europe's global empires. By 1800 Europe was on its way to world domination, based in part on the servitude and suffering of countless African slaves.

CHAPTER
REVIEW

Putting It in Perspective

European intrusions in Africa, and the resulting Atlantic slave trade, forged connections among disparate and distant cultures. Diverse societies in Europe, Africa, and the Americas were connected in an exploitative enterprise that brought wealth and power to some and enhanced the comfort of many, while subjecting millions of others to misery. The ancient practice of slavery, typically oppressive and cruel, was transformed into something even more onerous: a system of subjection that was racial, perpetual, and hereditary. African societies were also transformed, with power and wealth going mostly to Africans who sold other Africans as slaves. The

soil and resources of the Americas were exploited by Europeans, using the labor of these African slaves. And even Europe, though materially enriched, was morally diminished by its leading role in one of history's most infamous atrocities: the forced relocation and brutal exploitation of millions of human beings.

Indeed, in the long run, the slave trade's social impacts may have been its most destructive. Millions of victims were torn from their homelands and taken to distant lands under cruel conditions. Millions perished in the process; others survived to endure harsh lives in alien surroundings, with their descendants also sentenced to continued enslavement. Others, meanwhile, profited from these endeavors and even sought to excuse their actions by denying the humanity of those whose lives were destroyed. And even after the commerce in slaves and slavery itself were ended, a bitter legacy of racism and resentment continued to infect the societies of Africa, Europe, and the Americas, connected for centuries by the Atlantic slave trade.

Reviewing Key Material

KEY CONCEPTS

stateless societies, 514
slavery, 514
Middle Passage, 518
maroons, 519
African diaspora, 519
race, 519
racism, 519

Khoisan, 527
cassava, 528
matrilineal, 529
matrilocal, 529
polygyny, 529
bridewealth, 529

KEY PEOPLE

Nzinga Mbemba
  (Afonso I), 512
Ibn Khaldun, 515
Sonni Ali, 521
Askia Muhammad al-Turi
  (Muhammad I Askia), 521

Idris Alawma, 522
Diogo Cão, 523
Anna de Sousa Njinga
  (Njinga of Ndongo),
  524

ASK YOURSELF

1. How did the Atlantic slave trade originate? Why did Europeans use slaves from Africa to work their sugar plantations?
2. How did slavery in the Americas differ from slavery in Africa and the Muslim world?
3. What were the Atlantic slave trade's impacts on West Africa, Central Africa, and East Africa? Why did it have differing impacts on each region?
4. What were the benefits and detriments of the Atlantic slave trade for people in Europe, in Africa, and in the Americas?
5. How did the Atlantic slave trade contribute to a global shift in wealth and power?

GOING FURTHER

Ajayi, J., and M. Crowder, eds. *A History of West Africa.* 1985.
Barendse, R. J. *The Arabian Seas: The Indian Ocean World of the Seventeenth Century.* 2002.
Berger, Iris. *South Africa in World History.* 2009.
Berger, Iris, and E. Frances White. *Women in Sub-Saharan Africa.* 1999.

Coclanis, P., ed. *The Atlantic Economy during the Seventeenth and Eighteenth Centuries.* 2005.
Conniff, M. L., and T. J. Davis. *Africans in the Americas.* 2002.
Curtin, Philip D. *The Rise and Fall of the Plantation Complex.* 1998.
Edgerton, Robert B. *Warrior Women: The Amazons of Dahomey and the Nature of War.* 2000.
Ehret, Christopher. *The Civilizations of Africa: A History to 1800.* 2001.
Eltis, David. *The Rise of African Slavery in the Americas.* 2000.
Engerman, Stanley, et al. *Slavery.* 2001.
Fredrickson, George M. *Racism: A Short History.* 2002.
Gould, Philip. *Barbaric Traffic: Commerce and Antislavery in the Eighteenth-Century Atlantic World.* 2003.
Horton, M., and J. Middleton. *The Swahili: The Social Landscape of a Mercantile Society.* 2000.
Isichei, Elizabeth. *A History of African Societies to 1870.* 1997.
Klein, Herbert S. *The Atlantic Slave Trade.* 1999.
Lovejoy, Paul. *Transformations in Slavery: A History of Slavery in Africa.* 2000.
Manning, Patrick. *Slavery and African Life.* 1990.
Mariners Museum. *Captive Passage: The Transatlantic Slave Trade and the Making of the Americas.* 2002.
Middleton, J. *The World of Swahili: An African Mercantile Civilization.* 1992.
Mintz, Sidney W. *Sweetness and Power: The Place of Sugar in Modern History.* 1985.
Northrup, David. *Africa's Discovery of Europe, 1450–1850.* 2002.
Northrup, David, ed. *The Atlantic Slave Trade.* 2002.
Oliver, Roland, and Anthony Atmore. *The African Middle Ages, 1400–1800.* 2003.
Pilcher, Jeffrey M. *Food in World History.* 2006.
Robertson, Claire, and M. Klein. *Women and Slavery in Africa.* 1983.
Rodney, Walter. *How Europe Underdeveloped Africa,* 1981.
Searing, J. F. *West African Slavery and Atlantic Commerce, 1700–1860.* 1993.

Segal, R. *The Black Diaspora.* 1995.

Shillington, Kevin. *History of Africa.* Rev. 2nd ed. 2005.

Solow, Barbara. *Slavery and the Rise of the Atlantic System.* 1991.

Thomas, Hugh. *The Slave Trade: The Story of the Atlantic Slave Trade, 1440–1870.* 1997.

Thornton, J. *Africa and Africans in the Formation of the Atlantic World, 1400–1800.* 1998.

Tomich, Dale W. *Through the Prism of Slavery: Labor, Capital, and World Economy.* 2004.

Key Dates and Developments

1300s	Kongo Kingdom emerges		**1570s**	Angola colony started by Portuguese
1400s	Mutapa kingdom emerges		**1575**	Mutapa kingdom allows Portuguese to mine gold
1440s	West Africans begin selling slaves to Portuguese		**1591**	Moroccans crush the Songhai Empire
1468–1473	Sonni Ali defeats Mali and creates the Songhai Empire		**1623–1663**	Njinga reigns in Ndongo
1482–1483	Kongo Kingdom first visited by Portuguese		**mid-1600s**	English and Dutch move in on the Atlantic trade
1503–1507	East African cities attacked by Portuguese		**1652**	Dutch begin Cape Town settlement in South Africa
1520	Ethiopia visited by Portuguese mission		**1698**	Arabs from Oman drive Portuguese out of East Africa
1529–1541	Muslims and Portuguese struggle over Ethiopia		**1700s**	Height of Atlantic slave trade

PEARSON
myhistorylab Connections

Reinforce what you learned in this chapter by studying the many documents, images, maps, review tools, and videos available at www.myhistorylab.com.

Read and Review

✓• Study and Review Chapter 23

📖 Read the Document

Leo Africanus Describes Timbuktu, p. 521

Letters from the King of Kongo to the Kings of Portugal p. 523

🔍 View the Map

Map Discovery: Atlantic Slave Trade, p. 518

Map Discovery: European Empires, ca. 1660, p. 529

🔍 View the Image

West African Slave Market, p. 516

Research and Explore

👁 Watch the Video

Atlantic Connections: Sugar, Smallpox, and Slavery, p. 516

👁 Watch the Video

From Triangular Trade to an Atlantic System: Rethinking the Links That Created the Atlantic World, p. 517

((•• Listen to the Chapter Audio for Chapter 23 on myhistorylab.com

24

Absolutism and Enlightenment in Europe, 1600–1763

((•─Listen to the **Chapter Audio** for Chapter 24 on **myhistorylab.com**

■ What made absolute government so attractive to European rulers in the 17th and 18th centuries? Why did England reject the French model in favor of limited monarchy?

■ What new ideas about science and the role of reason reshaped European intellectual life in the 16th and 17th centuries?

■ How did the European Enlightenment affect ideas about governance?

The Hall of Mirrors, Palace of Versailles

The Hall of Mirrors in Louis XIV's magnificent palace at Versailles (page 535). This photo captures the wealth and power of the man who became Europe's most famous practitioner of royal absolutism.

As the first rays of the morning sun reflected off dozens of rectangular mirrors lining the long ceremonial hallway at the palace of Versailles, France's King Louis XIV was already awake. In the royal bedroom, as he dressed, he was attended by a dozen people, some of whom were his trusted servants. Others, however, were among the most distinguished nobles of France. The Duke of Rohan tied the king's shoes, the Count of Nevers handed Louis a freshly powdered wig, while the prince of Condé helped His Majesty into a richly brocaded jacket. Then Louis XIV, outfitted for the morning's affairs, led his distinguished retinue into a large meeting room adjacent to the Hall of Mirrors (see page 534).

It was an ordinary day in the summer of 1685. Though the ritual of dressing might suggest that a momentous ceremony was about to take place, it was only one of many rituals performed each day as the king went about his daily business of rising, eating, working, playing, and sleeping. Ostentatious and elaborate, the ceremonies were intended to underscore the king's dominance over his nobility as well as his grandeur. They were an integral component of **royal absolutism**, a system of governance in which the ruler's authority is said to come directly from God and cannot be limited or challenged by any human institution. Developed most extensively in France, this system was also the model for Austrian, Prussian, and Russian rule in 17th-century Europe.

Europe

Even as Louis reigned supreme, however, the foundations of absolutism were under challenge. As scientists overturned long-held beliefs about the physical universe, other thinkers began to question prevailing ideas of governance, social justice, economics, and gender roles. The result was an intellectual revolution, based on assertions that authority and belief must be challenged by reason, that society must be structured by logic rather than tradition and religion, and that governing authority comes not from God but from the people being governed. Initiated in Europe by a small, educated elite, this revolution opened the way for global advances in science and technology and for people the world over to participate more fully in their society's political and economic life.

The Age of Absolutism

Although monarchies had governed Europe for centuries, royal power had been limited by hereditary aristocracies and church hierarchies. In the 17th century, however, the French monarchy undermined the power of both to establish a governance system based on royal absolutism. Europe's other monarchies, envious of France, sought to do likewise. Austria and Prussia achieved considerable success, but English rulers were compelled to share governing authority with Parliament.

The French Model of Absolute Government

Seventeenth-century French absolutism was a form of government in which no institution could check the power of the king (Map 24.1). This did not mean the monarch could do anything he wished; he was restricted by the kingdom's fundamental laws, derived from centuries of custom. For example, he could not change the national religion from Roman

View the **Map**

Atlas Map: Geographical Tour: Europe in 1714

on **myhistorylab.com**

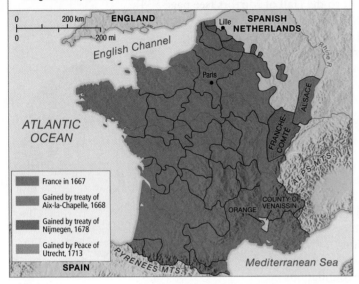

FOUNDATION MAP 24.1   France in 1715

A French proverb tells us, "The natural borders of France are these: the Rhine, the Alps, and the Pyrenees." Louis XIV dedicated much of his 72-year reign, and much of France's blood and treasure, to transforming that saying into reality. Notice that most of his acquisitions moved France in the direction of the Rhine River. Why was Louis XIV unable to achieve his goal of expanding France to its "natural borders"?

Legend:
- France in 1667
- Gained by treaty of Aix-la-Chapelle, 1668
- Gained by treaty of Nijmegen, 1678
- Gained by Peace of Utrecht, 1713

Catholicism to another faith, levy new taxes without the consent of representatives of society, or have someone executed without following legal procedures. The fundamental laws could not be changed, and the king was bound by them, as were all his subjects.

In practice, however, as long as the king respected the fundamental laws, he was nearly all-powerful. A French legislature existed in theory, but only the king could call it into session, and even then he was not bound by its decisions. No legislature was summoned between 1614 and 1789. There was a judiciary, but its members were appointed by the king, who controlled their salaries and had the power to exile them for life. Royal edicts had to be registered by judicial tribunals known as parlements (*pahr-luh-MAWN*), but in practice the king could compel the parlements to do his will. By the close of the 17th century, the French monarchy exercised immense power.

ROOTS OF FRENCH ABSOLUTISM. This accumulation of power was an outgrowth of the French Wars of Religion (1562–1594), after which

Fundamental laws set boundaries on the power of French kings

France's government was revived by King Henri IV, a former Huguenot who converted to Catholicism once he saw that France would not accept a Protestant king. Five years later he guaranteed Huguenots' rights in the Edict of Nantes (Chapter 20). But Henri, a charming and outgoing backslapper, governed France largely by the force of his attractive personality. It remained to be seen if a less appealing and talented monarch could rule France effectively.

Richelieu strives to create absolutism

In 1610, when Henri was succeeded by Louis XIII, the French monarchy was tested. Nine years old, sickly and shy, dominated by his unpopular Florentine mother, the new king never developed a taste for state affairs. Instead, he appointed a series of chief ministers to run the government. His early selections proved inept, but his last, Cardinal Richelieu (*RISH-lih-yoo*), turned out to be exceptionally competent. The cardinal devoted his 18 years in office to constructing the foundations for an absolute monarchy.

Richelieu.

Richelieu's main goal was to strengthen the monarchy to such a degree that even an incapable ruler would not harm the country. To achieve this goal, he sought to remove all obstacles to royal authority, thereby reducing the prospects for unrest should the king prove weak. The main obstacles were the Huguenots and the nobility.

Although he was a cardinal in the Catholic Church, Richelieu was no religious zealot; he was willing to allow Huguenots freedom of conscience and worship, guaranteed them by the Edict of Nantes. However, the edict had also granted them two hundred "places of safety," fortified towns in central and southern France protected by Protestant militia. To Richelieu, this threatened the monarchy: if Protestant forces invaded France, the fortified towns might support the enemy. So he convinced Louis XIII to annul this portion of the edict. The result was a Huguenot rebellion in 1627, supported by Protestant England. Richelieu led an army to crush the revolt, and a

1629 settlement allowed the Huguenots to retain civil and religious rights, but not their places of safety.

Richelieu also had no desire to destroy the French nobility; he was an aristocrat himself. But he wanted the nobles to support a strong monarchy and place the country's welfare above their own interests instead of promoting a weakened monarchy that they could manipulate. To undermine their power, Richelieu removed some of their privileges. He sent direct agents of the king throughout the country to assert the monarchy's control over local affairs, depriving nobles of much of their influence over ordinary citizens. To undercut noble control over the nation's defense, the cardinal suggested a permanent, or "standing," army, but at the time, France's treasury could not bear the expense. For the next French monarch, however, a standing army was both essential and financially possible. This ruler, King Louis XIV (1643–1715), came to epitomize royal absolutism.

Louis XIV was only five years old when his father died in 1643, and Richelieu had died five months earlier. On Louis XIV's behalf, the Queen Mother ruled as regent while Cardinal Jules Mazarin (*mah-zah-RAN*) served as chief minister. Regencies were always dangerous for a monarchy, as its foes might try to take advantage of inexperienced leadership. In this case a conspiracy of French nobles who hated Richelieu's policies used war with Spain as a pretext to remove Mazarin and reverse the trend toward absolutism. This rebellion, known as the **Fronde** (*FRAHND*), lasted from 1648 to 1653.

The Fronde drove Mazarin into exile in Switzerland, but the conspirators failed to intimidate the young king and the Queen Mother into supporting them. Reluctant to harm or overthrow Louis, they ruled France so badly that the exiled Mazarin found it easy to raise money to hire a mercenary army in Switzerland. This army then liberated the king and defeated the conspiracy.

Despite the Fronde's ultimate failure, the experience left a powerful impression on Louis XIV. Traumatized by the danger to himself and his mother, he emerged embittered at the nobility and convinced that its power must be broken. In 1661, at age 23, he began 54 years of directing French affairs himself, strengthening the monarchy by centralizing the government.

LOUIS XIV AND THE CONSOLIDATION OF ABSOLUTISM. Centralization of authority required a large bureaucracy. The king stood at its top, setting overall policy, sometimes intervening actively in decision making but leaving routine business to his ministers. Louis XIV appointed ministers to head various government departments, with each minister reporting to the king individually. Through such one-on-one sessions, the king maintained direct personal control over the operation of each department.

This degree of personal control was unprecedented in French history, and it gave Louis the means to undermine the power of the nobility. As ministers he appointed only commoners, whose advancement would depend upon him alone and whose loyalty would therefore be unquestioned. Nobles were never placed in influential positions that might enable them again to conspire against the king or obstruct the development of absolutism.

The nobles' opposition to this system was a threat to Louis, who addressed it with a carefully crafted program centered on construction of a magnificent palace in the Paris suburb of Versailles (*vehr-SIGH*). Completed in 1682, it testified to the greatness of Louis XIV, who now called himself the "Sun King." With accommodations for ten thousand people, gorgeously manicured grounds, a reflecting pool arranged to catch the rays of the sun on the summer solstice, and a fabulous Hall of

The Fronde attempts to reverse progress toward absolutism

((•─ **Listen** to the **Audio**
Louis XIV
on **myhistorylab.com**

Louis XIV moves against the nobility

Louis XIV.

Mirrors, the palace of Versailles even today remains so breathtaking that it is easy to overlook the political cunning behind its beauty.

Versailles was crucial to Louis's plans, because nowhere else in France could so many aristocrats be housed in luxurious surroundings. Nobles who lived there received honorary positions entitling them to wait upon His Majesty and look important while doing so. But while carrying rich allowances and boundless dignity, these positions provided no power. Moreover, by assembling the greatest aristocrats of the realm in one place, the king could have them spied on by his servants, who were ordered to report instances of treasonous behavior. The technique was similar to that of Japan's Tokugawa shoguns, who forced their daimyo to live in Edo (Chapter 21).

French commercial dominance proves crucial to absolutism

The French nobility was thus increasingly isolated from governance, and Louis worked tirelessly to accomplish just that. Presiding over Europe's wealthiest country, he appointed the astute Jean-Baptiste Colbert as minister of finance, charging him with organizing the economy to maximize tax receipts. Colbert shared Louis's conviction that absolutism could not be realized without the foundation provided by a powerful economy. The creation of a strong urban middle class would enrich the kingdom while providing the monarchy with a consistent revenue stream with which to implement royal policies. When Colbert succeeded, in part by encouraging overseas expansion through monopolistic trading companies (Chapter 22), Louis took the increased revenues and built the permanent army of Richelieu's dreams. The king could not prevent nobles from becoming officers, but he made sure that his war ministers were commoners. Moreover, Louis perfected Richelieu's system of direct royal agents, depriving aristocrats of most of their influence in local politics. Small wonder the nobility detested absolutism.

Read the **Document**

Jean Baptiste Colbert, "Mercantilism: Dissertation on Alliances"

on **myhistorylab.com**

Louis XIV sees religion as a component of absolutism

Louis XIV's efforts to subject France to his royal will extended into the religious sphere. His best-known motto, "I am the state," was complemented by "One faith, one law, one king." Considering the Huguenots heretics who must be removed from his kingdom, in 1685 he revoked the Edict of Nantes and insisted that all Huguenots convert to Catholicism. The result was a series of forced conversions, as well as a mass emigration of Huguenots to Prussia, Holland, or British North America in search of religious freedom. Louis's Huguenot policy damaged France economically, since many who fled were merchants or artisans. In the end, Louis's efforts to enforce "One faith, one law, one king" demonstrated that even an absolute monarch could not have everything his way.

Read the **Document**

Louis XIV Writes to His Son (1661)

on **myhistorylab.com**

Louis achieved much during his lengthy reign. He consolidated his authority as an absolute monarch and made France Europe's dominant power. But he also fought four wars that nearly bankrupted France, largely because he never got around to reforming its taxation system. This failure, even more than his intolerance of the Huguenots, threatened absolutism itself and eventually, in 1789, led to revolution.

Absolutism in Central Europe

Absolute monarchies develop elsewhere in Europe

France's power was the envy of other rulers, particularly in Central Europe, where the sprawling Holy Roman Empire dominated a region that included numerous small German states, the Netherlands, Austria, Bohemia, Switzerland, and parts of northern Italy. Its emperor, almost always from Austria's Habsburg family, was elected by local rulers who were largely autonomous in domestic matters. In the 17th and 18th centuries, however, absolute monarchies arose in Central Europe's two most powerful states: Austria and Prussia.

AUSTRIA'S MULTINATIONAL ABSOLUTISM. The Peace of Westphalia, which ended the Thirty Years War in 1648, destroyed the hopes of the Austrian Habsburgs to transform the Holy Roman Empire into a centralized German Catholic state (Map 24.2). Although they continued, with one exception, to be elected as emperors, they had little control

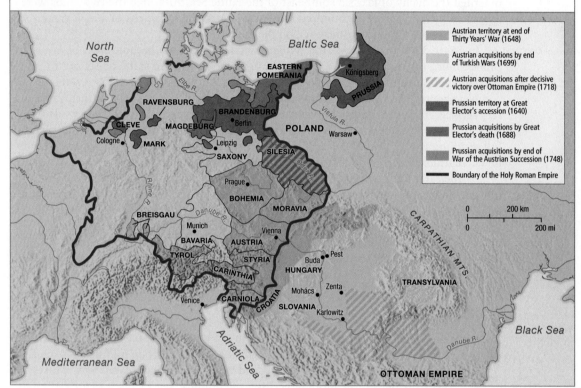

MAP 24.2 Growth of Austria and Prussia, 1648–1763

The Thirty Years War (1618–1648) prevented the Austrian Habsburg dynasty from reversing the Protestant Reformation and establishing Catholic religious and political control of Central Europe. Responding to this disappointment, the Habsburgs reemphasized their Austrian roots and worked toward the development of absolute monarchy. Note that their territorial gains in wars with the Ottoman Empire moved the Habsburg monarchy southeast, away from Germany and toward the Black Sea. How did the Great Elector of Prussia, Frederick William, react to Austria's southeastward orientation?

over most of the more than three hundred states that made up this so-called empire. But the Habsburgs were still hereditary rulers in Austria and Bohemia and were routinely elected kings of Hungary, most of which had been under Ottoman control since the 1520s. The Habsburgs sought to regain Hungary and tighten their domination over the areas they ruled directly, hoping to transform south-central Europe into an absolute monarchy.

Initially the Habsburgs had mixed success. They created a standing army but were nearly destroyed by the Ottoman Turks, who besieged Vienna in 1683. The Austrian capital's rescue by the king of Poland's multinational army marked a major turning point in Habsburg fortunes, as Austrian armies went on to drive the Turks from Hungary by 1699. In the process, the Habsburgs compelled the Hungarian nobles to accept them as hereditary rather than elective monarchs. A new empire was taking shape in Europe, one that was actually three distinct realms ruled by the same person. Austria, Bohemia, and Hungary each had its own separate assembly, its own language (respectively German, Czech, and Magyar), and its own laws and customs. The Habsburgs promised that as hereditary monarchs they would respect those different traditions. In return, they would rule as absolute monarchs, unconstrained by other institutions. Fearful of the growing power of Prussia, Russia, and France, the Bohemian and Hungarian nobles eventually

Habsburgs build a multinational form of absolutism

accepted this arrangement. By the early 18th century, a multinational form of absolutism had emerged in the Habsburg domains.

PRUSSIAN ABSOLUTISM: NOBILITY AND MONARCH. Another type of absolutism originated to Austria's north in Brandenburg, a medium-sized state centered on the city of Berlin. Its ruler was a member of the Hohenzollern (*HŌ-un-ZAH-lurn*) family, which in 1618 also inherited the duchy of Prussia southeast of the Baltic Sea. Although the two lands were separated by more than one hundred miles, they formed the nucleus of a new great power that would rise to prominence on the might of its army.

Prussia builds absolutism around its army

In 1640, 20-year-old Frederick William von Hohenzollern became ruler of Brandenburg-Prussia. Dismayed by the weakness of his divided state, he set out to strengthen his armies. He agreed to give his nobles, known as **Junkers** (*YOONG-kers*), complete control over their peasants and exemption from taxes in return for loyal military service. As a result, most Junker families furnished officers to the army, while the rest of the people were forced to pay very heavy taxes and the peasants were reduced to full serfdom. Before he died in 1688, Frederick William had brought his scattered lands under centralized rule and created a forty thousand–man army.

By the early 18th century, Prussia was moving rapidly toward absolutism. The Hohenzollern policy of cooperating with the Junkers in establishing serfdom gave these nobles a stake in a powerful monarchy. In exchange for tax exemptions and peasant labor services, they willingly granted the Hohenzollerns extensive political authority, although their control of the officer corps gave them significant leverage against the monarch. No legislature could check the kings of Prussia, but the army certainly could, a fact no Hohenzollern ruler could forget. Prussian absolutism, unlike the French version, was consolidated in a partnership between nobility and ruler.

Absolutism in Austria and Prussia is based on the aristocracy and serfdom

SOCIAL BASES OF EUROPEAN ABSOLUTISM. Absolutism in Austria and Prussia differed from that of France, largely due to differences in the ability of nobles to control the peasantry. France, where most peasants were free, had a strong middle class made up of educated urban professionals and wealthy merchant capitalists. These townsfolk helped the monarchy offset the nobility, serving as state officials and providing the ruler with money for hiring armies and bureaucrats. Austria and Prussia, by contrast, lacked strong middle classes, so their monarchs had to rely on nobles to collect the taxes, staff the bureaucracies, and run the armies. In return for such services, the nobles were given full authority over their peasants.

The result in Austria and Prussia was a mixture of absolutism with aristocracy: monarchs controlled the central government and exercised vast power, but nobles had almost total control over their estates. While peasants in France were legally free, those in Austria and Prussia were serfs. Technically they were not slaves, since they were attached to the soil and were not supposed to be bought and sold. In practice, however, they might as well have been slaves. They could not marry, or even leave the estate, without their lord's consent. They were typically forced to work three to six days a week on the lord's lands, or in some places to give him a share of their own crops. They were subject to the whim of the lord, who was free to impose penalties such as flogging that could lead to injury or death.

Despite its superficial similarity, then, absolutism in Austria and Prussia was not the same as in France. In France, where nobles were weak and peasants were free, the monarch's power rested on the shoulders of a strong urban middle class, but in Austria and Prussia executive power was based on the aristocracy and serfdom.

Prussian soldiers.

The English Alternative to Absolutism

In England, the monarchs, like those in France and Central Europe, sought to construct an absolute monarchy in the 17th century. They were blocked, however, by Parliament, a medieval legislature with a House of Lords made up of prominent nobles and a House of Commons representing wealthy commoners. In England, unlike elsewhere, the nobles and middle classes worked together to restrict the ruler, creating a **limited monarchy** that served as an English alternative to absolutism.

PARLIAMENT VERSUS THE KING. England's Parliament was summoned by monarchs whenever they needed money and soldiers. King Henry VIII (1509–1547) had skillfully manipulated Parliament during the English Reformation, and his daughter Queen Elizabeth I (1558–1603) had also done so during her conflicts with Spain (Chapter 20). Yet Parliament could and did restrict the power of the monarch, and it prevented the emergence of royal absolutism in England.

In Elizabeth's reign, Parliament was increasingly dominated by the House of Commons rather than the House of Lords. This shift reflected the growth of English commerce, which brought prosperity to merchants, bankers, and other commoners. Many such people purchased land in the country, established themselves as landed gentry, and represented rural constituencies in Parliament. Literate and vocal, they demanded influence proportional to their economic status.

England's Parliament limits the monarch's power

In 1603, Elizabeth I died unmarried and childless. The throne passed to King James VI of Scotland, son of her executed cousin Mary Stuart, thus initiating England's Stuart dynasty. Ruling in England as King James I (r. 1603–1625), he aimed to establish an absolute monarchy. But James was a spendthrift and a foreigner whose Scottish mannerisms irritated the English. A smart man who was not particularly practical, he repeatedly requested money from Parliament to finance recurring wars with Spain and interventions abroad on behalf of endangered Protestants. These requests were a source of tension between king and Parliament.

James's son Charles I (r. 1625–1649), frustrated by fiscal restrictions, sought to bypass Parliament and make his own laws. Distrusting the Stuarts, Parliament refused to approve new taxes, instead drawing up a "Petition of Right" that denounced the king's forcing wealthy people to lodge soldiers in their homes and imprisoning his subjects without due process of law. Religion complicated the tension, as many members of Parliament were Calvinist Christians who did not belong to the Anglican Church or recognize the authority of the king as its head. These **Puritans** considered Anglicanism too much like Roman Catholicism, and they developed their own simplified church. In sum, the Stuart kings stood for absolutism and Anglican supremacy; Parliament stood against both.

Financial disputes frustrate English kings' ambitions for absolute monarchy

In 1629, after four tense years, Charles and Parliament deadlocked. Since Parliament could meet only when called by the king, Charles sent it home and ruled without it until 1640. This **Eleven Years' Tyranny** violated centuries of English custom and alienated many. Charles hoped to apply in England the modern ideas of absolute monarchy evolving in France, but Parliament stood firm in asserting the medieval right of a legislative body to authorize taxation. These were important differences, and they may have been ultimately irreconcilable, but the failure of executive and legislature to engage in honest dialogue over such crucial matters eventually plunged England into civil war.

Charles I rules without Parliament

In his struggle with Parliament, Charles began in a strong position but made major mistakes. When he raised revenues by reviving old taxes, many considered this an effort to tax without parliamentary consent. When he attempted to impose the Anglican Church in Calvinist Scotland, where he was also king, he prompted a revolt by the Scots. To raise money to put down this revolt, he was forced to recall Parliament in 1640. By this time the possibility of reasoned discussion had ended.

THE ENGLISH CIVIL WAR AND PURITAN REVOLUTION. The new Parliament, which sat from 1640 to 1660, gave Charles the funds he requested but took action to restrain him. It passed a law requiring Parliament to meet every three years with or without the king's call, and another law prohibiting dissolution of Parliament without its own consent. These actions asserted new rights never before claimed by Parliament. When, in 1641, it drew up a list of grievances suffered during Charles's reign, the king ordered the arrest of five of its leaders. Parliament refused to hand them over, and civil war erupted.

Parliament's assertion of new rights forces a civil war

The king drew his soldiers from the rural north and west, while Parliament's forces came from the more urban and commercial regions in the south and east. To gain Scottish support, Parliament made Calvinist Presbyterianism the official religion of England, Scotland, and Ireland. Oliver Cromwell, a parliamentary leader, developed the Ironside Army, a military force driven by a nearly fanatical Puritanism. The Ironsides became the conflict's finest soldiers, forcing Charles in 1646 to surrender to the Scots, who turned him over to Parliament the next year.

View the Image

Allegorical View of Cromwell as Savior of England

on **myhistorylab.com**

Had Parliament wanted simply to remove Charles, it could have selected another family to rule England. But Cromwell and the army wanted more than a change of dynasty; they wanted a Puritan revolution. Fearing that a new king, to reclaim the monarch's religious authority, might restore the Anglican Church, they decided to try Charles for treason, execute him, and abolish the monarchy. Many in Parliament refused to go along with such extreme measures, so Cromwell purged it, reducing it to a Rump Parliament of about sixty members. This minority condemned and beheaded Charles I in 1649.

For the next four years, Cromwell governed with the Rump Parliament. In 1651 he invaded Ireland, massacring Catholics in retaliation for the butchering of Protestants in the northern region of Ulster ten years earlier. Protestant landlords were installed throughout the island, and the Catholic Church was driven underground. That same year Cromwell won naval engagements against the Dutch and Spanish, asserting English maritime commercial supremacy in the North Atlantic.

In 1653, Cromwell dismissed the Rump and effectively became a dictator, known as the Lord Protector. He was challenged, however, by extremist forces released by his own revolution, and he found no support among Anglicans, who despised him for displacing their church, or among royalists, who hated him for killing their king. His death in 1658 made it possible for the army in 1660 to restore the monarchy.

Oliver Cromwell.

THE STUART RESTORATION AND GLORIOUS REVOLUTION. A decade without a king convinced the English that, whatever its flaws, monarchy was a vital unifying institution. So they restored the Stuarts in the person of King Charles II (r. 1660–1685), son of the beheaded Charles I. Eager to keep his own head, Charles II generally respected parliamentary rights, while Parliament restored the Anglican Church and acknowledged the new king's authority. Tall, handsome, and courteous, he quickly earned the nickname "the merry monarch" for his love of parties, his reluctance to take himself too seriously, and his extensive familiarity with ladies' bedrooms. Even those who opposed his policies found him hard to dislike.

Charles II restores the Stuart dynasty

The great irony of Charles's reign was the religious question. His father, an Anglican, had faced a Parliament dominated by Puritans; now the Parliament was solidly Anglican, but Charles's sympathies lay with Catholicism (although he did not convert until he lay dying in 1685). Aware of these sympathies, in 1673 Parliament passed the Test Act, requiring that all office holders be Anglicans. The first to resign as a consequence was the Lord High Admiral, James, the king's younger brother, a declared Catholic and next in line for the throne, since Charles had no legitimate children. If and when James became king, renewed religious turmoil seemed a certainty.

When Charles II died in 1685, his Catholic brother became King James II. A man of limited intellect, James antagonized even his allies by his clear favoritism toward Catholics and his blundering dealings with Parliament. James, however, was already in his fifties, and most expected that the throne would eventually pass to his Protestant daughter Mary, wed to the Dutch leader William of Orange. But when, in 1688, James's second wife gave birth to a son, England faced the prospect of a continuous line of Catholic kings.

James II actually thought he could restore Catholicism, but Parliament resisted. Its leaders went to Holland and offered to help his daughter Mary seize the English throne. But her husband William, eager to lead England into an alliance against Louis XIV, insisted on becoming king. Once it was agreed that William and Mary could reign jointly, in 1689 they invaded England with a sizable army.

Parliament takes action against Catholic absolutism

These developments culminated in the **Glorious Revolution,** a cooperative effort by Parliament and the invaders to overthrow James II. The king was removed with very little bloodshed. Unable to find support in England, he fled to Ireland and raised a Catholic army, which was defeated in 1690 by the new King William III. James then fled to France, where he and his heirs launched claims to the English throne for decades.

In 1689, Parliament passed a **Bill of Rights,** a written document specifying the rights that William and Mary were required to endorse as conditions of their rule. No taxes could be levied without parliamentary approval; the monarchs could not ignore or violate any law passed by Parliament; no one could be imprisoned without due process of law. These conditions created a contractual relationship between the ruler and Parliament, defining England as a limited monarchy.

The Bill of Rights defines England as a constitutional monarchy

To many Europeans, the English alternative of limited monarchy seemed an outmoded, ineffective concept, reflecting old medieval notions of power shared between king and nobles. But the notion that government has a contractual duty to ensure people's rights, embedded in the English alternative, was soon regarded as a modern, progressive concept, owing to an intellectual revolution that was challenging many beliefs about science and society.

Europe's Intellectual Revolution

In the 16th and 17th centuries, while Western society was still in the turmoil of religious upheavals and witch hunts, innovative European thinkers, their horizons broadened by discoveries in the Americas of plants, animals, and human societies previously unknown in Europe, began an intellectual revolution. Using new approaches and techniques, they achieved dramatic breakthroughs in science and advanced new ideas about governance, human rights, economics, and gender roles. At first, the new concepts, confined mainly to the educated elite, had little effect on common people's lives or thinking, still largely shaped by family, farming, and faith. In time, however, Europe's intellectual revolution had a profound and global impact.

The Scientific Revolution

For many centuries, scientific understanding in the West derived largely from connections with Islamic societies, whose scholars had rediscovered and developed the ideas of earlier cultures. In the 16th and 17th centuries, however, Western thinkers both built upon and challenged these ideas to develop a new science, based on mechanical laws that were said to govern the physical universe.

ASIAN AND ISLAMIC CONNECTIONS. Prior to the 17th century, almost everything known about science in the West came from Africa, Asia, and the Islamic world. The great Muslim scholars of earlier centuries, such as Ibn Sina and al-Khwarizmi (Chapter 12), had rediscovered and translated works on science and mathematics from ancient Egypt, India, and Greece. Building on these works, they had developed philosophical systems to explain the world around them and mathematical systems (such as Arabic numerals and algebra) that would prove essential to scientific study. Technological advances such as paper and printing, gunpowder weapons, water-clocks, magnetic compasses, and other navigational instruments, developed in China and India, were likewise improved upon and spread westward by Muslims.

Islamic connections make Europe's scientific revolution possible

Muslim astronomers also studied the movements of the stars and planets, based mainly on a model developed by the great ancient Greek philosopher Aristotle, in which the earth sat unmoving at the center of the universe surrounded by transparent paths on which the sun, moon, stars, and planets revolved. In the second century C.E., the Egyptian astronomer Ptolemy (*TAH-luh-mē*), charting the irregular movements of the planets, proposed that they followed separate paths in moving around the earth. For centuries astronomers sought mainly to perfect this model by making minor adjustments, but in the 13th century the Persian Muslim scholar Nasir al-Din al-Tusi challenged the belief that the earth was unmoving and devised a mathematical model of circles rotating within circles to better explain the irregular paths of the planets. Contacts and connections with the Muslim world helped acquaint Western thinkers with the works of these and other scholars, providing a basis for scientific study in the West.

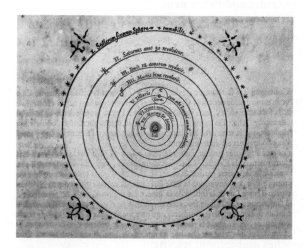

A 1667 representation of the Copernican view of the universe.

The Copernican system revolutionizes science

NEW SCIENTIFIC PERSPECTIVES. Then, in 16th-century Europe, a Polish monk named Nicholas Copernicus (*kō-PUR-nih-kus*), troubled by the cumbersome complexity of Ptolemy's system and perhaps inspired by al-Tusi's ideas, advanced the radical notion that the earth was not the center of the universe. Perhaps, he argued in a work published in 1543, the paths of planets seem irregular because they orbit the sun, not the earth, which is itself a planet circling the sun. The other planets do not really change directions; from the earth they just seem to do so, since the earth is moving, too. At first almost everyone rejected the Copernican hypothesis. Christian leaders, Catholic and Protestant alike, saw it as denying their basic belief that humans are the center of God's creation. Common sense, moreover, seemed to show that the earth could not be moving; if it were, things would fly off. Without a concept of gravity, Copernicus could not explain why planets orbit the sun. Since scientists as yet had no instruments to test the hypothesis, and since its presumption of circular orbits failed to fully clarify the movements of planets, it was not generally accepted.

In the early 17th century, however, the German astronomer Johannes Kepler revised the hypothesis by proposing that planetary orbits are elliptical, not circular. He also suggested that there is a precise mathematical relationship between a planet's speed and its distance from the sun: the closer it gets to the sun, the faster it travels. These observations revived the Copernican hypothesis and prepared the way for further discoveries.

In England, Francis Bacon, a lawyer and statesman with practical scientific interests, called for a new approach to scientific study. In his *Novum Organum* (*NŌ-voom or-GAH-noom*), roughly meaning "New Methodology," Bacon challenged scholars to focus on observing reality rather than on simply analyzing the works of past thinkers. To understand reality, he held, scientists must set aside traditional preconceptions and examine the world anew, using an empirical approach involving extensive observation and rigorous experimentation. He thereby helped lay the groundwork for the modern scientific method.

Like Bacon, René Descartes *(dā-KART)*, an enormously influential French philosopher, called for creation of a new science based on observation and experimentation. Unlike Bacon, however, Descartes foresaw that the new science would be grounded in mathematics, relying heavily on measurement, quantification, formulas, and equations. Descartes, moreover, developed a new system of understanding that was not based on the work of Aristotle or any other thinker. In his most important work, *Discourse on Method* (1637), Descartes subjected all previous knowledge to systematic doubt, concluding that the only thing he could be sure of was his own existence: he reasoned that since he was able to think, he must in fact exist. Beginning with the statement *cogito ergo sum (KŌ-jē-tō AIR-gō SOOM)*, "I think, therefore I am," he devised a new philosophy dividing all reality into two main entities: "thinking substance," or the subjective realm of the mind and spirit, and "extended substance," or the objective world of matter. By separating the study of material things that can be measured from spiritual things that cannot, he helped to separate science from religion and philosophy; by stressing mathematics, he inspired the search for mechanical laws that govern the material universe.

GALILEO'S DISCOVERIES AND NEWTON'S SYNTHESIS. This search for mechanical laws was decisively advanced by Galileo Galilei *(gal-ih-LĀ-ō gal-ih-LĀ-ē)*, an Italian scientist who discovered new laws of acceleration and motion and verified the Copernican hypothesis. The search was then carried further by the English scientist Isaac Newton, who blended the discoveries of Galileo and others into an overall synthesis depicting the universe as a mechanism that operates in accordance with mathematical laws.

Galileo grounds science in observation rather than revelation

Using his own inventions, such as the pendulum and telescope, to improve his measurements and observations, Galileo combined creative thinking with experimentation and mathematical logic, thus blending the approaches used by Copernicus, Bacon, and Descartes. Using a pendulum to time balls of different weights rolling down inclined planes, Galileo observed that falling bodies actually pick up speed as they fall and that they accelerate at the same rate no matter what they weigh. He concluded that the rate of acceleration of falling bodies is a constant that can be expressed in a precise mathematical formula.

Building on the work of Copernicus and Kepler, Galileo probed the heavens with his telescope. He observed, among other things, craters on the moon, thousands of previously unknown stars, and moons that orbited Jupiter. These discoveries demolished old beliefs that the heavens are perfect and finite, and that all heavenly bodies orbit the earth. In his classic *Dialogue on the Two Chief World Systems* (1632), Galileo ridiculed those who held these old beliefs, asserting instead that his observations validated the hypotheses of Copernicus and Kepler.

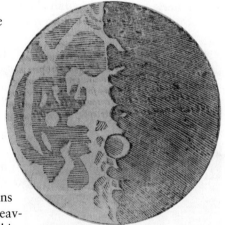

Galileo's view of the moon.

Galileo thereby brought upon himself the wrath of the Catholic Church, which in 1616 had condemned the Copernican hypothesis as contrary to Church teachings. Imprisoned and tried at age 68 by the Roman Inquisition, the Church's main agency for combating heresy, Galileo was forced to renounce his views. Devastated by the experience, ailing and later blind, he spent the rest of his days under house arrest, nonetheless continuing his mechanical experiments. But the impact of his work could not be suppressed. As others used their own telescopes and did their own mathematical calculations, they reached

Read the **Document**

Galileo Galilei, "Third Letter on Sunspots"
on **myhistorylab.com**

View the **Image**

Galileo's Views of the Moon
on **myhistorylab.com**

the same conclusions as Galileo. Their new science was based on observation and measurement, not revelation or religious authority.

Later in the 17th century, Isaac Newton assimilated and consolidated the work of Galileo and others, creating a new synthesis to explain how the universe functioned. In 1687 he published a monumental work called *The Mathematical Principles of Natural Philosophy*, often simply called the *Principia* (*prin-CHĒ-pē-uh*), from its Latin title. In it he showed that the force causing Galileo's falling bodies to accelerate at a constant rate was the same force that held the heavenly bodies in place and defined their orbits. He further concluded that this force, called gravity, can be measured and described in a concise mathematical formula, based on the mass of the objects involved and the distance between them. The universe, it appeared, was one huge mechanism that functioned according to natural laws, which were valid everywhere and always.

Newton's ideas were breathtaking and profound. His earlier work in optics had already marked him as a genius; now his discovery of the law of gravity raised him to the level of a new Aristotle. The poet Alexander Pope, a contemporary of Newton, paid him the supreme tribute: "Nature and nature's laws lay hid in night; God said 'Let Newton be,' and all was light."

Read the Document

Galileo Galilei, Letter to Madame Christine of Lorraine, Grand Duchess of Tuscany (1630s)

on **myhistorylab.com**

Newton explains the functioning of the universe

Read the Document

Isaac Newton, from Opticks

on **myhistorylab.com**

The Enlightenment

The European Enlightenment values reason above tradition

Read the Document

Immanuel Kant Defines the Enlightenment, 1784

on **myhistorylab.com**

The scientific achievements of the 17th century, along with growing global knowledge of varied lands and peoples, created great ferment among European intellectuals. By observing societies in Africa, Asia, and the Americas, they became open to new ways of thinking. By challenging traditional ideals, and by systematic observation and analysis, they began to develop a new kind of science. Now thinkers in areas such as politics, justice, economics, and gender roles sought to make similar advances. Their efforts produced the **Enlightenment**, a European intellectual movement inspired by boundless faith in human reason.

Title page of *Leviathan*.

NEW PERSPECTIVES ON GOVERNANCE. Rational reassessment of human governance was initiated by Thomas Hobbes, who in 1651 published a book called *Leviathan*. Horrified by King Charles I's beheading in 1649, Hobbes argued vehemently on behalf of absolute monarchy. He based his case not on religious authority but on secular reasoning, arguing that a single absolute power was essential for a stable society. According to Hobbes, humans are by nature selfish and violent, and human life in its original state was "solitary, poor, nasty, brutish and short," with each individual engaged in a chaotic "war of all against all." To escape this condition, he claimed, people surrender their freedom to the state in return for security and order, creating an unwritten contract between ruler and subjects.

Although Hobbes championed absolute power, his idea of a contract implied that the ruler was obliged to maintain order and protect the public welfare. But would the contract still apply if the monarch failed to do so? According to Hobbes it would: the danger of violence and chaos was so great the monarch's power must be unconditional, even if the actual ruler was incompetent, corrupt, or tyrannical.

Later thinkers took a different approach to Hobbes's concept of contract. One was John Locke, an immensely influential English thinker. In *Two Treatises of Government* (1689), Locke argued that all people are born with natural rights, which he identified as life, liberty, and property, and that government is obligated to protect these rights. If it fails to do so and instead proves abusive or despotic, it has broken the contract, and the people have the right to unseat it, forming a new government that better meets their needs. Governments, he implied, get their authority from the people they rule. Locke's *Treatises* seemed to justify the Glorious Revolution of 1688–1689, in which the English replaced a despotic ruler with new ones pledged to defend the people's rights.

Hobbes and Locke focus on contractual government

Locke also advanced the philosophy of knowledge. In his *Essay Concerning Human Understanding* (1690), he rejected the long-held assumption that people are born with ideas. Influenced by Ibn Tufayl (*too-FILE*), a 12th-century Muslim who wrote about a person growing up alone on an island, Locke asserted that at birth all minds are like a blank slate, or *tabula rasa* (*TAHB-yoo-lah RAH-sah*), and that ideas are shaped by environment and experience. In stark contrast to prevailing notions of nobility and race, Locke held that all humans are equal at birth; what each becomes is determined by interaction with the surrounding world (see "John Locke—Excerpts from *The Second Treatise of Civil Government*").

Read the **Document**

Thomas Hobbes, The Leviathan

on **myhistorylab.com**

Locke's ideas were enormously influential. European political philosophers, and later revolutionaries in the Americas and France, found inspiration in his notions that humans are born equal with natural rights, that governments have a duty to protect these rights, and that people are entitled to change or remove a regime that fails to do so. In 1776, in the American Declaration of Independence, Thomas Jefferson used Locke's views to inspire and justify the American Revolution (Chapter 26).

Another new perspective on governance was provided by Baron Montesquieu (*MONT-usk-yoo*), a French aristocrat who in 1748 published *The Spirit of Laws*. Using an empirical approach, he examined various political systems to determine what worked best. He concluded that no system was ideal and that the best form of government for any given state depended on its size, climate, economy, and traditions. Democracy, for example, seemed best for small city-states with homogeneous populations, while monarchy was best for large, diverse empires.

DOCUMENT 24.1 John Locke—Excerpts from *The Second Treatise of Civil Government*

Writing just before the Glorious Revolution in England, John Locke set forth an inspiring vision of a civil society in which government is legitimate only insofar as it protects the life, liberty, and property of the individual and enjoys the confidence of those who are governed.

The state of nature has a law of nature to govern it which obliges every one; and reason, which is that law, teaches all mankind who will but consult it that, being all equal and independent, no one ought to harm another in his life, health, liberty, or possessions . . .

Men being, as has been said, by nature all free, equal, and independent, no one can be put out of his estate and subjected to the political power of another without his own consent. The only way whereby any one divests himself of his natural liberty, and puts on the bonds of a civil society, is by agreeing with other men to join and unite into a community for their comfortable, safe, and peaceable living one amongst another, in a secure enjoyment of their properties and a greater security against any that are not of it . . .

The great and chief end, therefore, of men's uniting into commonwealths and putting themselves under government is the preservation of their property . . .

. . . when the government is dissolved, the people are at liberty to provide for themselves by erecting a new legislative, differing from the other by the change of persons or form, or both, as they shall find it most for their safety and good . . .

SOURCE: John Locke, "The Second Treatise of Civil Government" 1690.

DOCUMENT 24.2 Montesquieu—Excerpts from *The Spirit of Laws*

In 1748, the Baron de Montesquieu suggested that the separation of the executive, legislative, and judicial powers of government is essential to the maintenance of liberty and the avoidance of tyranny.

In every government there are three sorts of power: the legislative; the executive in respect to things dependent on the law of nations; and the executive in regard to matters that depend on the civil law.

By virtue of the first, the prince or magistrate enacts . . . laws, and amends or abrogates those that have been already enacted. By the second, he makes peace or war, sends or receives embassies, establishes the public security, and provides against invasions. By the third, he punishes criminals, or determines the disputes that arise between individuals. The latter we shall call the judiciary power, and the other simply the executive power of the state . . .

When the legislative and executive powers are united in the same person, there can be no liberty; because apprehension may arise, lest the same monarch or senate should enact tyrannical laws, to execute them in a tyrannical manner.

Again, there is no liberty, if the judiciary power be not separated from the legislative and executive. Were it joined with the legislative, the life and liberty of the subject would be exposed to arbitrary control; for the judge would be then the legislator. Were it joined to the executive power, the judge might behave with violence and oppression . . .

SOURCE: Charles de Secondat, Baron de Montesquieu, *The Spirit of Laws*, translated by Thomas Nugent, revised by J.V. Prichard. Based on a public domain edition published in 1941 by G. Bell & Sons, Ltd. London.

Montesquieu describes a government in which power resides in separate institutions that balance one another

Montesquieu nonetheless preferred a mixed system that drew on the best features of each form of government. Here his model was Britain, which to him seemed to have a fortunate combination of monarchy (the king), aristocracy (the House of Lords), and representative democracy (the House of Commons). Since the power of each was balanced by the other two, he concluded, this arrangement could prevent the sort of unchecked absolutism that had emerged in his native France. Montesquieu's ideas about the balance and separation of power (see "Montesquieu—Excerpts from *The Spirit of Laws*") later influenced the framers of the United States Constitution.

Illustration from the Encyclopedia.

THE PHILOSOPHES: PROGRESS AND SOCIAL JUSTICE. Montesquieu was one of the eminent French thinkers called **philosophes** (*FĒ-luh-ZŌF*) who dominated the Enlightenment in the 18th century. Philosophes espoused **deism**, a rational religion that viewed God not as a divinity involved deeply in human affairs but as a kind of master mechanic or "great watchmaker" who created the universe as a vast machine, established the laws by which it operates, and then mostly left it alone. But above all philosophes believed in reason and progress. They were convinced that society would steadily improve if great thinkers applied reason and scientific rigor to the study of human affairs and then published their work so others could build on it.

The spirit of the philosophes was exemplified by the great *Encyclopedia*, edited by the energetic philosophe Denis Diderot (*dē-deh-RŌ*). In a mammoth undertaking, Diderot and his colleagues gathered detailed articles by experts in numerous fields, from art to astronomy to political theory, and then published them in 28 large volumes (1751–1772) to make them available to all. Convinced of the power of education and publicity, the editors expected thereby to advance all areas of human endeavor.

But a philosophe called Voltaire, widely considered the Enlightenment's dominant figure, disputed this optimistic view. Raised in a middle-class French family and like Montesquieu an admirer of British ideas, Voltaire published works promoting the perceptions of Newton and Locke. Brilliant, sarcastic, and self-righteous, Voltaire was a passionate advocate of tolerance and freedom, an outspoken critic of France's monarchy and the Catholic Church, a crusader against injustice, and a champion of persons who had been abused by the wealthy and powerful. To Voltaire there was much that was wrong in the world, and a pressing need to combat injustice, ignorance, and oppression.

Like Voltaire, Jean-Jacques Rousseau (*roo-SŌ*), a Swiss-born French author and composer, was a champion of freedom and justice, but his ideas differed from those of other Enlightenment thinkers. Unlike Hobbes, who claimed that people were by nature selfish and violent, Rousseau believed that in the "state of nature" they were honest, unselfish, and free, and that greed, corruption, and oppression were introduced by organized society. Unlike Locke, who regarded property ownership as a natural right, Rousseau saw private property as a source of inequality and evil.

Rousseau's most famous work, *The Social Contract* (1762), began with the ringing phrase "All men are born free, but everywhere they are in chains" and went on to advocate a communal society based on harmony, equality, and virtue. Whereas Hobbes had depicted a contract *between* ruler and ruled, Rousseau envisioned one *among* all members of society. Whereas Locke had stressed individual rights, Rousseau stressed the common good as embodied in the "general will." Government's job was to determine and fulfill this will, not only responding to the desires of the majority but also embracing the genuine needs of all people (see "Jean-Jacques Rousseau—Excerpts from *The Social Contract*"). Later, believers in democracy and advocates of socialism found inspiration in Rousseau's ideas about community and equality.

The Enlightenment's leading economic thinkers, known as **physiocrats**, included the Frenchmen François Quesnay (*kā-NĀ*), a former court physician at Versailles, and Anne-Robert Turgot (*toor-GŌ*), France's comptroller general in the 1770s. Convinced that increased production and trade would enhance national wealth, they sought to free producers and merchants from artificial restraints imposed by governments and guilds. The physiocrats thus promoted **laissez-faire** (*leh-sā FARE*), a French term meaning "let do" (that is, "let them do as they choose"), a policy that governments should not intervene in economic affairs.

These ideas were systematized and expanded by the Scotsman Adam Smith, the "father of modern economics," who in 1776 produced his classic *Inquiry into the Nature and Causes of the Wealth of Nations*. Smith condemned mercantilism, the prevailing practice in which governments established colonies and regulated commerce to produce a favorable balance of trade. Instead he claimed that, if the economy were left alone, the forces of self-interest and competition would work as an "invisible hand" to increase overall prosperity. Consumers would naturally seek to buy quality goods and services at reasonable prices. Producers and merchants who met these objectives would prosper. Those who could make and sell good shoes, for example, at lower prices than competitors, would attract more customers and make more money, a powerful incentive for other producers to meet customers' needs. Supply and demand rather than government, he argued, should regulate production and prices. As demand increased it would drive

Voltaire.

Voltaire and Rousseau argue for liberty

((•—|**Listen** to the **Audio**
Enlightenment 2
on **myhistorylab.com**

|•—|**Read** the **Document**
The Encyclopedie, "Bakers (Boulanger)" (France) 1763
on **myhistorylab.com**

|•—|**Read** the **Document**
Voltaire, on Social Conditions in Eighteenth Century France
on **myhistorylab.com**

Adam Smith describes modern economic principles

DOCUMENT 24.3 Jean-Jacques Rousseau—Excerpts from *The Social Contract*

In 1762, Jean-Jacques Rousseau addressed the problem of the tension between the rights of the individual and those of the community. He found the answer in the concept of a social contract, by which people voluntarily submit to collective government, and in doing so, ensure their individual freedoms.

The problem is to find a form of association which will defend and protect with the whole common force the person and goods of each associate, and in which each, while uniting himself with all, may still obey himself alone, and remain as free as before. This is the fundamental problem of which the *Social Contract* provides the solution . . .

. . . each man, in giving himself to all, gives himself to nobody; and as there is no associate over whom he does not acquire the same right as he yields others over himself, he gains an equivalent for everything he loses, and an increase of force for the preservation of what he has . . .

Each of us puts his person and all his power under the supreme direction of the general will, and, in our corporate capacity, we receive each member as an individual part of the whole . . .

This public person, so formed by the union of all other persons formerly took the name of *city*, and now takes that of *Republic* or *body politic*; it is called by its members *State* when passive, *Sovereign* when active, and *Power* when compared with others like itself. Those who are associated in it take collectively the name of *people*, and severally are called *citizens*, as sharing in the sovereign power, and *subjects*, as being under the laws of the State . . .

SOURCE: Jean Jacques Rousseau, *The Social Contract or Principles of Political Right*, translated in 1762 by G.D.H. Cole.

---

prices up, but ambitious producers would soon respond by increasing supply, and prices would go down. Over time, quality would improve, prices would fall, and the public welfare would be secured. In promoting such ideas, Smith shaped modern arguments for free-market capitalism.

((•—Listen to the Audio
Enlightenment 3
on myhistorylab.com

GENDER AND THE ENLIGHTENMENT. With its focus on challenging traditional beliefs and securing people's rights, the Enlightenment also inspired discussion of what was then a revolutionary concept: the notion that women should have equal rights with men. Some philosophes, including the Marquis de Condorcet (*kōn-dor-SĀ*), argued that depriving women of such rights was irrational and unjust. Others, however, including Rousseau, saw it as unnatural for women to participate in public affairs.

Despite the persistence of such attitudes, some talented women played prominent roles in the Enlightenment. Condorcet's wife, Sophie, for example, translated Adam Smith's works into French and hosted a **salon**, a regular gathering where eminent thinkers and writers mingled with political and social leaders. Madame Geoffrin (*zhaw-FRAHN*), who used her husband's wealth to help finance Diderot's *Encyclopedia*, also held frequent influential salons. The Marquise du Chatelet (*shah-teh-LĀ*), Voltaire's longtime companion, was a gifted scientist and mathematician who translated Newton's *Principia* and other key works into French. And Madame de Pompadour (*pawm-pah-DOOR*), mistress of France's King Louis XV, was a dominant force in political and diplomatic affairs, a friend of the philosophes, and a generous patron of literature and the arts.

Women play an active role
in the Enlightenment

While these eminent French women benefited from ties with influential men and hosted salons attended mostly by males, in England some notable women rejected the patriarchal rules of their male-dominated society. Lady Mary Wortley Montagu (*MAHN-tug-yoo*), for example, refused to enter a marriage arranged by her father and promoted the radical notion that women should choose their own husbands. Mary Wollstonecraft, regarded today as a forerunner of modern feminism, was an ardent champion of sexual freedom and women's liberation from male domination. Determined to make her own way in life, she educated herself through extensive reading, then she worked as a governess and teacher before becoming a translator and publisher. In 1792 she published *A Vindication of the Rights of Women*, an impassioned and articulate call for equal education of women and men. Her work and a "Declaration of the Rights of Woman," published in France in 1791 by a writer called Olympe de Gouges (*aw-LAMP duh GOOZH*) (Chapter 26), were early milestones in the modern women's rights movement.

Absolutism and Enlightenment

Although absolutism by the 18th century was Europe's main form of governance, the Enlightenment generated an important shift in the attitudes and actions of some rulers. Intelligent monarchs, no longer content to base their authority mainly on religion and tradition, now sought to portray themselves as benefiting their people and to justify their power as a means for bringing enlightenment and reform. These monarchs met and corresponded with philosophes, published their own ideas, and sought to better the lives of their people through progressive reforms. This linking of absolutism with enlightenment, known as Enlightened Absolutism, flourished in Prussia and Austria as well as Russia (Chapter 25). In England and France, however, where monarchs lacked the interest and ability to carry out reforms, Enlightened Absolutism never took hold.

Absolutism and Enlightenment in Prussia and Austria

In the early 18th century, few European lands seemed less enlightened than Prussia. Its ruler, Frederick William I (1713–1740), was a crude, militaristic drillmaster king who loved his army above all else and had no use for enlightenment. Dressed in uniform rather than royal robes, he was known to patrol the streets of Berlin and beat the lazy and idle with his cane. But his son Frederick, heir to the throne, was a bright, sensitive lad who enjoyed poetry and drama, admired French philosophy, composed music, and even played the flute. These attributes, combined with his homosexual inclinations and indifference to the army, earned Frederick little but abuse from his father the king. Dismayed by this treatment, at age 18 the prince made plans to flee to England, but he was arrested and forced by his father to watch the beheading of the young man who was his accomplice and lover. The prince henceforth gave in, performed various military duties, and quietly looked forward to inheriting the throne.

Upon his father's death, King Frederick II (1740–1788), later called Frederick the Great, distinguished himself as an enlightened monarch. A friend of Voltaire and other philosophes, and an intellectual in his own right, Frederick undertook extensive reforms, calling himself the "first servant of the state." To promote justice, he codified laws and reformed the court system. To advance industry and commerce, he built roads and canals while lowering taxes on goods shipped within Prussia. To improve his people's welfare, he drained swamps, expanded agriculture, built schools, and promoted religious toleration. Reluctant, however, to offend the landed nobles whom he needed to lead his armies, he did not end serfdom.

Ironically, given his youthful disdain for the army, Frederick also proved an exceptional warrior. In a series of brilliant campaigns, he more than doubled the size and population of his country, earning a reputation as a military genius. He succeeded in establishing Prussia as one of Europe's great powers, mainly by fighting against the Austrian Habsburgs.

The Habsburgs, meanwhile, were trying to hold together their multinational empire in the absence of a male heir (Map 24.3). Since Maria Theresa, the 23-year-old monarch who inherited the Habsburg lands in 1740, was female, other rulers presumed her to be weak. In December 1740, Prussia's Frederick II boldly invaded the mineral-rich

Read the **Document**

Mary Wollstonecraft, Introduction to a Vindication of the Rights of Woman

on **myhistorylab.com**

Read the **Document**

Lady Mary Wortley Montagu, Letters

on **myhistorylab.com**

Enlightened Absolutism develops in Central and Eastern Europe

Frederick the Great rules by Enlightenment principles

Listen to the **Audio**

Enlightenment 1

on **myhistorylab.com**

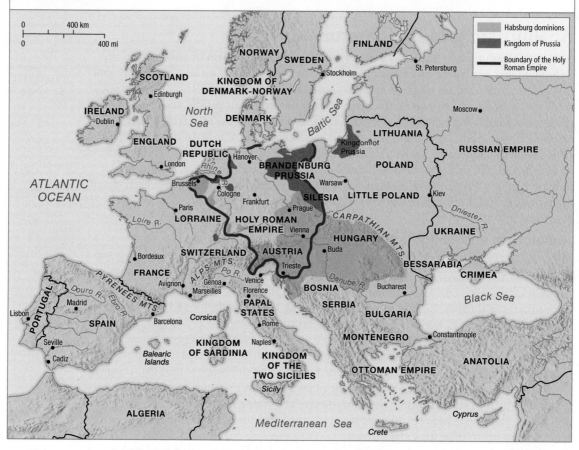

| MAP **24.3** | Europe in 1763 |

By 1763, Europe was clearly a continent in transition. The relentless expansionism of Louis XIV died with him in 1715, and France lost substantial territory overseas during the Seven Years War (1756–1763). Observe that the medieval Holy Roman Empire was becoming obsolete in an era of strong, absolute national monarchies and was now the subject of a struggle for control between Austria and Prussia. What might this trend toward absolute monarchies mean for a multinational state like the Ottoman Empire?

Habsburg province of Silesia, then France and others joined his war against Austria. Since the war was induced by a woman's succession to the Austrian throne, it was called the War of the Austrian Succession (1740–1748).

Maria Theresa proved more formidable than her foes had foreseen. In 1741 she took her newborn son (the future Emperor Joseph II) to Hungary and made a dramatic speech, holding him aloft for the Hungarian nobles to see and convincing them to pledge their support to both their beautiful young queen and their future king. Although unable to retake Silesia, she managed to turn back French and Bavarian efforts to create a puppet state in Bohemia.

Once the war ended in 1748, Maria Theresa set out to strengthen her realm. She and her advisers modernized and centralized the bureaucracy, unified the administration of Austria

Schönbrunn Palace in Vienna, the summer residence of the Habsburgs.

and Bohemia, and compelled their nobles to pay taxes. To better the lot of her subjects, she established an elementary school system and enacted reforms that reduced the nobles' power and improved the welfare of their serfs. Yet as a staunch Catholic who resisted religious toleration, she did not entirely qualify as an enlightened monarch.

Her son Joseph, however, fully fit this description. After his mother's death in 1780, Emperor Joseph II, dismayed by the suffering of his subjects, issued a series of radical decrees intended to impose Enlightenment ideals throughout Habsburg lands. In 1781 he abolished serfdom, empowered peasants to buy their own land, and even let them choose their own spouses. Later, despite vehement opposition from the pope, he proclaimed religious toleration and freedom of worship for his subjects. He also instituted freedom of the press, civil rights for Jews, equality before the law, and equality of taxation.

Joseph II imposes the Enlightenment on Austria

These actions did not always achieve the positive effects that Joseph intended. The nobles agitated against them, destabilizing the realm and confusing the peasants Joseph was trying to help. As rebellions against his reforms broke out in several regions, Joseph grew discouraged. He died disillusioned in 1790, after which his successors rescinded most of his reforms.

Unenlightened Monarchy in England and France

Ironically, neither England nor France—the Enlightenment's two main centers—experienced enlightened or effective monarchy in the 18th century. England, with a strong Parliament that could govern in the absence of a capable ruler, grew wealthier and stronger. France, plagued by unwise kings, drifted toward bankruptcy and political chaos.

The English monarchy was transformed by several key events in the early 18th century. In 1701, 12 years after removing King James II, Parliament passed an Act of Settlement excluding him and his Catholic heirs from the throne. In 1707 an Act of Union formally merged England and Scotland into the Kingdom of Great Britain. In 1714 the death of Queen Anne, the last non-Catholic member of the Stuart family, brought an end to the dynasty.

Anne was succeeded by a distant Protestant cousin, the ruler of a small German state called Hanover, who became King George I (1714–1727). As foreigners, he and his son King George II (1727–1760) relied heavily on their British ministers. From 1721 until 1742, the gifted politician Robert Walpole, the main leader of the House of Commons, effectively ran the government. The precedent he set established a crucial position, later called the **prime minister**, in which the same person serves as leader of both Parliament and the royal government, with both legislative and executive authority. The monarch, of course, was still head of state, but that role came to be largely ceremonial. Indeed, when King George III (r. 1760–1820) tried to play an active role in government, he ran into stiff opposition and eventually was labeled a tyrant by many of his subjects in Britain and North America.

The British Parliament asserts control of policy

Meanwhile, absolutism in France, so dynamic under Louis XIV, deteriorated once he was gone. Having outlived his oldest son and grandson, the Sun King was succeeded in 1715 by his 5-year-old great-grandson, who became King Louis XV (r. 1715–1774). While the new king was still a boy, France was ruled by a regent, who let the nobles regain much of the power they had lost under Louis XIV. Later, when Louis XV came of age, he proved a lazy and weak-willed ruler who made several attempts at reform but withdrew when he met opposition from the nobles. Lavish spending, costly wars, and failure to fix a financial system that exempted the nobles from taxation led the French government increasingly toward bankruptcy, creating the crisis that triggered the French Revolution of 1789.

France drifts toward bankruptcy

CHAPTER

REVIEW

Putting It in Perspective

In the 17th and 18th centuries, Western and Central Europe experienced great changes in approaches to government and society. Absolutism triumphed as the preferred form of government, and science and reason came to dominate all forms of intellectual thought.

Absolutism's triumph was based on interactions among monarchs, nobles, and wealthy middle classes. In France, absolutism triumphed because the monarchy, relying on support from the wealthy middle classes, managed to undermine the nobles' power while expanding their prestige. In Austria and Prussia, where there was no strong middle class, absolutism triumphed because the nobles supported it as a way to promote state power; in return, monarchs allowed the nobles to keep their privileges and control the peasants. In England absolutism did not triumph,

largely because the nobles and wealthy middle classes, as represented in Parliament, worked to limit the monarchy and force it to share power with Parliament.

The ascendancy of science and reason, meanwhile, was based on the challenges of innovative thinkers to prevailing views about science and society. These thinkers not only described laws that govern the universe but also provided new perspectives on governance, social justice, economics, and gender roles. In the short run, these perspectives prompted some rulers to become enlightened reformers; in the long run, they helped inspire the American and French revolutions of the late 18th century as well as the industrial and technological revolutions in the 19th and 20th centuries.

Reviewing Key Material

KEY CONCEPTS

royal absolutism, 535
Fronde, 537
Junkers, 540
limited monarchy, 541
Puritans, 541
Eleven Years' Tyranny, 541
Glorious Revolution, 543
Bill of Rights, 543

Enlightenment, 546
philosophes, 548
deism, 548
physiocrats, 549
laissez-faire, 549
salon, 550
prime minister, 553

Jean-Jacques Rousseau, 549
Adam Smith, 549
Madame de Pompadour, 550
Lady Mary Wortley Montagu, 550
Mary Wollstonecraft, 550

Olympe de Gouges, 551
Frederick William I, 551
Frederick the Great, 551
Maria Theresa, 551
Joseph II, 552
Robert Walpole, 553
Louis XV, 553

KEY PEOPLE

Louis XIV, 535, 537
Henri IV, 536
Louis XIII, 536
Cardinal Richelieu, 536
Cardinal Mazarin, 537
Jean-Baptiste Colbert, 538
Frederick William von Hohenzollern, 540
James I, 541
Charles I, 541
Oliver Cromwell, 542
Charles II, 542
James II, 543

William III and Mary, 543
Ptolemy, 544
Nicholas Copernicus, 544
Johannes Kepler, 544
Francis Bacon, 544
René Descartes, 545
Galileo Galilei, 545
Isaac Newton, 546
Thomas Hobbes, 546
John Locke, 546
Baron Montesquieu, 547
Denis Diderot, 548
Voltaire, 549

ASK YOURSELF

1. Why and how did France become an absolute monarchy in the 17th century? Why was the French model so attractive to rulers in Central Europe?
2. How did absolutism in Austria and Prussia differ from that in France? How did Central European society differ from that in the West? What impact did these differences have on governance?
3. What personal, political, social, and religious factors contributed to the failure of absolutism and development of limited monarchy in England in the 17th and 18th centuries?
4. What combination of circumstances and insights led to the great scientific advances of the 17th century? How

and why did these advances contribute to the quest for new perspectives on governance and society?

5. What were the central ideals of the Enlightenment, and how did they relate to governance, society, economics, and gender? How and why did 18th-century monarchs act as enlightened rulers?

GOING FURTHER

Anchor, Robert. *The Enlightenment Tradition*. 1987.

Ashley, M. *The House of Stuart: Its Rise and Fall*. 1980.

Beik, W. *Absolutism and Society in Seventeenth-Century France*. 1989.

Bergin, Joseph. *The Short Oxford History of Europe: The Seventeenth Century*. 2001.

Doyle, William. *The Old European Order*. 1978.

Dunn, John. *The Political Thought of John Locke*. 1990.

Fichtner, P. S. *The Habsburg Monarchy, 1490–1848*. 2003.

Gay, Peter. *The Enlightenment: An Interpretation*. 2 vols. 1966–1969.

Henry, J. *Scientific Revolution and Origins of Modern Science*. 1997.

Hunt, Margaret, and M. Jacob. *Women and the Enlightenment*. 1984.

Jacob, J. R. *The Scientific Revolution*. 1998.

Kenyon, J. P. *Stuart England*. 1978.

Koch, H. W. *A History of Prussia*. 1978.

Ladurie, Emmanuel Le Roy. *The Ancien Regime: A History of France, 1610–1774*. 1998.

Le Donne, John. *Absolutism and Ruling Class*. 1991.

Manning, B. *The English People and the English Revolution*. 1976.

McKay, D., and H. Scott. *Rise of the Great Powers, 1648–1815*. 1983.

Miller, John. *Absolutism in Seventeenth-Century Europe*. 1990.

Munck, Thomas. *The Enlightenment: A Comparative Social History, 1721–1794*. 2000.

Outram, D. *The Enlightenment*. 1995.

Rosenberg, Hans. *Bureaucracy, Aristocracy, and Authority: The Prussian Experiment, 1660–1815*. 1966.

Scott, H. *Enlightened Absolutism*. 1990.

Shennan, J. H. *Liberty and Order in Early Modern Europe*. 1986.

Speck, W. A. *The Revolution of 1688*. 1988.

Wiesner, Merry E. *Women and Gender in Early Modern Europe*. 2000.

Wilson, P. H. *Absolutism in Central Europe*. 2000.

Wolf, John B. *Louis XIV*. 1966.

Key Dates and Developments

Absolutism in France

1610–1643	Reign of King Louis XIII
1624–1642	Cardinal Richelieu as first minister
1643–1715	Reign of King Louis XIV
1643–1648	Ministry of Mazarin
1648–1653	Rebellion of the Fronde
1653–1661	Ministry of Mazarin
1661–1715	Active reign of Louis XIV
1682	Completion of the palace at Versailles
1685	Revocation of the Edict of Nantes
1715–1774	Reign of King Louis XV

Limited Monarchy in England

1603–1625	Reign of James I (first Stuart monarch)
1625–1649	Reign of Charles I
1629–1640	Eleven Years' Tyranny
1642–1647	English Civil War
1649	Execution of Charles I
1649–1658	Rule of Oliver Cromwell
1660–1685	Reign of Charles II
1685–1688	Reign of James II
1688–1689	The Glorious Revolution and Bill of Rights
1689–1702	Reign of William III (and Mary, until 1694)
1701	Act of Settlement
1702–1714	Reign of Queen Anne (last Stuart monarch)
1707	Formation of the Kingdom of Great Britain
1714–1727	Reign of King George I
1721–1742	Governance of Robert Walpole
1727–1760	Reign of King George II

Absolutism in Austria and Prussia

1640–1688	Reign of Frederick William, Great Elector in Brandenburg
1648	Peace of Westphalia (End of Thirty Years War)
1683	Lifting of the Siege of Vienna
1699	Expulsion of Ottoman Turks from Hungary
1701–1740	Reign of King Frederick I in Prussia
1740–1788	Reign of King Frederick II (the Great) in Prussia
1740–1780	Reign of Maria Theresa in Austria, Hungary, Bohemia
1740–1748	War of the Austrian Succession
1780–1790	Reforms of Joseph II in Austria, Hungary, and Bohemia

Europe's Intellectual Revolution

1543	Publication of the Copernican hypothesis
1620	Francis Bacon's *Novum Organum*
1632	Galileo's *Dialogue on the Two Chief World Systems*
1637	Descartes's *Discourse on Method*
1651	Hobbes's *Leviathan*
1687	Newton's *Principia*
1689	Locke's *Two Treatises of Government*
1748	Montesquieu's *The Spirit of Laws*
1751	Lisbon earthquake
1751–1772	Diderot's *Encyclopedia*
1759	Voltaire's *Candide*
1762	Rousseau's *Social Contract*
1776	Adam Smith's *Wealth of Nations*

PEARSON myhistorylab™ Connections

Reinforce what you learned in this chapter by studying the many documents, images, maps, review tools, and videos available at www.myhistorylab.com.

Read and Review

✔●─ **Study** and **Review** Chapter 24

▯●─ **Read** the **Document**

Jean Baptiste Colbert, "Mercantilism: Dissertation on Alliances," p. 538

Louis XIV Writes to His Son (1661), p. 538

Galileo Galilei, "Third Letter on Sunspots," p. 545

Galileo Galilei, Letter to Madame Christine of Lorraine, the Grand Duchesse of Tuscany (1630s), p. 546

Isaac Newton, from *Opticks*, p. 546

Immanuel Kant Defines the Enlightenment, 1784, p. 546

Thomas Hobbes, *The Leviathan*, p. 547

The Encyclopedie, "Bakers (Boulanger)" (France) 1763, p. 549

Voltaire, on *Social Conditions in Eighteenth Century France*, p. 549

Mary Wollstonecraft, Introduction to a Vindication of the Rights of Woman, p. 551

Lady Mary Wortley Montagu, Letters, p. 551

🔍─ **View** the **Image**

Allegorical View of Cromwell as Savior of England, p. 542

Galileo's Views of the Moon, p. 545

((●─ **Listen** to the **Audio**

Louis XIV, p. 537

Enlightenment 2, p. 549

Enlightenment 3, p. 550

Enlightenment 1, p. 551

Research and Explore

🔍─ **View** the **Map**

Atlas Map: Geographical Tour: Europe in 1714, p. 535

((●─ **Listen** to the **Chapter Audio** for Chapter 24 on **myhistorylab.com** ─

25

Russia's Eurasian Empire: Convergence of East and West, 1300–1800

- Why and how did Moscow arise as Russia's leading city in the 14th and 15th centuries?

- What were Muscovy's main trials and triumphs in the 16th and 17th centuries?

- Why and how did Peter the Great and his successors work to Westernize Russia?

- How and why was Russian society influenced by both East and West?

((•─Listen to the **Chapter Audio** for Chapter 25 on **myhistorylab.com**

Saint Basil's Cathedral, Moscow

Saint Basil's Cathedral, built on the edge of Moscow's Red Square to celebrate Russian expansion in the 1550s, is a striking symbol of Russia's Eurasian culture, combining and connecting contrasting features of Eastern and Western cultures.

In spring of 1697, there appeared in Europe a 250-member traveling entourage from Muscovy, a vast eastern domain that stretched across Eurasia from Poland to the Pacific. This "Grand Embassy" from Muscovy, which spent 16 months visiting such countries as Prussia, Holland, England, and Austria, created quite a stir. Many Europeans, having never seen Muscovites, were appalled by their heavy drinking and uncouth behavior. In England, for example, the Muscovites stayed three months in an elegant mansion, which they virtually destroyed. They drank around the clock, smashed the fine furniture, tore up the feather beds, used the prized paintings for target practice, and ran drunken races with wheelbarrows through the splendid gardens and hedges.

Russian
Empire

The embassy's most remarkable member was a young Muscovite who called himself Peter Mikhailov (*mik-HĪ-loff*). Handsome and strong, he stood 6 feet, 7 inches tall and spoke with a booming voice punctuated by wild arm gestures and twitches of the head. Word soon spread that he was really Peter Romanov, Muscovy's all-powerful tsar, who had come to Europe looking for ways to strengthen and enrich his country, while traveling under an assumed name as an apprentice shipbuilder. Largely unknown outside Muscovy, he would later gain renown as Russian emperor Peter the Great, a ruler who seemed larger than life in both stature and deeds.

Peter's Grand Embassy marked a major turning point in Russian history. Hitherto, although it had contacts with Europe, Russia's orientation had generally been Eastern, not Western. In the tenth through twelfth centuries, Russians had adopted Byzantine culture and Eastern Christianity. In the 13th and 14th centuries, they had been ruled by Mongols from the East. In the 15th century, led by the principality of Moscow, they had thrown off Mongol rule and formed a realm called Muscovy (the lands controlled by Moscow) that expanded east to the Pacific over the next two centuries. Now, on the eve of the 18th century, Peter had decided to reorient his country toward the West. In that century, he and his heirs would transform their realm into a great world power, blending elements of East and West, known as the Russian Empire.

Russia's Eastern Orientation

Early Russia's political and cultural orientation was shaped by its location at the edges of Europe and Asia, and by its adoption of Eastern Christianity, practiced in the Byzantine Empire. Battered by nomadic invasions across the Eurasian steppes, then conquered and ruled for more than two centuries by Mongols, Russians clung to their Byzantine heritage, including Eastern Orthodox Christianity. In the 15th century, as the Ottoman Turks destroyed the remnants of the Byzantine Empire, Russia emerged from Mongol rule as Muscovy, a principality led by Moscow, which claimed the Byzantine legacy and leadership of the Orthodox world. In the next few centuries, it expanded to the south and east, asserting control of the Eurasian steppes and all of northern Asia (Map 25.1).

Byzantine and Mongol Connections

Early Russia's tenth century conversion to Eastern Christianity (Chapter 10) had far-reaching results. It not only brought Russians the richness of Orthodox ritual; it also infused their society and culture with Byzantine ideals, including caesaropapism, which

Orthodox Christianity orients Russia eastward

Territorial expansion and East–West connections have been central to Russian history. Note that five centuries of Russian expansion created a vast realm that stretched from Eastern Europe to the Pacific. How was Russia affected by connections with both East and West?

Principality of Moscow, 1300
Expansion, 1300-1462
Expansion, 1462-1533
Expansion, 1533-1598
Expansion, 1598-1689
Expansion, 1689-1800

gave the ruler both political and religious authority. And it divided Russia from its western neighbors—Poles, Lithuanians, Germans, and Swedes—who embraced Western (Catholic) Christianity and culture. But it did not bring lasting political unity to Russia. By the 12th century, Russians were divided among rival principalities, leaving them open to Mongol conquest in the 13th century.

The Mongol conquest, by absorbing the Russians in a vast pan-Asian empire (Chapter 15), reinforced their Eastern orientation. Adapting to Mongol rule, they retained their Orthodox faith and Byzantine heritage, distinguishing them from both their Asian conquerors and their European neighbors. The Mongols wisely let the Russians keep their faith and culture, subjecting them to tribute rather than direct control. These practices helped Mongol rule in Russia last much longer (1237–1480) than in China or Islamic West Asia (where it ended in the 1300s). They also made Mongol rule more acceptable to Russians than the threat of conquest by the Catholic West. Indeed, in the 1240s, while pledging allegiance to the Mongols from the East, Russia's Prince Alexander Nevskii defiantly battled Catholic Swedish and German invaders from the West.

Mongols reinforce Russia's Eastern orientation

 View the **Map**

Atlas Map: The Four Khanates of the Divided Mongol Empire, ca. 1227–1350

on **myhistorylab.com**

The Rise of Moscow

In the 14th century, partly through collaboration with Russia's Mongol rulers, Moscow emerged as Russia's leading city and the headquarters of the Russian Orthodox Church. Using this strength and status, Moscow eventually overcame the Mongols, united Russian lands under its rule, and claimed the Byzantine legacy.

In the early 1300s, Moscow's princes, exploiting its location as a center of trade routes connecting many Russian cities, increased their power and wealth by working with the Mongols. Prince Ivan I, ruling Moscow from 1325 to 1340, helped the Mongols crush a rival Russian city, collected tribute from other Russians for them, and in 1328 got them to proclaim him grand prince, the overlord of other Russian princes. He also persuaded Russia's **metropolitan**, the head bishop of the Russian Orthodox Church, to settle in Moscow. Moscow thus became, and henceforth remained, Russia's religious center.

Ivan I's successors mostly retained the title of grand prince and support of the church while expanding the lands under Moscow's control. Aided by a commanding stone wall built in 1367 around the **Kremlin**—a fortified area in central Moscow housing churches, palaces, and government headquarters— Moscow thwarted attacks from the west by Lithuania and Poland. Alarmed by Moscow's growing power, in 1380 the Mongols sent an army to suppress it, but the Mongol army was ambushed and defeated by Moscow's Grand Prince Dmitri. The Mongols returned to sack Moscow in 1382, forcing it again to pay tribute, but the city's influence continued to grow.

In the next century, Grand Prince Ivan III (1462–1505), known as Ivan the Great, used war, intimidation, diplomacy, and bribery to annex and connect most other Russian lands, tripling Muscovy's size (Map 25.2). He granted lands and privileges to the **boyars**, Russia's landed warrior nobles, in return for their allegiance to Moscow. And he refused to pay tribute to the Mongols, who in 1480 finally sent an army, which confronted his forces across a river southwest of Moscow. As winter came and the river froze, Ivan's army packed up for retreat, fearing a Mongol assault across the ice. Assuming that Ivan was

The Kremlin in the 1400s.

Moscow emerges as Russia's religious center

MAP 25.2 Expansion of Muscovy, 1300–1533

From 1300 to 1533, while first assisting and later rebelling against Mongol rule, Moscow's princes greatly expanded their domain. Notice that it more than tripled in size under Ivan III, the Great (1462–1505). What methods did he and other Muscovite rulers use to conquer, absorb, and connect the Russian principalities?

Principality of Moscow in 1300

Expansion of Muscovy, 1300–1462

Expansion of Muscovy, 1462–1533

Ivan the Great unites
Russian lands and ends
Mongol rule

preparing an attack, and alarmed by reports of Russian raids elsewhere, the Mongols instead withdrew. This odd episode ended Mongol rule in Russia, marking Muscovy's emergence as a fully independent power.

Ivan also reinforced Russia's Byzantine connections. In 1453, before his reign began, the Ottoman Turks had conquered Constantinople (Chapter 17), long the center of Byzantine culture and Eastern Orthodox Christianity. As the Turks converted it into a Muslim metropolis, Moscow became by default the main city in the Orthodox world. In 1472, to enhance this status, Ivan married Zoe Paleologus (*ZŌ-ē pā-lē-AH-luh-gus*), niece of the last Byzantine emperor, who took the name Sofia and called herself empress. Ivan started calling himself **tsar**, a Russian version of the title "caesar" used by Roman and Byzantine emperors. In the Kremlin he built a new palace and three great cathedrals, staging elaborate ceremonies to stress his new majestic status.

📖▶ **Read** the **Document**

Filofei's Concept of the Third Rome (1515)

on **myhistorylab.com**

Moscow claims the heritage of Constantinople

Not long after Ivan's death, a key Russian cleric named Filofei advanced the notion of Moscow as the Third Rome. In this view, after Christian Rome fell to the Germans in 476, Constantinople, the Second Rome, became the center of the true Christian faith. Then, when Constantinople fell to the Turks in 1453, Moscow became Christianity's new center and thus the Third Rome. Religious in origin, this concept later had political connotations, implying that Russian tsars were the rightful successors to the Roman and Byzantine emperors.

Ivan the Terrible and His Impact

The first Moscow ruler actually crowned as tsar was Ivan III's grandson, Ivan IV, who reigned from 1533 until 1584. Inheriting the throne at age three, he was dominated first by his mother, who died when he was eight, and then by prominent boyars who fought each other for power. Witnessing brutal intrigues in which boyars arrested and killed each other, he grew to hate the leading boyars and, at age 13, ordered one of them slain. Further displaying a cruel streak, he allegedly threw dogs from the palace roof and trampled townsfolk during drunken horseback rides with wild friends. His erratic behavior, in which drunken revelry and cruelty alternated with piety and repentance, terrorized and convulsed his country later in his reign.

Ivan IV is crowned tsar,
linking him to caesars

IVAN'S REFORMS AND EASTWARD EXPANSION. In January 1547, still only 16 years old, Ivan held a majestic ceremony in which he was crowned tsar, symbolically aligning himself with the Roman and Byzantine caesars. The next month he married a young woman named Anastasia, from a minor boyar family called the Romanovs, who for a time helped to calm his stormy temperament. After a fire killed thousands in Moscow that June, Ivan publicly repented, promised to rule with compassion, and created a chosen council of advisors to assist him.

Muscovite cavalry.

For the next 13 years, until 1560, Ivan mostly kept his promise. Aided by his chosen council, he enacted reforms combating corruption, reducing boyar power, and bolstering his government's authority. A new law code improved judicial procedures, held local governors liable for subordinates' misdeeds, and imposed strict penalties for crime and corruption. A new fiscal system taxed farmlands based on productivity, ending a widely abused system whereby boyars and officials collected taxes at will, sending some revenues to Moscow while keeping the rest for themselves.

Ivan also reformed the Muscovite military and used it to expand his realm. He created Moscow's first standing army, with muskets and cannons, central control, and an elite royal guard. He used his army to attack the Mongols, whose lands by then had split into smaller khanates. Using cannons to pierce fortress walls, in 1552 his armies overran the Khanate of Kazan to Moscow's east, and in 1556 they conquered the Khanate of Astrakhan to the southeast (Map 25.3).

These conquests had momentous impact. They doubled Muscovy's size, opened the Volga River to its trade, and removed the main obstacle to its eastward expansion across Central Asia and Siberia. They reversed the earlier Mongol conquests, with Russians now subjugating Mongol lands to create a vast Eurasian empire. And they made Muscovy a multicultural realm, embracing many Mongols and Muslims, beginning a long process in which Russians came to rule numerous non-Russian (and non-Orthodox) peoples. Ivan IV's admirers started calling him Ivan *Groznyi*, roughly meaning Ivan the Formidable, later imprecisely translated as Ivan the Terrible.

To mark his military success, Ivan had a cathedral to the Virgin Mary built at the edge of Moscow's Red Square, a large plaza next to the Kremlin Wall. It eventually came to be called Saint Basil's Cathedral, after a wandering ascetic who criticized Ivan's later brutality. Composed of nine octagon-shaped structures, topped with candy-colored domes and golden crosses, it has stood ever since as a symbol of Russia's mystery and majesty (see page 556).

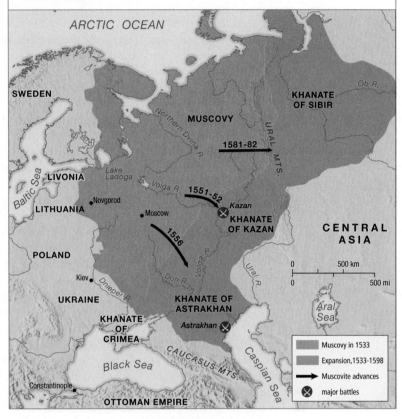

MAP 25.3 Expansion Under Ivan IV and Feodor I, 1533–1598

Under Ivan IV, the Terrible (1533–1584), and his son Feodor I (1584–1598), Muscovy expanded far to the east and southeast by conquering Mongol khanates. How did the conquest of these regions, populated mainly by non-Russians, change the Muscovite realm?

Muscovy expands into Mongol and Muslim lands

IVAN'S REIGN OF TERROR. Ivan's productive years ended in 1560 with the death of his beloved Anastasia, a personal tragedy that soon became Russia's tragedy as well. Deprived of his wife's restraining influence and sickened by suspicion that she had been poisoned, he turned against his chosen council and other officials. Some were arrested and executed; others fled into exile. In 1565 he unleashed a seven-year reign of terror, enforced by a cadre of six thousand thugs who, dressed in black and riding at night on black horses, destroyed homes and killed families of boyars that Ivan deemed disloyal. In 1570, hearing rumors of a plot against him in Novgorod, he took his forces to that city and conducted an orgy of violence, drowning, stabbing, spearing, roasting, and beheading thousands of people.

Ivan's last two decades were disastrous. Thousands of terrified peasants fled to the southern steppes, subverting Muscovy's agrarian economy and causing sporadic starvation. Ivan's armies, earlier so successful in the East, now proved inept in the West, losing ruinous wars to Sweden, Lithuania, and Poland. Three years before his own death, Ivan

Ivan IV terrorizes Russia and loses wars in the West

killed his oldest son (and heir) with a cane in a fit of rage. This tragedy eventually spawned a dynastic crisis called the Time of Troubles, in which Muscovy was torn apart by famine, civil war, and invasions.

THE TIME OF TROUBLES. Ivan was succeeded in 1584 by another son, named Feodor ($f\bar{e}$-$Y\bar{O}$-dur), a pious but inept man known as Feodor the Bellringer, who personally tolled Moscow's many church bells each morning. Feodor I's reign (1584–1598) nonetheless proved productive, owing to his talented advisor Boris Godunov ($g\bar{o}$-doo-NOFF), who sent armies to defeat the Swedes, regaining some territory lost by Ivan IV, and continued the eastward expansion begun under Ivan. And Godunov compelled the patriarch of Constantinople, overall leader of the Orthodox Church, to install Moscow's metropolitan as the Church's fifth patriarch, making him one of its five main leaders. This action affirmed Russia's central status in the Orthodox world, and the Russian church's status as an autonomous branch of the Orthodox faith.

Despite such successes, a bizarre episode in Feodor's reign foreshadowed troubles to come. In 1591 his nine-year-old half-brother Dmitri, Ivan the Terrible's only other surviving son, was found in a courtyard bleeding to death from a knife wound. The death was ruled accidental, but many suspected that Dmitri was murdered on the orders of Boris Godunov, so that Boris himself could become tsar after Feodor's death. This impression was enhanced in 1598 when Feodor died and Boris became tsar, elected by a **Zemskii Sobor** (z'YEM-sk$\bar{e}$ saw-BOR), a specially convened "Assembly of the Land" made up of delegates from Muscovy's various classes.

Boris's short reign (1598–1605) was beset by widespread famine, seen by many Russians as God's punishment for young Dmitri's murder. Then an adventurer from Poland appeared, claiming to be Dmitri, asserting that he had somehow survived and was thus the rightful tsar. Known to history as False Dmitri I, he promised ten years of freedom from taxation and raised an army that was enlarged by defections from Boris's forces. In April 1605, when Boris suddenly died, his remaining armies refused to support his 16-year-old son, Tsar Feodor II, who was soon deposed and murdered. Instead, they supported False Dmitri I, who was welcomed in Moscow as tsar. But the next year, when he angered Muscovites (who hated Poles and the Catholic Church) by marrying a Polish Catholic woman, ambitious boyars declared him an imposter and killed him. Then, dramatizing their hostility toward the Catholic West, they hacked apart and burned his body, put the ashes into a cannon, and fired it westward toward Poland.

Following Dmitri's grisly demise, Russia descended into chaos. A council of boyars claimed power, naming one of their own as tsar. But the prospect of boyar rule sparked a mass peasant revolt, followed by the emergence of another imposter (False Dmitri II) and by Polish and Swedish invasions that took advantage of the turmoil to seize Russian lands. In 1610 the Poles conquered Moscow and subsequently sought to install their king as Muscovite tsar.

Faced with the prospect of a Polish Catholic ruler, the Russians finally united in a national revival. Led by the 85-year-old Patriarch of Moscow, they raised a national army that drove the Poles out of the city in 1612. Then they called a new Zemskii Sobor, which in 1613 elected as tsar 16-year-old Michael Romanov, great-nephew of Ivan IV's beloved first wife Anastasia, and son of Filaret ($F\bar{E}$-lar-YET), a prominent Russian churchman imprisoned in Poland. Thus began the Romanov dynasty, which ruled Russia until 1917.

The Early Romanovs and the Russian Church Schism

Despite Tsar Michael's election, however, in 1613 Russia's future still seemed very uncertain. A weak young man chosen mainly because others found him nonthreatening, Michael ruled jointly with the Zemskii Sobor for years, as Muscovy fought off the Swedes, Poles, and groups of Russians who rejected Romanov rule. Only in 1619, after a truce with Poland allowed the return of Michael's father, Filaret, did the new regime's survival seem assured.

For the next 14 years, Michael ruled jointly with his father, who assumed the position of patriarch upon returning to Moscow. As corulers, the father–son team of patriarch and tsar gave a new twist to the Byzantine practice of uniting church and state. Filaret modernized the army and restored regular tax revenues, so by his death in 1633 his son Michael sat securely on the throne.

In 1645, when Michael died, his 16-year-old son became Tsar Alexis I (1645–1676). Reputedly a kind and gentle man, Alexis nonetheless had a violent reign marked by rebellions and conflicts, including a long war with Poland (1654–1667). But the reign's biggest crisis was a schism in the Russian Church.

The schism was triggered by the policies and personality of Patriarch Nikon (1652–1666), an authoritarian churchman who dominated the young tsar and for a time served as coruler. Convinced by Greek theologians that errors had crept into Russian church rituals, Nikon instituted changes in popular devotions, including how to make the sign of the cross and the number of communion wafers to use at Orthodox masses. Many Orthodox Russians, regarding the old rituals as central to salvation, saw Nikon's reforms as a threat to their eternal souls.

Soon millions of **Old Believers**, those who rejected Nikon's changes in Russian Orthodox practices, were openly defying church and state leaders, whom they saw as one and the same. In an effort to pacify the religious rebels, Nikon was removed as patriarch in 1666, but his reforms were left intact, so the revolt went on. Some Old Believers seized a monastery and for eight years held off Muscovite forces sent against them. Other Old Believers, rather than submit to a church and state they saw as directed by the devil, resorted to communal suicides, burning themselves to death in boats set ablaze on Russian rivers. Fueled by such zeal, the Old Belief gained millions of supporters, while church and state leaders eventually concluded that efforts to end it were futile.

An iconostasis with five rows of icons in a Russian Orthodox Church.

Schism divides the Russian Orthodox Church

Muscovite Culture and Society

The schism's vast impact reflected the importance of the Orthodox Church in Muscovite culture and society. Another key feature of this society was serfdom, which was firmly entrenched by the 1600s. These institutions affected almost every aspect of Muscovite life.

ORTHODOX AND ASIAN CONNECTIONS. Orthodox Christianity permeated Muscovy's culture. Muscovite music was church music, sung slowly and solemnly by all-male choirs without instrumental support, producing a tone sounding joyous to Russians but somber to many outsiders. Muscovite architecture was church architecture, exhibited in numerous ornate churches with onion-shaped domes, gilded crosses, and inner walls covered with elaborate frescoes. Muscovite artists produced mostly **icons**, stylized wooden paintings, typically depicting Christian holy persons, venerated as sources of grace and religious education and often displayed on an iconostasis (icon wall) separating the altar from the congregation in Orthodox churches. Muscovite writers and record keepers

Orthodox influence shapes Muscovite culture

were frequently Orthodox monks, who compiled chronicles that serve as key sources of information about early Russia.

Another key work composed by a cleric was the **Domostroi** (*DAW-muh-STROY*), or "Household Order," a manual on family life. Attributed to an Orthodox priest on Ivan IV's chosen council, the *Domostroi* counseled men to discipline their wives and children severely, beating them to instill obedience, and instructed wives to rely on their husbands for advice and support. It also said that diseases, as punishments from God for sins, should be treated by prayer, fasting, and religious rituals (see "Excerpts from the *Domostroi*").

As reflected in the *Domostroi*, Muscovite society was patriarchal. Each peasant village was run by an assembly of male elders, the patriarchs of each household. Women were excluded from village leadership and often from all public life. In Muscovy, as in India and Persia, women were secluded in the home—not supposed to go out in public unless accompanied by a man.

Document 25.1 Excerpts from the *Domostroi*

The Domostroi ("Household Order") sought to give Russians guidelines for living good Orthodox lives. What attitudes toward family, religion, and gender do these excerpts reflect?

How to instruct children and save them by fear: Punish your son in his early years and he will comfort you in your old age . . . Do not spare your child any beating, for the stick will not kill him, but will do him good; when you strike the body, you save the soul from death . . . If you love your son, punish him often . . . Raise your child in fear and you will find peace and blessing in him. Do not smile with him, do not play with him, for having been weak in little things you will suffer in great ones . . . Do not give him his will in his youth, but crush his ribs while he is not grown yet, or else he will harden and cease to obey you . . .

How to keep your house clean and well-ordered: In a good family, where the wife is careful, the house is always clean and well-arranged; everything is in order, put away in its right place, cleaned and swept. It's like going into paradise. All this is the wife's job . . . If she complies and does everything as it should be done, she deserves love and favor; but if she fails . . . to do the work . . ., let her husband discipline her and scare her in private; and after he should relent and speak kindly. Behave likewise with . . . children: punish their offenses, beat them for their faults, then relent . . . But if wife, son, or daughter pay no heed to word or instruction . . .,

if they refuse to do what they are told . . . they should be whipped according to their offense. Beat them in private, not in public; punish, then relent and say a loving word.

How Christians Are to Cure Diseases and All Kinds of Ailments: If God send any disease or ailment down upon a person let him cure himself through the grace of God, through tears, prayer, fasting, charity to the poor, and true repentance. Let him thank the Lord and beg His forgiveness, and show mercy and undisguised charity to everybody . . . Frequent the miracle-working and holy places, and pray there with a pure conscience. In that way you will receive from God a cure for all your ailments.

The Wife Is Always and in All Things to Take Counsel with Her Husband: In all affairs of everyday life, the wife is to take counsel with her husband, and to ask him, if she needs anything . . . By all means let her abstain from drinking liquor, for a drunk man is bad enough, but a drunk woman has no place in the world. A woman ought to talk with her lady-friends of handiwork and housekeeping . . . And if there is anything she does not know, let her politely inquire about it . . . Let not a woman rail at anyone, or gossip about others . . .

SOURCES: From *The Domostroi*, adapted by Dr. John Slatter (used with permission); *Excerpts from The Domostroi* (mid-16th century), http://www.dur.ac.uk/a.k.harrington/domstroi.html.

Unique to Muscovy's religious character were people called **holy fools**, radical ascetics who renounced worldly goods, wore few clothes, and spoke in seemingly nonsensical phrases deemed prophetic by many Russians. Unlike religious hermits who lived in wilderness caves, holy fools often lived in or near cities, brazenly urging urban dwellers to change their sinful ways. Some warned of cataclysms such as the Time of Troubles; others boldly scolded rulers such as Ivan the Terrible and Boris Godunov. According to legend, Blessed Basil, the holy fool for whom Saint Basil's Cathedral is named, once handed Ivan a piece of bloody meat to depict him as a butcher of Russians. Although often persecuted by Muscovite officials, holy fools persisted until the mid-1600s, when the Orthodox Church formally suppressed them.

Despite pervasive Orthodox influence, however, some key aspects of Russian culture arose from connections with Asian countries outside the Orthodox world. Chess, Russia's favorite game, came from Persia; its Russian name *shakhmaty* ("checkmates") derives from Persian for "the shah (king) is helpless." The balalaika (*bal-uh-LĪ-kuh*), a Russian stringed musical instrument, apparently developed from an earlier instrument used in Central Asia. Likewise from Central Asia came forms of dancing in which people dance alone, not with partners. The abacus, a calculating device on which beads are moved along wires, was adopted from China, as was tea, which became Russia's most widely consumed beverage.

Also widely consumed in Russia was vodka, a potent liquor first distilled in the 1300s. Noted for their heavy drinking, as reflected in the story that begins this chapter, Russians used alcohol to help them endure their harsh climate, rugged lives, and the rigors of peasant serfdom.

SERFDOM AND COLLECTIVE LIABILITY. In the 15th through 17th centuries, Muscovy's growth was accompanied by growing peasant serfdom. Russian peasants were subjected to harsh servitude, bound to the land and dominated by landlords.

In early Russia, peasants apparently lived in autonomous villages, raising wheat, oats, barley, cattle, and sheep in the surrounding fields. But over the years, in expanding their realm and fighting its foes, Muscovite rulers often bribed or rewarded noble warriors with lands encompassing peasant villages and fields. To support these warriors, who thus became their landlords, peasants were expected to supply labor and food, in return for military defense.

Initially peasants were free to move elsewhere if they were not in debt to their landlords. In the 1400s, however, to curb the disruption of peasants moving during growing season, peasant relocations were limited by law to a two-week period in late fall after the harvest. Then, during Ivan IV's reign of terror and the Time of Troubles, as thousands of peasants fled south from tyranny and famine, rulers began declaring "forbidden years," in which no peasants could leave their lord's estate at any time. By the early 1600s, most years were forbidden years. Finally, in 1649, the prohibition was made permanent: peasants and their descendants were bound in perpetuity to their landlord's estate.

Peasants were thus reduced to total serfdom, a status similar to slavery. With few restraints to deter them, landlords could beat their serfs, subject them to harsh labor, control every aspect of their lives, and even rape serf women. Peasants called serfdom the rule of the *knut* (*k'MOOT*), a flogging device made of strips of knotted leather used to punish them or keep them in line.

Serfdom was reinforced by **collective liability**, a practice whereby everyone in a community was jointly responsible for the obligations and actions of all members. Peasant villages, for example, were collectively taxed: if one village family either ran away or could not pay its share, the rest had to make up the difference. Similarly, if a runaway

Asian influences affect Muscovite culture

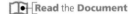 **Read the Document**

Adan Olearius: A Foreign Traveler in Russia (Early 17th Century)

on **myhistorylab.com**

Russian peasants are gradually subjected to serfdom

serf were returned to the village, the other villagers had to make sure this person did not flee again; otherwise, the rest could be severely punished. Villagers were also jointly responsible for services to their landlord and were obliged to turn in fellow villagers suspected of crimes.

Collective liability connects Russian serfs

Although it reinforced serfdom, collective liability also strengthened community, fostering cooperation and mutual support. Distinct from Western concepts of individual rights and duties, it served as cement that helped hold together the vast, diverse Russian society.

THE COSSACKS AND THEIR CONNECTIONS. To escape subjugation and serfdom, many Russians fled south to join the **Cossacks**, frontier adventurers dwelling in the open grassy steppes north of the Black and Caspian seas (Map 25.4). The early Cossacks were mostly peasants who, during Ivan IV's reign or the Time of Troubles, fled south beyond the reach of landlords and Muscovite rulers, forming fiercely independent, self-governing societies. Living in fortified camps, the colorful, hard-drinking, and hard-fighting Cossacks frequently hired themselves out as adventurers and soldiers, creating numerous conflicts and connections for Muscovy.

Always eager for a fight, the Cossacks were often disruptive. In the Time of Troubles, for example, they backed the False Dmitris and joined peasant revolts, adding to the era's instability. Decades later, many Cossacks supported a revolt by Stenka Razin (*rah-ZĒN*), a charismatic Cossack who moved north up the Volga River in 1670 with a growing rebel force, butchering landlords and freeing serfs, until finally crushed in 1671 by a Muscovite army.

Cossacks help unite eastern Ukraine with Muscovy

But Cossacks also performed useful services for Russia. In 1612, for instance, after adding to Muscovy's turmoil, they joined the Russian national army in driving out the Polish invaders. In 1654, after earlier rebelling against Polish rule in eastern Ukraine, the Cossacks turned to Moscow for support, triggering a war that brought this region under Muscovite rule. And in ventures stretching over a century, Cossack groups conquered Siberia, expanding Russia east across Asia to the Pacific Ocean (Map 25.4).

Russia's Expansion Across Asia

Far to the east of Moscow, extending across northern Asia from the Ural Mountains to the Pacific, is a vast region called Siberia, from the Mongol term *Sibir* (*sih-BEER*), meaning "sleeping land." Sparsely populated and bleak, known for bitter winters and short, hot summers, its forests and plains are drained by three great rivers flowing north to the Arctic Ocean. The harsh climate ruled out farming in all but the southernmost regions, so early Siberians lived by hunting and herding cattle or reindeer. But the forests teemed with fur-bearing mammals, such as mink, ermine, and fox, whose valuable furs were a source of wealth for Russian trappers and traders. Attracted by such riches and the lure of adventure in an untamed land, Cossack groups in the 1580s began moving into Siberia. By the 1700s, after clashing with China and crushing the Siberian peoples, Russians ruled the whole vast region.

THE COSSACK CONQUEST OF SIBERIA. The Russian conquest of Siberia was started by the Stroganovs, a wealthy merchant family eager to expand its trade in animal furs from the great Eurasian forests. In 1581–1582, a band of Cossacks, financed by the Stroganovs and led by an adventurer named Yermak, attacked the Khanate of Sibir, a Mongol realm across the Ural Mountains a thousand miles east of Moscow. Using firearms, Yermak's forces initially defeated the armies of the Sibir Khanate. But in 1584 Yermak drowned in

MAP **25.4**	Muscovite Expansion in the 17th Century

In the 17th century, thanks largely to Cossack adventurers, Muscovy expanded westward into eastern Ukraine and eastward to the Pacific. What factors contributed to Cossack expansion, and how did it inspire Russian conflicts and connections with Poland and China?

battle in Sibir while crossing a river, apparently weighted down by armor sent him as a gift from Ivan the Terrible. Even a well-meant present from Ivan proved deadly.

Eastward expansion continued under Boris Godunov, who as Tsar Feodor I's advisor sent troops to complete the Sibir conquest, and as tsar in 1604 ordered construction of a fortress farther east at Tomsk. The Time of Troubles then delayed the eastward drive, but Siberia nonetheless played a key role in restoring Russian stability: a large loan from the Stroganovs in 1613 and a tax in furs on Siberian residents helped rebuild Muscovy's treasury under Romanov rule.

In the 1620s and 1630s, eastward expansion resumed. Cossacks again set out across Siberia, founding fortress settlements along the way. One group reached the Pacific, more than four thousand miles from Moscow, in 1639. Another traveled far to the northeast, and in 1648 went by boat through the straits that separate Siberia from Alaska. A third moved toward Manchuria, eventually coming into conflict with the Chinese Empire.

Cossacks help connect Siberia with Muscovy

CONNECTIONS AND CONFLICTS WITH CHINA. In the 1640s and 1650s, these Cossacks set up fortresses northwest of Manchuria, plundering local peoples and clashing with Manchu outposts. The Manchus, who were then extending their rule over China (Chapter 21), treated the Cossacks as a nuisance, several times sending forces to destroy their strongholds. But each time the Cossacks returned to rebuild their fortresses.

Clashes continued for decades, as cultural and linguistic barriers hindered attempts at diplomacy. Envoys sent from Moscow refused to perform the kowtow, an East Asian

Cossacks connect and conflict with Manchus and Chinese

bow of respect that involved touching one's forehead to the ground, seeing that gesture as beneath their dignity. This refusal offended the Manchus and Chinese, as did letters from Moscow to Beijing, written in a blunt Russian style that came across as belligerent.

French Jesuits help arrange treaty between Russia and China

Finally, the Kangxi Emperor, China's great Manchu ruler, sent a large force in the 1680s to oust the Russians for good. It destroyed a Russian fortress at Albazin, killing its defenders and prompting the Russians to negotiate anew. Moscow this time sent a seasoned diplomat who could speak Latin to the outpost of Nerchinsk near the Manchurian border. China's negotiators included French Jesuits, friends of Kangxi from Beijing, who could also speak Latin and thus bridge the cultural and linguistic gap. By softening the language of both sides in the translation process, and by warning the Russians of more Chinese troops on the way, the Jesuits finally facilitated an agreement in 1689. The Treaty of Nerchinsk established a border between Russian and Chinese territory and gave Russians the right to send trading caravans to Beijing. One of history's most enduring accords, it remained in effect (with some modifications) for 170 years.

THE EXTENSION OF RUSSIAN RULE. Russia's expansion did not end at Nerchinsk, or even at the Pacific. In the 1700s, Russian explorers crossed from Siberia to Alaska and later moved down the American coast as far as northern California. Though their California presence proved temporary, the Russians held Alaska until 1867, when they finally sold it to the Americans.

Moscow extends governance over Siberia

Meanwhile, Muscovy sought to govern Siberia, home to several dozen distinct nationalities. Determined to control this immense but sparsely inhabited region, to populate it with Russians, and to continue collecting its rich fur revenues, Moscow sent governors, soldiers, and tribute collectors and encouraged some Russian farmers to resettle there.

In many ways, the Russians ruled Siberia harshly, using muskets to shoot Siberian peoples who resisted or rebelled. These attacks, and diseases such as smallpox, spread by Russian expansion, killed perhaps half the native population, paralleling the impact of European expansion in the Americas (Chapter 19). Later the Russians also used Siberia as a place to exile criminals and dissidents.

View the **Image**

Russian Views of "People of the Empire"

on **myhistorylab.com**

In other ways, however, the Russians were relatively lenient. They did not extend serfdom to Siberia, nor did they force the Orthodox faith on Siberians—especially since those who converted to it were exempt from the fur tax. Thus, despite its later reputation as a vast prison camp, Siberia was actually one of Russia's freest regions: a place where people seeking a new life could go to put some distance between themselves and Moscow's autocratic regime.

Russia's Western Reorientation

In the 18th century, even as their subjects were expanding and settling an enormous eastern empire, Russia's rulers reoriented their country and culture toward the West. This transition, begun by Tsar Peter I and continued under Empresses Elizabeth I and Catherine II, imposed Western values and views on the realm and expanded it far to the south and west.

Peter the Great: Westernization and War

Peter in his youth connects with Westerners near Moscow

Tsar Peter I, later called Peter the Great, began his reign in 1682. But since he was then only ten years old, the state was run for the next 12 years by regents—first his older half-sister, then his mother—leaving the young tsar uninvolved in government affairs. Restless and precocious, Peter spent his time in Moscow's German suburb, an enclave for visiting foreigners from Europe, whom Russians collectively called Germans. From them Peter heard about Europe's great cities, technologies, armies, and ocean fleets. He hoped someday to see these things firsthand, and to make his country a great power with cities, technologies, armies, and fleets matching those of the West. He also wanted to expand to the south, to take land from the Ottoman Turks and gain year-round ports on the Black Sea. So in 1697, after coming of age and taking charge of the government, he embarked on his Grand Embassy to the West, discussed at the start of this chapter. He did so partly to acquire Western technology and knowledge, and partly to garner support for a war against the Turks.

As a springboard for Westernizing Russia, Peter's trip was a success. Using an assumed name that scarcely concealed his identity, he visited cities and seaports, worked as a shipbuilder in Holland, observed European habits, styles, and governments, and enlisted numerous Western experts to help modernize his land.

In the next few decades, back in Russia, Peter enacted many Westernizing reforms. Some were cosmetic, such as making nobles shave their beards, smoke tobacco, and wear European clothes. Others were substantial: he ended the seclusion of women, adopted a Western calendar, simplified the Russian alphabet, introduced the printing press, founded schools, and started a newspaper. He expanded Russian industry and commerce, created Russia's first navy, and restructured his army and government along Western lines. He instituted a **service state**, requiring all nobles to serve in either the military or the bureaucracy, and replacing the old boyar status with a new noble standing based on government service. And he imposed a **Table of Ranks**, a 14-level organizational ladder, requiring state officials and military officers to work their way up the ranks through promotions based on performance rather than on heredity or prestige.

The most vivid symbol of Peter's new Russia was his new capital, Saint Petersburg, whose construction began in 1703. Built on swampy islands at the mouth of a river in northwestern Russia, with sturdy stone and stucco structures designed by Western architects, it cost thousands of laborers their lives. As a seaport on the Gulf of Finland, an arm of the Baltic Sea, Saint Petersburg connected Russia with Europe's great cities, among which it was soon counted. Peter called the city his "window on the West," signifying Russia's European future and his break with its Muscovite past.

Peter likewise expanded Russia, but not as he initially intended. The European powers, refusing to join him in war against the Turks, instead persuaded him to battle Sweden for lands along the eastern Baltic Sea. The result was the Great Northern War (1700–1721), a pivotal struggle pitting Muscovy, Poland, and Denmark against the Swedes, later joined by the Turks.

At first the war went dreadfully for Peter, as Sweden's young King Charles XII proved a brilliant warrior. With his forces outnumbered five to one, Charles routed the Russians in 1700 at Narva on the Gulf of Finland (Map 25.5). But then, disdaining Muscovites as unworthy foes, Charles focused on defeating Poland, delaying his invasion of Russia until 1708.

Mortified by the Narva defeat, Peter used this time to rebuild his army, improve its training and equipment, and construct a Baltic fleet. So when the Swedes invaded, he was ready, and in 1709 he defeated them decisively at Poltava (*pol-TAH-vah*) in

Peter the Great.

Peter brings Western ideas and ways to Russia

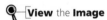**View** the **Image**

View of St. Petersburg from the First Russian Newspaper

on **myhistorylab.com**

Peter builds Saint Petersburg to enhance Russia's Western connections

View the **Map**

Atlas Map: Russia Under Peter the Great

on **myhistorylab.com**

Peter the Great's palace in St. Petersburg.

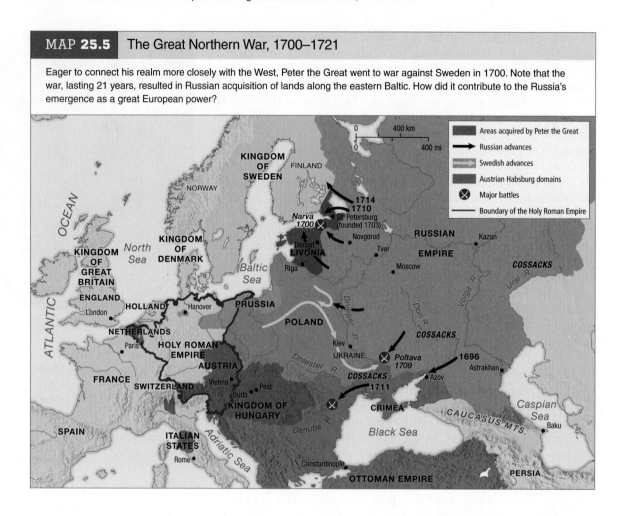

MAP **25.5**	The Great Northern War, 1700–1721

Eager to connect his realm more closely with the West, Peter the Great went to war against Sweden in 1700. Note that the war, lasting 21 years, resulted in Russian acquisition of lands along the eastern Baltic. How did it contribute to the Russia's emergence as a great European power?

Great Northern War connects Russia to Baltic Sea

View the **Image**

Battle of Poltava, 1709

on **myhistorylab.com**

Read the **Document**

Peter the Great, "Correspondence with Alexis" (Russia), 1715

on **myhistorylab.com**

Peter destroys son and fails to name a successor as Russian emperor

Ukraine. King Charles escaped to Turkey and fought on until his death in 1718, but the Russians ultimately won. The Treaty of Nystad (*NĪ-stad*) in 1721 sealed Peter's triumph by giving him control of the Gulf of Finland and the eastern Baltic shores. Peter was proclaimed Russian emperor, transforming the Tsardom of Muscovy into the Russian Empire, henceforth one of the world's great powers.

Peter's reign also had a darker side. An often cruel man, he imposed heavy taxes on the peasants and alienated nobles by making them work their way up the Table of Ranks. He undermined the Russian Church, abolishing its patriarch and placing it directly under state control. He melted church bells to make cannons and conducted an ongoing "Drunken Synod" in which he and his cronies dressed as clerics and held mock rituals that ridiculed religion.

Such practices made Peter many enemies, including his oldest son Alexis, suspected of secretly plotting with nobles, church leaders, and his mother (Peter's estranged first wife) against his father. Peter had Alexis tortured, resulting in his death in prison in 1718. Having thus, like Ivan the Terrible, destroyed his own heir, Peter enacted a new law that let the ruler name his own successor.

But Peter never named an heir. In November 1724, he was reportedly sailing in the Gulf of Finland when he saw a small boat that ran aground in a storm. Plunging into icy waters to rescue the victims, he caught a fever that aggravated earlier abdominal pains. In January 1725, as his condition worsened to the point of death, according to one account he called for a tablet and wrote "Give everything to . . . ." Then he dropped the pen, lapsed into a coma, and died the next morning.

Peter's failure to designate an heir almost undid his legacy. For the next 16 years, Russia was weakened by succession struggles and short reigns reminiscent of the Time of Troubles. But Peter's new state weathered these crises, and his legacy was finally ensured in 1741, when his able daughter Elizabeth seized the Russian throne.

Elizabeth I: Culture, Elegance, and Conflict

Like her father, Empress Elizabeth I (1741–1762) admired the West and thus continued his Westernizing ways. But she lacked his boundless energy and focused more on culture and elegance than on industry and technology. Glamorous, carefree, and single, she reportedly acquired more than fifteen thousand French dresses before her credit was cut off.

Her reign brought major cultural achievements. She transformed Saint Petersburg into a cultural center, bringing in artists, architects, and performers. She hired an Italian architect to build there a magnificent Winter Palace, which today houses the Hermitage, one of the world's great art museums. She sponsored the creation of the University of Moscow, founded in 1755 with the help of Michael Lomonosov (*luh-muh-NŌ-soff*), a universal genius who brought Western science and scholarship to Russia. She abolished capital punishment, imposed often by previous rulers, but did little to help the Russian serfs, enhancing instead the nobles' rights and powers.

In foreign affairs, Elizabeth saw Prussia's King Frederick the Great as a serious threat to Central Europe and Russia. So in 1756 she joined Austria, Sweden, and France in a war to defeat Frederick and divide up his domains. In this Seven Years War (1756–1763), Frederick fought heroically, displaying military genius against great odds, but he could not overcome the combined might of his foes. Russian armies routed the Prussians in several key battles and even sacked Prussia's capital, Berlin. By late 1761, facing utter defeat, Frederick considered suicide.

Then came a stunning twist of fate. In early 1762, on the verge of victory and in apparent good health, Elizabeth suddenly died and was succeeded by her nephew, Tsar Peter III. An unstable young man who idolized Frederick, Peter pulled Russia out of the war and allied with the Prussians. Russia was deprived of victory, and Frederick was rescued from defeat.

Catherine the Great: Enlightenment and Expansion

Russia's withdrawal saved Frederick the Great but doomed Peter III, enraging his forces by robbing them of their hard-won triumph. In summer 1762 he was deposed and later killed in a plot led by some of his guard officers, allied with his wife, a German princess from a tiny Central European state. Although she was not Russian, she quickly seized power and reigned 34 years as Empress Catherine II (1762–1796), one of Russia's most successful rulers.

Catherine the Great, as she is known, was an extraordinary empress. Brilliant, energetic, and ruthless, she worked to modernize Russia's culture, education, economy, government, and laws. Assisted by male advisors and indulged by male lovers, she was nonetheless the driving force for Russian reform and expansion.

A gifted intellectual and diligent monarch, Catherine saw herself as a shining example of the enlightened absolutism then fashionable in the West (Chapter 24). She brought Western scholars, musicians, architects, and art to Russia, corresponded with Europe's leading thinkers, and even wrote her own treatises and plays. Inspired by the European Enlightenment, in 1767 she composed a *Nakaz* (*Instruction*), a discourse on governance

Read the **Document**

Lomonosov: Panegyric to the Sovereign Emperor Peter the Great (1741)

on **myhistorylab.com**

Elizabeth brings Western culture to Russia

View the **Image**

Winter Palace at St. Petersburg

on **myhistorylab.com**

Elizabeth's death ends Russian march into Prussia

Catherine brings the European Enlightenment to Russia

Catherine's charter expanding rights of Russian nobles.

so filled with ideas of equality and liberty that it was banned in France by the French monarchy. In Russia she extended religious toleration, restricted torture, and started an education system.

Her passion for reform, however, began to wane in 1773, when southeast Russia was rocked by a mass revolt. It was led by Pugachev (*POO-gah-CHOFF*), a Cossack adventurer who promised to abolish serfdom, taxation, and military service, while claiming to be Peter III returning to retake his throne. Catherine finally crushed the revolt in 1774, but only by using armies she had to bring home from abroad. Thereafter, unsettled by the rebellion, she focused more on expanding her power than improving Russian lives. Her later reforms mainly strengthened her regime and enhanced the rights of nobles, reinforcing serfdom and leaving the peasants worse off than before.

Catherine's foreign ventures were far more effective. In a stunning series of diplomatic and military successes, she expanded westward, adding immensely to the Russian realm at the expense of Poland and the Ottoman Empire, long the dominant powers in Eastern Europe (Map 25.6). In 1764 she engineered the election of Stanislaw Poniatowski (*PON-yah-TOFF-skē*), her former lover, to the Polish throne. From 1768 to 1774, she fought a successful war against the Ottoman Turks, fulfilling the dreams of Peter the Great

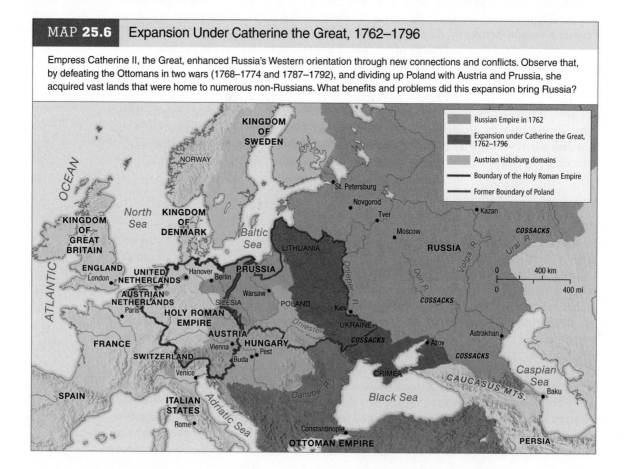

MAP **25.6**   Expansion Under Catherine the Great, 1762–1796

Empress Catherine II, the Great, enhanced Russia's Western orientation through new connections and conflicts. Observe that, by defeating the Ottomans in two wars (1768–1774 and 1787–1792), and dividing up Poland with Austria and Prussia, she acquired vast lands that were home to numerous non-Russians. What benefits and problems did this expansion bring Russia?

by conquering much of the Black Sea's northern shore. During the war Prussia's Frederick the Great, eager to acquire a slice of Poland that divided his kingdom, suggested that Austria and Russia join him in exploiting Polish weakness. The result in 1772 was the First Partition of Poland, which gave Russia, Prussia, and Austria each a part of the Polish kingdom.

But Catherine was not satisfied. She and Gregory Potemkin, her friend and former lover, later devised an elaborate "Greek Project" aimed at destroying the Ottoman realm and restoring the Byzantine Empire, which the Ottomans had ended in 1453. She even had her second grandson named Constantine, intending him to later rule this realm from Constantinople.

To further her aims, Catherine sought support from Emperor Joseph II, the Austrian Habsburg ruler. In 1787, she took him on a tour of Russia's new southern provinces, recently taken from the Turks, where Potemkin had developed numerous new settlements to showcase the prosperity Russia was supposedly bringing to the region. Impressed by these "Potemkin villages," some of which allegedly were façades built mainly for show, and swayed by Catherine's promises of success, Joseph joined her in a new war against the Turks.

In the second Russo-Turkish war (1787–1792), Russia won major victories but failed to achieve the empress's ambitious goals. Sweden, prompted by Britain and Prussia, declared war on Russia, creating a diversion in the north. Joseph II died in 1790, after which his successor, deeming Russians more dangerous than Turks, pulled Austria out of the war. In 1791 Potemkin died, leaving Catherine distraught and curtailing her interest in his and her Greek project.

That same year Poland's King Stanislaw Poniatowski, tired of being Catherine's puppet, approved a new constitution designed to make his country more autonomous. Seeing this move as a threat to her dominance of Poland, Catherine ended her war with the Turks in 1792, taking a bit more territory while freeing her forces for use against the Poles. Then, siding with Polish nobles eager to regain rights reduced by the new constitution, she invaded Poland and forced the king to revoke it. The next year Russia and Prussia conducted a Second Partition of Poland, taking much more land and greatly reducing Poland's size.

The enraged Poles rebelled in 1794 under Tadeusz Kosciusko (*tah-DĀ-oosh kos-CHOO-skō*), a Polish patriot who earlier fought in the American Revolution. Valiant but hopeless, the revolt was crushed by Russia and Prussia, who then joined with Austria in the Third Partition of Poland (1795), dividing up the rest of that country. Catherine died in 1796, having expanded Russia far to the west and southwest (Map 25.6).

Russia's Eurasian Society

In less than a century, then, the Tsardom of Muscovy, with its Eastern-oriented Byzantine Orthodox culture, had been transformed into the Russian Empire, infused with Western ways. Having gained vast territories stretching from the Black Sea to the Baltic, the Russian realm now extended deep into Europe, embracing many non-Russian nationalities and millions of Catholics, Protestants, and Jews. But Russia's underlying culture remained Eastern and Byzantine, characterized by serf agriculture and Orthodox Christianity. The result was a blended culture, combining elements of East and West in a complex, conflicted society rightfully called Eurasian.

COMMERCE, CULTURE, AND GENDER ROLES. Russia's 18th-century expansion was accompanied by great population growth—roughly from thirteen to thirty-six million people—and by sweeping economic, cultural, and social changes. Along with vast new lands and populations, Russia acquired an expanded and diversified economy, a complex

---

View the **Image**

Emelyan Pugachev Awaits Punishment for Leading Peasant Revolt

on **myhistorylab.com**

Catherine expands Russia to the west and southwest

View the **Image**

The Cake of Kings: First Partition of Poland, 1773 – Engraving

on **myhistorylab.com**

Catherine plots to revive the Byzantine Empire

Russia, Austria, and Prussia divide up Poland

Russian society blends East and West

Russian trader.

Russian learning and culture emulate the West

Russian women gain from Western influence

An early Russian newspaper.

new urban culture, and an increasingly open society with greater opportunities for women.

The empire's expansion spurred economic growth, partly by bringing Ukraine's rich farmlands fully under Russian rule, and partly by giving Russia access to trade through the Baltic and Black seas. The fertile new farmlands helped Russia better feed its growing population and also provided surplus grain to sell abroad, adding to the empire's already lucrative fur and timber exports. Russian iron goods and textile manufacturing likewise expanded immensely, with numerous new factories employing thousands of workers. Although many were servile laborers, effectively enserfed to factories rather than landowners, others increasingly were wage laborers, paid for their labor like workers in the West.

Changes in education and culture were equally significant. Eager to update Russian science and technology, Peter the Great sent hundreds of Russians to study in the West, opened Russian schools that focused on mechanics and navigation, adopted Arabic numerals in Russia, and founded the Russian Academy of Sciences—eventually one of the world's leading academic institutions. Stressing culture more than technology, Empresses Elizabeth I and Catherine the Great imported Western architects and artists, promoted poetry and drama, and supported literature and ballet—areas in which Russia later gained global preeminence. The University of Moscow, begun with Elizabeth's backing, offered degrees in medicine, philosophy, and law and published a newspaper for Moscow's literate elite. Catherine founded schools to train Russian teachers, laid the foundations for a network of elementary schools, and started Russia's first state school for women, later called the Smolny Institute. Although shortages of teachers and limited funding restricted the scope of such efforts, they did help to educate many young men—and, for the first time, young women.

Russia's Westernization also brought women other changes. Peter the Great ended their seclusion in the home, a Muscovite practice probably derived from Persia. Women were increasingly involved in public affairs, included in social functions, and even encouraged to adopt Western fashions. Although Muscovy at times had been governed by female regents, Peter made it possible for women to rule in their own right. His second wife, Catherine, a former peasant who reportedly held her own with him in carousing, briefly succeeded him as Empress Catherine I (1725–1727), the first of four empresses who ruled Russia in the 18th century.

The fourth of those empresses, Catherine II, the Great, embodied in her person a greatly expanded role for women, showing that she could exercise power as skillfully and ruthlessly as any male ruler had done. Dominating Russia with the forcefulness of an Ivan the Terrible or Peter the Great, she proved more capable and ambitious than most of her male predecessors. After disposing of her husband, she refused to simply serve as regent for her son, insisting instead on being empress in her own right. Enlightened and sophisticated, she nonetheless proved relentless in crushing unrest, enhancing her authority, and expanding the size and power of her adopted country. Her indulgence with numerous lovers, although it gained her a scandalous reputation, was another way in which she shared the practices of many male monarchs.

The changes in Russian commerce, culture, education, and gender roles, however, applied mainly to the upper classes—the landed nobles and urban elites—who attended operas and ballets, followed Western fashions and ideas, and spoke to each other in French as well as Russian. The rural peasant masses still lived in patriarchal villages, suffered from oppressive serfdom, and remained largely illiterate. Fortified by faith and often also by vodka, they toiled in drudgery through Russia's short summers and long winters, much as their Muscovite ancestors had done.

RELIGIOUS AND ETHNIC DIVERSITY. By the late 18th century, however, the empire's masses were far more diverse in culture and religion than in Muscovite times. Nearly half of the huge realm's subjects were now non-Russians, with dozens of different languages and cultures. Many were non-Orthodox as well, including millions of Catholics, Protestants, Jews, and Muslims living in the newly conquered lands.

These new subjects posed problems for the Russian state. Some, including many Poles and Ukrainians, deeply resented Russian rule and wanted their own independent homelands. Catherine responded with a combination of religious toleration and political repression, allowing non-Russians in Poland and elsewhere to worship as they chose but stifling all strivings toward political autonomy and crushing anti-Russian rebellions.

Equally vexing was the status of the Jews, millions of whom lived in the regions Russia took from Poland. In previous centuries, fleeing persecution in Central Europe and elsewhere, many Jews had moved to the Polish realm, where they were allowed to maintain their own customs and communities. The Kingdom of Poland, which then included Lithuania, Belarus, and Ukraine, had thus become the main homeland of European Jews. Now, suddenly, this homeland was part of Russia, where few Jews had hitherto lived, in part because of laws designed to shield Orthodox Russians from alien cultures and beliefs. Acting to sustain this situation, Catherine's regime restricted Jews to the newly conquered regions where they already lived, thus creating the **Pale of Jewish Settlement** (Map 25.7)—a broad band of lands along Russia's western borders where Jews were allowed to reside but increasingly subjected to legal limitations and abuses.

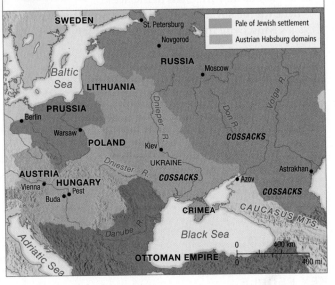

MAP 25.7 The Pale of Jewish Settlement, 1783–1917

In expanding westward the Russians took regions that were home to millions of Jews. Note that these lands included much of Poland and all of Ukraine. Why did so many Jews live there, and why did the Russians restrict the Jews to these regions?

Russian Empire incorporates numerous cultures and religions

CHAPTER

REVIEW

Putting It in Perspective

The Tsardom of Muscovy, emerging from Mongol rule in the 15th century, was centered on the city of Moscow, the Russian Orthodox Church, and peasant village agriculture, increasingly subject to serfdom. As the realm expanded to the east and south, conquering all of Siberia and a large segment of the steppes, it incorporated the peoples and cultures of those regions.

In the 18th century, Muscovy was transformed by its rulers into the Russian Empire, with governance systems, military forces, new technologies, and cultural features adapted from the West. The new capital, Saint Petersburg, elegantly showcased the new Western orientation, and the empire's conquests extended its rule over numerous non-Russians in the West.

Beneath the surface of Westernization, however, Russia's Muscovite foundations remained largely intact. In the countless rural serf estates, with their patriarchal villages and households, and in the myriad Orthodox churches, with their elaborate rituals and pious worshipers, Muscovite Russia lived on in the Russian Empire. The result was a realm that encompassed vast expanses of both Asia and Europe, with a blended society embracing many elements of both East and West, yet belonging fully to neither.

Reviewing Key Material

KEY CONCEPTS

metropolitan, 561
Kremlin, 561
boyars, 561
tsar, 562
Zemskii Sobor, 564
Old Believers, 565
icons, 565
Domostroi, 566

holy fools, 567
collective liability, 567
Cossacks, 568
service state, 571
Table of Ranks, 571
Pale of Jewish Settlement, 577

KEY PEOPLE

Ivan the Great, 561
Zoe (Sofia) Paleologus, 562
Filofei, 562
Ivan the Terrible, 562
Boris Godunov, 564
Michael Romanov, 564
Filaret, 564
Alexis I, 565

Nikon, 565
Peter the Great, 570
Elizabeth I, 573
Michael Lomonosov, 573
Catherine the Great, 573
Pugachev, 574
Stanislaw Poniatowski, 574
Gregory Potemkin, 575

ASK YOURSELF

1. How and why did Muscovy expand from a small principality into a vast Eurasian realm?
2. How did the Orthodox Church influence Muscovite politics, culture, and society? How and why did Muscovy claim the heritage of the Byzantine Empire?
3. How and why did serfdom develop in Muscovite Russia? How did collective liability reinforce serfdom? How did serf rebellions and Cossack ventures influence Russian history?
4. How did Peter the Great Westernize Russia and make it one of Europe's great powers?
5. How did Elizabeth I and Catherine II expand on Peter's work? What were the main impacts of Westernization and westward expansion on Russian culture and society?

GOING FURTHER

Alexander, John. *Catherine the Great: Life and Legend.* 1989.
Avrich, Paul. *Russian Rebels, 1600–1800.* 1976.
Blum, Jerome. *Lord and Peasant in Russia from the Ninth to the Nineteenth Century.* 1971.
Bobrick, Benson. *Fearful Majesty: The Life and Reign of Ivan the Terrible.* 1990.
Brennan, James F. *Enlightened Despotism in Russia.* 1987.
Bushkovitch, Paul. *Peter the Great.* 2002.
Clyman, T., and J. Vowles. *Russia Through Women's Eyes.* 1996.
Coughlan, Robert. *Elizabeth and Catherine.* 1975.
Crummey, Robert. *The Formation of Muscovy, 1304–1613.* 1987.
De Madariaga, Isabel. *Catherine the Great: A Short History.* 2nd ed. 2002.
Dixon, Simon. *Catherine the Great.* 2009
Dukes, Paul. *The Making of Russian Absolutism, 1613–1801.* 1990.
Evtuhov, Catherine, et al. *A History of Russia: Peoples, Legends, Events, Forces.* 2004.
Hughes, Lindsey. *Russia in the Age of Peter the Great.* 2008.
Kappeler, Andreas. *The Russian Empire: A Multiethnic History.* 2001.
Lincoln, W. Bruce. *Sunlight at Midnight: St. Petersburg and the Rise of Modern Russia.* 2001.
Massie, Robert. *Peter the Great: His Life and World.* 1986, 2009.
Michels, G. *At War with the Church: Religious Dissent in Seventeenth-Century Russia.* 2000.
Perrie, Maureen. *Pretenders and Popular Monarchism in Early Modern Russia.* 1995.
Poe, M. T. *A People Born to Slavery: Russia in Early Modern European Ethnography.* 2000.
Pouncy, C. *The Domostroi: Rules for Russian Households in the Time of Ivan the Terrible.* 1994.

Key Dates and Developments

1237–1480	Mongol rule in Russia
1328–1340	Reign of Moscow's Ivan I as grand prince
1453	Conquest of Constantinople by Ottoman Turks
1462–1505	Reign of Grand Prince Ivan III, the Great
1533–1584	Reign of Tsar Ivan IV, the Terrible
1598–1613	The Time of Troubles
1610–1612	Polish occupation of Moscow
1613	Michael Romanov elected tsar
1652–1666	Reforms of Nikon and Russian Church Schism
1682–1725	Reign of Tsar Peter I, the Great
1697–1698	The Grand Embassy to Europe
1700–1721	The Great Northern War
1703	Founding of Saint Petersburg
1721	Proclamation of the Russian Empire
1741–1762	Reign of Empress Elizabeth I
1762–1796	Reign of Empress Catherine II, the Great
1768–1774	First Russo-Turkish War
1772	First Partition of Poland
1787–1792	Second Russo-Turkish War
1793–1795	Second and Third Partitions of Poland

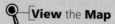

PEARSON myhistorylab™ Connections

Reinforce what you learned in this chapter by studying the many documents, images, maps, review tools, and videos available at www.myhistorylab.com.

Read and Review

✓ Study and Review Chapter 25

📖 Read the Document

Filofei's Concept of the Third Rome (1515), p. 562

Adan Olearius: A Foreign Traveler in Russia (Early 17th Century), p. 567

Peter the Great, "Correspondence with Alexis" (Russia), 1715, p. 572

Lomonosov: Panegyric to the Sovereign Emperor Peter the Great (1741), p. 573

🔍 View the Image

Russian Views of "People of the Empire," p. 570

View of St. Petersburg from the First Russian Newspaper, p. 571

Battle of Poltava, 1709, p. 572

Winter Palace at St. Petersburg, p. 573

Emelyan Pugachev Awaits Punishment for Leading Peasant Revolt, p. 575

The Cake of Kings: First Partition of Poland, 1773 – Engraving, p. 575

Research and Explore

🔍 View the Map

Atlas Map: The Four Khanates of the Divided Mongol Empire, ca. 1227–1350, p. 560

🔍 View the Map

Atlas Map: Russia Under Peter the Great, p. 571

((•)) Listen to the Chapter Audio for Chapter 25 on myhistorylab.com

The North Atlantic Revolutions, 1750–1830

((•—Listen to the **Chapter Audio** for Chapter 26 on **myhistorylab.com**

LA DESTRUCTION DE LA STATUE ROYALE A NOUVELLE YORCK

Toppling the Statue of King George III in New York

British North American colonists topple the statue of King George III in New York City shortly after the beginning of the American Revolution. Denounced in the Declaration of American Independence as a tyrant, George III's decision to use hired foreign mercenaries to suppress the rebellion earned him the hatred of many colonists (page 586).

- What intellectual and military factors prepared the way for the North Atlantic revolutions?

- Why was Britain unable to hold its thirteen colonies? What were the consequences of the American Revolution?

- What factors led to the French Revolution, and what factors turned it in a radical direction?

- How was the Haitian Revolution connected to the French Revolution? What were the consequences of the Haitian Revolution?

- How did Napoleon consolidate the reforms of the French Revolution? What factors caused the collapse of the French Empire?

- How did the Congress of Vienna attempt to restore Europe to its pre-French Revolution status?

- Why did the Congress System fail?

The French winter of 1788–1789 was unusually cold, but political discussion throughout the land was heated. Members of France's three classes—clergy, nobility, and commoners—gathered in churches, manors, shops, and taverns to elect delegates to the **Estates General**, a nationwide assembly summoned by the king for the first time in 175 years, to discuss the country's financial crisis. France was alive with rumors: the king would ask for new taxes; the clergy and nobility would resist; the absolute monarchy would be transformed into a limited, constitutional one; or the whole exercise would prove futile.

At the gatherings, each voter was asked to state his grievances, hopes, and demands. Their comments were recorded in small notebooks that the delegates elected to the Estates General took with them to Versailles. Collectively, the notebooks convey excitement and high expectation as the people of France spoke out to determine their destiny.

Across the Atlantic, others were determining their destiny that winter. In the French slave colony of Saint-Domingue (*SAN dō-MANG*), later known as Haiti, delegates were chosen for the French Estates General, setting in motion a series of events that would become the Haitian Revolution. Farther north, former British colonists, having recently won the American Revolution (1775–1783), held the first elections for their new United States government.

On both sides of the Atlantic, then, in the late 18th century, people were taking steps toward governing themselves through **revolution**, the overthrow or renunciation of one government or ruler and the substitution of another by those being governed. Although their situations differed substantially, the goals in each case involved greater freedom and equality, and the efforts to achieve them eventually involved violence.

United States
France
Haiti

The Background of the North Atlantic Revolutions

Enlightenment ideas and warfare prepare the way for the Atlantic revolutions

Two very different developments laid the foundation for the North Atlantic revolutions. One was the European Enlightenment, which produced a number of new ideas about government and society, including the notion that people have a right to decide their own form of government. These ideas eventually influenced societies around the world (Map 26.1). The other was Britain's victory over France in the Seven Years War, creating conditions that helped set in motion the American, French, and Haitian revolutions.

New Ideas About Government and Society

Europe's Enlightenment advances ideas of freedom

📖 Read the Document

John Locke, Essay Concerning Human Understanding

on **myhistorylab.com**

During the European Enlightenment, prominent thinkers developed political and social ideas challenging the foundations of absolute monarchy and hereditary nobility. English philosopher John Locke, for example, argued that governments get their authority, not directly from God, but from the people they rule. People have fundamental rights, he asserted, and governments have a duty to protect these rights; any regime that fails to do so can be replaced by its subjects. France's Baron Montesquieu proposed limits on absolute authority, advocating a separation of powers in which the ruler's power is checked by institutions that keep it from becoming oppressive. Swiss-born Jean-Jacques Rousseau, a passionate proponent of both liberty and equality, envisioned a society in which all members were free and equal in rights, working together for the common good.

FOUNDATION MAP 26.1   The North Atlantic World in 1750

By 1750, three Western European countries—Spain, France, and Britain—had claimed much of North America, often ignoring the cultures, traditions, and prior arrival of North American Amerinds. Notice that these colonial possessions had to connect with their mother countries across the North Atlantic. Those were difficult and often treacherous sea routes. How would this fact affect the chances that European powers could hold their colonial possessions over the long term?

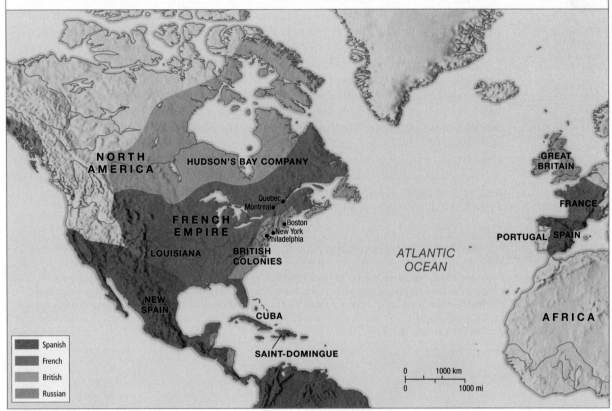

These ideas did not cause the North Atlantic revolutions, which arose from specific circumstances in America, Europe, and Haiti. But the new ideas did undermine the premise of absolutism, in which the ruler exercised unlimited power coming directly from God, and the premise of aristocracy, in which upper classes had rights and privileges not shared by common people. In time the new ideas inspired and justified revolutions around the world that aimed to secure people's rights and freedoms.

The Seven Years War

From 1689 to 1763, while Locke, Montesquieu, Rousseau, and others were advancing their ideas, Britain and France fought four major wars. Waged in Europe, North America, and the North Atlantic, involving colonial territories and Atlantic commerce, these were North Atlantic wars, not just European struggles.

The first three wars produced only minor territorial changes, but the fourth was decisive. Known in Europe as the Seven Years War (1756–1763), it was an effort by France, Austria, and Russia to combat the expansive ambitions of Britain and its ally, Prussia. In America, where growing British colonies sought to expand into regions claimed by France and inhabited by Amerinds (American Indians), British colonists called it the French and

Seven Years War becomes a global conflict

A powder horn of the type used during the French and Indian War.

Indian War. Since fighting also occurred in India (Chapter 22), this multifaceted conflict was actually a global war.

The North American phase of this war at first went badly for Britain. In 1754, in an effort to block the westward expansion of Britain's colonies into the Ohio River Valley, the French built a stronghold called Fort Duquesne (*doo-KĀN*) in what is now western Pennsylvania. The British sought to drive out the French, but in 1755 British forces were ambushed and slaughtered by the French and their various Amerind allies. In the next few years, the French won further victories in Europe and America.

Responding to this in 1756, Britain's King George II appointed William Pitt, a brash but brilliant politician, to serve as prime minister. By sending able soldiers to America while relying on Prussia to tie down the French in Europe, and by setting up a naval blockade to stop French ports from shipping supplies and soldiers to America, Pitt soon placed Britain in a more favorable position. In 1759 the British captured both Quebec, the capital of New France, and Fort Duquesne, which they renamed Fort Pitt (later Pittsburgh) in honor of the architect of victory. When the conflict ended in 1763, France was forced to surrender almost all its American empire, keeping only a few small islands and the Caribbean colony of Saint-Domingue. Britain's triumph was complete, and French humiliation was immense (Map 26.2).

| MAP **26.2** | Territorial Changes in North America Resulting from Seven Years War, 1756–1763 |

In losing the Seven Years War, France lost most of its North American empire, keeping only a few small islands and the Caribbean slave colony of Saint-Domingue. Britain took over French Canada and French claims east of the Mississippi River, while Spain took French claims to the west of that waterway. Note that to prevent clashes between its colonists and Amerinds, Britain issued a 1763 proclamation prohibiting its colonists from moving west of the Appalachian Mountains. How did British colonists react to this Proclamation of 1763?

The American Revolution

Britain's sweeping victory in the Seven Years War transformed the situation on both sides of the Atlantic. It altered Europe's **balance of power**, a situation in which no one nation would be strong enough to impose its will on the others. France, sensing that the balance of power had been changed in Britain's favor, was resentful and eager for revenge. The war ended the French threat to Britain's colonies, reducing their need for British military protection and thereby decreasing the colonists' dependence on their mother country. At the same time, it greatly increased Britain's state debt, leading its officials to seek ways to make colonists pay a share of the financial burden. And it brought France's former colonies under British rule, potentially putting them and their Amerind inhabitants at the mercy of British colonists eager for new landholdings.

Tensions Between Britain and Its Colonists

Up to this point, tensions between Britain and its colonists had been few. Under British protection, with low taxes and ways of getting around British trade restrictions, the colonies grew and prospered. The northern ones were dotted with thriving farms and cities, while the South was covered with prosperous plantations, worked by more than half a million African slaves. The colonists had elected their own assemblies (modeled in part on Britain's parliament) and had grown accustomed to running their own affairs.

In 1763, however, relations began to deteriorate, due to a conflict called Pontiac's Rebellion and Britain's subsequent efforts to halt colonial expansion. In the Midwest a group of Amerind nations, trading partners with the French for decades, rebelled at the prospect of living under British rule. Pontiac, chief of the Ottawa nation, led a five-month siege against the British at Detroit, while other Amerinds attacked and destroyed Britain's various frontier outposts. The British responded with deception and atrocity. During what were supposed to be peace talks at Fort Pitt, they gave the Amerind negotiators a "gift" of blankets infested with smallpox. This instance of biological warfare produced an epidemic that, combined with the force of British arms, put an end to the uprising.

Amerinds rebel at the prospect of British rule

Meanwhile, to prevent future clashes between colonists and Amerinds, in 1763 the British issued a proclamation closing the frontier and forbidding colonial settlements west of the Appalachian Mountains. This edict angered many colonists, who had dreams of developing the newly acquired lands in that region for themselves.

Equally disturbing to the colonists were Britain's attempts to raise revenue. The Seven Years War doubled Britain's debt and left its people burdened by heavy taxation. Recognizing that colonists paid few taxes even though they relied on British troops for protection, in 1765 Parliament passed a Stamp Act, taxing colonial documents and newspapers by requiring that they be stamped with a royal seal. Since this tax was not approved by their colonial assemblies, many colonists perceived it as "taxation without representation"—a denial of their rights as English subjects to be consulted in such matters. Nine of the thirteen colonies sent delegates to a Stamp Act Congress that declared the tax illegal. The Congress declared a boycott of British goods, hoping to force repeal of the tax. Ominously for Britain, the colonies for the first time were uniting in a common cause.

In response to the protest, the British government repealed the stamp tax but insisted on Parliament's right to tax the colonies. In 1767 Parliament passed the

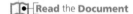

Read the **Document**

Benjamin Franklin and the British Parliament, "Proceedings Regarding The Stamp Act"

on **myhistorylab.com**

Funeral procession for the Stamp Act following its repeal.

THE REPEAL. — *or the Funeral Procession, of* MISS AMERIC-STAMP.

Townshend Acts, which increased customs duties on colonial imports of glass, lead, paper, paint, and tea. But the colonists, having won the struggle over the stamp tax, imposed another boycott, and in 1770 London removed all these taxes except the one on tea. By this time, however, feelings on both sides had hardened.

Clashes in the Colonies

Colonists rebel against Parliament's tea taxation scheme

View the Image

Boston Tea Party Revolution

on **myhistorylab.com**

View the Image

The Bostonians: Paying the Excise Man – Cartoon

on **myhistorylab.com**

In 1773, aiming to improve the declining fortunes of the British East India Company, Parliament allowed it to sell tea directly off its ships to consumers in ports such as Boston. Since this practice would lower the cost of tea to the colonists, company officers and British officials expected little resistance. But colonists saw the plan as a scheme to conceal the tea tax while undercutting colonial merchants, who could no longer compete with the company's inexpensive tea. When company ships docked in Boston, colonists disguised as Mohawk Indians climbed aboard on a December evening and dumped the tea into the harbor.

The British reacted to this colonial protest, known as the **Boston Tea Party**, by enacting in 1774 the Coercive Acts, called by the colonists Intolerable Acts, closing the port of Boston, and turning elected Massachusetts officials into royal appointees. These measures further angered and united the colonists. In 1774, a Continental Congress, with delegates from 12 colonies, met in Philadelphia. It declared the acts illegal and called on Massachusetts to form a rival government. The British government then declared Massachusetts to be in a state of rebellion. In April 1775, British troops sent to confiscate weapons clashed with colonial militia at Lexington and Concord near Boston.

The Boston Tea Party.

Read the Document

John Adams, Thoughts on Government

on **myhistorylab.com**

Read the Document

Thomas Paine, "Common Sense"

on **myhistorylab.com**

Even after this fighting, many colonists still hoped to avoid a break with the mother country. They simply wanted respect for their rights and for Britain to once again leave the colonies alone. But a Second Continental Congress, convening the next month, created a continental army, and King George III decided to crush the rebels by sending in German hired troops (see page 581).

Finally, in July 1776, the Congress issued a Declaration of Independence in the name of all 13 colonies, linking them together as the "United States of America" and transforming the colonial conflict into a revolution. Drafted by Virginia's Thomas Jefferson and reflecting the concepts of John Locke, the Declaration eloquently proclaimed the revolutionary ideals of individual rights and government by the people:

> We hold these truths to be self-evident, that all Men are created equal, that they are endowed by their Creator with certain unalienable Rights, that among these are Life, Liberty, and the Pursuit of Happiness—That to secure these Rights, Governments are instituted among Men, deriving their just Powers from the Consent of the Governed, that whenever any Form of Government becomes destructive of these Ends, it is the Right of the People to alter or to abolish it . . .

Read the Document

The Declaration of Independence (1776)

on **myhistorylab.com**

The Declaration gave the colonists an inspiring cause to fight for. In time, it changed the way people around the world viewed governance. The American Revolution had begun.

The Revolutionary War

The colonists, of course, needed more than words to fight Great Britain, one of the world's foremost powers. With their separate assemblies and inadequately trained militias, the colonies lacked coherence and experience. Britain, on the other hand, had vast resources, a well-trained army, and a splendid navy that ruled the seas. Britain also had support from numerous **Loyalists**, colonists who opposed the revolt against their mother country, and Amerinds, who feared that a colonist victory would reopen the frontiers, bringing masses of settlers into Amerind country.

The colonists had advantages, however. First, they were fighting on familiar terrain and had learned from the Amerinds to harass British positions while avoiding open-field battles, at which the British excelled. Second, the war was unpopular in Britain, whose people were weary of high taxes and prolonged conflicts. Third, British troops were fighting far from home with no real war aim except to crush the colonists. And finally the French, humiliated by defeat in the Seven Years War, decided to take revenge and restore the balance of power by assisting the rebels.

In the early fighting, British forces took the initiative, seizing New York City in 1776. They then planned to move north to Albany, where they would link up with another British army moving south from Canada. This maneuver would have cut the New England colonies off from the rest, dividing the rebels. The British commander in New York, however, instead moved south to attack Philadelphia, the rebels' capital city. Unsupported, the British army coming from Canada was soundly defeated in fall 1777 by colonial forces at Saratoga, north of Albany (Map 26.3).

The Battle of Saratoga changed the war's momentum. Now convinced that the colonists could win, France joined the war on their side in 1778. On land, the colonial commander, General George Washington, proved very capable, while at sea Captain John Paul Jones and the small United States Navy did surprisingly well. In 1781, with the help of French forces, Washington forced the surrender of a British army at Yorktown, Virginia. Extended negotiations followed, and the Treaty of Paris formally ended the conflict in 1783.

The British are supported by Loyalists and Amerinds

French soldiers and navy help the colonists defeat the British

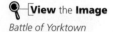

View the **Image**
Battle of Yorktown
on **myhistorylab.com**

Surrender of British forces at Yorktown.

The Consequences of the American Revolution

The obvious winners of the revolution were the colonists, who gained independence and all lands east of the Mississippi River, south of British Canada, and north of Spanish Florida. These were exciting times for the former colonies, now connected as autonomous states under Articles of Confederation drawn up during the war. But the new confederation soon found it lacked the unity needed to deal with collective problems.

To remedy this situation, a convention at Philadelphia in 1787 drafted the Constitution of the United States, a document based on Enlightenment principles and Montesquieu's notion of separation of powers. It created a federal republic in which the states and national government shared power. The national, or federal, government had an elected executive called the president, a two-house legislature called Congress, and an independent judiciary headed by a Supreme Court. In 1789, after ratification by the states, the new constitution went into effect. War hero Washington was elected the first president.

The apparent losers were the British, whose humbling defeat cost them their most prosperous North American colonies. But Britain's loss was not as devastating as it

MAP **26.3** United States of America in 1783

In 1783, having lost the American Revolution, Britain ceded to its former colonies all of its claims south of Canada and east of the Mississippi River, thereby forsaking its Amerind allies by consigning their lands to the expansive new United States of America. Many British Loyalists fled to Canada (British North America), where they became rivals of the descendants of the earlier French settlers. Observe that while the Ohio country (present-day Ohio, Michigan, Indiana, Illinois, Wisconsin, and Minnesota) remained unstructured, states like Virginia, North Carolina, and Georgia claimed land as far west as the Mississippi River. What issues would need to be resolved before additional states could be added to the United States of America?

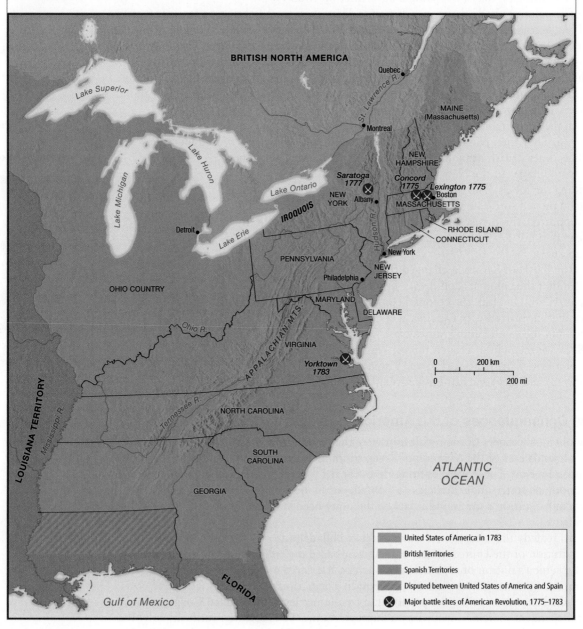

Legend:
- United States of America in 1783
- British Territories
- Spanish Territories
- Disputed between United States of America and Spain
- Major battle sites of American Revolution, 1775–1783

appeared. In the wake of the war, some sixty thousand Loyalists relocated from United States territory to Canada, counterbalancing that colony's French Catholics with English-speaking Protestants, thus consolidating Britain's hold on its newest and largest possession. And British trade with America actually increased, as commercial and cultural ties continued to link the mother country with its former colonies. Indeed, slave-grown raw cotton from the United States provided an important raw material for the industrial revolution in Britain, adding immensely to that country's wealth and power (Chapter 27).

Far more severe were the losses of North American Amerinds, whose hopes of preventing white settlers from moving west of the Appalachians were crushed when the British signed the peace treaty giving these lands to the new American nation. The victors ruthlessly punished those Amerinds, including many who had fought on the British side: their villages and farms were deliberately destroyed and their people scattered. But even Amerinds who did not fight the colonists were similarly treated. As more and more white settlers, now calling themselves Americans, expanded across the continent, the original Americans were largely dispossessed. Drastically diminished by diseases, and driven from their ancestral homelands, Amerinds who survived were eventually forced to live on reservations—marginal lands set aside for them by the United States government. There some strove to retain a hint of their heritage, with mixed results.

The most surprising losers were the rulers of France, which fought on the winning side. Aside from the satisfaction of helping to beat Britain, the French government gained little from the war but debt, already enormous as a result of earlier wars. Essentially, France was bankrupt. Within a few years, its efforts to address this financial crisis by taxing its nobles set off another revolution. This struggle, monumental in its impact, justified the destruction of the monarchy in France with some of the same ideals that had inspired the American Revolution.

The French Revolution

France faced serious problems. Its monarchy was wasting away under King Louis XVI, a well-meaning but barely competent ruler who would rather repair clocks than handle state affairs. Its ability to raise revenues to pay down its debts was hampered by a tax system that relied for most of its revenue on a land tax, then exempted the wealthiest two classes—the clergy, or First Estate, and the nobility, or Second Estate—who together controlled more than half of the country's land. The burden of taxation thus fell on the peasants and bourgeoisie, who made up the Third Estate and who resented the privileged position of the other two classes. Yet France was a wealthy country, whose flourishing farmlands and thriving businesses made it the envy of Europe. It had the resources to resolve its fiscal crisis, if only the tax system could be changed.

The Estates General and the Onset of Revolution

As described at the start of this chapter, in 1788, Louis XVI, faced with impending French bankruptcy, summoned the Estates General, an assembly of delegates from all three estates, to meet the following spring. Since the Estates General could restrict the king's power, no king had convened it since 1614, but since it alone could change the tax system, Louis had little choice. He wanted the nobles to give up their tax exemptions and they were inclined to do so, but only in return for a greater role in governance. The Third Estate's leaders likewise wanted more authority, but they sought a written constitution that would guarantee political participation to all people.

Margin notes

Watch the **Video**
The American Revolution as Different Americans Saw It
on **myhistorylab.com**

Amerinds are displaced and dispossessed by the new United States

Debts from war in America deepen France's financial crisis

Louis XVI summons Estates General to deal with fiscal crisis

Read the **Document**
French Peasants, Cahiers des Doléances (Grievances) (France), 1789
on **myhistorylab.com**

REVEIL DU TIERS ETAT.

A commoner awakens on a pile of weapons, frightening a clergyman and an aristocrat.

View the **Image**
Oath of the Tennis Court
on **myhistorylab.com**

In Paris, a mob attacks the Bastille

The National Assembly issues a Declaration of Rights

Read the **Document**
Declaration of the Rights of Man and the Citizen 1789
on **myhistorylab.com**

Women march to Versailles and force the king to go to Paris

In May 1789, amid great excitement, the Estates General assembled at Versailles, in the grandiose 17th-century palace built by Louis XIV. But the Third Estate, constituting 98 percent of the population, had only half the delegates. Moreover, since the king and first two estates insisted the estates must meet separately, as in the past, with each estate having one collective vote, the Third Estate could easily be outvoted 2 to 1 by the clergy and nobility. When Third Estate delegates protested this traditional system and refused to meet separately, they took the first step toward revolution.

Faced with this bold opposition, Louis XVI wavered. On June 17, sensing his weakness, the Third Estate declared itself the National Assembly of France and invited the other two Estates to join. Only a few clergy from the First Estate actually did so, but the Assembly nonetheless claimed to speak for the entire French people. Three days later, barred from their meeting hall by order of the king, Assembly delegates crossed the street to an indoor tennis court and there swore the **Tennis Court Oath**, vowing not to go home until France had a written constitution.

On June 27, after many more clergy and even some nobles joined the National Assembly, Louis appeared to give in, ordering all three estates to meet as one. But his order was only a delaying tactic. During the next two weeks he summoned loyal soldiers from outlying areas to Versailles to disperse the Assembly. By July 10 they began to arrive.

In Paris, only seven miles from Versailles, news of the troops' arrival touched off riots. To protect the Assembly and themselves, mobs of citizens sacked arsenals and stole firearms. On July 14, thousands of them surrounded a prison called the **Bastille**, a large medieval fortress where guns were supposedly stored. When the prison commandant panicked and lowered the drawbridge, the crowd surged into the courtyard, sending the guards fleeing and killing the commandant. The rioters then started tearing down the prison stone by stone.

When word of the Bastille's fall reached Versailles, the king panicked. Assuming that a mob big enough and well-armed enough to seize such a fortress could easily overwhelm his troops, he came to Paris on July 17 and endorsed what was now called the French Revolution: the end of absolutism and its replacement by a government in which power would be shared between king and National Assembly. On August 4, in a frenzy sparked by news of peasant uprisings against noble landowners throughout rural France, the Assembly formally abolished all class privileges. On August 26 it issued a Declaration of the Rights of Man and the Citizen, proclaiming that "Men are born and remain free and equal in rights." Nothing, however, was said about rights for women (see "Excerpts: Declaration of the Rights of Man and the Citizen").

In September, considering these developments far too radical, the king once again ordered troops to Versailles. Paris reacted violently. On the cold, rainy morning of October 5, six thousand women, unable to buy bread because of supply shortages, marched the seven miles to Versailles to confront the king. The **March of the Women** threatened physical harm to the royal family, forcing the king to move with his family to the Tuileries (*TWĒ-luh-rēz*) Palace in Paris, where he was kept under supervision to stop him from trying to reverse the revolution. Many nobles, aghast at such spectacles and angered at their loss of status, fled the country and plotted against the revolution from abroad.

The Constitutional Monarchy and Its Demise

Meanwhile, with mixed success, the National Assembly confronted major challenges, including France's financial crisis, the opposition of many Catholic clergy, and the resistance of a treacherous king.

The Assembly turned first to France's immense debt. Since land was the main source of wealth in France, the Assembly confiscated all land used by the Catholic Church for nonreligious purposes. The aim was to auction these lands and use the proceeds to pay France's debts while also creating a class of small landowners who would have a stake in supporting the new government. But selling so much land would take years, so in the meantime the assembly issued bonds called *assignats* (*ah-SEN-yaht*), which could be used as money and redeemed after the lands were sold. Unfortunately, however, by increasing the amount of money in circulation, the issuing of the *assignats* resulted in runaway **inflation**, a situation in which money declines in value and prices of goods and services rise. This weakened the French economy further and caused suffering in the general population, especially among poor people.

An assignat.

Having taken the Church's income-producing property, the Assembly then made the clergy civil servants with salaries paid by the government. This action ensured their financial well-being but also required them, like other civil servants, to swear an oath of allegiance to the state. Some clergy took the oath, but others refused to swear support for a revolutionary government. The Church split into friends and enemies of the revolution.

The Assembly subordinates clergy to the state, alienating many in the Church

In 1791, having created serious inflation and divided the Church, the Assembly issued France's first written constitution. It gave the king an absolute veto and the authority to appoint ministers and conduct diplomacy but also forced him to share power with an elected Legislative Assembly. A strong, clever king could have dominated such a government, but Louis XVI was neither. Rather than accept the constitution, he decided to escape to the lands of the Holy Roman emperor, Leopold II, brother of Louis's queen, Marie Antoinette. There Louis hoped not only to find sanctuary but to convince Leopold to invade France and restore absolute monarchy.

In June 1791, the king, queen, and their two children fled Paris under cover of darkness and headed for the border. However, since Louis was identifiable from his images on French money, and since he insisted on stopping at an inn to dine, he was recognized and arrested about twenty miles from the border. The royal family was returned to Paris.

The flight of the king crippled the Constitution of 1791. Louis and his ministers tried to pretend it was all a misunderstanding, but no one believed them. Clearly France was a constitutional monarchy ruled by a king who opposed the constitution. Then, fearing that other monarchs might invade France to stop the spread of revolution before it reached their countries, the Legislative Assembly in the spring of 1792 called for war against Austria and Prussia. Louis gladly approved, hoping for a French defeat that would restore him to absolute power.

Beset by inexperienced leadership, since many of its former officers were nobles who had fled the country, France's army at first fought poorly. In August 1792, interpreting French defeats as a sign that Louis was conspiring with the enemy, radical workers in Paris stormed the Tuileries Palace, almost killing the king and his family. Louis survived, but a search of his apartments revealed that he had indeed worked for France's defeat. The discovery destroyed the constitutional monarchy.

French defeats spark a new uprising

The National Convention and the Reign of Terror

The Assembly now summoned a National Convention to meet in September to draft a new constitution. Formally abolishing the monarchy, the Convention moved to put Louis on trial for treason. At the same time, French armies finally halted the

A new National Convention abolishes the French monarchy

DOCUMENT 26.1 Excerpts: Declaration of the Rights of Man and the Citizen

After the fall of the Bastille (July 14, 1789) and the revocation of the privileges of the nobility (August 4, 1789), the National Assembly drafted, approved, and published a declaration of rights, inspired to some extent by the English Declaration of Rights of 1689 (Chapter 24) and designed to safeguard the liberties of the French people against arbitrary actions by the executive power. Excerpts from this declaration follow.

APPROVED BY THE NATIONAL ASSEMBLY OF FRANCE, AUGUST 26, 1789 The representatives of the French people, organized as a National Assembly, believing that the ignorance, neglect, or contempt of the rights of man are the sole cause of public calamities and of the corruption of governments, have determined to set forth in a solemn declaration the natural, unalienable, and sacred rights of man, in order that this declaration, being constantly before all the members of the Social body, shall remind them continually of their rights and duties; in order that the acts of the legislative power, as well as those of the executive power, may be compared at any moment with the objects and purposes of all political institutions and may thus be more respected, and, lastly, in order that the grievances of the citizens, based hereafter upon simple and incontestable principles, shall tend to the maintenance of the constitution and redound to the happiness of all. Therefore the National Assembly recognizes and proclaims, in the presence and under the auspices of the Supreme Being, the following rights of man and of the citizen:

Articles:

1. Men are born and remain free and equal in rights. Social distinctions may be founded only upon the general good.

2. The aim of all political association is the preservation of the natural and imprescriptible rights of man. These rights are liberty, property, security, and resistance to oppression.

3. The principle of all sovereignty resides essentially in the nation . . .

4. Liberty consists in the freedom to do everything which injures no one else; hence the exercise of the natural rights of each man has no limits except those which assure to the other members of the society the enjoyment of the same rights. These limits can only be determined by law.

5. Law can only prohibit such actions as are hurtful to society. Nothing may be prevented which is not forbidden by law, and no one may be forced to do anything not provided for by law . . .

7. No person shall be accused, arrested, or imprisoned except in the cases and according to the forms prescribed by law . . .

9. As all persons are held innocent until they shall have been declared guilty, if arrest shall be deemed indispensable, all harshness not essential to the securing of the prisoner's person shall be severely repressed by law.

10. No one shall be disquieted on account of his opinions, including his religious views, provided their manifestation does not disturb the public order established by law.

11. The free communication of ideas and opinions is one of the most precious of the rights of man. Every citizen may, accordingly, speak, write, and print with freedom, but shall be responsible for such abuses of this freedom as shall be defined by law.

SOURCE: Declaration of the Rights of Man – 1789 (The Avalon Project at Yale Law School, 1996–2007) http://www.yale.edu/lawweb/avalon/rightsof.htm

Austrians and Prussians well inside France's borders, giving the Convention time to try the king.

Louis XVI's trial reflected the new governance concepts embodied in the Enlightenment and American Revolution. Under the old concepts, the people served the king, who was thus considered incapable of treason because that crime was defined as "an act against the king." Under the new concepts, however, the government served the people, whom Louis had betrayed by conspiring with France's enemies. The only real suspense, then, involved the method of punishment. By a vote of 361 to 360, the Convention condemned Louis to death. On January 21, 1793, Louis was executed by **guillotine**, a scaffold devised to release a heavy blade that instantly beheaded its victims. His queen, Marie Antoinette, was guillotined later that year.

Having thus renounced one-person rule, the Convention formed committees to run the government. Most notable was the **Committee of Public Safety**, a group of officials given broad powers to protect France from enemies foreign and domestic. By July 1793 it was under the control of an outspoken radical named Maximilien Robespierre (1758–1794).

Execution of Louis XVI.

The Committee of Public Safety issues a mass call-up to service

To deal with foreign foes, the Committee enacted a *levée en masse* (*luh-VĀ awn MAHSS*), calling the whole country into service: "The young men shall go to battle; the married men shall forge arms and transport provisions; the women shall make tents and clothing and serve in the hospitals." This mass call-up created a new type of army: untrained and inexperienced, but huge and enthusiastic, it dwarfed the small, professional armies of France's enemies. The *levée* also drafted many talented men who would not otherwise have enlisted, providing effective officers to replace the nobles who had fled. By 1794, the new army had driven the forces of Austria and Prussia out of France.

To deal with internal foes, Robespierre and his Committee established revolutionary tribunals to try anyone suspected of opposing the Revolution. Before long these tribunals were conducting a **Reign of Terror**, condemning suspects by the thousands to the guillotine, crassly called the "national razor." By mid-1794 hundreds of thousands of people, including prisoners of war and some of the country's most notable politicians, had been killed by various methods. No one in France seemed safe.

By this time, however, with the Austrians and Prussians in retreat, and with most counterrevolutionaries either executed or in exile, the terror had outlived its usefulness. In July, known as Thermidor (the month of heat) on a new calendar created by the revolutionary regime, Robespierre was denounced by the Convention and sent to the guillotine himself. A "Thermidorian Reaction" followed, with conservative elements hunting down and killing his supporters. The Revolution's most radical phase was over.

The Thermidorian Reaction terminates the Reign of Terror

The Role of the Lower Classes

Along with these political upheavals, the French Revolution also involved social rebellion: a struggle by the common people to transform French society, historically structured unequally. To achieve "Liberty, Equality, Fraternity," the rallying cry of the French Revolution, the lower classes fought to destroy noble power and privilege, a struggle that proved difficult, traumatic, and bloody.

In seizing the Bastille in July 1789, the lower classes demonstrated that a determined mob could overcome the power of the king. The next month, peasants rose in revolt across rural France, burning the records of noble class privilege and sometimes the nobles' manors. Meanwhile, middle-class townspeople, also determined to destroy class privilege, seized control of provincial city governments. In October, the March to Versailles showed that even poor urban women could force change by taking revolutionary action.

Revolutionary leaders, seeing the danger of defying the masses, hastened to show solidarity with the *sans-culottes* (*SAHN coo-LAHT*), shopkeepers and artisans, "without culottes," who wore ordinary trousers instead of the culottes (knee-breeches) worn by

The working class *sans-culottes* assert their power

Clothing of a *sans-culotte*.

Napoleon.

((•─ Listen to the Audio
Napoleon
on **myhistorylab.com**

nobles. In 1792, as foreign armies neared Paris, the *sans-culottes* arose to arrest the king and install a more radical government. By 1793, as inflation ravaged France and food grew scarce under wartime conditions, these men and women blamed their economic ills on conspirators and traitors. The *sans-culottes* cried out for vengeance, and the Committee of Public Safety, itself determined to destroy France's internal enemies, obliged them with the Reign of Terror.

But commoners were not unanimous in demanding radical change. Louis XVI's execution provoked a massive peasant uprising in western France, where Catholic farmers were appalled at the murder of a ruler they regarded as anointed by God. Many of the Reign of Terror's worst atrocities, including the mass butchery of captured rebels, were committed in response by revolutionary soldiers, told by their leaders that the rebellious peasants were subversives and foreign agents.

The Directory and the Rise of Napoleon

The Thermidorian Reaction following Robespierre's fall ended the Reign of Terror but not the financial crisis. After rampant inflation sparked a working-class uprising in Paris in May 1795, the National Convention dispersed, and a new legislature chose a five-man Directory to run the country.

Hampered by weakness and corruption, the Directory sought to unite France against its foreign foes. These now included Britain and Spain, which had joined Austria and Prussia against France. The new coalition posed a grave threat to the new French army, which had great size and enthusiasm but lacked outstanding leaders.

Then the Directory found Napoleon Bonaparte, who proved to be the leader France needed. Born in 1769 on the Italian island of Corsica, which had come under French control in 1768, he had been sent as a young man to military school in France. A loner and outsider, a man who relied on immense brainpower rather than noble ancestry, he was commissioned an artillery officer in 1788. The wars against Austria and Prussia that began in 1792 provided ample opportunity for promotion based on talent, and few soldiers have been as talented as Napoleon. By late 1793 he was a 24-year-old general and a rising star.

Desperate for able generals, the Directory appointed him in 1796 to lead an invasion of Austrian-dominated northern Italy. Surprising the Austrians by crossing the Alps in early spring, Napoleon defeated them in 1796–1797 and seized northern Italy from Austrian control. Then he created three northern Italian republics under French puppet regimes, exceeding his authority and alarming the Directory. Napoleon was an obviously exceptional soldier, but he was also a politically clever and ambitious man. That combination of qualities made him dangerous.

Yet the Directory continued to find Napoleon useful, sending him north to examine the possibility of invading Britain across the English Channel. Napoleon decided that France lacked the naval power to do so. If the British fleet caught a French armada at sea, France could lose both army and navy in a single battle. Instead, he proposed invading Egypt as the first step toward an eventual French invasion of British India. The Directory gladly agreed: if Napoleon succeeded, it could take the credit; if he failed and was killed, it would be rid of a formidable rival.

Napoleon's invasion of Egypt in 1798 was a tactical triumph. He defeated Egyptian armies in the Battle of the Pyramids near Cairo and then marched his victorious forces throughout the region. He also advanced the science of Egyptology: archeologists accompanying him discovered what came to be known as the Rosetta Stone (Chapter 2), a slab inscribed in ancient times with Greek and Egyptian writing that enabled linguists to decipher Egyptian hieroglyphics. But the campaign against Britain was a strategic disaster. In the Battle of the Nile (1798), British Admiral Horatio Nelson destroyed the French fleet at Aboukir (*ab-oo-KEER*) Bay near Alexandria, stranding Napoleon's army. With escape impossible, the next year Napoleon abandoned his troops and sailed for France.

The Rosetta Stone.

The Consulate: Consolidation of the Revolution

Arriving in France at the same time as news of his first victories in Egypt, Napoleon received a hero's welcome. Conspirators seeking a stronger government turned to Napoleon, and in a comic-opera coup, in which Napoleon was knocked unconscious, his brother rallied the troops to overthrow the Directory. It was replaced with a three-person executive body called the Consulate, which Napoleon would dominate as First Consul. The plotters hoped the new regime could restore order, preserve the revolution's reforms, and defeat France's enemies.

Napoleon did not disappoint them. Abroad, he defeated the anti-French coalition, forcing England to make peace in 1802. At home, he eased the financial crisis by creating the Bank of France, a private corporation empowered to issue currency and regulate the amount of money in circulation. *Assignats* were abolished and inflation controlled. He affirmed the revolutionary land settlement, letting peasants keep lands acquired from nobles who had fled France, thereby winning the devoted support of the rural masses. His codification of French Laws, known as the **Napoleonic Code**, ensured the integrity of private property while guaranteeing all male citizens equality before the law.

To implement these changes, Napoleon established a central bureaucracy, staffed by well-paid officials who depended on him for their positions and promotions. He also created a new nobility based on merit instead of heredity, granting titles as rewards for service, and opening careers to the most talented people.

Napoleon also healed the split in the French Catholic Church. Personally indifferent to religion, he nonetheless saw the Church as social cement that could bind the nation together. In 1801 he and the pope signed a *Concordat*, a treaty granting French Catholics freedom of worship. In return, the Vatican recognized the French clergy's status as civil servants. The Church was thereby enlisted in service to the state.

Napoleon's Concordat enlists the Catholic Church in the service of the state

Increasingly, however, Napoleon subverted the revolution's democratic spirit. He never stood for election, instead asking voters to approve his actions in votes held after the fact, and he largely disregarded France's elected assemblies. Disdaining free speech and a free press, he used censorship, propaganda, and police spies to ensure support for his regime, arresting numerous real and imagined foes. The Consulate (1799–1804) thus marked both the consolidation and the end of the revolution. Napoleon fulfilled many of its fondest hopes but also converted its hard-won democracy into a military dictatorship.

The Revolution and the Rights of Women

Women gain little despite their key role in the revolution

Napoleon's disdain for democratic ideals was likewise reflected in his attitude toward the rights of women. In this attitude, however, he was no different from the revolutionary governments preceding him.

Almost from the beginning, women had played a crucial role in the French Revolution, joining the crowds that propelled it forward, and radicalizing it by marching to Versailles in October 1789. Still, the various revolutionary regimes, controlled by middle-class men, did little to advance female status. Some early reforms increased their rights to inherit property and obtain a divorce, but women remained barred from holding government office and voting in national elections. Liberty and equality, as enshrined in the ideals and actions of the French Revolution, were reserved mainly for men.

▢▣ Read the **Document**

Olympe de Gouges, Declaration of the Rights of Woman and the Female Citizen

on **myhistorylab.com**

Attempting to call attention to this disparity, Olympe de Gouges (*aw-LAMP duh GOOZH*), a talented writer of political pamphlets, wrote a Declaration of the Rights of Woman and the Female Citizen in 1791. Amplifying the 1789 Declaration of the Rights of Man and the Citizen, de Gouges's document advocated equal rights for people of both sexes. "Woman is born free and lives equal to man in her rights," she declared, "male and female citizens, being equal in the eyes of the law, must be equally admitted to all honors, positions, and public employment according to their capacity and without other distinctions besides those of their virtues and talents" (see Excerpts: Declaration of the Rights of Woman and the Female Citizen).

Although Olympe de Gouges's arguments were democratic, her political sympathies were monarchist. Daughter of a butcher, neither her success as a self-made actress and journalist nor her impassioned feminism diminished her loyalty to the king. Her disturbing blend of monarchism and feminism made her suspect in the eyes of male revolutionary leaders. In 1793, after strongly criticizing Robespierre and his Committee of Public Safety, she was guillotined for treason.

The Napoleonic Code increases women's subjugation

The governments that followed the Committee of Public Safety proved even less flexible toward women. The Directory, focused mainly on restoring stability and defeating France's enemies, was neither interested in nor capable of radical reforms. Then Napoleon rolled back women's rights to their prerevolutionary status. The Napoleonic Code actually increased the subjugation of women, depriving them of the right to own property, execute written agreements, and maintain bank accounts—restrictions that endured in France until 1947.

The Haitian Revolution

Women in France were not the only French subjects lacking freedom and rights. Much worse was the condition of the African slaves who worked the plantations in France's Saint-Domingue colony.

American and French revolutionary ideals inspire opposition to slavery

The ideals of liberty and equality enshrined in the American and French revolutionary declarations implicitly challenged the age-old institution of slavery. In a hierarchical society, with rights and privileges determined by hereditary status, slavery could be accepted. But in a system based on freedom and equal rights, slavery contradicted core values. As ideals of liberty and equality spread around the world, so would a movement to end slavery. It began in the 1790s in Saint-Domingue, where slaves, inspired by the revolutions in America and France, decided to liberate themselves.

The Saint-Domingue Slave Colony

The French import African slaves to work Saint-Domingue plantations

In the 1600s, the western part of the Caribbean island of Hispaniola, a Spanish colony since the time of Columbus, came under French control and was named Saint-Domingue (Map 26.4). In the 1700s, eager to make a profit, French investors set up plantations

DOCUMENT 26.2 Excerpts: Declaration of the Rights of Woman and the Female Citizen

Following the publication of the Declaration of the Rights of Man and the Citizen, Olympe de Gouges, a skillful author of political pamphlets and a well-known figure in Parisian social circles, took exception to that document's implication that human rights were reserved for men alone. Her refutation of that position remains one of the most eloquent assertions of female rights ever written.

THE RIGHTS OF WOMAN Man, are you capable of being just? It is a woman who poses the question; you will not deprive her of that right at least. Tell me, what gives you sovereign empire to oppress my sex? Your strength? Your talents? Observe the Creator in his wisdom; survey in all her grandeur that nature with whom you seem to want to be in harmony, and give me, if you dare, an example of this tyrannical empire . . .

Man alone has raised his exceptional circumstances to a principle. Bizarre, blind, bloated with science and degenerated—in a century of enlightenment and wisdom—into the crassest ignorance, he wants to command as a despot a sex which is in full possession of its intellectual faculties; he pretends to enjoy the Revolution and to claim his rights to equality in order to say nothing more about it.

DECLARATION OF THE RIGHTS OF WOMAN AND THE FEMALE CITIZEN For the National Assembly to decree in its last sessions, or in those of the next legislature:

PREAMBLE Mothers, daughters, sisters [and] representatives of the nation demand to be constituted into a national assembly. Believing that ignorance, omission, or scorn for the rights of woman are the only causes of public misfortunes and of the corruption of governments, [the women] have resolved to set forth in a solemn declaration the natural, inalienable, and sacred rights of woman in order that this declaration, constantly exposed before all members of the society, will ceaselessly remind them of their rights and duties . . .

Consequently, the sex that is as superior in beauty as it is in courage during the sufferings of maternity recognizes and declares in the presence and under the auspices of the Supreme Being, the following Rights of Woman and of Female Citizens.

ARTICLE I Woman is born free and lives equal to man in her rights. Social distinctions can be based only on the common utility.

ARTICLE II The purpose of any political association is the conservation of the natural and imprescriptible rights of woman and man; these rights are liberty, property, security, and especially resistance to oppression.

ARTICLE VI The law must be the expression of the general will; all female and male citizens must contribute either personally or through their representatives to its formation; it must be the same for all: male and female citizens, being equal in the eyes of the law, must be equally admitted to all honors, positions, and public employment according to their capacity and without other distinctions besides those of their virtues and talents.

ARTICLE X No one is to be disquieted for his very basic opinions; woman has the right to mount the scaffold; she must equally have the right to mount the rostrum, provided that her demonstrations do not disturb the legally established public order.

ARTICLE XVII Property belongs to both sexes whether united or separate; for each it is an inviolable and sacred right . . .

POSTSCRIPT Woman, wake up; the tocsin of reason is being heard throughout the whole universe; discover your rights . . . Regardless of what barriers confront you, it is in your power to free yourselves; you have only to want to. . . .

SOURCE: From Women in Revolutionary Paris, 1789–1795: Selected documents Translated With Notes And commentary. Translated with notes and commentary by Darline Gay Levy, Harriet Branson Applewhite, and Mary Durham Johnson. Copyright © 1979 by the Board of Trustees of the University of Illinois Press. Used with permission of the editords and the University of Illinois Press.

MAP **26.4** Saint-Domingue and the Haitian Revolution, 1791–1804

Inspired by events in North America and France, and inflamed by brutal repression, slaves in France's Saint-Domingue colony rose in rebellion and beat back invasions by the British and French, finally proclaiming in 1804 the independent nation of Haiti. Note that Haiti occupies only 25 percent of the island of Hispaniola, sharing it with the Spanish colony of Santo Domingo (the present-day Dominican Republic). How did the success of the Haitian Revolution affect Spain's empire in the Western Hemisphere?

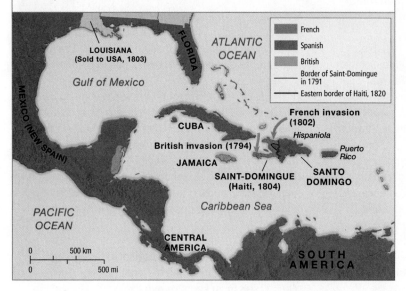

there, producing sugar, coffee, cotton, cacao, and indigo. Since the island's Arawak Indians had died from European diseases, the French imported African slaves to work the plantations.

After 1763, when defeat in the Seven Years War cost France its North American empire, Saint-Domingue emerged as France's most profitable colony. By the time of the French Revolution, it had more than three thousand plantations, accounting for well over half of French colonial investments. Its half million slaves made up almost 90 percent of its population; the rest of its inhabitants were divided between white French colonists and **people of color**—a term applied to former slaves and persons of mixed racial heritage, legally free but treated by the whites as social inferiors.

The Revolt of Toussaint L'Ouverture

Events in France triggered Saint-Domingue's revolution. When the Estates General was summoned in 1789, the colony's white settlers and people of color each sent separate delegations, the former hoping for greater independence from France, the latter seeking greater equality with white colonists. During the next few years of turbulence, as French radicals sided with Saint-Domingue's people of color, tensions between them and white colonists turned into civil war.

In 1791, as the colony's free people fought each other, the slaves of Saint-Domingue seized the opportunity to rebel. Led by François-Dominique Toussaint, who called himself Toussaint L'Ouverture (*too-SAN loo-vair-TOOR*), the rebels soon gained the advantage, helping themselves to the lands of the former slave owners. Toussaint, a former domestic slave, had been taught to read and write by a Catholic priest and quickly developed superb organizational and leadership skills. Escaping slaves flocked to his camps, and within two years he had constructed a cohesive, well-disciplined fighting force of twenty thousand men.

In 1793 two of France's European enemies intervened in the Saint-Domingue rebellion. The British feared that the slave revolt threatened their Caribbean holdings (especially Jamaica, with its three hundred thousand slaves), while the Spanish, who still controlled the eastern part of Hispaniola, hoped to take the whole island. Toussaint and his slave army were willing to support any regime that abolished slavery, but it soon became clear that neither invader cared much about abolition.

Toussaint's forces now allied with France, judging that their best hope for emancipation lay with the mother country, governed in 1793 by the radical National Convention. Their combined forces defeated the Spanish in 1794, but the British hung on, sickening and dying from yellow fever and malaria. They finally withdrew in 1798 after suffering

The French Revolution sparks the Saint-Domingue slave rebellion

View the **Image**

Slave Revolt in Saint Domingue, 1791

on **myhistorylab.com**

Britain and Spain intervene in Saint-Domingue

a hundred thousand casualties. Toussaint then had the delicate task of governing Saint-Domingue, supposedly on behalf of France, while preparing to oppose any French efforts to restore slavery. In France, after the Convention was dissolved in 1795, its successors, first the Directory and then Napoleon's Consulate, were far less supportive of abolition.

An assembly controlled by Toussaint proclaimed a constitution in 1801, making him governor-general for life and abolishing slavery. But it did not declare independence from France. By remaining a French colony, though a largely autonomous one, Toussaint hoped to avoid French intervention.

Napoleon, however, was by this time convinced that only the restoration of slavery and full French authority would make the colony profitable again. He was so contemptuous of the abilities of black soldiers that he assumed a small French army could defeat them in a few weeks. The British, of course, could have told him otherwise. French soldiers died by the thousands of yellow fever and malaria and also encountered serious problems of supply and logistics. Napoleon counted on Jamaica and the United States to provision his expeditionary force, but both were suspicious of his motives, fearing he intended to expand French holdings in the Caribbean.

Toussaint L'Ouverture

The Success and Impact of the Revolution

For a time the French appeared to be winning. Defeated by invading French forces in 1802, Toussaint was arrested and sent to France, where he died the next year in a frigid prison. But his successor, Jean Jacques Dessalines (*des-sahl-LĒN*), was a relentless killer who hated Europeans and gave the French no mercy. When Britain declared war on France in 1803, plundering French possessions in the Caribbean as it did so, Napoleon decided to cut his losses in the Western Hemisphere. He sold to the United States the Louisiana territory, a vast stretch of central North America recently reacquired by France from Spain, and pulled his forces out of Saint-Domingue after suffering some forty thousand casualties. On January 1, 1804, Dessalines declared independence, renaming the new nation "Haiti," an Arawak word meaning "mountainous," succinctly describing the terrain.

Haiti was the second colony, after the United States, to break from its mother country. But the Haitian Revolution differed from the revolutions in North America and France: it was more social than political, and it was clearly racial, pitting black slaves against white slave owners as well as people of color against both. Moreover, its focus on land usage related more to the rebels' African origins (since most had been farmers in Africa) than to French notions of liberty and equality. The Haitians wanted to center their lives on the land rather than on abstract political ideals. Toussaint misunderstood the strength of this desire, and when he invited white planters to return and distributed confiscated plantations to his black generals, he lost the support of his ex-slave soldiers. It took a man like Dessalines, who understood those desires and worked ruthlessly to fulfill them, to consolidate Haiti's revolution.

The revolution's success transformed not only Haiti. In Britain, Haiti's liberation energized the antislavery movement led by William Wilberforce, who fought the slave trade with moral and religious fervor. In 1807, Parliament passed his bill banning the slave trade, and Britain's Royal Navy then pressured other nations to stop trafficking in human beings. The United States banned the trade in 1808. Although France first abolished, then restored slavery, increasingly the institution was condemned. By the end of the 19th century, it had been abolished throughout the world.

Dessalines defeats France and declares Haiti independent

The Haitian Revolution fuels global antislavery and liberation movements

Napoleonic forces in battle.

In Haiti itself, victory proved disappointing. The previously prosperous colony of Saint-Domingue lost nearly all its educated elite in the revolutionary wars. Its sugar, cotton, and coffee production were largely destroyed by warfare, leaving the new nation without the financial and educational resources needed to rebuild. But the Haitian Revolution, combined with the earlier American Revolution, helped inspire independence movements throughout Latin America (Chapter 28).

The Napoleonic Empire

Haiti's independence, important as it was for the Americas, had little impact on its former mother country. Even as he was reluctantly giving up his hopes for France's colonial empire in the Americas, Napoleon was building a French Empire in Europe. With his exceptional military skills and his powerful French army, he defeated France's enemies and conquered much of the continent. In the process, he proclaimed himself emperor. Eventually, however, his ambitions grew beyond his capacity, leading to his personal downfall and the end of his empire.

The Formation and Expansion of the Empire

Napoleon built his empire on military genius, especially his ability to make the most of mobility, deception, and surprise. His armies often appeared where no one expected and performed maneuvers few other forces could match. In the smoke and chaos of battle, Napoleon unfailingly chose the right time and place to attack the enemy's lines. Needing only three hours' sleep a night, he consistently outworked his opponents; with an exceptionally nimble mind, he constantly outthought them. His remarkable memory for names and details gave him an added advantage, which he embellished by cheating whenever possible. Fighting Napoleon was discouraging.

Napoleon expands French rule and crowns himself emperor

By 1804, after five years as First Consul, Napoleon had not only stabilized France and consolidated its revolution, he had also defeated most of its enemies and expanded its borders. France by then controlled most of Italy, the Netherlands, and Germany as far east as the Rhine River (Map 26.5). As the all-powerful ruler of a growing territorial empire, Napoleon decided that he needed a title to match his actual status. So in 1804, in an elaborate ceremony at Notre Dame Cathedral in Paris, he crowned himself Emperor of the French. Fifteen years after the onset of revolution and eleven years after the execution of Louis XVI, France again was a monarchy.

The British destroy French naval power at Trafalgar

France again also terrified its neighbors. In 1805, alarmed by Napoleon's seemingly boundless ambitions, Austria, Russia, Sweden, and Britain formed a new coalition against him. That October, Britain's fleet destroyed the French navy in the Battle of Trafalgar, off the Spanish coast near Gibraltar. But no one could figure out how to beat Napoleon on land. His talented subordinates, most of whom had been forced to join the army by the *levée en masse*, helped him win a crushing victory at Austerlitz, in east-central Europe, in December 1805. There, Napoleon, outnumbered by Russian and Austrian forces, maneuvered his armies brilliantly to divide and conquer his foes. The next year he established control over much of Central Europe, defeating Prussia and abolishing the Holy Roman Empire. In 1807 he routed the Russians again and then concluded a treaty of alliance with Tsar Alexander I. As the year ended, the 38-year-old Corsican upstart was master of Europe.

Napoleon defeats Austria, Russia, and Prussia to dominate Europe

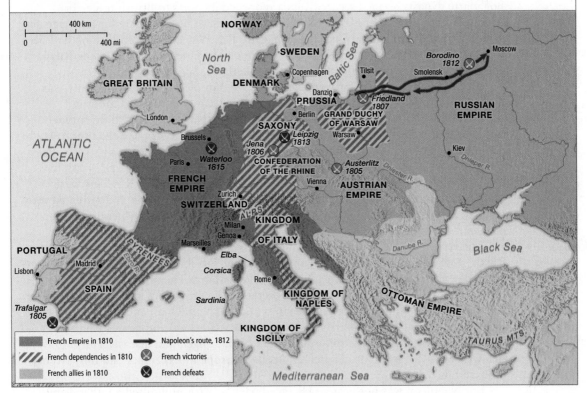

MAP 26.5   The Napoleonic Empire, 1804–1814

Having crowned himself emperor in 1804, Napoleon in the next few years defeated the forces of Austria, Prussia, and Russia, making him the master of Europe. But a British naval triumph that destroyed his fleet at Trafalgar in 1805, a debilitating campaign in Spain that began in 1808, and a disastrous invasion of Russia in 1812 eventually proved his undoing. Compare the size of Napoleon's empire with that of the Roman Empire (Map 8.4). Do you see any similarities in the eventual collapse of both these empires?

Yet Napoleon remained at war with Britain, whose naval triumph at Trafalgar had discouraged invasion by France. The French emperor turned to commercial warfare, and in 1806, hoping to undermine Britain's economy by cutting off its commerce, created the **Continental System.** Essentially a Europe-wide boycott of British goods by countries under French influence, the system damaged the British economy but failed to destroy it. Smugglers evaded the boycott, while Britain managed to gain new markets in Latin America, following one of Napoleon's worst blunders: invasion of Portugal and Spain.

When Portugal, linked with England since 1386 in one of history's most enduring alliances, refused to join the Continental System, Napoleon dispatched an invading force. It occupied Lisbon in 1807, while Portugal's royal family escaped to Brazil on British ships. Napoleon next tried to make Spain a puppet monarchy under his brother Joseph, but the French occupation of Madrid in 1808 was challenged by guerrilla forces loyal to Spain's Borbón dynasty. Joseph's coronation in turn prompted revolts in Spain's American colonies, which had no loyalty to this French usurper.

Britain took advantage of Napoleon's Spanish blunder. First, it shipped goods to Spanish America, capturing markets abandoned by Spain because of the war at home, thus helping Britain survive the Continental System. Second, it sent troops to help Spain's guerrillas fight the French, tying down Napoleon's best troops in a lengthy, debilitating conflict.

The Russian Campaign and the Empire's Collapse

Troubled Russia resumes ties with Britain

In 1810, however, Napoleon's Spanish mistake seemed only a minor annoyance. Confident in his control of Europe, he turned to domestic matters, divorcing his wife Josephine, with whom he had no children, and marrying Maria Louisa von Habsburg, daughter of the Austrian emperor. The marriage was designed to build ties between Austria and France; it also gave Napoleon an heir, born in 1811. Yet just as the Bonaparte dynasty seemed secure, Russia reopened its ports to British trade. Tsar Alexander was upset that Napoleon had spurned a Russian candidate for marriage and troubled by the Continental System's damage to Russia's economy, for Britain had been Russia's main trading partner. Napoleon responded in June 1812 by invading Russia with a Grand Army of six hundred thousand men.

The Russian campaign proved disastrous for Napoleon. His Grand Army was not nearly as powerful as it appeared. With more than two hundred thousand seasoned French troops tied down fighting in Spain, Napoleon had to draft two thirds of his soldiers from his satellite nations throughout Europe. Reluctant to lay down their lives for France, many deserted. Moreover, the Grand Army's sheer size actually worked against it. As always, Napoleon sought to come to grips with his foes and destroy them. Tsar Alexander's generals, noting that the Russians were outnumbered three to one, disobeyed his orders to fight Napoleon and retreated into Russia's interior. Had the Grand Army been smaller, the Russian generals would have had to stand and fight.

The French occupation of Moscow is followed by Napoleon's calamitous retreat

The retreat proved strategically sound, as Napoleon was drawn ever deeper into Russia. By September his forces occupied Moscow, but this did not force Alexander to surrender, as he was safe in the capital, Saint Petersburg. Then fires, which may have been deliberately set, burned much of Moscow to the ground. With no place to house his forces for the winter, Napoleon began withdrawing in October, retreating over the same route by which he had arrived. Lacking adequate food and beset by harsh weather, his men died by the thousands from cold, hunger, and disease. The Grand Army that crossed back into French-controlled Europe in December had only twenty thousand men.

But Napoleon was not beaten. He raced back to Paris and raised another army, rejecting an Austrian peace plan and thereby prompting Austria and Prussia to join with Britain and Russia. The new alliance then declared a war of liberation from French rule. In 1813, in the Battle of the Nations at Leipzig, Germany, the allies soundly defeated the French. In April 1814, Napoleon gave up his throne and was exiled to Elba, a Mediterranean island. King Louis XVIII, younger brother of the guillotined Louis XVI, was restored to the French throne by the victorious alliance (Louis XVI's only son, Louis XVII, disappeared in 1795 and was never found).

In early 1815, however, while allied leaders were meeting at Vienna to restructure Europe, they were interrupted by startling news: Napoleon had escaped from Elba and returned to France. Louis XVIII sent soldiers to arrest him, but they deserted to their former emperor. Louis then unwisely sent a whole army corps under one of Napoleon's former generals, who turned the entire corps over to his old leader. Napoleon then informed the king: "Sire, there is no need to send me more troops; I have enough."

Louis XVIII fled, and Napoleon reclaimed his throne, but his new reign lasted only a hundred days. The allies regrouped and Napoleon marched north to meet them. At the Belgian town of Waterloo, on June 18, 1815, he lost again. This time the allies sent the former emperor to the remote South Atlantic island of Saint Helena, where he died six years later of stomach cancer at age 51.

Restoration and Rebellion

Final victory over Napoleon enabled allied leaders at Vienna to complete a comprehensive peace settlement. Resolved to restore stability to a continent torn by decades of revolution and war, they worked to reestablish the old order that had existed before 1789. Although they developed plans to use force to suppress any future revolutions, they proved unable to extinguish the new ideas about equality and freedom that the North Atlantic revolutions had released.

The Congress of Vienna and the Congress System

Ably directed by Austria's foreign minister, Prince Klemens von Metternich, the Congress of Vienna (1814–1815) based its deliberations on three principles. First was *legitimacy*, the right of former rulers or ruling families to regain the positions they lost in the Napoleonic Wars. Second was *compensation*, the reimbursement of nations that had sacrificed lives and resources to defeat Napoleon. Third was an effort to maintain peace by establishing a *balance of power*, a situation in which no one nation would be strong enough to impose its will on the others, or to dominate Europe as France had under Napoleon.

To implement these principles, the Congress redrew the map of Europe (Map 26.6). France was returned to its 1789 borders, deprived of all the lands it had gained since the

The Congress of Vienna redraws European borders

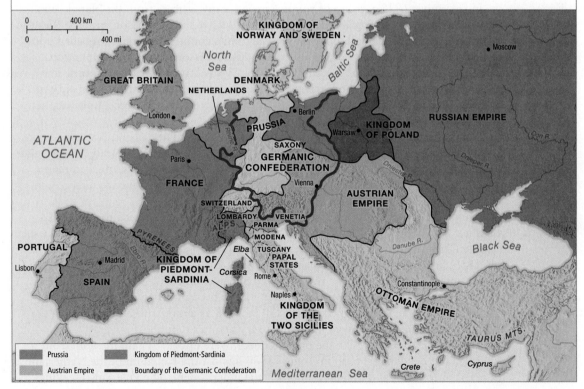

MAP **26.6**	Europe in 1815

Seeking to restore stability in Europe and establish a balance of power, the Congress of Vienna in 1815 returned France to its prerevolutionary borders, restored regimes that had been ousted by Napoleon, and created a Germanic Confederation in place of the old Holy Roman Empire. A Kingdom of Poland was restored in name but was still ruled by Russia's tsar. Observe that both Germany and Italy were fragmented, while the rest of Europe was composed of unified states. What difficulties would this pose for 19th-century Germans and Italians?

revolution. In Spain and Italy, regimes that had ruled before Napoleon were restored to power. The Holy Roman Empire, abolished in 1806, was replaced by a new Germanic Confederation. Prussia received some German territory west of the Rhine River, and Russia gained control of Finland.

Aiming in part to balance France's power by forming a strong nation to its north, the Congress created a Kingdom of the Netherlands, uniting Belgium (formerly the Austrian Netherlands) with the Dutch Netherlands under Dutch rule. The Congress also reconstituted Poland, earlier partitioned among Russia, Prussia, and Austria (Chapter 25) but agreed to let Russia's tsar serve as Poland's king, effectively making it a Russian satellite.

To further sustain stability and peace, Metternich persuaded the Congress to establish an ongoing mechanism known as the **Congress System**. It called for Europe's main powers to hold periodic meetings to deal with pressing problems and thus to preserve order by preventing wars and revolutions. Congresses were held at various European cities in 1818, 1820, 1821, and 1822; among other things they authorized armed interventions by Austria in Naples and by France in Spain to crush rebellions and restore royal rule.

Renewed Attempts at Revolution

Revolt in Greece creates tensions among the powers

In 1821, however, a Greek rebellion against the Ottoman Turks began to divide the powers. In Britain and France, the Western parliamentary monarchies, the revolt was seen as a heroic bid to liberate Greece, the cradle of Western culture, from Islamic rule. But the Eastern absolute autocracies—Austria, Prussia, and Russia—fearing the appeal of freedom, opposed all efforts at revolutionary change. Even Russia, despite its view of the Turks as foes and the Greeks as fellow Orthodox Christians, initially opposed the revolt, and by mid-1822 the Turks seemed to have suppressed it. But the rebels persisted, and the situation changed.

Western ideals prompt a failed rebellion in Russia

In December 1825 a group of young Russian army officers from the Napoleonic Wars, viewing their country as backward and repressive in comparison with the Western European countries they had marched through while conquering France, rebelled upon the death of Tsar Alexander I, hoping to force his successor to grant a constitution. Their brief insurrection, the "Decembrist Revolt," was crushed by loyal troops. The new tsar, Nicholas I, reacted by striving for the next 30 years to maintain the old order in Russia through police state mechanisms and military force. In Greece, however, he was willing to intervene to advance Russia's interests.

Hoping that a liberated Greece would be Russia's friend and client, Nicholas broke with Austria and Prussia to support the Greek rebels. In 1827, the Russian, French, and British navies challenged the Turks, and the next year Russian armies attacked them. The resulting Russo-Turkish War of 1828–1829 brought independence to Greece and inspired revolts in 1830 in France, Belgium, and Poland.

Revolution spreads in 1830 to France, Belgium, and Poland

France's revolt was an aftershock of the 1789 revolution. Realizing that its ideals could not be wholly obliterated, Louis XVIII, who reigned from 1814 to 1824, had issued a charter affirming such rights as liberty, equality, property, and freedom of religion. In July 1830, however, his reactionary successor, King Charles X, issued ordinances aimed at undermining these rights. The result was an upheaval in Paris deposing Charles. But instead of ending the monarchy, the July Revolution brought to power a royal cousin, King Louis Philippe, who reigned from 1830 to 1848 as a moderate. Remembering the Reign of Terror, the French were not ready to try another republic.

The other two revolts, like the one in Greece, were efforts to gain freedom from foreign rule. The Belgians rebelled in August 1830 against the Kingdom of the Netherlands; the revolt succeeded, and Belgium soon became independent. The Poles, also seeking independence, arose in November against Russian rule, but Nicholas I's army ruthlessly crushed them. The struggle between old and new orders unleashed by the North Atlantic revolutions was by no means over.

Putting It in Perspective

The North Atlantic revolutions, although they occurred in North America, Europe, and Haiti, had implications and repercussions far beyond these regions. By challenging such entrenched institutions as monarchy, aristocracy, colonialism, and slavery, they helped introduce a new vision of society, centered on ideals of political liberty and social equality.

The American Revolution, and subsequently the United States Constitution, established the precedent that people could decide their own form of governance, discarding structures they deemed oppressive and creating new ones that better served their needs. In freeing themselves from colonial rule, Americans set an example for freedom-seeking colonies in Latin America, and later throughout the world. And in forming a republic with elected officials accountable to the people and governing institutions limited by separation of powers, the United States proved that Enlightenment principles could be put into practice.

The French Revolution showed not only that kings could be overthrown and nobles disinherited, but also that common people could play a key role in shaping their own destiny. In fighting for liberty and equality, the rebels undermined monarchy and aristocracy, first in France and later throughout

Europe and Latin America. Napoleon curtailed democratic freedoms and formed a military dictatorship, but he also promoted equality under law and careers based on talent, spread these concepts across Europe by his conquests, and opened the way to Latin American liberation by invading Portugal and Spain.

The Haitian Revolution demonstrated not only that the American and French experiences could be repeated elsewhere, but also that slaves could liberate themselves by organizing to expel their oppressors. African slaves also proved they could defeat European armies while skillfully playing off Europeans against one another. In blending European ideas of freedom and equality with African concepts of land use, the Haitians took significant steps toward ending both colonialism and slavery.

The North Atlantic revolutions, nonetheless, marked only the onset of a long struggle between the old and new orders. Monarchs and aristocrats, backed by supporters of stability and tradition, sought forcefully to restore their status after Napoleon's defeat. But their efforts were soon challenged by a new wave of rebellions and ultimately subverted by an industrial revolution, already under way in Britain, that in time would revolutionize the entire world.

Reviewing Key Material

KEY CONCEPTS

Estates General, 582
revolution, 582
balance of power, 585
Boston Tea Party, 586
Loyalists, 587
Tennis Court Oath, 590
Bastille, 590
March of the Women, 590
inflation, 591

guillotine, 593
Committee of Public Safety, 593
Reign of Terror, 593
sans-culottes, 593
Napoleonic Code, 595
people of color, 598
Continental System, 601
Congress System, 604

KEY PEOPLE

William Pitt, 584
Thomas Jefferson, 586
George Washington, 587
King Louis XVI, 589
Marie Antoinette, 591
Maximilien Robespierre, 593
Napoleon Bonaparte, 594
Horatio Nelson, 595

Olympe de Gouges, 596
Toussaint L'Ouverture, 598
Jean Jacques Dessalines, 599
William Wilberforce, 599
Tsar Alexander I, 600
Prince Klemens von Metternich, 601

ASK YOURSELF

1. How did the ideals of the Enlightenment, and Britain's victory in the Seven Years (French and Indian) War, contribute to the American, French, and Haitian revolutions?

2. In what ways were these three revolutions similar, and in what ways did they differ? What impact did each of them have on events in the other two countries?

3. What roles did the working classes and women play in the French Revolution? How did they help make it increasingly radical from 1789 to 1794?

4. In what ways did Napoleon advance the ideals and consolidate the accomplishments of the French Revolution, and in what ways did he violate its ideals and undermine its accomplishments?

5. How did Napoleon rise from obscurity to become the master of Europe? How and why was he eventually defeated? How did his conquerors try to restore Europe's peace and stability?

6. How do the North Atlantic revolutions compare and contrast with earlier rebellions elsewhere, such as the major lower-class revolts in China (Chapter 21) and Russia (Chapter 25)? Why did the Atlantic revolutions have a greater global impact?

GOING FURTHER

Bailyn, B. *Ideological Origins of the American Revolution.* 1992.

Connelly, O. *The French Revolution and Napoleonic Era.* 3rd ed. 2000.

Countryman, Edward. *The American Revolution.* 2003.

Doyle, W. *The Oxford History of the French Revolution.* 1989.

Eccles, William J. *France in America.* 1990.

Ellis, Geoffrey. *Napoleon.* 1997.

Englund, S. *Napoleon: A Political Life.* 2004.

Fick, Carolyn. *The Making of Haiti.* 1990.

Furet, François. *The French Revolution, 1770–1814.* 1996.

Graymont, Barbara. *The Iroquois in the American Revolution.* 1972.

Hampson, Norman. *Prelude to Terror.* 1988.

Hunt, Lynn. *Politics, Culture, and Class in the French Revolution.* 1986.

James, C. L. R. *The Black Jacobins: Toussaint L'Ouverture and the San Domingo Revolution.* 1989.

Landes, J. *Women and the Public Sphere in the Age of the French Revolution.* 1988.

Lefebvre, Georges. *The Coming of the French Revolution.* 1989.

Levy, D., et al., eds. *Women in Revolutionary Paris.* 1979.

Liss, P. K. *Atlantic Empires: The Network of Trade and Revolution, 1713–1826.* 1983.

Lyons, M. *Napoleon Bonaparte and the Legacy of the French Revolution.* 1994.

Nash, Gary. *Urban Crucible: The Northern Seaports and the Origins of the American Revolution.* 2006.

Norton, Mary Beth. *Founding Mothers and Fathers: Gendered Power and the Forming of American Society.* 1996.

Rudé, George. *The French Revolution.* 1996.

Schama, S. *Citizens: A Chronicle of the French Revolution.* 1989.

Tackett, T. *When the King Took Flight.* 2003.

Wills, Gary. *The Unknown American Revolution.* 2005.

Key Dates and Developments

1756–1763	Seven Years War (French and Indian War)
1763	Pontiac's Rebellion; proclamation closing the frontier
1775–1783	American Revolutionary War
1787–1789	Composition and ratification of U.S. Constitution
1789	Outbreak of French Revolution
1791	Flight and capture of Louis XVI
1791–1803	Haitian Revolution
1792	Onset of French wars against European powers
1793	Execution of Louis XVI
1793–1794	Committee of Public Safety's Reign of Terror
1795–1799	The Directory

1796–1799	Napoleon's victories in Italy and Egypt
1799–1804	The Consulate
1804	Haiti declares independence
1804–1814	The Napoleonic Empire
1806	Creation of the Continental System
1807–1808	Invasions of Portugal and Spain
1812	Invasion of Russia
1814	Napoleon's defeat and exile to Elba
1814–1815	Congress of Vienna
1815	Napoleon's return and defeat at Waterloo
1821–1829	Greek rebellion against Ottoman Turks
1825	Decembrist Revolt in Russia
1830	French, Belgian, and Polish revolts

PEARSON myhistorylab Connections

Reinforce what you learned in this chapter by studying the many documents, images, maps, review tools, and videos available at www.myhistorylab.com.

Read and Review

✓●─[Study and **Review** Chapter 26

📖●─[Read the **Document**

John Locke, *Essay Concerning Human Understanding*, p. 582

Benjamin Franklin and the British Parliament, "Proceedings Regarding The Stamp Act," p. 585

John Adams, *Thoughts on Government*, p. 586

Thomas Paine, "Common Sense," p. 586

The Declaration of Independence (1776), p. 586

French Peasants, Cahiers de Doléances (Grievances) (France), 1789, p. 589

Declaration of the Rights of Man and the Citizen 1789, p. 560

Olympe de Gouges, Declaration of the Rights of Woman and the Female Citizen, p. 596

🔍●─[**View** the **Image**

Boston Tea Party Revolution, p. 586

The Bostonians: Paying the Excise Man – Cartoon, p. 586

Battle of Yorktown, p. 587

Oath of the Tennis Court, p. 590

Slave Revolt in Saint Domingue, 1791, p. 598

((●●─[Listen to the **Audio**

Napoleon, p. 594

Research and Explore

👁●─[Watch the **Video**

The American Revolution as Different Americans Saw It, p. 589

─── ((●●─[Listen to the **Chapter Audio** for Chapter 26 on **myhistorylab.com** ───

27

Industry, Ideology, and Their Global Impact, 1700–1914

((•─[Listen to the **Chapter Audio** for Chapter 27 on **myhistorylab.com**

- What factors and assets facilitated Britain's Industrial Revolution?

- Where and how did industry spread and what were its social impacts?

- What were the origins and main concepts of the new 19th-century ideologies?

- Why and how was Europe transformed by industry, liberalism, and nationalism?

- What were the main global impacts of the new industries and ideologies?

Cotton Mill Machinery

Industrial machines, such as these power looms used to mass produce cotton textiles, played a crucial role in the Industrial Revolution, which transformed the lives and labor of people all over the world.

On April 20, 1812, in the English town of Middleton, several thousand angry men assembled at a textile factory that had been replacing its workers with steam-powered machines. Intent on destroying the machines that were taking their jobs, the men started throwing rocks through the factory windows. Guards employed by the factory owner soon appeared and fired at the crowd, killing three men and dispersing the rest. But the next day, enraged by the bloodshed, the angry men reassembled. Carrying a straw dummy they called "General Ludd," the mythical leader of their movement, they set fire to the factory owner's home. Then guards again dispersed them, killing five more men.

The Middleton disorder was one of many that occurred in England between 1811 and 1816, as workers called **Luddites** attacked factories and machines they blamed for taking their jobs. They were reacting to **industrialization,** a momentous shift from a rural agrarian economy, in which people lived off the land and made goods by hand, to an urban manufacturing economy, in which goods were made in urban factories by machine.

For many millennia, since the advent of agriculture, most people lived by farming or herding. Work was performed by human or animal power, and most people had to raise food in order for all to survive. Goods, such as clothing and tools, were produced by hand in homes or artisans' workshops. Most people lived in villages or towns; only a small minority lived in cities.

By the early 1800s, however, society in England was changing. New farming methods enabled fewer people to produce more food, while new machines and energy sources greatly accelerated production of goods. People increasingly worked in factories and lived in cities rather than farming villages. This process, later called the Industrial Revolution, spread from Britain to Europe and America, transforming their societies, generating radical new political and social ideas, and giving Western nations the power and wealth to dominate the world. Other nations, responding to this domination, eventually embraced the new methods and ideas, altering lives and labor the world over.

Early Industrial Regions

The Industrial Revolution in Britain

Industrialization is by no means inevitable. To industrialize, a society needs not only the talent and desire to do so, but also certain key assets. These include a large labor force, ample food to sustain it, abundant raw materials, machines to make them into finished goods, energy to run the machines, receptive markets, reliable transportation, and capital to fund industrial ventures. Before the 19th century, various societies, including China, India, and France, had at times acquired many of these assets and developed thriving commerce. But their economies remained primarily agrarian. Not until the 1800s did economies develop in which most people worked in industry or commerce rather than raise their own food. The first place to develop such an economy was Britain.

Agricultural Advances and Population Growth

Britain's ample food supply was based on agricultural methods earlier developed in the Netherlands. Rather than leave some land untilled each year to regenerate the soil, Dutch and British farmers employed crop rotation, alternating grains such as wheat and barley with soil-enriching crops such as turnips and clover, thereby using all the land every year. By feeding the turnips and clover to sheep and cattle, and selectively breeding these animals to produce larger livestock, farmers likewise increased the meat and dairy supply. More and better-fed animals also produced more manure, which was used to fertilize crops, thus enhancing their yield. These techniques, along with draining of swamps to increase farmland, helped Britain quadruple its food production in the 18th and 19th centuries.

The new techniques helped subvert the age-old system in which peasant families pastured animals and farmed strips of land near their villages in open communal fields, often surplus lands of large landowners who let peasants use them. By the 1700s in Britain, these fields were increasingly closed off to peasants by large landowners who used fences or hedges to enclose the land, initially to pasture their sheep and later to implement the new farming methods on a larger scale. When local peasants objected, the large landowners often got Parliament (which they controlled) to pass laws approving these **enclosures**. Unable to subsist on their own without access to communal lands, many peasants became wage laborers, often working for large landowners engaged in large-scale commercial farming for profit. These workers formed a growing **proletariat**: a large class of landless laborers, many of whom eventually moved to cities to work in urban factories.

Thus enlarged by farmers driven off the land, Britain's urban labor force was also increased by population growth. From 1750 to 1850, despite extensive emigration to America, the British population grew from roughly six million to twenty million—a growth attributed largely to declining childhood mortality. New crops and farming methods provided a stable food supply and healthier diet, and public health advances, such as **vaccination** to immunize people against diseases such as smallpox, helped more children survive to adulthood and have their own children.

Population growth and new farming methods enlarge British labor force

The new farming methods, meanwhile, reduced the need for farmers and farm workers, since large-scale farms could now produce more food with fewer workers. Combined with rising population, the reduced need for farmers added to the numbers of landless poor people willing to work in factories for low wages. Many such people also came from Ireland, where widespread cultivation of the potato, imported from the Americas in the 16th century and capable of feeding more people using less land than grain crops, had also supported a huge population increase. Together these developments supplied a low-cost labor force for Britain's Industrial Revolution.

Cotton and Its Connections

Britain's ready access to vast resources helps to explain why it became the first industrial nation. Especially important were its rich deposits of iron, used to build industrial machines and later railways and bridges, and coal, used to smelt iron into steel and to fuel steam-driven machines. Another key resource, readily available to Britain because of its location and shipping prowess, came not from British mines but from India, Egypt, and American slave plantations.

In the 1700s, British production and use of cotton textiles rapidly expanded. This boom arose partly from convenience and taste: cotton clothes were lighter, cooler, easier to clean, and more comfortable than traditional wool or flax (linen) garments, while dyed and printed calico (cotton cloth from India) was more colorful and attractive. But the boom resulted mainly from mechanization: sturdy cotton fibers worked much better than fragile wool or flax in new machines designed to spin thread. And these machines were central to the Industrial Revolution.

For several centuries, in Western Europe, cloth had been produced through the "putting out" system, often called cottage industry (Chapter 20). Merchant capitalists supplied spinning wheels and weaving looms, along with raw wool or flax, to peasant cottages, where in winter when farm work was light, women spun the fibers into threads that men wove into cloth. This system benefited peasants, who were paid a set price for each piece of cloth produced, and merchant capitalists, who sold it at a profit.

But in the 18th century, cotton transformed this system. In the 1720s, to protect their business from the growing demand for cotton clothes, Britain's wool producers got Parliament to outlaw calico imports from India. So the British East India Company instead shipped from India raw cotton, whose fibers—softer yet tougher than raw wool—soon proved ideal for use in machines. In 1733, British machinist John Kay invented the flying shuttle, a hand-powered weaving device that sped up weaving but also created an imbalance, since now it took several spinners (mostly women) to supply enough thread for one weaver (usually a man). In 1767, to correct the imbalance, English weaver James Hargreaves invented another hand-powered device he called the spinning jenny (after his wife), allowing one woman to spin many threads at a time.

Two years later inventor Richard Arkwright patented the water frame, a water-powered spinning machine, and in 1779 Samuel Crompton devised the spinning mule, a cross between the spinning jenny and water frame. Powered by mill wheels turned by river currents, water frames and spinning mules were far more productive than hand-powered spinning wheels and jennies, but they were also large, complex, and expensive. The workers who ran them could no longer work at home: they had to go to mills and factories built along rivers and owned by wealthy industrialists. This shift from home to factory production marked the onset of the industrial age.

Britain's cotton industry took off, undercutting producers in India and elsewhere whose hand-woven cottons could not compete in quantity or price with machine-made cloth. By 1800, output of cotton textiles in Britain increased 800 percent, and by 1830 they accounted in value for half of all British exports. This boom sparked a huge demand for raw cotton from America, where the cotton gin, invented in 1793 by Eli Whitney to mechanically separate cotton seeds from fibers, had boosted supplies of raw cotton and cut costs. By increasing the profitability of cotton cultivation, however, the cotton gin also increased the demand for slave labor on American plantations. Britain's cotton boom thus expanded slavery in America, where African-Americans were ruthlessly exploited to furnish the precious fibers, and Amerinds were driven from their native lands as cotton cultivation pushed inexorably westward.

Cotton from India helps to transform British textile production

A water frame.

British demand for cotton sustains American slave plantations

Coal, Iron, Steam, and Their Connections

But industry needed more energy than slaves or paid workers could supply, and machines more flexible than water-driven ones that had to be set along rivers. These needs were met by the steam engine, a coal-powered steam-driven machine invented in 1712 by Thomas Newcomen to pump water from mines and improved in the late 1700s by Scottish engineer James Watt.

By 1800 steam engines were used not just in mines but also in factories and foundries, revolutionizing iron production. Employing steam-powered bellows to produce a hotter burn, iron-makers could smelt with coke (made from coal, which was plentiful in England) rather than charcoal (made from wood, which was growing scarce), thereby enhancing both quality and fuel supply. By using steam-driven hammers and rollers, manufacturers could now shape iron and steel for countless uses, including improved steam engines

Steam engines transform iron production and transportation

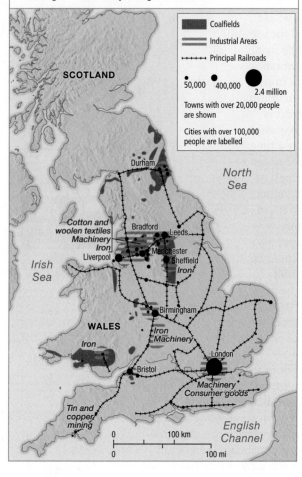

MAP **27.1** Industrial Development in England by 1840

England took advantage of many assets to become the first industrialized nation. Notice that its railway network linked coal-fields with industrial areas and factory towns. Why did these towns grow dramatically during industrialization?

and other machinery. Factories using these engines were built in towns and cities, which grew rapidly as people moved there from rural regions to find work (Map 27.1).

Steam engines also supplied a new means of transport. As an island nation with a large ocean fleet, navigable rivers, and numerous canals built mainly in the 1700s, Britain was already well equipped to ship goods and resources by water. But land transportation was still very slow and costly. In 1801, however, a mechanical engineer named Richard Trevithick invented a steam-powered carriage, and by the 1820s George Stephenson, another English engineer, developed a locomotive that ran on sturdy rails forged in iron foundries. In 1825, when a rail line linked Stockton coalfield to the town of Darlington, the railway era was born. Within decades, Britain was crisscrossed with railroads on which trains carried freight efficiently—and passengers at exhilarating speeds approaching a mile a minute. The blend of speed and power captured the public fancy, and railways became the sinews and symbols of the industrial age.

The new engines even transformed water transport. By the 1840s, British steamships with metal hulls were replacing sailing ships on the seas, while steamboats were traveling up and down inland rivers. No longer dependent on winds and currents, vessels now ran on fixed schedules, greatly reducing the duration and uncertainty of water travel.

Industrial Britain: Workshop of the World

As a prosperous country with a global empire extending from Canada to India and Australia, Britain already had large markets for its goods at home and abroad. But industry, by producing abundant low-cost goods, opened new mass markets. Historically, for example, unless they were wealthy, families made their own clothes, and underwear was a luxury reserved for the rich. Now, as textile mills produced more and more cheap cotton clothing, more and more people could afford more and more clothes, vastly increasing both market size and industrial profits.

Low-cost cotton textiles generate mass markets

These profits in turn expanded capital for industrial investment, supported by England's strong banking and credit institutions. Using profits from their agricultural estates, many British nobles invested in industry, as did merchants and bankers seeking greater wealth and power. Their resources, along with vast fortunes made in textile mills, helped finance the huge start-up costs of iron and railway industries. Industrialization thus produced enormous wealth and a powerful new class of industrial capitalists.

In 1851 an Exhibition of the Works of Industry of All Nations opened in London, with hundreds of machines displayed in a Crystal

The Crystal Palace.

Palace built of iron and glass. Millions came to marvel at Britain's industrial accomplishments. By then Britain had the world's strongest economy, producing over half of its iron and cotton goods and two-thirds of its coal. Once scorned by Napoleon as a "nation of shopkeepers," industrial Britain had become the "workshop of the world."

View the **Image**
Architectural Iron Works
on **myhistorylab.com**

Industry's Early Spread and Social Impact

Britain's industrial superiority did not last. Eager to duplicate British success, industries elsewhere imported British capital and machinery, copied British ideas, and hired British engineers. Envious of Britain's wealth and power, governments elsewhere created and assisted industries, built railways to enhance commerce, and imposed tariffs (surcharges on foreign imports) to protect their industries from foreign competition. By the second half of the 19th century, industry was expanding in Western Europe and North America and altering economies in much of the rest of the world.

Industrialization in Europe and North America

First to industrialize after Britain was the southern Netherlands, which in 1831 became the Kingdom of Belgium. Longtime leaders of craftsmanship and banking, Belgians benefited from early agricultural advances, large coal and iron deposits, and ready access to workers and technology from nearby Britain. Starting in the 1830s, Belgium's government built railways, while Belgian banks provided credit to finance industrial ventures. For most of the 19th century, Belgium ranked second to Britain in industry.

France, long Europe's wealthiest nation, initially lagged behind. In the late 1700s and early 1800s, France lacked both the political stability and the large iron and coal supplies needed to industrialize. But in the mid-1800s, government subsidies for railways and industries, iron and coal discoveries in Alsace-Lorraine in northeast France, and an influx of workers from Britain fueled French industrial expansion. By 1900, France was one of Europe's industrial leaders.

Industrialization spreads to Belgium and France

German industry at first was hampered by disunity: the dozens of independent German states each had their own tariffs and economic policies, hindering trade and preventing the development of a national German economy. A customs union, or *Zollverein* (*TSAWL-fuh-rīn*), initiated by Prussia in 1818 and expanded across Germany in 1834, reduced this problem by eliminating tariffs among many German states. Later, after political unification in 1871, Germany industrialized rapidly. Government support for railways (built partly to aid troop movements), a compulsory education system that supplied a literate workforce, and laws enabling corporations to collaborate in setting prices and production quotas boosted Germany's industrial output. By the early 1900s, it surpassed even that of Britain.

German customs union fosters industry and national unity

By then other nations, including Italy, Austria, Russia, and Japan, were also industrializing (Map 27.2). But world industrial leadership was shifting to North America, where a new industrial giant was surpassing all the others. The United States of America, a huge nation that by 1850 had expanded across the continent, had enormous assets and boundless industrial potential. In the early 1800s, as the North began to industrialize, the South remained largely agrarian, prospering on slave-grown cotton for British textile mills and blocking federal government support for northern industries (Chapter 28). The ensuing civil war (1861–1865), won by the North, opened the way for stunning industrial growth. Aided by vast natural resources, a government that now supported industry, and a huge labor force expanded by massive immigration from Europe, U.S. manufacturing soared. By 1914 the United States was far and away the world's industrial leader.

Industry spreads to Italy, Austria, Russia, Japan, and North America

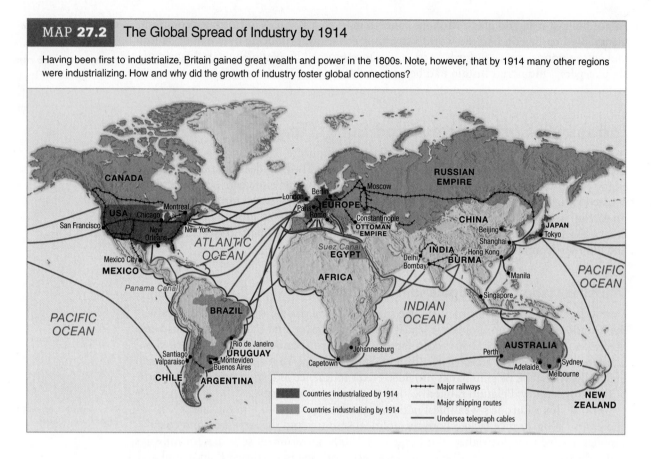

MAP 27.2 The Global Spread of Industry by 1914

Having been first to industrialize, Britain gained great wealth and power in the 1800s. Note, however, that by 1914 many other regions were industrializing. How and why did the growth of industry foster global connections?

Mechanization and Urbanization

Industry transformed society everywhere it took hold. The lives of common people, centered for centuries on farms and families, came to be dominated by machines, located largely in urban factories. More and more people moved to cities to take factory jobs, disrupting age-old working and living patterns.

One key aspect of industry was mechanization. Machines replaced people and steam replaced muscle in manufacturing goods. The machines were marvelous mechanisms, multiplying the goods produced while reducing their cost. But machines were also large and expensive, too big for the average home, and far beyond the average family's means. Machines were thus installed in factories, rather than homes and workshops, so workers had to go to factories to do their jobs.

For ten thousand years, since the origins of agriculture, most people's life and labor had been governed by the seasons and the sun. Farmers and artisans could work at their own speed and set their own schedules. Work, home, and family were intertwined.

But the factory system subjected workers to a burdensome new discipline. They had to be at work by a set time each morning, when the work whistle sounded. They worked long hours at repetitive tasks, with machinery dictating their pace, and coal-fired steam engines fouling the air they breathed. Work was hazardous, injuries were common, and breaks were few until the evening whistle blew. Machines seemed to run the workers' lives.

Workers also lost connection with the things they made. Traditional artisans and villagers could take pride in what they produced with their hands, but factory workers running machines were alienated from the results of their work. They might make just

Machines come to dominate factory workers' lives

one part—such as soles for a shoe—and never see the whole finished product. Often they felt like servants to machines.

The machines, of course, furnished employment, as the new factory system provided jobs for millions. Work was long, pay was low, and conditions often dangerous. But in an age of rapid population growth and declining need for farm labor, workers had little alternative.

Nor did they have job security. Machinery created many jobs, but it also took some away. In the 1780s, for example, as early British spinning machines produced abundant thread, handloom weavers who made thread into cloth were in great demand. As pay and status grew, thousands joined this profitable trade. But a new power loom, invented by Edmund Cartwright in 1785 and improved a few decades later, eventually displaced the handloom weavers. As wages fell and jobs vanished, numerous proud, once-prosperous men were destitute.

Weavers were not the only casualties of industry. In trade after trade, machines replaced skilled artisans, who thus could no longer earn a living from their traditional crafts. Blaming machines for their plight, some displaced workers, such as the Luddites described at the start of this chapter, attacked factories and machines in England and elsewhere.

Industry also brought mass dislocation and urbanization. As millions of people moved from farming villages to live near the factories that employed them, small towns grew into large cities around these factories. In the 1770s, Britain had four cities with over fifty thousand people; by the 1850s it had more than thirty. Manchester, a booming new factory town, grew in these years from twenty-five thousand to five hundred thousand people. By 1900 over half of England's people lived in cities and towns, compared with one in six a century earlier. As industry spread to Europe, America, and elsewhere, other countries, too, experienced urbanization.

Conditions in early factory towns were appalling. Families were crammed into tenements or shacks, often in one room, with dozens sharing an outhouse. Narrow, muddy streets and tiny courtyards teemed with garbage and sewage, which attracted rats and bred disease. Water from street-side pipes was often impure, and air was polluted with soot and steam from the factories.

Machines create new jobs but displace skilled artisans

Towns and cities grow as masses move there for factory jobs

((•—[Listen to the **Audio**
Industrial Revolution
on **myhistorylab.com**

Industry disrupts and divides families

Family and Society in the Industrial Age

Industry's impact on family and society was immense. As millions of people raised in rural villages were uprooted and relocated in crowded and alien cities, age-old social and family structures started to break down.

Long accustomed to working as a unit in their cottages and fields, family members now labored separately in factories or mines—often on different shifts, 12–14 hours a day, six days a week. Men, traditionally expected to support their families, typically took the better-paying jobs such as weaving and metalwork. But many early industries hired women and children, since they would work for much less than men. Women, as traditional spinners of thread, were employed in large numbers in early textile mills, usually at very low wages. Children, whose small size made them useful in narrow mineshafts and cramped factory settings, were paid even less.

Industry thus disrupted the functioning of families. Unlike rural mothers who mostly worked at home, mothers in factories could not take breaks to rest during pregnancy, nurse babies, tend children, or care for household needs. Fathers working long hours

Women workers in a British cotton mill.

Young boy at work in a textile mill.

Crowded in cities, workers connect as an exploited class

((•—[Listen to the **Audio**

Urbanization

on **myhistorylab.com**

Urban advances and factory reforms improve working-class lives

Urban street scene.

in factories were often unable or unwilling to help with the young ones. Many working-class parents, rather than leave their children untended, sent them to work in mines or mills, sometimes at ages as young as seven or eight. Eventually, however, the social dynamics of industrial cities, where poverty and affluence existed side by side, inspired efforts to end such abuses.

Peasant farmers had often been impoverished, and many historians hold that urban workers were initially no worse off—and eventually better off—than their rural cousins. But country folk, scattered in small villages, had little contact with others in their situation and were largely unseen by urban elites. Now industrial cities highlighted the gulf between rich and poor, creating a new class consciousness among both "haves" and "have-nots." Crowded in squalid cities with thousands in the same predicament, workers and their families identified as an exploited class—the urban proletariat. Increasingly aware of their vast numbers, they banded together to improve their lives, forming labor unions, organizing strikes, and staging demonstrations to enforce their demands.

Though residing in the same cities, the workers and the urban middle classes—often called the bourgeoisie—seemed to live in different worlds. In working-class areas, drunkenness, gambling, and promiscuity were common among the poorly fed and poorly educated people. In middle-class neighborhoods, well-fed people lived in tidy, well-furnished homes, husbands went to work in suits, wives stayed home to manage the household, and children attended fine schools.

Since they shared the same towns, however, rich and poor could not ignore each other. Envious of middle-class comforts and politicized by emerging labor movements, workers pushed for urban reforms. Appalled by the squalor surrounding them and fearful of urban crime and disease, many members of the bourgeoisie eventually supported such reforms.

Over time, as a result, urban conditions improved. Underground sewers, water sanitizing systems, indoor plumbing, and garbage collections helped curb filth and disease. Electric generators, developed in the 1830s by England's Michael Faraday, eventually powered trams and trolleys to transport urban dwellers and—after America's Thomas Edison invented the incandescent lamp in 1879—electric streetlights to light their way at night. Police forces protected people from crime, school systems educated their children, and urban parks provided recreation. Although slums, crime, and pollution still plagued industrial cities, by the early 1900s many were quite livable.

Factory conditions also improved. Governments passed laws to limit work hours, improve safety, ensure regular pay, and correct abuses. Wages steadily increased, while mass production of low-cost goods made them increasingly affordable to working-class families, helping millions lead more comfortable lives.

Women, however, gained little. Indeed, as women's employment in factories came to be seen as exploitative and threatening to the family, women's work outside the home became increasingly unfashionable. Especially in urban middle classes, but even among working classes, husbands came to consider themselves failures if their wives worked for wages. Labor thus divided along gender lines, with husbands going to work by day while wives stayed home to tend the children and household. This arrangement freed women from the need to get jobs but also deprived them of the chance to do so, leaving wives financially dependent on their husbands.

Industry exploits and marginalizes women

New Ideas and Ideologies

Faced with the transforming effects of the Atlantic and Industrial Revolutions, Europeans sought new ideas to explain the new realities. Supporters of the old order, determined to retain past structures and ways, were called **conservatives**—also called the *right* because of where their delegates sat in France's National Assembly. Advocates of change—also called the *left* for the same reason—developed new **ideologies**, systems of thought intended to explain and transform society in accordance with certain political, social, and cultural ideals. Dominant among them, in Europe and later elsewhere, were liberalism, socialism, nationalism, and romanticism.

Liberalism and Socialism

Liberalism, as its name implies, was based on the concept of liberty. Its political values, arising from the Enlightenment and Atlantic Revolutions, called for constitutional governments (limited monarchies or republics) with restricted powers, elected legislatures, and safeguards protecting people's rights. It stressed individualism and individual rights, championed career advancement based on talent rather than birth, and generally reflected the values of the bourgeoisie. Early liberals favored limited democracy, with voting rights for middle-class men who had some wealth or property and education, but not necessarily for women or working-class men.

Liberals promote political and economic freedom

In economics, liberals were disciples of Scottish economist Adam Smith (Chapter 24) and promoters of free-market capitalism. To them competition was the key to prosperity, encouraging manufacturers to produce high-quality goods at low prices to outsell competitors in an open market. Liberals thus urged governments to take a hands-off, *laissez-faire* approach to the economy, letting the forces of supply and demand regulate production and prices. Some liberal economists even saw poverty as inevitable: Thomas Malthus claimed population always grew to the point where there was not enough food for everyone, while David Ricardo's "iron law of wages" said population growth always drove down workers' pay to bare survival levels. Liberals' support for limited government, elected assemblies, individual rights, and free-market economies placed them in opposition to authoritarian governments everywhere.

Read the **Document**

Thomas Malthus, Excerpt from Essay on the Principle of Population

on **myhistorylab.com**

Read the **Document**

David Ricardo, On Wages, "The Iron Law of Wages"

on **myhistorylab.com**

Socialism was in many ways the antithesis of liberalism. While liberals favored liberty, socialists stressed equality, asserting that freedom meant little to those who had no means to enjoy it, and advocating more equitable allocation of society's wealth. Repulsed by the gulf between rich and poor, socialists sought to redistribute income, improve workers' wages, enrich their lives, and enhance their political power. While liberals prized individualism, socialists valued community, with people sharing resources and duties. While liberals praised competition, socialists extolled cooperation, encouraging collective work for the common good and rejecting capitalism as promoting selfishness and greed. While liberals advocated *laissez-faire* governance, socialists demanded public welfare policies to support the poor.

Socialists promote political, social, and economic equality

Some early socialists formed model communities based on these ideals. Robert Owen, a wealthy British industrialist who had worked as a child in a textile mill, created a model factory town at New Lanarck in Scotland, paying good wages and providing workers with decent housing, schools, and stores that sold low-cost goods. Later he founded a short-lived

Karl Marx.

Communists promote
working-class revolution

cooperative community at New Harmony in Indiana. Charles Fourier (*foor-YĀ*), an eccentric French idealist, promoted "phalansteries," communities of 1,620 people, with each member doing a job he or she enjoyed. Although such communities rarely lasted long, they reflected a widespread reaction against the worst aspects of industrialization.

Other socialists, called **Communists**, promoted violent overthrow of the existing order. In 1844 Friedrich Engels, son of a wealthy German industrialist, published *The Condition of the Working Class in England*, a fierce critique accusing capitalists of mass exploitation and murder. Four years later he joined with Karl Marx, son of a German lawyer, to write the *Communist Manifesto*, a ringing, radical pamphlet urging "working-men of all countries" to unite in a "communist revolution" (see "Excerpts from the *Communist Manifesto*").

According to Marx and Engels, societies pitted rich against poor in ongoing class struggles. The basis of any society was its economy, so the class controlling the economic resources also controlled the political, legal, religious, and military institutions. In pre-industrial Europe, for example, the economy was based on agriculture, so the main resource was land. Those who controlled it—the nobles—were the government officials, judges, church leaders, and military officers. But in industrial economies, the main resources were factories, and economic life was centered in cities. So the bourgeoisie became the dominant class, taking charge of politics, law, and religion. But the bourgeoisie inadvertently promoted its own demise: by bringing the workers together in factories and cities to exploit them, it united them as an exploited class. Eventually this huge new class, the urban proletariat, would overthrow the bourgeoisie, establish a pro-letarian dictatorship, and create a classless socialist society.

Communism, also called Marxism, provided a compelling explanation for industrial Europe's turmoil, and a vision of a brighter future for the exploited masses. It gained many followers, attracting idealists, radicals, and workers. The *Manifesto* claimed, in 1848, that Europe was haunted by the specter of Communism. That specter eventually haunted the whole world.

Nationalism and Romanticism

Far more pervasive than Communism was **nationalism**, an intense devotion to one's own cultural-linguistic group, and to its embodiment in a unified, independent state. In the 1780s Johann Herder, a German Protestant pastor, reacting against widespread emulation of French ideals, asserted that Germans must develop their own national identity. Each nationality, he declared, had its own unique *Volksgeist* (*FŌLKS-gīst*), or "people's spirit," rooted in its language, literature, customs, and culture. Although Herder did not regard one nation's spirit as better than others, later German thinkers viewed the German *Volksgeist* as nobler than the rest.

Meanwhile, the French Revolution, in undermining monarchy, helped to transfer people's allegiance from the person of the ruler to the abstract concept of the nation. *La Marseillaise* (*mahr-sā-YEHZ*), a stirring new French anthem composed in 1792, appealed to the people not as subjects of the king but as "children of the fatherland," urging them to unite in shedding the "impure blood" of "savage" foreign invaders. Although Napoleon, a Corsican by birth, banned this anthem when he became French emperor, he fostered France's national pride by conquering most of Europe. Then, to his dismay, other Europeans rallied their own national pride to fight against him. Russian resistance to his 1812 invasion was called the Great Fatherland War, and his 1813 defeat at Leipzig was known as the Battle of the Nations.

The Industrial Revolution, by moving rural people to cities and towns, also promoted national awareness. People increasingly identified with their nation, rather

DOCUMENT 27.1 Excerpts from the *Communist Manifesto*

According to the Communist Manifesto, first published in 1848, industrialization divided society into two hostile classes: the bourgeoisie, a small group of wealthy people who controlled the means of production, and the proletariat, a huge group of very poor people who worked in urban industry and were exploited by the bourgeoisie. What were the main views, values, and goals expressed in the Manifesto?

A spectre is haunting Europe—the spectre of communism . . .

It is high time that Communists should . . . publish their views, . . . and meet this nursery tale of the spectre of communism with a manifesto of the party itself . . .

The history of all hitherto existing society is the history of class struggles. Freeman and slave, patrician and plebian, lord and serf, guild-master and journeyman, in a word, oppressor and oppressed, stood in constant opposition to one another . . .

The modern bourgeois society . . . has not done away with class antagonisms. It has but established new classes, new conditions of oppression, new forms of struggle . . . Our epoch, the epoch of the bourgeoisie, possesses, however, this distinct feature: it has simplified class antagonisms. Society as a whole is more and more splitting up into two great hostile camps . . .— bourgeoisie and proletariat . . .

The bourgeoisie . . . has played a most revolutionary part . . .

The bourgeoisie has subjected the country to the rule of the towns. It has created enormous cities, has greatly increased the urban population . . ., and has thus rescued a considerable part of the population from the idiocy of rural life . . .

The bourgeoisie keeps more and more doing away with the scattered state of the population, of the means of production, and of property. It has agglomerated population, centralized the means of production, and has concentrated property in a few hands . . .

The bourgeoisie . . . has created more . . . colossal productive forces than have all preceding generations together. Subjection of nature's forces to man, machinery, application of chemistry to industry and agriculture, steam navigation, railways, electric telegraphs, clearing of whole continents for cultivation . . .

Modern bourgeois society, . . . a society that has conjured up such gigantic means of production and of exchange, is like the sorcerer who is no longer able to control the powers . . . he has called up by his spells . . . [N]ot only has the bourgeoisie forged the weapons that bring death to itself; it has also called into existence the men who are to wield those weapons—the modern working class—the proletarians . . .

At this stage, the laborers still form an incoherent mass scattered over the whole country . . .

But with the development of industry, the proletariat not only increases in number; it becomes concentrated in greater masses, its strength grows, and it feels that strength more . . .

The advance of industry . . . replaces the isolation of the laborers . . . by the revolutionary combination . . . What the bourgeoisie therefore produces, above all, are its own grave-diggers. Its fall and the victory of the proletariat are equally inevitable . . .

. . . The immediate aim of the Communists is . . . : Formation of the proletariat into a class, overthrow of the bourgeois supremacy, conquest of political power by the proletariat . . .

In short, the Communists everywhere support every revolutionary movement against the existing social and political order . . .

The Communists disdain to conceal their views and aims. They openly declare that their ends can be attained only by the forcible overthrow of all existing social conditions. Let the ruling classes tremble at a communist revolution. The proletarians have nothing to lose but their chains. They have a world to win.

Proletarians of all countries, unite!

SOURCE: Karl Marx and Frederick Engels, *Manifesto of the Communist Party* (1848) http://www.anu.edu/polsci/arx/clasics/manifesto.html

than their clan or village, as public education, newspapers, and elections broadened their knowledge of national issues. Playing on this growing national pride among an expanding electorate, politicians sought to win mass support with patriotic rhetoric and forceful foreign policies backed by strong standing armies.

Nationalists promote unified, independent national states

Nationalists idealized the nation-state, a political domain embracing all who shared a common language, heritage, culture, and ethnicity. In practice this ideal often meant oppression, exclusion, or forced assimilation of ethnic and religious minorities who did not fully "fit." Among Germans and Italians, whose lands were divided into numerous small states, nationalism manifested itself as a crusade for unification. Among subject nationalities, such as Irish, Hungarians, and Poles, it took the form of a quest for liberation. The goal, however, was the same: self-rule for each national group in a unified, strong, and independent homeland.

Romantics stress emotion, passion, heroism, nature, and beauty

Romanticism, like nationalism a reaction against the Enlightenment, was a cultural movement pervading Western art, literature, poetry, and music in the late 1700s and early 1800s. Rejecting the Enlightenment's intense rationalism, romantics stressed emotion, passion, exuberance, heroism, and the beauty of nature. French novelist Victor Hugo wrote works such as *Les Miserables* (*la mēē-zeh-RAH-bl'*) and *The Hunchback of Notre Dame,* full of sweeping drama and pathos. German painter Caspar Friedrich captured on canvas the wonder and power of nature, while French artist Eugène Delacroix (*oo-ZHEN deh-lah-KWAH*) dramatized the passion and heroism of the masses in paintings such as *Liberty Leading the People.* In music, the age's dominant figure was German composer Ludwig von Beethoven (*BĀ-tō-ven*), whose work deeply stirred the romantic soul. His Third Symphony, the *Eroica* (*ā-RŌ-ē-kah*), written for Napoleon, glorified heroism, while his Sixth celebrated nature. And the stunning climax of his splendid Ninth Symphony was a rousing choral rendition of the *Ode to Joy,* an exuberant romantic verse by German poet Friedrich Schiller.

Liberty Leading the People, by Delacroix.

Although primarily cultural, romanticism was sometimes linked with nationalism and revolution. The brothers Jacob and Wilhelm Grimm, to promote German national heritage, collected and published German folk stories as *Grimms' Fairy Tales.* Walter Scott, in novels and narrative poems, celebrated heroes and events of Scotland's past, thereby evoking Scottish national pride. William Wordsworth, England's exuberant poet of nature, spent a year in revolutionary France and later wrote: "Bliss was it in that dawn to be alive, But to be young was very heaven!" And his countryman Lord Byron, a talented poet and satirist, died in Greece while striving to help it gain national independence.

English novelist Mary Wollstonecraft Shelley blended ideology and industry. Her mother, Mary Wollstonecraft, author of *Vindication of the Rights of Women,* was a forerunner of modern feminism (Chapter 24). Her husband, Percy Bysshe Shelley, was a romantic poet whose works included "Ode to the West Wind," which exalted the power of both nature and revolution. And Mary Shelley herself wrote *Frankenstein,* the tale of a scientist who creates from lifeless matter an uncontrollable monster, symbolizing both the promise and peril of industry and technology.

The European Impact of Industry and Ideology

The Atlantic and Industrial Revolutions, and the ideologies they spawned, created in Europe a cataclysmic clash between past and future. Despite conservative efforts to preserve the past, the forces of change, relentless as the West Wind in Percy Shelley's poem and frightful as Frankenstein's monster in Mary Shelley's novel, could not be completely contained.

Reform and Revolution in Europe, 1832–1849

In Britain, where industrialization caused mass dislocation, Parliament sought to prevent rebellion by enacting reforms. The Reform Act of 1832, passed under pressure from the king, who was frightened by urban riots, shifted seats in the House of Commons from depopulated rural areas to new industrial towns and extended voting rights to urban middle classes. The Factory Acts of 1833 and 1847 restricted child labor and corrected other abuses, relieving some of the workers' distress.

Tensions nonetheless remained. In 1838, a coalition of liberals and industrialists began to press for repeal of the Corn Laws, which protected landed nobles from foreign competition by restricting grain imports from abroad. By keeping food prices high, however, these laws compelled industrialists to pay higher wages so workers could feed their families, leading to a clash between the old agrarian and new urban economic interests.

Parliament's landed nobles at first resisted reform, but their efforts were undermined by disaster in Ireland, where the potato crop had become the primary source of sustenance. In 1845 and 1846 a blight that devastated this crop led to mass starvation. At least a million Irish people died, while two million others fled to the United States, Canada, Australia, and Britain's factory towns. Faced with this human catastrophe, and fearful that it could raise prices and cause starvation in England, in 1846 Prime Minister Robert Peel got Parliament to revoke the Corn Laws, thus allowing both England and Ireland to import cheap foreign grain. Since bad Irish roads hindered grain distribution, this liberal victory did not at once end the Irish famine, but it did advance free trade, henceforth a central principle of Britain's liberal economy.

Irish famine brings mass starvation and prompts migration to America

Meanwhile, the working class was pushing for electoral power. In 1838 a "People's Charter," drafted by reformers later called Chartists, promoted **universal male suffrage** (voting rights for all men), secret ballots, annual elections, equal electoral districts, an end to property qualifications for membership in Parliament, and pay for its members so workers could afford to serve. But Britain's bourgeoisie, having recently won some power, were not prepared to share it with proletarians. Three times in the next ten years, the Charter was sent to Parliament, with petitions bearing from one million to five million signatures. Each time it was rejected, and in 1848 it was discredited when Parliament declared most of the signatures invalid. The spirit of Chartism nonetheless endured: over the next six decades, most of its demands were enacted into law.

Chartists promote full political democracy

France, meanwhile, with its own parliamentary monarchy, was also becoming an industrial society. King Louis Philippe (1830–1848), backed by the bourgeoisie, acted like one of them. Wearing a business suit and black coat, he walked to work from his apartment and backed policies supporting French industry. Aware that industry needed literate workers, his government enacted an Education Law in 1833, requiring each community to have a school. A Child Labor Law of 1841 banned factory work by children under 8 and obliged working children between 8 and 12 to also attend school. But such reforms did not prevent revolution.

French reforms advance education and curb child labor

In 1848, liberal and nationalist revolutions rocked France and Central Europe (Map 27.3). Governments toppled like buildings in an earthquake, while riots raged in the streets of major cities. For a while it seemed that liberalism and nationalism would triumph, but in time most revolts were crushed by conservatives who controlled the armies, while the middle classes were stunned into submission by the brutal spectacle in the streets.

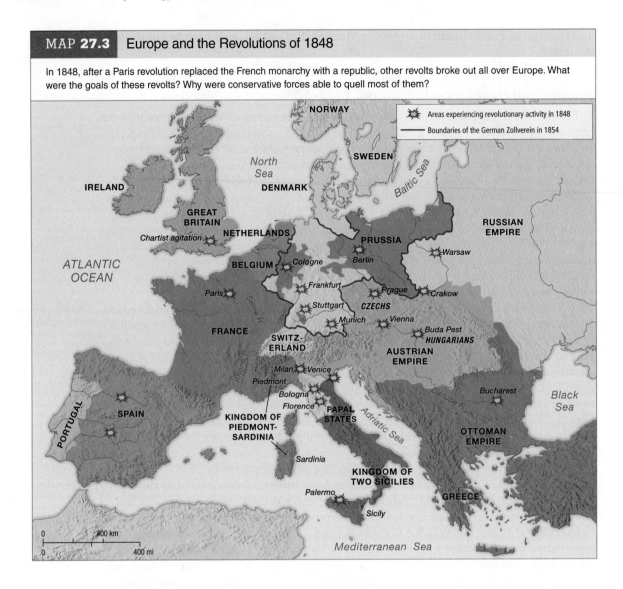

MAP **27.3** Europe and the Revolutions of 1848

In 1848, after a Paris revolution replaced the French monarchy with a republic, other revolts broke out all over Europe. What were the goals of these revolts? Why were conservative forces able to quell most of them?

The first revolt came in France, where economic depression and high unemployment fueled discontent among workers. In February 1848, facing mass protests, Louis Philippe summoned the National Guard to keep order. But the guards, drawn mostly from the working classes, rioted against the bourgeois regime. Intimidated by the rioters, the king abdicated, and the legislature declared a republic based on universal male suffrage.

1848 French Revolution produces Second Republic

The Second French Republic, like the first one in the 1790s, was turbulent. Prompted by socialist minister Louis Blanc, it started state-funded National Workshops to employ the jobless and held elections for an assembly to draft a new constitution. But conservatives, who won these elections because voters resented new taxes imposed by the new government, soon ended the workshops, leading to renewed worker riots in Paris. After the bloody repression of these riots, the assembly approved a constitution creating a powerful presidency. In December 1848, voters elected to this office Napoleon's nephew, Louis-Napoleon Bonaparte, whose name reminded them of France's glory days.

Nationalist revolts in Central Europe are defeated

France's uprising sent shock waves through Central Europe, where nationalism more than liberalism triggered upheavals. Inspired by events in Paris, Hungarians, Italians, and Czechs in the Austrian Empire rebelled for independence, while students and workers fought soldiers in Vienna, the imperial capital. But Austria was not yet industrialized, so its working class was too small to sustain the revolt. The army soon crushed all rebels except the Hungarians, who resisted until Austria's rulers finally asked Russia for help. Fearful that revolution might spread to his country, the Russian tsar sent a hundred thousand troops, repressing the Hungarian rebels in 1849.

In the German states, rebels fought for a united Germany under a liberal constitution. After riots in Berlin forced the frightened king of Prussia to promise a constitution, the German states sent delegates to an assembly in Frankfurt to discuss unification. The Frankfurt Assembly drafted a liberal constitution for a unified German Empire, offering the post of emperor to the Prussian king. But the conservative king, disdaining the liberal delegates, pointedly declined "to pick up a crown from the gutter" and later sent Prussia's army to disperse the assembly.

Liberalism, Nationalism, and Industrial Growth, 1850–1914

These setbacks destroyed neither liberalism nor nationalism. From 1850 to 1914, industry and ideologies made inroads all across Europe.

PROSPERITY AND REFORM IN BRITAIN. In the mid-1800s, Britain was the world's main industrial power. It also stood as an example of successful governance, as Parliament prudently enacted reforms to avoid the sort of uprisings that shook much of Europe. But in the early 1900s, Britain's stability was shaken by unrest among its workers, its women, and its Irish subjects.

Between 1850 and 1880, Britain produced 50 percent of the world's iron, steel, and cotton goods, 66 percent of its coal, and 40 percent of its machinery. English entrepreneurs built railways and bridges in Britain, South Asia, Latin America, and Africa. Until the century's last decades, when Germany and the United States emerged as formidable competitors, Britain dominated global markets in chemicals, machine tools, and electrical goods.

British dominate global trade and enhance global connections

Britain's great industrial age coincided with the reign of Queen Victoria (1837–1901), who gave her name to the "Victorian Era" and its prevailing values. Victorian morality focused on family and formation of individual character. Bible reading, prayer, Sunday worship, and strict parental discipline taught Britons to believe that God was on their side and that they must serve him by leading righteous lives. These values were typically fostered by mothers, who dominated home and family life, while men dominated the world of work outside the home.

Victorians praised, and often practiced, sobriety, diligence, and hard work. The upper and middle classes, perceiving the poor as drunken and dissolute, attributed these conditions to poverty itself and sought to alleviate them with charity and philanthropy. Organizations such as the Salvation Army and Methodist Church tried to turn the poor to God by preaching temperance and providing social assistance. Victorians taught their children to play fair, serve others, control their sexual desires, and lead good moral lives.

Victorian values combat poverty and immorality

Victorian morality thus helped reduce poverty and unrest in England's industrial cities. Private charity and government reforms helped improve working-class conditions, while growing prosperity raised living standards for all but the very poor. As workers demanded more democratic rights, Parliament passed the Reform Act of 1867, tripling the size of the electorate by extending voting rights to urban working-class males. Then, aware that electoral success now depended on working-class votes, Parliament legalized labor unions in 1871 and four years later permitted workers to picket during strikes. The subsequent growth of labor unions dramatically improved wages and working conditions. British workers now had an alternative to Marxist revolution: peaceful reform through parliamentary action, collective bargaining, and strikes. And Parliament had learned it could maintain stability by meeting working-class demands.

In the early 1900s, however, instability resurfaced. Britain's economic growth slowed, as Germans and Americans overcame its lead and cut in on its trade. After rising 35 percent from 1870 to 1900, real wages in Britain fell by 8 percent from 1900 to 1914, triggering worker unrest. From 1911 to 1914, led by radical labor leaders, workers staged massive strikes, bringing modest gains in wages and working conditions, but disrupting Britain's troubled economy.

Labor unions improve workers' lot, but unrest rises after 1900

Meanwhile, supporters of **women's suffrage**, a movement that worked for years to gain voting rights for women, lost patience with the legislative process. Dismayed that Parliament gave the vote to most males while refusing it to females, some women turned to violence. Beginning in 1910, activists known as suffragists, led by Emmeline Pankhurst and her daughters Sylvia and Christabel, planted bombs, vandalized museums, set fires, and staged hunger strikes when arrested. In 1913, to dramatize her crusade, a suffragist threw herself under the racing horses' hoofs at England's famous Epsom Derby. These methods called attention to the suffragist cause, but British women did not get the vote until after the Great War.

Suffragists press forcefully for women's voting rights

Suffragist parade.

Even more unsettling was the **Irish Home Rule** movement. Angered by centuries of British rule, Irish Nationalists, mostly Catholic, demanded domestic self-governance. Britain's Liberal Party took their side and finally got an Irish Home Rule Bill through Parliament in 1914. But Protestants in northern Ireland rebelled against the prospect of being ruled by Ireland's Catholic majority, and by summer 1914 Ireland verged on civil war. The outbreak of the Great War that August (Chapter 31) delayed resolution of the issue. But in 1921 most of Ireland became an independent Irish Free State, while Northern Ireland remained part of Britain's United Kingdom.

Irish Home Rule Movement divides Britain and Ireland

EMPIRE AND REPUBLIC IN FRANCE. The years 1850 to 1914 were difficult for France. Its government alternated between republic and empire, while its industrial growth, though impressive, lagged behind that of Britain, Germany, and the United States. And a series of diplomatic and military setbacks cost France the dominant position it had long held in Continental Europe.

The unwitting agent of France's undoing was Louis-Napoleon Bonaparte, nephew of the great Napoleon. As president of the Second French Republic (1848–1852), he consolidated control by pleasing business leaders and Catholics, while also showing sympathy for workers, presenting himself as a compassionate idealist with moderately socialistic views. But the constitution did not permit reelection, so in December 1851, after a skillful propaganda campaign depicting him as the only alternative to radicalism and chaos, he overthrew the Second Republic. The next year he formed a Second Empire with himself as Emperor Napoleon III (not Napoleon II, since the heir to that title, Napoleon I's son, had died in exile in 1832).

Napoleon III ends France's Republic and forms its Second Empire

Napoleon III then enacted a comprehensive modernization program, based on state support for business and industry. His government subsidized telegraph lines and canals, regulated railways, limited Sunday labor, cleared slums, beautified Paris, and enacted Europe's first pure food and drug laws. His efforts fueled a decade-long economic boom, in which French productivity grew more rapidly than that of any other nation.

Like his uncle Napoleon I, Napoleon III was repressive. He curbed freedom of the press, banned public political debate, and manipulated legislators by adjusting their pay. His regime was a dictatorship, led by a man who suppressed dissent and enacted popular reforms. As long as prosperity lasted, however, he enjoyed broad support.

Napoleon III combines popular reforms and repression

But prosperity did not last. By 1862 the American Civil War was depriving French textile mills of cotton from southern states and restricting the rich U.S. market for French exports, hurting France's economy and its emperor's popularity. His reputation was also hurt by the Maximilian Affair, a rash attempt to create a French satellite empire in Mexico under Austrian archduke Maximilian. Battled by Mexican patriots and weakened by French problems supporting an army overseas, the Mexican empire fell in 1867 after the United States, no longer distracted by its civil war, pressured Napoleon III to withdraw his forces.

A far more fatal blunder was Napoleon's failure to block Prussia's move to unify Germany. Assuming that Austria would defeat Prussia in an 1866 war, he failed to support Austria and then watched victorious Prussia unite all northern Germany. Belatedly seeing his mistake, Napoleon led his army against Prussia in the Franco-Prussian War (1870–1871) but was captured in combat, ending the Second French Empire. Paris demonstrations then led to creation of a Third French Republic, but it surrendered in 1871. Prussia established a unified German Empire, which annexed France's rich Alsace-Lorraine region and replaced France as Europe's dominant power.

Franco-Prussian War ends Second Empire and brings in Third Republic

Defeat left France in turmoil. Radical socialists in Paris formed a revolutionary regime called the Paris Commune, which governed the city from March until May of 1871, when the Third Republic's forces crushed it, killing more than twenty-five thousand people. For the next twenty years, monarchists intrigued against the Third Republic, which excluded them from key government positions. In the 1890s, a prolonged crisis over the conviction of Alfred Dreyfus, a French military officer accused of spying for Germany, deepened the divide between his liberal defenders and the military, backed by conservatives and the French Catholic Church. The fact that Dreyfus was Jewish fueled prejudices and passions, and it took 12 years to clear this innocent man.

France's Third Republic survives despite serious crises

Inflamed by the Dreyfus Affair, antimilitary ministries governed France from 1898 to 1906, persecuting officers and enacting anti-Catholic legislation. But by 1910, a "nationalist revival" renewed support for the military, as France faced the growing power of unified Germany.

NATIONAL UNIFICATION IN ITALY AND GERMANY. In the 1800s, Italy and Germany, long divided into numerous rival states, emerged as unified nations. Italian and German liberals and nationalists, fighting for national unity, were joined by industrialists, who hoped unified governments would aid commerce by ending internal trade restrictions and building roads and railways, and by strong leaders in prominent states seeking to expand their power.

Italy's unification was inspired by Giuseppe Mazzini, a romantic nationalist who fought to form a united Italian republic, but led by Count Camillo di Cavour after Mazzini's efforts failed. As prime minister to Victor Emmanuel II, King of Piedmont-Sardinia (northwest Italy's Piedmont region plus the island of Sardinia) from 1852 to 1861, Cavour sought first to acquire Lombardy and Venetia, which were ruled by Austria. Knowing that Piedmont-Sardinia alone could not defeat Austria, Cavour secretly courted France's Napoleon III, promising him lands (Savoy and Nice) in return for French help. Together they fought Austria and liberated Lombardy in 1859. But when Prussia threatened to intervene against France, Napoleon III pulled out of the war, leaving Venetia still under Austrian rule. The next year, however, the duchies of Parma, Modena, and Tuscany (Map 27.4) joined Piedmont-Sardinia and Lombardy in a northern Italian federation.

The initiative then passed to Giuseppe Garibaldi, a flamboyant Italian nationalist who had fought for Uruguayan independence in the 1840s, for an abortive Roman Republic in 1848–1849, and for Piedmont-Sardinia in the war against Austria. He recruited a thousand Italian volunteers, mostly under age 20, to sail to Sicily and fight for Italy's unification from the south.

Cavour and Garibaldi combine to unify Italy

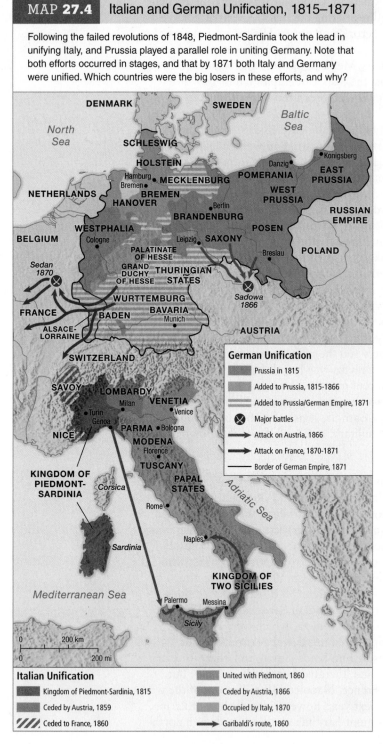

MAP **27.4**   Italian and German Unification, 1815–1871

Following the failed revolutions of 1848, Piedmont-Sardinia took the lead in unifying Italy, and Prussia played a parallel role in uniting Germany. Note that both efforts occurred in stages, and that by 1871 both Italy and Germany were unified. Which countries were the big losers in these efforts, and why?

German Unification

- Prussia in 1815
- Added to Prussia, 1815-1866
- Added to Prussia/German Empire, 1871
- ⊗ Major battles
- → Attack on Austria, 1866
- → Attack on France, 1870-1871
- — Border of German Empire, 1871

Italian Unification

- Kingdom of Piedmont-Sardinia, 1815
- Ceded by Austria, 1859
- /// Ceded to France, 1860
- United with Piedmont, 1860
- Ceded by Austria, 1866
- Occupied by Italy, 1870
- → Garibaldi's route, 1860

Garibaldi's invasion captured the imagination of Italian nationalists, who flocked to join his forces, known as Redshirts, after they won several battles. By September 1860 they had taken Sicily and southern Italy. Garibaldi planned to march on Rome, where the pope ruled the Papal States that dominated central Italy. But a French garrison protected Rome, so Cavour intervened to prevent war with France, sending forces south to head off Garibaldi while avoiding Rome. Blocked by Cavour's maneuver, Garibaldi gracefully gave the lands he had won to Victor Emmanuel II, who became king of Italy in 1861 when an all-Italian parliament proclaimed a unified Italian kingdom under Sardinia-Piedmont's constitution. Venetia was added in 1866, when Italy joined Prussia in defeating Austria, and Rome was finally included in 1870, when France withdrew its garrison during the Franco-Prussian War. The pope was left with less than a square mile on Rome's Vatican Hill.

As a constitutional monarchy with an elected parliament, Italy moved toward democracy and prosperity. By 1914 electoral reforms had extended the vote to most adult males, while expanding industry brought growing wealth to northern Italian cities. But worker unrest, as elsewhere, accompanied industrial growth, while poverty plagued the rural south. And, as self-described "prisoners in the Vatican," the popes refused to recognize the new nation until 1929, when Italy agreed to pay the papacy for the lands it had lost.

Germany's unification was led by Otto von Bismarck, a 6 foot, 5 inch man of enormous appetite and talent, who became Prussia's prime minister in 1852. A conservative who hated parliaments, he quickly clashed with Prussia's, which had rejected a bill to strengthen and reform the Prussian army. Backed by the king and army, he enacted the army reform anyway, igniting a constitutional crisis that outraged liberals and nationalists. But he knew they would forgive him if he could, in his words, use "blood and iron" to achieve what parliamentary speeches and votes could not: the unification of Germany.

Bismarck uses Prussian army to unify Germany

In 1866 he used the Prussian army against Austria, defeating this other major German power in the Seven Weeks War. He then united all northern German states in a North German Confederation led by Prussia. South German states remained outside the union, so Bismarck in 1870 provoked a conflict with France, foreseeing that the south would join the north in fighting the French. In the Franco-Prussian War (1870–1871), led by Prussia's modernized army, they did in fact join forces to defeat France. In January 1871, Bismarck proclaimed a united German Empire.

As chancellor to Prussia's king, who was now also German Kaiser (emperor), Bismarck governed Germany for the next two decades. In foreign affairs, having unified Germany through war, he now pursued peace, forming alliances to isolate France, which by itself was not strong enough to defeat Germany. In domestic affairs he first sought to weaken German Catholics and socialists, neither of whom he trusted. Then he made peace with the Catholics and tried to outflank the socialists by enacting the world's first comprehensive social security program. Yet Germany's Social Democratic Party, supported by an expanding working class, continued to grow, becoming the country's largest party—and the world's largest socialist party—by 1912.

Meanwhile, Germany's industrial economy boomed. By 1914, it led the world producing chemicals, electrical goods, and machine tools—and ranked second only to America in overall economic output. Workers' wages and buying power doubled between 1871 and 1914. But they still worked an average of 57 hours a week, lived in cramped slum housing, and endured high levels of illness, alcoholism, and family violence.

Otto von Bismarck.

Bismarck runs unified Germany, which becomes industrial power

Read the Document

A Letter from Otto von Bismarck (1866)

on **myhistorylab.com**

NATIONALISM AND COMPROMISE IN THE AUSTRIAN EMPIRE. Europe's other German power, the Austrian or Habsburg Empire, embraced many different nationalities (Map 27.5). For centuries it had thrived by adapting to changing conditions, but in the 1800s nationalism threatened its unity, leading subject nationalities to exalt their own cultures and eventually seek independence. Notable was the Slavic Revival, a movement among Eastern Europe's Slavic peoples (including Poles, Czechs, Slovaks, Slovenes, Serbs, Croats, and Ruthenians) to revive their cultural heritage, long submerged by Europe's dominant French and German cultures.

After Austria survived the revolutions of 1848–1849, including nationalist revolts by Czechs, Hungarians, and northern Italians, Emperor Francis Joseph (1848–1916) sought to suppress such nationalism and transform his diverse domains into a centralized state. His regime promoted modernization, subsidizing industries and railways, fostering free trade within the empire, reforming the judicial system, and ending serfdom wherever it still existed.

MAP 27.5   Ethnic Composition of the Austrian Empire, 1850

Although ruled by Austrians (who were Germans), the Austrian Empire was composed of many different nationalities with their own languages and customs. With the *Ausgleich* of 1867, the Austrians agreed to share power with the Hungarians, who were given control in the east. Why did this arrangement upset other nationalities and bolster their nationalist movements?

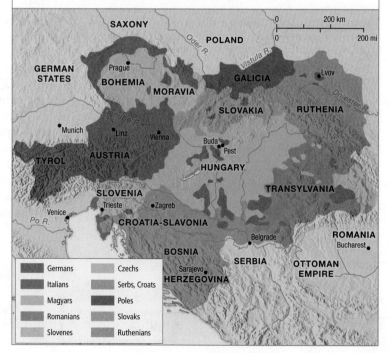

Legend:
- Germans
- Italians
- Magyars
- Romanians
- Slovenes
- Czechs
- Serbs, Croats
- Poles
- Slovaks
- Ruthenians

Austrian Empire's efforts to modernize fail to halt its erosion

But these efforts were undone by external events. In 1859, as noted above, Austria lost Lombardy in northern Italy to Piedmont-Sardinia, which was aided by France. Then, defeated by Prussia in the Seven Weeks War of 1866, Austria was shut out of German unification and lost Venetia as well. This defeat also compelled Austria to accept the **Ausgleich** (compromise) of 1867, granting Hungarians their long-sought autonomy by dividing the Habsburg realm into coequal self-governing Austrian and Hungarian sections. Each had its own constitution, parliament, ministries, and domestic policy, but they were linked by joint ministries of finance and foreign affairs, a combined military, and a common monarch, Francis Joseph. The Austrian Empire thus became the Dual Monarchy of Austria-Hungary.

Compromise with Hungary preserves empire amid growing nationalist unrest

The Ausgleich fully satisfied no one. The Habsburg regime survived, but only through power sharing. Hungary gained autonomy but fell short of full independence. The empire's other nationalities, emboldened by nationalist triumphs elsewhere, became ever more determined to gain autonomy. And, as Hungarians imposed their language and rule on national minorities in their part of the empire, these minorities came to despise Hungarians even more than Austrians. The Habsburgs held the empire together by promoting judicious reforms and economic progress—until it disintegrated at the end of World War I.

View the Image

The Clemency of the Russian Monster – British Cartoon, 1832

on **myhistorylab.com**

REFORM AND REACTION IN THE RUSSIAN EMPIRE. Russia in 1850 was Europe's most conservative power, reacting strongly against liberalism and nationalism inside and outside its borders. Tsar Nicholas I (1825–1855) used Russian forces to repress a Polish revolt in 1830–1831, help the Ottomans defeat an Egyptian rebellion in 1832–1833, and crush the Hungarian revolt against Austria in 1849. By 1850, Nicholas, widely considered Europe's handsomest and harshest monarch, had earned a reputation as the "Gendarme of Europe."

The tsar's brutality in stifling dissent, however, unsettled other European powers, which came to see Russia as more dangerous than the declining Ottoman Empire. In 1853, when the Ottomans rejected a Russian attempt to dictate their internal policies, Nicholas provoked war. The next year, France and Britain, fearing Russia might win, take Constantinople, and then dominate the eastern Mediterranean, entered the contest on the side of the Ottomans. Fought mainly in the Crimea, a peninsula jutting from southern Russia into the Black Sea (Map 27.6), the conflict came to be called the Crimean War (1853–1856).

The war, which Russia eventually lost, left a complex legacy. It inspired Britain's Florence Nightingale and other English women, appalled by high death rates resulting from disease and inadequate care, to professionalize the practice of nursing, which later provided career opportunities for women. It introduced new rifles that loaded at the breech rather than the muzzle to permit quicker refiring. It reinforced changes in the Ottoman Empire, discussed in Chapter 30. And it prompted the next Russian tsar to institute momentous reforms.

Tsar Alexander II, who succeeded Nicholas in 1855 and ended the war the next year, soon decided to abolish serfdom in Russia, where

MAP 27.6   The Crimean War, 1853–1856

Fearing Russia's growing power, Britain and France joined the Ottoman Turks against Russia in the Crimean War. Note that Piedmont-Sardinia, seeking French support in Italy, also joined the anti-Russian coalition. What were the war's main impacts, in Russia and elsewhere?

25 million peasants still lived in bondage to landlords. He was prompted by Russia's defeat, exposing its army of serf soldiers as unfit for modern war, and by concern that a serf-based economy could not compete with the industrial West. The global antislavery movement (Chapter 30) and persistent serf revolts in Russia also helped persuade him to end serfdom "from above" to avoid its abolition by rebellion "from below."

So in 1861, after several years of government discussions, Alexander signed the Emancipation Edict. To ensure that freed peasants could support themselves, the edict provided them with land. To maintain the support of noble landlords, the state compensated them with long-term bonds for the lands they ceded to peasants. And to reimburse the state for these bonds, peasants were required for 49 years to pay annual taxes known as redemption dues.

Other reforms followed, as the Russian regime sought to deal with its newly freed subjects. In 1864 it created in each county and province a *zemstvo* (*z'YEMST-vuh*), an assembly elected to manage such needs as roads, schools, medicine, and emergency food supplies. Later that year a new judicial system was established, with independent judges and trials by jury—concepts borrowed from the West. And an 1874 military reform, modernizing Russia's armed forces, reduced terms of service from 25 years to 6 and mandated basic education for soldiers.

Russia's Great Reforms were impressive. They peacefully provided 25 million serfs with freedom, land, legal rights, and local governance, while it was taking a bloody civil war to free four million U.S. slaves (Chapter 28). But the reforms raised expectations that could not be met. As living standards failed to improve and population growth left many families without enough land to feed themselves, discontent and poverty plagued the rural masses, while in the cities radical youths formed revolutionary groups.

In 1879, a group of young rebels called the "People's Will" sought to spark revolution by killing the tsar. Initially they failed: explosives they placed under a bridge did not detonate when the tsar's carriage crossed, and a bid to kill him as he traveled by railway exploded the wrong train. In 1880, a rebel employed at the tsar's Winter Palace blew up its dining room with dynamite at dinnertime, but that day the tsar was not there. In 1881 rebels threw a bomb at his carriage, but it bounced off and exploded in the road behind him. When he got out to survey the damage, however, they threw another bomb at his feet, and this one finally took the life of the acclaimed Tsar Liberator.

Rather than sparking a revolt, however, Alexander II's murder brought a forceful reaction from his son, Tsar Alexander III (1881–1894). The new tsar crushed the revolutionaries and rolled back his father's reforms, asserting state control over *zemstvos* and judges. He oppressed Jews and other non-Russians in his realm, hoping to suppress their nationalist aspirations. He also promoted industrialization by appointing the talented Sergei Witte (*VIT-tuh*) as minister of finance in 1892. Over the next decade, using huge sums borrowed from abroad, Witte subsidized industries and built railways to help exploit Russia's vast resources.

By the early 1900s, then, Russia had a growing industrial proletariat, a free but destitute and discontented peasant class, and large numbers of oppressed non-Russians. This volatile mix soon resulted in revolutions (Chapter 31).

Industry, Ideology, and Growing Global Connections

Although mechanized industries and secular ideologies arose first in Europe, eventually they affected the whole world. Armed with new technologies, inspired by new ideologies, and eager to find resources and markets for their new industries, Western nations in Europe and North America came to dominate the globe. The rest of this chapter discusses

Defeat, revolts, and economic weakness prompt Alexander II to end serfdom

Read the **Document**
Emancipation Manifesto (1861)
on **myhistorylab.com**

Great Reforms transform Russia but fail to end unrest

Tsar Alexander III promotes repression and industrialization

Georgian peasants in southern Russian Empire.

the foundations of Western domination and the main ways non-Western nations responded. Succeeding chapters examine in depth the impact of industry and ideology on the Americas, Asia, and Africa.

Industry, Technology, and Global Trade

Industrialization provided both the impetus and means for Western global domination. Industry's demand for resources and markets spurred European economic and political expansion, while advances in technology helped Westerners impose their will on the rest of the world.

Quest for industrial resources spurs global trade

As European nations industrialized and competed economically, they increasingly looked beyond Europe for resources, markets, and investment opportunities. Eager to secure their own supplies of cotton, coal, and iron, and eventually other industrial resources such as rubber, chromium, nitrates, and petroleum, Western industrialists sought to secure access to the resources of Asia, Africa, and the Americas. And as competition saturated domestic markets, European investors used their surplus wealth to seek potential profits overseas.

These efforts were aided by new steel and transportation technologies. The Bessemer steel-making process and Siemens-Martin "open-hearth" method, developed in the 1850s and 1860s, made steel more flexible and durable and less expensive. World steel production increased by 5,600 percent between 1870 and 1900, with 75 percent of it produced in the United States, Germany, and Britain. The steel boom also revolutionized transport and trade, as cheap, high-quality steel was used to make rails, railway cars, ships, bridges, and eventually automobiles.

Railways, steamships, canals, and cables enhance global connections

Railway construction benefited immediately. In the second half of the 19th century, railways were built extensively in the United States, Canada, France, Germany, Russia, Japan, Mexico, Argentina, and elsewhere. New lines connected previously isolated regions, helping to unite nations. They also aided commerce by connecting producers with markets, providing farmers and manufacturers with speedy, efficient, low-cost transport for their products.

Shipping also profited immensely. Steel-hulled ships using steel propellers powered by increasingly efficient engines grew in size and range of service. Soon freight, mail, and passengers were transported over great distances in voyages lasting days instead of weeks. In 1869 the Suez Canal opened, linking the Mediterranean Sea with the Red Sea and Indian Ocean; 45 years later the Panama Canal connected the Atlantic and Pacific Oceans across Central America. By 1900, a network of undersea steel telegraph cables enabled companies and governments to exchange information rapidly with distant lands.

Such developments transformed global trade. Railways moved goods and produce quickly and cheaply to ports, from which steamships moved them around the world. Quicker transport lowered prices dramatically, making many goods affordable to global consumers for the first time. Europeans, for example, bought beef from Argentina and wool from Uruguay and New Zealand, while exports of European manufactured goods enhanced industrial profits. British shipping companies moved goods for numerous nations, and British bankers financed railways and harbors around the world. Never before had remote regions been so closely connected.

The Great Global Migrations

Growing population and industry spark mass global migrations

Connections forged by industry, railways, and steamships also facilitated history's largest mass human migrations (Map 27.7). In the 1800s Europe's population grew from roughly 188 to 432 million, continuing an increase begun in the previous century. But actual growth

| MAP **27.7** | Global Migrations, 1815–1930 |

From 1815 to 1930, in history's greatest global mass migrations, millions left their homelands to settle in distant places. Notice that most left Europe for the Americas, but that some also went to Australia and New Zealand, while several million Asians also migrated to work on railways, in mines, or on plantations. What factors inspired so many people to migrate?

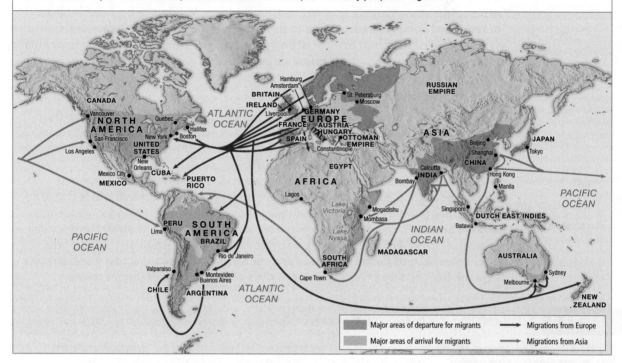

was even greater, since more than sixty million people left Europe between 1815 and 1930. Most of the migrants went to North and South America, Australia, and New Zealand. North America's population grew more than tenfold in these years.

Most migrants were young, ambitious men and women eager to improve their lives through hard work in spacious lands with limitless opportunities. By contrast, Europe was overcrowded, its industrial growth bringing not only jobs but also squalid slums that bred disease and crime. Urban steel mills spewed smoke that darkened the sky and caused respiratory diseases, while chemical plants making textile dyes, fertilizers, and explosives poisoned rivers and lakes, exposing people to toxic materials that increased cancer rates. No wonder many people chose to leave.

Some migrants, such as Russian Jews, fled persecution; others, like Irish Catholics, were escaping poverty and hunger. Some, like southern Italians and German Catholics, left because they disliked the results of national unification. Others, like Italian and Spanish peasants, commuted between South American and European harvests, which came in opposite seasons. Some migrants returned to Europe, but most never went back.

Migrants left Asia in far smaller numbers than from Europe—about three million between 1815 and 1920. Asians worked on South American plantations, at North American railway construction sites, and in South African gold mines,

Italian immigrants at Ellis Island, New York.

typically encountering racial discrimination. Opportunities for Asians were better in Southeast Asia's British, French, and Dutch colonies, where "overseas Chinese" often began as petty retailers and developed profitable business careers.

European and Asian migrations enhance global cultural connections

The great migrations established new cultural connections. South America became more European in culture, while North America was made more diverse by Irish, Italian, German, and Slavic Catholics, as well as Russian Jews. Millions of migrants brought "old country" concepts and customs to their new homes, while their letters to relatives in Europe helped to spread new social and political ideas from the Americas. Even after the migrations subsided, cross-fertilization continued.

Industry, Technology, and Imperialism

As global commerce and competition grew, European nations, eager to enhance their wealth and power, sought ever more forcefully to expand their economies and secure their raw material sources. In the process they practiced **imperialism,** using force to colonize and exploit the people and resources of Africa and Asia (Map 27.8).

👁 **Watch the Video**

The Origins of Modern Imperialism and Colonialism

on **myhistorylab.com**

New technologies aided imperial exploitation. Steamships helped Europeans transport goods and people all over the globe, independent of seasonal winds that hitherto governed sea travel. Steam-driven vessels traveled up rivers into Asian and African interiors, helping Westerners access resources and assert military control. Development of dynamite in the 1860s by Swedish scientist Alfred Nobel (who later endowed the Nobel Prizes) helped them blast mines and cut roads and railways across harsh terrain. Telegraph lines and undersea cables aided their administration of distant colonies.

MAP **27.8** European Imperial Expansion by 1914

By 1914, Europeans ruled most of Africa and southern Asia, while people of European heritage dominated the Americas, Australia, and New Zealand. Even China was penetrated by Western economic interests, while Japan adapted many Western ways. How did industrial growth and mass migrations also contribute to Europe's global domination?

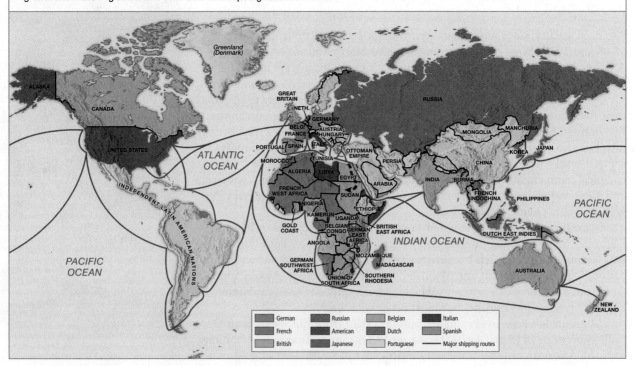

New weapons further aided imperial aggression. The breech-loaded rifle, developed in 1843, was far more accurate and quicker to reload than the old muzzle-loaded musket, giving Westerners a powerful edge over Asian and African armies. And the new Maxim machine guns, remarkable rapid-fire weapons developed in the 1880s, let small groups of Europeans, shooting from safe distance, kill Asians and Africans with appalling efficiency.

Industry, technology, and weaponry advance imperialism

Nationalism, Liberalism, and Racism

European ideologies also inspired and rationalized global domination. Europeans came to see imperial expansion as a matter of national pride and a means of spreading Western ideals.

Belligerent popular nationalism fuels imperialism

In the 1800s growing nationalism reinforced European rivalries, as Western nations competed to show the superiority of their institutions and armies. Liberal reforms heightened the competition: as more Europeans gained voting rights and education, and as newspapers boosted public awareness of world affairs, many people took warlike pride in their countries' colonial conquests. This bellicose popular nationalism was called **jingoism,** after a song sung in English pubs asserting, "We don't want to fight, but *by jingo* if we do, we've got the men, we've got the ships, we've got the money too!" Jingoism pervaded Britain, where people wanted to "paint the map red" (the color usually assigned to British possessions), and also infected other Western nations.

Liberalism and nationalism, moreover, joined with Christian compassion to help Europeans idealize imperial activity. Western missionaries, doctors, and teachers went to Asia and Africa seeking to spread Christianity, administer Western medicine, suppress slavery, and "uplift" Asians and Africans by teaching them Western ways. "The White Man's Burden," an 1899 poem addressed to Americans by Britain's Rudyard Kipling, illustrates this mixture of idealism and arrogance, depicting imperialism as a blend of compassion, duty, and service (see "The White Man's Burden").

Read the Document

Karl Pearson, "Social Darwinism and Imperialism"
on **myhistorylab.com**

Social Darwinism and racism rationalize imperialism

The ascendancy of science, and a growing "cult of progress," also supplied some support to European imperialism. In 1859 British biologist Charles Darwin published *The Origin of Species*, promoting his theory that evolution occurs through a process of natural selection, in which organisms best adapted to their environment are most likely to survive and reproduce. Soon thinkers called Social Darwinists, led by English sociologist Herbert Spencer, applied the notion of "survival of the fittest" to human societies, portraying human progress as a product of struggle between the strong and weak. Europeans then used these ideas to rationalize their expansion as part of a global struggle for survival and progress.

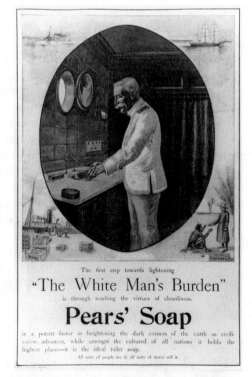

Such rationales were reinforced by racism, developed by some Europeans into a pseudo-science. In the 1850s a French aristocrat, Joseph-Arthur, Comte de Gobineau (*gaw-bē-NŌ*), published a four-volume *Essay on the Inequality of Human Races* that classified humans into distinct races, claimed races should never be mixed, and ranked white Europeans as a superior "Aryan" race. Others would later use his ideas to explain and justify Europe's global domination.

The first step towards lightening

"The White Man's Burden"

is through teaching the virtues of cleanliness.

Pears' Soap

is a potent factor in brightening the dark corners of the earth as civilization advances, while amongst the cultured of all nations it holds the highest place—it is the ideal toilet soap.

All sorts of people use it; all sorts of stores sell it.

Responses to Western Domination

Non-Western responses to Western domination ranged from resistance to cooperation to wholesale imitation. Each response involved painful choices and consequences.

Racist ad for soap to teach cleanliness to nonwhite peoples.

DOCUMENT 27.2 "The White Man's Burden" and "The Brown Man's Burden"

In his 1899 poem, "The White Man's Burden," Rudyard Kipling idealized imperialism as a form of service to colonized peoples. But Henry Labouchere soon responded with "The Brown Man's Burden," an ironic poem that ridiculed Kipling's by portraying imperialism as greedy, duplicitous, and murderous. Which perspective seems more accurate, and why?

Excerpts from *The White Man's Burden*
by Rudyard Kipling

Take up the White Man's burden—
Send forth the best ye breed—
Go bind your sons to exile
To serve your captives' need;
To wait in heavy harness,
On fluttered folk and wild—
Your new-caught, sullen peoples,
Half-devil and half-child.

Take up the White Man's burden—
In patience to abide,
To veil the threat of terror
And check the show of pride;
By open speech and simple,
An hundred times made plain
To seek another's profit,
And work another's gain . . .

SOURCE: Rudyard Kipling, *The White Man's Burden*

Excerpts from *The Brown Man's Burden*
by Henry Labouchere

. . . Pile on the brown man's burden;
And, if ye rouse his hate,
Meet his old-fashioned reasons
With Maxims up to date.
With shells and dumdum bullets
A hundred times made plain
The brown man's loss must ever
Imply the white man's gain . . .

Pile on the brown man's burden,
And if his cry be sore,
That surely need not irk you—
Ye've driven slaves before.
Seize on his ports and pastures,
The fields his people tread;
Go make from them your living,
And mark them with his dead . . .

SOURCE: *Truth* (London); reprinted in *Literary Digest* 18 (Feb. 25, 1899).

Asian and Muslim societies initially resist Western impact

One response, resistance to Western influence, was most evident in regions with long-established complex societies, such as China, India, and many Muslim lands. Such societies, where Westerners were often seen as "barbarians" or "infidels," initially opposed European intrusion, fighting to maintain traditional institutions and economies.

These societies soon found, however, that Western weaponry and technology, combined with the West's insatiable quest for raw materials and markets, made resistance futile. During the Opium Wars of 1839–1842 and 1856–1860, for example, Chinese forces, long dominant in East Asia, proved unable to defeat Western forces and prevent the infusion of Western goods and ideas (Chapter 29). It became apparent that nations failing to industrialize would fall far behind the West in power and wealth, leaving them increasingly vulnerable to Western economic penetration and imperial control.

Asian, African, and American regions supply industrial resources

A second alternative, attractive to countries rich in raw materials required by Western industry, was to seek wealth by selling their resources to industrial nations. This response emerged first in regions that produced raw cotton, such as Egypt, India, and the southern United States, and later in areas with other useful raw materials. Nitrates, for example, used in fertilizers and explosives, brought prosperity to Chile in the late 1800s. Rubber, used in vehicle tires and drive belts for machines, brought substantial income to Brazil and later to exploiters of Central Africa and Southeast Asia. Chromium, used in making stainless steel, an alloy whose resistance to heat and corrosion soon made it a key component of most machines and

A busy port in Chile in the early 1900s.

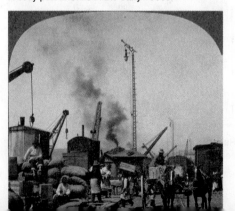

weapons, did the same for Turkey, southern Africa, and India. And the export of petro-leum, used initially to lubricate machines and later to fuel them, eventually brought wealth to the Persian Gulf and other oil-rich regions, especially after oil surpassed coal as the dominant energy source in the 20th century.

This alternative, however, also had major drawbacks. Frequently the fields and mines producing these resources were owned and exploited by Europeans, who paid local work-ers minimal wages, used the profits to benefit European industry, and flooded local mar-kets with cheap goods that undermined local artisans and traditional commerce. Unless and until these countries gained control of profits from the sale of their resources and used these profits to build their own industries, they remained economic subordinates of the West, serving mainly as suppliers of raw materials for Western industrial nations.

A third alternative was **Westernization**, the adoption by non-Western nations of Western-style industries, technologies, institutions, and ideologies. In time this would prove the only choice that gave these nations sufficient wealth and power to maintain or regain freedom from Western control. But Westernization created a painful predicament, since it involved transforming and even undermining the society's own traditional ideas and institutions.

Some societies adopted only ideas and institutions they found useful in opposing Western domination. In the early 1800s, for example, Latin Americans used liberalism and nationalism to support and validate their fight for freedom from Spanish and Portuguese rule (Chapter 28). Decades later in India, British-educated Indian profession-als began a movement, also based on Western-style liberal and nationalist ideals, to press for Indian independence from British colonial control (Chapter 29). Latin America and India, however, were slow to adopt Western industries and technologies, and thus to compete with Western wealth and power.

Non-Western nations adapt industry and ideologies to resist Western rule

Other countries, eager to compete with Western power and wealth, opted for wholesale Westernization. First to do so was Egypt, led from 1805 to 1848 by Muhammad Ali, a rebellious Ottoman viceroy who used profits from Egypt's cotton exports to build Western-style industries and armies, while also using liberal and nationalist ideals to push for freedom from the Ottoman Turks (Chapter 30). But the British, determined to retain their supremacy in the textile industry, supported the Ottomans against him and forced him to remove tariffs protecting Egypt's industries from competition with low-cost British goods. Egypt thus remained, like India, a supplier of raw cotton for England's textile mills.

More successful in imitating the West was Japan. Forced in the 1850s by Americans and Europeans to open ports to Western trade, the Japanese responded by adapting Western industries and ways to meet their needs. As government policies encouraged the development of textile mills, railways, shipping lines, mines, and factories, Japan emerged as a burgeoning industrial nation by the early 1900s. It also adopted nationalist ideals, a liberal constitution, and Western-style imperialism to become an expanding regional power (Chapter 29).

CHAPTER

REVIEW

Putting It in Perspective

Industrialization promised abundant wealth, inexpen-sive goods, and marvelous machines, while new ideologies offered bright visions of liberty, equality, and national self-rule. But the transition proved terribly traumatic, as early industry also fostered dislocation, destitution, and violence.

These impacts came first to Europe, where the industrial age was born. Conservatives fought to retain control, haunted by fears of revolutionary instability. But the engines of innovation, as loud and relentless as machines in the great mills, pushed the West ever forward into the unknown. Buoyed and buffeted by liberalism, nationalism, and industrial change, societies across the continent were transformed. In Western Europe, long led by Britain and France, the forces of change brought industrial growth, social stress, and political liberalization. In Central Europe, long divided into many small states, these forces promoted Italian and German unification and Germany's emergence as Europe's leading economic and military power. In Eastern Europe, long ruled by large multicultural empires, the forces of change proved divisive: as subject nationalities pushed for greater rights and self-rule, Austrian Habsburgs compromised to keep their realm from crumbling, and Russian rulers tried repression and reform in hopes of avoiding upheaval.

Meanwhile, the forces of change were affecting the rest of the world. Industry spread to North America, Japan, and eventually other regions. Rapid and efficient worldwide trade expanded global connections. The great migrations forged new connections among world cultures and continents. And imperialism extended Western rule over much of Asia and Africa. Envious of Europe's affluence, alarmed by its power, intrigued by its technology, and inspired by its ideals, other world cultures increasingly had to endure Western domination or adopt Western methods and machines.

Reviewing Key Material

KEY CONCEPTS

Luddites, 609
industrialization, 609
enclosures, 610
proletariat, 610
vaccination, 610
conservatives, 617
ideologies, 617
liberalism, 617
socialism, 617
Communists, 618
nationalism, 618

romanticism, 620
universal male suffrage, 621
women's suffrage, 624
Irish Home Rule, 624
Ausgleich, 628
zemstvo, 629
imperialism, 632
jingoism, 633
Westernization, 635

KEY PEOPLE

Richard Arkwright, 611
James Watt, 611
Richard Trevithick, 612
Friedrich Engels, 618
Karl Marx, 618
Johann Herder, 618
Mary Shelley, 620
King Louis Philippe, 621
Emmeline Pankhurst, 624
Napoleon III, 624
Alfred Dreyfus, 625

Giuseppe Mazzini, 625
Camillo di Cavour, 625
King Victor Emmanuel II, 625
Giuseppe Garibaldi, 625
Otto von Bismarck, 626
Emperor Francis Joseph, 627
Florence Nightingale, 628
Tsar Alexander II, 628
Herbert Spencer, 633

ASK YOURSELF

1. What assets are needed for industrialization? How did Britain possess each of them in the late 18th century? How and why did industry spread to Europe and America?

2. How did industrialization affect the lives and work of ordinary people? What were its main impacts on family and society?

3. Describe and explain the new ideologies that arose during early industrialization. What were the main impacts of these ideologies?

4. How did Britain avoid revolutions in the 19th century? Why did Continental Europe experienced several such upheavals?

5. Why did nationalism promote unification in Central Europe but disunity in Eastern Europe? How did liberalism and nationalism threaten both the Austrian and Russian Empires?

6. How did industry and technology facilitate global migrations and Western imperialism? What other factors fostered imperialism, and why? What choices and consequences did non-Western nations face in dealing with the Western challenge?

GOING FURTHER

Abernethy, D. B. *Global Dominance: European Overseas Empires*. 2000.

Anderson, Benedict. *Imagined Communities*. 1991.

Ashton, Thomas S. *The Industrial Revolution, 1760–1830*. 1997.

Bayles, Derek, and E. F. Biagini. *The Risorgimento and the Unification of Italy*. 2nd ed. 2002.

Berend, I. *History Derailed: Central and Eastern Europe in the Long Nineteenth Century*. 2003.

Broers, M., *Europe After Napoleon: Revolution, Reaction, and Romanticism, 1814–1848*. 1996.

Cranston, M. *The Romantic Movement*. 1994.

Curtain, Philip. *The World and the West*. 2000.

Feuchtwanger, E. *Bismarck*. 2002.

Fisher, D. *The Industrial Revolution*. 1992.

Flanders, J. *Inside the Victorian Home: A Portrait of Domestic Life in Victorian England*. 2004.

Fuchs, Rachel. *Gender and Poverty in Nineteenth Century Europe*. 2005.

Gildea, Robert. *Barricades and Borders: Europe, 1800–1914*. 3rd ed. 2003.

Himmelfarb, Gertrude. *The Idea of Poverty: England in the Early Industrial Age*. 1984.

Hobsbawm, Eric J. *The Age of Revolution*. 1996.

Horn, Jeff. *The Industrial Revolution*. 2007.

Inkster, Ian. *Technology and Industrialization*. 1998.

Landes, David. *The Unbound Prometheus: Technological Change and Industrial Development in Western Europe from 1750 to the Present*. 2nd ed. 2003.

Lane, Penelope, et al., eds. *Women, Work, and Wages in England, 1600–1850*. 2004.

Lindemann, A. *A History of European Socialism*. 1983.

Lyons, Martin. *Postrevolutionary Europe, 1815–1856*. 2006.

Malia, Martin, and Terrence Emmons. *History's Locomotives: Revolutions and the Making of the Modern World*. 2006.

Marks, R. *The Origins of the Modern World: A Global and Ecological Narrative*. 2002.

McLellan, David. *Karl Marx: His Life and Thought*. 4th ed. 2006.

McMillan, John. *Napoleon III*. 1991.

Meyer, David. *The Roots of American Industrialization*. 2003.

Mommsen, Wolfgang. *Imperial Germany, 1871–1914*. 1995.

Morgan, Kenneth. *The Birth of Industrial Britain*. 2004.

Pflanze, Otto. *Bismarck and the Development of Germany*. 2nd ed., 3 vols. 1990.

Pollard, S. *Peaceful Conquest: Industrialization of Europe*. 1981.

Pomeranz, Kenneth. *The Great Divergence: China, Europe, and the Making of the Modern World Economy*. 2002.

Sheehan, James. *Germany, 1770–1866*. 1989.

Sked, Alan. *The Decline and Fall of the Habsburg Empire*. 1989.

Sperber, Jonathan. *The European Revolutions, 1848–1851*. 2nd ed. 2005.

Stearns, Peter. *The Industrial Revolution in World History*. 3rd ed. 2007.

Taylor, B. *Eve and the New Jerusalem: Socialism and Feminism in the Nineteenth Century*. 1983.

Tilly, Louise A. *Industrialization and Gender Inequality*. 1993.

Tilly, Louise A., and Joan W. Scott. *Women, Work, and Family*. 1978.

Wolf, Eric. *Europe and the People Without History*. 1982, 1997.

Key Dates and Developments

1600s	Onset of Dutch and English agricultural advances
1733	John Kay's flying shuttle
1767	James Hargreaves's spinning jenny
1769	Arkwright's water frame and Watt's steam engine
1785	Cartwright's power loom
1801	Trevithick's steam-powered carriage
1811–1816	Luddite unrest in England
1825	Stephenson's steam locomotive; Darlington-Stockton railway
1832	Parliamentary Reform Act in Britain
1834	Customs Union (*Zollverein*) among German states
1838–1848	Chartist movement in Britain
1840–1930	European imperialism and global migration
1845–1846	Irish potato famine; British Corn Laws repealed
1848	*Communist Manifesto*
1848	Revolutions in France, Austria, Hungary, Italy, Germany

1851	Crystal Palace exhibition in London
1852	Creation of the Second French Empire
1853–1856	Crimean War
1859	Austro-Sardinian War
1860–1861	Formation of the Kingdom of Italy
1861–1874	Emancipation and Great Reforms in Russia
1862–1867	French intervention in Mexico
1865–1914	Post–Civil War American industrial boom
1866	Austro-Prussian Seven Weeks War
1867	*Ausgleich* produces Dual Monarchy of Austria-Hungary
1867–1884	Reform Bills in Britain
1870–1871	Franco-Prussian War, onset of France's Third Republic
1871	Formation of German Empire
1871–1890	Bismarck governs Germany as chancellor
1894–1906	Dreyfus Affair in France
1911–1914	Suffragist protests in Britain
1912–1914	Irish Home Rule Crisis in Britain

PEARSON
myhistorylab Connections

Reinforce what you learned in this chapter by studying the many documents, images, maps, review tools, and videos available at www.myhistorylab.com.

Read and Review

✓●─ **Study** and **Review** Chapter 27

📖●─ **Read** the **Document**

Thomas Malthus, Excerpt from *Essay on the Principle of Population*, p. 617

David Ricardo, *On Wages*, "The Iron Law of Wages," p. 617

A Letter from Otto von Bismarck (1866), p. 627

Emancipation Manifesto (1861), p. 629

Karl Pearson, "Social Darwinism and Imperialism," p. 633

🔍●─ **View** the **Image**

Architectural Iron Works, p. 613

The Clemency of the Russian Monster – British Cartoon, 1832, p. 628

British Empire Poster, "Growing Markets for Our Goods," p. 630

((●─ **Listen** to the **Audio**

Industrial Revolution, p. 615

Urbanization, p. 616

Research and Explore

👁●─ **Watch** the **Video**

The Origins of Modern Imperialism and Colonialism, p. 632

─── ((●─ **Listen** to the **Chapter Audio** for Chapter 27 on **myhistorylab.com** ───

28

Nation Building in the Americas, 1789–1914

((•●—Listen to the **Chapter Audio** for Chapter 28 on **myhistorylab.com**

- What were the principal causes of the Revolutions of Latin America?

- How did Mexico's failure to institutionalize affect its progress as an independent nation?

- How did Argentina and Chile handle the problem of institutionalization?

- How did the Brazilian Empire differ from other independent governments in Latin America?

- What major developments made possible the expansion of the United States?

- How did Canada overcome obstacles to its expansion and consolidation?

The Constitution of the United States of America

In 1787, the recently independent United States replaced its Articles of Confederation with a Constitution designed to strengthen the authority of the central government (page 655). This document, with its accompanying 27 amendments, proved to be not only an extraordinarily durable charter of authority, but also an effective protector of the rights of the people against government intrusion in their lives.

In September 1789, George Washington, first president of the United States, received a curious gift from the Marquis de Lafayette, his French comrade in arms from the American Revolutionary War. Inside a box of polished hardwoods, lying on a red velvet lining, was a large, rusty key. This, it turned out, was the key to the Bastille, the notorious Paris prison and symbol of royal tyranny, destroyed the previous July 14 in one of the defining moments of the French Revolution. At once the president understood the symbolism: the American Revolution, which had unlocked the door of liberty for English colonists in America, had inspired Lafayette and others in France to unlock that door for their own people. Who better to keep the key than the first president of the new American republic?

North America

South America

Two decades later, on a warm April evening in 1810, a Spanish-American aristocrat named Simón Bolívar (sĭ-MŌN bō-LĒ-vahr) sat at his desk in Caracas, Venezuela. Most of Europe was controlled by Napoleon, Spain was occupied by French troops, and the Spanish Empire in America was hanging by a thread. Bolívar opened a worn, leather-lined port-folio. Inside were two copies of the same doc-ument, one in English and one in Spanish: the Constitution of the United States. Having found the inspiration that would help him deal with the massive problems confronting South America, Bolívar took up his pen and began to write. The notes he made that evening would form the basis of his speech to a meeting in Caracas a few weeks later, a speech that would launch his remarkable political and military career.

Inspired by ideals of liberty and constitutional governance, in the 19th century the peoples of the Americas, led by revolutionaries such as Bolívar, fought to achieve independence from European colonial powers and then labored to build new nations and modernized societies. They looked to ideals that originated in Europe, and to the experience of the United States, where independence from colonial control had produced a nation whose founding documents implemented those ideals. But in Latin America, the revolutions were regional. Independence came in different ways at different times, and nation building began in different places under different circumstances. The result was a series of new nations rather than a unified continent, or a federation like those of the United States and Canada.

The degree of success that the new nations of the Americas achieved depended largely on their ability to overcome social and geographic divisions, establish effective economies, and build enduring political and social institutions. Generally, those nations that founded their futures on laws and institutions achieved considerable success; those controlled by forceful personalities proved less fortunate.

The Revolutions of Latin America

By the early 1800s, the Spanish and Portuguese empires in the Western Hemisphere had existed for more than three hundred years. They had endured many challenges and crises but had shown resilience in the face of changing times. Their sudden collapse, between 1808 and 1824, was set in motion by Napoleon's conquest of the Iberian Peninsula.

((•⌐ **Listen** to the **Audio**

Latin America

on **myhistorylab.com**

Preconditions for Revolution

Criollos resent
discrimination by
peninsulares

The rebellions that erupted in Spanish America early in the 19th century were grounded in animosity between two kinds of Spaniards (Chapter 19). *Criollos*, Spaniards born in America, were distrusted by the Spanish kings, who had never met them and could not directly control them through their families and property. *Peninsulares*, Spaniards born in the Iberian Peninsula, monopolized the highest offices in the Americas, but they had little interest in the Spanish Empire other than the wealth they could extract from it and carry back to Spain. Of 170 viceroys in Spanish America, only four had been born there—all to high-ranking Spanish officials living temporarily in America. Most key positions in the military and the Church likewise went to *peninsulares*. *Criollos*, excluded from these posts by the place of their birth, resented the arrogance of the *peninsulares*. Similar prejudices irritated those born in Portuguese Brazil.

In the 18th century, these grievances were reinforced by the ideas of the French Enlightenment. Only a few Latin Americans could read pamphlets written by French *philosophes* such as Voltaire and Rousseau, but those who did came to consider their exclusion from high position not only unfair but irrational. Such ideas undermined the traditional acceptance of Iberian rule.

Enlightenment ideas had this subversive effect even under the governance of an enlightened absolutist. Carlos III, who ruled Spain from 1759 until 1788, was a modern king who considered himself a servant of his people. He instituted reforms in administration, financial management, and imperial commercial policies, aiming to modernize his empire and improve the lives of its citizens. Although these reforms succeeded in many respects, their tendency to centralize authority in Madrid alienated *criollos*, who were accustomed to considerable local autonomy. They responded by demanding more radical changes than Madrid was willing to permit. By the early 19th century, many Spanish Americans considered their government unresponsive to their needs and indifferent to their opinions.

Yet many more remained loyal to Spain. The benefits of Carlos III's reforms were real, and at the time of his death in 1788 the Spanish Empire had never been more effectively governed or more prosperous. Spain and Portugal had ruled their American colonies for more than three centuries without professional military garrisons, except in a few areas where they were needed to guard against foreign invasion or Amerind raids. In all those years, there was not a single uprising that suggested irreconcilable differences with Madrid or Lisbon.

Despite occasional
uprisings, Iberian America
remains essentially
content with colonial status

There had, however, been uprisings. More than fifty Amerind revolts took place between 1740 and 1780, culminating in a large-scale rebellion between 1780 and 1783 that claimed more than a hundred thousand lives. Its leader, an Amerind who called himself Tupac Amaru II after the last Sapa Inca, called for specific reforms, including the removal of corrupt colonial officials, the end of forced labor service, and better working conditions in mines. But neither he nor his followers sought to challenge the legitimacy of Spanish colonial rule or to expel Spain from America, and Carlos III gave them no chance to change their minds. A Spanish army was quickly dispatched to Lima to put down the Tupac Amaru Rebellion.

Similarly, the 1781 *comunero* revolt in New Granada protested specific issues, in this case significant tax and price increases designed to raise funds to defend the region against possible British attack. Royal authorities deceived a rebel army of several thousand men by appearing to agree to reforms even as they assembled a loyal force. This army then caught the rebels by surprise and defeated them.

Neither the Amerind revolts nor the taxpayer rebellions were directed against Spanish rule. Spain's authority in America remained unquestioned, and few thought that open revolt would stand any chance of military success. In ruling a far-flung empire with a very small number of professional soldiers and considerable political skill, Spain enjoyed great success that might have lasted even longer had it not been for Napoleon Bonaparte.

Most Latin American nations owe their liberation to a chain of events set in motion by Napoleon. His armies invaded Portugal in November 1807 and Spain in March 1808 because those kingdoms had violated France's Continental System. When France removed King Carlos IV from the Spanish throne, *criollos* saw a startling opportunity: they could carry out conservative revolutions, breaking away from the puppet regime that Napoleon had established in Madrid while claiming loyalty to the true king of Spain. Since the Spanish American empire until recently had been the king's personal possession, rather than part of a centralized state, there was significant public sympathy for efforts to "defend" the deposed king's lands against a French conqueror.

In 1810 matters came to a head, as town meetings in major cities such as Caracas and Buenos Aires formally refused allegiance to the French puppet regime and appointed **juntas** (*HOON-tahs*), or provisional governments, to rule on behalf of imprisoned King Carlos. These meetings and the actions they took mark the beginning of the Latin American revolutions.

The Napoleonic Wars alter the relationship between Iberian kingdoms and their colonies

▣ ▸ Read the **Document**
On Constitutional Government (Early 19th Century) Simon Bolivar
on **myhistorylab.com**

Regional Character of the Spanish American Revolutions

The 1810 uprisings against Spanish rule occurred within regional contexts that eventually helped shape the boundaries of the new nations. As of 1776, Spain's American empire was administered through four viceroyalties—New Spain, Peru, New Granada, and La Plata (See Map 28.1 on page 644)—further subdivided into 12 *audiencias* located in major cities such as Mexico City, Lima, Caracas, Bogotá, and Buenos Aires. Viceroys attempted to ensure compliance with royal edicts throughout a viceroyalty, while *audiencias* could more easily supervise and execute laws on a regional level.

When revolutions broke out in 1810, some were spearheaded by local elites in major cities such as Caracas and Buenos Aires, while others were opposed by elites in similar cities, such as Mexico City and Lima. In either case, initial fighting took place within the region controlled by that city, not across Spanish America as a whole. Formidable topographical barriers, such as the Andes Mountains, the Atacama Desert, and the dense rain forests of Central America, worked to regionalize conflict further.

Revolutions in Iberian America occur regionally

These conditions meant that the revolutions were fought and won in one region at a time, rather than as a general war for independence of the kind that took place in Britain's North American colonies. It also meant that newly independent governments would begin building new nations at different times, in different regions, under different circumstances, with populations that did not consider themselves "Latin Americans," but citizens of individual regions.

((•▸ Listen to the **Audio**
Revolutionary Thought 2
on **myhistorylab.com**

Independence Movements in South America

In northern South America, fighting focused on Venezuela. There a wealthy young *criollo* named Simón Bolívar became the improbable hero of Latin American liberation. Educated in Europe, Bolívar considered himself an enlightened admirer of the reforms of the French Revolution. Both the 1812 Spanish Constitution of Cádiz and the 1787 Constitution of the United States inspired him with a vision of what a liberated Spanish America might look like, as the story at the beginning of this chapter indicates. Bolívar exploited that inspiration to dominate the movement for Spanish American independence.

FOUNDATION MAP 28.1 — Iberian America in 1810

The Spanish American and Portuguese American empires covered three quarters of the land surface of the Western Hemisphere in 1810. Notice that nearly all of this territory was divided into five enormous viceroyalties, ruled by viceroys who were the personal representatives of their kings. When King Jõao VI of Portugal was forced to flee to Brazil, and King Carlos IV of Spain was thrown into a dungeon by Napoleon Bonaparte, the viceroys lost much of their leverage over their colonists, and Spanish and Portuguese Americans began to talk seriously about independence. How did the overthrow of these kings help to stimulate the independence movements?

Spanish colonies
- Viceroyalty of New Spain
- Viceroyalty of New Granada
- Viceroyalty of Peru
- Audiencia of Chile
- Viceroyalty of Rio de la Plata

Portuguese colony
- Viceroyalty of Brazil

Disputed territory
- Disputed by Great Britain, Spain, and Russia

Bolívar had a shaky grasp of military strategy, but he was a bold leader who never knew when he was beaten. He lost most of his battles, but persevered, winning the *last* battles and thereby gaining final victory. Along the way he got vital support from the black cowboys of the Venezuelan backlands, superb fighters whose ruthless tactics destroyed the Spaniards. He marched his men across the Andes into what is today Colombia and won the battle of Boyacá in 1819, an astonishing feat still studied in military academies. He drafted laws, wrote constitutions for more than one Spanish American country, and created institutions of government. Bolívar did not win independence by himself, but like George Washington in British North America, he proved an indispensable leader (see "Excerpt from Simón Bolívar: The Jamaica Letter").

Farther south, the rebel junta in Buenos Aires found itself ignored by Madrid. Argentina is more than eight thousand miles from Spain, and the Spanish kings never appreciated its potential. So the junta, freed from having to defend itself, set out to export revolution to the surrounding Spanish colonies. Crucial to its efforts was an Argentine-born professional military officer, José de San Martín (*hō-SĀ dā sahn mahr-TĒN*), who in 1810 was serving with Spanish forces fighting Napoleon in Europe.

San Martín returned to Buenos Aires and became a revolutionary. He was convinced that the key to Spanish domination of the continent was the viceroyalty of Peru; rebel victory there, he believed, would guarantee independence for all of Spanish South America. San Martín asked the junta for a post in western Argentina, from which he raised an army and conquered Chile after a dangerous crossing of the Andes. Then he invaded Peru by sea, aided by a first-rate mercenary sailor, Thomas Lord Cochrane, an adventurous British aristocrat who hated authority and loved money and war. Together they gave revolutionary forces a foothold in Peru. Bolívar then used that position to complete the liberation of Spanish South America by 1824 (See Map 28.2 on page 646).

Simón Bolívar.

Bolívar and San Martín lead independence movements

DOCUMENT 28.1 Excerpt from Simón Bolívar: The Jamaica Letter

. . . It is a grandiose idea to think of consolidating the New World into a single nation, united by pacts into a single bond. It is reasoned that, as these parts have a common origin, language, customs, and religion, they ought to have a single government to permit the newly formed states to unite into a confederation. But this is not possible. Actually, America is separated by climatic differences, geographic diversity, conflicting interests, and dissimilar characteristics . . .

Among the popular and representative systems, I do not favor the federal system. It is over-perfect, and it demands political virtues and talents far superior to our own. For the same reason I reject a monarchy that is part aristocracy and part democracy, although with such a government England has achieved much fortune and splendor . . . Do not adopt the best system

of government, but the one that is most likely to succeed . . .

When success is not assured, when the state is weak, and when results are distantly seen, all men hesitate; opinion is divided, passions rage, and the enemy fans these passions in order to win an easy victory because of them. As soon as we are strong and under the guidance of a liberal nation which will lend us her protection, we will achieve accord in cultivating the virtues and talents that lead to glory. Then will we march majestically toward that great prosperity for which South America is destined . . .

SOURCE: Simon Bolivar, "The Jamaican Letter" in Vicente Lecuna and Harold A. Bierck, Jr., editors, Selected Writings of bolivar, Volume I (New York: Colonial Press, 1951).

MAP **28.2**	Independent Latin American Nations After 1825

Once independence was achieved, three of the five Spanish American viceroyalties (Map 28.1) split into multiple individual states. Gran Colombia, the former Viceroyalty of New Granada, hung together until 1830, after which it divided into Venezuela, Colombia, and Ecuador. The Viceroyalty of the Rio de la Plata split into the United Provinces (or Argentina), Bolivia, Paraguay, and Uruguay. The Viceroyalty of New Spain became Mexico but lost its southern portion to the United Provinces of Central America, which later subdivided further. Note that the Viceroyalties of Peru and Brazil remained largely intact. What factors might account for the ability of these two regions to remain united?

Failure and Eventual Success in Mexico

Spain's most valuable possession in the Americas was Mexico, called New Spain. Its *criollo* elite was just as resentful of peninsular domination as its counterparts in Caracas and Buenos Aires, and perhaps with greater reason, since *peninsulares* were more likely to settle in New Spain than in any other Spanish American colony. But when a radical priest, Father Miguel Hidalgo (*mih-GWEL hih-DAHL-gō*), organized a peasant and Amerind rebellion in the fall of 1810, he failed to gain *criollo* support. A revolt of the poor and the colored carried little attraction for the wealthy and white. Hidalgo was captured and executed by Spanish loyalist forces in 1811. His successor, another priest named José María Morelos (*mō-REH-lōs*), followed him to the firing squad four years later.

Mexican independence did not appear likely, but a liberal revolt in Spain in 1820, forcing the king to call a representative parliament, changed the situation dramatically. When this news reached New Spain, conservative *criollos* and *peninsulares*, both alarmed at the idea of a progressive government in Spain, united against Spanish rule. Important officers of Mexico's Spanish garrison joined the cause, led by Agustín de Iturbide (*ē-TUR-bē-dā*), who assured conservatives that the new nation would remain a Catholic monarchy (with Iturbide himself as emperor) and that there would be neither revenge nor discrimination against *peninsulares*. These reassurances ensured the revolution's success, and New Spain became independent Mexico in 1821.

From Colony to Empire in Brazil

The final important new Latin American nation was Brazil, which had been ruled by Portugal, not Spain. In 1807, hours before Napoleon's occupation of Lisbon, the Portuguese prince regent and his court escaped to Brazil on British ships. Their arrival, which brought European royalty to American shores for the first time, was not without its comic side. Society women of the colonial capital, Rio de Janeiro, flocked to dockside to welcome the court and observe the latest European fashions. The lengthy shipboard voyage, with insufficient fresh water for bathing, had led to infestations of lice, so the women on board had shaved their heads to get rid of the critters. When the ladies of the court disembarked, colonial matrons, at first astonished, promptly went home to shave their heads, imitating what they assumed was fashionable among European royalty.

Humorous misunderstandings aside, the transfer of the monarchy to Brazil was a shocking event, as if King George III had decided in 1770 to run the British Empire from Boston. Prince Regent Jõao (*ZHWOW*), who became King Jõao VI in 1816, fell in love with Brazil, judging that its size and resources made it potentially much stronger than Portugal. When Napoleon's defeat restored Portugal's independence, Jõao stalled for years, but by 1821 he was forced to return or lose the throne. Before leaving for Portugal, he appointed his son Pedro regent of Brazil and told him not to return to Portugal to become king in his turn, but to declare Brazil independent, keeping both countries under the rule of the same royal family. When called to Portugal in 1822, Pedro obeyed his father, formally separating Brazil from Portugal. Resistance from Portuguese troops in Brazil was fierce but brief.

Thus by 1825, all but a few tiny areas of Latin America were independent of Europe. The difficult task of nation building, already under way, aimed to construct strong and stable societies on the foundations laid during the independence period. But many of the new nations were ruled by **caudillos**, strong and often unscrupulous personalities, and they failed to achieve either enduring institutional stability or sustained economic growth.

Read the **Document**

Jose Morelos, Sentiments of the Nation (Mexico), 1813

on **myhistorylab.com**

Social revolutions fail in Mexico, but a conservative uprising succeeds

Brazil separates from Portugal

Mexico from Santa Anna to Díaz

Mexico was unfortunate. By the time it gained independence in 1821, 11 years of fighting had wrecked its mines, destroyed its businesses, and impoverished its peasants. More than five hundred thousand of its six million people had perished. Its leader, Iturbide, was an unprincipled adventurer whose misrule as Emperor Agustín I ended in 1823. After that various caudillos who had dominated the revolutionary years vied for power.

A powerful caudillo dominates Mexico

The victor was Antonio López de Santa Anna, who claimed to establish a republic but pushed Mexican political development in a strongly authoritarian direction. He strengthened executive power in ways that made it immune to elections, limits on terms of office, or the actions of other branches of government. When congress, for example, objected to his dictatorial rule, he dismissed it by force and replaced its elected legislators with men whose careers and salaries depended on his generosity. Santa Anna excelled during the revolution against Spain but later lost half his country to the United States in the Mexican-American War of 1846–1848. By the time he was overthrown in 1854, he had crippled Mexico's prospects for balanced government.

La Reforma

La Reforma, the revolutionary movement that overthrew Santa Anna's dictatorship, was in trouble from the outset. Composed of politicians and lawyers influenced by the Enlightenment and by liberalism (Chapter 27), it sought to reduce the privileges of the country's conservative churchmen, landowners, and military leaders. In 1857, when the reformers instituted a liberal constitution, the military rebelled and the government fled from Mexico City. The fugitive reform government, led by President Benito Juárez (*WAH-rez*), a lawyer and a Zapotec Indian, fought a three-year civil war—the War of the Reform—against the conservative forces.

Juárez established his rump government in Veracruz, a stronghold of liberalism and Mexico's main seaport. From there he could control shipping into and out of Mexico and secure the customs duties that formed the bulk of government revenues in a nation without income or property taxes. He then used the money to purchase weapons abroad while denying arms shipments to his enemies. Even more important for Mexico's future, Juárez issued the Reform Laws, creating an institutional framework on the foundation laid by the Constitution of 1857. Juárez offered a government of laws rather than one of privilege and force, and his vision and his economic stranglehold prevailed. By 1860 the war was over and he was back in Mexico City.

Juárez wins a civil war and defeats French intervention

Then Juárez blundered, refusing to honor the debts his former opponents owed to foreign banks. His refusal was legally justified, but it provided French Emperor Napoleon III with an excuse for invading Mexico to collect the debts and installing a puppet regime under Maximilian von Habsburg. The Maximilian Affair provoked a five-year guerrilla war in a country already devastated by civil strife. Juárez and his government won again when France withdrew in 1867, but Mexico was bankrupt, and in a vain attempt to rebuild his shattered nation, the formerly liberal Juárez found himself ruling as a dictator until his death in 1872.

Social Structure and the Porfiriato

The dramatic events of Juárez's rule had little impact on Mexico's social structure. The country's governance systems and its mostly rural society remained colonial. Its native peoples lived in isolated villages called pueblos linked by dirt roads or no roads at all, largely unchanged since the days of Cortés. Huts were constructed of adobe or split reeds and usually shared among people, pigs, chickens, and dogs. Schools were nearly nonexistent, and most Amerinds could neither read nor speak Spanish.

By contrast, the capital, Mexico City, had wide, well-swept, well-lit streets and a population that by 1850 exceeded 170 thousand. Many schools and churches dotted its residential districts, and lovely public parks provided recreational opportunities for the well-to-do. Yet even in urban areas, desperate poverty existed alongside the wealth enjoyed by a privileged few.

Ladies of high social station led pampered lives, presiding over luxurious homes, discussing literature or the opera with friends, and attending balls and theatrical performances. But most Mexican women were far less fortunate. In rural areas they kept house and worked long hours in the fields; in towns and cities they worked in textile mills, in restaurants, or in wealthy households as servants.

Mexicans' lives changed little until 1876, when Porfirio Díaz (*DĒ-ahz*), a general who had supported the constitutional forces, emerged as a military hero intent on saving his country from chaos. He ruled Mexico until 1911 in the **Porfiriato**, a period of political repression and rapid economic development. The massive foreign investment he attracted from England, Belgium, Germany, France, and the United States caused critics to accuse him of selling the nation's resources to foreign exploiters, while supporters praised his modernization of a backward land. His government paved roads, extended power lines, laid railways, and developed water and sewage systems. His notorious "rural guards," a ruthless government police force, stamped out banditry and crime with on-the-spot executions.

Women in 19th-century Mexico making sacks for coffee.

The Porfiriato begins to modernize Mexico

None of these efforts, however, brought real help to the lower classes. Rural laborers continued to be plagued by poor nutrition, low wages, rates of infant mortality that approached 80 percent in some areas, and a life expectancy of 30 years. Most were tied to the farms through debts that kept them and their descendants virtually enslaved in menial jobs. In 1910, as Mexico approached the centenary of Hidalgo's 1810 revolution, 50 percent of all the nation's dwellings were classified as unfit for human habitation by Mexico's admittedly lax standards. Only 20 percent of the population was defined as "literate," and many of those could do little more than sign their names.

By then Díaz was in his eighties, but his reluctance even to discuss a successor helped create a liberal coalition dedicated to his overthrow. The coalition united behind Francisco Madero (*mah-DĀ-rō*), a wealthy landowner's son, who believed that democracy could cure all of Mexico's ills. His opportunity to test his belief came in 1911, when Díaz was forced to resign in the face of a bloody revolution. But that revolution was social as well as political, and Mexico's problems were not easily solved.

Argentina and Chile: Contrasts in the Southern Cone

Two new nations dominated South America's Southern Cone, so called because the continent's southern portion is cone shaped. Argentina endured decades of dictatorship before developing durable institutions and modernizing its economy and society. By 1914 it was reasonably prosperous. Chile, in contrast, enjoyed stable government for 60 years without being plagued by caudillos. But its deeply rooted social inequalities combined with its economic volatility to imperil its institutions in the Revolution of 1891.

Argentina from Rivadavia to Rosas

Porteños and gauchos dominate different portions of Argentina's economy

At the time of independence, Argentina was a sparsely populated agricultural land with a literate elite clustered in Buenos Aires, the nation's principal seaport. The city's residents, known as *porteños* (*pōr-TĀN-yōs*) or "port dwellers," considered themselves superior to the illiterate **gauchos** (cowboys) of the backlands and the ranchers who dominated the country's agrarian economy. Bernardino Rivadavia (*rē-vah-DAH-vē-ah*), a *porteño* who led the government in the 1820s, attempted to provide Argentina with such basic institutions as a parliament, postal service, national bank, budget office, and judiciary. But like Bolívar and Juárez, he was influenced by the Enlightenment, which had little impact on the uneducated majority of Argentines. He offended them with his policies of religious toleration, encouragement of immigration, and political centralization, and their rebellion in 1827 forced him into exile.

View the **Image**

An Argentine Gaucho, ca. 1870

on **myhistorylab.com**

Rosas reverses Rivadavia's efforts at institutionalization

Rivadavia had institutionalized Argentina before its citizens were ready for modern government. His successor, Juan Manuel de Rosas (*RŌ-sahs*), was both a clever executive and a brutal gaucho, a man whose business and administrative skills were offset by a tendency to use violence as a tool of governance. Unlike Mexico's Santa Anna, Rosas was a man of genuine ability; but like Santa Anna, he retarded his nation's political development by dismissing legislatures rather than working with them to create balanced government. His overthrow in 1852, led by a Brazilian-financed coalition of rivals, opened the path to modernization.

Modernization: Society, Women, and the Economy

After a decade of strife between Buenos Aires and rural backlands was settled by compromise, Argentina entered a period of dramatic change. Its newly stabilized government promoted public works and addressed issues such as the status of Amerinds and women, education, immigration, and economic expansion.

Under a succession of presidents of high ability, Argentina built railways and telegraph lines, installed a sewer system in Buenos Aires, and laid a transatlantic, suboceanic cable. Argentina's flatness made it ideal for railroads, and their rapid development opened the interior to settlement. The gaucho disappeared in the 1880s, replaced by immigrants who rode the new trains to previously remote regions of the country.

The Argentine army subjugates native peoples

Once there, the new arrivals worked land previously belonging to Amerinds. As recently as 1876, an Amerind raid within 60 miles of Buenos Aires had carried off 500 prisoners and 300 thousand head of cattle. In 1879, however, the Argentine army, which had grown significantly during a recent war with Paraguay, embarked on what was called the "conquest of the wilderness." Soldiers swept across western and southern central Argentina, killing many Amerinds and confining the survivors to reservations. This campaign against the Amerinds was similar to those undertaken in the same years by Chile and the United States. Argentina's interior lands lay open to white development.

The cosmopolitan elite that encouraged the conquest of the wilderness also felt the country could not fully modernize until women became literate. In Spanish America prior to 1810, women had been the preservers of traditional Spanish culture, passing on to their children European Catholic attitudes about religion, morality, and proper conduct. Now Argentina's leaders wanted modern, progressive attitudes instilled in the nation's youth. If women were going to transmit such attitudes, the men reasoned, they would have to be educated.

Schooling for women was a difficult struggle despite strong presidential leadership. Conservatives feared that educated women would become too independent and abandon their traditional roles of child rearing and homemaking. In fact, middle-class women seemed to be doing just that, creating a feminist movement that in the late 19th century began agitating for equal access to higher education. By 1914 Argentina had the most advanced education for both men and women in Latin America, but opportunities for women remained limited. Educated in separate, single-sex schools, women studied a more limited curriculum and thus could not enter the male-dominated professions of law, medicine, and engineering. This educational situation did not improve significantly until the 1940s.

Meanwhile, agriculture remained the foundation of Argentine prosperity. The country's export economy had initially centered on sheep: in the 1850s the United States purchased huge quantities of Argentine wool, and by 1880 sheep outnumbered people in Argentina by thirty to one. Although wool exports declined after the U.S. Civil War, because of a high protective tariff instituted in the United States in 1867, that decline coincided with an agricultural revolution that by 1890 made Argentina a principal world producer of wheat, corn, barley, and oats.

Argentina becomes a major agricultural exporter

Then, after 1900, Argentine cattle ranching was revitalized by new technologies developed by Chicago meat-packing companies such as Armour and Swift. Chilling beef for transport rather than freezing it improved the texture and flavor, creating a huge new market in Europe. Chilled beef soon became Argentina's most profitable export, tying the nation's economic fortunes to its European markets. By 1914, Argentina's per capita income rivaled those of Germany, Belgium, and Holland, and its foreign trade exceeded Canada's.

Argentina's prosperity attracted a huge number of immigrants from Spain, Italy, and Germany, nearly six million between 1871 and 1914, more than half of whom became permanent residents. These immigrants almost overwhelmed a country whose population in 1869 had been only 1.8 million. One result was a dramatic increase in Argentina's literacy rate, from 22 percent in 1869 to 65 percent in 1914, since most European immigrants could read and write.

Argentina's economic expansion attracts millions of immigrants

The booming economy, however, did not benefit all. Argentine landowners and commercial leaders remained extremely wealthy, while 80 percent of the workers (most of them foreign-born) lived with their families in one-room tenements or shacks. Because of the country's agricultural revolution, they enjoyed a more nutritious diet than did the laboring classes in Mexico and Chile, but Argentina's social structure perpetuated the economic and political subordination of the immigrant population. Even the immigrants who settled the interior did so not as landowners but as hired workers on the estates of the wealthy. Moreover, Argentina's political structure, in which most authority resided in the executive, was not designed to be responsive to the needs of an immigrant population.

Immigrant hotel, Buenos Aires.

Chilean Institutionalization

The executive dominance characterizing Argentine government was also present in Chile, Argentina's western neighbor. The remotest of Spain's former colonies, Chile in 1825 had a population of only half a million people, most living in rural areas. Mining was the basis of its economy, and most miners worked in dangerous conditions and lived in desperate poverty. Clearly Argentina had a more desirable location, but Chile quickly developed governmental institutions that achieved political stability following independence.

This was accomplished by Diego Portales (*pōr-TAH-lez*), a businessman-turned-politician who dominated Chilean politics in the 1830s. Portales considered it his duty to impose order on a disorganized and illiterate population, but he wanted a strong state to

Portales initiates Chilean institutionalization

rest on stable institutions rather than personal loyalties. He succeeded so thoroughly that Chile avoided caudillismo altogether. The Constitution of 1833, which he wrote, provided for an indirectly elected president and congress, with suffrage limited to property-holding, literate males over age 25. This document furnished Chile with a highly centralized government in which municipal and provincial authorities were subject to direct control by the president.

Portales's successful institutionalization of Chile was envied throughout Latin America. Chile's first three presidents each served two complete five-year terms, but this stability was achieved by manipulating elections at all levels and retaining the loyalty of the military through pay raises and professional advancement. Then in 1857, the Conservative Party, which had elected the first three presidents, split over the issue of religious toleration for non-Catholics, and the Liberals, who favored toleration, came to power in the election of 1861.

The Liberals took control at a time of significant change. Chilean wheat farmers had prospered greatly during the California gold rush of 1849, as Chile was the only wheat-producing country on the Americas' Pacific coast and sold enormous quantities of grain to feed California's booming population. Increased tax receipts financed gas lighting for Santiago, Chile's largest city, which grew to a population of 150,000 by 1875. Chile also attracted British financiers, whose Pacific Steam Navigation Company dispatched passenger ships as far as Seattle and Liverpool. In 1874 the company's gross tonnage made it the equal of the entire U.S. Navy.

Prosperity also made possible Chile's national railway network. In a country shaped like a 3,200-mile-long shoestring, with an impassable desert in the north, dense forests in the south, the Andes Mountains in the east, and the Pacific Ocean in the west, oxcarts were inadequate for modern development. New railways provided rapid, inexpensive transportation for agricultural products, minerals, and manufactured goods. They fostered the creation of a national economy linking all parts of Chile. Following Chile's decisive victory over its northern neighbors in the War of the Pacific (1879–1883), its new national economy took off.

Social Stratification and Inequality

The War of the Pacific brings tremendous benefits to Chile

The source of conflict in the War of the Pacific was the nitrate-rich regions north of Chile, owned by Peru and Bolivia but developed primarily by Chileans. When Europeans began seeking nitrate for fertilizer and explosives, Peru and Bolivia became aware of the valuable resources they had formerly ignored. Their efforts to tax Chilean mines in violation of treaty agreements and to prevent Chile from seizing all the nitrate fields led to war. Chile's victory over its rivals made it the dominant military power on South America's western seaboard, deprived Bolivia of its seacoast, and launched a lengthy economic boom grounded in the lucrative nitrate fields.

Chilean social inequality excludes many from nitrate-based prosperity

Yet a booming economy did little to alter Chile's rigid social stratification. Plenty of jobs became available, but pay was low and working conditions horrible. The rich became richer, as mining companies and landowners profited from improved transportation systems. In some respects Chile was progressive: professional schools were opened to women in 1879, and Latin America's first female doctor and lawyer were both Chileans. But these high-profile advances obscured the lack of meaningful opportunity for women and men of modest means. Chile's population was less than three million in 1895, and most Chileans were impoverished.

Devastating public health conditions only made matters worse. Malnutrition and disease cut Chile's average life expectancy to 35 years in 1900. Only the wealthiest sections of Santiago and Valparaiso had clean water and sewage systems, while the working poor lived in squalor, with up to eight people in one unventilated 15-by-25-foot room. Typhoid fever raged unchecked through city slums, and in the early 1900s Chile's suicide rate was the highest on earth.

While the poor suffered, much of the country's newfound wealth went into the military. Previously small, the Chilean army grew tremendously during the War of the Pacific, and the government used it in 1883 to subjugate the Araucanian (*ar-ow-KAH-nē-uhn*) Amerinds in the far south, who had retained their independence since the Spaniards arrived. Peruvian and Bolivian bitterness over the war's outcome led to border disputes that kept the Chilean military on alert. The army hired German officers to modernize Chilean military education, while the navy expanded using increased appropriations from a national budget flush with unprecedented surpluses.

One unanticipated effect of this military expansion was the Revolution of 1891, in which both parties to a political dispute called on armed support. President José Manuel Balmaceda (*bahl-mah-SĀ-dah*) alienated Conservatives by pushing an ambitious program of public works and social reform, at the same time antagonizing Liberals by increasing executive power at the expense of Congress. In 1890 Congress refused to pass Balmaceda's budget, but he announced that he would spend the money anyway. This action split the military: the army sided with Balmaceda, and the navy sided with Congress, which voted in January 1891 to depose the president.

An eight-month civil war followed, but given Chile's long coastline the outcome was never in doubt: a government opposed by the navy could not survive. The army's German supervisors went over to the navy's side, and Balmaceda committed suicide one day after his presidential term expired. The Revolution of 1891 ended any chance for the restoration of a strong presidency in Chile. Thereafter Congress dominated government in this most institutionally stable of all Latin American republics.

An Araucanian chief.

The Revolution of 1891 ensures legislative domination in Chile

Brazil's Experiment with Empire

After independence, Brazil charted a course different from those of the other new nations of Latin America. In 1822, when Prince Regent Pedro declared independence from Portugal, he established a European monarchy in the Americas. As Emperor Pedro I, however, he quickly ran into problems. Brazil was a constitutional monarchy, but Pedro was temperamentally autocratic. The country's *criollo* elite resented the peninsular-born Portuguese whom Pedro trusted and promoted to high office. Then Brazil lost an entire province (afterward known as independent Uruguay) in a disastrous war with Argentina (1825–1828). With that Pedro lost the confidence of his subjects, and in 1831 he abdicated in favor of his young son, who reigned nearly 60 years as Emperor Pedro II.

Brazil adopts a four-branch system of government

Pedro II.

The Long Reign of Pedro II

Unlike his father, Pedro II had the right temperament to rule a nation like Brazil. Tall and rangy, with a long beard, domed forehead, and gentle manner, he was a well-read, contemplative man who considered himself an enlightened monarch. The Brazilian Constitution of 1824 provided for four branches of government: executive, legislature, judiciary, and *poder moderador* (moderative power), the last of these giving the emperor a veto over legislation, the right to dissolve Congress, and power to appoint governors, judges, and bishops. The moderative power was designed to give the emperor authority to reconcile disputes between branches and prevent extreme swings of the electorate in one direction or another. Pedro II exercised that power judiciously, balancing liberals

with conservatives and steering a moderate political course. His conduct was largely responsible for the longevity of the Brazilian Empire.

Brazil's modernization began in the 1850s, facilitated by an immense boom in coffee production as coffee drinking became popular in Europe and North America. Bankers raised capital for massive public works, including telegraph lines, railways, and a transatlantic cable linking Brazil to Europe. By 1870 Rio de Janeiro was a thriving metropolis of six hundred thousand, four times the size of Mexico City, with paved streets, gas lighting, and a vibrant social life.

Brazil's interior, however, remained mostly undeveloped, largely because its dense rain forests, steep mountain ranges, and turbulent rivers made travel there nearly impossible. When the transatlantic cable was completed in 1874, Pedro II could communicate with London almost immediately, while sending a letter from his palace in Rio to the upper Amazon could take months. Nevertheless, by 1876 the country was so successful, and Pedro so widely respected, that he was given the honor of helping to ring the Liberty Bell in Philadelphia on the centennial of the U.S. Declaration of Independence.

Slavery, Society, and Imperial Collapse

The future of Pedro's monarchy, however, was threatened by the question of slavery. The Atlantic slave trade had been suppressed, but Brazil's huge slave population did not need imports to sustain itself. Under international pressure for abolition, in 1871 the country enacted the Law of the Free Womb, freeing all children born of slave mothers on or after September 28, 1871. This was a gradual emancipation that would have ended slavery only over the course of decades, and even that limited intent was evaded. For years slave owners registered the birthday of slave babies as September 27, 1871.

Outrage over slavery undermines the emperor's authority

Amid widespread moral outrage, culminating in the army's reluctance to pursue fugitive slaves, Pedro sailed for Europe to have surgery early in 1888. In his absence, his daughter, Princess Isabel, signed the Golden Law of May 13, 1888, emancipating all slaves in Brazil immediately and without compensation to landowners. In so doing, she brought Brazil into line with international expectations and basic human decency.

But she also signed the empire's death warrant. Emancipation without compensation alienated Brazilian landowners, as their bank loans, which had used slaves as collateral, were now jeopardized. Others, too, were disaffected. Pedro's dedication to religious toleration had already alienated the Catholic Church, and in Congress an active republican minority opposed his monarchy. The army turned against the regime when the high command's pay and benefits were reduced in 1889. As troops occupied the government buildings, no one stepped forward to defend the monarchy. Pedro II abdicated quietly and went into exile in Europe, where he died in 1891. This bloodless revolution ended the Western Hemisphere's only successful monarchy, initiating a transition to what seemed a stable republic.

European immigration changes Brazil

To some extent, slavery and the empire had been undermined by economic and social changes, inspired by the coffee boom and increased immigration from Europe. Paid workers proved 50 percent more efficient than slaves in cultivating coffee, reducing the utility of slave labor. Moreover, as prosperity and warm weather attracted huge numbers of immigrants from Portugal, Spain, Italy, Germany, and Russia, Brazil was Europeanized. Immigrants brought European concepts, labor unions, and political parties—and a European love of soccer—and they overwhelmed the native and black populations. In 1890, 44 percent of Brazil's population was white; in 1940 the figure had risen to 63 percent. The shift resulted not only from European immigration but also from high mortality rates among black people.

Regrettably, with a flood of literate immigrants the government saw no need to educate the Brazilian-born lower classes; its failure to modernize primary education retarded social mobility throughout the 20th century. A small but growing feminist movement—an outgrowth of the crisis over slavery in the 1870s—began working to secure basic rights for women, including education, voting rights, and access to professional careers. But their efforts often met resistance from many of the men who had worked with them to end slavery, continuing to delay meaningful advances for women and the poor.

The Trials and Triumphs of the United States

As Latin American nations struggled to achieve stability, the United States underwent struggles of its own. In 1783, after the American Revolution, the United States of America was an assortment of 13 semi-independent states, connected by a weak central government under Articles of Confederation. Of its three million people, living mainly near the Atlantic coast, about 20 percent were slaves, and most of the rest were of British ancestry. Amerinds, living mainly in the interior, belonged to their own nations, a status soon recognized by treaties. There was little industry: most Americans were farmers, and only about 5 percent of the population lived in cities.

By 1914, on the eve of World War I, the United States was a huge, prosperous nation, spanning the continent from Atlantic to Pacific, with a strong central government. Home to more than 100 million people, including many from Southern and Eastern Europe, Africa, Latin America, and Asia, the country had become the world's industrial leader, with almost half its people living in cities. Slaves had been freed, and many Amerinds had been forced onto government-controlled reservations. America's remarkable transformation involved four major processes: unification, expansion, industrialization, and immigration.

Unification and Consolidation

The first step toward unification was adoption of a federal constitution. By the mid-1780s, leaders of the new republic had recognized that the government created by the Articles of Confederation was too weak to deal with the nation's problems. So in 1787, in Philadelphia, a constitutional convention met to create a new form of government. After extensive debate and several key compromises, it produced an impressive result. The United States Constitution (see page 640), which went into effect in 1789 while revolution raged in France, established a strong federal government with authority to conduct war and foreign relations, regulate trade, impose taxes, and enforce laws. It was led by a powerful official called the president, who served as head of state, chief executive, and commander-in-chief of the military forces.

The president's power was extensive but limited. It was shared with a two-house legislature called Congress, which was responsible for making laws, and an independent judiciary led by a Supreme Court to interpret those laws. Federal power was also restrained by substantial authority reserved to the states, and by a Bill of Rights, adopted in 1791 as the constitution's first ten amendments, which guaranteed specific liberties for all citizens and explicitly stated that all powers not delegated to the federal government belonged to the states themselves, or to the people. In practice, the constitution's division of powers between the authority of the federal government and the rights of the states created a tension between the two. It was not clear in the nation's early history whether it would develop into a single country with a strong federal union or an association of autonomous states. After the southern states, which claimed the right to withdraw from the Union, lost the Civil War of 1861–1865, the issue was resolved in favor of a strong federal union. Tensions between states' rights and federal powers nonetheless continue to the present day.

The U.S. Constitution provides for balanced power

Expansion and Social Division

The expansion of the United States began in 1803, when Napoleon Bonaparte offered to sell the Louisiana Territory to the young republic. He was eager for funds and flexibility to pursue his war against Britain and frustrated by French inability to crush the Haitian revolt. Louisiana, recently obtained by France from Spain, was as large as the original United States, but its vast treeless plains, vital to Amerinds for food and other resources, were of dubious value to France. Only later, long after President Thomas Jefferson's government had purchased Louisiana from France for 15 million dollars, did it become apparent that the "Great American Desert," now called the Great Plains, contained some of the world's most productive farmland.

The Louisiana Purchase, which doubled the size of the United States, was only the beginning of American expansion (Map 28.3). In 1819, beset by rebellions throughout its Latin American empire, Spain gave in to American pressure and agreed to cede Florida and establish a clear boundary between U.S. and Spanish territory in the West.

In practice this boundary meant little to Americans. In the 1820s, settlers from the southern states began moving into Texas, a vast, sparsely populated part of the new nation of Mexico, which won independence from Spain in 1821. At first Mexicans

---

MAP **28.3**   The Expansion of the United States, 1783–1853

The new American republic spread westward and southward throughout the first half of the 19th century, eventually connecting the center of the North American continent "from sea to shining sea." Notice that these acquisitions more than doubled the territory of the original United States. Although the newly acquired lands had once been claimed by European nations like Britain, France, Spain, and Russia, very few people of European descent lived in them. What challenges would this pose for territories seeking eventual admission as new states of the American Union?

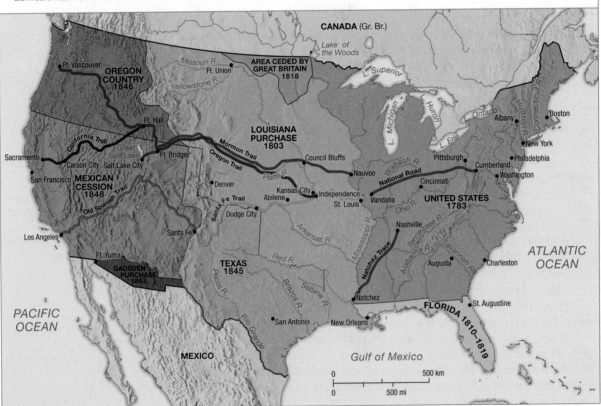

welcomed the newcomers, who were attracted by cheap land good for growing cotton, but by the 1830s these "Texicans" had proved neither loyal to Mexico nor interested in adopting Mexican ways. Led by Sam Houston, in 1836 they rose in rebellion, captured Mexico's president in battle, and forced him to grant Texas independence. The new "Lone Star Republic" then requested annexation by the United States.

At first the U.S. government was hesitant to take this step, knowing it might lead to war with Mexico; but in the 1840s an expansionist nationalism began to reshape American policy. Inspired by self-righteous optimism, many Americans had long seen themselves as God's instruments in building a New World society free from the problems and corruption of the Old. Now they came to see it as their divine right, or **manifest destiny**, to expand and control the whole continent. In 1844, they chose James Polk, a committed expansionist, as president. The next year Congress approved the annexation of Texas.

The United States expands under the principle of "manifest destiny"

Polk proceeded to fulfill his expansionist goals. In 1846 he settled a dispute over the Pacific Northwest (then called the Oregon territories) by agreeing to divide it with Britain along the 49th parallel, bringing the region south of that line under U.S. control. That same year the Mexican-American War began, driven both by American expansionism and Mexican resentment over the annexation of Texas. It ended two years later in American victory. By the Treaty of Guadalupe Hidalgo in 1848, the northern half of Mexico, from Texas to California, became the American Southwest. In less than half a century, the United States had almost quadrupled its size, and the federal republic now spanned the continent "from sea to shining sea."

The Mexican-American War adds extensive territories to the United States

But expansion intensified two grave social rifts that already divided the nation. In acquiring Mexico's land, the United States acquired the Mexicans who lived there, and in expanding westward it claimed the homelands of numerous Amerind nations. Mexicans were subjected to vicious stereotypes and ethnic discrimination, often treated as aliens in their own ancestral lands. Amerinds were driven from their lands and slaughtered in wars or herded onto reservations. The brutal treatment of these people, victims of manifest destiny, contradicted the presumption that Americans were shaping a superior society unstained by the Old World's sins.

Even more divisive was the issue of slavery, which had confounded the republic from its inception. By the time of the Mexican-American War, slavery had caused increasing bitterness and mistrust between North and South. The acquisition of vast new lands, and the question of whether slavery would be extended to them, helped transform this divisive dilemma into a violent conflict.

North Against South

Increasing disparities between North and South compounded the dispute over slavery. For decades, owing partly to regional differences and partly to Britain's Industrial Revolution, North and South had developed in different directions. The North was beginning to industrialize as factories and businesses helped cities grow. Northerners looked to the federal government for measures to support these new industries, such as tariffs to protect them against foreign competition. Nationalistic northerners increasingly took pride in the growth and strength of their nation, identifying less with their region or states than with the United States as a whole.

An 1884 lithograph of a cotton plantation on the Mississippi River.

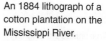

The South, meanwhile, as the main supplier of cotton for textile mills in Europe and New England, had remained an agrarian society based on plantations and slaves. Enormous demand for cotton and

Sectional interests differentiate North and South

the exploitation of slave labor provided southern planters with a healthy income to support their aristocratic lifestyle; they had little need for industry or interest in urbanization. Slaves manufactured what was needed on the plantations, and the South's cities were small, primarily ports from which cotton and other agricultural products were shipped. Southerners opposed tariffs because they increased the cost of imports, particularly manufactured goods from England and luxury items from France. They, too, were proud of their nation, but they were even more attached to their states, promoting states' rights over the interests of the country as a whole.

Though they dominated southern politics, planters were but a small minority of southern males. In 1860, only 25 percent of southerners owned slaves, and most owned only two or three. The majority of the South's white people owned no slaves at all but supported the slave system because it was the foundation of the southern economy. In the South, slaves represented wealth, and many families who did not have them aspired to purchase them. Farmers who opposed slaveholding would not be allowed to use the planter's dock for shipping goods downriver or be able to call on the planter for help in time of drought or flood. Finally, planters and farmers may have been far apart in wealth and social standing, but their white skin gave them a common interest in keeping slaves in their place and in reinforcing racial barriers.

Slavery becomes the principal issue dividing North and South

Increasingly, then, northern industrialism conflicted with southern agrarianism, while northern nationalism clashed with southern sectionalism. As the interests and cultures of North and South diverged, slavery became the flashpoint. In the first half of the 19th century, a worldwide antislavery movement had led to global prohibition of the slave trade, abolition of slavery throughout the British Empire, and a vocal abolitionist movement in the northern states. Southern whites, seeing their lifestyle as dependent on slavery, passionately defended this ancient institution.

Although the federal government lacked authority to outlaw slavery in the existing states, northern politicians tried to keep it from spreading to the western territories (Map 28.4). Southern slave states, fearful that their influence would decline as they became increasingly outnumbered by northern and western free states, resisted these efforts and began to think that they might be better off outside the Union. An elaborate compromise in 1850 helped postpone the break (see "Four Perspectives on the American Union"). But in 1860 former Illinois Congressman Abraham Lincoln, running on a platform that opposed the expansion of slavery into the new territories, was elected president in a vote divided along sectional lines. By the time he took office the next March, seven southern states had formally seceded, claiming the right to freely withdraw from the Union, much as they had freely joined it seven decades earlier. When Lincoln, a dedicated Unionist, asserted that the southern states were in rebellion and made clear his intent to crush this secession by force, four more states seceded, joining the other seven in a new Confederate States of America. The War Between the States had begun.

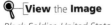

View the **Image**

Black Soldier, United States Civil War

on **myhistorylab.com**

The Civil War affects the United States profoundly

An ironclad warship of the Union Navy during the American Civil War.

Since industrial technology helped decide its outcome, the U.S. Civil War (1861–1865) was in many ways the first truly modern war. It involved mass production of weapons, the use of railways to move supplies and troops, the sending of messages by telegraph, and the use of ironclad ships and early types of submarines, trench warfare, repeating rifles, and early machine guns. Although the South had talented generals and brave soldiers, the North's industrial wealth and power secured its victory.

The northern triumph in the Civil War had several crucial results. It preserved the Union, establishing conclusively that the United States was a single nation, not an association of autonomous states. It ended slavery, provisionally through Lincoln's Emancipation Proclamation issued during the war and

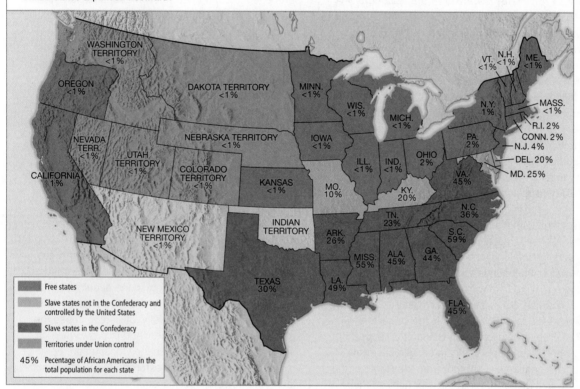

MAP 28.4 Slavery and Civil War in the United States, 1820–1861

The enslavement of African Americans, taken for granted by the Constitution of 1787, eventually tore the young republic apart. Note the sharp geographic division between southern "slave states" and northern "free states." Southern states, fearful that Congress would eventually contain a majority of free states and then would vote to outlaw slavery throughout the nation, insisted that for each free state admitted to the Union after 1815, one slave state must be admitted to balance voting in the Senate. This compromise broke down in the early 1850s and led quickly to civil war. Why did the compromise fail as the United States expanded westward?

permanently by the 13th constitutional amendment, ratified in 1865. By resolving the threat of disunity and ensuring the predominance of northern economic interests, the war also removed the last obstacles to the growth of American industry.

The Civil War did not, however, resolve the status of liberated slaves. Northern efforts at **Reconstruction**, designed to reintegrate the South into the Union, deeply embittered southern whites while providing southern blacks with little means to secure their rights and welfare. Many former slaves, most of whom had no land and little money or education, eventually became **sharecroppers**, farming the lands of white landowners in return for half their harvest. Beginning in the 1880s and 1890s, once Reconstruction had ended, African Americans were systematically deprived of the vote and segregated in public places by notorious **Jim Crow laws** that institutionalized racial discrimination in the southern states.

Industry, Immigration, and Overseas Commitments

In the North, spurred by enormous wartime demand for manufactured goods, industry in the 1860s began growing explosively. Exploiting extensive natural resources—including coal, iron, cotton, timber, waterpower, minerals, and oil—and supported by a government

Read the Document

African-American Emancipation Songs: (a) "Many Thousands Gone;" (b) "Kingdom Coming"

on **myhistorylab.com**

DOCUMENT 28.2 Four Perspectives on the American Union

In 1850, the Missouri Compromise, carefully crafted in 1820 to preserve the balance between free and slave states in the federal system of the United States, fell apart over the question of the disposition of the vast territories acquired in the Mexican-American War (the Mexican Cession). Did this mean that the American Union was headed for dissolution over the issue of slavery in the newly acquired territories? Four of the leading statesmen of the day offered these perspectives between 1850 and 1858.

In 1850 Senator Henry Clay of Kentucky, "the Great Compromiser," offered yet another compromise designed to save the Union. His Compromise of 1850 tilted toward the South, admitting California as a free state at the expense of permitting the extension of slavery to New Mexico and Utah. Arguing for his proposal, Clay raised the specter of southern secession:

Mr. President, I am directly opposed to any purpose of secession, of separation. I am for staying within the Union and fighting for my rights—if necessary, with the sword—within the bounds and under the safeguard of the Union . . . Here I am within it, and here I mean to stand and die . . . within it to protect myself . . . Will there not be more safety in fighting within the Union than without it? . . . The dissolution of the Union and war are identical and inseparable; they are convertible terms . . .

I conjure gentlemen, whether from the South or the North, by all they hold dear in this world, by all their love of liberty, by all their veneration for their ancestors, by all their regard for posterity, by all their gratitude to Him who has bestowed upon them such unnumbered blessings, by all the duties which they owe to mankind and all the duties they owe to themselves, by all these considerations I implore them to pause—solemnly to pause—at the edge of the precipice before the fearful and disastrous leap is taken in the yawning abyss below which will inevitably lead to certain and irretrievable destruction.

SOURCE: Henry Clay, "Compromise Resolutions"
31st Congress, 1st Session, February 6, 1850.

Four weeks later, Senator John C. Calhoun of South Carolina responded to Clay's appeal with a warning that the South would secede from the Union unless the North agreed to extend slavery to all the new territories, and to a constitutional amendment restoring the balance of power between North and South:

The prospect, then, is that the two sections in the Senate, should the efforts now made to exclude the South from the newly acquired territories succeed, will stand before the end of the decade twenty Northern states to twelve Southern (considering Delaware as neutral), and forty Northern senators to twenty-eight Southern. This great increase of senators, added to the great increase of members of the House of Representatives and electoral college on the part of the North, which must take place over the next decade, will effectually and irretrievably destroy the equilibrium which existed when the government commenced . . . What was once a constitutional federal republic is now converted, in reality, into one as absolute as that of the Autocrat of Russia, and as despotic in its tendency as any absolute government that ever existed . . .

How can the Union be saved? . . . The North has only to will it to accomplish it: to do justice by conceding to the South an equal right in the acquired territory, and to do her duty by causing the stipulations relative to fugitive slaves to be faithfully fulfilled; to cease the agitation of the slave question; and to provide for the insertion of a provision in the Constitution, by an amendment, which will restore to the South in substance the power she possessed of protecting herself before the equilibrium between the sections was destroyed by the action of this government . . . At all events, the responsibility of saving the Union rests on the North and not on the South . . .

SOURCE: John C. Calhoun, "Either Slavery or Disunion"
31st Congress, 1st Session, March 4, 1850.

Three days after Calhoun's speech, Senator Daniel Webster of New Hampshire rose to answer him. His lengthy address, known to history as the Seventh of March Speech, confounded antislavery forces in New England by urging northerners to accept the Compromise of 1850:

Mr. President, I wish to speak today, not as a Massachusetts man, but as an American . . . I speak today for the preservation of the Union. Hear me for my cause . . .

(continued)

DOCUMENT 28.2 *continued*

Secession! Peaceable secession! Sir, your eyes and mine are destined never to see that miracle. The dismemberment of this vast country without convulsion! . . . Who is so foolish, I beg everybody's pardon, as to expect to see any such thing? . . . No, Sir! I will not state what might produce the disruption of the Union; but, Sir, I see as plainly as I see the sun in heaven what that disruption itself must produce; I see that it must produce war . . .

Sir, I may express myself too strongly, perhaps, but there are impossibilities in the natural as well as in the physical world, and I hold the idea of a separation of these States, those that are free to form one government, and those that are slave-holding to form another, as such an impossibility. We could not separate the States by any such line, if we were to draw it. We could not sit down here today and draw a line of separation that would satisfy any five men in the country . . .

SOURCE: Daniel Webster, "The Seventh of March Speech" 31st Congress, 1st Session, March 7, 1850.

The Compromise of 1850 became law, but it did not end the debate over slavery and secession. As the decade moved along, the Kansas-Nebraska Act of *1854 repealed the Missouri Compromise and laid northern territories open to slavery, while the Supreme Court's 1857 ruling in the case of Dred Scott v. Sandford held that even free blacks were not entitled to citizenship, and that Congress had no power to prohibit the extension of slavery anywhere in the United States. Responding to the widening gulf between North and South over these matters, Abraham Lincoln, a candidate for a Senate seat in Illinois, spoke these prophetic words on June 16, 1858:*

"A house divided against itself cannot stand." I believe this government cannot endure, permanently, half slave and half free. I do not expect the Union to be dissolved; I do not expect the house to fall; but I do expect it will cease to be divided. It will become either all one thing, or all the other. Either the opponents of slavery will arrest the further spread of it and place it where the public mind shall rest in the belief that it is in the course of ultimate extinction, or its advocates will push it forward till it shall become alike lawful in all the states, old as well as new, North as well as South . . .

SOURCE: Abraham Lincoln, "Speech to the Republican State Convention at Springfield, IL," June 16, 1858.

---

clearly sympathetic to their needs, American capitalists and consumers created an industrial superpower over the next half century. America's numerous rivers and lakes, and especially its new railways, linked the nation. U.S. farmers transformed the Great Plains into wheat- and cornfields that fed the country's rapidly growing workforce.

Labor came from within the country, as Americans left farms to take new jobs in the cities, but especially from abroad, as millions of Europeans were drawn by America's promise of freedom and prosperity. Immigration soared in the 1840s with the failure of Ireland's potato crop, the sole source of sustenance for most of that island's population, and the resulting emigration of a million starving people. By 1900 tens of thousands of people came each year from Southern and Eastern Europe. Between 1860 and 1914, almost 30 million immigrants arrived in the United States, a mass migration unprecedented in world history. Many immigrants took factory jobs, swelling the population of the great northern cities, while others worked in mines and built railways. Laboring long hours, often for low wages, these immigrant laborers helped transform the American nation into an industrial giant.

U.S. economic expansion attracts millions of immigrants

But immigrants were not always warmly welcomed. Many Americans resented the newcomers and their unfamiliar customs, beliefs, and languages. America's Protestant majority, alarmed by the numbers of incoming Irish, Italian, and Polish Catholics, as well as Russian Jews, often treated these new groups with hostility. Concerns that low-paid immigrant workers were taking jobs from Americans who had been in the country longer sparked ethnic conflicts in the industrial North and violent hostility

Nativism develops as a reaction to massive immigration

U.S. anti-immigration poster: Laborers of many ethnic groups build a wall to keep out Chinese immigrants.

🔍 **View** the **Image**

U.S. Field Hospital in the Philippines, Philippine-American War

on **myhistorylab.com**

The United States becomes a world power

to Chinese workers in the West. **Nativism**, as anti-immigrant sentiment was called, led to the enactment in the 1880s of a ban on immigrants from China, and in the 1920s of strict numerical limits on those from Southern and Eastern Europe.

Massive numbers of foreigners further complicated the nation's racial problems. Many new arrivals, themselves victims of nativist bigotry, sought to boost their status by adopting racist attitudes toward former slaves, who remained at the bottom of the social and economic structure. At the same time, white supremacist groups such as the Ku Klux Klan, a secret, nativist, racist group first organized in the South, directed violent fury against Catholics, Jews, and African Americans.

Despite these tensions, the United States was becoming a world power. Although Americans traditionally avoided overseas commitments, some of them were eager to join the imperialist ventures that Western industrial nations engaged in toward the end of the 19th century. In 1898, aroused by Spanish efforts to crush a revolt in Cuba, one of the last colonies in Spain's once-great empire, the United States fought and won the Spanish-American War. Cuba gained independence from Spain but effectively became an American protectorate, while Puerto Rico and the Philippine Islands were transferred from Spain to the United States, essentially as colonies. Born of revolt against colonial control, America now had its own colonial empire.

By the early 20th century, the United States was a unified, wealthy nation with the world's largest industrial economy, an abundant supply of resources and food, and a vast, diverse population marked by regional, racial, and ethnic tensions. It was on its way to becoming the planet's most powerful and influential nation.

The Consolidation and Expansion of Canada

North of the United States, during the 19th century, Canada also emerged as a vast new nation. Although its development in some ways paralleled that of the United States, Canada avoided violent upheavals. Yet it also experienced ethnic strife, the product of a colonial heritage that was both French and British.

French and British Colonization of Canada

In the 17th century, while England was establishing colonies along the Atlantic coast, French explorers, trappers, and traders were creating a huge empire to the north and west. Unlike the British to the south, however, the French did not come in large numbers, numbering no more than ninety thousand by the mid-1700s.

Britain takes Canada from France in 1763

The events of the Seven Years War (1756–1763), also called the French and Indian War in North America, were disastrous for France, depriving it of its North American empire, much of which was taken over by Britain. Later, the American Revolution (1775–1783) cost Britain its original colonies but left it in control of Canada, to which thousands of British loyalists fled from the new United States. These immigrants, anxious to remain British subjects, gave Canada for the first time a sizable English-speaking population.

Canada is divided into two colonies

Accustomed to British ways, the newcomers pressed for a representative assembly similar to those that had existed in their former colonies. Fearful of conflict between them and the French Canadians, in 1791 Britain's Parliament divided Canada into two

MAP 28.5   The Expansion of Canada, 1867–1873

Canada became a self-governing dominion of the British Empire in 1867. Suspecting that the United States might feel that its philosophy of "manifest destiny" entitled it to expand northward, Prime Minister John A. MacDonald purchased the largely empty Northwest Territories from the trading companies that owned them. Then Canada's Parliament admitted Manitoba, British Columbia, and Prince Edward Island as additional provinces. Observe that MacDonald's actions changed Canada from a small, Atlantic-oriented country to the second largest nation on earth, spanning the continent and exceeding the United States in size. What challenges might arise from such rapid expansion into largely empty lands?

colonies, giving each an elected assembly and an appointed governor. The French Catholic area (later called Québec) became Lower Canada, since it lay in the lower valley of the Saint Lawrence River, while the English Protestant region (later called Ontario) became Upper Canada (Map 28.5). Unrecognized were Amerind nations, whose interests were dismissed by the British. Some, like the Inuit, lived in remote northern latitudes in which Europeans had no interest. Others, like the Huron, saw their claims pushed aside by British military power.

Dominion, Expansion, and Ethnic Anxieties

By 1837, however, severe tensions between the two colonies, and between the governor and assembly within each colony, produced violent revolts. Fearful that each might declare independence, or perhaps be annexed by the expansive American republic to the south, the British sent the respected Lord Durham to examine the situation. His 1839 *Report on the Affairs of British North America* became the blueprint for **dominion government** in a number of British colonies. This "Durham

Canada becomes a single colony in 1840

Report" called for self-governance by cabinets and prime ministers accountable to elected assemblies, and for federation of adjacent colonies into larger and stronger dominions. In response to these recommendations, Parliament's Canada Act of 1840 united the two colonies under a single two-house legislature. Although Britain retained control of trade and foreign policy, Canadians henceforth ran their internal affairs.

In the 1860s, two key Canadian leaders, appalled by the U.S. Civil War and anxious to prevent a similar conflict in Canada between people of French and British heritage, developed a compromise plan for nation building. One was George-Étienne Cartier (*zhorzh-Āt-YEN kart-YĀ*), committed to preserving French-Canadian culture; the other was John A. MacDonald, dedicated to fostering Canadian nationalism in a unified nation. At several key conferences in 1864, they helped write a Canadian constitution that combined a British-style parliamentary government with a federal union like that of the United States. The constitution secured British political structures while allowing the French-speaking province of Québec enough autonomy to protect its heritage. To reduce the potential for the kind of states' rights conflicts that had torn apart the United States, the Canadians agreed that any powers not listed in the constitution would belong to the federal government rather than the provinces. In 1867, Britain's Parliament passed the British North America Act, creating the Dominion of Canada. It included not only Upper and Lower Canada, now called Ontario and Québec, but also two former maritime colonies, New Brunswick and Nova Scotia. In most respects an independent nation, Canada retained its allegiance to the British monarch, represented by a governor-general.

Prime Minister John A. MacDonald spearheads Canadian expansion

MacDonald, who served as prime minister for most of the period between 1867 and 1891, expanded the country with breathtaking speed. In 1869 he negotiated with the British Hudson Bay Company to buy the Northwest Territories, an enormous expanse of wilderness and Amerind land stretching across the northern part of the continent. The province of Manitoba, established on some of this land, was added in 1870 to the federation. In 1871, MacDonald persuaded the large western colony of British Columbia to become a Canadian province; two years later he did the same with the small eastern colony of Prince Edward Island. By 1873 the Dominion of Canada, like the United States, extended from ocean to ocean.

MacDonald's great achievement, however, was not just to acquire vast tracts of land but to link them into a unified nation. The key to unity was construction of the Canadian Pacific Railway, completed in 1885, a magnificent engineering feat that not only connected the east with the west but also opened up the country's interior. In the years that followed, thousands came to Canada from Central and Northern Europe: some settled in eastern industrial cities such as Toronto and Montreal; others took westbound trains to Canada's plains, which became a fertile grain-producing region. The Canadian economy thrived, aided by the explosive growth of American industry and its need for the natural resources that Canada could provide.

As in the United States, however, expansion heightened tensions within Canada. As more and more English-speaking provinces were added to the dominion, French Canadians in Québec felt increasingly alienated from the rest of the country and concerned that their political and economic influence was declining. In the 20th century, they sought to enhance their status, some by having large families to increase their numbers, and others by forming a separatist movement and threatening to secede. Despite its internal tensions and dual culture, however, Canada remained a united country.

Putting It in Perspective

By 1820, most regions in the Americas had achieved independence from Europe's colonial powers, and by 1900, the new nations had diverged widely. The United States, with its durable constitution, abundant natural resources, and unprecedented immigration, succeeded in surmounting sectional strife to grow into a stable and prosperous industrial giant. Similarly, Canada, aided by Britain's desire to keep it from being annexed by its expansive southern neighbor, established enduring institutions and a thriving economy while expanding across the continent.

Mexico, once Spain's largest and wealthiest colony, experienced caudillismo, social strife, territorial loss, and foreign intervention and failed to sustain either stability or prosperity. Argentina, after some initial turmoil, developed stable political institutions.

Chile and Brazil enjoyed decades of stability, although military interventions at the end of the 1800s signaled upheavals ahead. Several smaller states, plagued by chronic instability and caudillismo, moved from government to government with little continuity.

Nonetheless, in the course of the 19th century, the Americas had undergone an incredible transformation. A host of new nations, large and small, had replaced the vast European empires that earlier ruled these lands. Although they separated themselves politically from Europe, these new nations adopted European ideas and welcomed millions of European immigrants. But despite their independence and innovations, the peoples of the Western Hemisphere experienced uneven levels of prosperity and were often vexed by problems derived from their European heritage.

Reviewing Key Material

KEY CONCEPTS

manifest destiny, 657	juntas, 643
Reconstruction, 659	La Reforma, 648
sharecroppers, 659	Porfiriato, 649
Jim Crow laws, 659	*porteños*, 650
nativism, 662	gauchos, 650
dominion government, 663	*poder moderador*,
caudillo, 647	653

KEY PEOPLE

Simón Bolívar, 641, 643	Benito Juárez, 648
King Carlos III, 642	Porfirio Díaz, 649
Tupac Amaru II, 642	Bernardino Rivadavia, 650
Napoleon Bonaparte, 643	Juan Manuel de Rosas, 650
José de San Martín, 645	Diego Portales, 651
Miguel Hidalgo, 647	Emperor Pedro II, 653
King João VI, 647	Abraham Lincoln, 658
Antonio López de	John A. MacDonald, 664
Santa Anna, 648	

ASK YOURSELF

1. Why did many Latin American revolutions have conservative roots? In what ways were they based on European ideas?

2. How did caudillismo rather than institutionalization affect the independent development of Mexico and Argentina?

3. How did immigration affect the national development of Argentina, Brazil, and the United States?

4. How did the doctrine of manifest destiny affect the growth of both the United States and Canada?

5. How did the victory of the North in the Civil War facilitate the economic development of the United States?

GOING FURTHER

Adelman, J. *Republic of Capital: Buenos Aires and the Legal Transformation of the Atlantic World.* 1999.

Bailyn, B. *The Ideological Origins of the American Revolution.* 1992.

Bauer, K. J. *The Mexican-American War, 1846–1848.* 1976.

Bushnell, D., and N. Macaulay. *The Emergence of Latin America in the Nineteenth Century.* 1995.

Collier, S., and W. Sater. *A History of Chile.* 1994.

Da Costa, E. V. *The Brazilian Empire: Myths and Histories.* 2005.

Davis, D. *Slavery and Human Progress.* 1984.

Foner, E. *Reconstruction: America's Unfinished Revolution, 1863–1877.* 1988.

Fox, G. *Hispanic Nation: Culture, Politics, and the Construction of Identity.* 1997.

Haring, C. *Empire in Brazil*. 1947.

Kinsbruner, J. *Independence in Spanish America*. 1994.

Lynch, J. *Simón Bolívar: A Life*. 2006.

Martin, G., ed. *The Causes of Canadian Confederation*. 1990.

McPherson, J. *Battle Cry of Freedom: The Civil War Era*. 1988.

Meyer, M., and W. Sherman. *The Course of Mexican History*. 2002.

Morris, R. *Founding of the Republic*. 1985.

Nugent, W. *Crossing: The Great Transatlantic Migrations, 1870–1914*. 1992.

Pike, Douglas. *Australia*. 1969.

Rock, D. *Argentina 1516–1987*. 1987.

Rodriguez, J. *The Independence of Spanish America*. 1998.

Rodriguez, J. *The Origins of Mexican National Politics*. 1997.

Stevens, D. *Origins of Instability in Early Republican Mexico*. 1991.

Telles, E. *Race in Another America: The Significance of Skin Color in Brazil*. 2004.

Voss, S. *Latin America in the Middle Period, 1750–1920*. 2002.

Key Dates and Developments

1789	Adoption of the United States Constitution		**1831–89**	Pedro II reigns as emperor of Brazil
1791	Canada divided: Upper and Lower Canada		**1833**	Chilean Constitution, drafted by Portales
1803	U.S. purchases Louisiana Territory from France		**1839**	Durham's *Report on the Affairs of British North America*
1807–08	Napoleon invades Portugal and Spain; Portuguese Prince Regent Jõao flees to Brazil		**1840**	Canada Act unites Upper and Lower Canada
1810	Latin American revolutions begin		**1846–48**	Mexican-American War
1818	Chile gains independence		**1854–72**	La Reforma in Mexico
1819	Bolívar wins the Battle of Boyacá		**1861–65**	Civil War in the United States
1820	San Martín lands in Peru		**1862–67**	French intervention in Mexico
1821	Iturbide leads Mexico to independence		**1867**	British North America Act creates Dominion of Canada
1821–27	Rivadavia tries to institutionalize Argentina		**1876–1911**	The Porfiriato in Mexico
1822	Meeting between Bolívar and San Martín in Ecuador; Pedro I proclaims Brazilian independence		**1879–83**	War of the Pacific
			1888	Abolition of slavery in Brazil
1824	Bolívar completes liberation of Spanish America		**1889**	Overthrow of the Brazilian Empire
			1898	Spanish-American War
1824–54	Santa Anna dominates Mexico			

PEARSON

myhistorylab Connections

Reinforce what you learned in this chapter by studying the many documents, images, maps, review tools, and videos available at www.myhistorylab.com.

Read and Review

✓● Study and Review Chapter 28

📖● Read the Document

On Constitutional Government (Early 19th Century) Simon Bolivar, p. 643

Jose Morelos, *Sentiments of the Nation* (Mexico), 1813, p. 647

African-American Emancipation Songs: (a) "Many Thousands Gone;" (b) "Kingdom Coming," p. 659

🔍● View the Image

U.S. Field Hospital in the Philippines, Philippine-American War, p. 662

((●● Listen to the Audio

Latin America, p. 641

Revolutionary Thought 2, p. 643

Research and Explore

🔍● View the Image

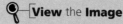

An Argentine Gaucho, ca. 1870, p. 650

🔍● View the Image

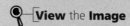

Black Soldier, United States Civil War, p. 658

29

New Connections and Challenges in Eastern and Southern Asia, 1800–1912

((•─[Listen to the **Chapter Audio** for Chapter 29 on **myhistorylab.com**

- What factors and developments destabilized China in the 19th century?

- How did India succumb, adapt, and respond to British rule?

- What challenges faced 19th-century Japan and how did Japan adapt?

- How did imperialism affect Asian countries and how did they respond?

- How and why did Chinese and Japanese responses to imperialism differ?

New Connections Challenge Asians

In the 19th century, new connections with the Western world created challenges for Asians. This color print shows Japanese people observing an American steamship.

In 1793, at China's bustling port of Tianjin (*t'YEN-JIN*), a large ship arrived from a distant land. Aboard were diplomats, scientists, artists, musicians, and translators, led by Lord George Macartney, representing Britain's King George III. Hoping to persuade China's leaders to open their ports to British goods, Macartney's mission brought six hundred cases of his country's finest wares, including textiles, carpets, cutlery, clocks, musical instruments, and scientific gadgets.

South and East Asia

But the mission soon ran into problems. Macartney, a proud aristocrat, refused to perform the kowtow, a humble bow that involved touching one's forehead to the floor, and thus was at first denied an audience with China's Qianlong (*ch'YEN LŌNG*) Emperor. The Chinese treated the British goods as tribute from a lesser nation, while Macartney, observing conspicuous poverty and crude weapons, saw China as backward and weak. When finally allowed to visit Qianlong at his summer palace, Macartney was awed by pavilions full of exquisite Chinese products and learned of the ruler's disdain for Western goods. "Our celestial empire possesses all things in prolific abundance," the emperor proclaimed in a letter to King George III. China had "no need to import the manufactures of outside barbarians."

Six decades later, in 1853, a similar encounter occurred in Japan. Here the visitors were Americans, arriving in steam-powered warships, with a letter from their president insisting that Japan open its ports to U.S. trade. After an awkward standoff, Japanese officials agreed to take the letter to Japan's military leader, the shogun. The visitors departed but promised to return the next year. Awed by America's warships and large guns, but facing resistance from his samurai warriors to the U.S. demands, the shogun agreed in 1854 to open two small ports. At the agreement's ceremonial signing, Japanese sumo wrestlers entertained their Western guests, while Japanese officials rode a scale-model train the Americans brought to impress them.

These two encounters exemplify the challenges posed to Asian nations by new connections emerging in the 1800s. Having long seen Westerners as inferior "barbarians," Asians first tried to limit these connections, then to exploit them by selectively adapting Western technologies and ways. Some adapted better to these new challenges than others.

Instability and Endurance in China

In the 1800s the Chinese Empire, long dominant in East Asia (See Map 29.1 on page 670), endured disasters that shattered its power and prestige. Resulting largely from problems in China itself, they were worsened by outside intrusions that aggravated and exploited China's instability.

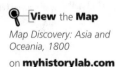

View the **Map**

Map Discovery: Asia and Oceania, 1800

on **myhistorylab.com**

China's Internal Problems

After conquering China in the 1600s and creating the Qing (*CHING*) dynasty, China's Manchu rulers brought stability and prosperity, leading most Chinese to accept the rule of these outsiders from Manchuria (Chapter 21). By the early 1800s, however, stability and prosperity were waning.

FOUNDATION MAP 29.1 East and South Asia Around 1800

In 1800 China dominated East Asia, with neighboring nations paying it tribute for protection and trade. Notice, however, that Western commercial interests controlled parts of India and Indonesia. Why did China and Japan seek to minimize connections with the West?

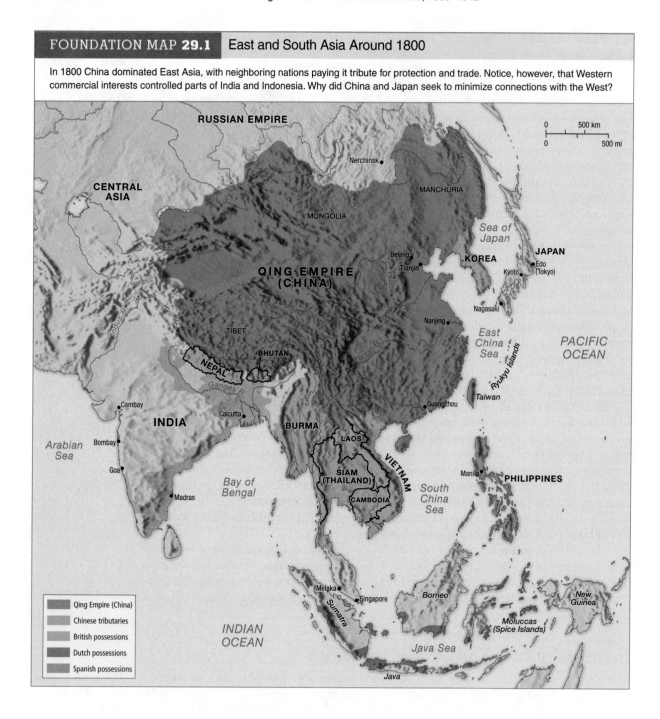

Southeast Asian and American crops spur Chinese population growth

One destabilizing factor was population growth. Agricultural advances, including fast-growing rice from Southeast Asia and sweet potatoes from the Americas, along with irrigation and fertilizer use, produced abundant food in early Qing China. But this abundance also helped double China's population, from about 150 million in the mid-1600s to more than 300 million by the early 1800s, while food production failed to keep pace. Farmers labored to produce more food, tilling marginal lands and clearing forests, but such practices often led to soil erosion and flooding. As land parcels shrunk and food grew scarce, some Chinese families practiced female infanticide, killing infant girls so there would be fewer mouths to feed, while countless young men joined bandit gangs and rebel groups that sought land and food by attacking the estates of large landowners.

A second factor was bureaucratic corruption. Local officials, who rarely got enough resources from the Qing regime to run their regions, often padded their revenues through bribes and extortion, taxing the peasants far beyond what the regime required and pocketing the excess. This practice, aptly called the "squeeze," sapped the common people's scant resources, while the emperor and his favorites drained the treasury to live in lavish splendor.

The upshot was widespread discontent, especially in southern and western China, where corruption and poverty were acute. One manifestation was the White Lotus Rebellion (Chapter 21), a vast peasant uprising that disrupted western China from 1796 to 1804. Another was growing discontent with the Qing dynasty, once more seen by many Chinese people as a foreign regime.

Poverty and corruption fuel Chinese discontent with Qing regime

The Opium Connection

Meanwhile, China's Western connections were growing. Since the mid-1700s, the Qing regime had limited trade with Westerners (mostly Dutch and British merchants) to the southern port city of Guangzhou (*GWAHNG-JŌ*), which the British called Canton. Even there this trade was controlled by the **Cohong**, the city's merchant guild, a group of Chinese firms that the regime authorized to conduct commerce with foreigners. Despite this constraint, the British built a lucrative trade, buying Chinese goods and then selling them in the West at huge profit. But the trade was one-sided: Europeans readily bought China's tea, silk, and porcelain, but the Chinese bought little in return, so the foreigners had to pay for their purchases mostly in silver. In 1793, frustrated by this situation and the growing silver drain, Britain sent the Macartney mission, described at the start of this chapter, to urge the Chinese to buy more British goods. But the British made little headway, as China's emperor insisted that his realm already possessed "all things in prolific abundance." (See "Excerpts from Qianlong's Letter to King George III")

Chinese trade restrictions frustrate the British

Opium smuggling helps British reverse trade imbalance

There were, however, some things China did not have in prolific abundance. One was industrial technology: the machines and weapons that soon made little Britain mightier and wealthier than enormous China. Another was **opium**, an addictive narcotic drug, made from poppies that grew profusely in India, which produced a sense of euphoria when ingested or smoked. Although opium was illegal in China, the British smuggled it in by sea from India, and its addictive properties soon created a growing demand among the Chinese people. Opium thus gave the British an insidious but effective way to redress the trade imbalance.

And redress it they did. From 1800 to 1840, the amount of opium smuggled each year into China increased more than tenfold. Its value soon exceeded that of all Chinese goods sold to the British, shifting the trade balance in Britain's favor and causing silver to flow *out* of China—a serious problem since Chinese taxes were paid mainly in silver. The spread of opium addiction, moreover, weakened China's army and bureaucracy and created a public health crisis in its urban slums. No wonder many Chinese saw the British as "barbarians" and "foreign devils."

To confront the opium crisis, in 1839 China's Daoguang (*DOW-GWAHNG*) Emperor sent Lin Zexu (*LIN DZUH-SHOO*), a conscientious official, to Guangzhou to halt the opium trade. Lin used drastic measures, seizing and destroying more than twenty thousand chests of British opium and sending Britain's Queen Victoria a letter threatening

Lin Zexu oversees destruction of British opium.

DOCUMENT 29.1 Excerpts from Qianlong's Letter to King George III

In 1793, hoping to get China to buy more British goods, Britain's King George III sent a mission under Lord Macartney to meet China's Qianlong Emperor. What does his response, excerpted below, reveal about China's attitude toward foreign goods and cultures?

You, O King, live beyond the confines of many seas, nevertheless, impelled by your humble desire to partake of the benefits of our civilisation, you have dispatched a mission respectfully bearing your memorial . . .

I have perused your memorial: the earnest terms in which it is couched reveal a respectful humility on your part, which is highly praiseworthy. In consideration of the fact that your Ambassador and his deputy have come a long way with your memorial and tribute, I have shown them high favour and have allowed them to be introduced into my presence. To manifest my indulgence, I have entertained them at a banquet and made them numerous gifts . . .

Our dynasty's majestic virtue has penetrated unto every country under Heaven, and Kings of all nations have offered their costly tribute by land and sea. As your Ambassador can see for himself, we possess all things. I set no value on objects strange or ingenious, and have no use for your country's manufactures . . .

You, O King, from afar have yearned after the blessings of our civilisation . . . I have already taken note of your respectful spirit of submission, have treated your mission with extreme favour and loaded it with gifts . . .

Yesterday your Ambassador petitioned my Ministers to memorialise me regarding your trade with China, but his proposal is not consistent with our dynastic usage and cannot be entertained. Hitherto, all European nations, including your own country's barbarian merchants, have carried on their trade with our Celestial Empire at Canton. Such has been the procedure for many years, although Our Celestial Empire possesses all things in prolific abundance and lacks no product within its own borders. There was therefore no need to import the manufactures of outside barbarians in exchange for our own produce. But as the tea, silk and porcelain which the Celestial Empire produces, are absolute necessities to European nations and to yourselves, we have permitted, as a signal mark of favour, that foreign *hongs* [merchant firms] should be established at Canton, so that your wants might be supplied and your country thus participate in our beneficence. But your Ambassador has now put forward new requests which completely fail to recognise the Throne's principle to "treat strangers from afar with indulgence," and to exercise a pacifying control over barbarian tribes, the world over. Moreover, our dynasty, swaying the myriad races of the globe, extends the same benevolence towards all. Your England is not the only nation trading at Canton. If other nations, following your bad example, wrongfully importune my ear with further impossible requests, how will it be possible for me to treat them with easy indulgence? Nevertheless, I do not forget the lonely remoteness of your island, cut off from the world by intervening wastes of sea, nor do I overlook your excusable ignorance of the usages of our Celestial Empire. I have consequently commanded my Ministers to enlighten your Ambassador on the subject, and have ordered the departure of the mission . . .

SOURCE: Emperor Qian Long, *Letter to George III, 1793,* in E. Backhouse and J.O.P. Bland, Annals and Memoirs of the Court of Peking (Boston: Houghton Mifflin, 1914) 322–331.

to execute opium-smuggling "barbarians" by "decapitation or strangulation" (see "Lin Zexu's Letter to Queen Victoria"). Enraged at the destruction of their "property," and maintaining that China had no authority to prosecute British subjects, British merchants appealed to their home government, which in turn sent warships to blockade Guangzhou.

Chinese effort to halt opium trade results in Opium War

The resulting conflict, the First Opium War (1839–1842), was a humiliation for China. The British, with modern warships and weapons, easily defeated China's outmoded forces, occupied Chinese ports, and even sent a 70-ship armada led by an iron-hulled steamship up the Yangzi River to demonstrate their naval superiority (Map 29.2).

The Treaty of Nanjing (1842), which ended the war, required China to abolish the Cohong monopoly, pay Britain a huge indemnity, and cede it Hong Kong island (southeast of Guangzhou). It also gave the British full commercial access to five major Chinese ports

DOCUMENT 29.2 Lin Zexu's Letter to Queen Victoria

In 1839, Lin Zexu, the Chinese official tasked with stopping British opium smuggling into China, composed a letter to Britain's Queen Victoria. What arguments did Lin use in his bid to get British aid in ending this practice? Why did they prove ineffective?

The kings of your honorable country . . . have always been noted for their politeness and submissiveness . . . For this reason the Celestial Court in soothing those from afar has redoubled its polite and kind treatment . . .

But after a long period of commercial intercourse, there appear among the crowd of barbarians both good persons and bad, unevenly. Consequently there are those who smuggle opium to seduce the Chinese people and so cause the spread of the poison to all provinces . . . His Majesty the Emperor, upon hearing of this, is in a towering rage . . .

Suppose there were people from another country who carried opium for sale to England and seduced your people into buying and smoking it; certainly your honorable ruler would deeply hate it and be bitterly aroused. We have heard heretofore that your honorable ruler is kind and benevolent. Naturally you would not wish to give unto others what you yourself do not want . . .

Suppose a man of another country comes to England to trade, he still has to obey the English laws; how much more should he obey in China the laws of the Celestial Dynasty?

Now we have set up regulations governing the Chinese people. He who sells opium shall receive the death penalty and he who smokes it also the death penalty. Now consider this: if the barbarians do not bring opium, then how can the Chinese people resell it, and how can they smoke it? The fact is that the wicked barbarians beguile the Chinese people into a death trap. How then can we grant life only to these barbarians? He who takes the life of even one person still has to atone for it with his own life; yet is the harm done by opium limited to the taking of one life only? Therefore in the new regulations, in regard to those barbarians who bring opium to China, the penalty is fixed at decapitation or strangulation. This is what is called getting rid a harmful thing on behalf of mankind.

Now we . . . have received the extraordinary Celestial grace of His Majesty the Emperor, who has redoubled his consideration and compassion. All those who from the period of the coming one year (from England) or six months (from India) bring opium to China by mistake, but who voluntarily confess and completely surrender their opium, shall be exempt from their punishment. After this limit of time, if there are still those who bring opium to China then they will plainly have committed a willful violation and shall at once be executed according to law, with absolutely no clemency or pardon. This may be called the height of kindness and the perfection of justice . . .

After receiving this dispatch will you immediately give us a prompt reply regarding the details and circumstances of your cutting off the opium traffic. Be sure not to put this off . . .

SOURCE: Reprinted by permission of the publisher from "Lin Tse-hsu's Moral Advice to Queen Victoria" in *China's Response to the West: A Documentary Survey, 1839–1923*, by Ssu-yu Teng and John King Fairbank, pp. 24, 26–27, Cambridge, Mass: Harvard University Press, Copyright © 1954, 1979 by the President and Fellows of Harvard College, Copyright renewed 1982 by Ssu-yu Teng and John King Fairbank.

and exempted British subjects from Chinese jurisdiction. Before long, France and America, eager to get in on the China trade, pressured the Qing regime to grant them similar rights.

These Western intrusions exacerbated China's problems. The opium trade and result- ing health crisis continued to grow unchecked. A cruel new "**coolie trade**" developed, as Western merchants hired or kidnapped Asian workers, disparagingly called "coolies," and shipped them abroad to serve as laborers in places such as Cuba, Peru, and California. These involuntary migrants helped fill a labor shortage created by the banning of the slave trade (Chapter 30), working in mines and building railways that added to the wealth of the West. But wages were so low and conditions so brutal that "coolies" were often little better off than slaves.

China's defeat opens door to further Western connections

Discredited by defeat and weakened by opium abuse in its army, the Qing regime found it harder than ever to deal with growing discontent. Its problems were compounded

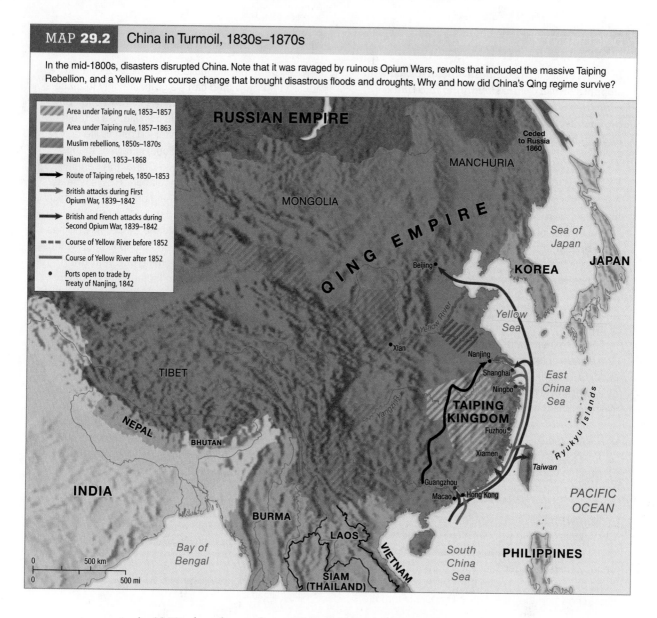

MAP 29.2 China in Turmoil, 1830s–1870s

In the mid-1800s, disasters disrupted China. Note that it was ravaged by ruinous Opium Wars, revolts that included the massive Taiping Rebellion, and a Yellow River course change that brought disastrous floods and droughts. Why and how did China's Qing regime survive?

in 1850 when the prudent and frugal Daoguang Emperor died, leaving the throne to his dissolute 19-year-old son, who reigned from 1850 to 1861 as the Xianfeng (*shē-YAN FUNG*) Emperor. As floods and famines ravaged the land, the Qing dynasty appeared to have lost the Mandate of Heaven.

The Taiping Rebellion and China's Disintegration

But who would gain Heaven's Mandate? For a while it looked to be Hong Xiuquan (*HŌNG shē-Ō choo-WAHN*), a tempestuous young man from southern China, who led a vast uprising called the **Taiping Rebellion** (1850–1864). Fueled by anti-Manchu hostility and Western religious ideas, this massive revolt, together with natural disasters and other uprisings, produced colossal devastation in China.

Hong, who belonged to an oppressed minority called Hakka, initially aspired to a career in China's civil service. In 1837, however, after three times failing the civil service

Hong Xiuquan blends Hakka and Christian ideals

exams, he became very ill. By his own account, he lapsed into a 40-day coma, during which he had visions. Later, influenced by Christian writings and Western Protestant missionaries, he concluded that he had been taken up to heaven, given a new heart that made him the younger brother of Jesus Christ, and commanded by God to smite the foreign devils who were destroying China. Inspired by this experience, Hong formed a new faith that embraced puritanical Christian values, banning opium, alcohol, adultery, gambling, and foot binding. Defying China's patriarchal traditions and social stratification, his "Society of God Worshipers" also stressed ideals popular among the Hakka, such as gender equality, communal property, and an end to social classes. It thus attracted many poor and oppressed men and women.

In 1850, concluding that the foreign devils he must smite were China's Manchu rulers, Hong Xiuquan assembled a devout and disciplined militia, made up of both men and women, who were treated as equals. By 1853 they had defeated a large Manchu army, captured the city of Nanjing, and declared it the capital of a new realm called the Taiping (*TĪ-PING*) Kingdom. For the next decade, it ruled much of central China (Map 29.2).

Although Taiping means "Great Peace," the Taiping Rebellion brought horrific violence, as Taiping forces fought Manchu armies in a bloody civil war that lasted until 1864. Muslim revolts in southern and western China added to the chaos, as did the Yellow River's sudden change of course in 1852, causing drought and famine in its former path and devastating floods in its new one. This wreckage in turn sparked an uprising called the Nian Rebellion, in which starving peasants, led by secret rebel bands called Nian, seized a large segment of northeastern China, terrorizing landlords and attacking towns with a quick-striking cavalry militia. Taking advantage of this turmoil, Britain and France launched a Second Opium War (1856–1860) to further impose their will on the Qing regime. From 1850 to 1864, as rebellions, famine, disease, and war took perhaps 20 million lives, China's once-illustrious empire fell into disarray.

Revolts, disasters, and foreign incursions devastate China

The Dynasty's Survival and Regional "Self-Strengthening"

The Qing dynasty nonetheless survived. Chinese Confucian officials, terrified by the rebels, rallied to its support, while the Taiping Kingdom was weakened by internal conflicts. Furthermore, after 1860, having won the Second Opium War and forced the Qing regime to grant them new privileges, the Western powers supported its survival in order to protect their gains. The regime itself, desperate to restore order, allowed some officials to form regional armies to combat the rebels. One such army, led by an eminent Confucian named Zeng Guofan (*DZUNG GWŌ-FAHN*), defeated the Taiping forces in 1864 and, after Hong Xiuquan committed suicide, massacred his followers in Nanjing. Another regional army, formed by Zeng's protégé Li Hongzhang (*LĒ HŌNG-JAHNG*), crushed the Nian rebels four years later, and the Muslim revolts in the west were finally quelled in the 1870s.

The dynasty thus endured, but momentum shifted to regional leaders with their own armies and officials. Distressed by China's vulnerability to the Western powers, they worked to modernize its industry and military in a series of "self-strengthening" efforts. Before his death in 1872, for example, Zeng Guofan built shipyards, military schools, and munitions factories, and he sent young men to America to study engineering and science. Li Hongzhang created his own industrial empire of railways, factories, and mines. He negotiated treaties with Britain and France, bought warships built in the West, and used Western experts to help run his railways and mills. As head of his own army and China's leading industrialist, he amassed great power and wealth.

Regional "self-strengthening" efforts adapt Western ideas

The dynasty, meanwhile, came to be led by a woman called Cixi (*TSUH-SHĒ*). Formerly one of emperor Xianfeng's many concubines, she had borne him a son in 1856

Corruption and conservatism hamper China's modernization

and, after Xianfeng died in 1861, used her status as the new child emperor's mother to become China's regent and effective ruler. Fourteen years later, when her son the emperor (allegedly weakened by syphilis acquired in sexual debaucheries) died at age 19, she intrigued to keep her power by placing her four-year-old nephew on the throne.

Known as the Empress Dowager (widow empress), Cixi worked tenaciously from 1861 until her death in 1908 to preserve her own power and that of the Qing regime. To restore stability after the rebellions, she and her officials granted tax relief, repaired roads and canals, and built grain storage facilities to protect against famine. But she also used her position to enhance her lavish lifestyle and prevent social or political change.

China thus failed to modernize enough to resist continued foreign intrusion. Its traditional disdain for foreign goods and ways hampered efforts to buy Western weapons and build industries that might compete with the West. Corruption also diverted resources needed for modernization, and Cixi herself used funds for updating China's navy to finance lavish personal projects, including a solid marble houseboat. Even Li Hongzhang, the most notable regional leader, took bribes and often seemed more eager to enhance his wealth and power than to strengthen China.

The Empress Dowager Cixi.

Subordination and Resistance in India

In the mid-1800s, while foreign connections contributed to China's woes, foreign rule was helping to unite and transform India. British connections, at first primarily commercial, expanded to include political rule, as the British sought not only to exploit the subcontinent but also to impose Western ways. Many of India's autonomous states were consolidated into a huge British colony, administered largely by British-educated Indian professionals, some of whom would later lead the quest for a united, independent India.

Commercial Connections and Cultural Conflicts

India historically was not a unified state, but rather an assortment of independent realms, connected by commerce, culture, and Hindu religion. In the 1500s, however, much of India had come under the Mughals, Islamic rulers who initially let native culture and Hinduism flourish but later oppressed them and imposed Muslim domination (Chapter 17).

Then, in the 1700s, as the Mughal regime declined, large parts of India came under the sway of the British East India Company, a commercial venture that held a monopoly of Britain's trade with southern Asia (Chapter 22). In some regions, which it had conquered using **sepoys** (*SĒ-poyz*)—Indian soldiers trained and commanded by the British—the company's rule was direct. In others it was indirect, exercised through pacts with Indian princes.

The British East India Company gains influence in India

At first British sway mattered little to most people in India. Foreign domination was nothing new to them; indeed, they had accepted early Mughal rulers as long as they tolerated Indian culture and beliefs. And the British East India Company, whose major concern was trade, initially seemed much less oppressive than the most recent Mughal rulers, who imposed harsh taxes and restrictions on India's Hindu majority. So in the early years of company control, common people in India were scarcely aware of their new foreign overlords.

British connections have growing impact on India

But in the 1800s, the British connection caused problems. First, cheap slave-grown cotton from America and inexpensive cotton clothes from England's textile mills ended India's traditional dominance of the global market for cotton goods. Second, the British began imposing Western values on India. They took steps to abolish such practices as **sati** (*suh-TĒ*), a custom by which upper-caste Hindu widows were sometimes burnt to death on their husband's funeral pyre, and ***thagi*** (*thuh-GĒ*), the work of professional bandits (or "thugs") who attacked and strangled travelers as religious ritual. Dismissive of Indian institutions, British reformers sought to establish Western-style educational and judicial systems in India. One of them, historian Thomas Babington Macauley, even asserted that "a single shelf of a good European library is worth the whole native literature of India."

Meanwhile, to protect their commercial and strategic interests, the British extended direct control over other parts of India (Map 29.3). During the Napoleonic Wars (1799–1815), fearing a French attack on the Indian subcontinent, the British seized the state of Mysore (*mī-SOR*) in southern India (1799). Several years later they invaded the lands of the Maratha (*mah-rah-TAH*) Confederacy in western and central India, finally annexing them in 1818. In 1839–1849, to counterbalance Russian expansion in Central Asia, the British took control of the Sind and Punjab (*pun-JAHB*) regions in the northwest. By the 1850s, the British dominated most of the Indian subcontinent.

The Indian Revolt of 1857

Over the years, as the British role in India expanded, Britain's government had become concerned that the company, a commercial enterprise, was wielding too much political and military power. Reacting to reports of plunder and abuse of Indians by company officials, the British Parliament passed an India Act in 1784, setting up a board of control to oversee company operations. Parliament then restricted the company's commercial monopoly in 1814 and ended its privileged status altogether in 1833. Increasingly, control of India shifted from company to crown, that is, from the British East India Company to Britain's royal government.

The expansion of British rule, and British insensitivity to Indian ways, led to the Indian Revolt of 1857. Begun as an insurrection by Indian sepoy soldiers against their British commanders, in Britain it is also called the "Sepoy Mutiny."

The revolt was triggered by British introduction of accurate new rifles for the sepoys and by rumors that, to use the cartridges for these rifles, they had to bite off a protective wrapping greased with cow fat or pig fat. Both Hindu soldiers (who considered cows sacred) and Muslim soldiers (who considered pork unclean), upset that they might violate their faith by tasting a forbidden substance, refused to use the new cartridges. Although the British eventually withdrew the order that sepoys must bite off the wrapping, they chained and imprisoned many sepoys for refusing to follow this order.

Enraged at this treatment of their comrades, hundreds of sepoys rebelled, killing British officers and many other Britons, including women and children. Others in northern India, including former landowners and

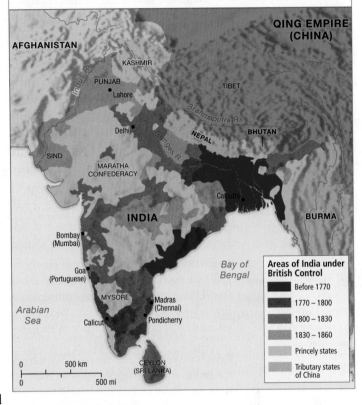

MAP 29.3   Growth of British Power in India, 1770–1860

Between 1770 and 1860, the British extended their rule over most of India. Observe that in 1770, British connections in India were coastal and commercial, but by 1860 most of India was under direct or indirect British rule. How did this rule help unite India and promote Indian nationalism?

Britain expands control over much of India

Read the Document
Arrival of the British in the Punjab (Mid-19th Century)
on **myhistorylab.com**

Indians revolt against British domination

British troops crushing Indian Revolt.

regional rulers who had been displaced by the British, joined in the revolt. Angered by the slaughter of their people, British officials ruthlessly crushed the revolt in 1858, burning whole villages and executing rebels by hanging them or shooting them with cannons. Superior weapons, and loyal sepoys brought from elsewhere in India, helped the British prevail.

After the revolt the British enterprise in India, begun as a commercial venture, was fully converted into imperial rule. Determined both to assert full control and provide more effective governance, Britain abolished the East India Company, imposing crown rule through a viceroy who governed in the name of the British monarch. Many Indian soldiers, their loyalty no longer trusted, were replaced with British troops. Local Indian rulers were formally subordinated to Britain's Queen Victoria, whom the British Parliament in 1876 proclaimed Empress of India.

The Rise of Indian Nationalism

In strengthening control over India, however, Britain inadvertently advanced Indian nationalism. By unifying India's diverse states under direct and indirect British rule, for example, and by creating a uniform civil service and a network of railways and telegraph lines, the British helped to unite India politically and economically. And by encouraging Indians to learn British ways to reinforce this rule, the British helped to foster a sense of Indian national unity.

Since the 1700s, a number of Indians had studied English language and ways, partly to participate in commerce and partly to incorporate Western science and technology into India's long tradition of mathematical and scientific expertise. Now the British, eager to instill their ideals, further encouraged such study, helping to develop a British-educated, English-speaking Indian elite. Many of its members attended British universities and then returned to play leading roles in Indian society.

In time some members of this elite formed an Indian nationalist movement. In learning British ways, they also learned Western liberal and nationalist ideals, which they adapted for India. If liberal ideals such as freedom and self-rule were vital to the British people, reasoned these Indian leaders, should not such ideals also apply to the people of India? If European nationalists took great pride in their historic institutions and beliefs, should not Indians do likewise?

In 1885, a group of British-educated Indian leaders convened the first session of what became the Indian National Congress. Based on earlier regional political groups in India, and modeled in part on British political parties, the Congress pushed for greater involvement of Indians in their own governance. Over the next few decades, faced with British resistance, it became increasingly assertive, developing into a full-blown nationalist movement. One faction, led by Gopal Krishna Gokhale (*GŌ-kuh-lā*), a moderate educator and political leader, called for greater Indian autonomy within the British Empire. Another faction, led by Bal Gangadhar Tilak (*TĒ-lahk*), a noted mathematician and radical nationalist whom the British at one point deported for sedition, pressed for full independence. Later, under the leadership of Mohandas Gandhi (Chapter 32), the Indian National Congress led a sustained nonviolent struggle for a united, independent India.

Read the **Document**

Amrita Lal Roy, English Rule in India, 1886

on **myhistorylab.com**

Indian elites adapt Western liberal and nationalist ideas to India

Read the **Document**

An Indian Nationalist on Hindu Women and Education (Early 19th Century)

on **myhistorylab.com**

Indian National Congress pushes for Indian self-rule

Challenges and Adaptations in Japan

Japan, too, was plagued by unwelcome foreign connections in the 1800s. Unlike India, Japan avoided foreign rule, but it did not avoid foreign cultural and technological influence. Indeed, to defend itself from Western powers, Japan adapted its traditional ways and institutions, borrowing ideas and technologies from its antagonists. As the Asian nation that most successfully resisted Western rule, Japan also became the most Westernized major Asian nation.

The Tokugawa Shogunate and the Western Challenge

By the mid-1800s, Japan had experienced over two centuries of rule by the Tokugawa family, whose leaders governed from the city of Edo as shoguns. As Japan's highest military official, overlord of the daimyo (regional warlords) and samurai warriors, the shogun was far more powerful than his nominal superior, the emperor, who reigned in the ancient city of Kyoto as a godlike religious figure lacking political power.

U.S. forces in Japan, 1853.

Japan minimizes Western connections for two centuries

Since the early 1600s, to protect Japan from unwelcome influence, the Tokugawa shoguns had banned most contact with Westerners, except for limited commercial and cultural connections with the Dutch, who had a small trading post near the southern port of Nagasaki (*NAH-gah-SAH-kē*). In the 1850s, however, a new Western power, the United States of America, decided to open relations with Japan. As American whaling ships and merchant vessels increasingly traveled the Pacific, the U.S. government came to see Japan as a potential refuge for stranded whalers and refueling point for American steamships traveling to and from China. In 1853, as described at the start of this chapter, an American squadron with steam-powered warships arrived near Edo and transmitted to the shogun a letter calling for open trade relations.

Americans press Japan to open new connections

This naval visit, led by Commodore Matthew Perry, triggered a crisis in Japan. Japanese law forbade most contact with Westerners under penalty of death, but the Americans had mighty ships with powerful weapons Japan lacked. When Perry returned with a larger force in 1854 and demanded a response, the shogun tried to compromise, agreeing to open two small ports to trade with the United States.

 **View** the **Image**

Japanese Views of Commodore Perry's Mission, 1853, I and II,

on **myhistorylab.com**

This compromise satisfied no one. It went too far for many samurai, who wanted to fight the Americans and felt the shogun dishonored his country by dealing with "barbarians." But it did not go far enough for the United States and other Western powers, who soon forced Japan to sign unequal treaties, like those imposed on China, that opened more ports to Western trade and exempted Westerners in Japan from Japanese jurisdiction. By 1859, not only the Americans, but also the Dutch, Russians, British, and French, had imposed such treaties, fully opening Japan to Western connections.

Western powers impose trade treaties on Japan

Civil War and Meiji Restoration

The shogun's submission to Western demands created a dilemma for many samurai warriors. They believed that his action had betrayed Japan and compromised his moral authority, but, according to their samurai code, they were honor bound to serve him loyally. If they defied him, they dishonored themselves, and for the samurai dishonor meant death.

Read the **Document**

The Views of Tokugawa Nariaki, 1841

on **myhistorylab.com**

To resolve this dilemma, some samurai launched a movement to "honor the emperor" and "expel the barbarians." Inspired by Yoshida Shoin (*YŌ-shē-dah SHŌ-ēn*), a passionate young patriot who earlier tried to hide on one of Perry's ships to study Americans first hand, these samurai declared that their ultimate loyalty was not to the shogun but to the emperor, the shogun's divine overlord and rightful Japanese ruler. They claimed they could best honor the emperor by defying the shogun and fighting the foreigners.

Although Yoshida was beheaded in 1859 for plotting to murder an agent of the shogun, in the 1860s Yoshida's admirers helped to trigger civil wars in which some daimyo and their samurai remained loyal to the shogun, while others sought to overthrow him and restore the emperor to full power. The Western powers, perplexed by these upheavals, responded to occasional attacks on their ships by shelling some coastal fortresses but did not intervene

Rebellious samurai depose shogun and restore emperor

The Meiji Emperor.

To strengthen Japan, the Meiji regime adapts Western ideas

directly. Finally, in 1868, the forces supporting the emperor prevailed, defeating the shogun and abolishing his office.

To emphasize the end of the shogunate, the victorious samurai had the young emperor Mutsuhito (*moot-soo-HĒ-tō*), who had recently inherited the throne, move from Kyoto to the shogun's former palace at Edo. That city, replacing Kyoto as Japan's imperial capital, was renamed Tokyo, or "eastern capital." Since Mutsuhito's reign was given the title Meiji (*MĀ-jē*), meaning "Enlightened Rule," he was called the Meiji Emperor, and the reestablishment of the emperor as head of Japan's government came to be known as the Meiji Restoration.

Centralization and Western Adaptations

To protect their country from the West, the emperor's advisors, a gifted group of young samurai from the factions that defeated the shogun, soon decided that they must unite and adapt to Western ways: in order to "expel the barbarians," Japan must first emulate them. During the Meiji reign (1867–1912), Japan pursued both centralization and selective adaptation of Western ideas and technologies.

The Meiji regime moved quickly to concentrate its power and unite Japan in the face of the foreign threat. It required the various daimyo warlords to surrender their troops and domains to the emperor and then to move to Tokyo and become imperial officials. It also moderated Japan's rigid class distinctions, curtailing samurai class privileges and ending regular stipends to the samurai. The regime then began in 1873 to create a new military system, based on French and German models, replacing the old class-based samurai armies with a large army made up mainly of commoners drafted into service. Armed with modern rifles rather than samurai swords, the new army was controlled by the central government, rather than by local lords.

Some samurai rebel against the end of class privilege

Knowing they could not face the foreign threat as separate forces with outmoded weapons, most daimyo and samurai accepted these reforms, but some were deeply distressed at the loss of their status. In 1877, after the regime ordered the samurai to discard the fabled swords that symbolized their status, about forty thousand samurai staged a mass revolt led by Saigo Takamori (*SĪ-gō tah-kah-MAW-rē*), a heroic warrior who had helped defeat the shogun in 1868. Saigo fought bravely, but he and his forces could not overcome the new army's superior size and weaponry. Defeated and branded a traitor, Saigo reportedly bled to death from a bullet wound. But a legend arose that he instead regained his honor by committing seppuku, the samurai suicide ritual, making him a romantic symbol of the bygone samurai era.

Japan adapts Western ways to fit its culture

In the ensuing decades, anxious to replicate the power and wealth of the industrial West, Japan adapted many Western ways to fit its East Asian society. To spur industrial growth, the government built railways, textile mills, factories, and mines, and then sold them to wealthy families to raise money. Thus arose the **zaibatsu**—distinctive Japanese family-owned conglomerates, each typically having its own banks, shipping lines, railways, mines, factories, and retail outlets. To provide the knowledge needed for industrial society, the Meiji regime established a new system of mandatory education, modeled on those in America and France, combining Western-style technical knowledge with traditional Japanese literature and learning. In 1889 the regime adopted a Western-type constitution, establishing a two-house parliament and a cabinet, while reserving vast authority for the emperor, to whom the cabinet and military were directly responsible. Culturally, the Japanese imitated Western forms of dress, dining, architecture, art, and entertainment, blending them with traditional Japanese styles.

By the 1890s, Japan was emerging as a blend of East and West, a Western-style industrial power on the edge of Asia. Two ominous factors were also emerging. One

Read the Document

Emperor Meiji, The Constitution of the Empire of Japan

on **myhistorylab.com**

was the absence in the new constitution of effective checks on the power of the military, which reported directly to the emperor, enabling it at times to act without approval of the civilian government. Another was the reality that Japan, so favored by climate and rich in beauty, lacked large deposits of mineral resources—such as iron and petroleum—essential for industry. These two factors would dominate Japanese policies for the next half-century, as Japan embarked on increasingly audacious efforts, from 1894 until 1945, to gain control of such resources through military expansion.

The Impact of Imperialism in Asia

Japan was not the only power seeking to expand in Asia. In the 19th century, the British, French, and Dutch, exploiting China's declining ability to protect the smaller nations to its south, increasingly brought these nations under their control. China held its own in Central Asia against British and Russian expansion, but in the 1890s Japan bested China in a war for control of Korea, and European powers forced the Qing regime to grant them zones in China for economic exploitation. For a time it seemed as if the "foreign devils" would dismantle the Celestial Empire.

Southeast Asia and the West

Mainland Southeast Asia, the region east of India and south of China, was so influenced by both that it was often called "Indochina." Its various states, although politically autonomous, derived their main beliefs and institutions from the Indian and Chinese traditions. Most were also Chinese tributaries: states paying tribute to China for its trade and protection. For centuries, this region, populated mainly by Buddhist village farmers who grew rice in the hot, rainy climate, attracted scant attention from European visitors, most of whom focused on the profits they could make by trading with India, the East Indies, and China (Map 29.4).

Southeast Asian states pay tribute to China

From 1771 until 1802, however, a massive revolt called the Tay-Son Rebellion rocked Vietnam, Southeast Asia's easternmost state, leading a young prince named Nguyen Anh (*n'WEN AHN*) to seek outside assistance (Chapter 21). The French, hoping to regain some influence in Asia after their ouster from India by the British, provided him with soldiers and weapons, helping him crush the revolt and found the Nguyen dynasty (1802–1945). Reigning until 1820 as Emperor Gia Long (*j̄e-AH LAWNG*), he did not promote trade with France but did allow the French to send some Catholic missionaries, who in time made a number of Vietnamese converts.

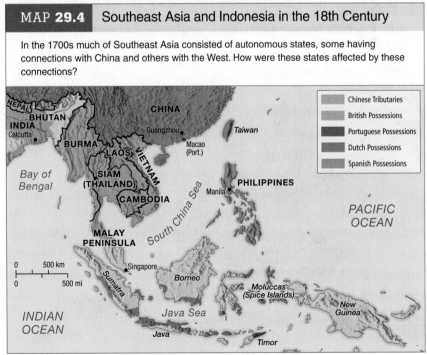

MAP 29.4 Southeast Asia and Indonesia in the 18th Century

In the 1700s much of Southeast Asia consisted of autonomous states, some having connections with China and others with the West. How were these states affected by these connections?

Chinese Tributaries
British Possessions
Portuguese Possessions
Dutch Possessions
Spanish Possessions

In the 1850s, alarmed at the growing number of Catholics in this largely Buddhist land and angered by a French priest's alleged involvement in a plot to overthrow him, Emperor Tu Duc, who reigned from 1847 to 1883, executed thousands of Vietnamese Catholics and several dozen French priests. France responded in 1858 by sending forces to occupy cities in southern Vietnam. China, engulfed at this time by the Taiping Rebellion and Second Opium War, was unable to help Vietnam, despite the fact that it had long paid tribute to China for trade and protection.

France exploits China's weakness to expand in Southeast Asia

Five years later a revolt in Cambodia, Vietnam's western neighbor, allowed France to further extend its sway in Southeast Asia. Despite the fact that Cambodia's king neither sought nor desired French assistance, France sent in troops and proclaimed Cambodia a French **protectorate**: a country controlled by an outside power claiming to provide security. In the 1870s France also sent forces to combat rebels in northern Vietnam, declaring it a French protectorate in 1883. At the urging of Vietnam's emperor, China finally sent an army to attack the French, but superior weapons helped France beat Chinese forces in the Franco-Chinese War of 1883–1885. Finally, in 1893, the French took over neighboring Laos, completing the formation of a large new colony called French Indochina, encompassing Vietnam, Cambodia, and Laos (Map 29.5).

Meanwhile Britain was also moving into Southeast Asia. To guard their sea route between India and China, over which traveled such valuable items as opium, tea, and silk, in 1819 the British occupied Singapore, a port on the straits connecting the Indian Ocean and South China Sea. In the 1870s, as France expanded its control over Vietnam and Cambodia, the British extended their influence northward from Singapore to protect that port. They took over several small sultanates on the Malay peninsula, soon a key source of industrial resources such as tin, and later rubber—after rubber trees were planted there by Britons who smuggled seeds from Brazil. In the 1880s, to prevent the French from expanding toward British India, Britain conquered Burma, now called Myanmar (*mē-AHN-mar*), rich in oil and teakwood.

Thailand exploits Western rivalries to maintain its independence

In all Southeast Asia, only Thailand, then called Siam, escaped colonization, partly because neither Britain nor France would let the other gain control there. Two talented Thai kings, Rama IV (1851–1868) and Rama V (1868–1910), cleverly exploited the British-French rivalry to keep Thailand independent. To further reinforce their realm, these kings centralized the state bureaucracy, established an educational system, and introduced such technologies as printing presses, railways, and telegraphs. Modernized by its monarchs and spared the disruption of foreign rule, Thailand emerged as Southeast Asia's most stable and prosperous nation.

MAP 29.5 Southeast Asia and Indonesia in the Early 20th Century

By the early 1900s, Southeast Asia was largely under Western rule. Note that Britain and France controlled most of mainland Southeast Asia, the Dutch ruled most of Indonesia, and America had replaced Spain in governing the Philippines. How did Siam, now called Thailand, escape Western domination?

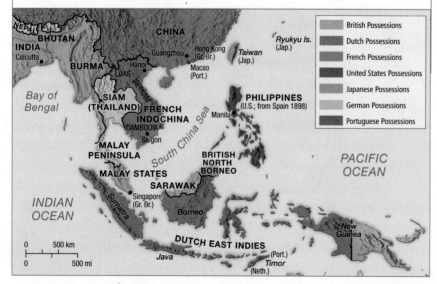

British Possessions
Dutch Possessions
French Possessions
United States Possessions
Japanese Possessions
German Possessions
Portuguese Possessions

NEPAL
BHUTAN
INDIA
Calcutta
CHINA
Guangzhou
Hong Kong (Gr. Br.)
Macao (Port.)
Taiwan (Jap.)
Ryukyu Is. (Jap.)
BURMA
Hanoi
LAOS
Bay of Bengal
SIAM (THAILAND)
FRENCH INDOCHINA
CAMBODIA
Saigon
PHILIPPINES (U.S.; from Spain 1898)
Manila
MALAY PENINSULA
South China Sea
MALAY STATES
Singapore (Gr. Br.)
BRITISH NORTH BORNEO
SARAWAK
PACIFIC OCEAN
INDIAN OCEAN
Sumatra
Borneo
New Guinea
DUTCH EAST INDIES
Java
Timor (Port.) (Neth.)

0   500 km
0   500 mi

Indonesia and the Dutch

The East Indies, a long string of islands today known as Indonesia ("Indian Islands"), stretching from Southeast Asia toward Australia, had a past that in many ways paralleled India's. Like India, it included many diverse realms, most of which had been influenced by Hinduism and Buddhism; like India, by the 1500s, it had come largely under Muslim

control. In the next few centuries, much as parts of India came under the sway of the British East India Company, parts of Indonesia came to be controlled by the Dutch United East India Company, a similar enterprise that monopolized trade between the Netherlands and East Indies from 1602 until 1799.

In the 1800s, the Kingdom of the Netherlands expanded Dutch influence in Indonesia, first by forging agreements with local rulers, then by requiring Indonesian villagers to set aside one fifth of their land to grow export crops such as sugar, pepper, coffee, tea, and tobacco. By collecting these globally popular products as a form of taxation, and then selling them abroad at huge profits, the Dutch gained vast wealth while most Indonesians remained very poor. By the early 1900s, as the islands also supplied industrial resources such as rubber, tin, and oil, the Dutch ruled most of Indonesia as a large and lucrative colony called the Dutch (or Netherlands) East Indies.

Japan Versus China in Korea

Meanwhile, noting China's inability to protect its tributary neighbors, Japan had begun to expand. In 1872, influenced by expansionist advisors, the new Meiji regime in Tokyo laid claim to the Ryukyu (*rē-YOOK-yoo*) Islands, a chain of small isles south of Japan, the largest of which is Okinawa (*ō-kē-NAH-wah*). The Chinese, who had long received tribute from the Ryukyu king, refused to recognize this Japanese claim. So Japan moved the king to Tokyo in 1879, proclaimed him a Japanese nobleman, and declared the Ryukyus officially part of Japan (Map 29.6). The Qing regime in China, facing

Indonesia is subjected to Dutch connections and control

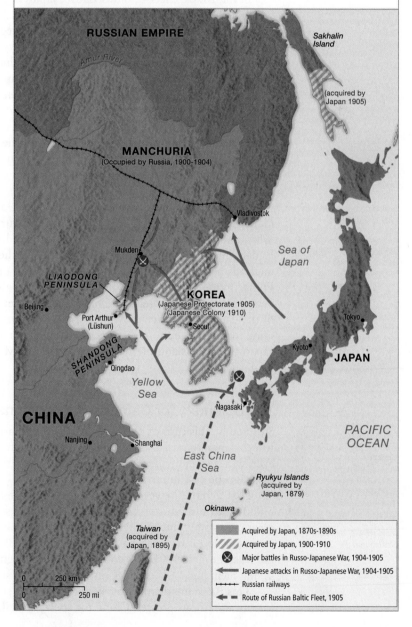

MAP 29.6   Japanese Expansion in Asia, 1870s–1912

Beginning in the 1870s, Japan created an empire in East Asia. Notice that Japan annexed the Ryukyu Islands in 1879, acquired Taiwan in the Sino-Japanese War (1894–1895), and gained southern Sakhalin Island, a protectorate in Korea, and influence in Manchuria as a result of the Russo-Japanese War (1904–1905). What key factors facilitated Japan's imperial expansion?

Japan exploits China's weakness to annex Ryukyu Islands

France's challenge in Southeast Asia and not yet fully recovered from the calamities of the 1850s and 1860s, could do little more than protest.

Far more troubling to the Qing regime was Japan's challenge in Korea, a former Chinese colony and longtime tributary, whose cultural ties to China were so strong that it even had its own version of China's Taiping movement. In 1860 a man named Ch'oe Che-u (*CHEH CHĀ-OO*), having repeatedly failed the Korean civil service exams, claimed that he was commanded by God to start a new religion. Known as Tonghak ("Eastern Learning"), this messianic creed combined Buddhist, Daoist, Confucian, and Christian ideas, calling for creation of an earthly righteous kingdom in which all would be equal under God. Its radical egalitarianism attracted many poor Korean peasants, frightening the government, which executed Ch'oe as a heretic subversive in 1864. The Tonghak movement nonetheless continued underground.

Tonghak movement in Korea blends Eastern and Western beliefs

In the 1870s, eager to industrialize, Japan began to covet Korea's natural resources, which included sizable coal and iron deposits. In 1875, in a move reminiscent of the U.S. opening of Japan two decades earlier, the Meiji regime sent a fleet to Korea to compel it to trade with Japan. The overmatched Koreans, advised by their Chinese overlords to negotiate, agreed the next year to let the Japanese conduct commerce at three Korean ports.

Japanese inroads in Korea trigger conflict with China

But in the 1880s, anxious to forestall any further expansion of Japanese influence in Korea, Chinese industrialist Li Hongzhang decided to take action. To counterbalance Japan, he urged Korea to open relations with the Western powers and even for a time sent troops into Korea commanded by his protégé, Yuan Shikai (*yoo-AHN shur-KĪ*). Japan, however, also sent in troops, so Li and the Japanese in 1885 agreed to a mutual withdrawal. But in 1894, when the Tonghak movement resurfaced in a mass rebellion, China and Japan again sent troops, allegedly to crush the revolt. Quickly these forces came into conflict with each other.

Japan defeats China in conflict over Korea

The resulting Sino-Japanese War (1894–1895) exposed the inadequacy of China's modernization. Corrupt Chinese officials had purchased inferior weapons from the West, pocketing what they saved by not buying higher-priced arms. Chinese military leaders, moreover, had not learned how to use the new weapons or employ new naval methods. And some of them, angered because Li Hongzhang had not helped them fight France in the 1880s, refused now to help him fight Japan. The Japanese, better led and better equipped, defeated the Chinese at sea, then overran Korea and the southern part of the Chinese province of Manchuria. As Japanese forces moved toward Beijing, the Qing regime agreed to terms, recognizing Korea as fully independent and ceding to Japan both the island of Taiwan and southern Manchuria's Liaodong (*lē-OW DŌNG*) Peninsula (Map 29.6).

The Scramble for Chinese Concessions

Western powers pressure Japan to give up gains in Manchuria

Stunned by this turn of events, Russia, France, and Germany quickly intervened and forced Japan to return the Liaodong Peninsula to China. Their **Triple Intervention**, however, was not really meant to help China, but rather to protect their own ambitions for exploitation of China.

First to move in were the Russians, who were building the **Trans-Siberian Railway**, a 5,800-mile railroad stretching from European Russia to Russia's Pacific coast. Intended as a great new trade route linking East and West, it was also designed to aid Russian industry by providing access to Asia's natural resources. In 1896, with a large bribe to Li Hongzhang, the Russians gained China's consent to build a segment of this railway through Manchuria, saving them hundreds of miles of track and huge sums of money.

China agrees to let Russia build railway through Manchuria

This Russian advance sparked a three-year **scramble for concessions**, in which European nations pressed China for special privileges, called concessions, that permitted their economic exploitation of key Chinese regions (Map 29.7). In 1897, France demanded and received railway and mining privileges in southern China, adjacent to French Indochina. Later that year, after two German missionaries were killed by a Chinese anti-Christian mob in northeastern China's Shandong (*SHAHN-DŌNG*) peninsula, Germany seized the Chinese port of Qingdao (*CHING-DOW*), then negotiated a 99-year lease on the port and mineral rights to the whole region. Soon Russia got a similar lease on Port

China forced to grant Western powers economic exploitation zones

| MAP **29.7** | East and South Asia in the Early 20th Century |

By the early 1900s, China no longer dominated East Asia. Observe that most of its neighbors had come under Western or Japanese rule, and China had been forced to grant concessions (economic exploitation zones) to Western countries and Japan. Why was China unsuccessful in resisting Western and Japanese expansion?

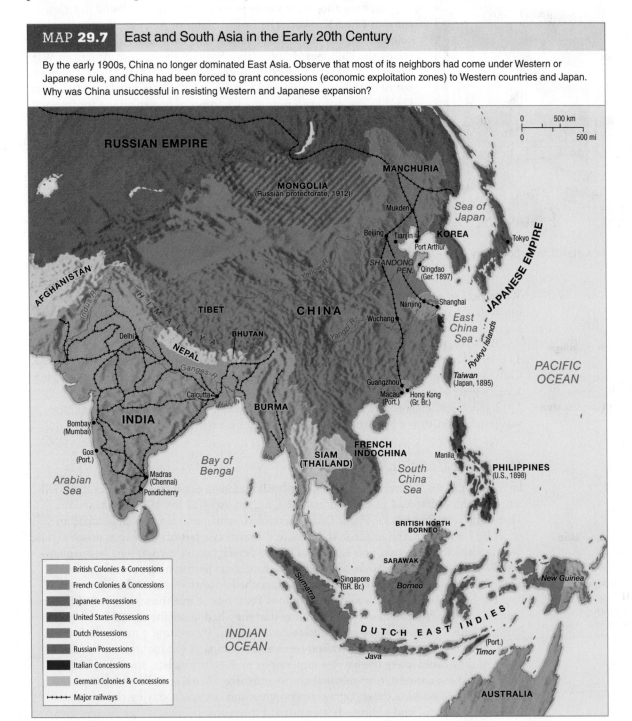

Cartoon depicting U.S. Open Door Policy.

U.S. Open Door Policy helps deter dismemberment of China

View the **Image**

American Cartoon on Western Powers Carving up China

on **myhistorylab.com**

Arthur (now Lüshun) at the Liaodong Peninsula's southern tip. By 1899 France and Germany had extended their concessions, Britain had extracted a huge new concession in the Yangzi River valley, and even Italy had secured a concession along China's eastern coast. For a while it appeared that Western concessions would divide up much of China.

But then another Western power, flexing its newfound muscles, came to China's rescue. The United States of America, despite its anti-colonial origins, in 1898 had acquired its own East Asian possession, taking the Philippine Islands from Spain in the Spanish-American War. Concerned that the European concessions in China might cut Americans out of the Chinese trade, in 1899 the United States proclaimed an **Open Door Policy**, issuing a note to each imperial power calling for free and equal trade with China and preservation of China's territorial integrity. One by one the other powers, worried that China's dismemberment might lead to wars among them, agreed in principle to the U.S. demands, and by 1900 the scramble for concessions was over.

The Chinese and Japanese Response

The events of the 1890s brought humiliation and anger to both China and Japan. The Chinese were humiliated by their loss to Japan in the Sino-Japanese War and angered at the concessions allowing Westerners to exploit regions of China. The Japanese were humiliated by the Triple Intervention, which forced them to return the Liaodong Peninsula to China, and angered at the Russians who then moved into Manchuria themselves.

Both reacted by waging war against Western powers: China's Qing regime supported an internal anti-Western uprising, and Japan's Meiji leaders started a conflict with Russia. China's efforts proved futile, as did last-ditch reforms that failed to save the regime, while Japan's were successful, bringing new status and global respect to the island nation. By 1912 Japan had emerged as East Asia's foremost power, while China's ancient empire was gone, overthrown by revolution and replaced by a republic.

The Boxer Uprising in China

In 1898, amid the Western scramble for concessions, China experienced devastating floods, renewing the widespread perception that the Qing dynasty had lost Heaven's Mandate. That same year, Empress Dowager Cixi, determined to maintain her power, blocked an effort by her nephew, the emperor, to institute Western-style reforms. She then arrested him, declared him too ill to rule, and again proclaimed herself regent, even though her nephew was 27 years old. The next year, angered at the foreigners partitioning her realm, she aligned with a secret martial arts society that launched an anti-Western rebellion.

The Society of Righteous and Harmonious Fists, whose members were called Boxers, blamed the floods on the Europeans, saying that they had upset the sacred earth by violating it with their railways, mines, and telegraph poles. By reciting a magic oath three times, then breathing through clenched teeth and foaming at the mouth, the Boxers believed they could make themselves impervious to Western bullets. In early 1900, with Cixi's tacit consent, they rebelled across northern China, smashing railways and telegraph lines, burning down Christian churches and convents, slaying thousands of Chinese Christians, and killing a few hundred Europeans. In June, as the Boxers invaded

View the **Map**

Map Discovery: China in the Late Qing Era

on **myhistorylab.com**

Boxer Uprising attacks Western interests in northern China

Beijing and laid siege to the Legation Quarter, a section of the city housing foreign embassies, Cixi's regime declared war on the imperialist powers—Britain, France, Germany, Russia, Japan, and the United States.

The Boxer War was short and bloody. For two months the Western embassy guards, numbering less than five hundred, held out against about two hundred thousand rebels, who found that they were not immune to Western bullets. Meanwhile, the Western powers and Japan assembled a force of thirty thousand soldiers, who then stormed Beijing and lifted the siege, bringing the war to an end.

The empress dowager nonetheless survived. Having fled in a peasant cart to the ancient city of Xi'an, she called on the foreigners to help her crush the Boxers, pretending that she had not backed them and declared war on the West. Her rival Li Hongzhang, who had opposed

Western forces combat Boxer Uprising.

the war and remained on good terms with the Western powers, persuaded them to go along with her pretense. Eager to restore order and exploit their concessions, and seeing no viable alternative to Cixi's continued rule, the invading nations agreed to the fiction that they had merely helped her defeat the rebels.

The Russo-Japanese War

Meanwhile, tensions mounted between Russia and Japan. During the Boxer Uprising, the Russians sent troops to Manchuria to protect their railway interests, further angering Japan, which was already irate at having been forced to give China back the Liaodong Peninsula. Now, fearing that Russia's presence in Manchuria would hinder their access to its ample coal and iron deposits, which they considered crucial to their industrial growth, the Japanese resolved to force the Russians out.

Russia occupies Manchuria and resists Japan's pressure to withdraw

Japan began with skillful diplomatic maneuvers. Having boosted its status with the Western powers by joining them in crushing the Boxers, it exploited growing fears of Russian expansion to conclude an "Anglo-Japanese" alliance with Britain in 1902 (Chapter 31). Bowing to international pressures, Russia agreed to withdraw from Manchuria by the end of 1903.

Japan attacks Russia and wins Russo-Japanese War

But the Russians did not actually withdraw. Instead, they began intruding into Korea, using a commercial enterprise designed to exploit Korean timber resources. Then, as the deadline for withdrawal neared, Russia offered to negotiate with Japan to divide Manchuria and Korea into Japanese and Russian economic exploitation zones.

Sensing that Russia was merely stalling to keep its troops in Manchuria, Japan prepared for war. On February 8, 1904, in a predawn surprise strike, Japanese torpedo boats devastated the Russian Pacific fleet at Port Arthur, beginning the Russo-Japanese War (1904–1905). Having thus crippled Russian sea power, Japan landed troops in Korea and Manchuria, defeating the Russians in several big land battles. Russia then sent its Baltic Sea fleet on a six-month journey to East Asia around Europe and Africa. But the Japanese navy, with ample time to prepare, ambushed and destroyed the Russian fleet off Japan's southwest coast in May 1905.

American-sponsored peace talks at Portsmouth, New Hampshire, that August ended the war. The defeated Russians returned Manchuria

Russian and Japanese diplomats with President Theodore Roosevelt (*center*) at Portsmouth peace talks

to China, while Japan gained primary influence in Korea, a leasehold on the Liaodong Peninsula, railway rights in southern Manchuria, and the southern half of Sakhalin (*SAH-kuh-LĒN*) Island (north of Japan). Five years later, Japan annexed Korea, making it a colony of the Japanese Empire (See Map 29.6 on page 683).

Japan's defeat of Russia has global implications

The Russo-Japanese War, though fought in East Asia, had a profound global impact. Shattering the myth of European superiority, Japan demonstrated that Western ways and weapons could be used to defeat a major Western power. Japan's victory thus gave hope to millions of Asians and Africans who had come under European rule. It also convinced the Japanese that military expansion was a good way to gain access to industrial resources. And it showed them that staging a surprise attack was a good way to fight a great power.

The End of the Chinese Empire

China belatedly tried to imitate Japan's modernization. Both to help her regime survive and to relieve Chinese poverty, which she had witnessed while fleeing the Boxer War in a peasant cart, Empress Dowager Cixi at last agreed to reforms. From 1901 until 1908, her regime worked to replace the old Confucian civil service exams with a new Western-style education system and to create an imperial parliamentary system like Japan's and Germany's. After Li Hongzhang died in 1901, she also gave his protégé, Yuan Shikai, the means to modernize China's military.

These reforms, designed to save the dynasty, may have hastened its end. Since the time of the Taiping Rebellion, when regional leaders were allowed to form their own armies, some had grown accustomed to acting with considerable autonomy. Now that the regime, with its reforms, seemed to be trying to recentralize power, regional leaders resisted. Even Yuan Shikai, rather than upgrading the entire Chinese army, focused on strengthening the forces directly loyal to him, making him a threat to the regime. So after Cixi and her nephew the emperor died in 1908, the regents of the new emperor, a three-year old boy called Puyi, forced Yuan Shikai to retire.

Chinese Revolution blends anti-Manchu fervor with Western ideologies

By then, a revolutionary movement, aimed at replacing the Qing regime with a parliamentary republic, had emerged. Its main spokesman was Sun Yixian (*SUN Ē-shē-AHN*), also known abroad as Sun Yatsen (*YAHT-SEN*) and in China as Sun Zhongshan (*JONG-SHAHN*). A peasant from southern China, he had lived in Hawaii as a youth with his brother, become a Christian, and studied Western medicine in British Hong Kong. Blending anti-Manchu hatred of the "foreign" Qing regime with Western-style liberal and nationalist ideals, he had returned to China to press for political change. But in 1896, to avoid arrest by the regime, he had fled abroad. For the next 15 years, he had traveled the world promoting a democratic Chinese revolution. Then, while in Denver, Colorado, in October 1911, he learned that a rebellion had begun in China.

The revolt started by chance. At Wuchang (*WOO-CHAHNG*), a provincial capital in central China (Map 29.7), a group of rebels were discovered by police after accidentally blowing up their hideout with a bomb. On October 10, 1911, as police began rounding up some rebels, others seized a local weapons arsenal, prompting the regional governor to flee. Large-scale riots soon erupted throughout China, while disaffected regional leaders did little to aid the regime. In December, Sun Yixian returned and declared a Chinese revolutionary republic.

Revolt leads to end of Qing dynasty and creation of Chinese Republic

In desperation, the young emperor's regents summoned Yuan Shikai from retirement, seeing him as the only one who had the military skills and standing to restore order. But rather than crush the rebels, Yuan negotiated with both them and the regents. As a result of these talks, the boy ruler Puyi abdicated his throne on February 12, 1912, and in March Yuan Shikai became president of a new Chinese Republic, with Sun Yixian leading its main political opposition party. China's long-dominant Celestial Empire thus came to an inglorious end.

Putting It in Perspective

Before 1800, Asian peoples had few direct connections with the West. Commerce was limited to places such as Nagasaki in Japan, Guangzhou in China, and trading posts established by the British in India and the Dutch in Indonesia. Few Asians knew about Westerners, and those who did often saw them as "barbarians" from inferior cultures seeking the riches of Asian civilizations.

In the 1800s this dynamic changed. Empowered by new technologies and weapons, Europeans extended their connections throughout Asia, adding to the challenges faced by Asian societies. Already beset by poverty, corruption, and population growth, China was further challenged by opium addiction, foreign wars, famines, and rebellions. Japan was tested by foreign intrusion, civil war, and sweeping social changes. India was rocked by rebellion and transformed by British rule. Indochina was exploited by the French, and Indonesia by the Dutch. By the early 1900s, many Asian nations were adapting Western ways to their own, partly to meet the challenges intensified by these connections, and partly because, as the Japanese showed, Asians could adapt Western ways to resist and defeat the West.

Reviewing Key Material

KEY CONCEPTS

Cohong, 671
opium, 671
coolie trade, 673
Taiping Rebellion, 674
sepoys, 676
sati, 676
thagi, 676

zaibatsu, 680
protectorate, 682
Triple Intervention, 684
Trans-Siberian Railway, 684
scramble for concessions, 684
Open Door Policy, 686

KEY PEOPLE

Lin Zexu, 671
Hong Xiuquan, 674
Zeng Guofan, 675
Li Hongzhang, 675
Cixi, 675
Gopal Krishna Gokhale, 678
Bal Gangadhar Tilak, 678
Matthew Perry, 679

Yoshida Shoin, 679
Meiji Emperor, 680
Saigo Takamori, 680
Emperors Gia Long and Tu Duc, 681, 682
Kings Rama IV and Rama V, 682
Ch'oe Che-u, 684
Yuan Shikai, 684
Sun Yixian (Sun Yatsen), 688

ASK YOURSELF

1. What factors and events contributed to China's instability from 1796 to 1864? How and why did the Qing dynasty survive?
2. How did commercial connections with Britain lead to India's subjugation? How did Indians respond? How did British policies expedite Indian resistance to British rule?
3. What factors account for the Meiji Restoration in Japan and the rise of Japanese imperialism?
4. How did China and Japan respond to Western intrusions? Why was Japan more successful in its efforts than China? What factors contributed to the end of the Chinese Empire?
5. How did people in each key Asian country adapt Western ways to fit their Asian cultures and to resist the West?

GOING FURTHER

Austin, Michael. *Negotiating with Imperialism: The Unequal Treaties and the Culture of Japanese Diplomacy.* 2004.

Bello, David A. *Opium and the Limits of Empire.* 2005.

Bergere, M. C. *Sun Yat-Sen.* 2000.

Bose, S. *The Indian Ocean Rim: An Inter-Regional Arena in the Age of Global Empire.* 2003.

Chang Hsin-pao. *Commissioner Lin and the Opium War.* 1964.

Duus, Peter. *The Rise of Modern Japan.* 2nd ed. 1998.

Ebrey, Patricia B., et al. *East Asia: A Cultural, Social, and Political History.* 2006.

Esherick, J. *The Origins of the Boxer Uprising.* 1987.

Fairbank, John King, and Merle Goldman. *China: A New History.* 2nd ed. 2006.

Fay, Peter Ward. *The Opium War, 1840–1842.* 1975.

Ferguson, N. *Empire: The Rise and Demise of the British World Order.* 2003.

Hane, Misiko. *Peasants, Rebels, Women, and Outcastes: The Underside of Modern Japan.* 2003.

Hibbert, C. *The Dragon Wakes: China and the West, 1793–1911.* 1970.

Huber, T. *The Revolutionary Origins of Modern Japan.* 1981.

Hunter, J. *The Emergence of Modern Japan.* 1989.

Janson, M. B., ed. *The Emergence of Meiji Japan.* 1995.

Karl, R. E. *Staging the World: Chinese Nationalism at the Turn of the Twentieth Century.* 2001.

Keene, D. *Emperor of Japan: Meiji and His World.* 2000.

Masani, Zareer, ed. *Indian Tales of the Raj.* 1988.

Masselos, Jim. *Indian Nationalism: A History.* 5th ed. 2004.

McClain, J. L. *Japan: A Modern History.* 2002.

Polachek, James M. *The Inner Opium War.* 1992.

Preston, D. *The Boxer Rebellion.* 2001.

Schirokauer, C., and D. N. Clark. *Modern East Asia: A Brief History.* 2004.

Spence, J. D. *God's Chinese Son: The Taiping Heavenly Kingdom of Hong Xiuquan.* 1996.

Spence, J. D. *The Search for Modern China.* 2nd ed. 1999.

Steinberg, John W., ed. *The Russo-Japanese War in Global Perspective: World War Zero.* 2005.

Taylor, Jean G. *Indonesia: Peoples and Histories.* 2003.

Têng, S. Y. *The Taiping Rebellion and the Western Powers.* 1971.

Wakemann, F., Jr. *The Fall of Imperial China.* 1975.

Waley, Arthur. *The Opium War Through Chinese Eyes.* 1968.

Walthall, Anne. *Japan: A Cultural, Social, and Political History.* 2006.

Wild, A. *East India Company.* 2000.

Wilson, George M. *Patriots and Redeemers in Japan.* 1992.

Wolpert, Stanley. *A New History of India.* 5th ed. 1997.

Key Dates and Developments

1771–1802	Tay-Son Rebellion in Vietnam		1877	Samurai Rebellion in Japan
1793	Macartney mission to China		1883–1885	Franco-Chinese War over Vietnam
1799	Dissolution of Dutch United East India Company		1885	Formation of the Indian National Congress
1839–1842	First Opium War		1889	Japanese Constitution
1850–1864	Taiping Rebellion in China		1894–1895	Sino-Japanese War and Triple Intervention
1853–1854	Perry's visits to Japan		1896–1899	Scramble for concessions in China
1856–1860	Second Opium War		1899–1900	Open Door Policy
1857–1858	Indian Revolt		1900	Boxer Uprising in China
1859	French occupation of southern Vietnam		1902	Anglo-Japanese alliance
1860–1864	Tonghak Movement in Korea		1904–1905	Russo-Japanese War
1868	Meiji Restoration in Japan		1911–1912	Chinese Revolution: end of Chinese Empire
1876	Britain's Queen Victoria declared Empress of India			

PEARSON
myhistorylab Connections

Reinforce what you learned in this chapter by studying the many documents, images, maps, review tools, and videos available at www.myhistorylab.com.

Read and Review

✔—Study and **Review** Chapter 29

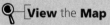Read the **Document**

Arrival of the British in the Punjab (Mid-19th Century), p. 677

Amrita Lal Roy, English Rule in India, 1886, p. 678

An Indian Nationalist on Hindu Women and Education (Early 19th Century), p. 678

The Views of Tokugawa Nariaki, 1841, p. 679

Emperor Meiji, The Constitution of the Empire of Japan, p. 680

View the **Image**

Japanese Views of Commodore Perry's Mission, 1853, I and II, p. 679

American Cartoon on Western Powers Carving up China, p. 686

Research and Explore

View the **Map**

Map Discovery: Asia and Oceania, 1800, p. 669

View the **Map**

Map Discovery: China in the Late Qing Era, p. 686

((•—Listen to the **Chapter Audio** for Chapter 29 on **myhistorylab.com**

30

New Connections and Challenges in West Asia and Africa, 1800–1914

((●─ **Listen** to the **Chapter Audio** for Chapter 30 on **myhistorylab.com**

- How did Ottoman decline and reforms affect West Asia and North Africa?

- Why and how did new regional states emerge in Africa in the early 1800s?

- How did each main African region come under foreign rule?

- How did Africans adapt to and resist foreign rule?

- What were the main impacts of foreign rule on African societies and how did they respond?

The Opening of the Suez Canal

In the 19th century, as reflected in this image of the ceremonial opening of the Suez Canal in 1869, new commercial and imperial connections created new challenges for West Asia and Africa.

In 1819, the Zulu, a warlike clan in southeastern Africa, fought a fierce two-day battle against a neighboring clan. Outnumbered nearly two to one, the Zulu emerged victorious, using new tactics devised by Shaka (*SHAH-kuh*), their innovative young ruler. Rather than throwing long spears from a distance, a traditional tactic typically producing few casualties, the Zulu attacked with short stabbing spears at close range, systematically slaughtering their enemies. Under Shaka the Zulu would create a mighty empire, defeating all who resisted them.

Six decades later, Zulu king Cetshwayo (*kech-WAH-yō*) waged war against outsiders from Britain. At first the Zulu did well, killing more than a thousand British soldiers in one 1879 battle. But later that year, the British attacked Cetshwayo's capital, Ulundi. The Zulu, with fifteen thousand warriors, had a three-to-one edge, but the British had a bigger advantage: modern artillery and Gatling machine guns that could fire three thousand rounds a minute. The Zulu thus could not get close to the British, whose deadly weapons mowed down their foes from 75 yards away. The British left behind a field full of corpses to mark the bloody Battle of Ulundi.

Africa and West Asia

These two conflicts reflect dramatic changes in Africa and West Asia in the 19th century. At the century's outset, connections in these regions typically fit long-established patterns (Map 30.1). Most of North Africa and West Asia belonged to the Ottoman Empire, a multinational realm created centuries earlier. Much of sub-Saharan Africa was organized into clans led by local chiefs, sometimes dominated by a regional kingdom. Along the coasts were seaports that conducted commerce in gold, ivory, various other goods, and slaves.

During the 1800s, however, the slave trade was suppressed and replaced by new commercial enterprises. Several new regional powers, including the Zulu, also emerged early in the century. But the biggest challenges came toward the century's end, when European powers, driven by new industries and ideologies (Chapter 27), carved up Africa among them, using new weapons against which Africans had little defense. By the early 1900s, the Ottoman Empire was a shrunken remnant of a once-great realm, while most of Africa was divided into European colonies. As a result, the economic, social, cultural, and political connections that had long prevailed in these regions were substantially transformed.

New Connections and Challenges in West Asia and North Africa

West Asia and North Africa had long been connected religiously and culturally by Islam. To Muslims, North Africa was the **Maghrib** (*MUH-grib*), Arabic for "the West," as it was the western part of the Islamic world. And to Muslims, West Asia, which (along with Egypt) Westerners knew as the Near East—now called the **Middle East**—was the center of Islamic civilization.

Since the early 1500s, most of West Asia and North Africa had also been connected politically by the empire of the Ottoman Turks (Map 30.1). From their capital

FOUNDATION MAP 30.1   Africa and West Asia Around 1800

In the early 1800s, as in centuries past, the Ottoman Empire connected West Asia and North Africa. Note, however, that no such realm connected sub-Saharan Africa, which featured various states and seaports and countless farming villages. What commercial and cultural connections linked parts of Africa into the global economy?

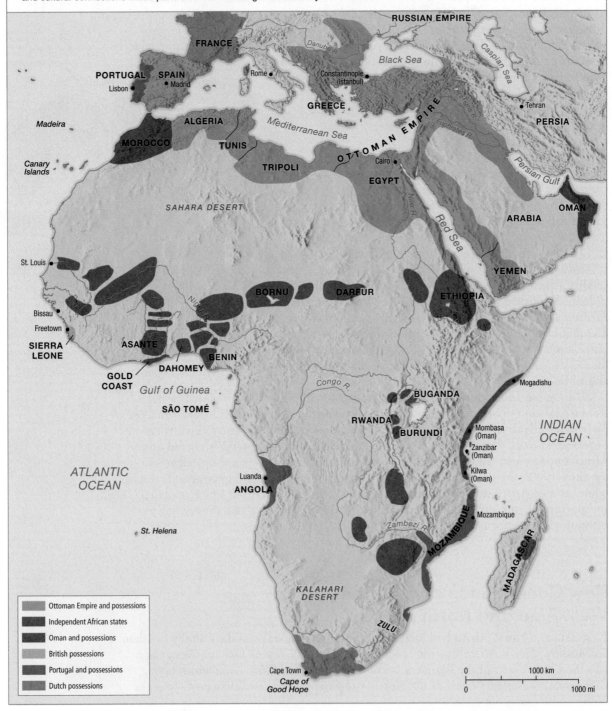

Ottoman Empire and possessions
Independent African states
Oman and possessions
British possessions
Portugal and possessions
Dutch possessions

at Constantinople, which the Turks also called Istanbul, Ottoman sultans had ruled with a blend of pragmatism, flexibility, and toleration (Chapter 17). Straddling parts of Europe, Asia, and Africa, and sitting astride the trade routes that connected them, the Ottoman Empire long had been one of the world's wealthiest and mightiest realms.

By the late 1700s, however, the Ottomans had fallen on hard times, as Russia repeatedly defeated them and took away chunks of territory. Lagging behind Europe militarily and industrially, in the 1800s the Ottomans tried to reform their realm but failed to halt its disintegration. North Africa gained freedom from Ottoman rule, only to come under European domination.

Scene from Russian-Turkish conflict, 1787.

Reform and Rebellion in the Ottoman Empire

Sultan Selim (*seh-LĒM*) III, reigning from 1789 to 1807, sought to centralize his power and enact reforms to reverse his realm's decline. But in 1798–1799, Napoleon's French forces conquered Egypt, one of the Ottoman Empire's most valuable provinces. Although the French withdrew in 1801 to fight elsewhere, and Egypt nominally returned to Ottoman rule, the sultans never regained real control there.

French occupation of Egypt spurs Ottoman reform efforts

In 1805, impressed with Napoleon's armies, Selim ordered a modernization of the Ottoman forces. But it threatened the privileged status of the Janissaries, elite slave soldiers who formed the Ottoman army's premier corps, and they responded with a fierce revolt in Ottoman Southeastern Europe. Selim survived this mutiny, in part by retracting his reforms, but in 1807 another armed revolt resulted in his imprisonment and eventual strangulation.

The empire's troubles continued under Sultan Mahmud (*mah-MOOD*) II, who reigned from 1808 to 1839. Defeat by Russia in 1812 cost the Ottomans more land in Southeastern Europe and boosted Russian influence there. Buoyed by the success of the Russians, their fellow Orthodox Christians, the Greeks rebelled against the sultan in 1821. Although at first contained by Ottoman forces, the rebellious Greeks eventually gained independence with help from the Russians, who once again defeated the Ottomans in 1828–1829 (Chapter 26).

Russians help Greeks gain independence from Turks

Faced with his realm's disintegration, Mahmud initiated new reforms. In 1826 he began a major military reorganization, which again prompted a Janissary rebellion. This time, however, the regime prevailed. Mahmud declared war on the Janissaries and eventually had cannons fired into their barracks, massacring them by the thousands. He then abolished the Janissary corps and began forming a new army trained in Western methods, armed with modern weapons, and based on Western-style mass conscription. Mahmud also moved to assert state control over law and education, co-opting the ulama (*oo-lah-MAH*)—learned religious leaders who traditionally dominated law and education in most Muslim countries—and reducing their influence.

The Tanzimat and the Young Turks

Mahmud's successors followed with the **Tanzimat** (*tahn-zē-MAHT*), or "reorganization," a set of reforms, enacted from 1839 to 1876, designed to modernize and Westernize the Ottoman Empire (see "Excerpts from the Tanzimat Rescripts"). An admirer of Britain and France, Grand Vizier (chief minister) Mustafa Reshid (*reh-SHĒD*)—awarded the honorary title pasha (*pah-SHAH*) and hence called Reshid Pasha—avidly promoted the reforms. They established regional representative assemblies, a secular school system, a more equitable tax structure, and a new set of laws modeled in part on France's Napoleonic Code. The Tanzimat also included a further restructuring of the military and a promise of equal rights for all men in the empire, including its non-Muslims (mostly Christians and Jews).

Tanzimat reforms adapt Western ideas to Ottoman society

👁 **Watch** the **Video**

The Ottoman Tanzimat Period (1839–1876): The Middle East Confronts Modernity

on **myhistorylab.com**

DOCUMENT 30.1 Excerpts from the Tanzimat Rescripts

The Tanzimat reforms were embodied in rescripts (edicts), excerpted below, issued by Ottoman sultans. Why were these reforms enacted? What impact would they have on Ottoman society?

THE RESCRIPT OF GÜLHANE (3 NOVEMBER 1839)

All the world knows that in the first days of the Ottoman monarchy, the glorious precepts of the Kuran and the laws of the empire were always honored. The empire in consequence increased in strength and greatness . . . In the last one hundred and fifty years a succession of accidents and . . . causes have arisen which have brought about a disregard for the sacred code of laws . . . , and the former strength and prosperity have changed into weakness and poverty; an empire in fact loses all its stability so soon as it ceases to observe its laws . . .

Full of confidence, therefore, in the help of the Most High, and certain of the support of our Prophet, we deem it right to seek by new institutions to give to the provinces composing the Ottoman Empire the benefit of a good administration.

These institutions must be principally carried out under three heads, which are:

1. The guarantees insuring to our subjects perfect security for life, honor, and fortune.
2. A regular system of assessing and levying taxes.
3. An equally regular system for the levying of troops and the duration of their service . . .

From henceforth . . . the cause of every accused person shall be publicly judged . . . , and so long as a regular judgment shall not have been pronounced, no one can secretly or publicly put another to death . . .

Each one shall possess his property of every kind, and shall dispose of it in all freedom . . . These imperial concessions shall extend to all our subjects, of whatever religion or sect they may be; they shall enjoy them without exception . . .

RESCRIPT OF REFORM (18 FEBRUARY 1856)

The guarantees promised on our part by the [Rescript] of Gülhane, and in conformity with the Tanzimat, to all the subjects of my Empire, without distinction of classes or of religion, for the security of their persons and property and the preservation of their honour, are today confirmed and consolidated . . .

Every distinction or designation tending to make any class whatever of the subjects of my Empire inferior to another class, on account of their religion, language, or race, shall be for ever effaced . . .

As all forms of religion are and shall be freely professed in my dominions, no subject of my Empire shall be hindered in the exercise of the religion that he professes . . .

. . . All the subjects of my Empire, without distinction of nationality, shall be admissible to public employments, and qualified to fill them according to their capacity and merit . . .

All the subjects of my Empire, without distinction, shall be received into the Civil and Military Schools of the Government if they otherwise satisfy the conditions as to age and examination . . .

Steps shall also be taken for the formation of roads and canals to increase the facilities of communication and increase the sources of the wealth of the country. Everything that can impede commerce or agriculture shall be abolished.

SOURCE: Boğaziçi University, Atatürk Institute of Modern Turkish History.

The reforms, applying mainly to men, did little to enhance women's status. Marriage and family were still governed largely by religious law, and women were still excluded from political and professional affairs. They were even typically excluded from the new textile industries, where men ran machines that made clothing, traditionally a woman's role. Still, the reforms helped to foster a new "enlightened" atmosphere that allowed the formation of several schools for women and increased participation by women in literature and art.

The Tanzimat, enforced by new state law courts rather than the ulama, upset the Islamic elite by ending its traditional control of law and education. But it impressed the British and French, who began to see the Turks as far more enlightened and less dangerous than the Russians, whose tsar reportedly disparaged the Ottoman realm as the "sick man" of Europe. In 1854–1856, Britain and France joined with the Turks to defeat the Russians in the Crimean War (Chapter 27).

The Tanzimat culminated in 1876 with the proclamation of a liberal constitution by Sultan Abdulhamid (*ahb-dul-hah-MĒD*) II (1876–1909), followed the next year by the opening of a Turkish Parliament. Eventually, however, unwilling to accept limitations on his authority, Abdulhamid shut down the parliament and suspended the constitution. He then ruled with an iron fist, imposing strict censorship and using secret police to repress dissent.

Dissent nonetheless continued. Defeat in another war with Russia (1877–1878) humiliated the Ottomans and cost them more lands in Southeastern Europe (See Map 30.2 on page 698). Fueled by liberal and nationalist ideals, some Turkish college students plotted against the sultan in 1889. Then, when their plot was discovered, they fled to Paris and started preparing a new revolution. These youthful reformist rebels, later called **Young Turks**, collaborated with dissident Ottoman army officers to rebel in 1908, forcing Abdulhamid to restore the constitution and parliament. The next year they replaced him with his mild-mannered brother, who as Sultan Mehmet V (1909–1918) mostly let the Young Turks run the show. They promoted industrialization and Turkish national pride, hoping to match the West's power and wealth by adapting its industries and ideologies. But they sided with Germany in the Great War, which proved a disastrous mistake, and their rabid Turkish nationalism during that war fueled distrust of the empire's non-Turks and atrocities against its Armenian Christians (Chapter 31).

Read the **Document**

An Ottoman Government Decree Defines the Official Notion of the "Modern" Citizen, June 19, 1870

on **myhistorylab.com**

The Transformation of Egypt

Meanwhile, Ottoman decline had enabled ambitious North African leaders, still under Ottoman rule, to assert autonomy. Most notable was Muhammad Ali, a former soldier in the Ottoman army sent to resist Napoleon's invasion of Egypt in 1798–1799. In a power struggle following France's 1801 withdrawal, Muhammad Ali rose to prominence, and in 1805 he was appointed Ottoman viceroy in Egypt. From then until 1848, he was effectively Egypt's ruler, transforming its economy, building a powerful military, and starting a dynasty that reigned until the 1950s.

To secure his power, Muhammad Ali disposed of all potential foes. He massacred the Mamluks, the class of former slave soldiers who had long served as Egypt's ruling elite, and brutally repressed several peasant revolts. He also dispossessed the old landowners, converting their lands into state property and making him the country's main landlord.

Determined to modernize Egypt's agriculture and commerce, he compelled the peasants to forsake subsistence farming (growing food for their own consumption), and instead to grow **cash crops** they could sell for money to buy food and goods. The most valuable cash crop was cotton, which grew very well in the Nile River Valley and produced healthy profits for the regime when sold to industrial Europe. Muhammad Ali then used these profits to create a modern army and navy, to start a Western-style public school system, and to begin industrializing Egypt by building factories and textile mills.

By the 1830s, as a result, he had gained greater wealth and power than his overlord, the Ottoman sultan, and actually proceeded to fight two wars against the Ottomans. In the first conflict (1831–1833), his (possibly adopted) son Ibrahim (*ib-rah-HĒM*) Pasha seized much of Syria and then governed it for most of the decade. In the second war (1838–1841), when Ibrahim's forces again defeated the Ottomans, it looked as if Egypt might gain full independence. But the European powers, fearful that a powerful new Egypt would replace the weak Ottomans astride the vital East–West trade routes, forced

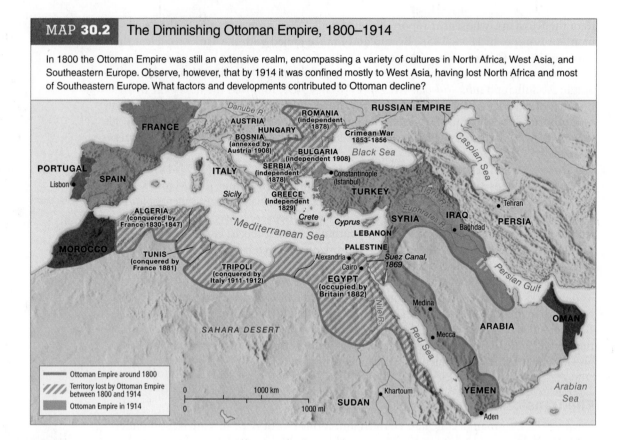

MAP 30.2 | The Diminishing Ottoman Empire, 1800–1914

In 1800 the Ottoman Empire was still an extensive realm, encompassing a variety of cultures in North Africa, West Asia, and Southeastern Europe. Observe, however, that by 1914 it was confined mostly to West Asia, having lost North Africa and most of Southeastern Europe. What factors and developments contributed to Ottoman decline?

Commerce and culture in Cairo, Egypt, in the 1800s.

Muhammad Ali to end Ibrahim's rule in Syria and to continue Egypt's nominal submission to the Ottoman sultan.

In economic affairs, Europeans also thwarted Egypt's industrialization. To protect its industrial preeminence, Britain compelled Muhammad Ali to remove protective tariffs he had placed on imports of Western industrial goods. Egypt's new industries then could not compete with inexpensive European imports that flooded local markets and undercut local producers. Thus, although Muhammad Ali did much to modernize Egypt, quintupling its commerce and vastly enhancing his own wealth, he was stymied in his efforts to make it an independent industrial power.

The Suez Canal and Its Impact

Muhammad Ali's grandson, Abbas Hilmy (*ah-BAHSS HILL-mē*) I, viceroy in Egypt from 1848 to 1854, was a conservative Muslim who sought to undo his grandfather's reforms. Resenting European influence, he closed the Western-style schools and factories started by Muhammad Ali, and opposed a French plan to construct a canal across the Isthmus of Suez.

The French had long hoped to build a canal there to shorten the sea route between Asia and Europe, over which traveled such valuable items as spices, tea, and cotton. The route around Africa was long, expensive, and perilous, and it had been dominated by the Dutch and British since the 1600s. Having occupied Egypt in 1798–1799, Napoleon explored the possibility of building a Suez Canal. But the task had seemed too daunting, given the region's hot, arid climate and the need to conscript thousands of workers, using picks and shovels, to dig a trench roughly 30 feet deep, 200 feet wide, and 100 miles long.

The development of steam-powered excavators and dredgers during Europe's Industrial Revolution, however, made a canal project feasible by the time of Sa'id Pasha (*sah-ĒD pah-SHAH*), a French-educated, pro-Western Egyptian leader who replaced Abbas Hilmy and reigned from 1854 to 1863. Organized by Ferdinand de Lesseps (*duh LESS-ups*), a former French diplomat who had served in Egypt, the Suez Canal Company began construction in 1859. Beset by labor problems and a cholera epidemic, the project took ten years.

Industrial advances facilitate construction of Suez Canal

But these delays did not dampen the excitement when the Suez Canal finally opened in November 1869. A grand ceremony, presided over by Sa'id's successor Ismail (*iss-MAH-ēl*) and French Empress Eugenie (*oo-zhā-NĒ*), and witnessed by dignitaries from Africa, Asia, and Europe, featured steam and sailing ships parading through the wondrous new waterway. The canal cut travel time from Europe to Asia in half, from more than a month to less than two weeks, substantially lowering East–West shipping costs. It bolstered global commerce and industry, and seemed to promise a flourishing future for Egypt, which owned 44 percent of the Suez Canal Company shares. But six years later, his regime deeply in debt, Ismail sold these shares to the British—a disaster for Egypt that within a decade would subvert its long-held hopes for independence (see "Global Trade and the Occupation of Egypt" section on page 709).

Suez Canal enhances connections between East and West

Ships parade through new Suez Canal, 1869.

The Origins of Arab Nationalism in West Asia

Islamic West Asia, including Palestine, Lebanon, Syria, Iraq, and much of Arabia, had likewise long been part of the Ottoman Empire. But in the 1800s, the region's Arab peoples grew restive under Turkish rule. Inspired by Egypt's resurgence, influenced by Western connections, and troubled by Turkish reforms, some Arabs started dreaming of self-rule and fostering Arab nationalism.

Egypt was both an example and impetus for West Asian Arab nationalism. Having begun to modernize and assert its autonomy, Egypt provided a model for other Arab lands. And by conquering and ruling Lebanon and Syria in the 1830s, Egypt connected them through commerce with the industrial West. Western connections were later strengthened by Lebanon's Maronite Christians, members of an ancient Lebanese church affiliated with Roman Catholicism, who worked with Western educators to establish schools in Lebanon, including a French Jesuit college. Such connections exposed many Arabs to Western-style nationalism and liberalism, and by the century's end some had started to agitate against Ottoman rule.

Enhanced connections with the West promote Arab nationalism

Meanwhile, the Turkish Tanzimat, by strengthening Ottoman administration and granting legal equality to non-Muslims, produced an anti-Turkish reaction among other Arabs. Fearful of being engulfed by Ottoman Westernization and secularization, some Arab Muslims started pushing for political autonomy, and eventually for full independence from Ottoman rule.

Ottoman reforms provoke anti-Turkish Arab nationalism

The Plight of the Maghrib

West of Egypt, the Maghrib encompassed four North African Muslim countries, collectively called the Barbary States (possibly because their original people were Berbers). In the early 1800s, only one of them, Morocco, an Islamic kingdom on Africa's northwest coast, was fully independent. The other three—Tripoli (today part of Libya), Tunis, and Algeria— were autonomous provinces of the Ottoman Empire (Map 30.2), recognizing its sultan as overlord but running their own affairs. Like Egypt, these countries hoped to benefit from Ottoman decline; like Egypt, they found their hopes thwarted by outside interference.

United States and Britain suppress North African piracy

The Barbary States provoked this interference by profiting from piracy. For centuries the notorious Barbary pirates had preyed on Mediterranean shipping, and their rulers collected tribute from countries trying to buy immunity from piracy. But in 1801, Tripoli's ruler, upset that Americans refused his demands for higher tribute, declared war on the United States, which then won the Tripolitan War (1801–1805) and ended Tripoli's tribute system. Ongoing efforts by the British and American navies, culminating in British bombardment of Algeria in 1816, terminated the tribute extortions of the other North African states.

Although diminished by such efforts, piracy persisted, giving France a pretext to invade Algeria. In 1827, Algeria's ruler, angered by unpaid French debts, supplied another pretext when he smacked the French consul with a fly swatter. The French regime of Charles X, eager to employ the many jobless veterans of the Napoleonic Wars and hoping for a quick victory to revive its flagging fortunes, invaded Algeria in July of 1830—three weeks before Charles was deposed by France's July Revolution (Chapter 26).

Algerians valiantly resist French takeover but fail

The French soon conquered northern Algeria, but their hopes for quick victory were dashed by Abdelqadir al-Jazairi (*ab-dul-KAH-dur al-jah-ZAH-ih-rē*), a young Algerian leader who took charge in 1832. He created a new state in the interior, rallying his people in a spirited resistance that forced France for a time to make concessions. But the French eventually launched a massive assault, devastating Algeria and compelling Abdelqadir to surrender in 1846. Highly respected, nonetheless, by friend and foe alike, he came to be called the "father of modern Algeria."

France's conquest of Algeria marked the beginning of the end of North African autonomy. In 1835, taking advantage of the turmoil, the Ottoman sultan sent forces to reoccupy Tripoli, subjecting it to direct Ottoman rule. Tunis survived as an autonomous Ottoman province, and Morocco as an independent state, until they were engulfed by momentous changes that affected the whole continent later in the century.

New Connections and Challenges in Sub-Saharan Africa

South of the Sahara, by 1800, certain economic and political connections had prevailed for centuries. Along the coasts and the desert's southern edge were urban centers and independent kingdoms, many involved in trading slaves and commercial goods. In the interior were mostly farming villages, connected by clans and run by local chiefs and elders. But after 1800, some connections started changing. The slave trade was banned, resulting in efforts to replace it with new economic enterprises, and to continue it illegally by procuring captives from East Africa. And several new regional states arose, creating new political connections.

The Banning of the Slave Trade

From the 16th through 18th centuries, the Atlantic slave trade ravaged Africa's western coastal regions and interiors (Chapter 23). Millions of Africans, mostly men and boys, were shipped overseas, robbing these regions of labor and talent, upsetting the gender balance, and wreaking havoc on family and economic structures. Some Africans nonetheless gained wealth and power by selling slaves to Europeans, often in return for firearms, which were used to conquer other Africans and acquire more captives.

By 1800, however, a growing international movement sought to outlaw the slave trade and eventually end slavery itself. The European Enlightenment and the Atlantic revolutions advanced ideals of equality and liberty that hardly harmonized with human bondage. Haiti's slave rebellion in the 1790s, and numerous smaller slave revolts, highlighted the evils and dangers of slavery, which were further emphasized by Christian missionaries and antislave abolitionists.

Global antislavery movement arises by 1800

Equiano memoir spreads antislavery sentiment

Among the most effective early abolitionists was Olaudah Equiano (Ō-LOUD-*ah ek-wē-AH-nō*), a former slave who claimed to have been kidnapped in West Africa at age 11, shipped across the Atlantic to the West Indies, then sold to a Virginia plantation owner and later to an English sea captain. Having gained some education and purchased his freedom, he later wrote his memoirs, publishing them in England in 1789. Although research has cast doubt on his African origins, his personal account of the evils of slavery was convincing to many of his contemporaries. His book sold widely in Europe and America, strengthening the antislavery movement, ably led in Britain by William Wilberforce, a devout Christian member of parliament.

Meanwhile, Britain's Industrial Revolution was producing new machines that reduced demand for human muscle, and it was showing that paid workers using these machines were far more productive than slaves. Industrialists, moreover, were coming to see Africa mainly as a source of raw materials, not slaves. Slavery, it seemed, was neither morally defensible nor economically efficient.

In 1803, responding to such perceptions, Denmark outlawed the slave trade, followed in 1807 by Great Britain. They were joined in 1808 by the United States, and during the next decade by Sweden, France, and the Netherlands. After 1815, British ships, with help from Americans and others, patrolled the West African coast, stopping slave ships, arresting slave traders, and freeing their captives. These efforts did not end slavery—millions of slaves were already in the Americas, where slavery was still legal—but they did help to transform African economic patterns.

Olaudah Equiano.

New Commercial Connections

One result of the banning of the slave trade was the development of new commercial connections to replace it. Eager to continue trade with Europe for textiles, tobacco, alcohol, and guns, enterprising Africans soon provided products to fill the slave trade's void. Some, such as gold and ivory, had long been part of African commerce. Export of these items, and of commodities such as coconuts and cloves, increased with the slave trade's decline.

Meanwhile, Europe's growing industries added value to other African products. One was raw cotton, grown in Egypt and East Africa to help supply Europe's booming textile mills. Another was gum arabic, a substance extracted from certain West African trees, which was used to make glues and dyes for these textile mills. A third was palm oil, long used to make candles and soaps, which became the leading lubricant for Europe's industrial machines. It emerged as one of West Africa's main commercial exports, until it was replaced by petroleum in the 20th century.

Ironically, however, cotton and cloves were grown on slave plantations, while gum arabic and palm oil production also involved slave labor. Male slaves, for example, were

Supplying products for industry strengthens slavery within Africa

forced to climb tall palm trees, cut down heavy palm nuts, and then, after female slaves extracted the oil by pummeling the palm nuts, convey the bulky liquid downstream in huge log dugout canoes. Paradoxically, then, the banning of the overseas slave trade helped strengthen slavery in Africa.

Another ironic outcome of the ban was the fact that it resulted, not in a quick end to the slave trade, but in its relocation from West to East Africa. To avoid the British and American ships patrolling the Atlantic coast, many slave traders transferred their activities to Africa's eastern shores, where coastal city-states had long conducted Indian Ocean slave commerce. Now they added to their business by selling slaves to traders bound for the Americas, where slavery was still practiced even though the slave trade was illegal.

Captives freed from a slave ship, East Africa, 1884.

The Atlantic slave trade thus lasted for decades after it was banned. Indeed, by decreasing the supply of slaves and making their transport more dangerous, the ban helped to increase their market value. Traders willing to run the risk could thus buy slaves in East Africa, transport them to the Americas, and reap a huge profit if they avoided detection. Between 1800 and 1870, despite efforts to suppress the slave trade, at least a million more captives were shipped from Africa to the Americas.

Illegal slave trading thus continued as long as slavery itself remained legal. And, although outlawed in 1833 in all British possessions and 15 years later in French colonies, slavery was legal in the United States until 1865, in Cuba until 1886, and in Brazil until 1888. Only when slavery itself was banned did the demand decline, eventually curtailing the cruel commerce that brought misery to millions of Africans.

The Rise of New Regional States

Commercial changes coincided with the rise of new regional states (Map 30.3). In West Africa, an extensive new Islamic domain called the Sokoto (sō-KŌ-tō) Caliphate arose in the interior, while several new settlements for returning former slaves were formed on the Atlantic coast. In East Africa, the island state of Zanzibar became the center of a huge trading empire, and smaller commercial realms developed farther inland. In South Africa, the new Zulu Kingdom created by Shaka, described at the start of this chapter, was challenged by other new states, including some formed by intruders of European ancestry.

West Africans historically blend Islam with local faiths

THE SOKOTO CALIPHATE. West Africa's most dynamic new state arose from a movement to purify Islamic practice in that region. For centuries Islam had flourished among the ruling classes and educated people in West African cities, but farmers and herders in rural areas often retained their age-old polytheistic beliefs. Muslim rulers long had tolerated these traditional beliefs, partly because they were thoroughly entrenched and partly because they enhanced the rulers' power by portraying them as semidivine (Chapter 13). Rural religion in West Africa thus often blended Islam with such traditional beliefs.

Fulani launch a "holy war" to purify West African Islam

In the 1700s, however, the **Fulani** (*FOO-LAH-nē*), a pastoral people from West Africa's grasslands, were attracted to Sufism—perhaps because this mystic strain of Islam (Chapter 12) provided a communal spirituality and elaborate ritual that adapted well to their rural lifestyle. By 1800 Usman dan Fodio (*oos-MAHN dahn fō-DĒ-ō*), a charismatic Fulani mystic, had clashed with local rulers, whom he accused of betraying

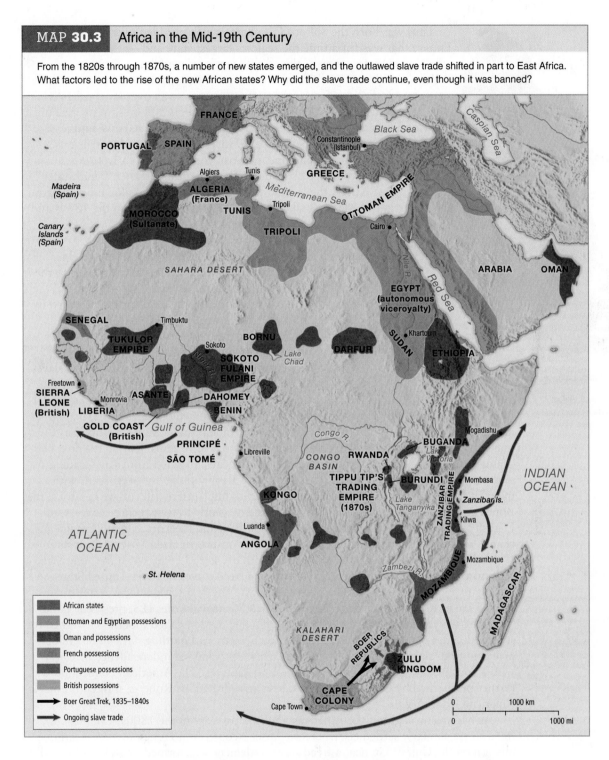

MAP 30.3 Africa in the Mid-19th Century

From the 1820s through 1870s, a number of new states emerged, and the outlawed slave trade shifted in part to East Africa. What factors led to the rise of the new African states? Why did the slave trade continue, even though it was banned?

Islam by tolerating "paganism" among their people. Hailed by his followers as both caliph (successor to the prophet Muhammad) and "commander of the faithful," in 1804 he declared a "jihad of the sword," a holy war to defend Islam against "unbelievers." In 1809, after his inspired armies had won several battles, the caliph's headquarters were established at a new town called Sokoto.

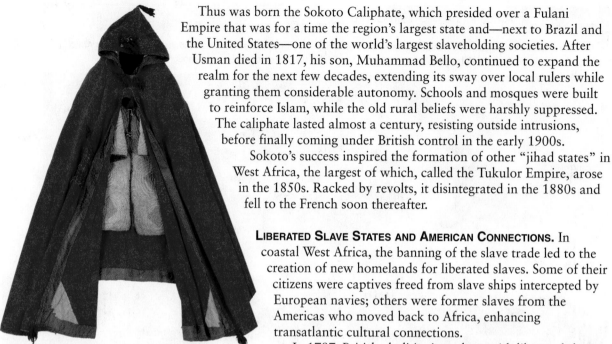

Fulani cavalry uniform.

Thus was born the Sokoto Caliphate, which presided over a Fulani Empire that was for a time the region's largest state and—next to Brazil and the United States—one of the world's largest slaveholding societies. After Usman died in 1817, his son, Muhammad Bello, continued to expand the realm for the next few decades, extending its sway over local rulers while granting them considerable autonomy. Schools and mosques were built to reinforce Islam, while the old rural beliefs were harshly suppressed. The caliphate lasted almost a century, resisting outside intrusions, before finally coming under British control in the early 1900s.

Sokoto's success inspired the formation of other "jihad states" in West Africa, the largest of which, called the Tukulor Empire, arose in the 1850s. Racked by revolts, it disintegrated in the 1880s and fell to the French soon thereafter.

LIBERATED SLAVE STATES AND AMERICAN CONNECTIONS. In coastal West Africa, the banning of the slave trade led to the creation of new homelands for liberated slaves. Some of their citizens were captives freed from slave ships intercepted by European navies; others were former slaves from the Americas who moved back to Africa, enhancing transatlantic cultural connections.

Freed slaves in Sierra Leone blend African and European ways

In 1787, British abolitionists, along with liberated slaves from the Americas, founded a settlement called Freetown in Sierra Leone (*sē-AIR-uh lē-ōN*), long an outpost for trade between West Africans and Europeans. In 1808, the year after Britain's Parliament banned the slave trade, the British navy started using the site as a base from which to combat this commerce, and as a home for African captives that British sailors freed from slave ships. During the next half-century, perhaps a hundred thousand **recaptives**, Africans liberated from slave-trading vessels, were resettled in Sierra Leone. Partly to create a community out of Africans with many different languages and cultures, and partly to implant English culture in Africa, the British government and Anglican Church worked diligently to transform recaptives into English-speaking Christians. In time a number of them and their descendants became merchants, missionaries, doctors, and lawyers, forming a Europeanized West African elite.

Freed slaves in Liberia bring American ideals to Africa

A different venture began in 1821, just south of Sierra Leone, when the American Colonization Society, established earlier to bring freed slaves from the United States to Africa, acquired some land on West Africa's coast. The first settlers from America arrived the next year and founded a town called Monrovia (after U.S. president James Monroe), which in time became the capital of a new nation called Liberia. Governed for several decades by the American Colonization Society, and battling African neighbors profiting from slavery and the slave trade, Liberia proclaimed independence in 1847, with a constitution modeled on that of the United States. The American connection was further personified by Liberia's first president, Joseph Jenkins Roberts, a freeborn black American from Virginia.

French and Latin American freed slaves blend African and Western ways

As nations throughout the Americas abolished slavery in the 1800s (Chapter 28), freed slaves similarly settled elsewhere on Africa's coast. At a French fort and Catholic mission on the Gulf of Guinea, a freed slave settlement was formed in 1849 at Libreville (*LĒ-bruh-vill*)—the French equivalent of Freetown—influenced by French culture and Catholicism. Liberated slaves from Latin America also came back to Africa in chartered ships, bringing Latin American cultural values. Coastal West African cities thus displayed Western cultural connections, including European languages, Christian beliefs, and fashions in architecture and dress from the Americas.

African-American cultural connections worked in both directions. Although thousands of former slaves returned to Africa, most of those born in the Americas stayed there. They became an influential **African diaspora**: descendants of transplanted Africans who enriched American societies with features from their African cultures. They infused American Christianity, for example, with elements of African spirituality, such as spirited worship, exuberant music, and visions of heaven as a place for reunion with departed loved ones. Popular Latin dances, such as mambo and conga, arose out of African roots. And striking new forms of music, including especially jazz, combined African rhythms with European harmonies and instrumentation.

THE ZANZIBAR COMMERCIAL EMPIRE. As slave trading shifted to East Africa, the island of Zanzibar emerged as the center of this traffic. About twenty miles off the East African coast, Zanzibar had been established as a trading post in the late 1600s by Arabs from the Persian Gulf sultanate of Oman. Under the energetic rule of Sa'id ibn Sultan (*sah-ĒD ib'n sool-TAHN*), also called Sa'id Sayyid (*sah-ĒD SĪ-yid*), from 1806 to 1856, Zanzibar formed a commercial empire that controlled coastal cities and parts of the interior. So wealthy did it become, in fact, that Sa'id Sayyid moved his headquarters there from Oman in 1828.

Zanzibar's empire was built on commerce interconnected with slavery. The island's main exports were slaves, captured in the African interior by warriors; cloves and coconuts, produced on slave plantations; and ivory, from elephant and rhinoceros tusks carried from inner Africa by slaves. Eventually, under British pressure, the sultan restricted the slave trade, which was formally suppressed in 1857. But the use and sale of slaves in the interior continued till the 1870s.

In the interior, enterprising merchants formed personal empires based on the Zanzibar trade. Most famous was Tippu Tip, a part-Arab, part-African entrepreneur who used European guns to control and exploit the upper Congo River basin in the mid-1800s. He gained great wealth but ravaged the region, killing much of its wildlife in his relentless hunt for ivory. Northwest of Lake Victoria, in what is now Uganda, a small realm called Buganda grew into a regional power, enriched by such pernicious but profitable pursuits.

THE ZULU KINGDOM AND THE BOER REPUBLICS. In southeastern Africa in the early 1800s, a different sort of empire emerged: a warrior kingdom based on military innovation and capability in combat. Created by the Zulu, one of many Bantu-speaking South African peoples (Chapter 13), it became the region's dominant power, until challenged by descendants of Dutch colonists.

Led by Shaka, the warrior king depicted at the start of this chapter, the Zulu carved out a sizable realm by conquest, killing thousands and scattering many others who fled in the face of their assaults. Shaka, who reigned from 1816 to 1828, organized Zulu youth into regiments and trained them in Zulu traditions, building their loyalty to him and to their people. His innovations also helped transform South African warfare from a relatively restrained rite in which warriors threw light spears at each other from a distance, into a fierce form of close combat in which disciplined soldiers equipped with ox-hide shields and short, stabbing spears systematically slew their foes.

Shaka was ruthless, but his detractors may have amplified his reputation for cruelty. The assertion that his wars depopulated whole regions, for example, was later made by Westerners eager to discredit the Zulu and colonize these regions. The claim that Shaka mourned his mother's death in 1827 by having numerous women killed, so their sons would share his grief, may have been advanced by his successor Dingane (*din-GAH-neh*) to justify his assassination of Shaka in 1828. Dingane's reign (1828–1840) was marked by internal conflicts among the Zulu, and by intrusions into their lands of Dutch South Africans called Boers.

African diaspora blends African and American cultures

Ivory tusks, Zanzibar.

Zanzibar commerce connects and exploits much of East Africa

Watch the **Video**
Zanzibar
on **myhistorylab.com**

Listen to the **Audio**
Africa/Zulus 1
on **myhistorylab.com**

Zulu kingdom connects much of southeastern Africa by conquest

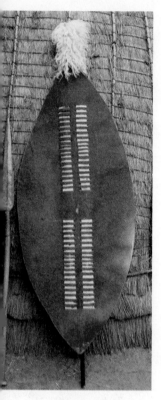

Zulu shield and spear.

Boers prevail in conflicts
with Zulu

The Boers, later called **Afrikaners** (*af-rih-KAH-nurz*), were descendants of Dutch and other European immigrants who settled in southernmost Africa, near the Cape of Good Hope, after the Dutch East India Company founded a station there for Asia-bound ships in 1652 (Chapter 23). Far from the liberal ideals of the European Enlightenment and Atlantic Revolutions, the Boers developed a society based on farming, ranching, slavery, racism, and rigid Calvinist Christianity. Perceiving themselves as God's chosen race in the wilderness, they dismissed local Africans as godless, subhuman heathens. As *trekboers* (Dutch for "wandering farmers"), the colonists organized patriarchal pastoral communities, speaking a language called Afrikaans (a South African variant of Dutch) and clashing repeatedly with neighboring South Africans.

In 1806, during the Napoleonic Wars, Britain seized the Cape settlement and eventually made it the British Cape Colony. At first the Boers, used to being left alone, paid little heed to the new regime. But soon Britain's relatively liberal attitude toward black South Africans upset them. In 1835, a few years after Britain banned slavery throughout its empire (including the Cape Colony), thousands of Boers began the **Great Trek**, a mass migration northeast from the Cape Colony into South Africa's interior. Comparing themselves to Biblical Hebrews entering the "Promised Land," they eventually formed two republics: the Orange Free State (in the Orange River region) and Transvaal (north of the Vaal River).

They also clashed with the Zulu. In February 1838, alarmed by the intrusion of white settlers into Zulu territory, Zulu king Dingane invited some Boers to his village and then had them killed. In December a new Boer leader, Andries Pretorius (*pruh-TOOR-ē-oos*), heading a force armed with muskets and cannons, avenged these killings by routing the Zulu at the Battle of Blood River—so named because the water ran red with Zulu blood. In the 1850s he helped gain British recognition of Boer independence, and Transvaal's capital was later named Pretoria in his honor.

At first the Boer republics had little contact with the outside world. Eventually, however, the discovery of diamonds and gold in this region would shine a global spotlight on the Boers, engulfing them in an imperialist wave that swept across the whole continent.

The Age of Imperialism in Africa

From the mid-1400s through the mid-1800s, connections between Africans and Europeans were limited largely to the African coasts. Some Europeans had ventured inland to capture and transport slaves, but Africans had conducted most such operations. Europeans in this era did little to colonize Africa: as late as 1875, their holdings in Africa included only the British Cape Colony, Portuguese Angola and Mozambique, French Algeria, and various coastal outposts. Outsiders had made few inroads into Africa's interior (Map 30.3).

Between 1880 and 1914, however, this situation changed. Armed with new technologies, impelled by new ideologies, and inspired by age-old motives such as curiosity and greed, Europeans brought most of Africa under their control, increasing their holdings from under 10 percent to over 90 percent of the African continent (Map 30.4).

Factors That Facilitated Imperialism

As noted in Chapter 27, the Industrial Revolution provided Europeans with the wealth and technology to dominate the world, the impetus to control its natural resources, and the means (including railways and steamships) to transport them. As further noted in that chapter, nationalism and racism were factors in European imperialism, as was a desire to impose Western ways on Asians and Africans. In Africa, however, several additional factors fostered European imperialism.

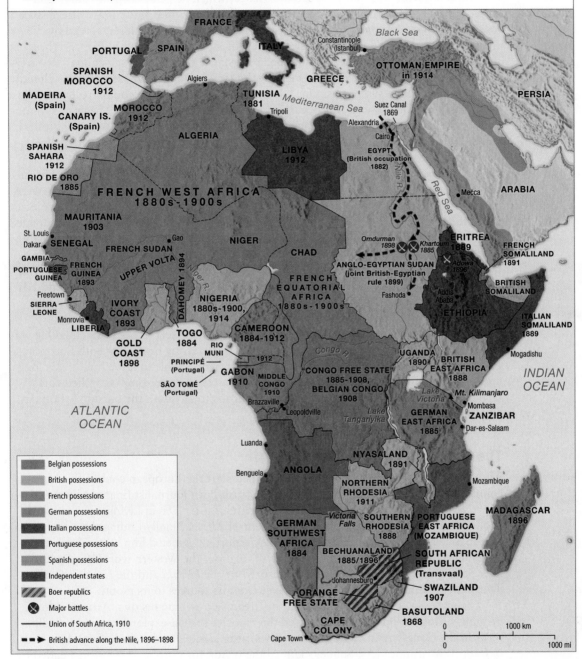

MAP 30.4   Colonization of Africa, 1880–1914

From 1880 to 1914, European powers colonized most of Africa, forming new boundaries with little regard for traditional cultures and commerce. Notice that by 1914 the only remaining independent states were Ethiopia and Liberia. How and why did they remain independent as the rest of Africa was colonized?

Legend:
- Belgian possessions
- British possessions
- French possessions
- German possessions
- Italian possessions
- Portuguese possessions
- Spanish possessions
- Independent states
- Boer republics
- ⊗ Major battles
- Union of South Africa, 1910
- ▪▪▶ British advance along the Nile, 1896–1898

One was the interaction between exploration and journalism. Seeking fame and fortune, and stirred by scientific curiosity, 19th-century Western explorers sought out Africa's natural wonders. They traced the courses of the Niger and Congo Rivers, found the sources of the Nile, and sighted such marvels as Mount Kilimanjaro (*kill-uh-mun-JAH-rō*),

Explorers and journalists enhance Western interest in Africa

Lake Tanganyika (*tan-gun-YĒ-kah*), and Victoria Falls (Map 30.4). The popular press in Europe and America, where such wonders were previously unknown, eagerly reported the explorers' adventures. By arousing public interest in Africa, and conveying detailed knowledge of its interior, these exploits helped to lay foundations for European colonization.

Another factor was new medical knowledge, which helped Europeans survive in tropical Africa's interior. For centuries it was called the "white man's graveyard," since Westerners who went there often died within a few years from malaria, spread by Africa's abundant mosquitoes, and sleeping sickness, carried by tsetse (*TSĒ-tsē*) flies. In the early 1800s, chemists isolated **quinine**, a substance derived from cinchona (*sing-KŌ-nuh*) trees, found mainly in South America's Andes Mountains, whose bark was already used to treat malaria symptoms. Once doctors found that quinine could prevent, not just treat, this often-fatal disease, Europeans in Africa started taking it while healthy, substantially reducing their chances of getting malaria. Quinine was also used to make "tonic water," which Europeans mixed with gin to consume as "gin and tonic." A drug for sleeping sickness was later developed in the early 1900s.

A third factor favoring Europeans was their modern weaponry. For centuries Africans had bought guns from Europeans, often trading slaves to get them, but those guns were old-style muskets, unreliable and slow, as they had to be loaded by pushing the projectile down the barrel. As Western inventors perfected new rifles that could quickly be reloaded by inserting a cartridge in the breech (a chamber behind the barrel), Europeans mostly kept these **repeating rifles** out of African hands. The same was true of new rapid-fire machine guns, including the hand-cranked Gatling gun, first used in the U.S. Civil War, and the fully automatic Maxim gun devised in the 1880s, each of which fired hundreds of rounds per minute. By the late 1800s, the outsiders had a vast firepower advantage, frequently making African resistance futile.

Even when Africans got modern weapons, they often faced other obstacles. One was a lack of ammunition, which they could only get by defeating or dealing with Europeans. A second was the fact that most Africans were farmers, unable to leave their fields long untended to fight wars, and vulnerable to European crop-destroying "scorched-earth" tactics. A third was the willingness of some Africans to ally with the outsiders, hoping to gain an edge over African foes.

The Colonization of the Congo Basin

An American newspaper's publicity stunt helped start the European contest for African colonies. In 1871, Henry Morton Stanley, a British-born journalist financed by the *New York Herald*, conducted a highly publicized search for Dr. David Livingstone, a noted explorer and missionary presumed lost in Central Africa. Finally finding the ailing physician in a village by Lake Tanganyika, Stanley reportedly greeted him, "Dr. Livingstone, I presume,"—soon a celebrated salutation throughout the Western world. Five years later Stanley led another expedition, sponsored by the *Herald* and the *London Daily Telegraph*, which followed the Congo River from its sources to its mouth.

Enthralled by these adventures, and by dreams of owning his own African colony, Belgium's King Leopold II in 1878 hired the reporter-turned-explorer to set up trading posts in the Congo basin. Within a few years, after signing trade treaties with hundreds of Central African leaders, Stanley claimed the region for European investors headed by Leopold II, who ruthlessly exploited its resources and people (see "The Imperial Scramble" section below).

In 1880, the French, concerned that the claims of Leopold and Stanley might exclude them from Central Africa, sent a mission to the region just north of the lower Congo River. Anxious also to protect French settlements in nearby Gabon, the French concluded

Quinine enables more Europeans to survive in Africa

Modern weapons give Europeans advantage over Africans

Maxim gun.

Stanley's search for Livingstone boosts Western interest in Africa

Sketch by famed explorer and missionary, Dr. David Livingstone.

their own treaties with local African rulers. The groundwork was thus laid for a group of colonies called French Congo, later consolidated as French Equatorial Africa (Map 30.4).

Global Trade and the Occupation of Egypt

Meanwhile, in Northeast Africa, the 1869 opening of the Suez Canal focused global attention on Egypt. By cutting in half the shipping distance between West and East, the canal gave a boost to both global trade and the new coal-powered steamships, whose usefulness in the East–West trade had been limited by the costs and burdens of carrying enough coal for the long route around South Africa. Britain, with its numerous steamships and extensive trade with India, soon became the canal's main user and began to take special interest in Egyptian affairs.

Britain's interest was further enhanced by the imprudence of Ismail, who governed Egypt from 1863 to 1879, using the title khedive (*keh-DĒV*), or "prince," granted him by the Ottoman sultan. To finance his ambitious modernization projects, which included roads, industries, and railways in addition to the Suez Canal, Ismail borrowed huge sums of money from European creditors, increasing Egypt's national debt by 1,400 percent. In an effort to avoid bankruptcy, as noted above, in 1875 he decided to sell his 44 percent interest in the canal. When the French unwisely declined to buy these shares, British Prime Minister Benjamin Disraeli jumped at the chance to do so, and Britain thereby became one of the canal's key shareholders.

In 1876, concerned that Khedive Ismail might still default on his loans, Britain and France compelled him to let foreigners manage his finances. But foreign fiscal control, resulting in high taxes and military pay cuts, offended nationalist Egyptian army officers, who rebelled against the khedive. The Ottomans removed him in 1879, but the revolt continued. Finally, in 1882, to protect their investments and secure the canal, the British sent an army to occupy Egypt and crush the rebellion. Although their stated intent was to stay only until order was restored, the British remained in Egypt for decades and controlled the canal until 1956.

The Imperial Scramble

Soon other European powers, fearful that Africa might be partitioned before they secured their share, scrambled to get colonies of their own. Seeking to set some ground rules, German chancellor Otto von Bismarck hosted a conference at Berlin in 1884–1885. Here the powers agreed that, rather than merely negotiate treaties with local African leaders, a European nation must henceforth establish "effective occupation" to claim a region. This provision meant that the European country must actually colonize the area, establishing a political presence as well as an economic one. The powers also promised to end slavery in their colonies and keep them open to trade with other countries.

Pledging to follow these rules, Belgium's King Leopold II expanded his control of the Congo region, creating a "Congo Free State" under his personal rule. Obsessed, however, with producing a profit by exploiting the region's rich resources—ivory, palm oil, copper, and especially rubber—Leopold instead made Congo a hell on earth. Beginning in the 1890s, when the newly invented inflatable tire sparked a global rubber demand, his agents imposed rubber quotas through forced labor. His private army enforced his rule through flogging, torture, hostage-taking, murder, and mutilation—including the widespread cutting off of hands. According to some accounts, more than half the region's estimated 30 million people perished under Leopold's rule, due to wars, rebellions, killings, starvation, and disease. After 1900, reports of these atrocities provoked international outrage (see "Report on Conditions in Congo"), prompting

Read the **Document**

H. M. Stanley in Uganda (1870s)

on **myhistorylab.com**

Suez Canal halves East–West shipping distance, boosting global trade

British occupy Egypt to protect their canal interests

At Berlin Conference Europeans set rules for colonizing Africa

Read the **Document**

Carl Peters, "A Manifesto for German Colonization"

on **myhistorylab.com**

**View** the **Image**

Belgian King Crushing the Congo Free State – Cartoon

on **myhistorylab.com**

Belgium's King Leopold II ruthlessly exploits Congo region

DOCUMENT 30.2 Report on Conditions in Congo

In 1903, British diplomat Roger Casement visited the Congo Free State to investigate reports of atrocities there. His report to Parliament, published in 1904, included the excerpts below. Why were such atrocities committed? How does this report compare with the image of the "White Man's Burden" (Document 27.3)?

. . . I visited two large villages in the interior . . . wherein I found that fully half the population now consisted of refugees . . . They went on to declare, when asked why they had fled (their district), that they had endured such ill-treatment at the hands of the government soldiers in their own (district) that life had become intolerable; that nothing had remained for them at home but to be killed for failure to bring in a certain amount of rubber or to die from starvation or exposure in their attempts to satisfy the demands made upon them. . . .

. . . [O]n the 25th of July (1903) we reached Lukolela, where I spent two days. This district had, when I visited it in 1887, numbered fully 5,000 people; today the population is . . . less than 600. The reasons given me for their decline in numbers were similar to those furnished elsewhere, namely, sleeping-sickness, general ill-health, insufficiency of food, and the methods employed to obtain labor from them by local officials and the exactions levied on them.

. . . At other villages which I visited, I found the tax to consist of baskets, which the inhabitants had to make and deliver weekly as well as, always, a certain amount of foodstuffs. (The natives) were frequently flogged for delay or inability to complete the tally of these baskets, or the weekly supply of food. Several men . . . showed broad [welts] across their buttocks . . . One, a lad of 15 or so . . . , showed several scars across his thighs, which he and others around him said had formed part of a weekly payment for a recent shortage in their supply of food.

. . . A careful investigation of the conditions of native life . . . confirmed . . . that the great decrease in population, the dirty and ill-kept towns, and the complete absence of goats, sheep, or fowls—once very plentiful in this country—were to be attributed above all else to the continued effort made during many years to compel the natives to [supply] rubber . . . During the course of these operations there had been much loss of life, accompanied, I fear, by a somewhat general mutilation of the dead . . .

. . . Two cases (of mutilation) came to my actual notice while I was in the lake district. One, a young man, both of whose hands had been beaten off with the butt ends of rifles against a tree; the other a young lad of 11 or 12 . . . , whose right hand was cut off at the wrist . . . . Of six natives (one a girl, three little boys, one youth, and one old woman) who had been mutilated in this way during the rubber regime, all except one were dead at the date of my visit.

SOURCE: *British Parliamentary Papers*, 1904, LXII, Cd. 1933.

Belgium's parliament to take over the region from Leopold in 1908. His worst abuses were curtailed, and the region became a colony called the Belgian Congo.

Meanwhile, other European powers carved up almost all the rest of Africa. Britain and France were the biggest imperialists, dividing most of the northern half of Africa between them, while Britain also gained vast domains in the south. Germany took Cameroon and Togo on the Gulf of Guinea and established protectorates over German East Africa, today united with Zanzibar as Tanzania (*tan-zuh-NĒ-uh*), and German Southwest Africa, now called Namibia (*nuh-MIB-ē-uh*). Italy took much of Somaliland in East Africa, Eritrea (*er-uh-TRĒ-uh*) on the Red Sea, and Tripoli in North Africa, while Portugal expanded its earlier holdings. By 1914, Africa's only independent states were Liberia, the small West African republic settled by former American slaves, and Ethiopia, the ancient Christian kingdom in East Africa (Map 30.4).

View the **Map**

Interactive Map: Colonization in Africa

on **myhistorylab.com**

The Roots of African Resistance

Ethiopia preserved its independence with Western weapons and anti-Western national fervor, providing a model for African resistance to colonial control. In the 1890s, after Italy sought to make his country its protectorate, Ethiopian King Menilek

(*MEN-uh-leck*) II (1889–1913) raised a large army to confront the intruders. Fired by national pride, and armed with modern rifles supplied by the French to thwart their Italian rivals, the Ethiopians defeated the Italians at Adowa (*AH-duh-wuh*) in 1896. This stunning victory showed the world that Africans, when armed with modern weapons and inspired by nationalist zeal, could hold their own against European armies.

Ethiopians routing Italians at Adowa.

Other Africans also sought to resist the Europeans. South of Egypt, in Sudan, a radical anti-Western Muslim movement emerged in the 1880s. It was led by a Muslim mystic who claimed to be al-Mahdi ("the divinely-inspired one"), a messianic leader many Muslims believed God would send to restore the true faith and herald the end of time. Early in 1885, al-Mahdi and his armies captured Sudan's capital, Khartoum (*kar-TOOM*), massacred its British-led Egyptian garrison, and set up headquarters across the Nile River at Omdurman.

Mahdi movement clashes with British interests in Sudan

But the British later got revenge. In the 1890s they set out to amass a string of possessions linking northern and southern Africa—from Cairo, Egypt, to the Cape of Good Hope—and to connect the continent by constructing a "Cape to Cairo" railway. They thus decided to subdue Sudan, then controlled by **Mahdists**, disciples of al-Mahdi, who had died in 1885. So in 1896 a British force led by General Horatio Kitchener began moving south from Egypt, armed with modern weapons and building a railway as it went. In September 1898, when Kitchener arrived at Omdurman, his army met a large force of Mahdist warriors. Inspired by religious zeal, but lacking modern weapons, the Mahdists repeatedly charged the British positions but were slaughtered by continuous fire from machine guns, repeating rifles, and cannons. Unlike the Ethiopians, who had modern weapons, the Mahdists were destroyed.

Several weeks later an odd episode almost triggered war between Britain and France. A small French expedition, traveling overland from the west, had arrived in July at Fashoda (*fah-SHO-duh*) on the Nile, 400 miles south of Omdurman, and claimed the area for France. When Kitchener, delayed by the Battle of Omdurman, arrived at Fashoda in September, he encountered the French expedition. Having got there first, the French insisted that the land was theirs, sparking a brief war scare between the two powers. But France's government, aware that Britain had a much larger army on the scene, eventually backed down and ordered its small force withdrawn. Britain thus gained control of the whole Nile Valley (Map 30.4).

Diamonds, Gold, and Diversity in South Africa

British expansion in South Africa met stiffer resistance. Imperialism there was tied to precious minerals, located largely in lands claimed by Boers (Map 30.5), attracting global interest and bringing to the region a growing diversity of peoples.

The history of South Africa, far removed from the centers of global wealth and power, was altered forever in 1867 when a Boer farmer, living near the Orange Free State's southwest border, saw children playing with small sparkling stones. Intrigued, he took one to a nearby town, where it was appraised as a diamond. Within a few years, thousands more were discovered, and numerous outsiders poured into the region, driven by "diamond fever."

In 1871, allegedly to protect local Africans from racist Boers, the British annexed the diamond field area, angering the Boers, who considered it theirs. Britain then imposed its own oppression on the local Africans, using modern weapons to demolish

Diamond mine in South Africa.

Discovery of diamonds fuels conflicts between British and Boers

MAP **30.5**	The Struggle for South Africa, 1867–1910

By the early 1900s, the British controlled South Africa, having conquered the Zulu and the Boers, among others. Note that in 1910 the former Boer republics (Orange Free State and Transvaal) were united with Britain's Cape Colony, Natal, and Zululand to form the Union of South Africa. Why and how did the British gain control of the Boer Republics? In what sense did the Boers nonetheless prevail?

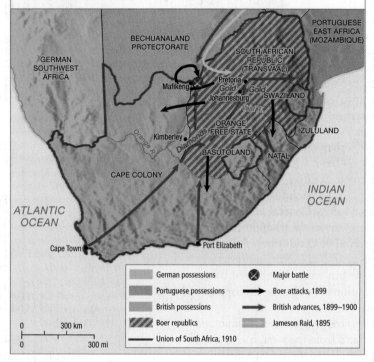

African armies—including those of Zulu King Cetshwayo, as described at the start of this chapter. By 1888 a British company called De Beers Consolidated Mines, led by English entrepreneur Cecil Rhodes, had gained control of the region's whole diamond business, making him one of the world's richest men.

But diamonds were only part of South Africa's riches. In 1886, along a ridge called the Rand in Transvaal, an even more spectacular find disclosed vast deposits of gold. Soon fortune-seekers from Europe, Australia, and America came in large numbers to Transvaal, while laborers were brought from all over Africa and India to work South African gold and diamond mines. The region's population thus became increasingly multicultural and multiracial.

Deeply resenting the diverse newcomers, the Boers restricted their rights. In 1895 Cecil Rhodes, by then prime minister of Britain's Cape Colony, sent a small force led by his agent Jameson to invade Transvaal, hoping to spark a revolt among the newcomers that would topple its Boer regime. No such rebellion ensued, and the Boers repulsed the raid, but tensions escalated into war between the Boers and the British in 1899.

The South African War (1899–1902), known in Britain as the Boer War, pitted the world's mightiest power against two small Boer republics, but it was resolved neither easily nor quickly. Armed with modern rifles and resolved to defend their realm, the Boers battled the British with guerrilla tactics. Finally the frustrated British sent a huge army under General Kitchener, who broke Boer resistance by burning their homes and fields and forcing their women and children into concentration camps, where thousands died of disease and malnutrition.

The Boers surrendered in 1902, but their defeat was only a temporary setback. Eventually their Afrikaner descendants dominated the Union of South Africa, formed in 1910 when Britain gave a measure of self-rule to the region's white minority. Within decades, this white minority, descended mainly from Boer and British settlers, imposed a racist regime upon the region's large black African majority (Chapter 37).

Gold discovery brings people from around the world to Transvaal

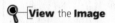

View the **Image**

Cecil Rhodes Astride Africa – Cartoon

on **myhistorylab.com**

Read the **Document**

Cecil Rhodes, "Confession of Faith"

on **myhistorylab.com**

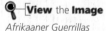

View the **Image**

Afrikaaner Guerrillas

on **myhistorylab.com**

The Impact of Empire on Africa

Before the coming of colonialism, Africans had a variety of political, economic, religious, and social systems. Some lived in large kingdoms or thriving urban centers, with powerful rulers, commercial economies, educated elites, Islamic institutions, and often warrior nobilities. Many others, however, lived in villages led by elders and chiefs, raised crops and tended herds, worshiped local deities, and centered their lives on patriarchal families and clans.

Imperialism disrupted these traditional systems. Eager to exploit Africa's human and natural resources, and smugly assuming that African ways were inferior to their own, Europeans sought to impose their economic outlooks, social structures, religious views, and political systems. European influence thus permeated Africa, mixing, and often clashing, with traditional ways.

View the **Map**
Map Discovery: Africa, 1915
on **myhistorylab.com**

Economic and Social Implications

Economically, under imperial rule, Africans had to adapt to new ways of life. Europeans turned some of Africa's best pastures and farmlands into plantations, then compelled Africans to produce commercial exports—such as cotton, palm oil, coconuts, cocoa, and cloves—on lands where Africans had long raised their own animals and food. Europeans also imposed taxes to be paid in cash, rather than in food or goods, thus forcing Africans to work for wages on plantations, in mines, or on railways, often at great distance from their villages. And colonial borders created by imperialists, often without regard for grazing lands, clan domains, or African ethnic and linguistic boundaries, disrupted traditional economic, social, and political patterns, resulting in regional conflicts that still endure.

Colonial rule transforms Africa's agrarian economy

These developments had sweeping implications for African societies. Traditional African social structures, based on patriarchal families and clans, were undermined as men had to work far from their villages, leaving their wives and children to tend crops and livestock alone. A new hierarchy arose, with Europeans on top, Western-educated Africans in the middle, and exploited African workers at the bottom. Clan structures and family ties broke down, while long-held customs and traditions waned.

Colonial rule undermines African family and social structures

Women's lives were acutely altered. Mass production of inexpensive clothes by Europe's textile mills, for example, destroyed the market for handmade clothing, one of the few trades traditionally open to African women. And the mass relocation of men from African villages forced women to work the fields while also performing their customary household and caregiver duties. But with so many men gone from the villages, women also started playing larger roles in local governance, running the villages and making key decisions. And some were even able to get an education and acquire new skills, in schools and missions started by Europeans.

Colonial rule alters African women's roles

The Impact of Western Ideals and Institutions

Traditional African ways thus blended with new ideas, promoted by Christian missionaries who built churches and hospitals, and by European educators who set up Western-style schools. Some Africans, learning to read and write European languages, eventually formed educated elites that, while still subordinate to Europeans, attained substantial wealth and power over other Africans. Many Africans converted to Christianity, the faith of their foreign rulers, while others adopted Islam, which had deeper roots in Africa and fewer ties to colonialism.

Africans blend traditional cultures with Western and Muslim ways

In seeking to impose law and order, and thus protect their political and commercial interests, Europeans also introduced new concepts of administration and justice, based on centralized bureaucracies and judicial systems. Some Europeans tried governing through local African rulers; others imported and appointed their own officials; but most eventually trained African lawyers, managers, soldiers, and police to run the colonies under European supervision. In many areas, the old African order of elders, clans, councils, and kings was blended and assimilated into Western-style government bureaucracies, staffed by Africans but controlled by European imperialists.

Africans being baptized as Christians.

View the **Image**

Christian Missionaries in Africa, Late 19th Century

on **myhistorylab.com**

View the **Image**

Dinizulu, King of the Zulus

on **myhistorylab.com**

Africans adapt Western weapons and ideals to combat European rule

African Resistance to Colonial Rule

Although Africans were often defenseless against Western weaponry, they were not necessarily passive or compliant. Many resisted the alien occupation, fighting fiercely to protect their ways. The Zulu, for example, battled the Boers in numerous wars and were beaten by the British in 1879 only after years of stalwart struggle. The Mahdists of Sudan destroyed a British-Egyptian force at Khartoum in 1885 and then fought courageously until finally crushed at Omdurman in 1898 by Kitchener's superior weapons. And in repulsing the Italians in 1896, the Ethiopians showed that African soldiers equipped with modern rifles could defeat European troops.

Eventually, colonial rule provided new motives and methods for African resistance. The brutality of European imperialism, by nature oppressive and exploitative, helped unite Africans against the outsiders. And as Africans learned European ways, they adapted them for use against colonial rulers. Africans who studied in Europe or America, for example, often were inspired by ideals of liberalism and nationalism to work for their people's freedom and self-rule, while Africans who fought in European wars acquired skills and training that would be useful in fighting for their own liberation. In the 20th century, these factors would help build independence movements across the African continent.

CHAPTER

REVIEW

Putting It in Perspective

In the 19th century, new connections transformed West Asia and Africa. The international slave trade was banned and eventually replaced with new kinds of commerce. Traditional subsistence farming, long the foundation of most African economies, was widely supplanted by cash crops such as cotton and cloves, by increased production of items such as palm oil, coconuts, and ivory, and by mining of valuable minerals such as diamonds and gold.

In West Asia and North Africa, as the Ottoman realm sought to halt its decline by adapting some Western ways, it alienated Arab Muslims and lost its North African dominions, which eventually came under European sway. In sub-Saharan Africa new states emerged, forged by religious fervor, commercial

connections, or military might, but they likewise were overwhelmed by the advance of European imperialism.

In West Asia and North Africa, Islamic cultural and social structures continued, but they increasingly coexisted with new Western-style laws and education systems. Throughout sub-Saharan Africa, traditional clan and village societies were replaced by structures imposed by Europeans and staffed with Western-educated Africans. European languages, Christian values, and Western ideologies such as liberalism and nationalism also influenced many Africans. These Africans, adapting Western ideals and modern weapons into their African heritage, in the 20th century would lead the liberation of Africa from European rule.

Reviewing Key Material

KEY CONCEPTS

Maghrib, 693
Middle East, 693
Tanzimat, 695
Young Turks, 697
cash crops, 697
Fulani, 702
recaptives, 704

African diaspora, 705
Afrikaners, 706
Great Trek, 706
quinine, 708
repeating rifles, 708
Mahdists, 711

KEY PEOPLE

Shaka, 693, 705
Cetshwayo, 693, 712
Sultan Mahmud II, 695
Mustafa Reshid Pasha, 695
Sultan Abdulhamid II, 697
Muhammad Ali, 697
Ibrahim Pasha, 697

Khedive Ismail, 699
Abdelqadir al-Jazairi, 700
Olaudah Equiano, 701
William Wilberforce, 701
Usman dan Fodio, 702
Joseph Jenkins Roberts, 704

ASK YOURSELF

1. How did the banning of the slave trade impact Africa's economy? How did the ban help reinforce slavery and the slave trade?

2. How did new regional states emerge in Africa in the early 1800s? How did they differ in their origins and operations?

3. How did Ottoman decline and reform efforts influence the various regions of West Asia and North Africa? What were the main elements and impacts of Egypt's modernization?

4. How did each of Africa's main regions come under European rule? How did Africans try to resist and adapt?

5. What were imperialism's main effects on African societies? How did it help foster African resistance?

GOING FURTHER

Achebe, Chinua. *Things Fall Apart*. 1958.

Ahmad, Feroz. *The Young Turks*. 1969.

Ajayi, J., and M. Crowder, eds. *A History of West Africa*. 1985.

Alpers, Edward. *Ivory and Slaves in East Central Africa*. 1975.

Boahen, A. Adu. *African Perspectives on Colonialism*. 1987.

Cleveland, W. L. *A History of the Modern Middle East*. 2000.

Collins, R., ed. *Historical Problems of Imperial Africa*. 1994.

Coquery-Vidrovitch, C. *African Women: A Modern History*. 1997.

Curtin, Philip. *The World and the West: European Challenge and Overseas Response in the Age of Empire*. 2000.

Curtin, Philip, et al. *African History: From Earliest Times to Independence*. 1995.

Delius, Peter, *The Land Belongs to Us*. 1984.

Findley, C. V. *Bureaucratic Reform in the Ottoman Empire*. 1980.

Findley, C. V. *The Turks in World History*. 2005.

Flint, John E. *The Cambridge History of Africa*. Vol. 5. 1976.

Getz, Trevor. *Slavery and Reform in West Africa*. 2004.

Getz, Trevor, and Streets-Salter, H. *Modern Imperialism and Colonialism*. 2010.

Guy, J. *The Destruction of the Zulu Kingdom*. 1979.

Hopkins, A. G. *An Economic History of West Africa*. 1973.

Hothschild, Adam. *King Leopold's Ghost*. 1998.

Julien, Charles A. *A History of North Africa*. 1970.

Kinross, J. P. D. B. *The Ottoman Centuries*. 1977.

Lapidus, I. *A History of Islamic Societies*. 1988.

Law, Robin. *From Slave Trade to "Legitimate" Commerce*. 1996.

Lewis, David Levering. *The Race to Fashoda*. 1995.

Lovejoy, Paul. *Slow Death for Slavery*. 1993.

MacKinnon, Aran. *The Making of South Africa*. 2003.

Marcus, Harold. *A History of Ethiopia*. 1994.

Miers, S., and R. Roberts. *The End of Slavery in Africa*. 1988.

Mitchell, T. *Colonizing Egypt*. 1988.

Northrup, David. *Africa's Discovery of Europe, 1450–1850*. 2002.

Omer-Cooper, John D. *The Zulu Aftermath*. 1966.

Packenham, Thomas. *The Scramble for Africa, 1876–1912*. 1991.

Robinson, R., and J. Gallagher. *Africa and the Victorians*. 1969.

Rodney, Walter. *How Europe Underdeveloped Africa*. 1981.

Rotberg, Robert I., ed. *Africa and Its Explorers*. 1970.

Sheriff, Abdul. *Spices and Ivory in Zanzibar*. 1987.

Shillington, Kevin. *History of Africa*. Rev. ed. 2005.

Thompson, Leonard. *A History of South Africa*. 1995.

Toledano, E. *State and Society in Nineteenth Century Egypt*. 1990.

Vandervort, B. *Wars of Imperial Conquest in Africa*. 1998.

Vatikiotis, P. J. *The History of Modern Egypt*. 1991.

Warwick, Peter, ed. *The South African War*. 1980.

Wesseling, H. L. *The European Colonial Empires, 1815–1919*. 2004.

Worden, Nigel. *A History of Modern South Africa*. 1995.

Key Dates and Developments

1798–1801	French occupation of Egypt
1803–1818	Banning of the slave trade
1804–1809	Formation of Fulani Empire (Sokoto Caliphate)
1805–1848	Transformation of Egypt under Muhammad Ali
1806–1856	Commercial empire in Zanzibar under Sa'id Sayyid
1816–1828	Zulu conquests under King Shaka
1821	Formation of freed slave settlement in Liberia
1830–1847	French conquest of Algeria
1835	Beginning of the Boers' Great Trek
1839–1876	The Tanzimat: reforms in the Ottoman Empire
1867	Discovery of diamonds in South Africa

1869	Opening of the Suez Canal
1871	Stanley's search for Livingstone
1875	British purchase of Egyptian canal shares
1878–1884	Stanley's acquisition of Congo region for Leopold II
1882	British occupation of Egypt
1884–1885	Berlin Conference on Africa
1885–1908	Leopold II's brutal rule of "Congo Free State"
1885–1914	Scramble for colonies in Africa
1886	Discovery of gold in South Africa
1896	Ethiopian defeat of Italians at Adowa
1898	British massacre of Sudanese Mahdists at Omdurman
1899–1903	South African War (Boer War)

PEARSON
myhistorylab Connections

Reinforce what you learned in this chapter by studying the many documents, images, maps, review tools, and videos available at www.myhistorylab.com.

Read and Review

✓●─ **Study** and **Review** Chapter 30

📖─ **Read** the **Document**

An Ottoman Government Decree Defines the Official Notion of the "Modern" Citizen, June 19, 1870, p. 697

H. M. Stanley in Uganda (1870s), p. 709

Carl Peters, "A Manifesto for German Colonization," p. 709

Cecil Rhodes, "Confession of Faith," p. 712

🔍─ **View** the **Map**

Interactive Map: Colonization in Africa, p. 710

Map Discovery: Africa, 1915, p. 713

🔍─ **View** the **Image**

Belgian King Crushing the Congo Free State – Cartoon, p. 709

Cecil Rhodes Astride Africa – Cartoon, p. 712

Afrikaaner Guerrillas, p. 712

Christian Missionaries in Africa, Late 19th Century, p. 714

Dinizulu, King of the Zulus, p. 714

((●─ **Listen** to the **Audio**

Africa/Zulus 1, p. 705

Research and Explore

👁─ **Watch** the **Video**

The Ottoman Tanzimat Period (1839–1876): The Middle East Confronts Modernity, p. 695

👁─ **Watch** the **Video**

Zanzibar, p. 705

──── ((●─ **Listen** to the **Chapter Audio** for Chapter 30 on **myhistorylab.com** ────

The Great War and the Russian Revolutions, 1890–1918

((•—[Listen to the **Chapter Audio** for Chapter 31 on **myhistorylab.com**

- Why did competing alliance systems promote war rather than preventing it?

- Why did the Great War become a stalemate between 1914 and 1916?

- What factors led to revolutions in Russia in 1917?

- What were the main reasons for Allied victory in 1918?

- How did the Great War affect civilians?

Over the Top

U.S. infantry goes "over the top," emerging from a trench on the Western Front of the Great War in 1918. Trench warfare became the most memorable feature of this traumatic, bloody conflict (page 727).

The Path to War and Revolution   **719**

It was Sunday, June 28, 1914. Archduke Franz Ferdinand, Crown Prince of Austria-Hungary, paid a state visit to Sarajevo (*sah-rah-YĀ-vō*), capital of the Austrian province of Bosnia. As his motorcade entered the city, a terrorist seeking to free Bosnia from Austria threw a bomb at Franz Ferdinand's car. The assassin's aim was off, and the bomb blew up the car behind the Archduke's. Enraged, Franz Ferdinand shortened his visit by several hours. As he was leaving the city, however, his car took a wrong turn and stalled on a small side street. Watching from a nearby café was another assassin, who walked up to the car and murdered the Archduke and his wife with a revolver. Within five weeks all Europe was at war.

At the palace of Versailles in France, precisely five years after the shots at Sarajevo, European leaders met in solemn assembly to sign a treaty formally ending the conflict triggered by those shots, then known as the Great War. It had killed more than nine million people in combat, devastated much of Europe, helped spark momentous revolutions in Russia, and spread fear across the globe. The experience was so horrifying that the peacemakers at Versailles hoped not merely to end the Great War, but to abolish war forever.

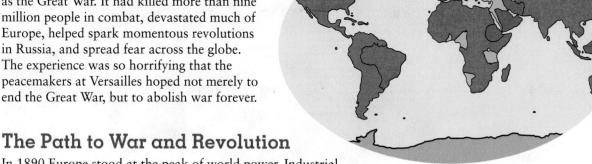

Allied and
Associated Powers
(Red)

Central Powers
(Tan)

Neutrals (Green)

The Path to War and Revolution

In 1890 Europe stood at the peak of world power. Industrial modernization and the technologies it generated gave Britain, France, and Germany unprecedented wealth and dominion, with global empires encompassing much of Africa and Asia. Italy and Belgium also gained African colonies, as industrial nations competed for possessions and access to raw materials. But the Russian, Austrian, and Ottoman Empires, for centuries dominant in Eastern Europe and beyond, had been slow to industrialize and had fallen behind. Liberalism and nationalism also threatened these three multinational realms, as their various peoples pressed for greater freedom and autonomy. After 1890 rivalries among all these powers intensified as each sought to improve its status and security. Europe divided into powerful and hostile alliances, leading to a series of crises that eventually culminated in catastrophic conflict.

The Diplomatic Revolution of 1890–1907

In 1890 Europe was also at peace. The wars of Italian and German unification, fought decades earlier, had altered the balance of power in favor of a newly unified Germany. But under Chancellor Otto von Bismarck, that new nation had emerged as a conservative power, maintaining its position by preserving the status quo. France, humiliated and hoping to regain Alsace and Lorraine, provinces lost to Germany in the Franco-Prussian War (1870–1871), was kept isolated and powerless by Bismarck's skillful diplomacy. He engineered a series of alliances designed to isolate France and keep Austria and Russia from fighting each other in the Balkans.

Between 1879 and 1882, at Bismarck's initiative, Austria, Italy, and Germany put aside past animosities to sign the **Triple Alliance**, a defensive pact in which each promised to assist the others in the event of unprovoked attack by a third party (Map 31.1). Then, in 1887, a Reinsurance Treaty with Russia gave Germany additional leverage in the Balkans: in the event of war in that region, Germany would oppose whichever nation it considered the aggressor. Since neither Russia nor Austria alone

*Bismarck's alliances
maintain peace in Europe*

FOUNDATION MAP **31.1** European Alliances and Crises, 1905–1914

The Diplomatic Revolution of 1890–1907 divided Europe into two approximately equivalent alliance systems: the Triple Alliance and the Triple Entente. Observe that the Triple Alliance occupied a central position on the continent, surrounded by the nations of the Triple Entente. Between 1905 and 1914, a series of international crises, clustered in Southeastern Europe and North Africa, brought Europe ever closer to armed hostilities. Yet between 1905 and 1913, each of these crises was settled peacefully. How did this succession of peaceful resolutions actually make war more rather than less likely in 1914?

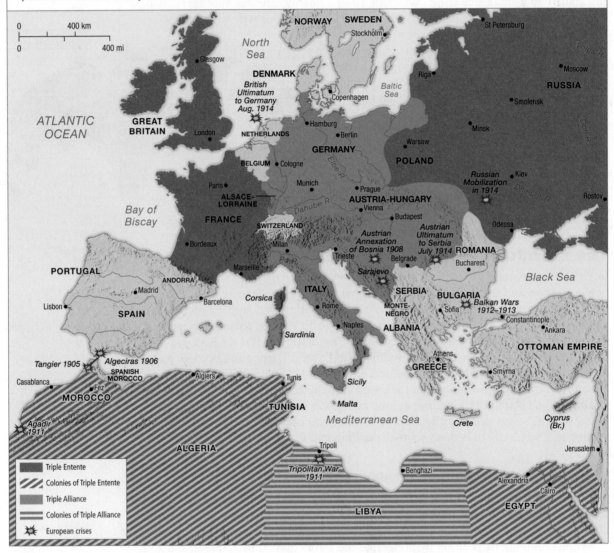

William II, Kaiser of Imperial Germany.

could win a war against Germany, Austro-Russian tensions in the Balkans were effectively frozen in place. Moreover, since Italy, Austria, and Russia were each allied with Germany, France was left isolated on the continent with no anti-German allies. These twin pillars of Bismarck's diplomacy—isolation of France and prevention of Balkan war—kept Europe at peace throughout the 1870s and 1880s.

REVERSAL OF BISMARCK'S DIPLOMACY. But starting in 1890, Bismarck's efforts were undone by a new German Kaiser. William I died in March 1888 at age 91; his son Frederick III died three months later of throat cancer. The throne passed to 29-year-old William II, a brash young man who dismissed Bismarck in 1890, regarding him as out of touch with contemporary problems. The new Kaiser wanted to play the leading role in German foreign affairs.

This prospect was dangerous for Germany because, although quick-witted, William II was an erratic ruler with no temperament for the hard work required of a monarch who wished to govern as well as reign. Lacking Bismarck's ruthlessness and skill, William took ill-considered actions that quickly compromised Germany's dominant position in Europe. He and his new ministers felt that Germany's Reinsurance Treaty with Russia (1887) violated the spirit of the Triple Alliance of 1882 (Germany, Austria-Hungary, and Italy) by making it unclear whether Germany would support Austria or Russia in a Balkan war. They therefore refused to renew the Reinsurance Treaty when it expired in 1890.

The decision for nonrenewal destroyed both of Bismarck's pillars. With one stroke it tilted Germany toward Austria in the Balkans and prompted Russia, which considered nonrenewal a hostile act, to negotiate an alliance with France. This ended France's isolation and compromised Germany's dominant position in Europe. War became a realistic possibility, and if it occurred, Germany would have to fight a two-front war against Russia in the East and France in the West.

The implications of the Franco-Russian alliance were not lost on William II, but he blamed Germany's weakened position on his enemy's intrigues rather than learning from his mistake. Certain of the purity of his motives, he was insensitive to how they were perceived by other governments. Thus in 1898, when he authorized a huge naval expansion so that Germany's fleet could rival Britain's and ensure German access to its overseas colonies, he was astounded to learn that London feared this buildup. As an island nation that had to import food, Britain responded with its own massive increase in naval production. The hugely expensive naval arms race that followed embittered both sides.

Germany unwittingly initiates a Diplomatic Revolution

Abandoning their historic avoidance of peacetime alliances, the British sought allies to counter the German threat. In 1902 Britain and Japan, both alarmed by German and Russian expansionism in East Asia, concluded an alliance. Now Japan's large Pacific fleet could protect the British Empire in Asia, relieving Britain's Grand Fleet for action in European waters. Even more unprecedented was the Anglo-French Alliance of 1904, in which these longtime enemies agreed to respect each other's African domains and consult one another should a third party (such as Germany) threaten the peace.

Mistrust of Germany leads Britain to seek alliances

Stunned by these developments, but considering Franco-British animosities too deep to permit genuine partnership, German leaders tested the alliance by provoking a crisis over Morocco. But the Anglo-French Alliance held together against German belligerence, and as Germany's international position deteriorated, that belligerence grew. German leaders perceived the empire to be encircled by the Franco-Russian Alliance (which its own diplomatic ineptness had done so much to create), excluded from choice colonies in Asia and Africa that the older British and French empires had already seized, blocked by the British Grand Fleet from access to the colonies it did possess, and barred by British merchants and contracts from markets to which its rapidly expanding industrial might entitled it. Sensing its increasing isolation, Germany became more assertive with each rebuke. Meanwhile, this assertiveness continued to cause other European nations to draw together. In 1907 Britain and Russia, each aligned with France, concluded an accord with each other. This development, unthinkable only a few years earlier, was made possible by dramatic developments in Russia.

Germany's sense of isolation intensifies its assertive conduct

RUSSIA AND ITS CHALLENGES. In the early 1900s, Russia suffered from many internal problems. Rapid population growth, which shrunk the average peasants' land allotments, threatened their self-sufficiency. Rising nationalism among non-Russian nationalities, which constituted roughly half the realm's inhabitants, threatened the empire's cohesion. Its slowness to industrialize left it lagging behind the West and threatened its great power status. And its ruler, Tsar Nicholas II (1894–1917), rigidly opposed to reforms that would limit his powers, lacked the decisiveness needed to exercise those powers effectively.

🔍 **View** the **Image**
Early Russian Factory
on **myhistorylab.com**

Russia wrestles with the dilemma of modernization

Convinced, nonetheless, that Russia must modernize in order to survive, Sergei Witte (*VIT-tuh*), minister of finance from 1892 to 1903, promoted industrialization through government action. He borrowed vast funds abroad (particularly from Russia's new ally, France) to support new enterprises and build railways, especially the monumental trans-Siberian line, which provided access both to Asian markets and to Siberia's abundant resources, including timber and oil. His policies brought impressive increases in Russia's state revenues and industrial output.

But his policies also destabilized Russia. As thousands of peasants moved to cities to work in factories, their dislocation strained the social structure. Uprooted from their villages, crowded into urban slums, and compelled to work long hours at low wages in dangerous, monotonous jobs, Russian factory workers became a powerful force for change. Poor harvests and a weak economy added to the general discontent, as did the empire's efforts to "Russify" its ethnic minorities by forcing them to adopt Russian language and ways.

A textile mill in Tashkent, Russian Central Asia, around 1900.

As social unrest increased, various revolutionary groups emerged. *Liberals* wanted a Western-style parliamentary regime with a constitution and capitalist economy. *Socialist revolutionaries*, rejecting capitalism, wanted a socialist revolution based on the peasant masses. *Marxists*, or *social democrats*, saw the industrial working class as the backbone of a socialist revolution that would transfer ownership of the means of production to the workers. In the early 1900s, growing social unrest was manifested in student demonstrations, industrial strikes, peasant uprisings, and political assassinations that rocked the Russian Empire. Minister of Interior Viacheslav Plehve (1902) and the tsar's uncle, Grand Duke Sergei (1904), were blown to bits by bomb-throwing assassins. Industrial growth, intended to build Russia's wealth and power, seemed to be tearing it apart.

The Russo-Japanese War (1904–1905) complicated the unrest. At first Japan's attack prompted a patriotic surge that quieted revolutionary activity. But when military setbacks discredited the tsarist regime, factory workers rebelled against extended work hours and pressures to boost production. In January 1905, a sincere but naive Orthodox priest organized a massive workers' march in Saint Petersburg. The marchers called for shorter workdays, expanded civil rights, and an end to the war. Although they carried icons and sang patriotic hymns, imperial troops opened fire on them, slaughtering several hundred.

Bloody Sunday, as this event was labeled, stunned Russia's people and undermined support for Nicholas II. Within months Russia was engulfed in revolution as strikes and demonstrations spread throughout the land. By October 1905, as massive general strikes—in which all workers, rather than just those in a particular industry, walked off the job—shut down major cities, Saint Petersburg was controlled by a council, or **soviet**, of elected workers' delegates.

The Revolution of 1905 forces Nicholas II to make political concessions

Threatened by these events, the tsar ended the war and issued an "October Manifesto," promising a constitution and an elected parliament, or **Duma**. This action satisfied liberals, splitting the opposition and helping to save the regime. Radicals and socialists continued to rebel, but tsarist forces, reinforced by loyal troops returning from the war, eventually crushed the remnants of the revolt.

The tsar thus survived the Russian Revolution of 1905 by agreeing to share power with the Duma. His new constitution, however, severely restricted this parliament, and his government shut it down when it seemed too radical. In 1907 his prime minister imposed a new electoral system that ensured a loyal majority. The revolution thus did little to limit the regime's power. But it gave Russian workers a brief taste of freedom, taught them how to organize soviets, and provided revolutionaries with experience that they would put to use in revolutions to come.

The war and revolution also helped Russia and Britain overcome their longstanding animosity. Russia's defeat by Japan convinced the British that Russia was less dangerous than Germany, and Russia's reformed government seemed superficially similar to Britain's parliamentary monarchy. Mutually fearful of Germany's growing power, in 1907 the two countries signed an Anglo-Russian Entente, reconciling their claims to colonies and spheres of influence in Asia.

Mistrust of Germany connects Russia and Britain

The Crises of 1908–1913

The Anglo-Russian Entente completed the **Diplomatic Revolution of 1890–1907**, creating a **Triple Entente** (Britain, France, and Russia) to offset the Triple Alliance of Germany, Austria-Hungary, and Italy. Europe had moved in 17 years from a continent dominated by Germany to one balanced precariously between competing alliance systems. This development was dangerous not only to Germany but also to European peace. Power relationships among nations are safest when they are *imbalanced*: war is unlikely when one side clearly dominates the other. When equilibrium exists, however, either side may be tempted to test its luck. Such would be the case in Europe after 1907.

The Triple Entente balances the Triple Alliance

In 1908 Austria's decision to annex the Balkan provinces (Map 27.5) of Bosnia and Herzegovina (*her-tseh-gō-VĒ-nah*), which it had administered since 1878 but which technically were owned by the declining Ottoman Empire, provoked a crisis with Russia, which claimed to be the protector of the provinces' Slavic peoples. Germany, supporting Austria, forced Russia to back down by threatening war. This **Bosnian Crisis of 1908–1909** tied Austria even closer to Germany and provoked Russia into funding an immense eight-year military buildup designed to prevent similar humiliations.

In 1911 Germany initiated another crisis, allegedly in an effort to obtain French concessions elsewhere in Africa in return for German recognition of a French protectorate over Morocco. But that aim initially was not clear and war seemed a real possibility. France's ally Britain starkly warned Germany not to treat Britain "as if she were of no account in the Cabinet of Nations." War was avoided when France agreed to the trade, but the crisis frightened Britain and France into concluding a 1912 naval agreement, pledging each to defend the other's interests in case of war. Once again, Germany's belligerence further united its foes.

A series of crises both frightens and reassures Europe

Italy, meanwhile, eager to expand its African holdings, took Tripoli from the Ottomans during a war fought in 1911–1912. Emboldened by the Ottomans' poor performance in this war, four small Balkan nations formed an anti-Turkish alliance. Much to the world's surprise, the Balkan allies drove the Ottomans from the Balkans in the First Balkan War (1912) but then fought among themselves over the spoils in the Second Balkan War (1913). Since the European powers assembled a conference to prevent these wars from spreading and arranged a compromise to safeguard the interests of Austria and Russia, these events actually reassured Europe. By the end of 1913, Europeans felt confident that any future crisis could be managed by negotiation, which had resolved every recent confrontation.

((•— Listen to the **Audio**
World War I
on **myhistorylab.com**

The Crisis of July 1914

Franz Ferdinand's murder provokes a European crisis

Watch the **Video**

Video Lectures: The Outbreak of World War I

on **myhistorylab.com**

Germany's unconditional support of Austria leads to war in Europe

On June 28, 1914, as described at the beginning of this chapter, the heir to the throne of Austria-Hungary, Archduke Franz Ferdinand, was murdered in Sarajevo by Gavrilo Princip (*PRIN-chip*), a Bosnian assassin trained and equipped in Serbia. Although Franz Ferdinand was not popular in Austria, in a Europe ruled mostly by monarchs the assassination of a crown prince was a very serious matter. The Serbian government was widely considered responsible, and the general expectation was that Austria would somehow punish Serbia.

Austria decided to go to war against Serbia but was uncertain of how Russia, Serbia's protector, might respond, and therefore asked for assurance of German support. Assuming that Tsar Nicholas II would sympathize with the family of the murdered Franz Ferdinand, and therefore considering Russian intervention unlikely, Kaiser William II promised to back any action Austria might take. This guarantee was the infamous **"blank check,"** a document that would allow Austria to lead Germany and the rest of Europe into war. Austria prepared a ten-point ultimatum, or set of strict demands, the refusal of any one of which would justify Vienna in breaking off diplomatic relations as a prelude to war. The harsh ultimatum was designed to prove unacceptable to Serbia and make war inevitable. But Serbia's reply was conciliatory, impressing even Germany's Kaiser with its effort to keep peace. It fell short of total acceptance, however, so on July 25 Austria broke off relations.

Serbia's moderate response pulled European opinion to the Serbian side. Britain, preoccupied with a dangerous crisis over Irish Home Rule (Chapter 27), assumed that Germany would be receptive to a conference like the one that had contained the Balkan Wars. This time, however, Germany was more interested in confrontation than cooperation. On July 28, Austria declared war on Serbia, and Russia, overcoming any sympathy the tsar may (or may not) have felt for Franz Ferdinand, prepared to rescue the Serbs. France resolved to stand by Russia, and Britain warned the Germans that it might not be able to stay neutral in a Franco-German war. Sobered by these developments, Germany sought on July 30 to restrain Austria, but it was too late. The need to move large numbers of troops on railways placed European armies on rigid timetables. This necessity was particularly pressing in Germany, which, threatened with a war on two fronts, planned to defeat France in six weeks and then turn to deal with Russia, whose less-developed transport system would slow its mobilization for war.

Needing to move before its enemies could prepare, Germany declared war against Russia on August 1 and France on August 3 (Map 31.2). The next day, as Germany's army invaded neutral Belgium on the way to attacking France, Britain, like Germany a guarantor of Belgian neutrality, entered the war on the side of France and Russia. All the great powers of Europe except Italy were now at war.

Archduke Franz Ferdinand (left) and Emperor Franz Josef of Austria-Hungary.

European powers choose war over peace

The July Crisis of 1914, unlike its predecessors, resulted in war for several reasons. Austria wanted to end Serbian ethnic agitation. Germany wanted to back its Austrian ally, assuming it would be better to risk war now than to wait until Russia completed its military buildup. Russia wanted to avoid humiliation like that of 1908–1909. France wanted to avenge the loss of Alsace-Lorraine and support its Russian ally. Britain wanted to avoid a French defeat that would give Germany control of France's ports on the English Channel. And all military leaders wanted to mobilize before their enemies did so. None of these "wants," however, made war inevitable. European nations had freedom of choice and could have opted against war in 1914. They did not.

| MAP **31.2** | The Great War in Europe and Southwest Asia, 1914–1918 |

The Great War quickly became a stalemate late in 1914. The Central Powers exploited their central position on the continent to attack on different fronts at different times, but trench warfare, barbed wire, and machine guns all favored the defensive posture of the Triple Entente. Note that German forces conquered an amount of Russian territory equivalent in size to all of Germany and Austria-Hungary combined. Despite this achievement, why did the Central Powers fail to win the war?

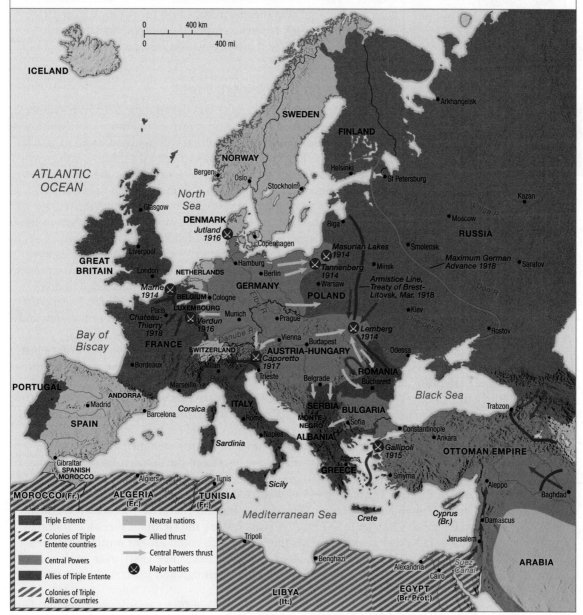

Deadlock and Devastation, 1914–1916

Why didn't the European nations decide against war? First, the military capabilities of the rival alliances were so closely matched that each side was willing to take a chance on victory. Second, each nation's leaders expected to win quickly. None of them expected the war to do what it did—come close to destroying European civilization. This helps

Both sides anticipate a short, victorious war

The most famous recruiting poster ever devised, featuring the face of British Field Marshal Lord Kitchener.

explain why they were willing to roll the dice at a time when their forces were so closely balanced. Third, many people in each country actually welcomed the prospect of war as an escape, in the words of poet Rupert Brooke, "from a world grown old and cold and weary," and believed it would be a purification that would create a stronger, cleaner world. So hundreds of thousands of young men, cheered by their families and sweethearts, marched off to war in August 1914, grateful for the opportunity to prove themselves, rejoicing with Brooke: "Now God be thanked who has matched us with His hour!"

Stalemate on the Western Front

Reality set in quickly, and reality was devastating. Belgian resistance slowed the German army, the British arrived in France more quickly than anticipated, and Russia mobilized with unusual speed to attack Germany in the East. But Germany's strategy for dealing with a two-front war was unrealistic in any case, as it relied for success on more top-flight combat divisions than the German army possessed. The Kaiser's forces won some impressive victories, bringing them close to Paris. But at the Marne River, having mobilized the city's taxis to transport their troops, the French outflanked the Germans and forced them to retreat. By mid-September the opposing armies were deadlocked. Meanwhile, in the East, a premature Russian advance into East Prussia, designed to relieve pressure on the French in the West, succeeded in doing that but ended in disaster. German Generals Paul von Hindenburg and Erich Ludendorff isolated and destroyed the entire Russian Second Army, ending the threat of invasion and saving Austria, which was being defeated farther south by the Russians.

In just a few months of warfare, losses were appalling. In three months France lost 306,000 soldiers, 3 percent of its military-age males, and more than the United States would later lose during all of World War II. Germany, with a military-age population three times larger than France's, had lost 241,000 men. Farther east, Russia and Austria had suffered catastrophic losses, with 1.5 million Russian and 1.268 million Austrian troops killed or captured. Russia's huge population could replace those losses, but Austria's could not. So the danger to Germany and Austria stemmed not only from Germany's failure to defeat France quickly but also from the destruction of the cream of the Austro-Hungarian armies. To prevent total collapse on the Eastern Front in 1915, Germany transferred sizable forces eastward and held the defensive in the West.

That defensive gave the Great War its most morbid characteristic: **trench warfare.** From the English Channel to the Franco-Swiss border, the Germans dug an elaborate system of parallel and angled trenches that the French could neither outflank nor pierce. France, perplexed, built trenches of its own. For the next three years, each of these opposing systems prevented any meaningful breakthrough and frustrated generals schooled in attacking rather than defending.

Trenches had been used before. In the American Civil War, Confederate general Robert E. Lee had employed so many of them that his men called him "the King of Spades." But prior to 1914, trenches had been dug to fortify positions for a battle or siege and then abandoned when it was over. In the Great War, trenches became permanent installations. Their permanence was attributable to barbed wire, which slowed offensives to a crawl, and especially to the machine gun. Capable of firing 11 rounds a second through water-cooled barrels, machine guns swept the entire field in front of a trench, cutting off attackers at the knees. Eventually, offensive technology would be developed to neutralize these factors.

The Western Front stalemates into trench warfare

DOCUMENT 31.1 Charles Hamilton Sorley, "When You See Millions of the Mouthless Dead"

The poetry of the Great War captured in vivid, unforgettable imagery the shocking hopelessness of the gruesome slaughters on the Western Front. Charles Hamilton Sorley was killed in action in 1915, but not before he had written what many have called the saddest poem of the war.

When you see millions of the mouthless dead

Across your dreams in pale battalions go,

Say not soft things as other men have said,

That you'll remember. For you need not so.

Give them no praise. For, deaf, how should they know

It is not curses heaped on each gashed head?

Nor tears. Their blind eyes see not your tears flow.

Nor honour. It is easy to be dead.

Say only this, "They are dead." Then add thereto,

"Yet many a better one has died before."

Then, scanning all the o'ercrowded mass, should you

Perceive one face that you loved heretofore,

It is a spook. None wears the face you knew.

Great Death has made all his forevermore.

SOURCE: Charles Hamilton Sorley, "When You See Millions of the Mouthless Dead" (1915).

For the moment, however, bewildered commanders launched repeated attacks "over the top" of the trenches (see page 718), sending soldiers surging into the barbed-wire traps of "no-man's land" between opposing lines in the vain hope of achieving a breakthrough.

Trench warfare consumed soldiers' lives at unprecedented rates, transforming war from violence carrying the prospect of glory into violence of unending degradation (see "Charles Hamilton Sorley, *When You See Millions of the Mouthless Dead*"). Men lived and died in ditches eight feet deep, standing in stagnant water, plagued by rats and vermin, and often living next to the decaying corpses of their comrades. The optimism of the 19th century died on the Western Front, as trenches scarred both the landscapes of northeastern France and the psyches of the men who occupied them.

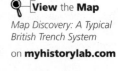

Read the **Document**

Excerpt from Four Weeks in the Trenches, Fritz Kreisler

on **myhistorylab.com**

Efforts to Break the Stalemate

As casualties mounted, each side added allies and sought to break the stalemate. Germany and Austria-Hungary, joined by Bulgaria and Ottoman Turkey in a coalition called the Central Powers, employed mass attacks and artillery bombardments, supplemented on land by poison gas and at sea by German submarine warfare. Britain, France, and Russia, joined by Britain's ally Japan and other nations in a combination called the Allied Powers, relied on mass attacks and a British naval blockade of Germany. Hoping to gain Austrian territory in a peace settlement, Italy joined the Allies in 1915, abandoning its prewar alliance with Germany and Austria.

View the **Map**

Map Discovery: A Typical British Trench System

on **myhistorylab.com**

OFFENSIVES IN THE EAST AND SOUTHEAST. As 1915 began, General Erich von Falkenhayn (*FAHL-ken-hīn*), chief of the German General Staff, argued for a Western offensive. Noting Britain's ability to draw reinforcements from Canada and Australia, he wanted to defeat France quickly. But although Falkenhayn outranked Hindenburg and Ludendorff, they, not he, had won Germany's only decisive victory in 1914, and they demanded an offensive in the East. So in the West, Falkenhayn settled for smaller

Austro-Hungarian soldiers wearing gas masks.

attacks using chlorine gas, a fearsome new weapon that, when inhaled, stimulated fluid production in the lungs to cause death by drowning. Eventually used by both sides, poison gas was limited in its usefulness by shifting winds, which sometimes blew the gas back on the side releasing it, and by the development of gas masks. It nonetheless killed tens of thousands of horses, on which all armies depended for transport, and heightened the impersonal doom of trench warfare.

Hindenburg's insistence on an Eastern offensive was logical. A victory there would prevent Austria's collapse and possibly force Russia, frighteningly short of rifles and artillery shells, to seek a cease-fire. From May to September 1915, the Central Powers' offensive captured more than 750,000 Russian prisoners. This saved the Austrian army, but the Russians withdrew into their vast interior and raised reinforcements to replace their losses, hoping their increasing output of industrial weapons would eventually enable them to expel the Germans. As in France in 1914, Germany won major victories in the East but lacked the overwhelming superiority required to win the war. Italy's entry on the side of the Allies further reduced German prospects, tying down Austrian forces in bloody, debilitating fighting for the remainder of the war.

The Allied landing at Gallipoli fails

If the Central Powers could not break the stalemate in the West or East, perhaps the Allies could break it in the southeast. Turkey's entry into the war late in 1914 on the side of the Central Powers closed Russia's southern seaports, since Turkey controlled entry to the Black Sea through the Dardanelles Straits. On April 25, 1915, an improvised landing force of Britons, Australians, and New Zealanders went ashore on the Gallipoli (*gah-LIH-pō-lē*) peninsula, hoping to force the Straits open and knock Turkey out of the war. But it was pinned on the beaches under Turkish artillery fire from defensive positions coordinated by Captain Mustafa Kemal (*moo-STAH-fah keh-MAHL*), who would go on to rule Turkey after the war. The British did not have sufficient troops for a full-scale invasion, and they had underestimated Turkish resistance. By January 9, 1916, the invaders evacuated Gallipoli. Both sides suffered losses in the hundreds of thousands, and the stalemate continued.

Troops from Australia and New Zealand at Gallipoli.

THE WAR AT SEA. By the end of 1915, although the Central Powers held a strong position in the heart of Europe, their impressive offensives had failed to defeat any of their enemies.

Germany, moreover, was increasingly deprived of food and supplies by a tight British naval blockade. The British Grand Fleet outmatched the German High Seas Fleet in both equipment and seamanship. It could maintain a tight blockade regardless of the number of merchant vessels sunk by German **U-boats** (submarines), a number that ranged from 50 to 100 per month but failed to stop supplies from reaching Britain.

British naval efforts were primarily defensive, forcing Germany to take the initiative or slowly starve. U-boat warfare raised German hopes but proved frustrating: rules of the sea required that a submarine give warning before launching torpedoes and allow crews and passengers to be rescued. Since this process exposed and endangered these small boats, they often ignored it, casting Germany in the role of an outlaw nation. The sinking of neutral vessels by mistake caused diplomatic crises, as did the sinking in 1915 of the British passenger liner *Lusitania*. That ship was carrying more than a thousand

The Lusitania while it was still afloat.

American passengers as well as a cargo of contraband munitions destined for Britain. The heavy loss of life almost forced the United States to break diplomatic relations with Germany, which thereafter temporarily restricted U-boat raids.

U-boat warfare damages Germany's relations with the United States

THE VERDUN, SOMME, AND BRUSILOV OFFENSIVES. By early 1916 the balance of forces was shifting to favor the Allies. Tremendous Russian industrial expansion provided adequate modern equipment for the tsar's armies; France mobilized unprecedented numbers of women for factory work, releasing men for combat duty; and Britain, whose army in 1914 had seven combat divisions, now fielded seventy. Made confident by this shift, Allied generals planned a summer offensive of their own, but Falkenhayn struck first, unleashing an offensive against the French at Verdun, a fortress in eastern France.

Verdun was selected for its symbolic significance: as a fortress town since Roman times, it represented France's will to resist. Falkenhayn, not realizing how much French factory work had been shifted to women, believed that France must be running short of military-age men. By besieging Verdun, he meant not to capture it but to force France to defend it by sending in more and more men. Eventually France would either lose Verdun or spread its remaining forces so thin that Germany could break through elsewhere on the Western Front.

Germany attacked Verdun on February 21 with a bombardment so enormous that the roar of the guns was heard in England. For a few days, it seemed the town would fall, but the French, deciding it must be held, appointed General Philippe Pétain (*PĀ-tan*) to hold it. Pétain entrenched his men in fortifications to wait out the shelling. Eventually, German infantry moved forward and were shot down. By the end of June, each side had lost more than two hundred thousand killed and wounded, and Verdun's crater-scarred landscape resembled the surface of the moon.

The 1916 offensives devastate the Western Front

Falkenhayn's failure at Verdun would cost him his command in August, but on July 1 he was still in charge as the Allies opened their offensive on the River Somme in northern France. They, too, placed their faith in overwhelming artillery fire, but they overestimated their own strength and underestimated German defenses. The British Army alone lost twenty thousand dead in the first eight hours, the largest one-day loss in British military history. By August 1 the combatants combined had lost more than 350,000 men, and the front lines had scarcely moved. The Somme offensive finally ended on November 19, with more than 1.2 million men killed or wounded.

Finally the lessons of trench warfare began to sink in. Throwing huge numbers of cloth-clad soldiers at positions protected by barbed wire and machine guns produced carnage without altering the tactical situation in any useful way. The foot soldiers cursed their generals; a popular analysis of the fighting is entitled *Lions Led by Donkeys*. But without technology that could overcome trenches, the generals had few options. Frustrated by their inability to break the stalemate, they could think of nothing more creative than to propel more and more men into the devastation of trench warfare. None of the generals yet advised their governments to seek a negotiated peace, although deadlocked wars in centuries past had been settled by negotiation.

The deadlock in the West did not, however, prevent movement in the East. Falkenhayn had attacked Verdun freely because he thought the 1915 German assault had ruined Russia's offensive capability. He was mistaken. In June 1916, Russian general Alexei Brusilov (*broo-SĒ-loff*) launched the Brusilov offensive, splitting the Austrian Seventh Army in two, taking four hundred thousand

Devastated landscape, northern France.

prisoners, and costing the Central Powers a million casualties. He lacked the rail and road systems to follow up his victories, but he pushed Austria to the brink of collapse. The Central Powers were running out of manpower and resources. It was time for statesmen to find a way to make peace.

The War Against Germany's Colonies

European issues, not colonial issues, caused the Great War. But colonial disputes had contributed significantly to the rising tensions between the new German Empire and the longer-established empires of France and Britain. Once war broke out, Germany fought on two fronts and was unable to defend its overseas possessions adequately. Forces from Britain, France, Belgium, Japan, Australia, and New Zealand picked off those possessions one by one, making the Great War truly global long before the 1917 intervention of the United States.

JAPAN OCCUPIES GERMANY'S PACIFIC EMPIRE. In Asia, the Anglo-Japanese Alliance of 1902 obligated Japan to come to Britain's aid if its possessions were attacked by a third party. On August 1, 1914, London informed Tokyo that it did not expect to ask for Japan's intervention. Three days later Japan declared itself neutral, but by August 6 Britain was having second thoughts. The Royal Navy wanted to blockade the German port of Qingdao on China's Shandong Peninsula while hunting German warships and armed merchant ships in order to keep Pacific sea-lanes safe for British commerce. These goals could not be achieved without sending additional British ships to the Pacific, and those ships were needed in the Atlantic. Britain therefore asked Japan for help in capturing or sinking armed German merchant ships, while German warships and the blockade of Qingdao would be handled by the Royal Navy.

Japan's entry creates a global war

This limited collaboration was inconsistent with neutral status. On August 7–8, the Japanese cabinet decided to declare war on Germany and eliminate German influence in China and the Pacific. That frightened China, which feared Japanese more than European expansionism. Britain, recognizing Japan's intent to partition China, urged Japan to remain neutral. But Tokyo argued that Japanese public opinion demanded war with Germany and that the government could not resist the will of the people. Neither claim was fully true, but with Britain preoccupied with Germany in Europe, on August 23 Japan entered the war on its own terms (Map 31.3).

Japan moved at once against the German garrison at Qingdao, ignoring China's neutrality in doing so. Sixty thousand Japanese soldiers, with one British and one Indian battalion, laid siege to the city in early September. Even so, it took until November 7 for the invaders to force the garrison of three thousand German marines to surrender. By that time all of Germany's Pacific holdings had been overrun. New Zealand troops occupied Samoa without resistance on August 29, and on September 15 the Australians accepted the surrender of German New Guinea and the Solomon Islands, where the Germans were led by an artillery captain who had no guns and an equestrian instructor who had no horses. Obviously Germany had never intended to defend the region vigorously. German defenses were no better in the Caroline Islands, the Marshall Islands, the Mariana Islands, and the island of Palau, all of which fell to the Japanese on October 6. Japan's entry into the Great War allowed it to conquer territories that could form an outer defense perimeter for the Japanese Empire in the event of a future conflict with a Pacific power such as the United States.

India makes an enormous contribution to the Allied war effort

India's small participation in the siege of Qingdao proved to be only the beginning of a major military commitment made by Britain's most valuable imperial possession. No fighting took place on the subcontinent, but 850,000 Indian soldiers fought beside

MAP **31.3**   The Great War in Asia, 1914–1918

When Britain asked Japan for assistance in tracking down armed German merchant vessels, Japan took the opportunity to declare war on Germany and occupy German possessions in East Asia and the Pacific. Notice that Australia and New Zealand occupied other German holdings on behalf of the British Empire. Farther west, India made significant contributions in men, horses, and supplies to the Allied war effort. Why was Britain more prepared than Germany to fight a global war on a global scale?

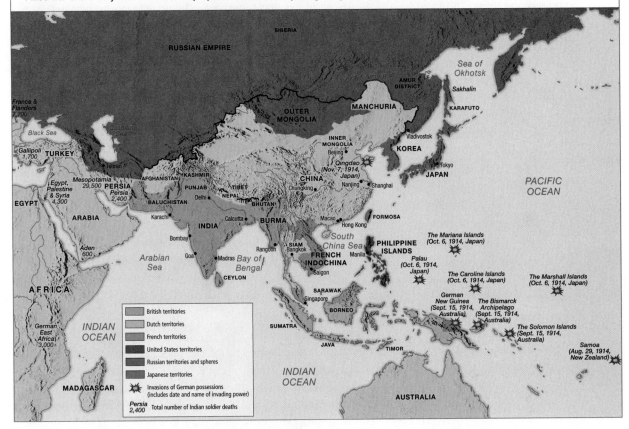

the British in Asia, Africa, and Europe. Nearly 50,000 died in those actions. India also contributed 150,000 horses and mules, 11,000 camels, 75,000 tons of timber, and 550 million rounds of ammunition. The extent of this assistance made Britain's refusal to grant meaningful autonomy to India after 1918 very difficult for Indians to accept.

DEVASTATION IN AFRICA. Germany's African colonies were not particularly valuable in themselves; they were table scraps left to the Germans after the British and French Empires had eaten their fill. But they could serve as staging areas for attacks on British and French interests, and their six important wireless stations could relay messages from Germany to its ships around the world. Britain and France wasted no time in attacking Germany in Africa.

The easiest Allied victory came in the West African territory of Togo (Map 31.4). Surrounded by the British

An ammunition factory in India.

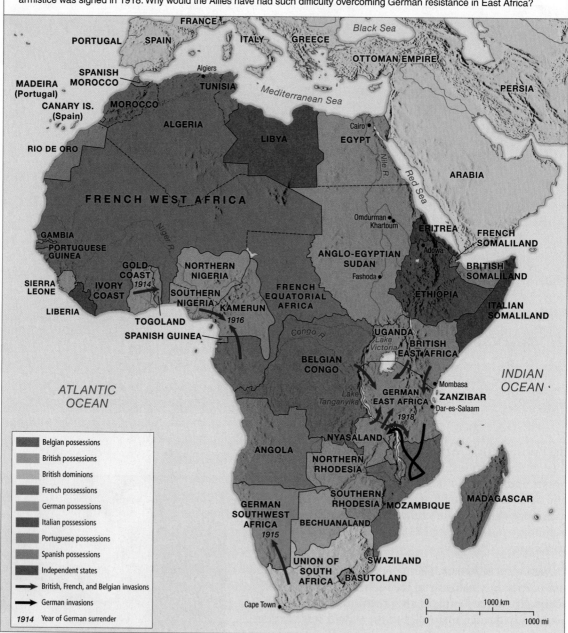

MAP 31.4   The Great War in Africa, 1914–1918

Germany's African colonies were lightly defended and could never have affected the fighting in Europe, but each of them contained at least one wireless station that could relay communications from Germany to German ships around the world. The Allies wanted to destroy these stations, and also to remove these colonies from German control. Observe that the stiffest fighting occurred in German East Africa, where forces under Colonel Paul von Lettow-Vorbeck remained in the field until after the armistice was signed in 1918. Why would the Allies have had such difficulty overcoming German resistance in East Africa?

Gold Coast and French West Africa, it fell to a joint invasion on August 27, 1914. The western Central African colony of Kamerun proved harder for the Allies. A combination of skillful German resistance, difficult topography, and the impossibility of fighting during five months of torrential rains delayed Allied victory into 1916. By that time German South-west Africa had already surrendered to a joint force of 60,000 Britons and Boers.

That left German East Africa, a sprawling colony as large as France, with a defense force of fewer than three thousand men commanded by Colonel Paul von Lettow-Vorbeck, a veteran of the Boxer Rebellion who had no intention of surrendering to anyone. Lettow launched raids into British East Africa (Kenya) and Uganda in 1914, raising the German flag beneath Mount Kilimanjaro and causing an uproar among Britain's colonists. His forces repelled a joint British-Indian offensive that November, after which he confined his efforts to guerrilla warfare, fighting and quickly withdrawing. After German resistance collapsed in southwestern Africa, experienced troops from that conflict arrived in East Africa and embarked on a 1916 campaign under the command of General Jan Christiaan Smuts, a master of unconventional warfare who had repeatedly frustrated the British in the Boer War.

Germans fight the Allies in East Africa

Smuts launched a multinational offensive from four different colonies at once, using British forces from Kenya and Nyasaland, Belgian troops from the Congo, and Portuguese soldiers from Mozambique, hoping to encircle Lettow and end the fighting in Africa. Lettow, however, now commanded more than 16,000 men, most of them native Africans who had enlisted in his cause and knew the terrain better than Smuts. Lettow divided his German-African forces, broke out southward into Mozambique, moved northward again around Lake Nyasa, and ended up in northern Rhodesia, where he finally surrendered his command on November 25, 1918. His bloodied but undefeated troops had fought the British as recently as November 12, one day after the Armistice was signed in France.

The battles over Germany's colonies devastated much of Africa. Campaigning in Kamerun lasted two years and wrecked much of the countryside. East Africa was ravaged by the constant fighting between Germany and Britain, which resulted in burned villages, loss of crops and stored food, and the drafting of more than one hundred thousand Africans to serve as soldiers and porters. Nearly 10 percent of Africans drafted died, mostly from malnutrition and disease. To make matters worse, the global influenza pandemic of 1918 killed over 3 percent of the entire population of East, West, and Central Africa. To Europeans, Africa was a sideshow to the main war, but to Africans it was everything they had. By 1918 they responded to the Allied victory with little more than exhaustion and relief.

The Great War creates chaos in Africa

European Civilian Life During the Great War

War's hardship lay heaviest on the soldiers, but noncombatants suffered, too, although in different ways. By the end of 1916, the war had disrupted civilian life in all warring nations. Military needs took precedence in distribution of food, clothing, and critical raw materials. Inevitable shortages at home were handled through rationing, which restricted each person or family to a fixed quantity of each item per month or year. Many families lost members to military service, while those remaining at home were often required to work up to 72 hours a week in war plants.

Women workers in a British shipyard.

Since Britain was not invaded, its people suffered least, but their lives were not easy. Britain imported much of its food, and U-boat raids jeopardized both agricultural and industrial imports. The British avoided malnutrition through strict rationing, and Germany's inability to sink the entire British merchant marine allowed imports to reach England, but birth weights declined and vitamin deficiencies afflicted many children. British soldiers were probably the war's best-fed troops, but at the expense of provisions for people at home.

France uses women in factories and on farms

In France, the huge casualty lists of 1914 led to the drafting of most able-bodied men and their replacement in factories and on farms by women. France lost a higher percentage of men aged 18 to 25 than any other warring nation, leaving many women without spouses and depressing the birthrate for the next two decades. German occupation of northeastern France cost that nation 80 percent of its prewar industry. New factories were established farther south, but the French people suffered severe shortages of manufactured consumer goods for the rest of the war.

Germany suffered tremendously, largely because of the slow strangulation imposed by the British blockade. Having counted on swift victory, the Kaiser's regime had no plans for allocating resources or feeding people at home in a lengthy war. Resource allotment was eventually handled by a central government agency, as the German economy shifted all production priorities to the war effort. More than a million women joined the industrial workforce, leaving children in the care of grandparents or aunts and necessitating rapid overhauling of workplaces—for example, through installation of women's lavatories on factory floors. Long hours of wartime work ruined the health of many malnourished women, unaccustomed to strenuous physical labor.

The British blockade causes malnutrition in Germany

Malnutrition was the principal challenge facing the German home front. Germany in 1913 imported one third of its food supply. The British blockade cut off food imports, and the harvests of 1916 and 1917 were awful because of fertilizer shortages and terrible weather. In the "turnip winter" of 1916–1917, turnips and other vegetables usually fed to livestock became main dishes on German dinner tables. Bread was made from one part flour and two parts sawdust, occasionally mixed with powdered limestone. Rations declined to 1,000 calories per day, although 2,280 is the average required for adult health. About 750,000 Germans died of malnutrition between 1914 and 1918, while many others fell to disease, their immune systems weakened by lack of food, the rationing of soap to one small bar per month, and the rationing of coal, which lowered household temperatures to levels dangerous in Germany's chilly climate.

In Russia, the government encouraged wartime sacrifice by banning the sale of vodka. At first the results were beneficial: criminal cases in Russia's capital declined 80 percent, and the incidence of poverty dropped by 75 percent as savings deposits grew. But consumption of tea and sugar increased tremendously, and by 1916 alcohol-starved Russians were drinking varnish and cologne. Russian farmers kept pace with food demand, but soldiers at the front were fed first. Russia's railway system eventually proved unable to supply both soldiers and cities in a country partially occupied by enemy forces, triggering cataclysmic revolutions in 1917.

Year of Revolution, 1917

The year 1917 proved pivotal for both sides. The Allies gained a long-term advantage with the entry on their side of the United States. But mutinies in France and revolutions in Russia hurt the Allied cause in the short run, giving the Germans the edge going into 1918.

The United States Enters the War

The United States tries to remain neutral

Woodrow Wilson, president of the neutral United States, tried to end the war late in 1916 by asking both sides to state the terms they needed to ensure their future security. The request was modest, but results were disappointing: each alliance presented uncompromising demands that were mutually exclusive. Reelected in November 1916 on the slogan "He kept us out of war," Wilson watched uneasily, fearing that unless the conflict ended soon, he would be unable to keep America out much longer.

On January 31, 1917, Wilson's apprehensions grew stronger. The Germans, faced with continuing military stalemate and starving from Britain's blockade, resumed unrestricted submarine warfare. The Kaiser's advisors argued that U-boats could strangle Britain and end the war quickly; they minimized the consequences of a break with the United States, whose small army would need months of expansion and training, and whose soldiers would have to be ferried to Europe in troop ships that U-boats could sink. Their argument was desperate rather than logical, but the longer the stalemate lasted, the weaker the Central Powers became and the more willing they were to grasp at any possible solution.

America's reaction to Germany's unleashing of its U-boats startled Berlin. On February 26, 1917, Wilson asked Congress for permission to arm merchant ships. Three days later the U.S. government published the **Zimmermann Note**, an intercepted effort by German diplomat Arthur Zimmermann to bribe Mexico into an alliance against the United States by offering to return Texas, New Mexico, and Arizona, lost in the Mexican-American War of 1846–1848, in the event of German victory. Public outrage over this offer and persistent U-boat attacks against American shipping led Wilson to ask Congress for a declaration of war on April 2, 1917. Congress complied four days later, but not until 1918 did large numbers of U.S. soldiers, transported across the Atlantic by naval convoys for protection against German U-boats, arrive in France. When they did, they brought new energy that helped defeat the Germans.

Anti-German propaganda.

Germany's actions bring the United States into the war

Mutinies in the French Army

In the meantime, however, widespread mutinies rocked France's war-weary armies. Following the failure of an April 1917 offensive, nearly half the units in the French army refused to participate in further attacks.

The French government took the mutinies seriously because they were national in scope, involving civilian as well as military discontent. French soldiers lived in terrible conditions, ate inadequate food, and received almost no leave time. Their families endured high prices, long workweeks, and grinding anxiety over loved ones at the front. Both soldiers and families suffered from the stress of an apparently endless war. The government responded by suppressing strikes at home, naming the controversial, passionately anti-German, 76-year-old Georges Clemenceau (*klā-mahn-SŌ*) as prime minister, and appointing as army chief General Pétain, hero of Verdun. Pétain improved the food, granted regular leaves, and punished thousands of mutinous soldiers. Most important, he suggested that future attacks would be mounted only if they had legitimate prospects of success. Building on his reputation as a general who never asked men to sacrifice their lives needlessly, he gradually restored discipline and ended the crisis.

France limits the impact of mutinies

The French mutinies were a lost opportunity for the Germans. Unaware of the protests, German commanders Hindenburg and Ludendorff, having reoriented German strategy eastward after replacing Falkenhayn in 1916, concentrated on the Eastern Front throughout 1917. That shift may have saved the French army.

The Russian Revolutions

Nothing, however, could save the Russian monarchy, battered by German advances and the breakdown of Russia's wartime food supply system. In March 1917, food shortages sparked a spontaneous revolt that overthrew the tsarist regime. For the next eight months, an ineffective transitional regime sought vainly to restore order and maintain the war effort, but it was overthrown in November by Marxist revolutionaries, committed to removing Russia from the war and establishing a socialist society.

STRESSES AND STRAINS OF THE GREAT WAR. The Great War was disastrous for Russia from the outset. In the war's first month, as Germany invaded France, the Russians had rushed to relieve their French allies by attacking Germany from the East. By prompting the Germans to divert troops from France, this assault helped the French hold on. But the unprepared and poorly led Russians were badly defeated and never fully recovered.

Russia staggers under the war's burdens

As the war continued and supplies of rifles, munitions, and food ran low, Russia's situation went from bad to worse. Russian forces fought well against Austria, but they were no match for the Germans, whose 1915 offensive pushed deep into the tsarist empire. Huge numbers of refugees, fleeing the German advance on foot, overwhelmed Russian roads and towns, undermining morale and further slowing the flow of supplies.

In August of that year, faced with a series of defeats, Tsar Nicholas II made a fateful decision: he assumed command of Russia's armies himself. His goals were to raise the soldiers' morale with his presence at the front, and to signal that Russia would stay in the war despite crippling setbacks. But the tsar's lack of military expertise soon made him a liability, and his absence from the capital left Russia reliant on his wife, Empress Alexandra, for governmental administration. And she was distracted and increasingly discredited by her connections with a dissolute Siberian "holy man" called Rasputin, who was apparently able to heal her son Alexis, heir to the Russian throne.

THE FALL OF THE RUSSIAN MONARCHY. Alexis had hemophilia, a congenital condition that kept his blood from clotting, so even the slightest cut or bruise could cause him to bleed to death. But Rasputin, apparently through prayer, seemed to be able to stop the bleeding. Seeing him as a savior sent by God, Alexandra came to trust him fully and rely on his advice.

Rasputin and Alexandra prove unable to lead Russia effectively

Unfortunately for the monarchy's public image, Rasputin also led a life of public drunkenness and debauchery. Moreover, Alexandra herself was originally from Germany, the hated enemies' homeland. And to protect her son, his condition was kept secret, so the public did not know why Rasputin enjoyed her favor. As she systematically replaced effective ministers with unscrupulous incompetents favored by Rasputin, Russia's internal order disintegrated. The result was scandal: while the tsar was at the front, it seemed, a treacherous German woman and her depraved friend were ruining Russia.

As the situation deteriorated, even loyal monarchists lost faith in the regime. Despite all efforts, the Duma could overcome neither the blunders of Russian officials nor the skills of German armies. Finally, in December 1916, a reactionary Duma deputy and two relatives of the royal family decided to murder Rasputin. First they fed him wine and pastries laced with cyanide poison. Then, when he remained unfazed, they shot him, clubbed him till he was unconscious, and drowned him in a canal.

The murder changed little. The Germans were still advancing, the inept ministers were still in office, internal order was still breaking down, and the distraught empress continued to hold power. Even as she conducted seances to communicate with her departed advisor, patriotic Russians and dedicated Duma deputies began to look for ways to replace their failing leaders with a more capable regime.

Meanwhile, a far deeper and broader revolt was taking shape among the Russian masses. By this time, runaway inflation, sparked by the printing of excess currency to pay for the war effort, had eroded people's meager incomes, while the hardships of continued conflict had pushed them to the breaking point. In the villages, from which most able men had long since been sent to the front, the remaining overstrained peasants refused to sell their grain in return for worthless currency. Cities ran out of bread, and as work hours increased to meet war demands while purchasing power fell, many urban workers went on strike. At the front, where millions of Russian troops had been killed, wounded, or captured, soldiers began questioning both the war and their orders. Pushed beyond all patience, the masses began to move.

Early in 1917 tensions exploded in Russia's capital, renamed Petrograd (Peter's city) during the war because Petersburg sounded too German. On March 8, International Women's Day, exasperated female textile workers started a mass demonstration. They were joined by throngs of women who were waiting in long lines for bread and by striking men from the city's other industries. By the next day, the whole city was on strike, and rioters controlled the streets. Away at the warfront, Nicholas responded by ordering local troops to disperse the demonstrators. On March 11 they did so, shooting into the rioting crowds and effectively clearing the streets. But that night the tormented troops, upset at being ordered to shoot their own people, resolved not to do it again, and some started to mutiny. On March 12 the rioting resumed, but when soldiers were ordered to fire at the crowds they shot their officers instead.

The tsar's authority had evaporated. On March 15, pressed by several Duma deputies and army officers, he renounced the throne for himself and his sickly son. Nicholas's brother, next in line, wisely refused to accept it. The 300-year-old imperial Russian monarchy silently ceased to exist.

DUAL POWER AND THE BOLSHEVIK CHALLENGE. In the midst of the revolution, two important bodies emerged to dominate developments for the next eight months. One was the **Provisional Government**, a temporary cabinet composed largely of Duma leaders, which assumed power until a new constitution could be enacted. Another was the **Petrograd Soviet**, made up of deputies elected by workers and soldiers, modeled on the soviet of 1905.

The Provisional Government, led by liberals, proclaimed democratic rights and freedoms for all, and promised to hold elections for a constituent assembly that would decide the future form of rule. But it alienated peasants by postponing major land reforms. It failed to fully restore internal order, or to solve Russia's economic problems. Most disastrously, it kept Russia in the war, determined to press on to victory despite the suffering of the people.

The Petrograd Soviet, led by socialists who believed Russia too economically primitive for a socialist regime, agreed to let the Provisional Government manage matters for the time being. Backed by strong popular support, however, the Soviet sought to shape policy, creating an ambiguous situation that Russians called "dual power." As the Petrograd Soviet called for broad reforms and peace "without annexations or indemnities," local soviets, elected by workers, soldiers, and peasants, sprang up all over Russia.

Following these events from afar was Vladimir Ilich Ulianov (*ool-YAH-noff*), better known as Lenin. Fifteen years earlier, as a rising socialist leader, he had challenged the orthodox Marxist view that industrial workers would eventually create a socialist revolution. The workers, he argued, would not do this on their own: they would merely form unions and settle for better wages and working conditions. Revolution, he asserted, must instead be made by a dedicated group of professional revolutionaries, acting as the workers' "vanguard." His views had split Russian Marxists into two factions: his supporters, who called themselves **Bolsheviks** ("those in the majority"), and their opponents, called Mensheviks ("those in the minority"). Having fled Russia to avoid arrest by tsarist police, Lenin had been attending a conference of European socialists in Switzerland when the Great War broke out. Switzerland was neutral in the conflict, and as part of its neutrality, it

The Russian monarchy breaks under the strain of war

View the **Image**
Soviet Poster, 1917
on **myhistorylab.com**

Burying the fallen, Petrograd, March 1917.

Dual centers of power cause chaos in Russia

Lenin.

prohibited political leaders and men of military age who were citizens of warring nations from leaving the country. Lenin was trapped in Switzerland along with other Russians in exile.

Now, suddenly, Russia was in revolution, and Lenin could not be part of it. His frustration grew as he learned that Soviet leaders, including some of his Bolsheviks, had let the Provisional Government take power rather than launch a socialist rebellion. In a sealed train provided by the Germans, who helped him return in hopes that his presence would weaken Russia's war effort, Lenin made his way to Petrograd in April. Once there, he stunned his socialist colleagues by demanding an immediate end to the "imperialist war" and the overthrow of the Provisional Government. He also called for the **nationalization** of all Russian land—the forced transfer of private property to state control. Later he simplified his views into slogans appealing to the Russian masses: "Peace!" "Land!" "Bread!" and "All power to the Soviets!"

Lenin's Bolsheviks appeal to ordinary Russians

Although Soviet leaders considered Lenin's ideas too radical, workers found them attractive and support for the Bolsheviks grew. So did their upper ranks. In May, Leon Trotsky, a brilliant Marxist orator and organizer who had helped lead the soviet of 1905, returned from exile in New York. Though a longtime political opponent of Lenin, he now joined him in pushing for immediate revolution, adding immensely to the energy and effectiveness of the Bolshevik leadership.

Confusion followed. In July radical workers and sailors, inspired by Lenin's ideas and angered at the Soviet's refusal to take power, rose in rebellion in Petrograd. Lenin, believing the uprising premature, at first tried to stop it and then reluctantly gave it his support. But the "July Days" revolt failed when Soviet leaders rejected its demands, and forces loyal to the Provisional Government, influenced by rumors that Lenin was a German agent, disarmed the rebels and arrested some Bolshevik leaders. When Lenin himself fled to Finland, it appeared that the Bolshevik movement would collapse.

Read the Document

Bolshevik Seizure of Power, 1917

on **myhistorylab.com**

THE BOLSHEVIK TRIUMPH. Then, in September, the Bolsheviks were inadvertently rescued by actions of Russian conservatives. Eager to strengthen the Provisional Government and shut down the Soviet, General Lavr Kornilov (*kor-NĒ-loff*), the army's commander-in-chief, began sending troops toward Petrograd. Russia's prime minister, Alexander Kerensky, fearing a right-wing coup, fired the general and called on the people to "save the revolution." Bolshevik leaders, including Trotsky, were released from prison and quickly took charge of the resistance, in which Bolshevik sailors and railway workers defeated the "Kornilov mutiny."

The Bolsheviks take power in Russia

Suddenly the Bolsheviks were heroes. As their support among workers grew, they gained a majority in the Petrograd Soviet and elected Trotsky its chair. Lenin returned in October, and together they planned a new revolution, timed to coincide with an All-Russian Congress of Soviets, convening in the capital on November 7, 1917. Early that morning, Bolshevik Red Guards seized the city's railway stations and other strategic locations. By afternoon, most of Petrograd was in their hands. That evening, with 390 of the 650 delegates, the Bolsheviks took control of the Congress of Soviets. When Mensheviks and others walked out in protest, Trotsky rhetorically relegated them to the "dustbin of history." The next day the Bolsheviks completed their coup by storming the headquarters of the Provisional Government.

The Bolsheviks move to fulfill their promises

Moving quickly to implement their program, the Bolsheviks formed a Soviet government with Lenin at its head. They issued a Decree on Peace, declaring an end to the war, and a Decree on Land, authorizing peasants to divide up nobles' estates. They nationalized banking and foreign trade and urged workers to take control of factories. After several weeks of fighting, they defeated the remnants of the Provisional Government, took charge of Moscow, and spread their power to other Russian cities. In November they permitted previously planned elections for the constituent assembly, but when it became clear they could not control the assembly, they shut it down in January 1918 after it met for only one day. They also adopted the Western calendar, moved the capital to Moscow, began to repress the Orthodox Church, and officially started calling themselves Communists.

Further actions by the new regime underscored its radical nature. It declared equal status for all Soviet citizens, without regard to social class or gender, making Soviet Russia the first major country to provide legal equality and full voting rights to all women. It also proclaimed equality for Russia's many ethnic minorities, some of whom, including Finns, Estonians, Latvians, Lithuanians, and Poles, gained independence at the end of the Great War. And, determined to get Russia out of the war and fulfill their Decree on Peace, Russia's new rulers began seeking a separate peace with Germany.

Bolshevik poster extolling the revolution.

Year of Decision, 1918

As 1918 began, the outlook for Germany appeared favorable. The Allies stood to gain eventually from the arrival of fresh American troops, but few had arrived thus far. In the meantime, by making peace with Russia, the Germans could move half a million battle-tested troops from the Eastern to the Western Front, giving them a huge advantage in northern France. It seemed that they might break the stalemate and win the war before the Americans could make much difference.

Barely noticed in all the turmoil was the use in November–December 1917 of a new technology that might favor the Allies. The British sent three hundred ungainly machines into combat at Cambrai in northern France and won a limited but highly significant victory. The perplexed Germans called these machines "power-driven mechanized vehicles on treads that destroy trenches." The more succinct British called them "tanks."

Russian Withdrawal from the War

On March 3, 1918, German and Soviet officials signed the Treaty of Brest-Litovsk, ending Russia's participation in the Great War. In a calculated risk of dazzling magnitude, the Bolsheviks gave Germany two thirds of Russia west of the Ural Mountains in return for peace. Lacking an army capable of stopping the Germans, and anxious to maintain worker support by keeping his 1917 promises, Lenin explained that the Bolsheviks needed peace to consolidate their power.

The Treaty of Brest-Litovsk gave the Germans access to huge supplies of timber, oil, and grain from western Russia, but more important, it freed fifty combat-ready divisions for immediate transfer to the Western Front. There Ludendorff and Hindenburg were preparing to batter the Allies into submission. The Americans were starting to arrive in force: three hundred thousand had debarked by March, and 1.3 million would land in France by August. But these raw recruits were not as militarily valuable as the five hundred thousand battle-toughened Germans transferred from East to West. If the war lasted until 1919, the influx of fresh Americans would eventually alter the balance in favor of the Allies, but no such alteration seemed possible in 1918.

The Treaty of Brest-Litovsk enables Germany to fight on one front

The Great March Offensive and Influenza Pandemic

The Great March Offensive began well for the Germans: 76 German divisions overran 28 British divisions, pushing them back toward Paris. Desperate to avoid catastrophe, the British agreed to serve under the French general Ferdinand Foch (*FŌSH*), whose appointment as overall commander of Allied forces on April 3, 1918, saved the situation by giving one man unconditional authority to allocate reserves.

Foch's efforts to stiffen Allied resistance were aided by Americans and by the flu. By late May, German forces stood only 56 miles from Paris, but there they were blocked by inexperienced American troops at Belleau Wood. This unexpected U.S. victory startled the Germans. Driven to the limits of their endurance, they soon fell victim to one of history's deadliest afflictions: the great influenza pandemic of 1918.

A pandemic of influenza kills many millions throughout the world

This disease, which incapacitated half a million German soldiers in June, was much more deadly than the varieties of flu that today kill more than 36,000 Americans each winter. Sweeping the globe in 1918, it targeted young, healthy people with vigorous immune systems, killing between 70 and 100 million people. Infected with catastrophic fevers and severe respiratory infections, many sufferers literally drowned in their own blood and fluids. Advancing German troops, exposed to the elements in an unusually wet spring and malnourished because of the British blockade, proved far more susceptible than well-fed Allies quartered in trenches, houses, and barns.

Unity of command enabled the Allies to exploit the German plight. On July 18, Foch committed Allied reserves to a surprising counteroffensive. The German lines shuddered and fell back. After four years of brutal war, they lacked the manpower reserves to blunt the Allied assault, and in technological development they had fallen fatally behind. Technology, which in 1914 had favored the defensive, now provided the attacker with the tank as a means of destroying trenches. The Allies had produced more than a thousand quality tanks, while the Germans had built about fifty inferior ones.

Bulgaria's surrender dooms the Central Powers

Ludendorff tried unsuccessfully to stabilize his front, but German forces were demoralized by defeat, weakened by disease, terrified by Allied tanks, and disheartened by the prospect of continuing American arrivals. Foch threw everything he had into a broad-front assault on September 26; two days later Ludendorff's nerve cracked, and he decided to ask the Kaiser to seek an armistice. One day after that, Germany's ally Bulgaria asked for an armistice on the Balkan Front. With Bulgaria out of the war, Allied forces could drive northwest from the Balkans into Austria-Hungary, defenseless there since it had committed all its troops to the Italian Front. Austria's collapse would open a "back door" into Germany, which lacked sufficient reserves to defend a new front. Bulgaria's surrender was the final blow. The war in Europe was nearly over.

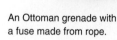

Decision in Southwest Asia

In Southwest Asia, the Great War was ending as well. In entering the war on the side of the Central Powers, the Ottoman Empire had committed itself to more than its limited infrastructure and industrial base could support. An Ottoman attack on Russia through the Caucasus Mountains in December 1914 proved disastrous, as more than thirty thousand Turks died of frostbite and the Russians counterattacked successfully. The campaign was catastrophic not only for the Ottomans but also for their Armenian subjects.

The Russian army's counteroffensive included a division of Christian Armenians, who reportedly massacred the inhabitants of several Turkish villages. This alleged atrocity, coupled with the April 1915 declaration of a secessionist Armenian government backed by the Russians, caused many Turks to doubt the loyalty of people of Armenian

An Ottoman grenade with a fuse made from rope.

descent. Between 1915 and 1918, according to many historians, half a million Armenians were deported to Mesopotamia, while more than a million were murdered outright or died of disease and starvation during forced marches across desert regions. The scholarly and political disputes over how many were killed and whether or not these actions constituted **genocide,** the deliberate and systematic destruction of an entire race or ethnic group, pale beside the immensity of the human tragedy that befell the Armenians.

The Turkish victory at Gallipoli in 1915 did not cure the vulnerability of the empire. Continuing warfare in the Caucasus brought many casualties and little gain. In 1916, Hussein ibn Ali, Sherif of Mecca, protector of the Holy Places of Islam, placed himself at the head of an Arab revolt that immediately threatened Ottoman control of Palestine and Arabia. A British liaison officer, Colonel T. E. Lawrence, offered tactical advice to the Arabs and rode into history as "Lawrence of Arabia." But the heavy fighting against the Ottomans was done by an army of Britons, Australians, and New Zealanders based in Egypt, and an army of Indians fighting in Mesopotamia.

Indian and British forces in Mesopotamia took Baghdad in 1917 and Mosul the following year, threatening Ottoman petroleum resources (Map 31.5). In Palestine, the Egyptian-based army of General Allenby took Jerusalem in December 1917 and by September 1918 was confronting Turkish forces at Megiddo, the "Armageddon"

The Ottoman Empire collapses

MAP **31.5**   The Great War in Southwest Asia, 1917–1918

The Ottoman Empire, attacked from three sides, finally cracked under the strain in 1918. Note that Indian and British troops, moving up the Tigris and Euphrates valleys, conquered Mesopotamia and compromised Ottoman petroleum supplies. An Arab army in Palestine and Syria weakened the southern flank and helped British forces, moving north from Egypt, to break through at Megiddo and force the Ottomans to capitulate on October 30, 1918. Why did the Ottoman Empire, known for a century as the "sick man of Europe," succeed in holding out for so long?

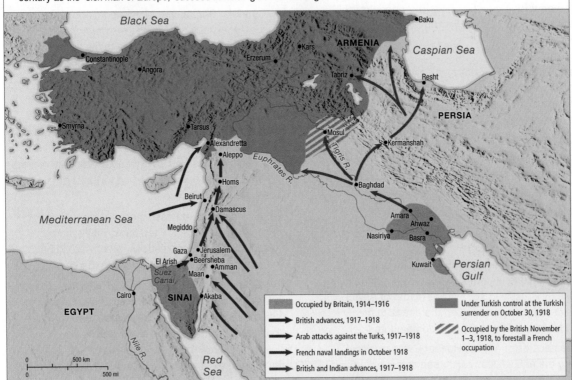

referred to in the Bible. Allenby's forces won at Megiddo, broke through Turkish lines, and forced the Ottoman Empire to sign an armistice on October 30. Together with Bulgaria's surrender in September, this left Germany and Austria-Hungary isolated and desperate.

The Path to the Armistice

Ending the war formally took until early November. The Kaiser decided to ask for a truce on the basis of the Fourteen Points, a plan for a just peace outlined by Wilson in January 1918 (see "Woodrow Wilson, The Fourteen Points"). But for Wilson, who had led America into the war "to make the world safe for democracy," no government led by an emperor could be sufficiently democratic. On October 16 he issued conditions that implied that the Kaiser should abdicate. William II, outraged, resisted until November 9. By then Austria-Hungary had also surrendered, and Germany's army continued to retreat toward its own frontier.

Now the weakening of German morale proved decisive. Sailors of Germany's High Seas Fleet mutinied when admirals asked them to put to sea to fight the British Grand Fleet and go down with honor. Faced with desertion and civil war, the German High Command informed the Kaiser that the army would no longer defend his regime. Disbelieving to the last, William went into exile in neutral Holland, where he lived quietly until 1941, dying a year after Nazi Germany invaded and subjugated the country that had welcomed him.

DOCUMENT 31.2 Woodrow Wilson, The Fourteen Points

In January 1918, U.S. president Woodrow Wilson outlined what he hoped would be viewed as the foundation upon which a just and lasting peace might be established. His outline became known as the Fourteen Points.

I. Open covenants of peace, openly arrived at, after which there shall be no private international understandings of any kind but diplomacy shall proceed always frankly and in the public view.

II. Absolute freedom of navigation upon the seas . . .

III. The removal, so far as possible, of all economic barriers and the establishment of an equality of trade conditions among all the nations . . .

IV. Adequate guarantees given and taken that national armaments will be reduced to the lowest point consistent with domestic safety . . .

VIII. All French territory should be freed and the invaded portions restored, and the wrong done to France by Prussia in 1871 in the matter of Alsace-Lorraine, which has unsettled the peace of the world for nearly fifty years, should be righted . . .

X. The peoples of Austria-Hungary, whose place among the nations we wish to see safeguarded and assured, should be accorded the freest opportunity to autonomous development.

XI. Rumania, Serbia, and Montenegro should be evacuated; occupied territories restored; Serbia accorded free and secure access to the sea; and the relations of the several Balkan states to one another determined by friendly counsel among historically established lines of allegiance and nationality . . .

XII. The Turkish portion of the present Ottoman Empire should be assured a secure sovereignty, but the other nationalities which are now under Turkish rule should be assured an undoubted security of life and an absolutely unmolested opportunity of autonomous development . . .

XIII. An independent Polish state should be erected which should include the territories inhabited by indisputably Polish populations, which should be assured a free and secure access to the sea . . .

XIV. A general association of nations must be formed under specific covenants for the purpose of affording mutual guarantees of political independence and territorial integrity to great and small states alike.

SOURCE: Woodrow Wilson, The Fourteen Points (1918).

Armistice talks were proceeding as William left. Having appealed for a truce on the basis of the Fourteen Points, the German government was appalled at the severity of the terms actually offered. Germany was required to evacuate all occupied territory, abandon German territory west of the Rhine River, repudiate the Treaty of Brest-Litovsk, surrender all its ships and massive amounts of military equipment, and agree to **reparations**, payments to compensate the Allies for war damages. These terms were imposed on a nation devastated by the influenza pandemic and literally starving from the effects of the British blockade, a continuing act of war for which no ending date was set.

That condition transformed the truce into an outright surrender. An **armistice** is a temporary cessation of hostilities between warring powers, but the continuing blockade, weakening Germany's ability to resist with each passing day, effectively made it impossible for Germany to resume fighting. When bells rang throughout Europe and America at 11:00 AM. Greenwich Mean Time on November 11—the eleventh hour on the eleventh day of the eleventh month of 1918—they tolled not merely an armistice, but the actual end of the Great War.

The Great War is ended by an armistice

CHAPTER
REVIEW

Putting It in Perspective

With the end of the Great War, later called World War I, Europe's long nightmare seemed over. The conflict's crushing impact had fallen mostly on Europe, which at the close of 1918 lay demoralized, devastated, and in many ways transformed. The royal houses of Germany, Austria-Hungary, and Russia had been overthrown, and the Ottoman sultan would soon follow. Austria-Hungary and the Ottoman Empire had broken apart, the former into small national states, the latter into a Turkish national state and regions that became virtual colonies of Britain and France. Marxism had come to power in Russia, frightening capitalist nations everywhere and heightening postwar anxieties. The war toppled dynasties and changed the way in which Europe was organized.

For more than nine million soldiers, the organization of Europe was irrelevant: they were dead. The casualty lists dwarfed even those of the Napoleonic Wars. But for many who had not served at the front, the death toll was less devastating than the living human wreckage. Men without limbs and without faces haunted the cities of Europe, surviving hideous wounds that in earlier wars would have killed them on the battlefield. Tens of thousands suffered from shell shock, a debilitating psychological condition stemming from prolonged exposure to artillery bombardment. Civilians, particularly in Germany, had suffered terribly from malnutrition and exposure, factors that fed the enormous death tolls in the influenza pandemic. The result was a demographic void, an absence of healthy young men between the ages of 18 and 35 that would scar Europe for two generations.

The physical destruction of land and property was unprecedented. Trench warfare wrecked vast areas of northeastern France. Unexploded shells and munitions lay in fields across Europe, maiming curious children into the 1960s. Livestock had been blown to bits or butchered for food in colossal numbers; replacing them would take decades. The task of rebuilding was daunting.

Finally, the prospect of another such war altered the perspectives of traumatized Europeans. Nearly everyone agreed that such a catastrophe must never be allowed to happen again, but how could it be prevented? Could the nations of Europe bury their hatreds along with their dead and learn to work together for stability and peace? The answers to these questions were not immediately apparent, and in the silence created by their absence, the nightmare lived on.

Reviewing Key Material

KEY CONCEPTS

Triple Alliance, 719

Bloody Sunday, 722

soviet, 722

Duma, 722

Diplomatic Revolution of 1890–1907, 723

Triple Entente, 723

Bosnian Crisis of 1908–1909, 723

blank check, 724

trench warfare, 726

U-boats, 728

Zimmermann Note, 735

Provisional Government, 737

Petrograd Soviet, 737

Bolsheviks, 737

nationalization, 738

genocide, 741

reparations, 743

armistice, 743

KEY PEOPLE

Franz Ferdinand, 719, 724

Otto von Bismarck, 719

Kaiser William II, 720

Tsar Nicholas II, 722

Sergei Witte, 722

Gavrilo Princip, 724

Paul von Hindenburg, 726

Erich Ludendorff, 726

Erich von Falkenhayn, 727

Mustafa Kemal, 728

Philippe Pétain, 729

Alexei Brusilov, 729

Paul von Lettow-Vorbeck, 733

Jan Christiaan Smuts, 733

Woodrow Wilson, 734

Georges Clemenceau, 735

Empress Alexandra, 736

Rasputin, 736

V. I. Lenin, 737

Leon Trotsky, 738

Lavr Kornilov, 738

Alexander Kerensky, 738

Ferdinand Foch, 740

Hussein ibn Ali, 741

ASK YOURSELF

1. Why wasn't the Crisis of July 1914 resolved peacefully, as so many earlier crises had been?
2. Why was the Great War so much more protracted than earlier wars in the 19th century? Why was it so much more deadly?

3. How did the strains of modernization and war weaken the Russian monarchy? Why did the Bolsheviks triumph in Russia in 1917?
4. Why did the Allies eventually win the Great War?

GOING FURTHER

Barry, John. *The Great Influenza.* 2003.

Beckett, Ian. *The Great War, 1914–1918.* 2001.

Eksteins, Modris. *Rites of Spring: The Great War and the Birth of the Modern Age.* 1989.

Ferguson, Niall. *The Pity of War.* 2000.

Ferro, Marc. *The Great War, 1914–1918.* 1993.

Fitzpatrick, Sheila. *The Russian Revolution, 1917–1932.* 2nd ed. 1994.

Florinsky, Michael. *The End of the Russian Empire.* 1961.

Fromkin, David. *Europe's Last Summer.* 2004.

Fussell, Paul. *The Great War and Modern Memory.* 1977.

Gatrell, Peter. *Government, Industry and Rearmament in Russia, 1900–1914.* 1994.

Gilbert, Martin. *The First World War: A Complete History.* 1996.

Hasegawa, Tsuyoshi. *The February Revolution: Petrograd, 1917.* 1981.

Holquist, P. *Making War, Forging Revolution.* 2002.

Joll, James. *The Origins of the First World War.* 2nd ed. 1992.

Keegan, John. *The First World War.* 1999.

Langer, William. *European Alliances and Alignments, 1871–1890.* 1977.

Neiberg, Michael. *Fighting the Great War: A Global History.* 2005.

Stevenson, David. *Cataclysm: The First World War as Political Tragedy.* 2004.

Strachan, Hew. *The First World War: To Arms.* 2001.

Tuchman, Barbara. *The Guns of August.* 1962.

Wohl, Robert. *The Generation of 1914.* 1979.

Key Dates and Developments

1890–1907	The Diplomatic Revolution
1894–1917	Reign of Nicholas II in Russia
1904	Anglo-French Entente
1904–1905	Russo-Japanese War
1905	Russian Revolution of 1905
1907	Anglo-Russian Entente
1908–1914	European crises
1914	The Great War begins Deadlock develops on Western Front
1915	Italy enters the war Sinking of the *Lusitania* Landing at Gallipoli

1916	Battle of Verdun The Somme Offensive The Brusilov Offensive
1917	Fall of the Russian monarchy (March) United States enters the war Mutinies in the French army Bolshevik Revolution in Russia (November)
1918	Treaty of Brest-Litovsk Great March Offensive Global influenza pandemic Armistice (November 11)

PEARSON myhistorylab™ Connections

Reinforce what you learned in this chapter by studying the many documents, images, maps, review tools, and videos available at www.myhistorylab.com.

Read and Review

✔• Study and Review Chapter 31

📖• Read the Document

Excerpt from *Four Weeks in the Trenches, Fritz Kreisler,* p. 727

Bolshevik Seizure of Power, 1917, p. 738

🔍• View the Image

Early Russian Factory, p. 722

Soviet Poster, 1917, p. 737

((•• Listen to the Audio

World War I, p. 723

Research and Explore

👁• Watch the Video

Video Lectures: The Outbreak of World War I, p. 724

🔍• View the Map

Map Discovery: A Typical British Trench System, p. 727

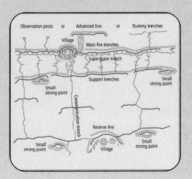

((•• Listen to the Chapter Audio for Chapter 31 on myhistorylab.com

Anxieties and Ideologies of the Interwar Years, 1918–1939

32

((•—[Listen to the **Chapter Audio** for Chapter 32 on **myhistorylab.com**

- What changes occurred in Western society and culture in the interwar years?

- What challenges disrupted Western societies and how did these societies respond?

- How and why did dictatorships arise in Italy, Russia, Germany, and elsewhere?

- Why and how did new forms of nationalism arise in Africa and Asia?

An Age of Anxiety

Anxieties abounded in the interwar years, as long-held standards of behavior, art, and science seemed to disappear. This famous "surrealist" painting, *The Treachery of Images,* proclaims in French that "This is not a pipe"—making the point that perceptions of "reality" are deceiving. It is, after all, a *painting,* not a pipe (see page 751).

In December 1918, Woodrow Wilson was greeted in Paris by seas of flags and flowers, and warmly cheered by enormous crowds as he rode in an open carriage. Earlier that year, declaring his objectives in the Great War, the American president had listed Fourteen Points (page 742). They included such idealistic goals as open peace talks, freedom of the seas, free trade, arms control, and **national self-determination**—the right of each nationality to freely decide its own political status. In November, Germany had agreed to a war-ending armistice based on his Fourteen Points. Now, as he arrived for the Paris Peace Conference that would shape the postwar world, Wilson was the man of the hour, a prophet whose idealism fed people's hopes for a fair and enduring peace. The hopes and dreams of a war-weary world rested on his shoulders.

Dictatorships

Soon, however, world events dampened these hopes and dreams. At the peace conference, beginning in January 1919, Allied leaders, bent on punishing defeated foes, resisted Wilson's idealism. Britain and France sought to weaken Germany by imposing huge reparations payments. The Italians demanded lands secretly promised them when they joined the war, and then went home enraged when Wilson and others rejected their demands. In April, in Amritsar, India, British-led troops shot hundreds of anti-British protesters, dimming hopes for self-determination in Europe's Asian colonies. In May, Chinese students in Beijing, angered that the conference permitted Japan to take over German claims in China, began a mass movement heralding the rise of Chinese nationalism and Communism. In June, outside Paris, at the Palace of Versailles, subdued German delegates signed a harsh treaty imposed by the conference, while flags across Germany flew at half-mast to mark the nation's resentment. In September, back in America, exhausted by futile efforts to promote the Versailles Treaty there, Wilson suffered a paralyzing stroke.

Western Democracies, Colonies, Dominions

Animosities enduring from the war—and from the peace imposed at Paris—would contribute two decades later to a Second World War. In the interwar era (1919–1939), nations East and West were torn by cultural and social changes, the global economy was rocked by depression, and radical new ideologies reshaped Europe, Africa, and Asia. So unsettling was this era that later observers called it the Age of Anxiety.

Western Society and Culture in an Age of Anxiety

The Great War devastated Europe, physically and emotionally. The lands where it was fought, strewn with mines and scarred by trenches, would take decades to recover, while the loss in human potential caused by its countless casualties was incalculable. Prewar faith in progress, driven by new technologies, died in the trenches as new technologies helped produce inhuman slaughter. As hope and idealism gave way to fatalism and cynicism, challenging new ideas, combined with social and cultural changes, added to the anxieties of the interwar years.

The Rise of Relativism and Relativity

((•—[Listen to the Audio

Post War 1

on **myhistorylab.com**

Especially unsettling was a growing attitude of **relativism**, the view that truth and morality vary from one person, group, or situation to another. People in the West had long presumed that absolute standards of truth and morality existed, and that human reason, aided by divine revelation, could distinguish fact from falsehood and good from evil. But by the 1920s, with faith in Western ideals shaken by the war, many were coming to feel that all certainties had vanished. Much as "beauty is in the eye of the beholder," what was true for one person might be false for another, and what was wrong in some cultures or conditions might be acceptable in others.

Some 19th-century thinkers (Chapter 27) had laid the foundations for such relativism. Karl Marx, for example, held that human society was based on class struggle, and that violent rebellion was not a moral evil but a necessary part of that struggle. Indeed, to many Marxists and followers of other ideologies, a statement's truth or an action's morality depended on whether or not it advanced their cause. Herbert Spencer and the Social Darwinists, who applied the notion of "survival of the fittest" to human societies, also saw struggle as essential, but unlike Marxists they claimed that the strong must naturally prey on the weak. To them, the struggle for survival, which justified almost any action advancing one's nation or race, superseded truth and morality. And German philosopher Friedrich Nietzsche, questioning the existence of objective truth and morality, proclaimed that "God is dead," by which he apparently meant that modern science and secular society had effectively killed Christianity and its moral values.

Relative thinking challenges traditional morality

In the 20th century, new understandings of human psychology further challenged conventional attitudes about truth and morality. Austrian psychiatrist Sigmund Freud (*FROID*), disputing the idea that human behavior is based on rational decisions, held that people are driven by unconscious instincts and impulses that conflict with the conscious mind. Freud's ideas—including his focus on human drives for sexual pleasure, his rejection of religious scruples, and his concept of a death wish that clashes with self-preservation instincts—suggested that, since human behaviors are induced by unconscious urges, there can be no absolute moral standards.

Another form of relativism revolutionized physics, whose laws had seemed so constant since the time of Isaac Newton. In 1905 and 1916, Albert Einstein, a German scientist of Jewish descent, published his theories of **relativity**, asserting that measurements of time, space, and motion vary with the perspectives of observers (see "Einstein on Relativity"). To explain his concepts, Einstein used

Albert Einstein.

DOCUMENT 32.1 Einstein on Relativity

In the excerpts below, Albert Einstein uses examples based on moving trains to help demonstrate his theories of relativity. How and why did his theories revolutionize science?

It is not clear what is to be understood . . . by "position" and "space." I stand at the window of a railway carriage which is travelling uniformly, and drop a stone on the embankment, without throwing it. Then, disregarding the influence of the air resistance, I see the stone descend in a straight line. A pedestrian who observes . . . from the footpath notices that the stone falls to earth in a parabolic curve. I now ask: Do the "positions" traversed by the stone lie "in reality" on a straight line or on a parabola? . . . With the aid of this example it is clearly seen that there is no such thing as an independently

existing trajectory . . . , but only a trajectory relative to a particular body of reference . . .

. . . In order to attain the greatest possible clearness, let us return to our example of the railway carriage supposed to be travelling uniformly . . . Let us imagine a raven flying through the air in such a manner that its motion, as observed from the embankment, is uniform and in a straight line. If we were to observe the flying raven from the moving railway carriage, we should find that the motion of the raven would be one of different velocity and direction, but that it would still be uniform and in a straight line . . .

SOURCE: Albert Einstein, *Relativity: The Special and General Theory (1920) III.* "Space and Time in Classical Mechanics"; V "The Principle of Relativity (In the Restricted Sense)".

Einstein asserts that measurements of time and space are relative

illustrations based on moving trains. If a man drops a stone from a moving train, for example, he will see the stone fall in a straight line (ignoring wind resistance), but an observer on the ground will see the stone fall in a curve. Similarly, if a bird flies by in a straight line, the man on the train will see it flying with a different speed and direction than observed by the person on the ground. The stone's path and the bird's speed and direction are thus relative to the location and movement of the two observers.

Einstein asserts that matter can be converted into energy

In his famous formula $E = mc^2$ (energy equals mass times the speed of light squared), Einstein proposed that matter could be converted into energy, asserting that each atom of matter contains enormous energy in its nucleus. By the 1940s, scientists would split the atoms of radioactive elements, such as uranium and plutonium, to release their nuclear energy and develop atomic bombs (Chapter 33). In showcasing science's vast creative and destructive powers, scientists helped to further blur distinctions between good and bad.

All these new ideas added to the age's uncertainties. If truth and morality varied according to one's situation and psychology, if time and space varied according to one's perspective, and if even solid-looking matter consisted of energy particles, how could humans ever trust their judgments? Human judgments, after all, had led to the Great War.

Technology and Popular Culture

New technologies transform Western popular culture

Meanwhile, as new ideas transformed people's perspectives, new technologies transformed their everyday lives. In the 1920s, especially in the West, the growing use of radios, phonographs, movies, telephones, electric appliances, and automobiles gave rise to whole new forms of popular culture. Radios, for example, enabled sports fans to follow their favorite teams, feeding a growing frenzy for spectator sports. Radios and phonograph records helped millions enjoy new forms of popular music, including blues and jazz. And millions went to movies each week—especially after 1927, when films with sound, pioneered by an immensely popular American movie called *The Jazz Singer*, began replacing silent films.

Telephones, refrigerators, and washing machines made life easier for many, but the most influential new mass-market product was the automobile. To expedite production, American automaker Henry Ford used the **assembly line**, making vehicles by conveying them in a continuous flow through a series of workstations that each performed a single function. This system enabled Ford to mass-produce millions of inexpensive cars, known as Model Ts, at prices affordable to ordinary people.

Mass-produced cars and trucks foster regional and global connections

As other manufacturers, following Ford's lead, used assembly lines to package foods and make appliances, mass-produced goods and vehicles transformed Western societies. Roads were paved and expanded to accommodate cars and trucks, and dotted with gasoline stations, supplying fuel from oil-rich regions such as Texas, the Dutch East Indies, and the Persian Gulf. Rural residents drove cars to town to shop or attend movies, while city people used cars for weekend drives to the countryside or beach. Farmers plowed fields with motorized tractors, while townsfolk ate produce brought daily by motor trucks. Nations were knit together by new technologies, as autos reduced distances and expanded regional contacts, while radio programs, newscasts, movies, and sports reached millions, helping to foster a sense of national culture.

New technologies also were used to build political support. Radio transmitted "fireside chats" by British prime minister Stanley Baldwin and U.S. president Franklin Roosevelt, as well as fiery speeches by Italian dictator Benito Mussolini and Germany's Adolf Hitler. In the 1920s, movies such as *Battleship Potemkin*, by Soviet film pioneer Sergei Eisenstein, rallied support for Communism by exalting Russia's revolutionary past; in the 1930s, films such as *Triumph of the Will*, by German female filmmaker Leni Riefenstahl, showcased mass glorification of Hitler.

Cars on Florida beach in the 1920s.

Changes in the Role of Women

Riefenstahl's filmmaking career was but one example of the new roles played by women in the postwar West. Following the Great War, women in Britain, Germany, Poland, Russia, and America received voting rights, partly in response to decades of activism promoting women's suffrage and partly in recognition of the work done by women who took jobs in industry when the men were off at war. Although most women gave up these jobs after the war, some stayed on to pursue careers in industry and business formerly closed to women, while those returning to the home often did so with a new assertiveness based on their wartime work experience.

Changing women's roles were also reflected in new fashions and behaviors. Freeing themselves from confining corsets that accentuated breasts and hips, some young women became "flappers" (or, in Mexico, "pelonas") sporting short hair, short skirts, and straight-fit styles emphasizing boyish figures. Liberated by automobiles from parental supervision, single young women and men went on dates to movies and dances, smoked cigarettes in public, and in cars engaged in sexual conduct their parents surely would have frowned on.

Expanding roles for women affect fashions and social conduct

Flapper fashions in 1920s included shorter swimsuits.

Architecture, Art, and Literature

New trends and technologies also affected architecture, art, and literature. By the early 20th century, growing use of cranes, elevators, structural steel, and reinforced concrete helped architects design larger and taller buildings than before. Devising new styles based on simplicity and function, architects such as Germany's Walter Gropius and his Bauhaus (*BOUW-house*) school created elegant but practical structures in cities from America to India. Cities became assortments of cubic structures, from large block-shaped buildings to soaring urban skyscrapers.

New art forms were likewise inspired by new urban realities and by global connections forged in the imperial age. Before the Great War, some European artists, influenced by Japanese art that disregarded perspective and realism, experimented with **impressionism**, depicting impressions made on the painter by scenes from nature and modern urban life. Inspired by cubic urban structures and by African art forms, Spanish-French painter Pablo Picasso created **cubism**, an artistic style using geometric shapes to produce bold images. After the war German artist Otto Dix used ghastly images to capture war's nightmare and postwar social decadence, while Picasso and others embraced **surrealism**—art that sought to challenge perceptions (see page 747) or to portray Freud's unconscious world of drives, fantasies, and dreams. As "modernism" rejected traditional values, and "modern art" depicted subjective impressions instead of objective reality, artistic standards, like moral norms and scientific theories, were revolutionized by relativism.

Global connections and urban realities impact architecture and art

Three Musicians, a cubist painting by Picasso.

New literary methods also violated traditional standards. In his novel *Ulysses* (1922), for example, Ireland's James Joyce used a stream of consciousness technique, later adopted by others, to depict the free and ungrammatical flow of a character's inner thoughts and impressions. And American poet e. e. cummings shunned such conventions as rhyme, meter, and capitalization.

Other writers and poets reflected the age's anxieties. In a two-volume work, *The Decline of the West* (1918 and 1922), German educator Oswald Spengler claimed that Western civilization, having undergone cycles of growth and development like other

Literature and poetry reflect new techniques and global anxieties great cultures before it, was now in decline and decay. In the 1929 novel *All Quiet on the Western Front*, German author Erich Maria Remarque depicted the ordeals of a group of young men who joined the German army in the Great War expecting to find honor and glory, but instead found only death, degradation, mutilation, and madness. In *The Waste Land* (1922), British-American poet T. S. Eliot provided bleak, grotesque images of desolation, death, and despair. And in *The Second Coming* (1921), Irish poet W. B. Yeats cogently captured the era's pervasive pessimism:

> Things fall apart; the center cannot hold;
>
> Mere anarchy is loosed upon the world,
>
> The blood-dimmed tide is loosed, and everywhere
>
> The ceremony of innocence is drowned;
>
> The best lack all conviction, while the worst
>
> Are full of passionate intensity.

Democracy, Depression, and Dictatorship

Yeats's pessimism proved prophetic. In the interwar years, efforts to achieve an enduring peace proved elusive. Hopes gave way to resentments, prosperity gave way to depression, and democracies gave way to dictatorships—often driven by men and ideologies full of passionate intensity.

The Versailles Settlement

In 1919 the victorious powers—led by U.S. president Woodrow Wilson, British prime minister David Lloyd George, and French premier Georges Clemenceau (*klā-mahn-SŌ*)—dominated the Paris Peace Conference cited at the start of this chapter. Excluded from the conference were the defeated powers, Germany and its allies, as well as the new Soviet Russia. The result was a settlement devised and imposed by the victors.

Great War victors impose harsh treaties on the vanquished

Although the victors imposed a treaty on each defeated country (Germany, Austria, Hungary, Bulgaria, and Ottoman Turkey), the centerpiece of the settlement was the Treaty of Versailles with Germany. A compromise between Wilson, who had promised a just peace, and his allies, who sought retribution from their defeated foes, it blamed the Germans for the war and forced them to pay huge reparations for war damage. Germany also had to reduce its army to one hundred thousand men, surrender land to Belgium, France, Denmark, and Poland, demilitarize its Rhineland region bordering Belgium and France, and give up all its overseas colonies. When the treaty was signed on June 28, 1919, exactly five years after the shots at Sarajevo that triggered the Great War, the starved, exhausted Germans bitterly resented the harsh pact forced upon them.

Treaties form League of Nations, but U.S. fails to join

At Wilson's insistence, the treaties also created the **League of Nations**, an international organization designed to maintain peace by cooperation among its members, intended eventually to include most of the world's nations. It opened in 1920 but was weakened by the absence of Wilson's own country. The U.S. Senate, wary of foreign commitments, rejected Wilson's dream by failing to ratify the Versailles Treaty. The world's richest nation thus did not join the League.

▶ Read the **Document**

The Covenant of the League of Nations, 1924,

on **myhistorylab.com**

Former German colonies and Ottoman provinces became **League of Nations mandates**, lands entrusted to victorious nations such as Britain, France, or Japan, allegedly to help prepare the people for self-rule. This formula allowed the victors to take over the possessions of the vanquished, including Arab lands in the Middle East, while paying lip service to Wilson's notion of national self-determination.

Britain and France manage former German and Ottoman possessions

Democracy and Dictatorship in Eastern Europe

Meanwhile, following the collapse of the Russian, German, and Austro-Hungarian empires during the Great War, numerous new nations emerged in Eastern Europe, formed by nationality groups long subject to these realms. The former Russian regions of Finland, Estonia, Latvia, and Lithuania became independent states. The Austro-Hungarian Empire was replaced by the smaller nations of Czechoslovakia, Austria, Hungary, and Yugoslavia, the last of which united the former empire's southernmost domains with its initial war enemy, Serbia. A new Poland, made up of lands from each of the three old empires, was linked to the Baltic Sea by a "Polish Corridor" that divided East Prussia from the rest of Germany. Prewar Romania doubled its size with territories taken from Russia and Austria-Hungary (Map 32.1).

The rise of these new nations at first appeared a triumph for democracy. All had democratic constitutions and elected parliaments. Even Hungary, after a short-lived

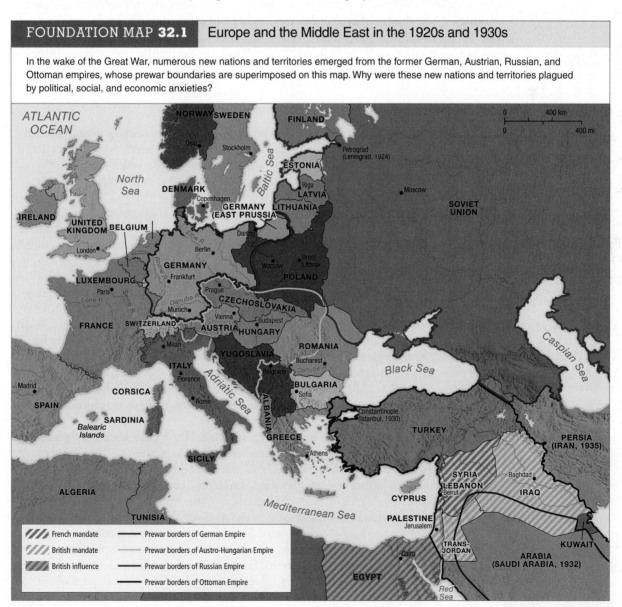

FOUNDATION MAP 32.1   Europe and the Middle East in the 1920s and 1930s

In the wake of the Great War, numerous new nations and territories emerged from the former German, Austrian, Russian, and Ottoman empires, whose prewar boundaries are superimposed on this map. Why were these new nations and territories plagued by political, social, and economic anxieties?

Communist regime in 1919, became a constitutional monarchy, as did Yugoslavia. But all had serious problems that soon subverted democracy.

Ethnic unrest and unemployment unsettle new democracies

One major problem was posed by ethnic minorities. Eastern Europe's nationalities were so intermingled that most of the new nations included many people who differed in language and loyalty from the majority. Poland and Czechoslovakia, for example, each contained many Germans, who often felt more loyal to Germany than to the country where they lived.

Another problem was unemployment, especially among former soldiers, some of whom formed bands of angry outcasts. With few skills other than fighting, they roamed the streets assaulting passers-by and staging periodic protests.

Fear of Communism aids the rise of dictatorships

The biggest problem, however, was fear of Communism. Living in the shadow of Soviet Russia, a huge realm that sought to promote Communist revolutions in other countries, most of the new nations soon deemed democracy too weak to combat the Soviet challenge. Fearful of Soviet power, and of Communist inroads among their own working classes, they restricted democratic rights and cracked down on dissent. By the early 1930s, all the new nations except Finland and Czechoslovakia were ruled by **dictators**, leaders who wielded total control, dominated weak elected institutions, and used the army and police to suppress dissent.

Fascism in Italy

Democracy's biggest setback in the 1920s came in Italy, a parliamentary monarchy and victor in the Great War. Many Italians felt betrayed by Allied leaders, who had secretly promised Italy some lands ruled by Austria when Italy joined the war, but failed at Versailles to fully honor this promise, on the grounds that secret agreements violated Wilson's Fourteen Points.

Anger at Allied "betrayal" and economic crises unsettle postwar Italy

Compounding Italian resentment was an economic crisis. High unemployment, especially among war veterans, led to working-class unrest, which Communists exploited to promote crippling strikes. When Italy's parliamentary democracy proved unable to control the situation, many Italians supported a new movement pledging to combat Communism and restore order.

This movement's leader was a former Socialist named Benito Mussolini, who became a rabid nationalist while serving in the Great War. Irate at the Allied snub of Italy in 1919, he formed a "fighting band," or *fascio di combattimento* (FAH-shō dē com-bat-ē-MEN-tō), of former soldiers like himself committed to combating Communism and advancing Italian nationalism. The term *fascio*, a bundle of rods like the ones ancient Romans used as symbols of their power, gave the movement its name. **Fascism** was an ideology that glorified the nation as an organic collective community under a powerful leader who embodied its will. Stressing military strength and repressing internal dissent, it subjected individual rights to the goals of the nation and its leader.

📖 **Read the Document**

Benito Mussolini, "The Political and Social Doctrine of Fascism"

on **myhistorylab.com**

Benito Mussolini.

Mussolini, a bald, burly, swaggering showman, sent his black-shirted fighting squads into the streets to beat up Communists and Socialists. These "Blackshirts" broke strikes and burned labor union headquarters, adding to the public crisis. In October 1922 Mussolini organized a "March on Rome" to intimidate the government. When King Victor Emanuel III, fearing civil war, refused to declare martial law so the army could fight the fascists, the prime minister and cabinet resigned. Anxious to restore order, the king then appointed Mussolini prime minister, confident that Italy's constitutional structure would keep him from gaining too much power.

The king was soon proven wrong. Granted emergency powers to restore order, Mussolini used them to enact a law giving two thirds of the seats in parliament to the party getting the most votes in an election. In 1924 elections, rigged by fascist thugs who threatened to beat up anyone who voted against fascism, his party got the votes it needed to govern alone. By the late 1920s, the fascists were the only party left.

Although he destroyed democracy, Mussolini was very popular. In place of political strife, he offered unity, efficiency, and popular programs. His "corporate state" divided the economy into 22 areas, each supervised by a "corporation" made up of business, labor, and government leaders, thus combining private ownership with state controls. He boasted of making trains run on time—although travelers frequently found them as late as ever. He provided public spectacles, including fiery speeches during which he often stripped to the waist and thumped his barrel chest as crowds chanted "Duce" (*DOO-chā*), Italian for "leader." In the 1930s, as economic depression rocked the world, his fascist methods were emulated elsewhere—most ominously, in Germany.

The Great Depression and Its Global Impact

By 1929, although suppressed in Italy and most of Eastern Europe, democracy remained strong in Western Europe and America. During the next decade, however, a disastrous economic depression threatened its survival even there.

The Great Depression of the 1930s was triggered by events in America, where an economic boom in the 1920s created an illusion of endless prosperity. Confident consumers bought autos, appliances, and other goods, frequently on credit. As businesses flourished, more and more people bought stocks, or shares in commercial enterprises. Often they did so "on margin," paying 10 percent of the stock's current price, borrowing the rest from their brokers, then selling the stock when prices rose, repaying their brokers and pocketing the profits.

Everyone seemed to make money—as long as prices rose. But in 1929, fears that stocks were overpriced led many investors to sell. The resulting decline in demand drove stock prices down, starting a chain reaction. As brokers lost money, they demanded full payment from their clients for stocks purchased on margin; to get the money, the clients had to sell stocks at a loss, further driving prices down. On October 24 ("Black Thursday") and October 29 ("Black Tuesday"), the bottom fell out of the New York Stock Exchange, with many stocks losing half their value.

The 1929 stock market crash shattered consumer confidence. Shaken Americans simply stopped buying, decreasing demand for goods, so manufacturers cut production and laid off workers—who thus no longer had incomes to buy goods, furthering the downward spiral. Banks were caught in the middle: ruined stock investors and laid-off workers could no longer make payments owed to banks for loans and mortgages, while cash-strapped depositors sought to withdraw all their money. Having loaned that money to others, from whom they could not collect, many banks were forced to close, causing many people to lose their life savings.

Other banks survived by demanding full repayment of loans made to European firms that had borrowed heavily from U.S. banks to finance the Great War and postwar recovery. To come up with the money, these firms laid off workers, resulting in mass unemployment—especially in Germany, where U.S. loans had been used extensively to finance reparations payments to France required by the Versailles Treaty.

Further American actions globalized the Great Depression. In 1930, to protect declining U.S. industries from foreign competition, Congress passed the Smoot-Hawley Tariff, placing huge duties on imports from other countries. Despite a signed appeal from a thousand American economists, warning that this tariff would ruin the world economy, President Herbert Hoover signed it into law. Globally sold goods, such as beef from Argentina, coffee from Brazil and Indonesia, and sugar from Brazil and the Caribbean, thus lost their American markets, causing economic crises in these countries.

Bread line during the Great Depression.

Depression and farming crisis deepen global suffering

View the **Image**

Migrant Mother, Great Depression

on **myhistorylab.com**

Depression undermines support for capitalism and democracy

Many regimes responded with **economic nationalism,** erecting tariff walls and trade barriers to protect their industries and products from international competition, and (in Latin America) with "import substitution industrialization," creating new industries to produce things they previously imported. The results were a further decline of world trade and global economic devastation.

The Great Depression thus became a global calamity. From 1929 to 1932, worldwide industrial production dropped 38 percent. In industrial countries unemployment ranged from 20 percent to 33 percent. Thousands lost homes as banks foreclosed on mortgages unpaid by jobless workers. In America, able-bodied people in the prime of life waited in line for rations of bread or sold apples for nickels on street corners; others committed suicide, or abandoned their families to become wandering, rootless "hoboes."

The suffering was worsened by a global agricultural crisis. Responding to food shortages in Europe during and after the Great War, North American farmers had expanded their output of wheat and other grains. But in the 1920s, as farming rebounded in Europe and agricultural advances brought higher crop yields, the resulting grain surplus caused prices to fall sharply. Then, in the 1930s, high rates of urban unemployment decreased demand for food, damaging agricultural economies and ruining farmers everywhere.

Capitalism and democracy were shaken. Support for radical movements grew the world over, as desperate people opted to sacrifice freedom for economic stability. Even in places with long traditions of political and economic freedom, people looked to government for solutions.

The New Deal in the United States

In America, where the crisis began, President Hoover was ill equipped to deal with the Depression. A staunch believer in free markets, he refused to support federal unemployment aid or economic intervention. Instead, he sought vainly to restore confidence by promising that prosperity was "just around the corner." As suffering mounted, he lost the 1932 election to Franklin D. Roosevelt, an engaging idealist who promised "a New Deal for the American people."

"FDR" proved a tireless activist whose infectious optimism and eloquence, enshrined in such memorable phrases as "the only thing we have to fear is fear itself," made him one of America's most effective presidents. Using government programs to relieve misery, increase buying power, and promote economic recovery, he infused new hope and created a consensus on behalf of activist government.

Roosevelt uses government intervention to combat Depression

Roosevelt proposed and Congress enacted numerous ambitious measures. A huge public works program, launched to provide jobs for the unemployed, built or rebuilt schools, highways, bridges, and public buildings. Subsidies to farmers helped them leave some fields unfarmed, reducing overproduction, which had undermined farm profits by driving prices down. Banks were regulated, deposits insured by the government, and buying stock on margin prohibited. A Civilian Conservation Corps sent jobless men into rural areas to plant trees and build hydroelectric dams on rivers such as the Tennessee and Columbia. Most enduring of all was the Social Security system, which provided government pensions for the aging and later also the disabled.

The results of the New Deal were mixed. On one hand, it may have saved American capitalism: the crisis was so severe that massive government spending was probably the only way to get money into circulation and reinvigorate industrial production. On the other hand, it did not end the Depression. Slow production gains were reversed by a 1937 recession. What ended unemployment in America was not the New Deal but World War II, which put millions to work producing war materials and serving in the armed forces.

The Civilian Conservation Corps at work, 1937.

But the New Deal's impact outweighed its failures. Vastly expanding the federal bureaucracy, it provided a new vision of democratic governance, summarized eloquently by Roosevelt himself: "Better the occasional errors of a government that cares about its citizens than the constant omissions of a government frozen in the ice of its own indifference." The New Deal abolished child labor, set minimum wages and maximum work hours, and guaranteed workers the right to bargain collectively. Its measures and methods, which mobilized government in support of the common people, endured and affected American society long after the Depression was over.

Roosevelt was loved and hated to a degree unmatched by other elected leaders. A wealthy man, he was reviled by the rich as a traitor to his class, while inspiring in ordinary people an affection so powerful it transcended politics. He styled himself "the champion of the forgotten man," and that description, endorsed by millions, gave him the moral authority to lead his nation through the Great Depression and Second World War.

Roosevelt's activism restores American hope

Democracy and Socialism in Western Europe

Unlike America, which before the Depression was averse to government activism and supremely self-confident, Western Europe had a history of social legislation (Chapter 27) and deep insecurities flowing from the Great War. European voters were thus open to socialist experiments.

Britain's new Labour Party, which had socialist ideals and labor union roots, twice won elections in the 1920s under Ramsay MacDonald, illegitimate son of a poor Scottish woman, who became Britain's first socialist prime minister. Assuming that role a second time in 1929, he, like Hoover, had to deal with the Great Depression. In 1931, as the crisis worsened, MacDonald formed at the king's request a coalition government of Labourites, Conservatives, and Liberals, abandoning radical socialism and splitting his own party. The new coalition adopted economic nationalism and cut spending on social programs, but these steps did not end the Depression. In 1935 the British turned to Stanley Baldwin, whose calm manner reassured them, but the economy did not recover until Neville Chamberlain, who replaced Baldwin as prime minister in 1937, increased defense spending, and introduced a military draft.

France in the interwar years, obsessed with recovery from the Great War and fearful of German resurgence, was beset by short-lived governments averaging less than a year. When depression hit in the early 1930s, fascist groups formed across the country, declaring democracy too weak to deal with the crisis, while scandals undermined the government's moral legitimacy.

In response came the Popular Front, a coalition of leftist parties that won the 1936 elections under Socialist Leon Blum. Elated workers launched a series of strikes that forced the new government to grant 12 percent wage increases, paid vacations, and a 40-hour workweek. But these progressive measures backfired, reducing production and scaring investors into withdrawing money from France's economy. The ensuing economic downturn undermined the Popular Front, and in 1937 Blum was voted out by the National Assembly. A series of weak coalition governments followed, leaving France ill equipped to meet the challenge of a resurgent Germany.

Western Europeans try various methods to restore prosperity

In Norway and Sweden, depression brought less misery than elsewhere. Elected socialist governments provided "cradle to grave" health and welfare benefits, supported by high taxes. Scandinavian socialism thus presented a viable democratic alternative to dictatorial Communism, practiced in Soviet Russia.

Communism in Russia

When Bolshevik Communists seized power in Russia in 1917, their aim was to spark an international revolution against world capitalism. But when no such upheaval occurred, they slowly transformed Marxist internationalism into Soviet nationalism: rather than promote a worldwide workers' rebellion, they focused on strengthening Soviet Russia as a socialist fatherland, tying Communism's global goals to Russia's national agenda.

THE RISE OF SOVIET NATIONALISM. The first step toward Soviet nationalism came in March 1918 when, ignoring his own party's pleas for an international Communist crusade, Soviet leader V. I. Lenin withdrew Russia from the Great War through the Brest-Litovsk Treaty with Germany. This action, designed to give the Soviets time to consolidate control in Russia, instead set off a Russian civil war. In it, a new "Red Army," created from scratch by Soviet War Commissar Leon Trotsky, fought the "White" armies, a coalition of anti-Communist Russians. The Allied Powers, hoping to get Russia back into the war against Germany, also sent troops to aid the Whites. But the various White armies were unable to coordinate their attacks, and Allied interest in Russia waned once the Great War ended. By early 1921, the Reds had emerged victorious.

Soviet poster from 1920s: "Bridge to a bright future."

But they had little to celebrate. The Great War and Russian civil war had totally ravaged Russia. Since 1913, its industrial output had dropped 80 percent, and farm output had been cut in half. Millions had died from war, disease, and starvation, capped by catastrophic famine in 1921.

Ever the realist, Lenin that year took another step back from global Communist revolution, instituting a New Economic Policy (NEP) that used capitalist methods to strengthen his Communist nation. Although the Soviet state kept control of foreign trade and major industries, which it had nationalized, NEP allowed smaller businesses (which made up most of the economy) to operate as private enterprises. Instead of seizing grain from peasants, as it did in the civil war, the regime imposed a tax in kind—a percentage of the harvest payable in grain. Peasants could sell what was left on the open market, giving them a potent (yet capitalistic) incentive to produce. Communist Russia also opened trade with capitalist Britain and Germany, acting like a traditional state, not a revolutionary regime. Indeed, in 1922, a new constitution created a federal state: the Union of Soviet Socialist Republics (USSR), or Soviet Union.

That year Lenin, only 52, suffered the first of several strokes that finally took his life in 1924. As he became incapacitated, many saw his most capable colleague, War Commissar Trotsky, as the likely new Soviet leader. But other Communists, annoyed by Trotsky's arrogance and fearful that he might use his control of the Red Army to become a military dictator, formed a coalition against him. It came to be dominated by Joseph V. Djugashvili (*joo-GAHSH-vē-lē*), general secretary of the Soviet Communist Party, who called himself the "Man of Steel": Stalin.

Joseph Stalin.

Stalin was a crude but effective organizer, good at getting things done. As general secretary, he set the party's agenda, ran its daily affairs, and appointed its local managers. While others grappled with major issues, he dealt with organizational affairs, quietly amassing power by staffing the party structure with his supporters. He also positioned himself as Lenin's heir by creating a cult to the late leader, marked by a marble mausoleum in Moscow and by the renaming of Petrograd (formerly Saint Petersburg) as Leningrad.

In 1925, after defeating and deposing Trotsky, the coalition crumbled. Afraid that Stalin was gaining too much power, his allies turned against him. But they were too late: with his control of the party, Stalin deftly ousted them, and by 1928 he had become a dictator.

Stalin's rise to dictatorship marked the triumph of Soviet nationalism. His defeated foes, as Marxist internationalists, saw NEP as a tactical retreat and were eager to resume the quest for world revolution. But Stalin, as a Soviet nationalist, insisted on **socialism in one country**, a program that focused on strengthening the USSR, while requiring Communists everywhere to put off world revolution and support the Soviet state.

Sidebar notes (left margin):

Civil war, won by Communists, devastates Russia

Lenin implements New Economic Policy to rebuild Russia

Lenin's illness and death set off a Soviet power struggle

Stalin's rise is a triumph for Soviet nationalism

Stalin nonetheless grew impatient with NEP. At first it had been successful, restoring production to prewar levels by the mid-1920s, but by 1928 economic progress had slowed. Fearful that the capitalist powers would soon move to crush his country, with its weak industrial base, Stalin decided that the USSR could not survive without rapid industrial growth.

Fearing capitalist powers, Stalin opts to industrialize rapidly

He also decided that he needed control of the grain harvest. Under NEP, like farmers in the West, Soviet peasants found that an oversupply of grain drove prices down. So rather than sell their grain at a loss, they hoarded it, hoping to push prices back up. This hoarding infuriated Stalin, who needed the grain to feed urban factory workers and to sell abroad for machines to build Soviet industry.

STALIN'S REVOLUTION. His response was the "Stalin Revolution," a mass campaign to reorganize farming and rapidly expand industry. It began in 1928 with the First Five Year Plan, an economic blueprint that set ambitious targets and timetables for industrial and agricultural output. In practice it produced a frenzied and forcible mobilization of Soviet society.

The agricultural reform, called collectivization, created a monstrous catastrophe. To gain control of the grain, Stalin forced peasants onto **collective farms**, multifamily farms supposedly owned by their members but actually run by the state, which took all the grain it needed to support industry. When self-reliant farmers resisted such collectivization, Stalin's regime called them "enemies of the people" and sent troops with machine guns to destroy them. As civil war swept Soviet Ukraine in the early 1930s, millions of resisters were shot or sent to prison camps in Siberia, where they were made to mine that region's resources under inhuman conditions. As the state's need for grain increased, moreover, it took most of the harvest, leaving farmers less than they needed for survival. The resulting forced famine killed five to ten million people.

Collectivization of farming causes catastrophic civil war and famine

Appalled by such atrocities, even loyal Communists began to see Stalin as a murderous monster. Fearful they might plot against him, in the mid-1930s the Soviet dictator decided to destroy them. His police arrested numerous Communists and charged them with fabricated crimes, such as collaborating with enemy countries or supporting Trotsky, whom Stalin had driven into foreign exile in 1929. During the **Great Purges**, Stalin's systematic efforts to eliminate opponents in 1936–1938, dozens of party and military officials were placed on trial, forced to make false confessions, and summarily shot. Millions of other people were arrested and shipped to Siberia. Finally, in 1940, a Stalin henchman, using an ice ax, murdered Trotsky in Mexico.

Stalin's industrialization and terror regiment Soviet society

By then, Stalin had both industrialized and terrorized his nation. Through superhuman sacrifices by Soviet workers, combined with machinery purchased abroad using grain taken from the farmers, the USSR had become an industrial giant. But it scarcely resembled the "worker's paradise" envisioned by early socialists. Workers and peasants, in whose name the revolution was made, now lived in fear of the regime, working long harsh hours in factories and collective farms under brutal state control. To make their nation an industrial power, they paid a terrible price.

Giant Soviet steel mill of the 1930s.

But to Stalin there had been no choice: in order to survive, the Soviets had to overcome their backwardness at any cost. In a 1931 speech, responding to requests that he slow the pace of industrialization, he used Russian nationalism and fear of foreigners to justify his frantic approach:

No, comrades . . . , the pace must not be slackened . . . To slacken the pace would mean to lag behind; and those who lag behind are beaten . . . We are fifty or a hundred years behind the advanced countries. We must make good this lag in ten years. Either we do it or they crush us.

Stalin's fear of foreign attack proves prophetic

The Soviet dictator was paranoid, obsessed with real and imagined foes, but his speech proved prophetic. Ten years later, in 1941, his newly industrialized nation would face his ultimate fear: a massive invasion by a resurgent Germany.

National Socialism in Germany

Germany's path to dictatorship, like Russia's, was marked by economic woes, fears and resentments of foreigners, and a desire to strengthen the nation against outside interference. After more than a decade of democracy, in the 1930s Germany came under the control of a nationalist, racist, and militarist movement known as National Socialism, supporters of which were called **Nazis**.

War reparations and multiple parties weaken German democracy

THE FAILURE OF GERMAN DEMOCRACY. German democracy, initiated after the Great War, faced obstacles from the outset. One was an overabundance of political parties, making it hard for any to win a majority of seats in the Reichstag (*RĪKS-tahk*), Germany's elected assembly. Governing cabinets thus were usually multiparty coalitions, and the chancellors who headed these cabinets often found it hard to keep their coalitions together. Another was the fact that many Germans detested their new Weimar (*VĪ-mar*) Republic (named for the city where its constitution was drafted in 1919) for accepting the hated Versailles Treaty and its crippling reparations.

By 1923, unwilling to further offend Germans by raising taxes to fund the reparations, the cash-starved Weimar government had stopped making payments to France. When France responded by occupying Germany's industrial Ruhr Valley, German workers struck in protest; France in turn closed off the region, preventing delivery of food and goods to the striking workers. The government, forced by public opinion to pay the strikers' unemployment benefits, printed vast amounts of paper money, resulting in horrific inflation. By August, a loaf of bread cost millions of times what it had earlier that year, and workers were paid with bales of worthless bills. Millions of Germans thus lost their life savings.

Hitler and Nazis try to grab power during inflation crisis

During this crisis, an obscure rabble-rouser made a bid for power. Adolf Hitler, an embittered young Austrian who had served bravely in Germany's army during the Great War, had since become leader of the **National Socialist German Workers' Party**, a fringe group later called the Nazis. A spellbinding speaker, he trumpeted the myth that "undefeated" Germany had been "stabbed in the back" by traitors who accepted the peace terms, and he urged Germans to rearm and avenge the humiliation of Versailles. In November 1923 he launched a *putsch* (attempted power grab) in a Munich beer hall, firing a shot into the ceiling to signal the start of his rebellion.

But German democracy survived the 1923 crisis. The "Beer Hall Putsch" was quickly crushed and Hitler was jailed for a year, while the Reichstag found a strong leader in Gustav Stresemann (*SHTRĀ-zuh-mahn*). A pragmatic nationalist, Stresemann raised taxes, cut government spending, revalued the currency, and negotiated long-term low-interest loans from the United States. The inflation ended, payments resumed, and France withdrew from the Ruhr. In 1925 Stresemann negotiated the Locarno Treaties with France, Belgium, Poland, and Czechoslovakia, agreeing that Germans would not use force to change the 1918 borders, and in 1926 he brought Germany into the League of Nations. By the time he died in 1929, Germany seemed stable and prosperous, and Hitler's Nazis had faded into insignificance.

German woman fuels stove with worthless money during inflation crisis.

Great Depression strengthens support for Communism and Nazism

Then came the Great Depression. As struggling U.S. banks called in their loans, the German economy collapsed. Millions of Germans, frightened and unemployed, began voting for extremist parties. Hitler's promises to rearm Germany, renounce Versailles, and expel the Jews, whom he blamed for Germany's suffering, struck a responsive chord—as did German Communist Party promises of a full-employment workers' state. By 1932 the Nazis and Communists were two of the Reichstag's largest parties. In January 1933, when German capitalists and nationalists, terrified of a Communist takeover, opted to support the Nazis as a lesser evil, Hitler was appointed chancellor, heading a coalition of Nazis and small right-wing parties.

HITLER AND THE THIRD REICH. Having come to power by democratic means, Hitler soon destroyed German democracy. In February 1933, when the Reichstag building burned down, he obtained emergency powers to deal with the crisis. Accusing Communists of setting the fire (although some evidence pointed to the Nazis), Hitler got the Reichstag to ban the Communist Party. Then he dissolved the other parties one by one. By July Germany was a one-party state, which Hitler called the Third Reich (Third Empire).

The Nazis then regimented the rest of German society. Labor unions were dissolved into the Reich Labor Front, an association of labor and management delegates dominated by Nazi agents. A "national" Lutheran church was formed with the support of the regime, and a pact was made with the Catholic Church to ensure its rights in Germany if it avoided politics. Dissenting ministers and priests were then suppressed and sent to labor camps. Youth groups were absorbed into the Hitler Youth (for boys aged 9–18) and League of German Girls. A Ministry of Propaganda, headed by Josef Goebbels (*GEH'r-bulz*), took control of newspapers, magazines, radio stations, and film studios. Within months the Nazis controlled almost every aspect of German life.

Although the Third Reich was a dictatorship, with strict controls and concentration camps to confine dissenters, Hitler was popular with Germans. He united them as one, with himself as their *Führer* (leader). He restored their national pride, lost after the Great War, declaring them a "**Master Race**" descended from ancient Aryans and destined to dominate "subhuman Slavic races" by conquering *Lebensraum* (*LĀ-behnz-raowm*)—living space for Germany's growing population—in Poland and the USSR (see "Excerpts from Hitler's *Mein Kampf*").

Hitler exploited people's fears by promoting anti-Semitism, anti-Jewish hostility long present in Christian Europe. But his attacks were racial, not religious: he vilified Jews as an impure race that must not be allowed to pollute the German Master Race through intermarriage or illicit sex. Nazi laws deprived Jews of German citizenship and forbade Jews under penalty of death from having sex with "pure" Germans. On *Kristallnacht* (the Night of Broken Glass), November 9–10, 1938, Nazis instigated anti-Jewish riots, burning synagogues across Germany, destroying thousands of Jewish-owned shops, and killing nearly one hundred Jews. Mass Jewish emigration, prompted by such actions and promoted by Nazis seeking to make Germany *Judenrein* (free of Jews), reduced its Jewish population from 560,000 in 1933 to under 300,000 in 1939.

Hitler, meanwhile, restored German prosperity, putting jobless men to work building military equipment and great highways (*Autobahnen*) on which to transport it. He urged women to leave the work force, to free up jobs for men and enlarge the Master Race by having Aryan babies. He financed his costly projects with ten-year government bonds, vowing to repay them by plundering nations later conquered by Germany. His plans were thus based on a new European war to restore German dominance and reverse the "shameful" verdict of Versailles. That conflict, later called World War II, was not long in coming.

Hitler becomes chancellor and destroys German democracy

Watch the **Video**
Conformity and Opposition in Nazi Germany
on **myhistorylab.com**

Hitler promotes nationalism, racism, and anti-Semitism

Synagogue being burned during *Kristallnacht*.

Hitler borrows to build Germany, based on future war

DOCUMENT 32.2 Excerpts from Hitler's *Mein Kampf*

In Mein Kampf *(My Struggle), which he composed in prison after the failed "Beer Hall Putsch" of 1923, Adolf Hitler set forth his racist ideology. How did he justify hatred of Jews and military expansion at Russia's expense?*

. . . Nature's restricted form of propagation and increase is an almost rigid basic law . . .

The stronger must dominate and not blend with the weaker . . . Only the born weakling can view this as cruel . . .

The fox is always a fox, the goose a goose, the tiger a tiger . . . [Y]ou will never find a fox who . . . might, for example, show humanitarian tendencies toward geese, as similarly there is no cat with a friendly inclination toward mice . . .

No more than Nature desires the mating of weaker with stronger individuals, even less does she desire the blending of a higher with a lower race . . .

Historical experience . . . shows with terrifying clarity that in every mingling of Aryan blood with that of lower peoples the result was the end of the cultured people . . .

[I]t is no accident that the first cultures arose in places where the Aryan, in his encounters with lower peoples, subjugated them and bent them to his will . . .

As long as he ruthlessly upheld the master attitude, not only did he really remain master, but also the preserver and increaser of culture . . .

. . . The great leaders of Jewry are confident that . . . the Jews will devour the other nations of the earth . . .

[T]he Jew knows very well that he can undermine the existence of European nations by a process of racial bastardization . . .

And again the National Socialist movement has the mightiest task to fulfill.

It must open the eyes of the people . . . and it must remind them again and again of the true enemy of our present-day world . . . It must call eternal wrath upon the head of the foul enemy of mankind as the real originator of our sufferings.

It must make certain that . . . the mortal enemy is recognized and that the fight against him becomes a gleaming symbol . . .

Only an adequately large space on this earth assures a nation of freedom of existence . . .

[W]e National Socialists must . . . secure for the German people the land and soil to which they are entitled on this earth . . .

And so we . . . stop the endless German movement to the south and west, and turn our gaze toward the land in the east . . .

If we speak of soil in Europe today, we can primarily have in mind only Russia and her vassal border states. Here Fate itself seems desirous of giving us a sign. By handing Russia to Bolshevism, it robbed the Russian nation of that intelligentsia which . . . guaranteed its existence as a state . . . For centuries Russia drew nourishment from this Germanic nucleus . . . Today it . . . has been replaced by the Jew. Impossible as it is for the Russian by himself to shake off the yoke of the Jew . . . , it is equally impossible for the Jew to maintain the mighty empire forever. He himself is no element of organization, but a ferment of decomposition . . . And the end of Jewish rule in Russia will also be the end of Russia as a state . . .

New Varieties of Nationalism in Africa and Asia

While Stalin blended nationalism with Communism, and Hitler combined nationalism with racism, Africans and Asians adapted nationalism to their own conditions and cultures. As a result, in the interwar years, new forms of nationalism arose across Africa and Asia.

Nationalism and Anticolonialism in Africa

African nationalism arises in resistance to colonial rule

The Great War and Versailles settlement aided African nationalism, which was rooted in **anticolonialism,** or resistance to colonial rule. Taught by their European rulers to use European weapons against other Europeans, and exposed to Wilsonian ideals of national self-determination, Africans concluded they could use these weapons and ideals to fight European rule. But Europeans were still better armed, as shown by French slaughter of the Baya people in French Equatorial Africa (Map 32.2), who rebelled against forced railway labor in 1928–1931. So interwar African nationalism aimed for eventual rather than immediate independence.

MAP **32.2**   Africa in the 1920s and 1930s

Although nationalism spread among Africans during the interwar years, most of Africa remained under European rule. Note that even Ethiopia lost independence when it was invaded by Italy in 1935–1936. How did the Great War help to promote African nationalist movements? Why did they have limited success in the interwar years?

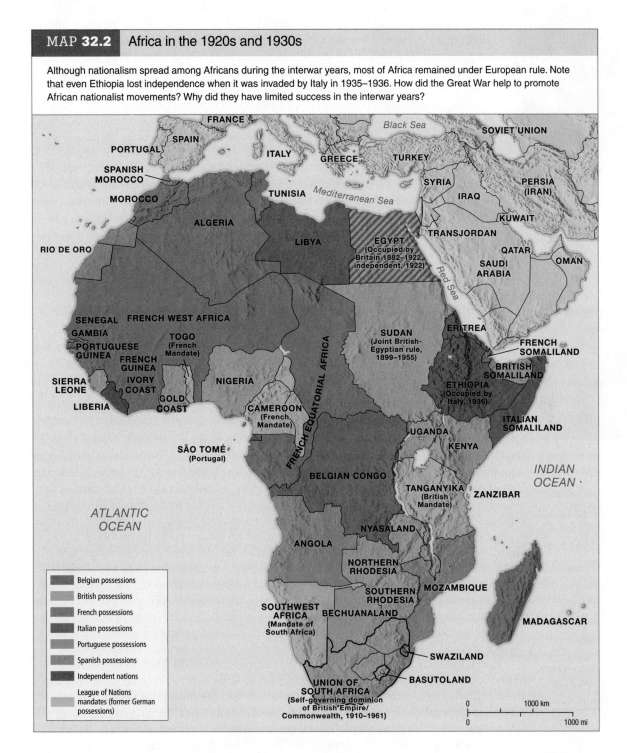

African workers and farmers strike against Europeans

Marcus Garvey.

Africans devise religious and cultural forms of nationalism

Some African workers and farmers went on strike against European employers. Strikes in British-held regions in the Gold Coast and the Northern Rhodesian copper belt achieved only modest gains, but in the 1930s Gold Coast cocoa farmers forced a significant price increase by withholding their produce from the markets. Nationalists led these protests, learning from them the prospects and limitations of collective action.

In the Belgian Congo, nationalism grew out of religion. Simon Kimbangu (*kim-BAHN-goo*) founded his own church in 1921 and proclaimed himself prophet. He taught that God would free the Congo peoples from Belgian bondage, so they need not pay taxes. The Belgians threw him in prison (where he died in 1951), but his church included future nationalist leaders such as Joseph Kasa Vubu (*kah-sah VOO-boo*), who became the first president of independent Congo in 1960.

Pro-African intellectuals developed other forms of nationalism. In the 1920s Marcus Garvey of Jamaica founded the Universal Negro Improvement Association, advocating "Africa for the Africans" and the end of European rule. Based in New York, Garvey never visited Africa, but his movement inspired several young Africans who led the anticolonial struggle after 1945. A culture-based alternative was offered by the Négritude movement, composed of French-speaking West African and Caribbean writers who celebrated African cultural traditions and their differences from Europe. One such scholar, Léopold Senghor (*SONG-or*), became the first president of independent Senegal in 1960.

In South Africa the **African National Congress** (ANC), founded in 1912 by educated black professionals to combat white racial repression, made little headway in the interwar years. But after World War II, when anticolonialism swept Africa, ANC became its strongest nationalist organization.

Secular and Islamic Nationalism in the Middle East

In the Middle East, the demise of the Ottoman Empire, in the wake of the Great War, boosted several different forms of nationalism. Turkey, the empire's main successor state, adopted a Western-style secular nationalism, promoting loyalty to nation above religion, while others in the region sought to merge nationalism with Islamic, and often anti-Western, ideals.

Kemal Atatürk promotes shift from Arabic to Latin script.

Mustafa Kemal fosters modernization and secular nationalism in Turkey

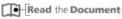

Read the **Document**

The Six Arrows of Kemalism: The Principles of the Republican People's Party (RPP), 1935

on **myhistorylab.com**

Watch the **Video**

Ataturk: Mustafa Kemal

on **myhistorylab.com**

Reza Shah Pahlavi tries to modernize and secularize Iran

In a 1919–1923 revolt, Turkish nationalists led by war hero Mustafa Kemal ousted the Ottoman sultan, who at Allied insistence had given up most of the realm's non-Turkish regions, and created a Republic of Turkey in what was left (Map 32.3). As president and virtual dictator until he died in 1938, Kemal revolutionized his country. Determined to reduce the role of Islam and have his people identify as Turks more than as Muslims, he replaced Islamic schools with secular ones and Islamic law (Shari`ah) with Western-style legal codes. He modernized industries, Westernized styles and fashions, and even replaced Arabic script with the Latin alphabet. He abolished the sultanate and caliphate, took the name Atatürk ("father of Turks"), and made Turkey a modern secular nationalistic state.

Equally revolutionary was his emancipation of women, who by 1920 had gained some access to secondary education and factory jobs. Hoping to further economic growth by doubling the talent pool, he vastly expanded women's opportunities. His reforms banned polygyny, gave women the right to vote and to serve in parliament, granted them equal access to divorce and child custody, and guaranteed their rights to education and employment.

Kemal's secular policies sent shock waves across the Middle East. In Persia Reza Shah Pahlavi (*PAH-luh-vē*), a military man who took power and reigned as shah (king) from 1925 to 1941, sought to imitate Kemal's reforms. He built railways and industries, reformed the legal system, and renamed his country Iran (after the ancient Aryans who had settled there). He even sought to end the seclusion and veiling of women, but stiff opposition from the country's powerful Shi'ite Muslim clerics limited his success.

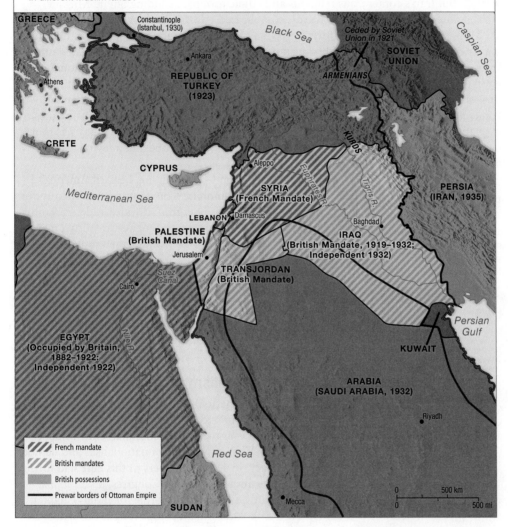

MAP 32.3   The Middle East in the 1920s and 1930s

In the Middle East, with the Ottoman Empire's demise, some of its lands became French and British mandates, others later became part of Saudi Arabia, and what was left became the Republic of Turkey, with its capital at Ankara. Notice that the old capital, Constantinople, was formally renamed Istanbul in 1930, and that Persia became Iran in 1935. Why and how did different forms of nationalism emerge in different Muslim lands?

GREECE

Constantinople (Istanbul, 1930)

Black Sea

Ceded by Soviet Union in 1921

SOVIET UNION

Caspian Sea

Ankara

ARMENIANS

REPUBLIC OF TURKEY (1923)

Athens

CRETE

KURDS

CYPRUS

Aleppo

Euphrates R.

Tigris R.

PERSIA (IRAN, 1935)

Mediterranean Sea

SYRIA (French Mandate)

LEBANON Damascus

Baghdad

PALESTINE (British Mandate)

IRAQ (British Mandate, 1919–1932; Independent 1932)

Jerusalem

Suez Canal

TRANSJORDAN (British Mandate)

Cairo

Persian Gulf

Nile R.

KUWAIT

EGYPT (Occupied by Britain, 1882–1922; Independent 1922)

ARABIA (SAUDI ARABIA, 1932)

Riyadh

French mandate

British mandates

British possessions

Prewar borders of Ottoman Empire

Red Sea

0   500 km
0   500 mi

SUDAN

Mecca

Elsewhere other Muslims, offended by such secularism, responded with forms of nationalism tied to Islam. In Egypt, which became an independent monarchy in 1922, the Society of Muslim Brothers, a militant Islamic nationalist group devoted to resisting secularism, emerged in 1928. In formerly Ottoman Syria and Palestine, nationalism took a pro-Islamic, anti-Western tone against France and Britain, which during the war had promised independence but then ruled these regions as League of Nations mandates. France further upset Muslims by carving from its Syrian mandate an area called Lebanon with a large Christian population, hoping to form a Christian-dominated nation. Britain angered Muslims by letting Jews settle in its Palestine mandate, based on the Balfour Declaration, a wartime pledge to help Jews form a national homeland there (Chapter 37).

Other Muslims embrace Islamic and anti-Western nationalism

French and British mandates create problems in Lebanon, Palestine, and Iraq

Faisal at Versailles with
T. E. Lawrence "of Arabia"
(*right*) and others.

Although Britain and France withdrew in the 1940s, their actions inflamed antagonisms that still plague the region.

In Iraq, made up of three former Ottoman provinces where Britain had a League of Nations mandate, the British tried to create a Muslim nation. After forming a monarchy in 1921 under King Faisal (*Fī-sul*), son of Hussein ibn Ali, Sherif of Mecca, who had led the Arab Revolt against the Ottomans in the Great War, Britain recognized Iraqi independence in 1932. But Iraq's contentious religious and ethnic groups, including Shi'ite Muslim Arabs, Sunni Muslim Arabs, and Kurds, complicated efforts to achieve national unity.

More successful were the efforts in Arabia of Abdul Aziz ibn Saud (*sah-OOD*), leader of a strict Muslim sect called Wahhabism (Chapter 22), who in the 1920s defeated other Arabs and in 1932 formed the Kingdom of Saudi Arabia. To create a Saudi national identity in a desert land dominated by Arab tribes, he imposed Wahhabism as the national form of Islam. He also forged connections with each tribe by marrying more than 240 women, divorcing most of them after two weeks, and sending them back to their tribes pregnant and laden with gifts. Ibn Saud was prolific—the House of Saud today has more than 7,000 princes—but his gifts were modest, usually a fine robe and a few goats, since his initial wealth was limited.

Then Charles Crane, head of America's Crane Plumbing Company, sent an engineer to search for underground water in desert Arabia. After 18 months, the engineer reported that Arabia had no such water, then resigned and went to work for Standard Oil of California. He had found not water but oil, which was on its way to surpassing coal as the world's main fuel. Saudi oil reserves would later prove the richest on earth, and Saudi Arabia would become one of earth's richest nations.

Nationalism and Nonviolence in India

Indian nationalism grew out of British rule, which united the diverse subcontinent and created a British-educated Indian elite influenced by Western notions of nationalism and democracy. In 1885, members of this elite had formed the Indian National Congress, a nationalist body advocating self-rule for India (Chapter 29). After Indian troops fought for Britain in the Great War, Woodrow Wilson's call for national self-determination raised hopes that the Allies would grant India self-rule as a matter of both gratitude and principle.

But the British were loath to let their lucrative colony go. They increased the role of Indians in its governance but imposed laws making Indians accused of anti-British activity liable to prison without trial, sparking demonstrations across India. In April 1919 in Amritsar (Map 32.4), a British commander had his Indian soldiers fire repeatedly on unarmed

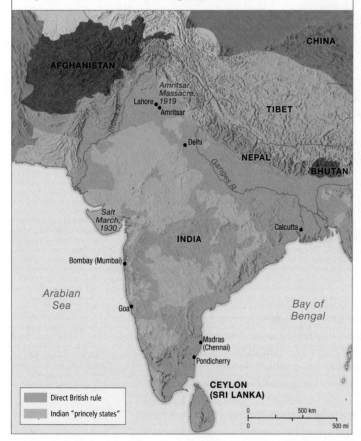

MAP **32.4** India Between the Wars, 1919–1939

Indian nationalists between the wars sought independence from Britain. Observe that Britain ruled much of India directly, but other parts indirectly through treaties with "princely states." Why were Gandhi's tactics, including the 1930 Salt March, effective against the British?

Direct British rule

Indian "princely states"

demonstrators, killing at least 379 and wounding more than a thousand. The Amritsar massacre shattered hopes for peaceful transition to self-rule and left India verging on rebellion.

At this point an unusual leader emerged. Son of a Hindu merchant, Mohandas K. Gandhi (1869–1948) had studied law in England and practiced it in South Africa. There, evicted from a "whites-only" train car and barred from "whites-only" hotels, he identified with South Africa's oppressed minorities. In time he developed **satyagraha** (*sut-YAH-gruh-huh*), or "truth force," a nonviolent way to combat oppression by refusing to cooperate with oppressors (see "Gandhi on Nonviolent Resistance"). Returning to India, he became a leader of the Indian National Congress.

In 1920, following the Amritsar massacre, Gandhi led a national boycott, urging Indians not to buy British goods, pay British taxes, or participate in British institutions. In 1922, when some of his followers defied him and turned to violence, Gandhi was arrested for inciting insurrection. Distressed, after two years in jail he withdrew from politics to work among the poor. But in 1930, outraged by British imposition of a heavy tax on salt, he reemerged to lead a mass nonviolent resistance campaign. Since most Indians lacked refrigeration, they needed salt to preserve their food, so he urged them to get their own salt from seawater. Under his leadership some fifty thousand Indians staged a sensational Salt March, walking two hundred miles to the seaside salt flats, where they peacefully endured brutal beatings ordered by British officials.

When reports of these beatings prompted an international outcry, British authorities, seeing that their use of force was futile, negotiated with Gandhi. The resulting Government of India Act, passed by Britain's parliament in 1935, gave India a constitution calling for an elected two-house national legislature. It was not full independence—the British still controlled the government's executive branch—but it was a major step toward self-rule.

One key factor in Gandhi's success was his conversion of Indian nationalism from an aim of the elite into a movement of the masses, who affectionately called him Mahatma ("great-soul"). Sparsely dressed in handwoven cloth he spun on a small spinning wheel, he identified with the outcastes and poor, inspiring in them dignity and pride. Another factor was his clever exploitation of Britain's self-interest. Realizing that imperial rule relied on Indian cooperation, he promoted noncooperation, seeking to show Britain that continuing its control would be more trouble and expense than letting go. A third factor was his aptitude for public relations and seizing the moral high ground. Reports of Indian nonviolence in the face of brutal beatings helped win sympathy in Britain for Indian self-rule.

Gandhi's success was incomplete, for he failed to calm the fears of India's Muslim minority. The 1937 elections held under the new constitution gave the Hindu-dominated Indian National Congress most legislative seats. Concerned that Indian independence would result in oppression of Muslims by the Hindu majority, Muhammad Ali Jinnah, leader of an association called the Muslim League, turned it into a separatist movement. But violent clashes between Hindus and Muslims then strengthened British imperialists, who portrayed these clashes as proof that India was not ready for self-rule. Indian independence was delayed until 1947.

Nationalism and Communism in China

China, too, was affected by nationalist reaction against foreign intrusion, by ideas adapted from the West, and by internal divisions. But China's divisions rested not on religion, as in India and the Middle East, but on ideology, as Nationalists and Communists fought over China's future.

Amritsar massacre leaves India on brink of anti-British rebellion

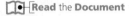Read the **Document**

Mohandas Gandhi, Satyagraha in South Africa on **myhistorylab.com**

Gandhi leads nonviolent resistance against British rule

Gandhi with spinning wheel.

1935 Constitution gives India a degree of self-rule

Gandhi's mass appeal and moral standing undermine British rule

Muslim League, fearing Hindu rule, leads separatist movement

DOCUMENT 32.3 Gandhi on Nonviolent Resistance

Gandhi portrayed violence as cowardly and nonviolence as courageous. How did his approach contrast with Hitler's (Document 32.2)? Why was it effective against Britain?

. . . I believe that non-violence is infinitely superior to violence, forgiveness is more manly than punishment . . .

Strength does not come from physical capacity. It comes from an indomitable will . . . We in India may in a moment realize that one hundred thousand Englishmen need not frighten three hundred million human beings . . . .

I am not a visionary. I claim to be a practical idealist. The religion of non-violence is not meant merely for the . . . saints. It is meant for the common people as well. Non-violence is the law of our species as violence is the law of the brute. The spirit lies dormant in the brute, and he knows no law but that of physical might. The dignity of man requires obedience to a higher law—to the strength of the spirit.

I have therefore ventured to place before India the ancient law of self-sacrifice. For *satyagraha* and its offshoots, non-cooperation and civil resistance, are nothing but new names for the law of suffering . . .

Non-violence in its dynamic condition means conscious suffering. It does not mean meek submission to the will of the evil-doer, but it means the pitting of one's whole soul against the will of the tyrant. Working under this law of our being, it is possible for a single individual to defy the whole might of an unjust empire . . .

Non-violence is not a cover for cowardice, but it is the supreme virtue of the brave. Exercise of non-violence requires far greater bravery than that of swordsmanship. Cowardice is wholly inconsistent with non-violence. Non-violence . . . is a conscious deliberate restraint put upon one's desire for vengeance. But vengeance is any day superior to passive, effeminate, and helpless submission. Forgiveness is higher still. Vengeance too is weakness. The desire for vengeance comes out of fear of harm, imaginary or real. A dog barks and bites when he fears. A man who fears no one on earth would consider it too troublesome even to summon up anger against one who is vainly trying to injure him . . .

Non-resistance is restraint voluntarily undertaken for the good of society. It is, therefore, an intensively active, purifying, inward force. It is often antagonistic to the material good of the non-resister . . . It is rooted in internal strength, never weakness . . .

SOURCE: Roger S. Gottlieb (editor) *Liberating Faith*. Copyright © 2003 Rowman & Littlefield. Reprinted by permission.

Sun Yixian forms the Guomindang as Chinese Nationalist Party

Yuan Shikai bans Guomindang and bids to become emperor

Regional warlords rule China after Yuan Shikai's death

Allied snub and May Fourth protests fuel Chinese nationalist fervor

THE RISE OF NATIONALIST CHINA. The father of Chinese nationalism was Sun Yixian (*SUN Ē-shē-AHN*), also called Sun Yatsen, a Western-educated Chinese doctor who had emerged in the early 1900s as a revolutionary leader against the imperial regime. But when that regime fell in 1912, Sun, lacking military support, stepped aside in favor of former general Yuan Shikai, who became president of a new Chinese Republic (Chapter 29). Sun then formed the Guomindang (*GWŌ-MIN-DONG*), or "National People's Party," a nationalist and democratic organization that won a majority of the seats in 1913 parliamentary elections.

But Yuan Shikai, a military man with imperial ambitions, soon outlawed the Guomindang, shut down the parliament, and schemed to make himself emperor. He was thwarted, however, by rebellion in the south, and humiliated when Japan used the Great War to seize the Shandong peninsula, a key coastal region in northeast China earlier leased by Germany.

When Yuan died suddenly in 1916, China dissolved into chaos. His regime still functioned in Beijing under his former aides, but in the provinces his governors and generals emerged as regional warlords, collecting taxes and commanding armies that fought each other and pillaged the land. China's "Warlord Era" lasted from 1916 to 1928.

Meanwhile, Sun, having fled abroad in 1913, returned to China in 1917 to rebuild the Guomindang. The Russian Revolution, occurring that same year, provided inspiration and support. Lenin's views, equating imperialism with capitalism, and Soviet pledges to back Asian nationalist movements, resonated in China—especially after May 4, 1919, when news reached Beijing that the Paris Peace Conference, ignoring China's pleas, had let Japan keep control of the Shandong peninsula. The resulting **May Fourth Protests**, which spread all across China, were directed both against the West (for letting Japan keep Shandong) and the weak Chinese regime (which had earlier acquiesced to Japan's presence there). They energized Chinese nationalism, which continued to grow long after Shandong was returned to China in 1922.

They also energized Chinese Communism. In Shanghai in 1921, Chinese Marxists founded the Chinese Communist Party, aiming to secure with Soviet support a socialist future for China. In 1924, at Soviet urging, the Chinese Communist Party joined the Guomindang, linking Communism with nationalism against capitalism and imperialism in a common effort to liberate China from the warlords and the West. Aided by Soviet agents, Sun reshaped the Guomindang as a Soviet-style revolutionary party with activist groups, or cells, in major cities. He also published an influential work, *The Three Principles of the People*, calling for nationalism, democracy, and "people's livelihood," often equated with socialism.

Chinese Communists and Nationalists combine in effort to unite China

But after Sun's death in 1925, power in the Guomindang passed to its military wing, led by Sun's disciple Jiang Jieshi (*jē-AHNG jē-EH-SHUR*), also called Chiang Kaishek (*jē-AHNG KĪ-SHEK*). Sun had tapped Jiang, who had studied Red Army methods in Moscow, to form a Guomindang army that could conquer the warlords. In 1926, having trained a large force, Jiang set out on a "Great Northern Expedition," moving north from his party's southern base to unite China under Guomindang rule (Map 32.5). He was backed by both Nationalists and Communists.

After Sun dies, Jiang Jieshi and the army dominate Guomindang

In April of 1927, Jiang and his forces arrived at Shanghai. Long a center of Western capitalist commerce, this port city teemed with poorly paid dock and factory workers, living in squalor and working long hours in unsafe conditions. Communists had organized these workers and persuaded them to take over the city to welcome Jiang as a liberator. But Jiang, in collusion with the capitalists, instead stunned the city by using his army to massacre Shanghai Communists.

Jiang turns against Communists and massacres them in Shanghai

Jiang had reasons for staging this **Shanghai Massacre**. He was concerned that the Communists, whose numbers were growing, might soon dominate his movement. He was alarmed by recently discovered evidence that the Soviets planned to use his revolution to bring China under Communist control. He was impressed by the power and wealth of Western capitalists, whose help he could use in rebuilding China. And he was shaped by his background as a soldier: like Yuan Shikai, he believed in using force against potential foes.

Jiang resumed the Great Northern Expedition, but his allies and aims had changed. He sided with Western capitalists, married a wealthy American-educated woman, and later (partly to please his new wife's mother) became a Christian. Rather than attack the warlords, he cut deals with them, letting them retain regional rule if they recognized his regime. By 1928, Jiang was China's main leader, heading a new Nationalist regime with its capital at Nanjing.

Jiang "unites" China by cutting deals with warlords and West

Despite its parliamentary institutions and Western ties, however, "Nationalist China" was a one-party state with limited strength. Jiang's power came from his army, his ties with the warlords, and appointment of his cronies as key officials to run China's economy. While Jiang focused on his military, these "bureaucratic capitalists" worked to modernize and industrialize China, while also gaining great wealth for themselves.

NATIONALISTS VERSUS COMMUNISTS. Jiang's dominion in China was far from complete. He controlled the cities and army, the standard centers of strength. But the Chinese masses neither lived in cities nor served in the army. Most were peasants who lived in villages

Chinese peasant masses wooed by Mao Zedong and Communistss

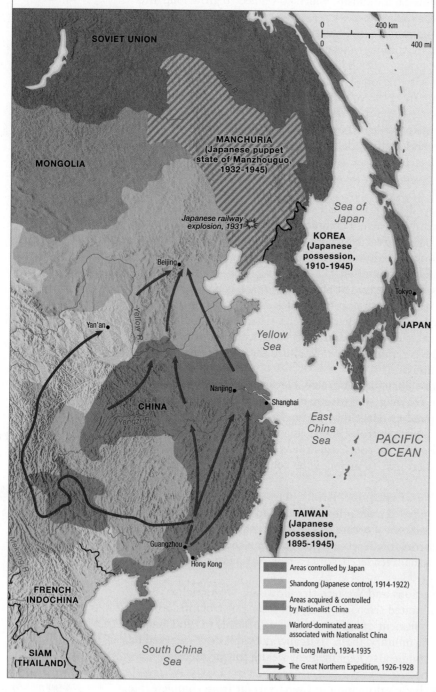

| | MAP **32.5** | Nationalist China and Expansionist Japan, 1926–1937 |

Chinese turmoil and Japanese expansionism marked the interwar years. Note that Nationalist efforts to unify China failed to dislodge the warlords, who cut deals with the regime, or the Communists, who survived by fleeing to Yan'an on the Long March. Why and how did Japan move into Manchuria?

SOVIET UNION

MANCHURIA
(Japanese puppet
state of Manzhouguo,
1932-1945)

MONGOLIA

Japanese railway
explosion, 1931

Beijing

Sea of
Japan

KOREA
(Japanese
possession,
1910-1945)

Tokyo

JAPAN

Yan'an

Yellow R.

Yellow
Sea

Nanjing

CHINA

Shanghai

Yangzi R.

East
China
Sea

PACIFIC
OCEAN

TAIWAN
(Japanese
possession,
1895-1945)

Guangzhou

Hong Kong

FRENCH
INDOCHINA

Mekong R.

SIAM
(THAILAND)

South China
Sea

Areas controlled by Japan

Shandong (Japanese control, 1914-1922)

Areas acquired & controlled
by Nationalist China

Warlord-dominated areas
associated with Nationalist China

The Long March, 1934-1935

The Great Northern Expedition, 1926-1928

with their extended families, tilling the soil as peasants had done for ages. China's Communists, shattered by the Shanghai slaughter, turned to these peasants as the basis for a new revolution, inspired by a gifted young Marxist named Mao Zedong (*MAOW zuh-DŌNG*).

Raised among peasants and influenced by both Sun and Lenin, Mao had become a Communist, but he had trouble relating to urban factory workers. In his native province, however, he saw peasants organize themselves to combat landlords and warlords. Rejecting the orthodox Marxist view that revolution must arise with the urban proletariat, in 1927 he published a radical report claiming that peasants could lead China to socialism. Unlike Jiang, who allied with the rich and strong, Mao looked to the poor and weak to help him transform society. But like Jiang, Mao felt the future must be shaped by force. "A revolution is not a dinner party," he wrote. "A revolution is an insurrection, an act of violence by which one class overthrows another."

In the next several years, Mao and his comrades mobilized peasants in south-central China, forming a "Chinese Soviet Republic" with its own institutions and army. But Jiang then sought to crush this movement with military attacks. Finally, in October 1934, Mao and about a hundred thousand supporters sought to escape. With the Nationalist army in pursuit, they fled on foot across mountains, plains, and rivers to the wilds of the west and north, fighting constant battles in a six thousand–mile retreat, later hallowed in Communist legend as the **Long March** (Map 32.5).

A year later, about twenty thousand survivors reached the relative safety of the remote northwest.

Communists flee on "Long March" from Jiang's attacks

There, protected by the region's rocks, hills, and isolation, Mao rebuilt his movement. Based in the town of Yan'an, he promoted socialism among the region's rural people, operating clinics, shops, and schools in caves to shield them from Nationalist attacks. His programs eventually won him broad support among China's peasants. Meanwhile, in 1936, Jiang was forced by one of his warlords to negotiate a truce with the Communists, so China could deal with a growing foreign threat: the military expansionism of imperial Japan.

Mao and Communists rebuild in remote Yan'an

Nationalism and Militarism in Japan

More than any other Asian nation, Japan had imitated the West in focusing on industry and military might. By defeating Russia in 1905, Japan had also emerged as Asia's leading power. But the island nation nonetheless lacked the fuel and raw materials to sustain modern industries and military forces. Japan thus sought dominion over nearby Asian regions rich in resources.

One such region was Korea, occupied by Japan in the Russo-Japanese War and formally annexed in 1910. Mixing modernization with repression, Japan built roads, factories, hospitals, and schools but also exploited Korea's resources and undermined its culture, forcing Koreans to speak Japanese and take Japanese names. Although Korean nationalists declared independence on March 1, 1919, sparking massive anti-Japanese demonstrations, Japan crushed the protests ruthlessly and continued to rule Korea until 1945.

Meanwhile, having joined the Allied Powers in the Great War, Japan seized China's Shandong peninsula, an iron-rich region the Germans had leased, and a number of German-held Pacific islands. Japan also profited commercially from the war, selling materials and supplies to the European Allies. In 1919 the Allies rewarded Japan, recognizing its rights in Shandong (which it kept until 1922) and giving it League of Nations mandates to govern the islands it had taken.

Japan expands into Korea and Shandong to gain resources

Despite a postwar recession and a 1923 Tokyo earthquake that took 130,000 lives, in the 1920s Japan expanded economically. Japanese *zaibatsu*—private industrial empires, such as Mitsui and Mitsubishi, that made and sold products ranging from textiles to steamships— emerged among the world's largest commercial conglomerates. By the 1930s, owing to urban industrial growth, almost half Japan's people lived in cities, up from only 12 percent in the 1890s. And many adopted a new urban culture, ignoring old Shinto and Buddhist values while embracing such modern amusements as movies, magazines, and sports.

Industry and democracy grow in Japan in 1920s

In these years Japan also grew more democratic. In 1925 it extended the vote to all men over 25, quadrupling the electorate, but still excluding women, who did not get voting rights until two decades later. New social legislation lifted restrictions on labor unions, limited work hours, and initiated a national health insurance program. By 1926, at the accession of Emperor Hirohito (1926–1989), Japan seemed to be evolving into a stable capitalist democracy.

Japanese youths in samurai dress reflect rising militarism.

But looming on the horizon were threatening clouds. One was a growing population, which rose from 40 million in the 1890s to 70 million in the 1930s, deepening demand for resources and space—thus adding to expansionist pressures. Another was the growth of foreign trade, which made Japan wealthy but also dependent on markets in the West.

Most ominous was the rise of **militarism**, an exaltation of the armed forces that promoted military might as central to the nation's character. Enthused by Japan's victory over Russia and success in the Great War, many Japanese revered their military, expecting it to secure land and resources while stressing traditional samurai values of courage, honor, loyalty, and toughness. Furthermore, as the constitution gave civilian leaders little power over the armed forces, military leaders could often act unhindered on their own.

Need for resources and space fuels Japanese militarism

Depression, Western tariffs, and crop failure devastate Japan

Adding to these anxieties was the Great Depression, which devastated Japan. In the early 1930s, as Western nations imposed import quotas and tariffs, Japanese exports steeply declined, undermining industries and causing mass unemployment. In 1931, moreover, disastrous crop failures brought starvation to the countryside. As civilian leaders proved unable to ease their distress, many in Japan looked to the military for solutions.

Japanese army creates puppet state in Manchuria

And the military looked to Manchuria, where Japan had based troops since the war against Russia. A huge Chinese province rich in coal and iron, it had ample land to provide food and space for Japan's growing population. In September 1931, Japanese officers conspired to blow up a Japanese-owned railway in Manchuria and blame the act on Chinese terrorists. Then the Japanese army, citing a need to defend Japan's interests, attacked Chinese forces and conquered Manchuria, creating there in 1932 a Japanese puppet state called Manzhouguo (*man-JOO-gwō*).

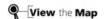 **View** the **Map**
Atlas Map: The Growth of Japan
on **myhistorylab.com**

The "Manchuria Incident" destroyed Japanese democracy. The civilian government, unable to restrain the military, resigned in futility at the end of 1931. A new prime minister, seeking to restrain the armed forces, was murdered by a militarist the next May. Concluding that only the military could control its own, the emperor then made an admiral prime minister, ending civilian rule. The new regime soon suppressed left-wing parties and eventually all opposition.

Military leaders come to rule Japan in 1930s

Japan exits the League and signs pact with Nazi Germany

The Manchuria Incident also damaged world peace. In 1933, censured by the League of Nations for aggression in Manchuria, Japan quit the League and grew more aggressive. In 1936 it signed the Anti-Comintern Pact, an agreement to collaborate with Nazi Germany against international Communism. The next year, as Japan began a new arms buildup, its forces in Manchuria provoked a war with China. This struggle later merged with conflicts in Europe into a Second World War.

CHAPTER
REVIEW

Putting It in Perspective

During the two decades that followed the Great War, Woodrow Wilson's dream of national self-determination turned into a nationalistic nightmare. The Versailles settlement, a compromise between Wilsonian ideals and Allied retributions, frustrated the hopes of both winners and losers, while cultural changes and new ideologies heightened global anxieties. In the 1920s, faced with economic and political instability, Italy and much of Eastern Europe turned from democracy to dictatorship. In the 1930s, shaken by the Great Depression, America and Western Europe retreated into economic nationalism, depriving other nations of Western markets and globalizing the crisis.

Russia and Germany both became brutal dictatorships, Stalin's based on Soviet nationalism and Hitler's on nationalistic racism.

Meanwhile, anti-Western anxieties and nationalistic ideologies fueled anticolonialism in Africa, secular and Islamic nationalism in the Middle East, nonviolent resistance in India, conflicts between Nationalists and Communists in China, and expansive militarism in Japan. By the late 1930s, it was clear that the Great War had not been "the war to end all wars," as Wilson and others had hoped. Instead, it had only been the First World War, soon to be surpassed in brutality and breadth by a second global conflict.

Reviewing Key Material

KEY CONCEPTS

national self-determination, 748
relativism, 748
relativity, 749
assembly line, 750
impressionism, 751
cubism, 751
surrealism, 751
League of Nations, 752
League of Nations mandates, 752
dictators, 754
fascism, 754
economic nationalism, 756
socialism in one country, 758

collective farms, 759
Great Purges, 759
Nazis, 760
National Socialist German Workers' Party 760
Master Race, 761
Lebensraum, 761
anticolonialism, 762
African National Congress, 764
satyagraha, 767
May Fourth Protests, 769
Shanghai Massacre, 769
Long March, 770
militarism, 771

KEY PEOPLE

Woodrow Wilson, 748, 752
Friedrich Nietzsche, 749
Sigmund Freud, 749
Albert Einstein, 749
Henry Ford, 750
Sergei Eisenstein, 750
Leni Riefenstahl, 750
Pablo Picasso, 751
David Lloyd George, 752
Georges Clemenceau, 752
Benito Mussolini, 754
Herbert Hoover, 755
Franklin D. Roosevelt, 756
Ramsay MacDonald, 757
Stanley Baldwin, 757
Leon Blum, 757
V. I. Lenin, 758

Leon Trotsky, 758
Joseph Stalin, 758
Adolf Hitler, 760
Gustav Stresemann, 760
Simon Kimbangu, 764
Marcus Garvey, 764
Mustafa Kemal, 764
Reza Shah Pahlavi, 764
King Faisal, 766
Mohandas K. Gandhi, 767
Muhammad Ali Jinnah, 767
Sun Yixian (Sun Yatsen), 768
Yuan Shikai, 768
Jiang Jieshi (Chiang Kaishek), 769
Mao Zedong, 770

ASK YOURSELF

1. Why did the Paris Peace Conference fail to provide a lasting peace? Why did the Versailles Treaty cause so much resentment?
2. Why was Western culture in turmoil in the interwar years? Why did many new democracies fail to survive?

3. Why did the U.S. stock market crash result in a global depression? What impact did the depression have on political changes in America, Western Europe, Germany, and Japan?
4. How did Mussolini, Stalin, and Hitler gain power? What methods and concepts did each use to control and strengthen his country?
5. What were the origins, ideals, and exploits of interwar nationalist movements in Africa, the Middle East, and Asia? How and why did these nationalist movements differ?

GOING FURTHER

Andelman, David. *A Shattered Peace: Versailles 1919 and the Price We Pay Today.* 2007.
Arnason, Harvey, and Peter Kalb. *History of Modern Art.* 2003.
Bosworth, R. J. B. *Mussolini.* 2002.
Brendon, Piers. *The Dark Valley: A Panorama of the 1930s.* 2000.
Bullock, Alan. *Hitler and Stalin: Parallel Lives.* 1993.
Burleigh, Michael. *Third Reich: A New History.* 2000.
Cleveland, W. L. *History of the Modern Middle East.* 2nd ed. 2000.
Davies, Sarah, and James Harris, eds. *Stalin: A New History.* 2005.
Dirlik, Arif. *The Origins of Chinese Communism.* 1989.
Evans, R. J. *The Coming of the Third Reich.* 2004.
Evans, R. J. *The Third Reich in Power, 1933–1939.* 2005.
Eyck, Erich. *History of the Weimar Republic.* 1962.
Fenby, Jonathan. *Generalissimo: Chiang Kai-shek and the China He Lost.* 2005.
Fitzpatrick, Sheila. *Stalin's Peasants: Resistance and Survival in the Russian Village after Collectivization.* 1995.
Freund, Bill. *The Making of Contemporary Africa.* 1999.
Fromkin, David. *A Peace to End All Peace: The Fall of the Ottoman Empire and Creation of the Modern Middle East.* 2001.
Gandhi, Mohandas K. *An Autobiography.* 1957.
Irokawa, Daikichi. *The Age of Hirohito.* 1995.
Isaacson, Walter. *Einstein: His Life and Universe.* 2007.
Kater, Michael. *The Hitler Youth.* 2004.
Kershaw, Ian. *Hitler: Nemesis.* 2000.
Kindelberger, C. P. *The World in Depression, 1929–1939.* 1986.
Lee, Stephen J. *European Dictatorships, 1918–1945.* 2nd ed. 2000.

Lewin, Moshe. *The Soviet Century*. 2005.

Mango, Andrew. *Ataturk: Biography of the Founder of Modern Turkey*. 2000.

Mann, Michael. *Fascists*. 2004.

McElvaine, R. *The Great Depression: America, 1929–1941*. 1984.

Medvedev, Roy. *Let History Judge: The Origins and Consequences of Stalinism*. 1989.

Mehta, V. *Mahatma Gandhi and His Apostles*. 1977.

Mussolini, Benito. *Fascism: Doctrine and Institution*. 1968.

Paxton, R. O. *The Anatomy of Fascism*. 2004.

Payne, Stanley G. *A History of Fascism, 1914–1945*. 1995.

Sato, Barb. *The New Japanese Women: Modernity, Media, and Women in Interwar Japan*. 2003.

Service, Robert. *Stalin: A Biography*. 2004.

Sheridan, James E. *China in Disintegration, 1912–1949*. 1975.

Shirer, William. *The Rise and Fall of the Third Reich*. 1960.

Snow, Edgar. *Red Star over China*. 1938.

Sontag, R. J. *A Broken World, 1919–39*. 1971.

Spielvogel, J. *Hitler and Nazi Germany*. 5th ed. 2005.

Stephenson, Jill. *Women in Nazi Germany*. 2001.

Terrill, Ross. *Mao: A Biography*. Rev. ed. 1999.

Thurston, Robert. *Life and Terror in Stalin's Russia*. 1996.

Tucker, Robert. *Stalin in Power, 1928–1941*. 1990.

Volkogonov, Dmitri. *Stalin: Triumph and Tragedy*. 1996.

Weitz, Eric. *Weimar Germany: Promise and Tragedy*. 2007.

Whittam, John. *Fascist Italy*. 1995.

Wolpert, Stanley. *Congress and Indian Nationalism*. 1988.

Wolpert, Stanley. *Gandhi's Passion: The Life and Legacy of Mahatma Gandhi*. 2001.

Wolpert, Stanley. *India*. 2005.

Zarrow, Peter. *China in War and Revolution, 1895–1945*. 2005.

Key Dates and Developments

1918–1921	Reds prevail in Russian Civil War
1919	Paris Peace Conference formulates Treaty of Versailles
1919	Japan crushes nationalist protests in Korea
1919	Amritsar massacre kills hundreds in India
1919	May Fourth Protests fuel nationalism in China
1919–1923	Kemal overthrows Ottoman sultan, creates Republic of Turkey
1920	U.S. Senate fails to ratify Versailles Treaty
1921	Lenin initiates New Economic Policy
1922	Mussolini takes power in Italy
1923	Inflation crisis rocks Germany
1923	Tokyo earthquake kills 130,000
1925	Reza Shah Pahlavi becomes ruler of Persia
1925	Locarno Treaties stabilize Central Europe
1927	Jiang Jieshi massacres Chinese Communists in Shanghai
1928	Stalin launches First Five Year Plan
1929	U.S. stock market crash triggers Great Depression
1930	Smoot-Hawley Tariff globalizes Great Depression
1930	Gandhi organizes Salt March in India
1930–1933	Civil war and forced famine kill millions in Soviet Ukraine
1931	Japanese army conquers Manchuria
1932	Ibn Saud forms Kingdom of Saudi Arabia
1932	Iraq granted independence under King Faisal
1933	Hitler comes to power in Germany
1934–1935	Mao leads Long March in China
1935	Persia is renamed Iran
1935	Britain grants India limited constitution
1936	Germany and Japan sign Anti-Comintern Pact
1936–1938	Stalin conducts Great Purges in Russia

PEARSON
myhistorylab™ Connections

Reinforce what you learned in this chapter by studying the many documents, images, maps, review tools, and videos available at www.myhistorylab.com.

Read and Review

✓•─ **Study** and **Review** Chapter 32

📖•─ **Read** the **Document**

The Covenant of the League of Nations, 1924, p. 752

Benito Mussolini, "The Political and Social Doctrine of Fascism," p. 754

The Six Arrows of Kemalism: The Principles of the Republican People's Party (RPP), 1935, p. 764

Mohandas Gandhi, Satyagraha in South Africa, p. 767

🔍•─ **View** the **Image**

Migrant Mother, Great Depression, p. 756

))•─ **Listen** to the **Audio**

Post War 1, p. 748

👁•─ **Watch** the **Video**

Ataturk: Mustafa Kemal, p. 764

Research and Explore

👁•─ **Watch** the **Video**

Conformity and Opposition in Nazi Germany, p. 761

🔍•─ **View** the **Map**

Atlas Map: The Growth of Japan, p. 772

))•─ **Listen** to the **Chapter Audio** for Chapter 32 on **myhistorylab.com**

33

World War II and the Holocaust, 1933–1945

((•— Listen to the **Chapter Audio** for Chapter 33 on **myhistorylab.com**

- What factors made it difficult for Britain and France to prevent the outbreak of war in 1939?

- Why was Germany unable to translate its early triumphs into final victory in 1941?

- What were Japan's objectives in beginning the Pacific War?

- How did World War II affect civilians?

- Why did Germany exterminate millions of European Jews?

- What were the main reasons for the eventual Allied victory over Germany?

- What were the main reasons for the eventual defeat of Japan?

- In what ways did World War II affect the world decades after its completion?

Japanese Attack on Pearl Harbor, 1941

A motor launch rescues a sailor from the water alongside the burning American battle-ship *West Virginia* during the Japanese attack on Pearl Harbor, December 7, 1941. The Japanese attack converted a major war in Europe into World War II, a truly global war (page 788).

On September 2, 1945, a solemn ceremony took place on board the *Missouri*, a United States Navy battleship anchored in Tokyo Bay, Japan. Thousands of uniformed military personnel lined the decks as General Douglas MacArthur, commander of American forces in the Pacific, read the terms of surrender. Then, conspicuous in their formal civilian attire of top hats and tails, representatives of the Japanese Empire stepped forward to sign the surrender papers. The entire ceremony took only a few minutes to end history's bloodiest war.

World War II was over. Sixty million people lay dead, the majority of them noncombatants caught in the gruesome clutches of a total war that made few distinctions between soldiers and civilians. In some respects, the war settled issues left unfinished from the Great War of 1914–1918. In other respects, it opened a new era in the evolution of the modern world. For many of those living at the time, 1945 signified a genuine turning point in history, both a completion of the past and an irrevocable break with it. They would carry the trauma of World War II with them the rest of their lives.

Allied Nations in Red

Axis Nations in Tan

Neutral or Occupied Nations in Green

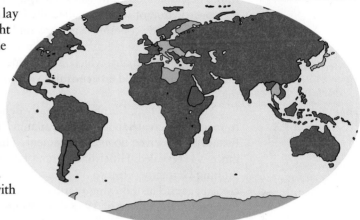

The Road to War

In the 1930s, most Europeans were trying to put the trauma of the Great War behind them. But for Adolf Hitler, Chancellor of Nazi Germany, that war had never really ended. He had come to power pledged to renew it, and the conflict he started would, until December 1941, be justifiably known as Hitler's War.

The Nazi worldview demanded huge additional territories, as *Lebensraum*, or "living space," for the German Master Race (Chapter 32). That space, according to Hitler, could be found to Germany's east, on the fertile plains of Poland and European Russia. Gaining it would require victory in a war for mastery of Europe. France must be defeated, since it would never permit such German expansion without a fight, but Britain, Hitler hoped, could be bought off with a promise to respect the British Empire. The Soviet Union would, of course, fight to save itself, but Slavs, whom Nazis considered subhuman, would be no match for the Aryan armies. Victory was not certain but was likely.

Hitler's program requires a major war

Germany Prepares, 1933–1936

Hitler's initial moves as chancellor mixed aggression with caution. Recognizing German military inferiority resulting from the Versailles Treaty, he worked to improve Germany's international position while confusing its enemies. In 1933 Germany withdrew from the League of Nations, protesting its members' failure to agree on universal disarmament while they kept Germany disarmed. Simultaneously, however, Hitler negotiated a ten-year nonaggression pact with Poland and renewed a 1926 economic treaty between Germany and Soviet Russia. This combination of combativeness with reassurance allowed observers to see what they wanted to see.

Hitler implements a two-track foreign policy

Hitler's double game was derailed in the summer of 1934, when he overreached by authorizing the Austrian Nazi Party to attempt to overthrow the Austrian government. The rebels succeeded in assassinating Austria's chancellor, Engelbert Dollfuss, but spent the rest of the evening drinking in Viennese bars and were soon arrested.

Benito Mussolini's forces mobilized on Italy's Austrian frontier, sending a clear signal that Italy would not tolerate German intervention in Austrian affairs. Hitler quickly backed down, claiming he had had nothing to do with the assassination, but his international image had clearly been damaged, and his relationship with Europe's senior fascist dictator, Mussolini, was shaky.

Then Hitler's luck improved. In 1935 Mussolini invaded Ethiopia, hoping to avenge Italy's defeat at Adowa in 1896 (Chapter 30) by conquering that nation and beginning the construction of what he called the "New Roman Empire." The League of Nations promptly placed economic sanctions on Italy—an embargo banning all exports to Italy except oil. Unable to purchase munitions and industrial equipment from League members, Italy turned to Germany, which as a nonmember could sell to Rome without penalty. Hitler thus was able to build a friendship with Mussolini while demonstrating the weakness of the League.

Outmaneuvering Britain and France, Germany remilitarizes the Rhineland

That same year, Germany formally denounced the Treaty of Versailles and proceeded to rearm and create an air force. An angry France discussed anti-German measures with Britain but received no encouragement. Three months later the reason for British reluctance was revealed: Hitler had purchased British silence by negotiating a naval agreement limiting Germany's fleet to 35 percent the size of Britain's. Hitler's double game had succeeded again. The following year he defied Versailles again by remilitarizing the Rhineland. Once more the victors of 1918 did nothing, in part because they believed that their citizens would not be willing to go to war to prevent Germany from rearming territory that everyone recognized was German in the first place. But the impression of weakness in the democracies was unmistakable.

Civil War in Spain, 1936–1939

British and French ineffectiveness was further highlighted by their response to the outbreak of civil strife in Spain. There a revolution in 1931 had exchanged a monarchy for an unstable republic. In February 1936 a leftist coalition won the Spanish general election; five months later, a group of fascistic military officers led by General Francisco Franco rose in revolt, invading Spain from its own Mediterranean and North African colonies. The leftist parties rallied to the republican cause as Spain plunged into a catastrophic civil war.

The Popular Front government found itself less well equipped than its rebellious army. Seeking to purchase weapons abroad, it was turned down by Paris and London, who sought to confine the crisis by committing all nations to a policy of nonintervention. This policy benefited the rebels not only because they were better armed than the government, but also because two of the three nations that violated the nonintervention agreement—Italy and Germany—backed Franco. The fascist dictatorships, claiming to defend Europe against Bolshevism, sent troops and equipment to the rebels, while Soviet Russia actually confirmed fascist charges by aiding the Spanish Republic. Britain and France merely stood by and watched the Spanish government collapse.

In a material sense, interventionist aid was overrated. The Soviets, more than a thousand miles from Spain, sent obsolete arms and aircraft accompanied by technicians and advisors. Some of these men helped, but others meddled in disputes within the Spanish Communist Party and actually weakened the republican cause. Germany sent planes that destroyed cities such as Guernica to test the effects of terroristic bombing on civilian populations. But in general Hitler held back, hoping that

Spanish Civil War poster.

a prolonged civil war might weaken his enemy France, which was divided over whether to intervene militarily on behalf of the Spanish Republic. Only Italy intervened in strength, sending more than fifty thousand soldiers and significant quantities of weapons. What the rebels really needed was an embargo on arms sales to republican forces, which in effect they got when Britain and France refused to sell arms to either side.

To most of the world, the lesson of the Spanish Civil War appeared to be that democracies were afraid to confront dictators, even though Britain and France might hide behind the moral superiority of nonintervention. Toward the end of the 1930s, the principal questions facing Europe seemed to be when and where—and even if—the democracies would resist.

The democracies respond inadequately to the civil war in Spain

Germany's Eastward Expansion

German intervention in Spain sealed Hitler's friendship with Mussolini, leading to a German-Italian alliance called the Rome–Berlin Axis. This fascist partnership seemed potentially stronger than the Anglo-French alliance, which lacked the American and Russian support it had enjoyed during the Great War. Along with Germany's earlier remilitarization of the Rhineland, the Axis gave Hitler the foundation he needed to take the initiative in European diplomacy. From February 1938 through March 1939, Germany acted while Britain and France reacted.

Italy joins Germany in the Rome–Berlin Axis

Germany's eastward expansion was implemented one step at a time, with careful attention to its flanks and rear. Geography dictated that Austria, on its southern flank, be handled first. In 1919, Austria had tried to unite with Germany rather than stand alone as a feeble remnant of the once-mighty Habsburg Empire. But that union, known as *Anschluss* (*AHN-schloose*), never had a chance because the victorious powers thought Germany should be penalized rather than rewarded for losing the war. Austro-German interest in *Anschluss* persisted, though, and after Hitler came to power in Germany in 1933, an Austrian version of the Nazi Party grew rapidly and worked toward union. In Vienna, Chancellor Kurt von Schusschnigg quietly sought to maintain Austrian sovereignty without needlessly antagonizing Hitler. This effort ended in February 1938 when Hitler ordered Schusschnigg to accept Austrian Nazis into his cabinet or face war. Hitler himself had begun in 1933 with only 3 Nazis in a cabinet of 11; clearly he meant to gain control of the Austrian government in a similar way.

Schusschnigg stalled for nearly a month. Then he announced, with four days' notice, a nationwide referendum on Austrian independence. Furious, Hitler ordered an immediate invasion, which succeeded without bloodshed because Austrian forces were instructed by their government not to resist (Map 33.1). German tanks and jeeps, caught with insufficient oil in their crankcases, broke down in embarrassing numbers on the road to Vienna, but nothing could dampen Hitler's joy at proclaiming the union of his homeland and his Third Reich.

Still Britain and France did nothing. They had no alliance with Austria, and their people were unlikely to support a war to prevent German-speaking Austrians from becoming Germans. Hitler had used the self-determination clauses of the Treaty of Versailles to his advantage. But Czechoslovakia was next on his list, and that nation had an alliance with France.

Again Hitler argued for self-determination. The western border region of Czechoslovakia, called the Sudetenland (*soo-DĀ-ten-land*), was populated mainly by Germans, and Hitler claimed Germany's right to annex the area. Throughout the summer of 1938, Hitler pressured the Czechs to cede him the Sudetenland, and the Sudeten Nazi Party increased the pressure by staging provocations and incidents. But the Czechs, counting on French support, stood firm. They knew that as the Sudetenland contained most of

After annexing Austria, Hitler turns on Czechoslovakia

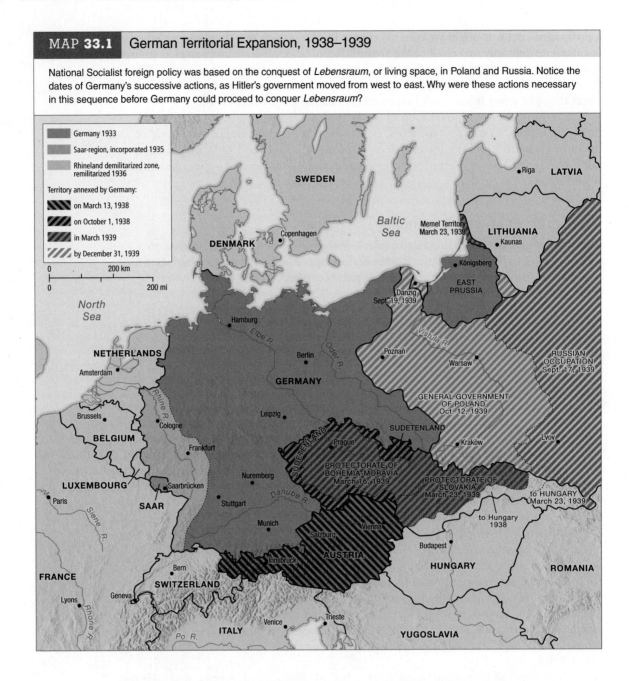

| MAP **33.1** | German Territorial Expansion, 1938–1939 |

National Socialist foreign policy was based on the conquest of *Lebensraum*, or living space, in Poland and Russia. Notice the dates of Germany's successive actions, as Hitler's government moved from west to east. Why were these actions necessary in this sequence before Germany could proceed to conquer *Lebensraum*?

Czechoslovakia's frontier fortifications against Germany, the rest of the nation would be defenseless without the region. British prime minister Neville Chamberlain, desperate to avert another European war that would doubtless involve his country, flew twice to Germany to meet with Hitler personally. But still the German leader insisted on annexation.

In late September war seemed likely, a fact that worried not only German military leaders (who thought Germany would lose a war against Czechoslovakia, Britain, and France) but also most ordinary Germans, who lacked enthusiasm for renewing the Great War. Mussolini, having no intention of taking Italy into such a war but reluctant to see Germany lose one, suggested a four-power conference at the last minute. Hitler agreed, hosting the conference himself in Munich on September 28–29, 1938. He came away with an Anglo-French agreement that Germany would annex the Sudetenland on October 1.

The Munich Treaty, with its concessions to Germany, was the triumph of **appeasement,** a policy of giving in to a potential aggressor to maintain the peace. Appeasement arose not out of cowardice but from a sincere desire to avoid another Great War by addressing German concerns over the severity of the Treaty of Versailles. Its fatal weakness was that the Nazi government was not so much interested in these concerns, which it viewed as pretexts, as in what could be gained by the threat of force or by force itself. Czechoslovakia rightly believed that it had been sold out to a bullying dictator. Chamberlain wrongly believed that he had secured "peace in our time"; what he had gained was peace for six months. On March 15, 1939, Germany invaded the remainder of Czechoslovakia, which was now a purely Slavic country with almost no German population. Clearly Hitler's intention was not to pursue self-determination or to adjust genuine grievances but to expand Germany eastward. Poland would be next on the list.

Temporarily the initiative passed to Britain and France, which issued a guarantee of Polish independence on March 31. But this commitment did not impress Hitler, who could not imagine that Britain and France would fight to defend a nation with a weak army when they had sold out Czechoslovakia, a well-fortified country with a strong one. His cynicism made him miss the point: the democracies now knew that his self-determination rhetoric was phony, and at last they resisted.

Pressure on Poland increased until, on August 23, Germany shocked the world by signing a nonaggression pact with the Soviet Union. Germany agreed to divide Poland with the Soviets and to grant Moscow other favorable adjustments along its western borders. In return, the Soviets guaranteed Germany regular shipments of grain, oil, and timber. British blockades had caused crippling shortages of food and supplies in Germany during the Great War, so this **Nazi-Soviet Pact** effectively rendered Germany blockade proof by giving it access to Russian food and resources. Hitler assumed this agreement would convince Britain and France that it was useless to fight over Poland, but when Germany invaded that country on September 1, London and Paris demanded German withdrawal by September 3. When the deadline expired, Britain and France declared war on Germany, beginning what would later be known as World War II.

The Munich Conference of 1938. Front row, from left to right: Chamberlain, Daladier, Hitler, Mussolini, Italian foreign minister Ciano.

The Munich Conference gives the Sudetenland to Germany

Read the **Document**
Neville Chamberlain, In Search of Peace
on **myhistorylab.com**

Read the **Document**
Adolf Hitler, The Obersalzberg Speech, 1939
on **myhistorylab.com**

View the **Map**
Interactive Map: German Expansion Under the Third Reich
on **myhistorylab.com**

Germany's invasion of Poland begins World War II

Hitler's War, 1939–1941

From September 1939 until December 1941, world leaders usually called the new conflict "the European War." In the newspapers, on radio broadcasts, and in everyday conversation, however, it was known as "Hitler's War." Adolf Hitler's actions had started the war, his ideology inspired it, and his leadership guided Germany to unprecedented territorial domination. By July 1940, German forces occupied most of the continent and intimidated the few neutral nations that remained. Europe's future appeared to be one of subjugation to the Master Race.

Listen to the **Audio**
World War II 1
on **myhistorylab.com**

From Poland to France

German conquest of Poland took only four weeks, featuring a new tactic called **Blitzkrieg,** or "lightning war." Striking more rapidly than the enemy was nothing new in warfare; what made Blitzkrieg so effective was the radio, which permitted instant communication

Blitzkrieg enables Germany to conquer Poland quickly

German mechanized warfare.

between armored units on the ground and dive-bombers in the air. The resulting coordination of modern mechanized units threw the more conventional Polish forces into disarray and gave the Germans a reputation for machine-like efficiency despite the fact that most of their transportation, like that of other European armies in 1939, was still handled by horses. After three weeks, fulfilling the terms of the Nazi-Soviet Pact, the Soviets invaded from the East to help Germany complete the division of Poland (Map 33.2). The USSR improved its borders in the Baltic region, taking territory from Finland in the Russo-Finnish War (November 1939–March 1940), and absorbing the Baltic states of Estonia, Latvia, and Lithuania in July 1940 through nonaggression pacts and internal subversion.

While the Soviets were occupying additional land, Germany was engaged in the so-called Phony War, a quiet seven-month period in which Hitler first tried to convince Britain to withdraw from the war, and then, having failed in this effort, looked for a strategy that would defeat France. Attacking westward in spring of 1940, Germany broke the French lines by driving armored units through the dense Ardennes Forest on the Franco-Belgian border. The French high command, having observed the effectiveness of Blitzkrieg in Poland, was for some reason unprepared for such tactics in France and had stationed no reserve forces with which to counter a possible breakthrough. Meanwhile, the British Expeditionary Force, trapped against the English Channel at Dunkirk, narrowly escaped to England when Hitler ordered a 48-hour halt for tank maintenance. France surrendered on June 24, 1940. General Charles de Gaulle, French under-secretary of state for war, flew to London and announced the formation of the Free French movement in hopes of attracting French volunteers to continue the fight against Germany, but few heard his radio broadcast of June 18 and even fewer responded to his call.

Hitler receiving news of France's surrender.

The conquest of France makes Germany master of Europe

The fall of France shocked the world. Until then the war had been a series of sideshows that, although important, could not settle the conflict. But France was a different matter. Nazi Germany had achieved in six weeks what Imperial Germany had been unable to accomplish in more than four years between 1914 and 1918. Hitler was master of most of the European continent, and any future challenge to his rule would necessitate an invasion of Europe from abroad. The French army had been considered the bastion of democracy against fascist aggression; its amazingly swift collapse demoralized those throughout the world who yearned for Hitler's defeat. Many feared that the Third Reich, as Hitler had boasted, really would last a thousand years.

The Battle of Britain

Yet Britain remained undefeated, and its morale showed no signs of weakening. Winston Churchill had replaced Neville Chamberlain as prime minister just before the Nazi attack on France. Passionately anti-German, referring to Hitler as a "bloodthirsty guttersnipe" and invariably pronouncing "Nazi" to rhyme with "nasty," Churchill employed his remarkable rhetorical skills to inspire his island nation and rebuild its confidence in ultimate victory (see "Address of Winston Churchill to Parliament, June 4, 1940"). In this mission he was indirectly aided by Hitler, who had no coherent plan for defeating Britain. Everyone,

MAP **33.2**   Hitler's War in Europe, 1939–1940

Once Germany had secured its southern and eastern flanks by absorbing Austria and Czechoslovakia, Hitler was free to initiate a European war. Observe that Germany and the Soviet Union collaborated to conquer Poland, and that Soviet support left Germany free to turn westward against Norway, the Netherlands, Belgium, Luxembourg, and France. How might Hitler's strategy have changed had the Soviet Union not supported his westward aggression?

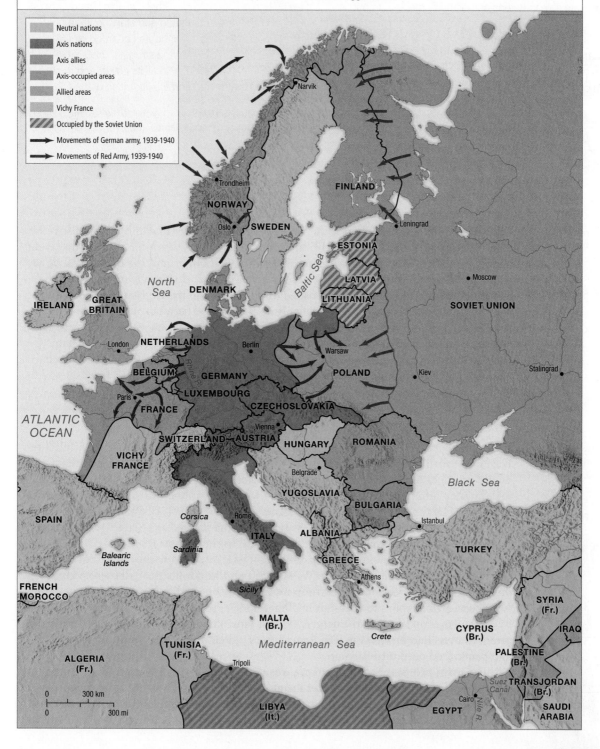

DOCUMENT 33.1 Address of Winston Churchill to Parliament, June 4, 1940

. . . I have, myself, full confidence that if all do their duty, if nothing is neglected, and if the best arrangements are made, as they are being made, we shall prove ourselves once again able to defend our Island home, to ride out the storm of war, and to outlive the menace of tyranny, if necessary for years, if necessary alone. At any rate, that is what we are going to try to do . . . Even though large tracts of Europe and many old and famous States have fallen or may fall into the grip of the Gestapo and all the odious apparatus of Nazi rule, we shall not flag or fail. We shall go on to the end, we shall fight in France, we shall fight on the seas and oceans, we shall fight with growing confidence and growing strength in the air, we shall defend our Island, whatever the cost may be, we shall fight on the beaches, we shall fight on the landing grounds, we shall fight in the fields and in the streets, we shall fight in the hills; we shall never surrender; and even if, which I do not for a moment believe, this Island or a large part of it were subjugated and starving, then our Empire beyond the seas, armed and guarded by the British Fleet, would carry on the struggle, until, in God's good time, the New World, with all its power and might, steps forth to the rescue and the liberation of the Old.

SOURCE: Address of Winston Churchill to parliament, June 4, 1940 from Robert Rhodes James, (ed.) *Winston S. Churchill: His complete Speeches, 1897–1963*, Volume VI (1935–1942) Copyright © 1974. Published by Chelsea House Publishers. Reprinted by permission of Curtis Brown, UK.

Britain frustrates Germany's bid for air superiority

including Churchill, knew that if the German army landed in England it would win the war, but everyone also knew that Britain's Royal Navy was powerful enough to prevent an invasion. The unavoidable logic in this thinking led Hitler into the unusual tactic of trying to destroy Britain's Royal Air Force so that his own *Luftwaffe* (the German air force) could keep the Royal Navy bottled up in port while the German army invaded.

This approach produced the Battle of Britain, a contest between air forces that the British won between August and November 1940. They used a new detection system called "radar," invented in Britain in 1938, to direct their fighters against incoming German raiders. Their pilots performed with such efficiency and heroism that Churchill claimed, "Never in the field of human conflict was so much owed by so many to so few."

The German Invasion of Russia

Germany invades Russia to fulfill Hitler's ideological dream

Frustrated by a war against an enemy he couldn't invade, Hitler turned east to fulfill the Nazi quest for living space in European Russia. He had promised his generals that he would not fight a two-front war, but since neither Britain nor Germany was capable of invading the other, he could plausibly claim that action on the British front was stalled. Besides, if Hitler's drive for living space were going to succeed, Germany would have to fight the USSR at some point. Hitler assumed that the Russians, a Slavic people scorned by the Nazis as "subhumans," would quickly fall to the Master Race.

The invasion of Russia began on June 22, 1941, and it took the Soviet government completely by surprise (Map 33.3). Washington and London repeatedly sent Moscow intelligence data concerning Nazi troop movements, but Stalin dismissed them as capitalist lies designed to split the Nazi-Soviet alliance. He apparently suffered a nervous collapse when the invasion began and emerged 11 days later shaken and grim. By July 16 German armored units had broken the Red Army's lines, taken more than a million prisoners, and penetrated deep into Russia.

The main problem facing Germany was the immensity of the Soviet Union, amounting to one sixth of the land surface of the globe. The primitive state of local roads slowed the German advance, but even if that advance had been swifter, Germany did not have enough soldiers to achieve victory over a country so large. In addition, the Red Army,

Fires burn in London during the Battle of Britain.

MAP **33.3**   Germany's Invasion of the USSR, 1941

Frustrated by his inability either to conquer Britain or to force it out of the war, Hitler turned on the Soviet Union in June 1941, intent on fulfilling the Nazi objective of acquiring *Lebensraum*. Note that numerous German thrusts enabled them to occupy immense areas of western Russia but left Moscow unconquered and most of the Soviet Union free of German control. Why was Germany unable to defeat the Soviet Union in 1941?

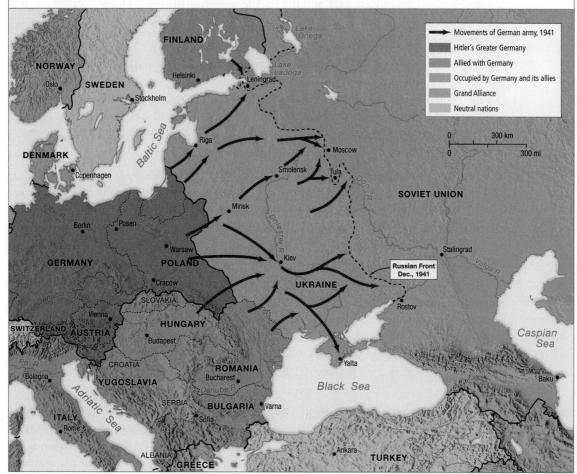

substantially larger than the German, drew on huge manpower reserves. German forces made their task much more difficult by treating non-Russian ethnic groups, which had initially welcomed them as liberators from Communist oppression, as Slavic subhumans. Finally, Hitler and his high command failed to define a single principal objective, choosing instead to drive simultaneously for the cities of Leningrad, Moscow, and Kiev.

Soviet resistance proved more persistent than Germany had anticipated. By November Kiev had been taken, Leningrad was besieged but could not be completely surrounded, and furious fighting engulfed the western approaches to Moscow. Acting out of sheer desperation, and believing a spy's report that Japan would move against the Americans, British, and Dutch in the Pacific rather than against Soviet Siberia, Stalin in late November transferred 250,000 Siberian troop reserves west to the Moscow front under Georgi Zhukov (*gay-ŌR-gē ZHOO-kawf*), his most successful commander. The resulting Soviet counteroffensive in early December caught the Germans off-guard and unprepared for winter conditions. The supposedly subhuman Russians then handed the German army a

Read the **Document**

Winston Churchill, "Their Finest Hour" (Great Britain), 1940

on **myhistorylab.com**

A Soviet counteroffensive surprises the German army

stinging defeat. The Germans stiffened and held their positions throughout the winter, but Hitler's chain of Blitzkrieg victories was over, and anti-Nazi forces gained new hope.

East Asia and the Pacific, 1937–1942

Meanwhile, events in East Asia and the Pacific were transforming Hitler's conflict into a Second World War. Japan had fought on the winning side in the Great War but had been treated with condescension by its allies after 1919. The Japanese government's request that the Versailles Treaty include a racial equality clause had been rejected by Britain, France, and the United States. At the Washington Naval Conference of 1921, Japan was forced to accept a treaty that limited it to only three large naval ships for every five built by the United States and five by Britain. In 1924, the United States Congress passed discriminatory immigration legislation that permitted 53,000 British immigrants to enter each year, but only 100 Japanese. Japan concluded that its former allies thought little of its wartime support.

Suffering economically from the Great Depression, Japan decided in 1931 to secure the natural resources it needed for its rapidly developing industrial capability by conquering China's resource-rich province of Manchuria. Six years later, on July 7, 1937, Japanese army units from Manchuria, staging provocative maneuvers in China, clashed with Nationalist Chinese troops at the Marco Polo Bridge, not far from Beijing.

The New Order in East Asia

Japanese aggression and atrocities endanger Asia

Japan followed up this incident by conquering northeast China, hoping to quickly force the Nationalists to accept peace terms. But Chinese president Jiang Jieshi (Chiang Kaishek), faced with overwhelming force, refused to surrender or to mount an all-out resistance. Determined to press forward, the Japanese struck south, capturing Shanghai in a bloody three-month battle and taking Nanjing in December. Japanese troops then went on a rampage in Nanjing, massacring as many as two hundred thousand people and raping thousands of women.

The Rape of Nanjing.

The international outcry that followed this **"Rape of Nanjing"** energized Chinese resistance to Japanese military occupation. It also inadvertently produced further atrocities. Hoping to satisfy their soldiers and prevent future international condemnation over mass rapes, the Japanese set up "comfort stations" near the front lines, forcing young Korean girls to serve as "comfort women," whom Japanese soldiers repeatedly raped each day. But the outcry over Nanjing did not slow Japan's advance. By the end of 1938, the Japanese had conquered most of eastern China (Map 33.4). Declaring a "New Order in East Asia," they portrayed themselves as liberators who were cleansing the region of Western imperialists and creating a prosperous new economic sphere dominated by Asians.

Still the Chinese refused to submit. The Chinese Communists, from their northwestern base at Yan'an, mounted an effective guerrilla campaign that tormented Japanese troops, sabotaged their systems of transport and supply by blowing up trucks and trains, and won the allegiance of many Chinese peasants. Meanwhile, the Nationalists, whose inability to stop the invaders rapidly eroded their public support, retreated to central China and hoped that Japan would blunder.

A few years later, their hopes were fulfilled. In 1940, after France surrendered, the French colony of Indochina was left unprotected. Attracted by that region's assets and

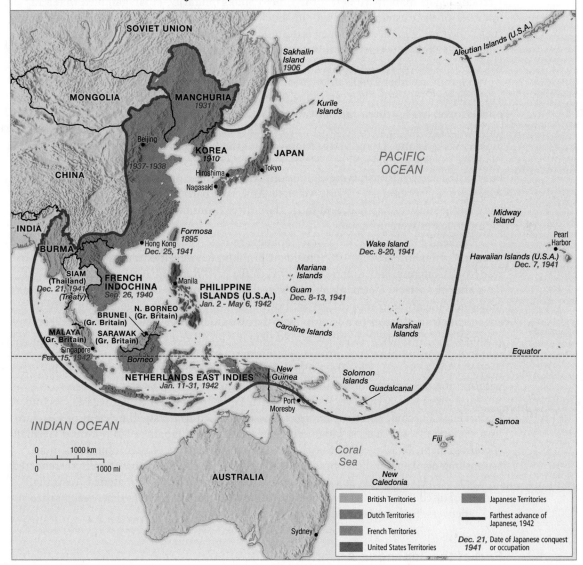

MAP 33.4 | Japanese Conquests, 1937–1942

From its island base, Japan in fewer than fifty years created an empire and expanded it to the line shown on the map. Notice that this expansion was achieved at the expense of Britain, China, the United States, France, and the Netherlands. None of the first three countries were willing to accept Japanese domination of the region, and Japan's strength was inadequate to force them to do so. What disadvantages did Japan face as a result of its rapid expansion?

awed by Nazi success, the Japanese joined the Axis, allying with Germany and Italy in the Tripartite Pact. Japan then began moving troops into Indochina. Hoping to force them to withdraw, the United States imposed an embargo in 1941, depriving Japan of American supplies, including oil. But this embargo only confirmed Japan's conviction that it must possess its own sources of fuel and raw materials.

Acting on this conviction, the Japanese planned a bold and spectacular operation: a campaign to conquer British Singapore and Malaya, the oil-rich Dutch East Indies, and the Philippine Islands, an American commonwealth. The action would start with

Japan decides to gain resources through conquest

a surprise assault on the U.S. Pacific Fleet, based in the Hawaiian Islands at a naval station called Pearl Harbor.

Japan Strikes in the Pacific

Recognizing its inability to defeat the United States militarily, Japan gambled that a rapid takeover of the western Pacific would shock the Americans and leave them unwilling to spend the time, blood, and money required to retake it. If this hoped-for scenario did not materialize, Tokyo was left with no plausible alternative to defeat. This desperate gamble led Japan to one of the most brilliant tactical victories of the war.

In late November 1941, an invasion fleet headed southward from Japan. Simultaneously, Japan's First Air Fleet, an innovative grouping of six aircraft carriers into a single attack force, left northern Japan heading east. In a carefully coordinated multipronged assault spread across thousands of miles of the Pacific, the southern force attacked Guam, Wake Island, Hong Kong, Malaya, and the Philippines on December 7–8, while the First Air Fleet attacked Pearl Harbor. American forces, anticipating the southern but not the eastern thrust, were caught unprepared in the greatest military disaster in American history (see page 776). All eight American battleships anchored in the harbor were either sunk or disabled, and more than three thousand casualties were inflicted. Japanese losses were minimal.

The Pearl Harbor attack boosted Japanese morale, but they lost their gamble. Rather than accept Japan's actions, U.S. president Franklin Roosevelt obtained a declaration of war from Congress, and Americans rallied to the cry "Remember Pearl Harbor!" Four days after the attack, Germany and Italy declared war on the United States. They were under no obligation to support Japan, but Hitler hoped to encourage the Japanese to engage the United States in a lengthy war that would distract America for years. He assumed that the American public would demand an all-out effort against Japan and that U.S. forces would make little impact on the war in Europe until after Germany defeated Soviet Russia. Therefore, Hitler believed, his declaration of war would be without practical effect but would further heighten the morale of the Japanese.

Hitler was wrong on several counts. First, Germany did not defeat Russia. Second, Roosevelt, Churchill, and their military advisors agreed to pursue the defeat of Germany first, making the war against Japan secondary. Finally, the Japanese did not need German encouragement. By May 1942 they had conquered every one of their objectives in an astonishing display of military boldness and skill. When the Philippines finally surrendered to Japan on May 6, 1942, Tokyo controlled the western Pacific, threatened Australia, and was poised to strike against the three American aircraft carriers that, being at sea on maneuvers, had not been destroyed at Pearl Harbor.

End of the Japanese Advance

Admiral Isoroku Yamamoto (*ih-sō-RŌ-koo yah-mah-MŌ-to*), architect of the Pearl Harbor strategy, designed another two-pronged plan to destroy the carriers. A massive six-carrier strike force would leave Japan bound for Midway Island, the only remaining American military possession west of Hawaii. On route, two of the six carriers would separate from the main body and head northeast, threatening an invasion of Alaska. Yamamoto reasoned that Admiral Chester Nimitz, commanding what remained of the U.S. Pacific Fleet, would be compelled to divide his forces to counter the threat, and his carriers would be isolated and sunk one by one.

But Nimitz, whose intelligence section was reading Japanese naval codes, knew that Midway was the principal target and did not divide his forces. The Americans were still

---

Margin notes:

Japan attacks Pearl Harbor to eliminate the U.S. Pacific Fleet

The Allies decide to deal with Germany before Japan

((•─ **Listen** to the **Audio**
World War II 2
on **myhistorylab.com**

Japan's strategy fails at Midway

outnumbered by four carriers to three, but a squadron of American dive-bombers took the Japanese carriers by surprise and destroyed all four. The Midway disaster ended Japan's string of victories and virtually guaranteed its ultimate defeat.

North Africa and Europe, 1942–1943

In the winter of 1941–1942, Hitler renewed his attack on the Soviet Union by driving southeast toward the oil-rich Caucasus region. That strategic decision was opposed by many of his military advisors. Some encouraged continuing pressure on Moscow, hoping to crack Soviet resistance there. Others, like Field Marshal Erwin Rommel, begged Hitler to push from North Africa through the Suez Canal and the Middle East, eventually linking up with Japan in the Persian Gulf and Indian Ocean. Such a strategy would deprive Britain of its oil and might force it to make peace.

Erwin Rommel, the "Desert Fox."

The Battle for North Africa

Rommel, one of the century's finest battlefield commanders, was in North Africa because of Italian military errors. Mussolini had become overconfident after Germany's defeat of France and committed his finest troops to Italy's African colony of Tripoli in an effort to push Britain out of Egypt. Instead, the British forces, outnumbered ten to one, invaded Tripoli and humiliated the Italians by forcing huge numbers of them to surrender. Fearful that Mussolini would abandon the struggle, Hitler decided to send Rommel at the head of two tank divisions, the "Afrika Korps," to reverse Italy's failure.

The North African desert turned out to be ideal terrain for tanks. German forces quickly pushed the British back into Egypt (Map 33.5). London naturally reinforced its position in order to defend the Suez Canal, but when Rommel asked for more troops

MAP **33.5**	World War II in North Africa, 1940–1943

Italy's 1940 attempt to conquer Egypt from its colony in Libya failed completely and forced Germany to send an expeditionary force under Field Marshal Erwin Rommel to North Africa to bail the Italians out. Observe that British and American landings in northwestern Africa coincided with a major British victory at El Alamein in 1942. Why did the Allied occupation of North Africa endanger Germany's hopes for victory in World War II?

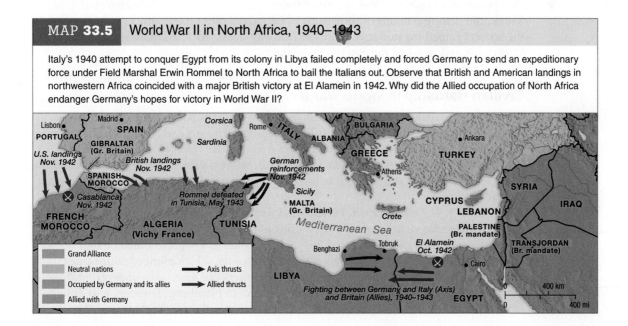

and equipment, as well as for a strategic decision to turn North Africa into a principal combat area, Hitler denied both requests. In both 1941 and 1942, Hitler focused on *Lebensraum* and the Soviet Union rather than the Middle East, thereby missing a reasonable chance at forcing Britain out of the war. Rommel, undersupplied and undermanned, proved tactically brilliant in desert warfare but unable to overcome Britain's material superiority.

Germany loses in North Africa

The British War Cabinet determined to capitalize on that superiority. In the summer of 1942, Britain's Eighth Army received its new commander, General Bernard Law Montgomery, a feisty Scot who believed in rigorous training and crushing material advantage. That October he attacked and defeated the Afrika Korps. Simultaneously, U.S. forces, having waited nearly a year to engage the Germans, landed in Morocco and Algeria. Caught between British and Americans, Rommel's troops fought skillfully but hopelessly. Ironically, now that it would do no good, Hitler insisted on reinforcing Rommel—over the latter's explicit objections. When the Afrika Korps surrendered on May 13, 1943, an additional 250,000 German soldiers needlessly became prisoners of war.

Stalingrad and Kursk

By mid-1943 the war in the east had also turned against Germany. Hitler's decision to drive toward the Caucasus was ill advised, dragging the German army into a house-to-house battle for the large city of Stalingrad. In November 1942, a Soviet counteroffensive penetrated a weak point in the German lines and encircled the city (Map 33.6). German forces trapped there were forbidden to try to break out until the armies invading the Caucasus could be withdrawn; otherwise more than a million men would have been captured. By the time the withdrawal was completed, it was too late to save Stalingrad. The German Sixth Army, reduced from 220,000 to 90,000 freezing, starving men, surrendered on February 2, 1943. It was the turning point of the war for the Soviet Union, and Stalin ordered nightlong fireworks over Red Square in celebration.

The Red Army takes the strategic initiative at Kursk

Germany still held the strategic advantage, however, and proved it by attacking the Soviets near Kursk in July. The weeklong fight was the largest tank battle in history to that point; astronauts can still see, from outer space, a large reddish-brown spot near Kursk, the rusting remains of thousands of destroyed tanks. Germany lost the battle and the Soviets gained the initiative. Like the Midway defeat for the Japanese, for the Germans Kursk marked the end of expansion.

Civilian Hardship in World War II

Many of the hardships the Great War imposed on civilians (Chapter 31) returned to plague the home fronts in World War II. Rationing reappeared as a means for managing shortages of food, fuel, clothing, and vital raw materials. Tens of millions labored six or seven days a week in defense plants. Once again, women took up work on farms and in factories as men were drafted. But new burdens appeared in the early 1940s to intensify civilian suffering.

In Britain, Germany, Japan, Poland, and Russia, aerial bombing destroyed homes and burned whole sections of cities. Air raids in the Great War had been sporadic and ineffective, but now they were relentless and devastating. People huddled behind drawn curtains in darkened rooms during nighttime blackouts, which plunged entire cities into darkness to make them less visible to bombers. Others crammed into underground shelters for protection. Sometimes there was no escape: in Hamburg, Dresden, and Tokyo, massive incendiary bombing created firestorms that raised surface temperatures to over

MAP **33.6** Soviet Victories at Stalingrad and Kursk, 1942–1943

Unable to take Moscow in 1941, the Germans turned south to the oil fields of the Transcaucasus in 1942. Their defeat at Stalingrad was a principal turning point in the war. But notice that the Red Army was unable to take the offensive until after the German defeat at Kursk in 1943 in the largest tank battle of the war. How did the Red Army then proceed to expel the Germans from Russia?

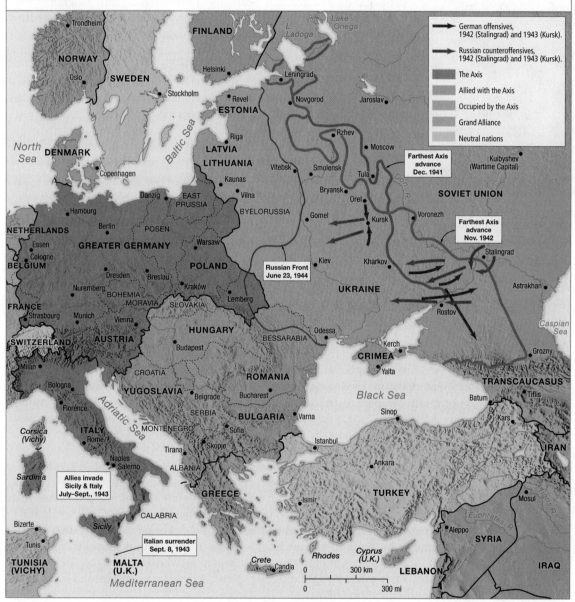

2,000 degrees. Some people caught outside shelters were trapped in asphalt as streets melted; others were boiled alive when they dove into canals to escape the heat; still others were melted into tiny pools of liquid fat.

Ground warfare was no less destructive. In Russia, advancing Germans totally destroyed more than nineteen thousand villages, often burning the inhabitants alive

World War II produces intense civilian suffering

Female welder at a munitions plant, 1942.

in synagogues or churches. When Soviet forces invaded Germany in 1945, they retaliated by crucifying German farmers on barn doors and raping and mutilating women. Japanese soldiers in Manila in 1944 slaughtered the patients and staff of entire hospitals and threw babies against walls to break open their skulls. In the Great War, British propaganda had accused Germans of atrocities against Belgian civilians, but most such accusations were fictional; in World War II, the brutality was both factual and unimaginable.

Many civilians caught in war zones did not survive. Tens of millions perished in China and Russia as battlefields shifted back and forth across major cities. The city council of Benghazi in North Africa posted street signs in both English and German; Benghazi changed hands five times in two years, each change more destructive than the one before. Even in places without armed conflict, death was never far away from civilians. In Bengal in eastern India, shipping shortages and British administrative failures combined in 1943 to produce a famine that killed 1.5 million people. Compared with those who suffered such horrors, civilians enduring shortages and lengthy workweeks seemed fortunate indeed.

Resistance to Nazi Rule

In Nazi-occupied Europe, as nations were systematically plundered to feed and enrich the conquerors, civilians suffered extensively from cold, malnutrition, and deprivation. These hardships, combined with Nazi treatment of conquered nationalities as inferior peoples, provoked desperate resistance to German rule.

Underground resistance organizations developed quickly in France, Yugoslavia, Greece, and Czechoslovakia, where rugged terrain aided concealment. Britain encouraged these groups by sending agents behind enemy lines and, in Yugoslavia, through air drops of men carrying money and weapons. Countries with level terrain, like Belgium and Holland, could not create complex resistance networks. But in Poland, a country with few mountains, an underground Home Army recruited three hundred thousand men and women between 1940 and 1944. These organizations carried out sabotage and spread anti-German propaganda in an effort to keep hope alive.

Resistance movements fail to cripple the German occupation of Europe

Yet the resistance movements did not seriously weaken Nazi control. When underground agents assassinated Reinhard Heydrich, Reich Protector of Bohemia and Moravia, in Prague in 1942, brutal Nazi retaliation served as a warning to all resisters. More than 1,300 Czech men, women, and children from two nearby villages were murdered, and the villages themselves were bulldozed and burned to the ground. Germany monopolized the heavy equipment required to conduct modern warfare; without such matériel, the Polish Home Army was cut to pieces when it revolted in Warsaw in August 1944. The Red Army, a few miles away, did not intervene, seeing an advantage to German slaughter of anti-Communist Poles.

Nazi Mass Murder

For millions of Jews and other innocent civilians, Nazi occupation meant mass murder. Before the war, in Germany itself, Nazi anti-Semitism had been characterized by vandalism, legal harassment, persecution, and beatings. But the German conquests of 1939–1940, and invasion of Russia in 1941, brought millions of Jews under Nazi control. In the summer of 1941, Hitler and the German leadership, obsessed with the Nazi vision of racial purification, decided to exterminate them all.

Extermination Camps

The methodology of mass murder evolved between 1939 and 1941. In September 1939, the Nazi regime started systematically killing people it considered unproductive or inferior. This campaign killed more than 120,000 mental patients, disabled people, terminally ill people, and severely wounded soldiers. A public outcry embarrassed the government and drove the slaughter underground in 1941, but two years of murder created a variety of extermination methods and an experienced corps of professional killers. In the following years, both the methods and the murderers were used throughout Europe against Jews and others the Nazis considered unworthy of life. Hitler was indifferent to moral considerations and unafraid of the condemnation of other nations. Referring to the slaughter of the Armenians in the Great War (Chapter 31), he observed on more than one occasion, "Who today remembers the Armenians?"

Nazi Germany embarks on a policy of genocide

Initially, Jews were shot or gassed with carbon monoxide in the back of vans. Those methods, however, proved time consuming and wasteful. By the fall of 1941, Germany had begun to experiment with mass gassings in detention camp buildings disguised as showers. Zyklon-B, a high-potency insecticide, proved effective in murdering hundreds of people at a time. On December 8, 1941, gassings in trucks with Zyklon-B began at Chelmno in Poland, the first of six designated extermination sites. Five others followed, all in Poland, including the largest and most infamous, Auschwitz-Birkenau, at which more than two million people were murdered (Map 33.7). By the end of the war, nearly six million Jews had perished from gas, brutalization, malnutrition, exposure, and disease in what later became known as the Holocaust.

Jewish Hungarian women at Auschwitz-Birkenau.

On January 30, 1942, in a villa in the Berlin suburb of Wannsee (*VAHN-sā*), Reinhard Heydrich, who was then head of the Security Service of the Nazi SS (Hitler's elite bodyguard), convened a conference of Nazi officials from across Europe to discuss the "Final Solution to the Jewish Question": mass murder. Heydrich's deputy and "Jewish specialist," Adolf Eichmann, an expert in train scheduling, explained how Jews from throughout Europe would be transported to camps in Poland. The journeys would take days in unheated and unventilated boxcars without sanitary facilities; food and water would be minimal or unavailable. Many Jews would die before reaching the camps; once there, the rest would die through overwork, exposure to cold, malnutrition, or outright murder. If any objections to this plan were raised at Wannsee, the minutes of the conference do not record them.

Nazi racial doctrine defined Jews as "race defilers" who schemed to destroy the Master Race through intermarriage and seduction. Many of those who assisted in the Holocaust, however, knew little of these ideas. For most ordinary Germans, as well as the Dutch, French, Latvians, Poles, Romanians, Ukrainians, and others who helped them, Jews were outsiders despised for various reasons—as killers of Christ, moneylenders, rivals for economic or educational advantage, or practitioners of mysterious rituals. Some Jews had been assimilated into Europe's dominant cultures, but many remained in cohesive communities and were feared and resented. The Holocaust was conceived and

MAP **33.7** The Holocaust in Europe, 1941–1945

In pursuit of its racist ideology, Nazi Germany created an intricate network of detention facilities, transit sites, and death camps across Europe. More than six million Jews were murdered, and they were not the only group processed through this system. Note that Soviet POWs, Polish Catholics, Sinti and Roma peoples, Serbians, homosexuals, Jehovah's Witnesses, and handicapped or politically undesirable Germans were also exterminated. What might account for the widely varying numbers of Jewish deaths from one country to another?

Total Deaths from Nazi Extermination Policies	
European Jews	6,183,000
Soviet POWs	3,000,000
Polish Catholics	3,000,000
Serbians	700,000
Sinti and Roma	250,000
Germans (political prisoners, resisters, and handicapped)	150,000
Homosexuals	12,000
Jehovah's Witnesses	2,500
TOTAL	**13,297,500**

Map legend:
- Greatest extent of Axis power, 1942
- *1,000* Estimates of Jewish deaths in the "final solution"
- ■ Main concentration camp, founded before 1940
- ■ Main concentration camp, founded from 1940
- ● Camp built for implementation of "final solution" from 1941
- ✕ Euthanasia center
- ◎ Transit camps for deportations to Auschwitz
- ▲ Mass murder site
- □ Major ghetto

planned by fanatical racists seeking to "purify" Europe of Jews and make it safe for the "Master Race," but it was carried out by ordinary people who did not like Jews and thought little of anyone who did. Some of those involved in the killings were sadists and criminals, but just as often they were otherwise normal people who behaved with unspeakable cruelty out of fear, a desire to conform and obey orders, a sense of their own superiority, or in the hope of gaining some sort of advantage.

The Implementation of Mass Murder

Beginning early in 1942, occupied Europe was "combed" of Jews from west to east. Of those who reached the camps alive, most were gassed within a few hours of arrival. The strongest were selected for forced labor on minimal rations; some were chosen for medical experiments, others for service as prostitutes. By early 1943 most Polish Jews had been gassed at Treblinka or Auschwitz, and most German Jews remaining after years of persecution were also dead. Much of the richness and beauty of European Jewish culture went with them.

Germany collects European Jews for extermination

In the rest of Europe, chances for survival varied widely from country to country. Most Dutch Jews were killed at Auschwitz, although some, like Anne Frank, a young Dutch girl whose diary was later found and published throughout the world, were moved from one camp to another. Nearly all the Jews of Denmark survived, protected by Danish authorities and eventually smuggled by boat into neutral Sweden. Italians considered exterminating Jews abhorrent, and not until Germany occupied much of Italy following Mussolini's overthrow in 1943 were most Italian Jews shipped to Auschwitz. Russian, Romanian, Latvian, and Lithuanian Jews were systematically exterminated, while Hungarian Jews were protected by Admiral Nicholas Horthy's pro-German dictatorship until he was forced to resign in 1944. Hundreds of thousands of them were then murdered. By that time, however, the Red Army was moving into Poland, where it liberated the death camps one by one. In advance, however, the Germans evacuated remaining prisoners to Germany by atrocious "death marches," in which tens of thousands died of maltreatment and cold. The survivors were imprisoned in camps in Germany, such as Dachau, Buchenwald, and Bergen-Belsen, where tens of thousands more, ill and malnourished, perished, including Anne Frank, who died in March 1945.

Jews were the primary targets of Nazi extermination policies, but they were not the only ones. Sinti and Roma people from Hungary and Romania, often called Gypsies, were depicted by Nazis as inferior racial stock, placed in camps, and often killed. In occupied Poland, those with college degrees, including doctors, lawyers, Catholic clergy, and military officers, were systematically shot in order to deprive the Poles of future leadership. Soviet and other Slavic prisoners of war were treated brutally; more than 90 percent of them died from overwork, starvation, and sadistic medical experiments. Homosexuals were singled out for isolation, persecution, and murder. Had Germany won World War II, none of the groups of people listed here would have survived.

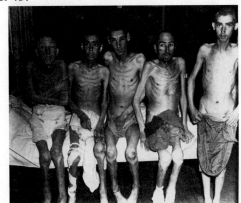

Concentration camp survivors.

The Question of Responsibility

Responsibility for the Holocaust rests with Nazi Germany

In the face of the scale of Nazi atrocities, not fully known until the war's end, people around the world anguished over the question of responsibility: could anyone have done anything to prevent these horrors? The Allied governments protested and publicized the atrocities, but their broadcasts reached few Germans and were not widely believed even in Britain and America. World War I atrocity propaganda had largely been proven false, and most people assumed that Hitler's alleged atrocities were Allied fabrications. The Allies, after all, were hardly neutral observers. After Pope Pius XII died in 1958, some suggested that this head of a neutral state and moral leader of global stature, who knew the details of the Nazi program through the Vatican's diplomatic network, should have spoken out against Nazi crimes. But there is no reason to believe that large numbers of German Catholics would have refused to cooperate with their government even had the Pope asked them to do so. Some suggested that the Allies should have bombed the camps, but by 1944, when Allied planes first came within bombing range of Auschwitz, the vast majority of Jews who would perish in the Holocaust were already dead. Moreover, had the camps been bombed, the Nazis would have found other ways to carry out their murderous agenda. In short, Roosevelt's consistently articulated position still seems the most practical: the best way to stop the killings was to win the war and destroy the Nazi regime.

When British and American troops liberated Buchenwald and Bergen-Belsen in spring of 1945, the films they made there shocked the world. Starving people sitting beside mounds of decaying corpses, bulldozers pushing heaps of naked bodies into mass graves, and the hollow-eyed stares of the barely living were shown in newsreels for months. One consequence of the Holocaust, as Hitler had intended, was the virtual destruction of Jewish culture in Europe. An unintended result was widespread pressure for the establishment of a Jewish state in Palestine as a place of refuge. Yet nothing could replace the hopes and lives destroyed in history's most extensive and appalling genocide.

American soldiers wade ashore at Omaha Beach in Normandy on D-day, June 6, 1944.

The Allies attack Germany from east and west

The Defeat of Germany, 1944–1945

By late summer of 1943, defeat of the Nazis seemed possible. Encouraged by its victories at Stalingrad and Kursk, the Red Army began the gradual liberation of Soviet soil. In Italy, a successful Allied landing and Mussolini's overthrow gave Germany a second front to defend. But much of Europe was still under Nazi occupation, and the Germans would not be defeated easily.

Squeezing Germany Between West and East

At a meeting that November in Tehran, the capital of Iran, Churchill, Roosevelt, and Stalin agreed on a third front: an Anglo-American invasion of France, across the English Channel, scheduled for May 1944 under the direction of U.S. general Dwight D. Eisenhower. Stalin promised to support this risky but necessary undertaking with a massive Eastern offensive to distract Germany and relieve the pressure on Allied beachheads. When the landings occurred in Normandy on **D-day,** June 6, 1944, they surprised the German military, which expected the invasion to come ashore near Calais, only 19 miles by ship from England (Map 33.8). Despite fierce resistance on Omaha Beach, the Allies held their ground. Stalin's promised Eastern drive began on June 22 (the third anniversary of the invasion of Russia) and achieved surprising gains. In mid-August, as Soviet pressure in Poland combined with an Allied breakout from Normandy, it appeared likely that the war in Europe would end in 1944.

Unexpectedly, however, the Germans regrouped and stabilized both fronts. Field Marshal Walther Model, known as "the Führer's Fireman," shuttled from one side of Germany to the other shoring up shattered lines. In Italy, the Allied invasion was stalled by difficult terrain, German defensive skills, and the poor performance of some American generals. Although it failed, a desperate German winter offensive in the West reminded Allied leaders that Germany's army remained intact and powerful.

The fighting finally ended with a crushing display of Allied superiority in manpower and matériel. The Red Army's January 1945 offensive tore huge gaps in the German lines and probably would have ended the war within weeks had Stalin been less sensitive to the concerns of his allies. At a February conference in Yalta, a southern Soviet resort town, the three Allied leaders—Churchill, Roosevelt, and Stalin—formally agreed to

| MAP **33.8** | The Allied Victory in Europe, 1944–1945 |

Between June 6, 1944 (the date of the invasion of Normandy), and May 8, 1945, Germany was squeezed from west and east. The bulk of the fighting was done by the Red Army, against which Germany deployed 80 percent of its forces, and which occupied most of Eastern Europe on its path toward Germany. Observe that the Eastern Front was twice the length of the Western Front. How might this disparity in deployment of soldiers and resources have affected Stalin's expectations of what Russia might gain from its victorious efforts?

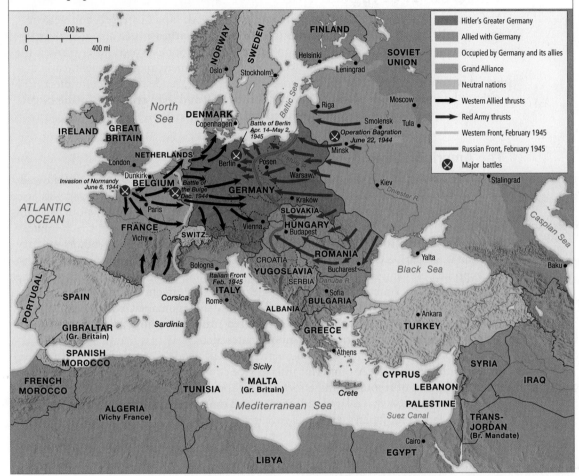

divide both Germany and its capital, Berlin, into military occupation zones at the close of the war. A Soviet conquest of Berlin at a time when British and American forces had not yet set foot on German soil might have worried and embarrassed the Western Allies.

Allied Victory in Europe

On March 7, 1945, the Americans and British finally crossed the Rhine and broke into Germany itself. Montgomery's British forces drove across the North German plain, American troops under Generals Omar Bradley and George Patton pierced central and southern Germany, and in the East, the Soviets resumed their offensive in mid-April. Outnumbered and outgunned, its tanks driven by 60-year-old veterans of the Great War and its fortifications manned by 13-year-old boys, the German army cracked. Roosevelt's death from a stroke on April 12 deprived him of the satisfaction of seeing the war end.

Watch the **Video**

Video: FDR on Winning the War

on **myhistorylab.com**

On April 30 Roosevelt's principal antagonist, Adolf Hitler, shot himself in his Berlin bunker as Soviet troops took the city one street at a time. Germany surrendered in the West on May 8 and in the East the next day, ending the Second World War in Europe.

The Defeat of Japan

As Germany's dreams of European domination collapsed, Japan's strategy for creating an empire by expelling Western powers from East and Southeast Asia also failed. That strategy was grounded in the assumption that the United States would never commit the money and troops necessary to conquer Japan. But the American government, capitalizing on widespread fury at Japan's surprise attack in 1941, made those commitments without hesitation. Once mobilized, the U.S. economy and industrial base, much larger than those of the Japanese Empire, secured eventual U.S. victory.

The American Strategy

View the **Image**
American Workers at B-17 Bomber Plant
on **myhistorylab.com**

The Americans attack the Japanese Empire by northern and southern routes

In the Pacific war, unlike the war in Europe, most combat took place at sea or followed the amphibious landing of soldiers from troop ships, and nearly all the fighting was done by Japanese and Americans. Late in 1942, the Americans, ready to take the offensive following their victory at Midway, had to choose a route along which to approach Japan. A northern route across tiny Pacific islands would rely on the U.S. Navy, but its military arm, the U.S. Marine Corps, might be too small for the land fighting required. A southern approach utilizing Australia and the Dutch East Indies would rely on the army rather than the navy, and American policy makers leaned in this direction. But that option would center on General Douglas MacArthur, a brilliant egomaniac whose defense of the Philippines had made him a hero in the United States but whose arrogance made him deeply unpopular with superiors and subordinates alike.

The solution was to choose the southern route but divide command between Admiral Nimitz and General MacArthur. This interservice compromise defied logic and led to mass duplication of resources and effort, but it thoroughly frustrated the Japanese, who were caught between two related yet independent offensives, each too powerful for them to defeat (Map 33.9). Japan's conquests gave it vast deposits of raw materials, but Japanese military industries benefited very little from them. Relentlessly, American submarines and surface vessels sank Japanese ships attempting to transport such materials.

Still, the Americans faced difficulties. Amphibious assaults upon Pacific islands proved deadly. Large parts of the Pacific remained unmapped in the early 1940s, and generals coordinating landings with tidal variations had to rely on guesswork provided by Pacific Islanders. Once ashore, ground forces faced well-entrenched, skillful Japanese infantry totally dedicated to their cause and willing to follow the ancient samurai code (Chapter 14) by dying to the last man. Poisonous insects and reptiles, stifling heat and drenching rains, and tropical fevers and diseases added to the burden of fighting. American and British forces fighting Japanese troops in the jungles of Burma and New Guinea suffered similarly.

The Japanese Empire Contracts

Gradually the Americans pushed the Japanese back. The names of battles on formerly unfamiliar Pacific islands became, for Americans, a litany of sacrifice; for the Japanese, the battles brought hostile forces ever closer to the Japanese home islands. During most of the war, only medium-range bombers were available, and they were hardly adequate

MAP **33.9**   World War II in the Pacific, 1942–1945

Between 1942 and 1945, Japan was attacked by British forces in Burma, by Chinese forces in China, and by American forces in the central and southern Pacific. Note that the Americans, unable to agree on a northern or a southern path to Japan, proceeded along both paths at the same time. The conquest of the Marianas in summer 1944 brought the Japanese home islands within range of American bombers, which then subjected Japan to a devastating bombing campaign, culminating in the use of atomic weapons. How did the intervention of the Soviet Union, which occurred at the same time as the atomic explosions, affect Japan's desire to continue the war?

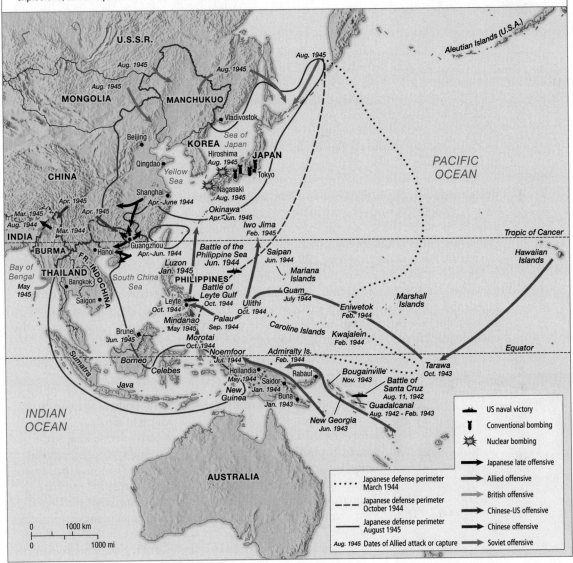

to cover the vastness of the Pacific. But in late 1944, the United States introduced the B-29 Superfortress. A pressurized cabin allowed the B-29 to reach altitudes up to 35,000 feet, putting it well beyond the range of enemy fighters and antiaircraft weapons. Now, as MacArthur's forces retook the Philippines, aided by the U.S. Navy's decisive victory in October at Leyte Gulf, attention shifted to the capture of two islands. Iwo Jima would place B-29s within range of Japan's home islands, and Okinawa could serve as a staging area for an amphibious assault upon Japan itself.

A U.S. Marine receives communion from a Catholic chaplain atop Mount Suribachi on Iwo Jima.

Gruesome combat engulfs Iwo Jima and Okinawa

Aerial bombing destroys Japan's largest cities

The fighting for Iwo Jima, a desolate volcanic island defended by 20,000 Japanese, began in February 1945 and lasted three hellish weeks. The Japanese dug in and died to the last man. They killed 6,000 Americans and wounded 25,000 more, making this the only Pacific battle in which American casualties (31,000) exceeded Japanese (21,000). The campaign for Okinawa lasted nearly three months (April–June 1945), but in that action Americans killed 110,000 Japanese while losing 7,000 of their own. In both battles, but especially at Okinawa, Japanese fighter pilots flew suicide missions, deliberately crashing their planes into American ships. These "kamikaze" fighters, named for the "divine winds" that thwarted the 13th-century Mongol attacks on Japan (Chapter 15), sank 55 ships and terrified Americans, who considered them evidence of unrelenting Japanese fanaticism. In fact, they were evidence of desperation. As most of Japan's best pilots were already dead, aviation fuel to train replacements was unavailable, and first-time pilots were usually killed at once by experienced Americans, Japan's leaders decided to send them to their deaths in a way that might inflict some real damage.

Kamikaze warfare and Japanese unwillingness to surrender in the face of certain death made Americans dread an amphibious landing on Japan. Aerial bombing, its advocates hoped, might force the Japanese into surrendering before a landing would be necessary. In February 1945, General Curtis LeMay, commanding the 20th U.S. Air Force, employed clusters of incendiary bombs in an effort to burn as much of Japan as possible. On March 9 a raid on Tokyo by 279 B-29s destroyed 40 percent of the city in three hours, killing 89,000 civilians and demolishing 267,000 buildings. By summer Japan's six largest cities were devastated, with two million buildings destroyed, 260,000 people killed, and 9 to 13 million more made homeless. LeMay's practice of dropping leaflets announcing his next target in advance produced panic. As millions of workers fled to the countryside, Japan's war economy, already deprived of raw materials, shut down.

The effects of the atomic bomb on Hiroshima.

Atomic Weapons

Some Japanese leaders realized there was no point in fighting on. In early July Japan asked the USSR, still neutral in the Pacific war, to inform the Americans of Japan's wish to surrender, so long as the emperor could be retained as head of state and symbol of national unity. Stalin, who had agreed at Yalta to declare war on Japan three months after Germany's defeat, passed the information to Harry Truman, president since Roosevelt's death in April. But the United States had insisted throughout the war on unconditional surrender, and by the time Japan's request reached Truman, he had learned of a fearsome new weapon that he hoped would make it unnecessary to invade Japan, bargain over surrender terms, or bring the Soviets into the Pacific war.

This weapon was the atomic bomb, a secret project initiated in 1942 with the intent of harnessing the immense power released by splitting the atoms of radioactive elements, a process called nuclear fission. American, British, and expatriate European scientists, working at sites in the United States, finally developed a workable device, successfully tested at Alamogordo, New Mexico, on July 16, 1945. Its enormous explosive power, equivalent to twenty thousand tons of dynamite in a single bomb, made it the most potent weapon yet developed. Its use against civilian targets raised serious ethical concerns among some of the scientists who helped create it, but there is no evidence that the United States government viewed it as anything other than a weapon of great power that would save lives by ending the war quickly.

After Alamogordo the Americans possessed enough fissionable material for only three bombs, and Truman ordered two of them sent immediately to the Pacific island of Tinian, where two specially configured B-29s with handpicked, highly skilled crews were waiting. On August 6 the first atomic bomb used in warfare fell on **Hiroshima**, destroying most of the city and instantly killing between seventy thousand and eighty thousand people. Thousands more died from burns and radiation sickness within weeks. On August 8, the USSR, fulfilling Stalin's Yalta promise, declared war on imperial Japan. On August 9, the Americans, having heard no response to their demands for immediate Japanese surrender, dropped a second bomb on Nagasaki, killing 35,000 people and leveling much of the city. The emperor then intervened and forced a Japanese surrender. With the signing of a formal surrender aboard the U.S. battleship *Missouri* in Tokyo Bay on September 2, history's deadliest war officially ended.

The United States uses atomic weapons against Japan

The Legacy of World War II

The Great War had brought drastic political changes, but those that followed World War II were even more shattering. Nazism, fascism, and Japanese militarism were abolished, replaced eventually by political systems imposed by the conquerors. Italy and Japan remained intact, while Germany and Austria were temporarily divided among four occupying powers—Britain, France, the Soviet Union, and the United States. The occupations lasted until 1955 in Austria and 1990 in Germany. The war in Europe was followed by more than four decades of hostility and tension between the USSR and its former allies, a debilitating, dangerous global confrontation known as the Cold War (Chapter 34). The League of Nations, now defunct, was replaced by a United Nations composed of all powers that had declared war against the Axis. It soon expanded to include the losers (although divided Germany remained outside until 1973), and it became a forum for Cold War disputes. The Grand Alliance of Britain, the United States, and the Soviet Union broke apart because of distrust between Communism and capitalism, and between Stalin and everyone else.

Terrible devastation complicated recovery efforts. Japanese cities, many almost totally destroyed, were rebuilt rapidly with American aid, largely because of Japan's importance as a potential ally in the Cold War. But Europe was divided between Soviet and Western zones of occupation and influence, and within those zones by national boundaries and ethnic hatreds. Millions of displaced persons, having lost their homes or countries, roamed the continent, seeking villages and towns that no longer existed, searching for relatives and loved ones killed in battle, murdered in the Holocaust, buried by collapsing buildings, crushed by tanks, or simply lost. Cities were clogged with corpses and rubble (Dresden, Germany, was not cleared of rubble until 1965), while hunger, disease, and poverty gripped the demoralized survivors. Harry Truman, having ridden through Berlin on his way to a conference in July 1945, arrived at his destination trembling. He had fought in the Great War and seen terrible suffering, he commented, but nothing like this. In the Second World War, 60 million people perished, two thirds of them in China and the Soviet Union combined.

The war's enormous devastation requires massive reconstruction

Yet these terrors were eventually overcome, in part because of other aspects of the war's legacy. The Cold War encouraged the Western allies to help rebuild the roads and bridges of their friends and former foes. The Allies were assisted in their task by the unprecedented authority the war had conferred on modern governments. To win the war, democracies such as Britain and America had employed such authoritarian techniques as seemed necessary for survival. Afterward, peacetime regimes retained that centralization of power, and they were able to work quickly to bring recovery and stability.

Eventually those aspects of wartime governance were institutionalized or replaced, but other legacies of the war, particularly in scientific and medical fields, had even more extensive and enduring impacts on human life. Radar, which had saved Britain in 1940, was now enhanced through microwave technology, making possible not only the postwar microwave oven but also tiny radar sets on aircraft, which in turn made postwar commercial aviation viable. Passenger aircraft came to be powered by jet engines, first used in wartime Germany and then modified in Britain and America for peacetime use. The world's first computer, which filled a huge room at the University of Pennsylvania after coming online in 1945, foreshadowed an information age previously unimaginable. Eventually, artificial earth satellites made possible intercontinental telephone and television communication, accurate weather forecasting, and Internet transmissions; they were placed in space by ballistic missiles, a technology developed in wartime Germany.

Wartime medical advances offer peacetime benefits

Medically, wartime advances proved tremendously helpful to humanity. The development of penicillin ushered in the age of antibiotics; together with sulfa drugs used to treat previously fatal infections, it saved the lives of many soldiers and allowed generations of children to grow up in relative freedom from life-threatening infectious disease. Residents of the tropics likewise benefited from the development of synthetic atebrine, providing better treatment for malaria. The creation of the potent insecticide DDT for use in the jungles of Asia and the South Pacific sharply reduced outbreaks of malaria and typhus after the war ended. In addition, battlefield perfection of techniques of blood transfusion rendered significant benefits to civilians after 1945.

So the world survived, and some of it prospered after its emergence from the destruction of war. Europe, torn apart by the two world wars, eventually attained unprecedented levels of stability and affluence, as did Japan and other parts of Asia. The war contributed to the fatal weakening of European overseas empires and exerted a direct impact on the decolonization movements that succeeded after 1945. The horrifying destruction of the war years gave way to rebuilding and rapid economic growth, and the technological and medical improvements of those years benefited nearly everyone. These benefits do not diminish the incalculable costs, both financial and human, of the savage conflict we call World War II, but they do testify to humanity's immense capacity for survival and growth, even in the most agonizing circumstances.

One aspect of the war's legacy, however, threatened to destroy not only what had managed to survive but also the very existence of human life on the planet. Nuclear power offered tremendous potential benefits in terms of energy and peaceful uses of radiation, but the mushroom clouds over Hiroshima and Nagasaki cast a shadow of fear over the postwar years. The Cold War that followed World War II was darkened from its outset by that shadow.

CHAPTER
REVIEW

Putting It in Perspective

In the 1930s it seemed unlikely that democracy could survive. The anxieties of the 1920s, culminating in the Great Depression, made many believe that only powerful authoritarian governments could deal with the

issues left by the Great War. Italy and Japan, which had fought on the winning side, and Germany and Russia, which had lost, shared deep dissatisfaction with the war's results and installed such dictatorships in an effort to reassert their claims. Democracies like Britain and France tried in vain to appease these dictators, while the world's largest democracy, the United States, withdrew from European affairs. In such a climate, rulers like Hitler, Mussolini, and Stalin flourished.

Eventually, however, the dictatorships grew impatient with appeasement. Germany started a major war in 1939 in pursuit of living space in the East and a racial paradise for the "Master Race." Italy joined the struggle in 1940, hoping to profit from Germany's victory over France at little cost to itself. Japan attempted to secure raw materials for its industrialized economy by conquering China and expelling Europeans and Americans from their holdings in the central and western Pacific. By early 1942, these Axis powers appeared to be winning what by then was known as World War II.

But the dictators had overreached. The Soviet Union, itself a dictatorship, at first appeased Hitler through the Nazi-Soviet Pact of 1939 but two years later found itself invaded by Germany. Its enormous reserves of manpower and huge expanses of territory proved too much for the German army to handle.

Britain survived the defeat of France in 1940 and refused to surrender. Its command of the Atlantic sea-lanes and the courage and skill of its fighter pilots saved it from German invasion. Finally, Japan's attack on Pearl Harbor brought the United States into the war. America's tremendous industrial capacity enabled the nation to fight major wars on two fronts, supply its allies with huge quantities of war matériel, and carry out the research and development required to produce atomic weapons. The devastating combination of Russia, Britain, and the United States provided the Grand Alliance with the overwhelming force necessary to win World War II.

The legacy of the war was mixed. Widespread destruction, the deaths of 60 million people, and the use of massive aerial bombing and atomic weapons marked World War II as the most terrible conflict in human history. But the war also brought dramatic scientific, technological, and medical advances that extended human life expectancy and improved the quality of life for billions of people. Out of the appalling suffering came hope for a better future and widespread resolve to avoid a third world war.

Reviewing Key Material

KEY CONCEPTS

Lebensraum, 777
Anschluss, 779
appeasement, 781
Nazi-Soviet Pact, 781
Blitzkrieg, 781

Wannsee Conference, 793
Luftwaffe, 784
Rape of Nanjing, 786
D-day, 796
Hiroshima, 801

KEY PEOPLE

Douglas MacArthur, 777, 798
Adolf Hitler, 777
Benito Mussolini, 778
Francisco Franco, 778
Neville Chamberlain, 780
Winston Churchill, 782
Joseph Stalin, 784
Jiang Jieshi, 786
Georgi Zhukov, 785
Franklin Roosevelt, 788
Isoroku Yamamoto, 788

Chester Nimitz, 788
Erwin Rommel, 789
Bernard Law Montgomery, 790
Reinhard Heydrich, 793
Adolf Eichmann, 793
Anne Frank, 795
Pope Pius XII, 795
Dwight Eisenhower, 796
Walther Model, 796
Omar Bradley, 797
George Patton, 797
Harry Truman, 800

ASK YOURSELF

1. Why did Germany absorb Austria and Czechoslovakia before invading Poland in 1939? What did Hitler's government hope to accomplish?
2. Why was Germany unable to conquer the Soviet Union?
3. Why did Japan attack the United States in 1941?
4. What strategies did the Allied powers use to defeat the Axis forces between 1942 and 1945? What factors made these strategies effective?
5. How and why did Germany murder millions of Europeans during World War II?

GOING FURTHER

Dallek, Robert. *Franklin D. Roosevelt and American Foreign Policy, 1932–1945*. 1979.
Dower, John. *War Without Mercy: Race and Power in the Pacific War*. 1986.
Erickson, John. *The Road to Berlin: Stalin's War with Germany*. 1983.
Glanz, David, and Jonathan House. *When Titans Clashed: How the Red Army Stopped Hitler*. 1998.
Hilberg, Raul. *The Destruction of the European Jews*. 2001.
Ienaga, Saburo. *The Pacific War, 1937–1945*. 1978.

Iriye, Akira. *The Origins of the Second World War in Asia and the Pacific*. 1987.

Keegan, John. *The Second World War*. 1990.

Kershaw, Ian. *Hitler*. 2 volumes, 1998 and 2001.

Prange, Gordon. *At Dawn We Slept: The Untold Story of Pearl Harbor*. 1981.

Rhodes, Richard. *The Making of the Atomic Bomb*. 1986.

Taylor, Telford. *Munich*. 1984.

Watt, D. C. *How War Came*. 1989.

Weinberg, Gerhard. *The Foreign Policy of Hitler's Germany*. 2 volumes, 1970 and 1980.

Weinberg, Gerhard. *A World at Arms*. 1994.

Yahil, Leni. *The Holocaust*. 1990.

Yamamoto, Masahiro. *Nanking: Anatomy of an Atrocity*. 2000.

Key Dates and Developments

1937	Japan invades China
1938	Germany annexes Austria Munich Conference: Germany annexes Sudetenland
1939	Germany takes Czechoslovakia Nazi-Soviet Pact Germany invades Poland; Britain and France declare war
1940	Germany conquers Norway, Holland, Belgium, and France Battle of Britain
1941	Germany invades the Soviet Union Japan attacks Pearl Harbor
1942	Japan conquers Dutch East Indies and Philippines Extermination of European Jews and others begins United States defeats Japan at Midway Island Allies invade North Africa
1943	USSR defeats Germany at Stalingrad Allies invade Italy
1944	Normandy invasion and Soviet offensive in the East
1945	United Nations Organization established Germany surrenders Atomic bombing of Hiroshima and Nagasaki Japan surrenders

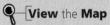 **myhistorylab** Connections

Reinforce what you learned in this chapter by studying the many documents, images, maps, review tools, and videos available at www.myhistorylab.com.

Read and Review

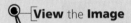 **Study** and **Review** Chapter 33

Read the **Document**

Neville Chamberlain, *In Search of Peace*, p. 781

Adolf Hitler, The Obersalzberg Speech, 1939 p. 781

Winston Churchill, "Their Finest Hour" (Great Britain), 1940, p. 785

View the **Image**

American Workers at B-17 Bomber Plant, p. 798

Listen to the **Audio**

World War II 1, p. 781

World War II 2, p. 788

Watch the **Video**

Video: FDR on Winning the War, p. 797

Research and Explore

View the **Map**

Interactive Map: German Expansion Under the Third Reich, p. 781

Listen to the **Chapter Audio** for Chapter 33 on **myhistorylab.com**

34

East Versus West: Cold War and Its Global Impact, 1945–Present

((•─Listen to the **Chapter Audio** for Chapter 34 on **myhistorylab.com**

■ Why and how did the Cold War originate?

■ How and why did it become a global confrontation?

■ What were the main Cold War crises and conflicts and why did they occur?

■ What were the West's main achievements and challenges in the Cold War era?

■ What were the Soviet Bloc's main achievements and failures?

■ How and why did the Cold War end?

Atomic Explosion

The mushroom cloud of a nuclear blast, such as this U.S. atomic bomb test in 1946, was a terrifying symbol of the Cold War, a 45-year struggle between capitalist West and Communist East, affecting the entire world.

July 24, 1945, was not a good day for Joseph Stalin.

Eight days earlier, arriving in Germany for a conference at Potsdam with British prime minister Churchill and U.S. president Truman, the Soviet leader had been in a dominant position. His country, having fought the most crucial battles and borne the brunt of the bloodshed, was the main Allied victor over Germany in World War II. His Red Army, occupying Eastern Europe and eastern Germany, was the world's mightiest military force. Even Truman, anxious to get Soviet help in the ongoing war against Japan, was initially deferential to the Soviet dictator.

But as the conference proceeded, Truman grew increasingly assertive. On July 24, he joined Churchill in denouncing Soviet repression in Eastern Europe. Then, as the session ended, Truman quietly informed Stalin that America had a new weapon of "unusual destructive force." Stalin's response, a vague assertion that it should be "put to good use against Japan," was so indifferent that Churchill wondered if the Soviet leader understood the weapon's significance.

Stalin indeed understood. His spies had informed him of U.S. efforts to build an atomic bomb, successfully tested in New Mexico on July 16. He knew this new weapon would make it harder to get concessions from his Western allies, who now had less need of his help against Japan. He knew the American bomb would offset his Red Army's might in any postwar contest for preeminence. And he knew he was no longer the world's most powerful man—that distinction now belonged to Truman, an untested newcomer on the world stage. That night, in his private quarters, Stalin ordered his lieutenants to accelerate Soviet efforts to develop atomic weapons. Later, back in Russia, he gathered his top scientists, slammed his fist on a table, and demanded: "Comrades, build me a bomb. The Americans have destroyed the balance of power."

The ensuing nuclear arms race, the ongoing Soviet occupation of Eastern Europe, and American efforts to stop the spread of Soviet Communism fueled an intense 45-year East–West struggle. The West, known to foes as the "imperialist camp" and friends as the "free world," included the capitalist democracies of Western Europe and North America, led by the United States. The East, also called the "Communist bloc," included the Communist countries of Eastern Europe and Asia, led by the USSR. Americans and Soviets confronted each other globally—through threats, propaganda, espionage, the arms race, and support for opposing sides in regional conflicts—but they did not engage in hot combat (armed warfare) directly against one another. The struggle between these two "superpowers" hence was called the Cold War.

Origins of the Cold War

The Cold War was rooted in ideological conflict between Communism and capitalism and in distrust between East and West stemming from their joint struggle against Nazi Germany. In Central and Eastern Europe, at the end of World War II, Stalin's objectives proved incompatible with those of his Western allies.

Communism and capitalism had always been hostile. Communists openly aimed to destroy world capitalism, with its stress on individualism and competition, and replace it

Capitalism and Communism have conflicting goals and ideals

with a global community based on collectivism and cooperation. Stalin had postponed, but by no means abandoned, this goal, while building Soviet socialism and resisting the Nazis. Capitalists, for their part, were determined to stop the spread of Communism, which they saw as a mortal threat to Western freedom and prosperity.

Even their joint struggle against Nazism had been fraught with distrust. Capitalists resented the Nazi-Soviet pact of 1939, which had enabled Germany, with Soviet assent, to overrun Poland and much of Western Europe. Communists were upset that the Western allies delayed their main anti-German offensive until June 1944, three years after the Nazi invasion of the Soviet Union, by which time the Soviets had driven out the Germans at an appalling price. Since the war cost the USSR 25–30 million lives, while Britain and America together lost fewer than a million, the Soviets felt they had endured more than their share of suffering. And since they freed Eastern Europe from the Nazis, the Soviets felt they had the right to decide that region's future.

Furthermore, by 1945, the whole western part of the USSR was devastated. Faced with massive rebuilding, and anxious to prevent future invasion, Stalin had several key goals: Germany must be incapacitated so it could not strike again; it must make huge reparations payments to rebuild the USSR; and the Soviets must be shielded from Germany by a buffer zone of friendly countries in Eastern Europe. While noting the Soviet need for security and reconstruction, however, the Western powers opposed massive reparations, and wanted free elections in Germany and Eastern Europe— which might well result in leaders unfriendly to the Soviet Union. Western goals were thus incompatible with Stalin's.

East–West tensions evolve during struggle against Nazis

Soviet and Western postwar goals prove incompatible

Stalin, Roosevelt, and Churchill at Yalta.

Western Allies make concessions to Soviets at Yalta

📖 **Read** the **Document**

The Charter of the United Nations (1945)

on **myhistorylab.com**

Allies divide Germany into occupation zones

The Yalta and Potsdam Conferences

In February 1945, while Allied armies were still fighting Germans, Stalin met with U.S. president Franklin Roosevelt and British prime minister Churchill at the southern Soviet city of Yalta to plan the postwar peace. By then, the Soviets, in ousting the Germans, had occupied much of Eastern Europe, including most of Poland. And, although in Europe the war's end was in sight, in Asia it was not, so Roosevelt and Churchill were willing to bargain for Soviet help against Japan.

Consequently, at Yalta, Stalin got much of what he wanted. His allies agreed to let Poland be ruled by a Soviet-installed regime, and to let the USSR keep the eastern part of prewar Poland, annexed in 1939. In return, Poland was to be compensated with territory from Germany, moving Polish borders westward (Map 34.1). Stalin pledged to let Poles elect their own leaders (a promise he would not keep) and, in a secret agreement, to declare war on Japan three months after the war in Europe ended (a promise he would honor precisely). He also cleared the way for the **United Nations** (UN), an international peacekeeping body created to replace the defunct League of Nations, by dropping his earlier demand that, since the USSR consisted of 16 (later 15) Soviet republics, it should have 16 seats in the UN General Assembly.

The allies agreed to divide Germany into occupation zones: a Soviet sector in the East, and British, American, and French zones in the West. But Roosevelt and Churchill, judging that reparations imposed on Germany after World War I had aided Hitler's rise, resisted Stalin's demand for reparations, so action on that issue was postponed. Otherwise, the Soviet leader had reason to be pleased with the Yalta accords.

Much had changed, however, by the next Allied meeting, held in Germany at Potsdam in summer 1945. Roosevelt had died in April and was replaced by Harry Truman, a blunt, combative man who disliked Communists as much as Nazis and had

FOUNDATION MAP 34.1 | European Boundary Changes and Occupation Zones, 1945–1955

The end of World War II brought territorial changes in Europe. Note that the USSR kept lands it had earlier claimed in Eastern Europe, including all of eastern prewar Poland, and that Poland was compensated with lands from prewar Germany, while the rest of Germany and Austria were divided into occupation zones. Why did Germany's occupation and division continue throughout the Cold War?

once said he hoped that war between them would "kill as many as possible." Germany had surrendered in May, removing the main reason for Allied cooperation, which was further strained by Soviet repression in Eastern Europe. And, in the midst of the Potsdam talks, Churchill was replaced as prime minister by Clement Attlee, a mild-mannered Socialist whose Labour Party won a stunning electoral upset by pledging to improve British workers' lives and decrease Britain's global commitments.

Attlee's pledge to reduce Britain's role meant that America would henceforth be the Western world's main leader. Emerging from the war with immense wealth and power,

Postwar America emerges as leader of the Western world

Americans had boundless faith in capitalist democracy and contempt for Soviet socialism. And, as news arrived in Potsdam about the successful atomic bomb test in New Mexico, Truman and his aides saw little need for further concessions to the Communists.

So the Americans stood up to Stalin at Potsdam. They agreed to let him take reparations from Germany, but only from the less-developed Soviet-occupied zone, whose factories would be disassembled and sent east by rail. Truman demanded free elections in Eastern Europe, which Stalin resisted, knowing that these would likely install anti-Soviet regimes. And, as noted at the start of this chapter, the president told the Soviet leader about the atomic bomb—then hastened to use it against Japan soon after the conference concluded.

Truman later said that he used the bomb to end the war without an invasion of Japan, which would have cost thousands of American lives. But historians have since asserted that he also had other goals: to demonstrate American strength to the Soviets and end the war before they could occupy part of Japan, much as they had occupied eastern Germany and Eastern Europe.

Americans, strengthened by A-bomb, resist Soviets at Potsdam

Divided Europe: The "Iron Curtain"

Soviet power in Eastern Europe by then was becoming entrenched. From 1945 to 1948, intent on securing his buffer zone of countries friendly to the USSR, Stalin used coercion and rigged elections to establish Soviet-dominated "satellite" regimes in Poland, Romania, Bulgaria, Hungary, and Czechoslovakia, forming a coalition called the **Soviet bloc**. Millions of ethnic Germans, whose families had lived in Eastern Europe for generations, were forcibly deported to Germany. In Yugoslavia, Communists gained and exercised power independent of the USSR.

Postwar Soviet expansion worries Western leaders

The West, having largely demobilized its forces following the war, increasingly felt threatened by Soviet power. The massive Red Army, renamed the Soviet Army in 1946, remained in occupation of Manchuria, northern Korea, northern Iran, Eastern Europe, and above all eastern Germany, where it stationed hundreds of thousands of soldiers. Judging that only America could block further Soviet expansion, former Prime Minister Churchill, speaking in Missouri in March 1946, evoked the image of a Europe divided by a line he called the "iron curtain," east of which lay countries imprisoned by Communism (see "Churchill's Iron Curtain Speech").

Churchill's speech helps persuade Americans to counter Soviet expansion

The iron curtain imagery, combined with Soviet belligerence, helped to arouse the Americans. They demanded that Stalin withdraw his troops, as previously promised, from occupied northern Iran; faced with forceful U.S. pressure, he eventually complied. Later that year, the Americans declared their intent to keep forces in western Germany indefinitely and to unite most of western Germany by merging their occupation zone with Britain's.

The Truman Doctrine and Marshall Plan

(⦿ Listen to the Audio
Cold War I
on myhistorylab.com

In the following year, 1947, major U.S. initiatives sought to counter Communism's spread. In March, reacting to a Communist insurgency in Greece and to Soviet pressures against Turkey, President Truman proclaimed a new policy, soon called the **Truman Doctrine**. Henceforth, he avowed, the United States must "support free peoples who are resisting attempted subjugation by armed minorities or by outside pressures"—leaving no doubt that he meant Communist minorities and pressures from Soviet Russia. And it soon became clear that American aid would go far beyond Greece and Turkey: in June Secretary of State George Marshall announced a massive program of U.S. economic

DOCUMENT 34.1 Churchill's Iron Curtain Speech

In March 1946, speaking in Fulton, Missouri, Winston Churchill used the image of an "iron curtain" to highlight Europe's division. What was the goal of his speech?

The United States stands at this time at the pinnacle of world power. It is a solemn moment for the American democracy. For with this primacy of power is also joined an awe-inspiring accountability to the future . . .

A shadow has fallen upon the scenes so lately lighted by the Allied victory. Nobody knows what Russia and its Communist international organization intends to do in the immediate future, or what are the limits, if any, to their expansive and proselytizing tendencies . . . It is my duty, however, . . . to place before you certain facts about the present position in Europe.

From Stettin in the Baltic to Trieste in the Adriatic, an iron curtain has descended across the Continent. Behind that line lie all the capitals of the ancient states of central and eastern Europe. Warsaw, Berlin, Prague, Vienna, Budapest, Belgrade, Bucharest, and Sofia, all these famous cities and the populations around them lie in what I might call the Soviet sphere, and all are subject, . . . not only to Soviet influence, but also to a very high and increasing measure of control from Moscow . . . The Communist parties, which were very small in all these eastern states of Europe, have been raised to preeminence and power far beyond their numbers and are seeking everywhere to obtain totalitarian control. Police governments are prevailing in nearly every case . . .

Whatever conclusions may be drawn from these facts, . . . this is certainly not the liberated Europe we fought to build up. Nor is it one which contains the essentials of a permanent peace . . .

SOURCE: Reproduced with permission of Curtis Brown, Ltd. London on behalf of The Estate of Winston Churchill. Copyright © Winston S. Churchill.

aid to all of war-torn Europe. Although billed a "European Recovery Program," the **Marshall Plan** was designed to preclude Communist expansion by strengthening Europe economically, thus advancing America's Cold War strategy.

In July, George F. Kennan, a policy planner in the U.S. State Department, gave the new strategy a name. In the journal *Foreign Affairs*, in an article signed "Mr. X" (since he lacked official permission to use his name), Kennan promoted "a long-term, patient but firm and vigilant containment of Russian expansive tendencies," claiming that Communism, if so contained, would eventually collapse. **Containment of Communism** hence became the central aim of U.S. Cold War policy. Over the next four decades, America provided political, economic, and often military support to almost any regime anywhere resisting Soviet influence, while the Soviets similarly aided forces resisting Western domination.

Americans adopt global strategy based on containment of Communism

▶ Read the **Document**
George F. Kennan, "Long Telegram," 1946
on **myhistorylab.com**

The Berlin Blockade and NATO

Stalin reacted angrily to the U.S. initiatives. Realizing that Marshall Plan aid would boost American influence in Europe, he ordered his Eastern European satellites to reject it and later formed a Council for Mutual Economic Assistance (Comecon) to advance their economic development. He also ordered them to rid their regimes of all remaining non-Communists. Accordingly, in February 1948, Communists took full control of Czechoslovakia, completing consolidation of the Soviet bloc. But the West could also consolidate: in June 1948, France merged its German occupation zone with the British-American sector, uniting western Germany and giving it a unified currency. On June 24, fearful that the West was moving to reunite and rebuild Germany, Stalin retaliated by blocking all road and rail routes from western Germany to Berlin.

Thus began the Berlin blockade, the Cold War's first great crisis. The German capital, like the whole country, had been divided into occupation zones by the four wartime

Stalin's blockade of Berlin triggers major Cold War crisis

The Berlin airlift.

American-British airlift overcomes Berlin blockade

NATO Alliance commits United States to defend Western Europe

allies (Map 34.1, inset). But since Berlin lay inside Soviet-occupied eastern Germany, 90 miles behind the "iron curtain," the city's British, French, and American sectors, collectively called West Berlin, depended upon food and supplies delivered from western Germany. Without such supplies, 2.5 million West Berliners could not long survive. The Western allies, Stalin figured, would have to either abandon Berlin or make concessions elsewhere to get him to reopen the routes.

Truman, however, rejected these options, along with a proposal for a U.S. armored force to fight its way to Berlin through Soviet-occupied eastern Germany. Instead, he opted, with British support, to supply West Berlin by air. For the next 11 months, American and British cargo planes flew food and supplies around the clock into West Berlin. Anxious to avoid an all-out war with the world's only nuclear power, the Soviets chose not to forcibly interrupt the airlift. They quietly ended the blockade in May 1949.

By then it was obvious that Stalin's blockade had backfired. Rather than abandon Berlin, the Americans abandoned their historic avoidance of peacetime military alliances. In April 1949, the United States, along with Canada, Iceland, and nine European nations, formed an alliance called **NATO** (North Atlantic Treaty Organization), designed to protect Western Europe against Soviet expansion. Warning that an "attack against one" member would be considered "an attack against them all," the alliance thereby served notice to the Soviets that any attempt to expand in Europe would mean war with the United States. Implicit in this warning was a nuclear threat.

The Global Confrontation

By 1949, then, deadlock had developed in Europe: Communists controlled the East, relying on Soviet power, and NATO defended the West, backed by American might. At the center of the standoff was Germany, where two separate states were created that year: capitalist West Germany in the zones occupied by Britain, America, and France, and Communist East Germany in the Soviet sector.

Cold War standoff in Europe grows into global confrontation

((•─Listen to the Audio
Cold War III
on **myhistorylab.com**

Soon, however, Communist advances elsewhere turned the stalemate into a global confrontation. The rise of Communist regimes in China and North Korea, and later in North Vietnam and Cuba, was met by forceful U.S. efforts to stop further Communist expansion. New leaders emerging in both East and West failed to solve the standoff, while both sides developed horrific new weapons that put the whole world at risk.

New Realities and New Leaders

Communist triumph in China stuns and alarms the West

On August 29, 1949, far ahead of Western expectations, the USSR successfully tested an atomic bomb, abruptly ending America's nuclear monopoly. Scarcely a month later, on October 1, 1949, Communists took control in China, the world's most populous nation, sending shock waves throughout the Western world. In June 1950, a Communist regime in North Korea, set up there by the Soviets, abruptly invaded non-Communist South Korea. Suddenly the Soviets had the bomb, and a relentless Red tide seemed to be engulfing the globe (Map 34.2).

Communists stalemate American-led coalition in Korean War

The unnerved Americans, resolving to stem the Communist tide, opted to defend South Korea. The ensuing Korean War (1950–1953), described in Chapter 35, pitted an American-led UN coalition against Soviet-supplied Communist forces, threatening to spark a new global conflict. But the United States, anxious not to weaken its defenses in Europe by pursuing an all-out Asian war, confined its campaign to Korea, even when Communist China sent hundreds of thousands of volunteer troops to help the North

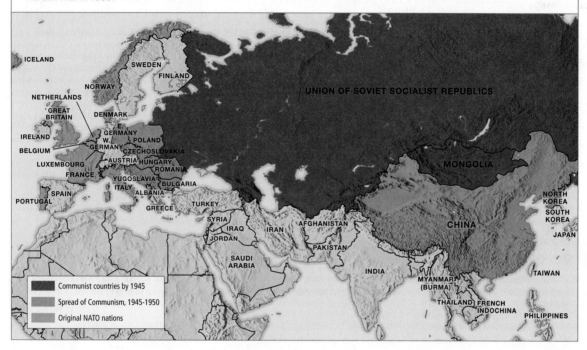

MAP 34.2   Communist Expansion in Eurasia, 1945–1950

In the wake of World War II, new Communist regimes came to power in Eastern Europe, North Korea, and China, creating the impression of a "Red tide" sweeping the globe. How did this impression influence the formation of NATO in 1949 and the Korean War in 1950?

Legend:
- Communist countries by 1945
- Spread of Communism, 1945-1950
- Original NATO nations

Koreans. And the USSR, although it gave arms to its Communist allies, avoided direct involvement. In July 1953, unwilling to risk another world war, both sides settled for a truce in Korea that simply sustained the stalemate.

By this time both the Americans and the Soviets had new leaders. In January 1953, General Dwight Eisenhower, the Allied commander in Western Europe during World War II, replaced Harry Truman as U.S. president. In March came the death of Joseph Stalin, followed by a succession struggle resulting in the rise of a new Soviet Communist Party leader named Nikita Khrushchev (*khroosh-CHOFF*).

Eisenhower, a popular war hero who had led the 1944 Normandy invasion, was committed both to combating Communism and to cutting U.S. defense costs, which had become immense. Seeking simultaneously to save money and strengthen U.S. defenses, his administration decided to reduce its armed forces and deter the Soviets mainly with nuclear weapons—a policy called "massive retaliation." By arming its new B-52 long-range jet bombers with hydrogen bombs (new nuclear weapons many times more powerful than the original atomic bombs), the United States could respond to a Soviet Army attack in Europe by dropping these "H-bombs" on the USSR. Faced with this threat, presumably, the Soviets would dare not attack, and America could avoid the huge expense of stationing numerous U.S. troops in Europe and Asia. The policy provided, in the words of one American official, a "bigger bang for the buck."

To cut defense costs, United States relies on global nuclear threat

But the new U.S. policy merely accelerated the arms race. Determined to neutralize the American atomic threat, the Soviets produced their own H-bombs and long-range bombers that could reach the United States. Soon Britain and France, doubting that America would risk its own destruction to defend Western Europe, were developing and

Soviets develop and expand nuclear forces to counter U.S. threat

📖 Read the **Document**

"The Kitchen Debate"
(1959)

on **myhistorylab.com**

🔍 View the **Image**

The "Kitchen Debate"
Between Nixon and
Khrushchev

on **myhistorylab.com**

enlarging their own atomic forces. By 1960 there were four nuclear powers and thousands of nuclear weapons, posing a threat to humanity's survival should there be an all-out global war.

Khrushchev, meanwhile, proved a formidable foe. The self-educated son of impoverished peasants, he was a firm believer in the virtues of Soviet socialism, which had enabled him to rise from obscurity to enormous power. He was convinced that Communists could win a prolonged global contest against capitalism, partly by strengthening Soviet power and partly by supporting the global movement against Western colonialism.

Decolonization and Global Cold War

Soviets aid Asians and
Africans emerging from
Western colonialism

The Cold War coincided with **decolonization**, a process whereby colonized peoples in Asia and Africa (Chapters 35 and 37) gained independence from Western imperial rule (Map 34.3), often through nationalistic "liberation movements." Communists since V. I. Lenin, depicting Western imperialism as an outgrowth of industrial capitalism and colonized peoples as allies of socialists in a global struggle against capitalist imperialists, had encouraged such movements. Now Khrushchev and his successors actively supported them and aided former colonies emerging from Western domination, hoping

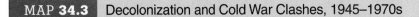

MAP **34.3** Decolonization and Cold War Clashes, 1945–1970s

The Cold War was interconnected with decolonization in Africa and Asia. Notice that by the mid-1970s most African and Asian colonies and mandates had gained independence from their former rulers. How did this process, combined with Soviet efforts to win allies in these regions, contribute to Cold War clashes?

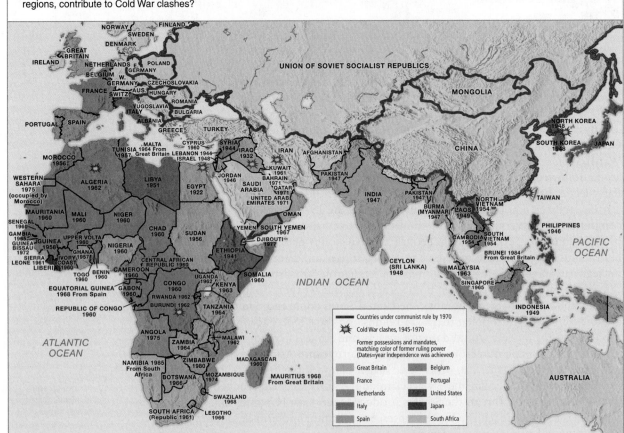

thereby to undermine the West and win friends for the USSR. To counter Soviet advances, America in turn aided anti-Communist elements in regions emerging from colonialism. Nationalists in Asia, Africa, and Latin America exploited the East–West rivalry to obtain weapons and resources from one side or the other, further globalizing the Cold War.

Asians, Africans, and Latin Americans exploit global Cold War rivalry

One example was India, freed from British rule in 1947 but split into two hostile states. The Republic of India, a Hindu-led Western-style democracy, took economic aid from the USSR, which hoped to expand its influence in South Asia. Pakistan, a Muslim military dictatorship, got military and economic assistance from the United States, which wanted a strong ally in the region to help resist Soviet inroads. Another example was the former Dutch East Indies, which became independent Indonesia in 1949. The Soviets supported Sukarno, a nationalist who led the new nation until the mid-1960s, ignoring the fact that he was more mystical and Muslim than Marxist. The Americans supported his successor Suharto, a military dictator who seized power in 1967, overlooking his regime's antidemocratic oppression and rampant corruption.

Soviets and West aid opposing sides in Asian and African conflicts

Similar situations emerged elsewhere. In the Middle East, eager to gain influence and undermine the West, the USSR aided Arab nationalists—even though they were monotheistic Muslims with no use for atheistic Communism. The United States, anxious to encourage pro-Western Arab forces and secure oil supplies, supported oil-rich Persian Gulf regimes—despite the fact that they were openly oppressive and undemocratic. In Central Africa, when Belgium abruptly freed its Congo colony in 1960, the Soviets supported its new president, pan-African nationalist Patrice Lumumba—prompting the Americans to consider him a Communist and oppose him. In Latin America, seeking to preclude Communist inroads in its own "backyard," the United States subverted elected left-wing leaders in Guatemala in 1954 and Chile in 1973 (Chapter 36).

Asia, Africa, and Latin America become Cold War battlegrounds

In general, then, while aiding decolonization and annoying the West, Soviet support for anticolonial nationalists did little to advance Communism. Although happy to take Soviet aid, these nationalists, anxious not to trade freedom from Western rule for Soviet domination, rarely joined the Communist camp. Two major exceptions were Vietnam, where a Communist-led insurgency ended French colonial rule in 1954, and Cuba, where an anti-American pro-Marxist regime came to power in 1959. In the 1960s these two nations became major Cold War battlegrounds.

Peaceful Coexistence and Its Problems

By then Khrushchev's efforts to strengthen his own empire had tarnished his anti-imperial image. In 1955, when NATO admitted West Germany, he responded by forming the **Warsaw Pact**, a Soviet-led alliance of East European Communist states (Map 34.4). It counterbalanced NATO and also rationalized continued Soviet Army presence in Eastern Europe. In 1956, when the Hungarians sought to leave the Soviet bloc, Khrushchev used troops and tanks to repress their rebellion, exposing the alarming brutality of Soviet imperial rule.

Even more alarming to the West were advances in Soviet rockets. In 1957, the Soviets successfully tested an **ICBM** (intercontinental ballistic missile), an unmanned rocket that could hit America with nuclear warheads from the USSR. The Soviets also beat the Americans into outer space, launching *Sputnik* (*SPOOT-nēk*), the world's first artificial earth satellite, in 1957, and sending cosmonaut Yuri Gagarin (*gah-GAH-rēn*) into orbit in 1961.

Early Soviet rocket.

These spectacular Soviet accomplishments stunned the Americans. Shocked that Soviet technology suddenly seemed superior to their own, they soon built their own fleet of ICBMs and embarked on an expensive space race that in 1969 would land U.S. astronauts on the moon.

Soviets develop long-range missiles, sparking rocket and space race with America

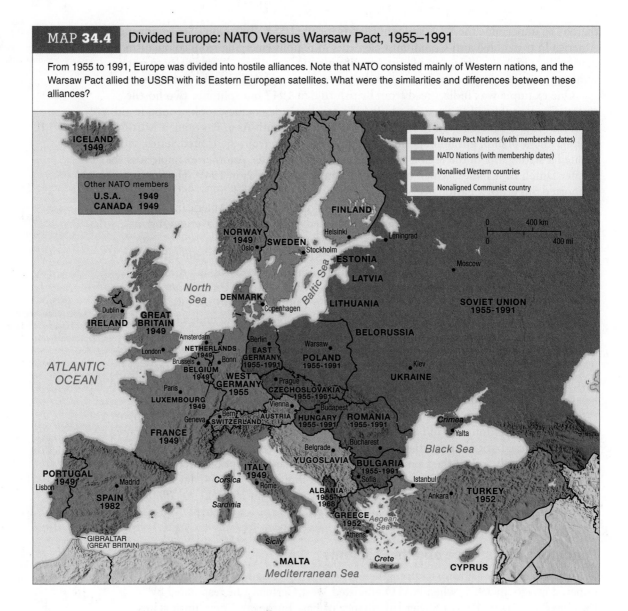

MAP **34.4**   Divided Europe: NATO Versus Warsaw Pact, 1955–1991

From 1955 to 1991, Europe was divided into hostile alliances. Note that NATO consisted mainly of Western nations, and the Warsaw Pact allied the USSR with its Eastern European satellites. What were the similarities and differences between these alliances?

This momentous achievement would eventually help to restore America's pride, but nothing could overcome its new insecurity. Protected from invasions by wide oceans, Americans had long assumed that wars were mostly fought elsewhere. Now Soviet possession of ICBMs, and periodic passes of Soviet earth satellites over the United States, made it painfully clear that Soviet rockets could reach the American homeland. Never again could Americans feel fully secure.

Khrushchev, nonetheless, had no desire for war against America. Acutely aware that a nuclear conflict could destroy the USSR, he rejected the Communist premise that capitalism made war inevitable. Instead, he pressed for "peaceful coexistence" between East and West, confident that, if war was avoided, Communism would eventually prevail as the superior system.

Khrushchev calls for peaceful coexistence and denounces Stalin

Eager to make the Soviet model more attractive, Khrushchev worked to end the worst abuses of the Stalinist system and improve Soviet life. In 1956, in an emotional "secret speech" in the middle of the night to a Communist Party Congress, he detailed and denounced the crimes of his paranoid predecessor (see "Khrushchev on Peaceful Coexistence and on Stalin's Crimes"). Stunned delegates wept as Khrushchev blamed Stalin for imprisoning, torturing, exiling, and murdering countless innocent people, including many loyal Communists.

The speech, a poorly kept secret that soon leaked out and was published in the West, was reinforced by other Khrushchev efforts to break with the Stalinist past. He relaxed Stalin's censorship, reduced internal oppression, freed political prisoners, and launched

---

DOCUMENT 34.2 Khrushchev on Peaceful Coexistence and on Stalin's Crimes

In February 1956, in his opening address to a Communist Party congress, Khrushchev called for peaceful coexistence with the West. At the end of the congress, in a secret speech in the middle of the night, he denounced Joseph Stalin and the crimes of the Stalin era. What did Khrushchev mean by peaceful coexistence? Why did he denounce Stalin?

EXCERPTS FROM KHRUSHCHEV'S REPORT TO THE 20TH PARTY CONGRESS . . . For the strengthening of world peace, it would be of tremendous importance to establish firm, friendly relations between the two biggest powers of the world, the Soviet Union and the United States . . . We want to be friends with and to cooperate with the United States in the effort for peace and security of the peoples as well as in the economic and cultural fields. We pursue this with good intentions, without holding a stone behind our back . . . If good relations are not established . . . , and mutual distrust exists, this will lead to an arms race on a still greater scale and to a still more dangerous growth of the forces on both sides . . .

The principle of peaceful coexistence is gaining increasingly wider international recognition. And this is logical, since there is no other way out of the present situation. Indeed, there are only two ways: either peaceful coexistence or the most devastating war in history . . .

As will be recalled, there is a Marxist-Leninist premise which says that while imperialism exists wars are inevitable. While capitalism remains on earth the reactionary forces representing the interests of the capitalist monopolies will continue to strive for war gambles and aggression, and may try to let loose war. But there is no fatal inevitability of war. Now there are powerful social and political forces, commanding serious means capable of preventing unleashing of war by the imperialists and—should they try to start

it—of delivering a smashing rebuff to the aggressors and thwarting their adventuristic plans . . .

EXCERPTS FROM KHRUSHCHEV'S SECRET SPEECH . . . After Stalin's death the Central Committee of the Party began explaining concisely and consistently that it is impermissible and foreign to the spirit of Marxism-Leninism to elevate one person, and to transform him into a superman possessing supernatural characteristics akin to those of a god . . . Such a belief about a man, and specifically about Stalin, was cultivated among us for many years . . .

Stalin originated the concept of enemy of the people. This term . . . made possible the usage of the most cruel repression . . . against anyone who disagreed with Stalin . . . This led . . . to the fact that many entirely innocent people . . . became victims.

. . . It became apparent that many party, Soviet and economic activists, who were branded . . . as enemies, were actually never enemies, spies, wreckers, etc . . . ; they were only so stigmatized, and often no longer able to bear barbaric tortures they charged themselves (at the order of the investigative judges-falsifiers) with all sorts of grave and unlikely crimes . . . Many thousands of honest and innocent Communists have died as a result of this monstrous falsification of cases . . .

. . . Stalin was a very distrustful man, sickly suspicious . . . This sickly suspicion created in him a general distrust even toward eminent party workers who had known him for many years. Everywhere and in everything he saw enemies, "two-facers," and "spies." Possessing unlimited power, he indulged in great willfulness and choked a person morally and physically . . .

SOURCES: "Krushchev on Peaceful Coexistence and on Stalin's Crime" *New York Times*, February 15, 1956, page 10, translation by the Soviet Information Bureau of TASS and United States Congress, The Congressional Record, 84th Congress, 2nd Session, Vol. 102, 1956, pages 9839, 9391, 9392, 9394 and 9395.

ambitious efforts to improve food and housing, with the stated goal of matching Western living standards by the 1970s. These reforms fell short of providing either freedom or prosperity, but they did demonstrate that the Soviet system was becoming less harsh.

In 1959, to bolster his peacemaker image, Khrushchev made a 12-day trip to America. He toured U.S. cities, met with politicians and entertainers, explored an Iowa cornfield, and even sought to visit California's Disneyland theme park—but was prevented from doing so by security concerns. His buoyant personality did much to ease American anxieties: a man who so obviously enjoyed life hardly seemed the sort to start a nuclear war. He and Eisenhower discussed ways to reduce world tensions and planned to meet again at a **summit conference**, a face-to-face meeting of the world's most powerful leaders, the following year in Paris. By early 1960, as Soviet and Western officials prepared for the Paris summit, the Cold War's end seemed in sight.

Khrushchev's trip to America paves way for Paris summit meeting

Such hopes, however, were dashed in May 1960, when an American U-2 spy plane, sent to take reconnaissance photos on the eve of the summit, crashed in the USSR. Assuming the pilot was dead, America issued a false claim that the craft was a weather plane accidentally flown off course. Khrushchev, who for four years had been angered by such spy flights over his country, now revealed that the U-2 pilot had been captured alive, and demanded an American apology. But Eisenhower, who admitted publicly that he had authorized the mission, refused to repent.

This **U-2 Affair** doomed the Paris summit. Blaming Eisenhower for endangering the peace, Khrushchev in Paris again demanded an apology. When none was forthcoming, he denounced the Americans and refused to negotiate. The summit ended in shambles, as did several years of work toward peaceful coexistence. Giving up on Eisenhower, whose presidency was nearing its end, Khrushchev waited to encounter the next American president.

Khrushchev's anger at U-2 Affair ruins Paris summit

Berlin, Cuba, Vietnam, and MAD

John F. Kennedy, who took office in January 1961, was handsome, rich, and eloquent, but inexperienced in foreign affairs. When he met Khrushchev at a summit conference in Vienna, Austria, that June, the Soviet dictator bullied the new president about Berlin. Since 1949 more than two million people—including many scientists and engineers—had escaped Communist East Germany by crossing from East Berlin to West Berlin. To stop this outflow, Khrushchev demanded that the Western powers leave the city. Failure to do so, he said, would result in war. Kennedy was shaken but refused to back down and went home expecting the worst.

Khrushchev and Kennedy clash about Berlin at Vienna

Summer 1961 was filled with foreboding, as Kennedy announced a military buildup, bracing for another Berlin blockade and perhaps even war. In August, however, the Communists stunned the world by building a barbwire barrier to seal off the border between East and West Berlin. Then, in the next few months, they replaced the barbwire with a wall.

Much to Berliners' dismay, Kennedy did not try to stop the wall's construction since it posed no real threat to the West. Indeed, by stopping the human outflow, the wall enabled the Soviets to accept continued Western presence in Berlin, eventually easing the crisis. But the Berlin Wall, which stood 28 years as an unsightly symbol of Communist oppression, further undermined the Soviet image. As Kennedy later claimed in a stirring speech to a huge crowd in West Berlin, "Freedom has many difficulties and democracy is not perfect. But we have never had to put a wall up to keep our people in."

Berlin Wall, built by Communists, symbolizes global East–West divide

Khrushchev, meanwhile, faced an even deadlier dilemma. As Kennedy accelerated the arms race by ordering production of a thousand new ICBMs, the Soviets, with fewer than a dozen, lagged far behind. The USSR lacked the wealth to build huge numbers of expensive missiles and still fund Khrushchev's ambitious plans to improve the domestic economy.

His thoughts turned to Cuba, 90 miles from American shores, where Fidel Castro, an anti-American revolutionary, had taken power in 1959. After America tried unsuccessfully to unseat him by landing armed anti-Castro Cubans in Cuba at the "Bay of Pigs" in April 1961 (Chapter 36), Castro began pressing for Soviet protection against another U.S. attack. In response, in spring 1962, Khrushchev came up with a perilous plan. He would secretly place Soviet mid-range nuclear missiles in Cuba, where they could target the United States. He could thus protect Castro, counter the U.S. missile buildup, and save the Soviet Union the huge cost of building numerous new ICBMs. Once the missiles were in place in Cuba, he planned to reveal their presence—and hopefully use them as leverage to secure withdrawal of Western forces from Berlin.

But in October 1962, before the Soviets had completely installed the missiles, American spy planes discovered their presence in Cuba. Kennedy demanded their removal and had the U.S. Navy blockade Cuba to halt further weapons shipments, provoking a superpower confrontation called the **Cuban Missile Crisis**. For several days the world watched in terror as the Soviets and Americans teetered on the brink of war. But Khrushchev chose not to challenge the blockade and Kennedy resisted pressure to bomb or invade Cuba. Finally, in return for a public U.S. promise not to invade the island, Khrushchev agreed to remove the missiles. Privately, Kennedy also pledged to remove from Turkey American mid-range missiles that were aimed at the USSR.

Stepping back from the brink of catastrophe, Kennedy and Khrushchev sought to reduce tensions, and in 1963 they agreed to a treaty banning all nuclear tests except those held underground. The Nuclear Test Ban Treaty helped curb atmospheric pollution from nuclear tests but did little to stop the arms race, since the agreement did not ban production of new weapons.

In November of that year, while in Dallas, Texas, President Kennedy was shot and killed by an assassin. His successor, Lyndon Johnson, sent increasing numbers of U.S. troops to Vietnam, divided after French defeat in 1954 into Communist North Vietnam and anti-Communist South Vietnam. For the next decade, the Vietnam War (Chapter 35) was a central Cold War battleground, with Americans fighting in South Vietnam against a Communist insurgency backed by the North, which was aided with supplies and weapons by the Soviets and Chinese Communists.

Meanwhile, the arms race intensified. In 1964, plagued by domestic and foreign policy failures, Khrushchev was ousted and replaced by a group of his former subordinates, led by a new party boss named Leonid Brezhnev. Blaming the Cuban fiasco on Soviet weakness, the new regime pursued a relentless naval and nuclear buildup. By the 1970s, each side had so many thousand nuclear weapons that the world lived in terror of a superpower conflict—possibly begun by miscalculation—that would incinerate millions. But the horror of such a war may have helped to prevent it: since an all-out conflict could annihilate both sides, each side sought to avoid one. This "balance of terror" was also called Mutual Assured Destruction, aptly abbreviated as **MAD**.

Khrushchev responds to U.S. missile buildup by placing Soviet missiles in Cuba

👁—**Watch** the **Video**
Cold War Connections: Russia, America, Berlin, and Cuba
on **myhistorylab.com**

Americans blockade Cuba and Soviets agree to remove missiles

Cartoon of Khrushchev and Kennedy fighting on "Cuban cliff."

U.S. troops sent to South Vietnam to fight Communists

Brezhnev regime replaces Khrushchev and accelerates arms race

The West in the Cold War Era

Despite such global tensions, the West achieved unparalleled prosperity during the Cold War. Western Europeans emerged from the ashes of World War II, rebuilt their economies with substantial U.S. help, and, as they lost their colonial empires, sought to strengthen their commerce and status through European unity. Americans used their abundant wealth and resources to cover costly Cold War endeavors, while dealing with difficult domestic divisions and societal changes.

The Revival of Western Europe

Western Europeans lose colonies but regain prosperity

The Cold War era was not easy for Western Europeans. Having long dominated the globe, they now found themselves dependent on America for military and economic support. Europe's Asian and African colonies, guided by growing nationalism, armed with modern weapons, and sometimes backed by Soviet support, increasingly claimed independence (Chapters 35 and 37). Britain, Belgium, and the Netherlands reluctantly released their colonies, while France and Portugal sought for years to hold on to theirs. Eventually, however, such efforts proved futile: by 1975, almost all of Asia and Africa were independent, and Europe's once-great global empires were gone (Map 34.3). The era of European domination was over.

Western Europe nonetheless survived and thrived. Aided by the U.S. Marshall Plan and protected by NATO, Europe's capitalist democracies enjoyed enormous economic expansion in the 1950s and 1960s. To foster growth, governments intervened in the economy, using planning commissions to set goals, supplying funds and tax incentives to businesses, and even controlling key industries. To improve the status of the working classes, and thus counter Communism's appeal, governments expanded social programs, providing health insurance, unemployment compensation, old-age pensions, public housing, and family allowances to help parents care for children. They thus combined elements of socialism with capitalist economies.

Western Europeans unite to increase economic strength

To strengthen themselves economically, and decrease dependence on America, European nations also began to unite in their own self-interest. Led by France and West Germany, in 1957 six of them formed the European Economic Community (EEC), also called the **Common Market,** reducing tariffs on each other's goods to foster commercial growth. EEC expansion was slowed in the 1960s by French president Charles de Gaulle, a fervent nationalist who blocked British membership for fear it would dilute French influence. He also asserted France's military independence, withdrawing from NATO's joint command but staying in the alliance.

In the 1970s, however, the European Community (EC), created in 1967 by merging the EEC with several other agencies, began to expand. By 1973 de Gaulle was gone, as were most of Europe's colonies, and an economic downturn had brought high unemployment and working class unrest. Anxious, therefore, to increase its markets and resources, the EC welcomed Britain, Ireland, and Denmark as members. By the 1980s, when three more nations were added, the EC encompassed more than 300 million people and over a quarter of the world's trade.

European Economic Community grows into European Union

Further integration and expansion followed. In 1993 the EC was incorporated into a new European Union (EU), which launched a common currency called the euro, replacing numerous old national currencies with a single monetary system. By 2007, the EU had grown to 27 nations (Map 34.5) with half a billion people, embracing even former Soviet satellites that had by then gained independence. In 2005, however, voters in France and the Netherlands, fearful that these countries could lose their political autonomy, refused to ratify a negotiated European Constitution, sidetracking efforts to augment Europe's economic integration with greater political unity.

Affluence and Anxieties in America

Global commerce and Cold War spending enhance American affluence

As Western Europeans dealt with their diminished status after World War II, America enjoyed unprecedented influence and affluence. But pressing Cold War concerns, and

MAP **34.5** Growth of the Common Market and European Union, 1957–2007

Founded with six members in 1957, the European Economic Community (EEC), or Common Market, eventually added many new members, growing into the European Community (EC) in 1967 and European Union (EU) in 1993. What were the advantages of membership? Why did some members resist political integration?

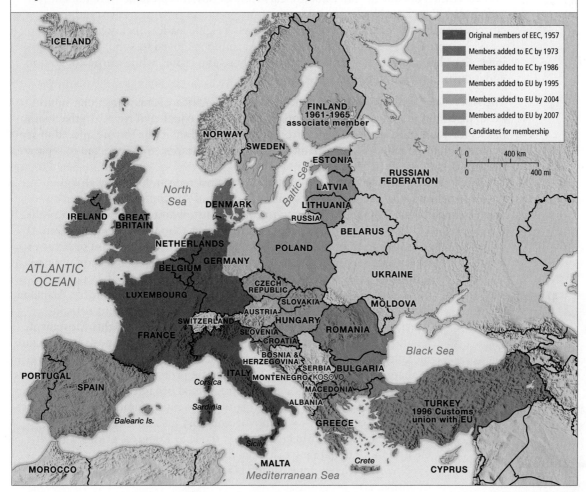

Legend:
- Original members of EEC, 1957
- Members added to EC by 1973
- Members added to EC by 1986
- Members added to EU by 1995
- Members added to EU by 2004
- Members added to EU by 2007
- Candidates for membership

deep divisions in American society, also produced intense anxieties in the "land of plenty."

America in the Cold War years experienced unparalleled abundance. A huge global and domestic demand for U.S. consumer goods, following years of shortage during World War II, combined with massive Cold War defense spending to generate an economic boom. As purchasing power more than doubled between 1945 and 1970, Americans rushed to buy houses, cars, and televisions, which soon replaced radios as the main form of home entertainment. Improved roads and incomes helped millions move from crowded cities, with closely packed dwellings and street-front stores, to sprawling suburbs, with neat neighborhoods of look-alike homes, shopping malls, and supermarkets. A vast interstate highway system, designed in part to aid military transport in the Cold War era, promoted commerce and mobility, while a changing economy and affordable air conditioning fostered mass migration to the sunny South and West.

Rows of look-alike houses in suburban America.

((⊶[**Listen** to the **Audio**

Cold War II

on **myhistorylab.com**

Urban problems and fear of Communism foster American anxieties

But anxieties persisted. The rise of Communist China and the Korean War helped trigger a "Red Scare" in the early 1950s. U.S. Senator Joseph McCarthy, using tactics later called "McCarthyism," made sweeping charges that Communists had infiltrated government, industry, and entertainment. McCarthy was discredited in 1954, but (as declassified documents later made clear) fears of Soviet espionage were not entirely unfounded. For years, the Federal Bureau of Investigation (FBI) secretly scrutinized citizens suspected of disloyalty, including even civil rights leaders (below).

Urban problems added to the insecurity. As millions moved to suburbs, decaying inner cities became breeding grounds of drug abuse and crime, while traffic congestion and industrial pollution fouled the air and water.

THE AMERICAN CIVIL RIGHTS MOVEMENT. Furthermore, African Americans, long subject to racial discrimination, began to press more forcefully for equal civil rights. In the South, blacks for years had been segregated from whites, denied the right to vote, placed in separate and poorly funded schools, denied service at restaurants, and restricted to separate restrooms.

By the 1950s, however, widespread reaction against racism, fueled by global revulsion against Nazi racist atrocities and by Asian and African struggles against Western imperialism, compelled America to confront its own racial divide. In 1954 the U.S. Supreme Court, faced with compelling evidence that schools for white children provided better education than schools for black children, ruled in the case of *Brown v. Board of Education* that separate education was inherently unequal and soon ordered schools to desegregate "with all deliberate speed."

Civil Rights Movement combats American racism

In 1955 a black boycott of segregated buses in Montgomery, Alabama, brought to the fore Dr. Martin Luther King, Jr., an eloquent African-American minister who emerged as leader of the **Civil Rights Movement**, a nationwide campaign for racial equality. Combining appeals to Christian morality and American democratic ideals with tactics used by India's Mahatma Gandhi (Chapter 32)—including protest marches, civil disobedience, and nonviolent resistance—King gained broad support among whites as well as blacks. With the backing of President Lyndon Johnson, a former Southern segregationist who now committed his administration (1963–1969) to fighting racism and poverty, the U.S. Congress passed a 1964 Civil Rights Act banning discrimination in jobs and public services, a 1965 Voting Rights Act ensuring blacks the right to vote, and an array of antipoverty programs.

Black American Rosa Parks on a Montgomery bus.

Ongoing racial and ethnic tensions deepen U.S. social unrest

Racism and racial tension nonetheless endured. Legal segregation was banned, but many whites still resisted sharing neighborhoods and schools with blacks. Violent upheavals in many U.S. cities showed that racial divisions persisted. As America grew increasingly diverse, people of Asian, Latin American, and Amerind backgrounds, who also experienced discrimination, similarly sought to gain equality by using the methods and ideals of the Civil Rights Movement.

DIVISIONS IN AMERICAN SOCIETY. Racial and ethnic tensions were not the only anxieties afflicting Cold War America. Protests against an unpopular war, and changing attitudes toward sex, gender, and family, also reflected deep divisions in American society.

Segregated facilities in America.

From 1965 to 1973, U.S. combat forces fought in the debilitating Vietnam War (Chapter 35). At first it enjoyed broad support, as part of the global anti-Communist struggle, but soon increasing casualties and troop call-ups convinced many Americans that the war was going badly—and that claims to the contrary by U.S. leaders were lies. By 1967 an antiwar movement was staging protests demanding U.S. withdrawal.

The movement attracted many members of the **baby boom** generation, Americans born during a huge surge in births following World War II. Raised in affluence and influenced by a youth culture that combined opposition to racism and violence with relaxed attitudes toward sex and drugs, many baby boomers joined both civil rights protests and antiwar protests. Many also resisted the draft, which made young men liable to military service, and some even left the country. In 1968, as civil rights leader Martin Luther King and antiwar candidate Robert Kennedy (the late president's brother) were assassinated, and riots disrupted the presidential nominating conventions, U.S. society seemed to be dissolving into chaos.

That same year, after promising to end the Vietnam War and to restore "law and order," Richard Nixon, a crafty Cold Warrior, was elected president. By gradually reducing the U.S. role in Vietnam, he restored some stability, but riots resumed in 1970 when he expanded the war into Cambodia. In 1973 he suspended the draft and secured U.S. withdrawal from the war, easing domestic tensions. But the "Watergate" scandal, exposing Nixon's efforts to obstruct justice following a break-in by his minions at the offices of his political foes in Washington's Watergate complex, created further turmoil, leading to his disgrace and resignation in 1974.

By then America was undergoing a social revolution. In the 1960s, a new women's rights movement, building on the work of the earlier crusade that helped women gain voting rights, inspired millions of women to pursue careers—such as law, public service, medicine, and management—hitherto open mainly to men. Divorce rates doubled between 1960 and 1980, as women who could earn a living felt less need to stay in unhappy marriages, and as divorce and remarriage became more socially acceptable. Sex outside of marriage likewise became more acceptable, as more and more unmarried and premarried couples cohabited. Abortions increased in the 1970s and 1980s, especially after a 1973 Supreme Court decision, in the case of *Roe v. Wade*, supported abortion rights for women. Alarmed by such developments, religious conservatives sought to outlaw abortion and restore "traditional family values," a set of moral standards condemning sex outside of marriage, denouncing homosexual relationships, and asserting that a wife's main career should be that of homemaker and mother.

Antiwar movement heightens unrest among American youths

Antiwar protesters with flowers confront U.S. soldiers.

Changing women's roles and sexual standards challenge U.S. society

The Soviet Bloc

Life in the Soviet bloc contrasted sharply with life in the West. Stalin, desperate to rebuild the USSR after World War II, reimposed harsh repression and ruthlessly exploited his new Eastern European satellites. Khrushchev, hoping to set a more attractive example, eased repression and tried to improve people's lives, ending Stalin's worst abuses and investing heavily in housing, agriculture, and consumer goods. But a series of poor harvests undercut his agricultural advances, and the Cuban crisis settlement ruined his bid to overtake America without a costly arms race. The Brezhnev regime (1964–1982), while also trying to improve living standards, cracked down on dissent and spent huge sums on an arms buildup. By the 1970s the USSR had surpassed America in numbers of long-range missiles, but its domestic economy lagged far behind.

Khrushchev visiting factory in Communist Albania.

Life Under Communist Rule

Communism did many things for its people. It supplied numerous social services, including free health care, day care for children, subsidized housing, low-cost food and consumer goods, cheap public transport, quality education, guaranteed employment, and extensive pensions. Soviet society was highly literate, while Soviet scientists and athletes ranked among the world's best. In the USSR and its satellites, more and more people enjoyed concerts, ballets, movies, sports, television, and even Western imports such as rock music and jazz.

Communism supplies social services but not freedom or abundance

But Communism provided neither freedom nor Western-style prosperity. Stalin's successors softened his system but continued to control both society and economy. Although Khrushchev relaxed censorship, artists, writers, and the state-run media were still expected to emphasize the country's successes in science, sports, and space, while ignoring such failures as its shortage of quality goods and housing. A centralized economy, with five-year plans that set specific quotas for every industry and enterprise, helped the regime focus resources on the arms race but regimented the rest of society. From Central Europe to the Pacific, Soviet bloc peoples lived in cramped apartments and waited in long lines to buy drab produce grown on dismal collective farms and shoddy goods made in industries plagued by alcoholism and absenteeism.

Nor did Communism create the classless society Marxists envisioned. While the masses endured a dreary existence, a privileged elite of high officials had superior housing and medical care, fancy vacations and country homes, and access to special stores selling luxury items such as caviar and imported liqueurs. Soviet women often held jobs in areas dominated by men in the West, such as medicine and engineering, but Soviet wives were still expected to shop, cook, and clean for their husbands and families. By the 1970s, Communist idealism had given way to cynicism and careerism, while aging Soviet rulers focused mainly on maintaining control.

"Classless" Communist societies produce new privileged elites

Similar conditions prevailed in other Communist countries, which typically had their own planned economies, privileged elites, and drab living conditions. The contrast was especially striking in the divided nations of Korea and Germany, where people in the Communist part endured poverty and oppression, while those in the capitalist part grew increasingly prosperous. But even in Communist China, where mass experiments meant to improve life instead provoked mass suffering, prosperity proved elusive until the 1980s and 1990s, when new leaders added capitalist incentives to Communist controls (Chapter 35).

Challenges to Soviet Authority

Soviets vainly struggle to suppress internal dissent

In the USSR, Communist control meant suppressing dissenters who dared to criticize or defy the regime. Aleksandr Solzhenitsyn (*sōl-zhih-NĒT-sin*), a brilliant Russian author who had spent years in a Stalinist prison camp, was accused of treason for writing *The Gulag Archipelago*, an account of the prison camp system, and exiled abroad in 1974. Andrei Sakharov (*SAH-kha-roff*), an eminent nuclear physicist who helped develop the Soviet H-bomb but then became an outspoken critic of Soviet human rights abuses, was confined in 1980 to a central Russian city to keep his message from the outside world. Other key dissidents were harassed by Soviet secret police, imprisoned on false charges, or confined in psychiatric wards. But despite such repression, a network of dissident writers and activists operated throughout the Brezhnev years, secretly typing and circulating works exposing Soviet failings.

Soviets control their satellites with force and fear

The Soviets also struggled to keep their satellites in line. In Czechoslovakia, in 1968, a Communist reformer named Alexander Dubček (*DOOB-chek*) introduced "socialism with a human face," lifting most restrictions on speech, press, and foreign travel. After watching warily for months, the USSR sent in troops and tanks to crush the reform movement, eventually removing Dubček and installing a repressive regime. The Soviet invasion of Czechoslovakia was justified by an assertion, later called the **Brezhnev Doctrine**, that the USSR had the right to intervene in other Communist countries to protect the global interests of socialism, as defined by Soviet leaders. In 1981, after an independent trade union called Solidarity staged strikes and protests in Poland, the Soviets again threatened to intervene in a satellite country. But Poland's Communist regime imposed martial law (emergency military rule) to restore order and outlawed the dissident union, thereby making a Soviet invasion unnecessary.

Clearly, then, the Soviet bloc was sustained by the threat of force. To millions of Eastern Europeans, and to non-Russians who made up half the USSR's population, the Soviet bloc was a replica of the old tsarist Russian empire, with Marxism serving as a new pretext for Russian imperial ways. Envious of Western affluence and aware that Europe's empires in Asia and Africa had crumbled, many Soviet subjects dreamed of the day that the Soviet empire would likewise fall apart. That day came much sooner than many expected.

The End of the Cold War Era

By the late 1960s, the Cold War was taking its toll on both superpowers. Through enormous efforts, the Soviets had managed to surpass the United States in numbers of ICBMs and to hold their vast empire together. But their economy was stagnant, and their friendship with Red China had turned into bitter rivalry, sparking deadly border clashes in 1969. The Soviet leaders thus agreed to talks with the Americans, mired in the Vietnam War and facing their own stalled economy, in an effort to ease anxieties and control the nuclear arms race.

((•─[**Listen** to the **Audio**
Communism
on **myhistorylab.com**

Détente and Its Demise

The result of these talks was an era of **détente** (*dā-TAHNT*), a relaxation of international tensions, during the 1970s. Early in the decade, when Soviet-American efforts to end the arms race bogged down, President Nixon reached out to Communist China, paying it a historic visit in February 1972. This trip not only opened dialogue between China and America, bitter foes for over two decades; it also raised Soviet fears of Chinese-American cooperation, prompting Soviet leaders to work out agreements with the United States. As a result, in May 1972 in Moscow, Brezhnev and Nixon signed treaties limiting the numbers of offensive and defensive missiles each side could have and endorsed several scientific and cultural agreements. The next year U.S. involvement in Vietnam ended and Brezhnev visited the United States. In 1975, after a dramatic orbital docking of American and Soviet space vehicles raised hopes for joint scientific endeavors, the two superpowers joined 33 other nations in signing the Helsinki Accords, a comprehensive set of agreements to stabilize Europe's security. Once again, the Cold War seemed to be ending.

Détente, however, had its limits. Hampered by huge military expenses, the Soviets were eager to end the arms race, but not their global efforts to spread Communism. The USSR thus kept aiding Vietnamese Communists, even after U.S. withdrawal, while also sending military aid to African Marxists in Ethiopia and Angola, and to Arabs fighting Israel in the

Cold War costs and nuclear fears prompt efforts at détente

"Stop the arms race" poster, 1978.

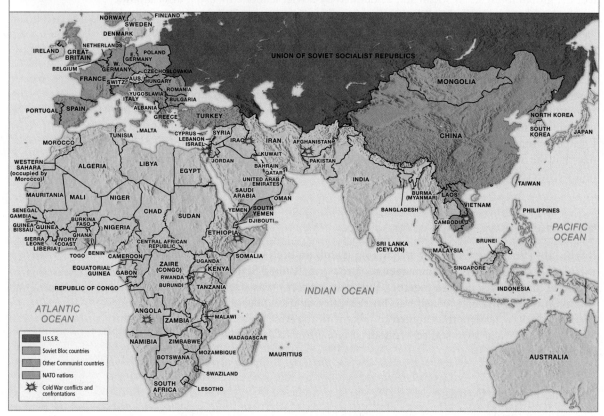

| MAP **34.6** | Cold War Clashes of the 1970s and 1980s |

Despite efforts at détente in the 1970s, the Cold War continued and intensified in the 1980s. Note that East and West remained locked into hostile alliances, and that Cold War clashes persisted in Africa and Asia. How did Soviet support for anti-Western movements and U.S. aid to anti-Communists fuel conflicts in these continents?

Clashes in Africa and Islamic world undermine efforts at détente

Middle East (Map 34.6). U.S. attempts to promote human rights provisions of the Helsinki Accords, especially those allowing Soviet bloc citizens access to Western publications and broadcasts, angered the Soviets, fearful of efforts to destabilize their bloc with anti-Soviet propaganda. A new arms control pact, signed in 1979, went unratified by the U.S. Senate after the USSR, to support a client regime endangered by revolt, invaded neighboring Afghanistan. This Soviet assault, beginning a lengthy Soviet-Afghan War (1979–1989), dealt a death blow to détente.

Seeing the Soviets' Afghan incursion as a threat to vital U.S. oil shipments from the Persian Gulf, President Jimmy Carter, whose administration (1977–1981) had earlier worked to end the arms race, now initiated anti-Soviet sanctions and a new American arms buildup. But U.S. voters, upset by a flagging economy and by Carter's inability to secure the release of American hostages seized in Iran in 1979, defeated him in the 1980 elections.

Alarmed by Soviet aggressiveness, America intensifies the arms race

Elected instead was Ronald Reagan, an ardent anti-Communist with a deep distrust of the USSR, which he later labeled an "evil empire." Asserting that the Soviets would cheat on any arms agreement, he and his advisors denounced détente and intensified the arms race, hoping thereby to bankrupt the USSR. Imitating Soviet support for anti-Western liberation movements, his administration aided anti-Communist insurgents in

Angola, Ethiopia, Nicaragua, and Afghanistan, and even supplied modern antiaircraft missiles to Afghan rebels fighting Soviet forces. The Cold War and arms race thus resumed with full force.

The Gorbachev Revolution

In Moscow, however, Leonid Brezhnev's death in 1982 opened the way for a major policy shift. His last years had been marred by economic stagnation, the rise of the anti-Soviet Solidarity union in Poland, and failures in the Afghan War, in which ragged rebel guerrillas were humbling the mighty Soviet Army and draining Soviet resources. His two immediate successors were aging and ailing bureaucrats who died before having much impact. But in 1985, power passed to a young, energetic new Soviet leader named Mikhail Gorbachev (*GOR-bah-CHOFF*), who was eager to make changes.

Conscious of the Soviet system's shortcomings, Gorbachev promoted *perestroika* (*p'YEH-reh-STRAW-ē-kah*), "restructuring" of Soviet society. To boost economic output, he experimented with Western-style profit and market incentives, granted greater autonomy for farmers and factory managers, and launched a drive against drunkenness by restricting alcohol sales. To improve government performance, he combated corruption, encouraged *glasnost* (*GLAHSS-nōst*), or open discussion of the USSR's problems, and allowed limited democratic elections.

To help cut military costs and support for Cold War clients, and thus free up resources for his reforms, Gorbachev also sought to ease international tensions. He held several summit meetings with Reagan who, despite his anti-Communism, decided he could deal with the new Soviet leader, and the two signed a 1987 treaty eliminating mid-range missiles.

Their efforts to reduce long-range weapons, however, were thwarted by Reagan's ambition to build a space-based missile defense system, officially called **SDI** (Strategic Defense Initiative) but widely known as "Star Wars" (after a popular film series featuring futuristic space weapons). Reagan depicted SDI as a "peace shield" that would render nuclear missiles obsolete by making it possible to intercept them in space. But the Soviets saw it instead as a weapon that would free the United States to attack the USSR without fear of retaliation. Gorbachev therefore denounced SDI, postponing his pursuit of further arms accords until after Reagan was replaced in 1989 by George H. W. Bush, a cautious president less wedded to SDI.

Collapse of the Communist Bloc

Meanwhile, Gorbachev took other striking steps. In 1988 he began withdrawing troops from Afghanistan, acting to end the war he called a "bleeding wound." Later that year, in a stunning speech at the United Nations, he called on all countries to renounce the use of force and announced sizable Soviet military cuts. And in 1989 he disowned the Brezhnev Doctrine, inviting Eastern European nations to pursue their own paths to socialism.

Since the threat of force was what held the Soviet bloc together, Gorbachev's words and deeds had vast repercussions. Eastern Europe's Communist regimes, no longer sure they could count on the Soviets to help them crush dissent, started taking steps to gain public support. The Polish government legalized the Solidarity union, suppressed since 1981, and created a new senate based on free elections, soon won by Solidarity. The Hungarian Communists scheduled free elections and, hoping to impress voters, tore down barbwire borders barring escape to the West, thereby opening a hole in the iron curtain.

Gorbachev seeks "restructuring" and improvement of Soviet economy

Read the **Document**

Mikhail Gorbachev on the Need for Economic Reform (1987)

on **myhistorylab.com**

Gorbachev seeks reduced global tensions to ease strain on Soviet economy

Gorbachev withdraws from Afghan War and renounces use of force

Poland and Hungary ease repression and proclaim free elections

East Germany opens its borders; Berliners tear down Berlin Wall

East Germans then proved especially creative. Thousands of them, hearing the news from Hungary, traveled there intending to escape to the West through the open borders. When East Germany's Communist rulers reacted by banning trips to Hungary, East Germans instead went to Czechoslovakia, and pressured the Czechs to provide them with trains to West Germany. Embarrassed by this spectacle, with no support from the Soviets, and with anti-Communist rallies arising throughout East Germany, the East German regime took a desperate gamble. On November 9, 1989, hoping to appease its people, it officially reduced its restrictions on travel to the West. Within hours exultant Berliners were tearing down the Berlin Wall.

Berlin Wall's fall sparks democratic revolts throughout Eastern Europe

These events, and Soviet failure to stop them, inspired uprisings across Eastern Europe, as most of its countries moved toward independence by the end of 1989. Bloodshed was limited, except in Romania, where Communist dictator Nicolae Ceausescu (*chow-SHESS-koo*) had police massacre protesters, until his forces rebelled against him and killed him on Christmas day.

German reunification signals end of Cold War

View the **Map**

Map Discovery: Reunified Germany, October 1990

on **myhistorylab.com**

In free elections held in East Germany in March 1990, voters overwhelmingly chose candidates who favored German unification. In return for a large West German loan to the Soviets that summer, Gorbachev agreed not to resist, paving the way for Germany's unification in October. West Germany's government took over the whole country, as East Germany's ceased to exist. By then, with Berlin's Wall gone, Eastern Europe free, and Germany reunited, few could doubt that the Cold War really was over.

Cartoon of Gorbachev and Soviet breakup.

Gorbachev tries to sustain USSR as republics assert independence

Disintegration of the USSR

Then came the collapse of the USSR. As the nation's economy, hampered by bad harvests and bureaucratic stagnation, continued to decline, Gorbachev's standing with his people plummeted. Using the new openness he allowed, many openly denounced him. Inspired by events in Eastern Europe, moreover, the USSR's 15 Soviet Republics, each dominated by a different nationality, began demanding national independence. By late 1990 all 15 had proclaimed some form of autonomy—including even Russia, the largest Soviet republic, encompassing three quarters of the USSR's land and over half its people (Map 34.7).

Hoping to halt the disintegration, in January 1991 the Soviets sent forces into Latvia and Lithuania, two small Soviet republics that had declared outright independence. Scrambling to save the situation, Gorbachev then promoted a new "union treaty" designed to give the republics internal autonomy while preserving the overall union in foreign and military affairs. The treaty, however, enraged Communist hard-liners, who wanted to preserve strong centralized control.

Hard-line coup attempt foiled by Yeltsin, head of Russian republic

On August 19, 1991, the day before the treaty was scheduled to be signed, eight hard-liners, including the defense minister and head of security police, attempted an ill-conceived coup. Visibly fortified with vodka, they publicly declared an emergency and ordered troops to occupy key cities. Having earlier detained Gorbachev, however, they failed to arrest Boris Yeltsin, outspoken head of the Russian republic. Climbing atop a tank in front of the Russian parliament in Moscow, Yeltsin boldly urged mass resistance to the coup. Thousands soon gathered in support, defying police and military forces assembled on the scene. When commanders, unsure of their troops' loyalty and anxious to avoid a bloodbath, decided the next day not to order an assault, the coup leaders had no way to assert control. Within a few days they gave in, ending the abortive August coup (derided by Russians as the "vodka putsch") and letting Gorbachev resume his duties.

Soviet Union crumbles as Russians and others withdraw

But momentum had passed to Yeltsin and the heads of the other republics, who each asserted more independence following the coup. Gorbachev strove to devise a new

MAP 34.7 Disintegration of the Communist Bloc, 1989–1992

In 1989 revolts in Eastern Europe brought independence to former Soviet satellites, and in 1991 the Soviet Union broke up into 15 separate countries. How did the 1989 Eastern European revolts help trigger the USSR's disintegration two years later?

union treaty, hoping to preserve some Soviet authority, but few paid any attention. After several months, Russia and many other republics formed a Commonwealth of Independent States, a loose coalition with no central control, and agreed to dissolve the USSR. On December 25, 1991, when Gorbachev reluctantly resigned his post, the once-mighty Soviet Union ceased to exist.

The World Transformed

The global situation thus was totally transformed. The Soviet bloc was gone, Germany reunited, and the USSR split into 15 separate states. Communism survived in China, Cuba, Vietnam, and North Korea, but none had the power of the former Soviet Union. In Asia, Africa, and Latin America, anti-Western regimes and rebels could no longer look for Soviet support. The Communists had lost the Cold War.

Russia still had formidable forces, but it lacked political and economic stability in the 1990s. Yeltsin, who served as its president from 1991 to 1999, was plagued by ill health and by challenges from the Russian parliament and from Chechnya, a small southern region that sought to break from Russia and form a separate republic. His successor, Vladimir Putin, a former officer in the Soviet security police, sought to crush the Chechnya revolt and suppress internal dissent, silencing critics and taking control of the media and provincial governors. In 2008, after serving as president for the lawful two-term limit, Putin engineered the election of Dmitri Medvedev, a colleague who then continued Putin's influence by appointing him prime minister.

Europe, no longer divided, moved toward even greater unity, as former Soviet satellites joined NATO and the European Union (Map 34.8). The breakup of Yugoslavia into smaller republics in 1991 led to bloody ethnic wars in Bosnia (1992–1995) and Kosovo (1998), but NATO involvement eventually brought a fragile peace to the region.

Read the **Document**
Constitution of Russia
on **myhistorylab.com**

View the **Map**
Map Discovery: Republics of the Soviet Union, 1991
on **myhistorylab.com**

Post-Soviet Russia tries democracy but soon becomes repressive

European Union and NATO admit former Soviet satellites

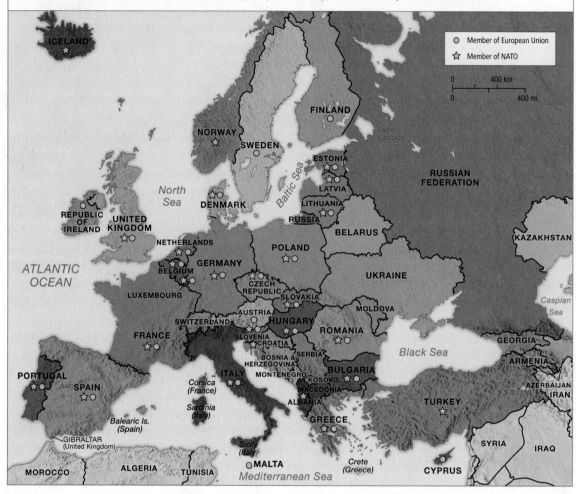

MAP **34.8** Twenty-First-Century-Europe: Fragmentation and Integration

In the late 20th and early 21st centuries, Europe experienced both fragmentation and integration. Note that the breakups of the USSR, Yugoslavia, and Czechoslovakia created many new nations, while expansion of NATO and the European Union connected many countries militarily and economically. Why did so many nations want to join NATO and the EU?

United States faces severe global challenges despite unrivaled power and wealth

The United States, as the sole surviving superpower, enjoyed unrivaled influence and prosperity. But in September 2001, angered at U.S. policies in the Middle East, Islamist terrorists used hijacked airliners to kill thousands of Americans (Chapter 37), leaving the nation feeling newly vulnerable. U.S. invasions in Afghanistan and Iraq, accused of harboring terrorists, resulted in long wars that divided America and damaged its global standing, as did a severe economic crisis beginning in 2008. The election that year of Barack Obama, the nation's first black president, led to sweeping health care and financial reforms and a costly economic stimulus intended to reduce unemployment. But these programs, combined with persistently high unemployment and mushrooming budget deficits, also sharpened political and social divisions.

Growing concerns about climate and environment likewise sharpened global anxieties. Evidence of extensive **global warming**, with increasing average temperatures and melting of polar ice caps, brought fears of impending environmental disaster, along with sharp debates about the cause and potential responses. These concerns were compounded by continuing global reliance on fuels made from petroleum oil, in part because their use created carbon emissions said to affect the climate, in part because demand for them contributed to regional conflicts, and in part because the search for new oil brought risk of environmental damage—as exhibited by a massive 2010 oil spill following an oil well accident in the Gulf of Mexico. But other energy sources also posed serious perils, as evidenced by hazardous radiation leaks from an earthquake-damaged Japanese nuclear power plant in 2011. With global tensions compounded by grave concerns about environment and energy, humanity faced an uncertain future in the 21st century.

CHAPTER
REVIEW

Putting It in Perspective

The Cold War divided the world into two immense armed camps, led by competing superpowers, driven by conflicting ideals, and characterized by contrasting political and economic systems. The capitalist West and Communist East struggled for supremacy through a series of crises, any of which could have led to all-out war, all the while striving to avoid such war since it would destroy them both. Stalemated in Europe, they battled for influence in Asia and Africa, where conflicts in such places as Korea, Vietnam, Cambodia, Ethiopia, Angola, and Afghanistan took millions of lives. For four decades humanity endured both the ongoing dread of unlimited war and the ongoing reality of limited wars occurring somewhere in the world.

Humanity nonetheless survived the Cold War. America achieved great prosperity while leading the West against Soviet Communism, but also was torn by divisions regarding race, gender, morality, and foreign policy. Western Europeans, while losing their colonies and looking to America for defense against the USSR, overcame age-old divisions to unite militarily and economically. The Soviets relied mainly on armed force, sacrificing prosperity to sustain their military might, while using the constant threat of force to keep subject peoples in line. When Gorbachev, hoping to refocus Soviet resources on economic growth, acted to reduce armed forces and remove the threat of force, the Soviet empire crumbled and the Cold War came to an end.

The Cold War had extensive global impact. It compounded anticolonial conflicts, aggravated regional upheavals, and complicated efforts to achieve stability in Asia, Latin America, Africa, and the Middle East. The next three chapters discuss these efforts and upheavals.

Reviewing Key Material

KEY CONCEPTS

United Nations, 808
Soviet bloc, 810
Truman Doctrine, 810
Marshall Plan, 811
containment of
    Communism 811
NATO, 812
decolonization, 814
Warsaw Pact, 815
ICBM, 815
summit conference, 818

U-2 Affair, 818
Cuban Missile Crisis, 819
MAD, 819
Common Market, 820
Civil Rights Movement,
    822
baby boom, 823
Brezhnev Doctrine, 825
détente, 825
SDI, 827
global warming, 830

KEY PEOPLE

Joseph Stalin, 807
Harry Truman, 807
Winston Churchill, 807
Clement Attlee, 809
George Marshall, 810
George F. Kennan, 811
Dwight Eisenhower, 813
Nikita Khrushchev, 813
Sukarno, 815
Suharto, 815
Patrice Lumumba, 815

Yuri Gagarin, 815
John F. Kennedy, 818
Fidel Castro, 819
Lyndon Johnson, 819
Leonid Brezhnev, 819
Charles De Gaulle,
    820
Joseph McCarthy, 822
Martin Luther King, Jr.,
    822
Richard Nixon, 823

ASK YOURSELF

1. Why did the Cold War begin? How did the differing ideals, aims, and actions of Soviet and Western leaders contribute to its onset?

2. Why did the Cold War expand into global confrontation? Why did the USSR aid anticolonial movements and former European colonies? Why did such aid often fail to advance the spread of Communism?

3. What were the main Cold War crises? Why did each occur, and how was it resolved? Why did efforts at peaceful coexistence and détente fail to end the Cold War?

4. How did life in the Soviet bloc differ from life in the West? What problems and divisions beset Soviet and Western societies?

5. What major strategies did each side adopt in the Cold War? What were each side's major strengths and weaknesses? Why did the West prevail?

6. What actions and decisions by Soviet and Western leaders led to the end of the Cold War and disintegration of the Soviet empire?

GOING FURTHER

Alperovitz, Gar. *Atomic Diplomacy*. Rev. ed. 1985.
Baylis, John, et al., eds. *The Globalization of World Politics*. 2004.
Beschloss, Michael. *The Crisis Years, 1960–1963*. 1991.
Brown, D. *Globalization and America Since 1945*. 2003.
Chafe, W. H. *The Unfinished Journey: America Since World War II*. 5th ed. 2003.
Crockatt, R. *The Fifty Years War*. 1995.
Dobbs, M. *Down with Big Brother: Fall of the Soviet Empire*. 1997.
Dockrill, M. *The Cold War, 1945–1963*. 1988.
Frankel, M. *High Noon in the Cold War: Kennedy, Khrushchev, and the Cuban Missile Crisis*. 2004.
Fursenko, A., and T. Naftali. *Khrushchev's Cold War*. 2006.

Gaddis, J. L. *The Cold War: A New History*. 2005.
Garthoff, R. *Détente and Confrontation*. 1985.
Gleason, A. *Totalitarianism: Inner History of the Cold War*. 1995.
Hitchcock, W. *The Struggle for Europe: The Turbulent History of a Divided Continent, 1945–2002*. 2003.
Hunt, Michael. *The World Transformed, 1945–Present*. 2004.
Isserman, M., and M. Kazin. *America Divided*. 2000.
James, H. *Europe Reborn: A History, 1914–2000*. 2003.
Judge, E., and J. Langdon. *The Cold War: A Global History with Documents*. 2011.
Khrushchev, Nikita. *Khrushchev Remembers*. 1970.
Kotkin, S. *Armageddon Averted: The Soviet Collapse, 1970–2000*. 2001.
LaFeber, W. *America, Russia, and the Cold War, 1945–1992*. 2002.
Lapidus, Gail. *Women, Work, and Family in the Soviet Union*. 1982.
McCormick, J. *Understanding the European Union*. 2005.
Pagden, A., ed. *The Idea of Europe*. 2002.
Paterson, T., et al. *American Foreign Relations*. 6th ed. 2004.
Perkins, Ray. *The ABCs of the Nuclear Arms Race*. 1991.
Reynolds, David. *One World Divisible: A Global History Since 1945*. 2000.
Rifkin, J. *The European Dream*. 2004.
Rosen, R. *The World Split Open: How the Modern Women's Movement Changed America*. 2000.
Roskin, M. G. *The Rebirth of Eastern Europe*. 2001.
Schaller, M., et al. *Present Tense: The United States Since 1945*. 2004.
Suny, Ronald. *The Soviet Experiment*. 1998.
Taubman, William. *Khrushchev: The Man and His Era*. 2003.
Turner, H. *The Two Germanies Since 1945*. 1987.
Walker, M. *The Cold War: A History*. 1993.
Westad, O. A. *The Global Cold War*. 2005.
Whitfield, Stephen. *The Culture of the Cold War*. 1991.
Wilkenson, J., and H. Stuart Hughes. *Contemporary Europe: A History*. 10th ed. 2004.
Yergin, Daniel. *Shattered Peace*. 1977.
Zubok, V., and C. Pleshakov. *Inside the Kremlin's Cold War*. 1997.

Key Dates and Developments

1945	Yalta and Potsdam conferences
1947	Truman Doctrine and Marshall Plan
1948–1949	Berlin blockade and airlift
1949	NATO Treaty, Communist victory in China
1950–1953	Korean War
1955	Warsaw Pact
1957	Soviet ICBM and *Sputnik*, European Common Market
1960	U-2 Affair
1961	Berlin Wall erected
1962	Cuban Missile Crisis
1965–1973	Direct U.S. involvement in Vietnam
1968	Soviet invasion of Czechoslovakia
1972	Nixon's China visit; Soviet-American arms control pact
1979–1989	Soviet involvement in Afghan War
1989	Fall of Berlin Wall, revolutions in Eastern Europe
1990	Reunification of Germany
1991	Disintegration of USSR
1993	Formation of European Union
2001	Terrorist attacks on America
2008	Global economic crisis

PEARSON

myhistorylab Connections

Reinforce what you learned in this chapter by studying the many documents, images, maps, review tools, and videos available at www.myhistorylab.com.

Read and Review

 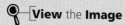 **Study** and **Review** Chapter 34

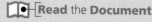 **Read** the **Document**

The Charter of the United Nations (1945), p. 808

George F. Kennan, "Long Telegram," 1946, p. 811

The Kitchen Debate (1959), p. 814

Mikhail Gorbachev on the Need for Economic Reform (1987), p. 827

Constitution of Russia, p. 829

View the **Map**

Map Discovery: Republics of the Soviet Union, 1991, p. 829

View the **Image**

The "Kitchen Debate" Between Nixon and Khrushchev, p. 814

Listen to the **Audio**

Cold War I, p. 810

Cold War III, p. 812

Cold War II, p. 822

Communism, p. 825

Research and Explore

Watch the **Video**

Cold War Connections: Russia, America, Berlin, and Cuba, p. 819

View the **Map**

Map Discovery: Reunified Germany, October 1990, p. 828

Listen to the **Chapter Audio** for Chapter 34 on **myhistorylab.com**

The Upheavals of Asia, 1945–Present

((•—[**Listen** to the **Chapter Audio** for Chapter 35 on **myhistorylab.com**

Modern Urban Asia

The era following World War II brought massive upheavals in Asia. Asians threw off Western domination, engaged in bloody regional conflicts, and transformed age-old rural ways of life by creating modern urban societies with global connections, as illustrated by this photo of Osaka, Japan.

- ■ Why and how did India and Pakistan develop as hostile and very different nations?

- ■ What factors account for Japan's revival and resurgence after World War II?

- ■ What factors account for Korea's conflict and its development as two very different nations?

- ■ What factors account for China's great upheavals and later economic growth?

- ■ How and why did the Cold War contribute to conflicts and upheavals in Southeast Asia?

- ■ Why and how have Asian societies been transformed since 1945?

On September 2, 1945, the day of Japan's surrender ending World War II, a small, frail man addressed a huge crowd in the Southeast Asian city of Hanoi. "All men are created equal," he asserted in Vietnamese. "They are endowed by their creator with certain inalienable rights; among these are life, liberty, and the pursuit of happiness." Noting that this "immortal statement" was from the U.S. Declaration of Independence, he went on: "In a broader sense, this means: All the peoples of the earth are equal from birth [and] have a right to live, to be happy and free." The speaker, Ho Chi Minh (*HŌ-CHĒ-MIN*), was declaring independence for his nation, Vietnam.

South and East Asia

Vietnam, like many Asian lands, had endured both Western and Japanese imperialism. It had been part of France's Indochina colony since the 1800s and part of Japan's empire since 1941. Now that Japan was defeated, Ho Chi Minh hoped that Vietnam could avoid the return of French rule by declaring independence and appealing to American ideals of freedom and human rights. But Ho Chi Minh was a Communist, and France, soon to be part America's anti-Communist alliance, was determined to restore its imperial control. So Indochina's quest for independence got caught up in the Cold War, bringing Southeast Asia three decades of almost constant conflict.

Ho Chi Minh's declaration and the ensuing conflicts exhibit the ideals and connections fueling upheavals in Asia after World War II. Adapting for their own purposes Western ideals such as democracy, nationalism, and socialism, Asians sought to escape Western domination, only to get enmeshed in global Cold War politics. India gained independence but divided into separate Hindu and Muslim nations, one courted by the Soviets and the other by the Americans. Japan arose from the ashes of defeat to become, with American help, a capitalist stronghold in Asia. China endured a brutal civil war won by Communists, who then combined calamitous experiments in mass mobilization with bitter hostility toward the West. Korea and Indochina became the Cold War's bloodiest battlegrounds, torn by civil wars that emerged as international conflicts between Communism and capitalism. By the early 21st century, although regional tensions persisted, economic growth and the Cold War's end finally brought stability and prosperity to much of Asia.

Independence and Conflict in India and Pakistan

After decades of struggle for independence, the Indian subcontinent (Map 35.1) was freed from British rule in 1947. But with independence came partition into two hostile states: the Republic of India, a Hindu-dominated democracy, and the Islamic Republic of Pakistan, which became a dictatorship. As both states grappled with poverty and population growth, they remained bitter foes, embroiled in Cold War politics and later endangered by each other's atomic weapons.

Independence and Partition

In the 1930s, led by Mahatma Gandhi, Indians had compelled Britain to grant them some autonomy (Chapter 32). By the 1940s, however, two key obstacles limited further progress. One was the Muslim League, representing India's large Islamic minority, which

FOUNDATION MAP 35.1 East and South Asia in 1945

After World War II, Asia's prewar rulers sought to maintain or restore their prewar power. Note that the British still ruled India, the Nationalists reclaimed China, the French sought to reassert control in Indochina, and the Dutch did the same in Indonesia. Why and how was each of these regions transformed?

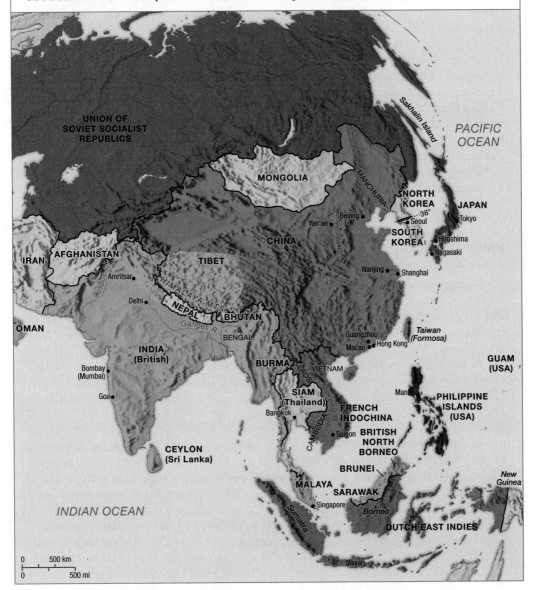

feared repression by the Hindu majority if India became independent. Another was World War II, which heightened tensions between India and Britain, especially after Britain committed India to war without consulting Indian leaders. Dismayed, Gandhi and his followers planned a new anti-British campaign, but Winston Churchill's government arrested them in 1942. A fierce foe of Indian independence, Churchill had long ago declared Gandhi's actions "nauseating" and "seditious."

The end of the war in 1945 brought India new hope and new problems. British voters swept Churchill's government from office, and his successors began moving to

View the **Image**
Mahatma Gandhi
on **myhistorylab.com**

India gains independence, but Muslim Pakistan splits off

📖 **Read** the **Document**

Jinnah, the "Father" of Pakistan (1947)

on **myhistorylab.com**

📖 **Read** the **Document**

Gandhi Speaks Against the Partition of India (pre-1947)

on **myhistorylab.com**

Mass relocation and violence mar Indian independence

grant India self-rule. But the Muslim League, led by Muhammad Ali Jinnah, organized protests pressing for a separate Islamic state. When these protests fueled violent clashes between Hindus and Muslims, Britain reluctantly agreed to partition the subcontinent. On August 15, 1947, two separate new nations emerged: the Republic of India and Pakistan (meaning "Land of the Pure"), itself divided into East and West sections on opposite sides of northern India. Saddened by his country's "vivisection," Gandhi predicted that "rivers of blood" would flow.

This prediction proved prophetic. Since Hindu and Muslim populations were often intermingled, the partition left millions of Muslims in Hindu-dominated India, and millions of Hindus in Islamic Pakistan. As Britain's rapid pullout resulted in a power vacuum, many Muslims, fearing Hindu repression, fled India for Pakistan, while many Hindus likewise fled Pakistan for India. Chaotic and violent mass migrations, involving up to 15 million people, were marked by forced expulsions and bloody clashes killing half a million or more. War erupted in the northern region of Kashmir, claimed by both Pakistan and India (Map 35.2), and eventually divided by a truce in 1949. By then Gandhi was gone, murdered in 1948 by a militant Hindu who resented his efforts to accommodate Muslims. The "rivers of blood" that Gandhi had foreseen thus included his own.

👁 **Watch** the **Video**

Video Lectures: Gandhi in India

on **myhistorylab.com**

Gandhi slain, but his ally Nehru leads nonaligned, democratic India

India: Democracy, Progress, and Problems

India adopted a British-style parliamentary system, with democratic rights guaranteed for all, regardless of sex, religion, or caste. Until 1964 it was led by Jawaharlal Nehru (*NĀ-roo*), Gandhi's longtime associate, who as prime minister used state-run industries and modernizing reforms to pursue prosperity. Principled and conscientious, he achieved modest success, but massive poverty and population growth continued to burden the new nation.

In foreign affairs, Nehru practiced nonalignment, rejecting U.S. pressures to join the anti-Communist camp and accepting Soviet aid. India thus became a leader of the **nonaligned nations,** a group of countries (including Indonesia, Egypt, and Yugoslavia) refusing to side with either superpower, hoping to get aid from both and avoid Cold War commitments.

📖 **Read** the **Document**

Jawaharlal Nehru, from The Autobiography of Jawarharlal Nehru

on **myhistorylab.com**

Indira Gandhi improves agriculture and curbs population growth

In 1966, two years after Nehru's death, his daughter Indira Gandhi (no relation to the Mahatma) became prime minister and dominated India for almost two decades. Talented and tenacious, she pursued programs providing the poor with housing and land. She also backed the **Green Revolution**, a global agricultural movement that used synthetic fertilizers and scientifically developed high-yield crops to enhance farm output. She attacked corruption and promoted male sterilization to slow population growth. These unpopular efforts brought electoral defeat in 1977, but three years later voters returned her to office. Increasingly rigid and self-righteous, she was challenged by the nation's Sikhs, a religious minority whose faith combined elements of Hinduism and Islam. In 1984, after Sikhs turned to violence in pushing for political autonomy, she ordered an attack on their Golden Temple at Amritsar, killing more than 450 people. Several months later her own Sikh guards murdered her in retribution.

Indira's son Rajiv Gandhi, a former airline pilot who replaced her as prime minister, focused on enhancing military strength and technological know-how—efforts that helped India eventually become a leader in computer technology. But tainted by charges that he took financial kickbacks from a Swedish firm that sold India weapons, Rajiv and his government were voted out in 1989. Two years later,

Persistence of poverty in India.

MAP 35.2   India and Pakistan Since 1947

In 1947, as India gained independence, it was split into two hostile states—Hindu-dominated democratic India and Muslim Pakistan. Note that they fought over Kashmir in the north, and that in 1971 East Pakistan became independent Bangladesh. Why was there such hostility between Pakistan and India? What was the Cold War's impact on their rivalry?

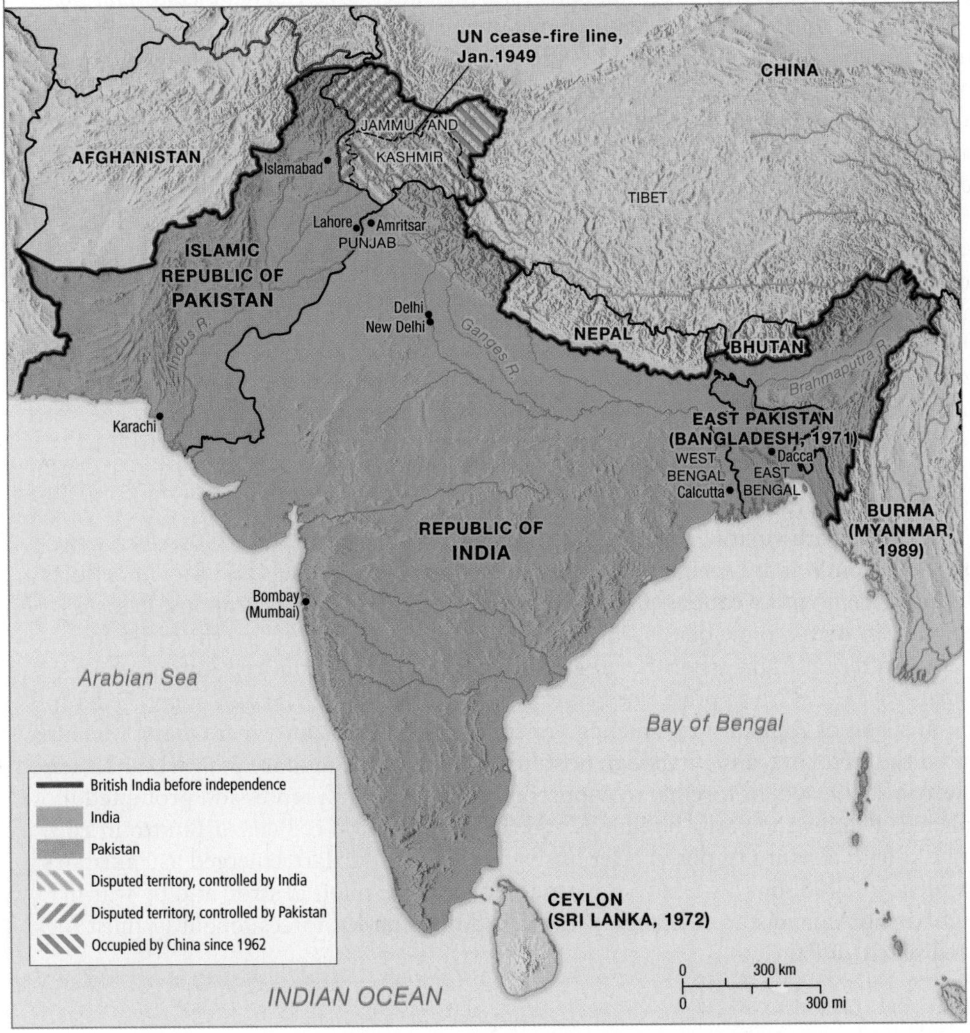

while campaigning for return to office, he and 16 others were blown apart by a woman, with a bomb in a basket of flowers, who allegedly had ties to a violent separatist movement. Sonia Gandhi, Rajiv's Italian-born widow, later became prominent in Indian politics, but legally could not be prime minister due to her foreign origins.

By the early 21st century, then, India was a land of contrasts. Its population of well over a billion made it by far the world's largest democracy, but its human rights guarantees failed to satisfy religious and ethnic minorities. Its agricultural and technical advances, especially its leadership in computer technology, brought prosperity to millions, but millions of others still lived in poverty. Its military strength, enhanced by successful nuclear tests in 1974 and 1998, made it a prominent power but also intensified problems with Pakistan.

Agricultural advances and technology increase Indian prosperity, but poverty persists.

Pakistan: Dictatorship and Division

Pakistan had problems of its own. Its partition with India left it with some of the subcontinent's poorest lands, lacking both mineral resources and industrial development. Its ongoing struggle with India over Kashmir, which erupted into periodic violence, taxed its resources and increased the influence of its army. Although it had parliamentary institutions, Pakistan by 1958 was a military dictatorship, remaining thereafter largely under dictatorial rule.

East Pakistan rebels and becomes independent Bangladesh

In 1970 East Pakistan's Bengali people, who shared West Pakistan's Muslim faith but differed in language and culture, voted for autonomy, unhappy being ruled by a regime a thousand miles to their west. The next year, when West Pakistan sent tanks and troops to crush Bengalis rioting for self-rule, India sent forces to help them resist. East Pakistan thus gained independence in 1971 as a new nation called Bangladesh (East Bengal), which nonetheless continued to be torn by poverty and instability.

Pakistan becomes military dictatorship and U.S. Cold War ally

What was left of Pakistan, in the west, benefited from Cold War politics. The United States, intent on containing Communism by forming alliances with countries near the Communist bloc, allied with Pakistan's repressive regime and gave it extensive economic and military aid. But the Pakistani army's political involvement repeatedly frustrated efforts at civilian rule, while corruption impeded attempts to achieve stability and prosperity. Zulfikar Ali Bhutto (*BOO-tō*), for example, who ruled the country through martial law during the 1970s, was arrested by his foes for electoral fraud and executed in 1979. His daughter Benazir Bhutto, the first woman to head a modern Muslim country, served twice as prime minister (1988–1990 and 1993–1996) and was twice dismissed on charges of corruption.

Afghan wars, atomic race with India, and unrest unsettle Pakistan

Tensions with volatile neighbors also troubled Pakistan. In the 1980s, during the Soviet-Afghan War, it became a base for Afghan anti-Soviet rebels and for U.S. efforts to supply them with weapons. In 1998, after India tested nuclear weapons, Pakistan exploded its own atomic device, raising fears of nuclear war between the bitter foes. In 2001, after an Afghanistan-based Muslim terrorist group attacked America on September 11, Pakistani president Pervez Musharraf (*moo-SHAH-ruf*) supported a U.S. invasion of Afghanistan—fueling violent unrest in Pakistan, where many Muslims shared the terrorists' anti-American hostility. Musharraf, a military man who had seized power in 1999, sought forcibly to suppress unrest. But harsh repression prompted more violence, including terrorist bombings and the assassination of Benazir Bhutto in 2007 as she sought a return to power. Her husband, Asif Ali Zardari, emerged as Pakistan's president in 2008, but his tenure was troubled by fierce internal strife and by war in neighboring Afghanistan (Chapter 37), where American-led forces fought Islamist foes based partly in Pakistan.

Revival and Resurgence of Japan

While India and Pakistan dealt with internal and external strife, Japan emerged from the ashes of World War II to become a U.S. Cold War ally and an economic powerhouse. Restructured with American help along democratic and capitalist lines, Japan came to rival the West in productivity and prosperity. But its economy was dangerously dependent on foreign markets and imported resources, while its society still struggled with contrasts between its Eastern traditions and modern Western values.

Japan's Economic Miracle

U.S. occupation and support promote Japanese prosperity and democracy

Japan's recovery was aided by postwar U.S. occupation, lasting from 1945 until 1952. Determined to rid Japan of militarism, Americans strove to remake it as a capitalist democracy. Under General Douglas MacArthur, the U.S. occupation commander, they helped Japan develop a new constitution and bill of rights that granted the vote and legal equality to both men and women. Japan's armed forces were limited in size, and its emperor was reduced to symbolic status. A war crimes tribunal set up by MacArthur tried and executed Japan's top wartime leaders but was relatively lenient to lower-ranking officials. Workers were encouraged to form unions with full rights to bargain and strike. Large estates owned by wealthy landlords were divided into small farms and sold at low cost to former tenants. Education was restructured along American lines, with a new emphasis on individualism challenging Japan's traditional collectivist approach.

Japan also gained from the Cold War. As the Soviet-American struggle intensified, and Communism spread to nearby North Korea and China, U.S. leaders came to see Japan as a bulwark against Asian Communism. America thus treated Japan more as an ally than a defeated foe, opening U.S. markets to Japanese products and giving Japan extensive economic aid. A 1951 treaty committed America to defend Japan militarily, allowing U.S. forces to maintain bases on its soil. Thus protected from foreign attack, and limited by its constitution to a small military force, Japan was able to focus its energies on economic growth.

Cold War divisions help Japan become a bastion of capitalist democracy

Japan's economic approach, blending market capitalism with central government planning, soon became a model for the rest of Asia. In collaboration with business, the government Ministry of International Trade and Industry (MITI) set production goals and quotas, granted cooperating firms low taxes and interest rates, and shielded them from foreign competition with tariffs and import controls. Japanese government and business thus worked together, competing in the global market almost like one huge enterprise, sometimes described as "Japan, Incorporated."

These efforts nourished Japan's "economic miracle." With government support, access to Western markets, and strong traditions of hard work and employee loyalty, Japanese businesses flourished. Some, such as Sony, Nissan, Toyota, and Honda, became global conglomerates, ranking among the world's largest corporations. They rewarded their workers with good pay and benefits, job security, and company-sponsored health and recreation programs. By the 1980s, Japan's living standards were among the world's highest, and its economy was second only to America's.

A science class in Japan.

Problems amid Prosperity

But for all its success, Japan faced serious problems. Some stemmed from its dependence on global commerce, others from a clash between its Westernized culture and traditional values.

Lacking mineral resources and reliant on foreign trade, Japan was vulnerable to actions by its trading partners, especially the United States, which in 1971 imposed a 10 percent import surcharge to protect U.S. businesses from growing imports of low-cost Japanese goods. A 1973 oil embargo by oil-rich Arab countries, imposed against America and its allies for supporting Israel in a war against Arabs (Chapter 37), created critical shortages in Japan, highlighting its dependence on imported fuels and spurring efforts to greatly improve its energy efficiency. A severe economic downturn in the 1990s, combined with increased competition from other Asian nations, Europe, and America, further damaged Japanese economic confidence.

Japan depends on global trade and energy imports

Meanwhile, Western culture's pervasive impact subverted Japanese traditions, including Shinto and Buddhist religious practice. Furthermore, although Japan's crime rate remained lower than those in the West, Japanese cities suffered from similar industrial blights—slums, traffic jams, urban sprawl, and air pollution. Even Japanese democracy, modeled on that of the West, was marred by corruption and scandal,

Western impacts and urban blight mar Japan's traditional culture

intensified by the longtime rule of the Liberal Democratic Party, which held power from 1955 until 1993.

Japanese women gain legal rights but male dominance persists

In gender matters, too, Japan was torn between tradition, which assigned women a submissive role, and modern expectations, which promoted equality. Japanese women now had full legal rights and growing employment opportunities, but Japan's corporations still often put them in subordinate positions, with lower salaries and fewer chances for advancement than men. And Japan's male-dominated government for decades concealed World War II atrocities against women by Japanese troops, including the use of Korean "comfort women" as sex slaves for Japanese soldiers (Chapter 33). In 1993 the government finally apologized, after women who survived these abuses came forth to publicize them, but some Japanese leaders continued to deny or minimize such wartime atrocities.

Japan in the 21st century was also challenged by Chinese economic growth and by natural disaster. Surpassed by China in 2010 as the world's second-largest economy, in 2011 Japan was rocked by a devastating earthquake and tsunami that killed thousands, left hundreds of thousands homeless, and resulted in radiation leaks from a damaged nuclear power plant.

These challenges notwithstanding, Japan nonetheless remained among the world's most prosperous and influential countries. Its neighbors at first were less fortunate.

Conflict and Division in China and Korea

Interactive Map: The Emergence of Modern China, 1919 to the Present

on **myhistorylab.com**

While Japan was rising from the ashes of World War II, China and Korea were plunging into conflict and chaos. In 1946 a civil war began between China's Communists and its Nationalist government, widely discredited by rampant corruption and poor performance in the war against Japan. In a stunning Cold War Marxist triumph, the Communists emerged victorious in 1949, controlling the Chinese mainland, while the Nationalists survived by moving their regime to the island of Taiwan. Then, in 1950, Asian peace was shattered again by conflict in Korea, which became a Cold War battleground. Three years of futile fighting left Korea, like China, with two hostile regimes, one Communist and one nationalist.

Civil War in China: Communists Versus Nationalists

China's Communists gain popular support during war against Japan

Map Discovery: Civil War in China, ca. 1947

on **myhistorylab.com**

((•—[Listen to the **Audio**

Communist China 1

on **myhistorylab.com**

Japan's defeat and U.S. aid restore Nationalist rule in China

On the surface, during China's long war against Japan (1937–1945), Chinese Nationalists and Communists were allied against the common foe. In reality, however, they waged simultaneous struggles against Japan and each other. Expanding from Yan'an, their remote northwestern base, the Communists waged effective guerilla war, tormenting the Japanese troops who occupied northern and eastern China. The Nationalists, meanwhile, hampered by corruption and incompetence, retreated from the Japanese, while striking out sporadically against the Communists. By 1945, the Communists, by vigorously resisting the invaders, had greatly enhanced their prestige, while the Nationalists under Jiang Jieshi (Chiang Kaishek) had lost much support.

When Japan surrendered in 1945, both sides in China scrambled for position. The Nationalists, aided by American vehicles, planes, and ships, soon reoccupied most of the territory vacated by Japan. Jiang seemed once again the master of China. Even Stalin recognized Jiang and signed a treaty with him regarding Manchuria, which the Soviets had occupied at the end of the war (and then largely looted of industrial resources to help rebuild the USSR).

Hoping to avoid a Chinese civil war, which the Soviets could exploit, the United States negotiated a truce between China's Communists and Nationalists, getting both to endorse a coalition government. The deal, however, was doomed. The

Communists, distrusting America as the capitalist world's leader and the Nationalists' main supporter, accepted the truce only to buy time. And Jiang Jieshi, with a huge army and access to U.S. arms, still intended to crush his Communist foes. By mid-1946 the truce had broken down, and China was engulfed in civil war.

Initially the Nationalists did well. Because they controlled China's cities, railways, factories, and mines, they were able to dominate industry and transportation. Their three-million-man army outnumbered the Communist forces by at least three to one. And their modern American weapons and vehicles gave them a big edge over the Communists, whose rifles were limited and who moved mainly on foot. By mid-1947, the Nationalists had moved across northern China and captured the Communist headquarters at Yan'an (Map 35.3).

Communist soldiers study artillery during Chinese Civil War.

MAP **35.3**   Communist Victory in China, 1948–1949

Early in the Chinese Civil War, the Nationalists seemed to have the advantage. Notice, however, that after earlier retreating to Manchuria, the Communists turned the tables in 1948 and defeated the Nationalists in 1949. What factors contributed to Communist victory? How and why did the Nationalists survive?

[Map showing China and Korea region, 1948–1949]

- U.S.S.R.
- MONGOLIA
- MANCHURIA
  - Oct. 1948
  - Nov. 1948
  - Nov. 1948
  - Nov. 1948
- NORTH KOREA
  - P'yongyang
- Sea of Japan
- JAPAN
- 38°
- Seoul
- SOUTH KOREA
  - Pusan
- Beijing — Jan. 1949
- Yellow R.
- July–Aug. 1948
- Yan'an (Captured by Nationalists, May 1947)
- CHINA
- Jan. 1949
- Oct.–Nov. 1948
- Nov. 1948–Jan. 1949
- Yellow Sea
- Mar.–Apr. 1949
- Nanjing
- Apr. 1949
- Shanghai — May 1949
- East China Sea
- Chongqing
- PACIFIC OCEAN
- U.S. Naval Patrols, beginning in 1950
- Taipei
- Oct. 1949
- Guangzhou
- Oct. 1949
- Taiwan
- REPUBLIC OF CHINA (Nationalist China) since 1949
- FRENCH INDOCHINA
- LAOS
- VIETNAM
- Gulf of Tonkin
- South China Sea
- 0   500 km
- 0   500 mi

⊗ Major battles
→ Major Communist advances

Communists benefit from guerilla tactics and broad peasant support

War refugees, China, 1949.

((•─ Listen to the **Audio**

Communist China 2

on **myhistorylab.com**

Communists create People's Republic and ally with USSR

Soviet and U.S. occupation zones result in divided Korea

Communist North Korea invades South Korea in 1950

But the Communists were far from beaten. In fighting Japan, they had honed their guerrilla tactics, learning to battle a better-armed foe by avoiding direct combat and relying on subversion and sabotage. In their years at Yan'an, they had won over the peasants by giving them land and abolishing social classes. The Nationalists controlled the cities and railways, but the Communists were aided and supplied by village peasants, who made up most of China's population.

Communist commander Lin Biao (*LIN b'YOW*) retreated with his "People's Liberation Army" to Soviet-occupied Manchuria, where he gained access to Soviet weapons and those left behind by Japan. Hoping to crush his foes, Jiang pursued the Communists into Manchuria, extending his supply lines and leaving his forces vulnerable. A Communist counterattack, aided by peasants who disrupted the Nationalists' supply lines and dug trenches to trap their tanks, turned the tide in 1948. The Communists won victory after victory, taking Beijing in January 1949 and Nanjing in April. By summer the Nationalist forces were in full flight.

Divided China: Taiwan and the People's Republic

But Communism's triumph proved incomplete. The Nationalists fled to the island of Taiwan, where they were protected by the U.S. Navy. Ruling only Taiwan, they nonetheless still called their regime the Republic of China, claimed with American backing to be China's legitimate government, and even held China's United Nations seat until 1971. Led by Jiang Jieshi, who ruled under martial law until his death in 1975, they dreamed of restoring control over China's mainland. But by 1987, when Taiwan finally lifted martial law and began moving toward democracy, this dream had long since disappeared. The future of mainland China lay in Communist hands.

The Communists, meanwhile, moved to consolidate their power. On October 1, 1949, at a grand ceremony in Beijing, their longtime leader Mao Zedong proclaimed a new regime called the People's Republic of China. The world's most populous country, its half-billion people constituting over a fifth of all humanity, was now under Communist rule.

Much to the dismay of the West, which refused to recognize the new regime and called it simply "Red China," early in 1950 Mao and his comrades concluded a treaty of friendship and alliance with the USSR. But even as China's new rulers moved to impose their ideals, they were faced with a complex conflict in Korea.

Occupation, Partition, and Conflict in Korea

Like China, Korea emerged in 1945 from Japanese occupation only to be divided between Communists and nationalists. In the waning days of World War II, after entering the war against Japan, the Soviets invaded northern Korea. As the war ended, worried that they might take all Korea, the United States insisted on dividing it at the 38th parallel of latitude into U.S. and Soviet occupation zones. In the North, within a few years, the USSR installed a Soviet-style government led by Kim Il-sung, a capable, ruthless Communist who had been active in anti-Japanese resistance. In the South, under U.S. influence, a right-wing nationalist named Yi Sung-man, widely known as Syngman Rhee, emerged in 1948 as president. The superpowers then removed their troops, leaving Korea split into hostile states.

The fragile peace did not last long. On June 25, 1950, with a large, Soviet-equipped army, North Korea launched a massive invasion across the 38th parallel, quickly overrunning most of the South (Map 35.4). But America, stunned by Communism's recent triumph in China, was not about to let another country "go Communist." After promoting a U.N. resolution calling for support for South Korea, the Americans helped create a U.N. military force. Eager to show that the new United Nations—unlike the old League of Nations—could resist aggression, 15 other countries joined in this effort, the U.N.'s first military action.

Led by America's General Douglas MacArthur, the U.N. force soon reversed the war's momentum. In September, with a surprise amphibious landing at the port of Inchon behind the lines of North Korean forces, MacArthur divided them and drove them from the South. In October, expanding beyond his initial objective of liberating the South, MacArthur pushed into North Korea, aiming to defeat the Communists and unite the country. By November he occupied most of the North and seemed on the verge of victory.

But again the war's momentum changed. As MacArthur's forces approached the Yalu River, which separates Korea from China, the Communist Chinese began to fear that he might invade their land. Without declaring war, they sent thousands of Chinese troops as "volunteers" to aid the North Koreans. Caught off guard, the U.N. forces retreated, barely escaping to the South, where they regrouped and continued the war.

As stalemate soon developed, not far from the 38th parallel, MacArthur demanded authority to attack Communist China. But his superiors, anxious to avoid an all-out Asian war, opted to limit the conflict to Korea and seek a negotiated truce. In 1951, when he openly questioned this policy, MacArthur was relieved of his command. The war dragged on in debilitating deadlock until July 1953, when an armistice finally ended the fighting. Over two million people had been killed, the majority of them Koreans, while countless others suffered from disease and dislocation as their country was ravaged. And yet Korea remained divided, separated by a heavily patrolled demilitarized zone (DMZ), two and a half miles wide, along the armistice line.

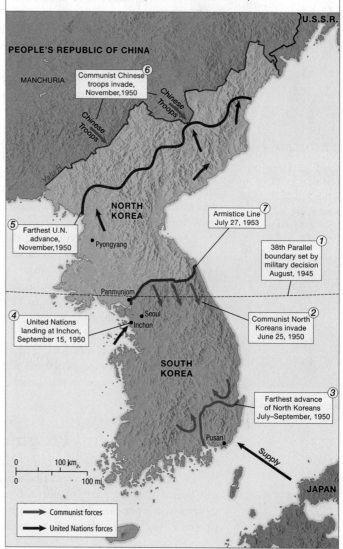

MAP 35.4   The Korean War, 1950–1953

After North Korea invaded South Korea in 1950, the war soon became an international conflict. Why and how did America and Communist China each get involved? Why did a stalemate develop?

Communist forces

United Nations forces

American-led U.N. forces drive Communist armies deep into North Korea

Communist Chinese troops help North Korea stalemate U.N. forces

Divided Korea: Communist North, Capitalist South

In the North for the next four decades, Kim Il-sung ruled a Stalinist police state, with a planned economy, state-run industries, and collective farms reflecting its Soviet roots. Relentlessly hostile to South Korea and America, it maintained good relations with both

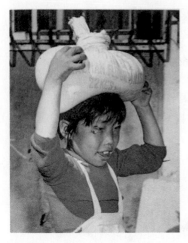

Korean child receiving food aid.

Repressive regimes rule South Korea, but U.S. backing helps bring prosperity

Communist China and the USSR, even when they eventually became bitter rivals. After Kim Il-sung died in 1994, his son Kim Jong-il continued the repressive regime. An eccentric recluse with a love of fast cars and a mortal fear of air travel, the younger Kim moved to develop nuclear weapons (and claimed to have succeeded in 2005), despite a faltering economy and widespread famine.

In the South, Syngman Rhee, whose American-backed regime was authoritarian and corrupt, ruled until 1960, when he was ousted by a student-led uprising. The next year, however, the military seized control and held power for the next three decades. General Park Chung-hee, as president from 1961 until his assassination in 1979, combined political repression with strong support for industry and economic growth. By the 1980s, with U.S. help and access to global markets, South Korea had become a capitalist powerhouse, with automaker Hyundai and electronics giant Samsung among the world's leading corporations.

The regime nonetheless remained repressive, rigging elections, censoring the press, and suppressing dissent. In 1980, Kim Dae-jung, leader of the democratic opposition, was arrested and condemned to death. Under U.S. pressure, the regime reduced his sentence to 20 years in prison and later let him go to America for medical care. In 1987, as South Korea prepared to host the 1988 Summer Olympic Games in its capital, Seoul, student-led protests captured world attention, compelling the government finally to allow free elections.

Democratic reforms followed, but corruption scandals and a short but severe Asian economic downturn in 1997 plagued the new democracy. Elections that year brought to power the widely admired Kim Dae-jung, who improved the economy, reduced corruption, and even reached out to the Communist North, meeting with North Korean leader Kim Jong-il in the year 2000. By the 21st century, despite ongoing corruption problems and dangerous tensions with the belligerent North, South Korean society was prosperous and democratic.

Seoul, South Korea's modern capital.

Radicalism and Pragmatism in Communist China

Communist China's radical reforms seek to aid peasants and women

China was less fortunate than South Korea. After driving out the Nationalists in 1949, the Communists formed a socialist state based on the Soviet model, with Mao Zedong as Chairman of the party's Central Committee, and Zhou Enlai (*JŌ EN-LĪ*) as the government's premier. The regime endeavored to transform the country and improve people's lives, but its efforts brought mass upheavals and extensive suffering.

Landowner trial, China, 1950s.

Early Radical Reforms

Seeking to remake China in accord with their Communist vision, Mao and his comrades initiated radical reforms and mass campaigns designed to end corruption and instill selfless socialist values. They transferred land from landlords to peasants, encouraged peasants to share farm animals and tools, and killed about a million former landlords and others labeled "enemies of the people." Radically breaking with the past, they promoted equality for women, easing access to day care for children so mothers could work outside the home. A 1950 Marriage Reform Law allowed women to inherit property and seek divorces, while inviting young people to choose their own spouses—subverting the age-old practice by which parents arranged their children's marriages. In the next five years, several million women divorced men they were earlier compelled to wed.

Following the Soviet example, China's Communists also centralized control over information, education, and the economy. They directly managed the media, using it to mobilize support for the party and attack practices they deemed harmful to society, such as drug abuse, corruption, prostitution, and religion. To educate the masses and instill Communist ideals, they took control of schools and colleges and required teachers to follow a curriculum imposed by Communist authorities. And in 1953, with Soviet assistance, they initiated a Five-Year Plan, designed to promote heavy industry and collectivize farming. By the mid-1950s, China seemed to be creating a Soviet-style socialist society.

China adopts Soviet-style central planning and control

But Mao's vision differed radically from the Soviet model. Whereas Soviet Communism, in line with Marxist doctrine, was based on the urban proletariat, Mao's version was founded on the rural peasants. Inspired by his peasant background and disdain for urban elites (Chapter 32), Mao aimed to create a rural egalitarian society. Moreover, while Soviets strove to transform society through economic planning and socialist programs, Mao sought to do so by changing the people themselves, using media control and mass campaigns to mold their minds, alter their attitudes, and mobilize the masses for heroic achievements.

Mao's peasant socialism and mass campaigns diverge from Soviet model

The Great Leap Forward and Its Failure

Although the Five-Year Plan fostered economic growth, for Mao, the rural revolutionary, it was too urban, timid, slow, and bureaucratic—too much like the Soviet system of centralized control by an elite managerial class. So in 1958 he launched the Great Leap Forward, a sensational campaign of mass mobilization designed to rapidly reshape China into a rural socialist society. Small collective farms were combined into huge communes of five thousand families, many of which had collective work brigades, communal dining halls, day care facilities, and even their own small factories. Industry was moved from cities to communes, where peasants produced goods in rural workshops and steel in small backyard furnaces. China's future, Mao insisted, must be fashioned by the rural masses, not by urban technocrats and bureaucrats. "Twenty years in a day" was his slogan, and the Chinese people strove valiantly to meet his ambitious goals.

Great Leap Forward forms huge rural communes throughout China

But the Great Leap Forward became a great catastrophe. Lack of industrial expertise resulted in shoddy goods, backyard furnaces produced inferior steel, and pressure to meet unrealistic goals led communes to overstate their harvests, creating a massive food shortage. In 1960, droughts, typhoons, and torrential rains resulted in horrendous famine, killing an estimated 20–30 million people.

Poor performance and natural disasters ruin Great Leap Forward

This catastrophe, moreover, fueled a growing rift between China and the USSR, which had supplied substantial aid. Offended by Mao's rejection of their model and loath to use their limited resources to support his disastrous Great Leap Forward, in 1960 the Soviets cut off aid. The Chinese, offended by Soviet efforts at "peaceful coexistence" with the West (Chapter 34), increasingly renounced them as collaboration with Communism's foes. By 1963 the two Communist giants were openly vilifying each other. In 1964 China tested an atomic bomb, adding to the fears of Soviet leaders, already alarmed that Mao saw nuclear war as a viable option.

Chinese split with Soviets and develop nuclear weapons

Meanwhile, moderate Chinese leaders, including Premier Zhou Enlai, tried to repair the damage from Mao's experiment. In 1960 they abandoned the Great Leap Forward, relaxed the pace of change, began dismantling the communes, and eased Mao Zedong into semiretirement.

The Great Proletarian Cultural Revolution

Mao's youthful Red Guards conduct a new radical mass campaign

But Mao, the "Great Helmsman" who had piloted the Communists to power, refused to sail silently into the sunset. Late in 1965, aided by Defense Minister Lin Biao and the People's Liberation Army, he launched his most spectacular venture: the Great Proletarian Cultural Revolution.

Seizing control of the media and denouncing moderates for following the "capitalist road," he urged young people to form **Red Guards**, radical militias aimed at restoring Maoist revolutionary fervor. Millions of high school and college students joined and then went on a rampage. Attacking "capitalist elitism," they disrupted businesses and closed universities, forcing managers and professors to labor in the fields with peasants. Scorning China's pre-Communist past, they destroyed countless cultural artifacts and historic buildings and books. At mass rallies exalting their leader, they waved copies of his "Little Red Book," *Quotations from Chairman Mao*, a collection of sayings they could recite by heart (see "*Quotations from Chairman Mao*"). This spectacle marked the high point of the cult of Mao and the ultimate expression of his radical populism in action. But it also echoed China's past: as Mao basked in mass exaltation, he almost seemed to have assumed the Mandate of Heaven, enjoying a regal status like emperors of old.

Mao's "Little Red Book."

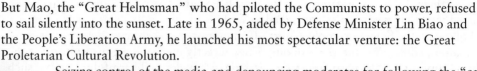

Listen to the **Audio** *Communist China 3* on **myhistorylab.com**

Cultural Revolution creates chaos and widens China's rift with USSR

But like the Great Leap Forward, the Cultural Revolution was a catastrophic failure: it created mass chaos, set the economy back years, and isolated China from the outside world, which watched in spellbound anxiety. Finally, in 1970, the radicalism subsided, schools and businesses reopened, and stability was restored. By 1971 the moderates were back in power and Lin Biao was dead, reportedly killed in a plane crash as he fled toward the Soviet Union following a failed coup attempt. According to a mythical but widely circulated account, when Mao learned that Lin Biao was escaping after his act of betrayal, the Great Helmsman stretched out his arm toward his former comrade's flight path, and at that instant Lin Biao's plane exploded. Such was the power attributed to Mao Zedong.

Nixon in China.

China's Opening to the West

But Mao's era was approaching its end. The aging chairman again faded into the background as moderates sought to end China's isolation. Premier Zhou Enlai, a gifted diplomat and nimble opportunist who retained his post throughout the Cultural Revolution, now engineered a stunning change in Chinese foreign policy. He helped open his Communist country to the capitalist West.

A dangerous deterioration in Chinese-Soviet relations preceded China's change of course. In 1967, rampaging Red Guards denounced the USSR and besieged its Beijing embassy. In 1968, the Soviets invaded Czechoslovakia and proclaimed the Brezhnev Doctrine, asserting their right to intervene in other Communist countries (Chapter 34). China reacted in horror, fearing it might be the next Soviet target. In 1969, Communist China and the USSR fought brief but deadly undeclared border wars along their frontier. Hoping to offset the threat from their Soviet neighbor, China's leaders started looking to improve relations with the West.

Moving to exploit this Chinese-Soviet hostility, the Americans began to seek dialogue with Communist China, whose existence they had never formally recognized. In 1971 the United States lifted restrictions on American travel to China. The Chinese then invited the U.S. table tennis team to play

DOCUMENT 35.1 *Quotations from Chairman Mao*

Mao's "Little Red Book" was a central symbol of the Great Proletarian Cultural Revolution, with youthful Red Guards committing it to memory and waving it at mass rallies. Based on these excerpts, what was the nature and attraction of "Mao Zedong Thought"?

A revolution is not a dinner party, or writing an essay, or painting a picture, or doing embroidery; it cannot be so refined . . . , so temperate, kind, courteous, restrained and magnanimous. A revolution is an insurrection, an act of violence by which one class overthrows another.

Every Communist must grasp the truth, "Political power grows out of the barrel of a gun."

. . . There are two winds in the world today, the East Wind and the West Wind . . . I believe . . . today that the East Wind is prevailing over the West Wind. That is to say, the forces of socialism have become overwhelmingly superior to the forces of imperialism.

The revolutionary war is a war of the masses; it can be waged only by mobilizing the masses and relying on them.

The atom bomb is a paper tiger which the U.S. reactionaries use to scare people. It looks terrible, but . . . the outcome of a war is decided by the people, not by . . . new types of weapon.

Every comrade must . . . understand that as long as we rely on the people, believe firmly in the inexhaustible creative power of the masses and hence trust and identify ourselves with them, we can surmount any difficulty, and no enemy can crush us while we can crush any enemy.

There is an ancient Chinese fable called "The Foolish Old Man Who Removed the Mountains." It tells of an old man who lived . . . long ago and was known as the Foolish Old Man of North Mountain. His house faced south and beyond his doorway stood . . . two great peaks . . . obstructing the way. With great determination, he led his sons in digging up these mountains hoe in hand. Another greybeard, known as the Wise Old Man, saw them and said derisively, "How silly of you to do this! It is quite impossible for you few to dig up these two huge mountains." The Foolish Old Man replied, "When I die, my sons will carry on; when they die, there will be my grandsons, and their sons and grandsons, and so on to infinity. High as they are, the mountains cannot grow any higher and with every bit we dig, they will be that much lower. Why can't we clear them away?" Having refuted the Wise Old Man's wrong view, he went on digging every day, unshaken in his conviction. God was moved by this, and he sent down two angels, who carried the mountains away . . . Today, two big mountains lie like a dead weight on the Chinese people. One is imperialism, the other is feudalism. The Chinese Communist Party has long made up its mind to dig them up. We must persevere and work unceasingly, and we, too, will touch God's heart. Our God is none other than the masses of the Chinese people. If they stand up and dig together with us, why can't these two mountains be cleared away?

SOURCE: Quotations from Chairman Mao Tse-tung (Foreign Languages Press, 1967).

---

in Beijing, where it was warmly welcomed by Zhou Enlai. This "Ping Pong diplomacy" foreshadowed a secret visit to Beijing that summer by President Nixon's national security advisor, Henry Kissinger, followed by a dramatic announcement from Nixon himself that he would soon visit China. Later that year the United Nations recognized Communist China, giving it the seat previously held by the Nationalists on Taiwan.

Communist China opens dialogue with America and gains U.N. seat

Nixon's visit to China in February 1972, parts of which were televised around the world, featured meetings with Zhou and Mao, attendance at banquets and a ballet, a presidential trip to China's Great Wall, and a joint statement pledging both sides to work for improved relations. But it did not at once bring normalized relations, since the Chinese insisted that America must first break relations with Taiwan. Only in January 1979, when America finally did so (while continuing military and economic support for Taiwan), were full diplomatic relations established between the United States and the People's Republic.

China hosts U.S. president and later establishes diplomatic relations

China After Mao: Economic Growth and Political Repression

By then the People's Republic had new leaders. In 1976 Zhou Enlai and Mao Zedong both died, and a new power struggle arose between radicals and moderates. Led by Mao's widow Jiang Qing (*jē-AHNG CHING*), a group of radicals, later called the **Gang of Four**, sought to seize power and renew the Cultural Revolution. They were defeated and imprisoned by moderates under Deng Xiaoping (*DUNG shē-YOW-PING*), an aging pragmatist who had worked to restore the economy after the Great Leap Forward, but then was denounced as a "capitalist road" follower and expelled from leadership during the Cultural Revolution. Back in power as vice premier in 1977, Deng ran the country through his protégés, whom he placed at the head of the government and Communist Party.

Deng and his protégés liberalized the economy. Breaking with Mao's radical collectivism, they allowed small profit-oriented private businesses, experimented with free enterprise in special economic zones, and sent Chinese students abroad to study business, science, and technology in Japan, America, and Europe. Using capitalist-style incentives and proclaiming that "to get rich is glorious," the regime let peasants farm small family plots and sell what they produced in open markets. It also patched up relations with the USSR, while wooing the West with prospects of lucrative trade—even as China flooded global markets with inexpensive watches, shoes, bikes, toys, and clothes made in Chinese factories using low-cost Chinese labor. These efforts increased China's stability and prosperity, tripling average family income by the 1990s.

But the changes did not bring freedom or democracy. After initially easing repression, Deng and his comrades in the 1980s faced growing demands for more democracy and less corruption, culminating in spring 1989 in mass student demonstrations in Beijing's vast Tiananmen Square. Fearing mass unrest, on June 4, 1989, the regime trucked in troops from the provinces, then used tanks and artillery to clear the square, killing hundreds, if not thousands.

The Tiananmen Square Massacre shocked the world but did no lasting damage to China's commerce. Eager to exploit the mass market of more than a billion Chinese, the West concluded that sanctions would do more harm than good. Even after Deng Xiaoping died in 1997 at age 92, his colleagues continued to combine economic liberalization with political repression. Under Jiang Zemin (*jē-AHNG zuh-MIN*), president of the People's Republic from 1993 to 2003, China expanded its domestic market economy and international trade, while sternly suppressing dissent.

By 2008, when western China had a catastrophic earthquake and Beijing hosted the Olympic Summer Games, China had achieved impressive economic growth. Its great urban centers sported skyscrapers, traffic congestion, air pollution, countless cell phone users, and a wide array of businesses large and small. Surpassing Japan in 2010 as the world's second-largest economy (behind the United States), and approaching America and Europe in economic output, China was resuming its historic role as a world economic leader.

But not everyone shared the new prosperity. Party officials and their families grew rich through commercial connections, but workers in some businesses lost their jobs due to capitalist competition, and peasants in remote regions still were often impoverished. Gender disparities resurfaced, as parents seeking to improve family incomes pulled daughters out of school to work in Chinese industry, where they were less likely than men to be promoted and more apt to be laid off. Such practices lifted millions of families from poverty, but also often reinforced abuses and inequities. The new China was a modern economic power, but it scarcely resembled the egalitarian peasant socialist society envisioned by Mao Zedong.

Deng and pragmatists liberalize economy and pursue global trade

((•⟶ **Listen** to the **Audio**
Communist China 4
on **myhistorylab.com**

Tiananmen Square Massacre reinforces political repression

Chinese pragmatists suppress dissent while liberalizing commerce

The old and the new in Shanghai, China.

The Agonies of Southeast Asia and Indonesia

South of China, upheavals also marked the postwar era in the former French colony of Indochina, embracing Vietnam, Laos, and Cambodia, and in the former Dutch East Indies, now called Indonesia. As people in these regions sought freedom from foreign rule, their efforts were entangled in the global Cold War between Communism and capitalism, spawning wars, rebellions, and genocide. Only after the Cold War's end did these areas achieve some stability.

Vietminh, France, and the First Indochina War

Indochina's strife was rooted in the era of French rule, from the mid-1800s until World War II, in which France governed masses of Buddhist village farmers through a French-educated, Catholic, urban elite. An independence movement against French rule arose, led by a Vietnamese nationalist called Ho Chi Minh ("he who brings enlightenment").

As a young man, after leaving Vietnam to work as a cook on a steamship, Ho Chi Minh traveled widely and lived for six years in France. There, dismayed by French refusal to give colonists the same rights as French citizens and attracted by the anti-imperialism of Russia's Marxist leaders, he became Communist. After sojourns in the USSR and China, he returned to Vietnam, where in 1930 he formed the Indochinese Communist Party. In 1941, as Japan occupied Indochina, Ho joined other nationalists in a coalition called **Vietminh**, the Vietnamese Independence Brotherhood League, which then conducted guerrilla war against Japanese occupation forces. As noted at the start of this chapter, on the day Japan surrendered to the Allies in September 1945, Ho Chi Minh proclaimed independence for Vietnam.

Ho Chi Minh fights to free Indochina from France and then Japan

But France had other ideas. Eager to restore its pride and great power status, damaged by four years of German occupation (1940–1944), it sought to restore its colonial empire. Needing a strong France to counter Soviet power in Europe, Britain and America provided tacit support.

France tries to restore imperial rule after World War II

The result was the First Indochina War (1946–1954), between the French and Vietminh. The Vietminh commander, former history teacher and gifted strategist Vo Nguyen Giap (*VAW n'WEN ZAP*), used guerrilla tactics to weaken the French until, with Chinese help, he amassed a well-equipped army. Then, in spring 1954, as the French wearied of war, he trapped and defeated them at a northern outpost called Dien Bien Phu (*dē-YEN bē-YEN FOO*) (Map 35.5).

Vietminh forces defeat France in First Indochina War

Meanwhile, French leaders met in Geneva, Switzerland, with Indochinese delegates and key officials from Britain, America, the USSR, and China in talks aimed at ending the Indochina War. In July 1954, they produced the **Geneva Accords**, ending French rule in Indochina and dividing it into Laos, Cambodia, North Vietnam, and South Vietnam. Laos and Cambodia would have neutral regimes, aligned with neither Communist East nor capitalist West. North Vietnam would be ruled by Vietminh (led by Ho Chi Minh and the Communists), and South Vietnam would soon have an anti-Communist Catholic president named Ngo Dinh Diem (*NOH DĒN dē-YEM*). Vietnam's partition into North and South was meant to be temporary: the Geneva Accords called for elections in 1956 to unite the country.

Geneva Accords split Indochina into Laos, Cambodia, North Vietnam, and South Vietnam

But those elections were not held. The United States, fearing that Vietminh's prestige would ensure its electoral victory, thus bringing all Vietnam under Communist rule, backed efforts by Ngo Dinh Diem to prevent the vote. Anxious to counter Communism, the United States opted to prevent elections Communists might win. America thus became the main supporter of an unpopular and dictatorial South Vietnamese regime.

U.S. support for South Vietnam paves way for Vietnam War

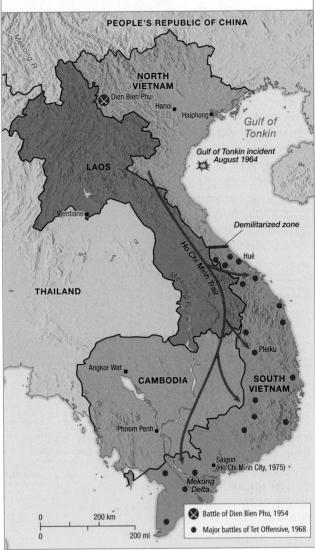

MAP 35.5 Vietnam, Laos, and Cambodia, 1954–1975

Despite massive U.S. military support for South Vietnam, North Vietnam won the Vietnam War (1964–1975) and united all Vietnam under Communist control. Note that Communist supply lines ran through Laos and Cambodia. How did the war and its outcome impact all these countries?

Vietnam becomes a major Cold War battleground

Vietnam, America, and the Second Indochina War

Ngo Dinh Diem's regime, moreover, was neither strong nor stable. By relying on France's old colonial structures and giving government jobs to the Catholic minority, he alienated both nationalists and Buddhists. Exploiting his unpopularity, Communists in South Vietnam formed a nationalist coalition called the National Liberation Front and guerrilla units called **Viet Cong**. By 1963 they were leading a full-fledged insurgency against him, with Buddhist monks burning themselves to death on city streets to protest his repressive rule.

The Americans, having supported Ngo Dinh Diem with military aid and advisors, finally conspired against him with his army, which killed him in November 1963. South Vietnam thus came under military rule, but even the army could not restore stability.

Capitalizing on the chaos, in 1964 Communist North Vietnam started sending armed units south to support the Viet Cong. That same year, in the nearby Gulf of Tonkin, a U.S. surveillance ship reported being shot at by North Vietnamese patrol boats. Although North Vietnam denied these reports, the second of which was never verified, the U.S. Congress passed a Gulf of Tonkin Resolution authorizing President Lyndon Johnson to take "all necessary measures . . . to prevent further aggression." It turned out to be a license to wage war. As American forces arrived the next year in large numbers, South Vietnam's insurgency became an international conflict.

For several years the war intensified. As America sent more and more troops, North Vietnam, supplied with arms and aid by the Soviets and Chinese, funneled in forces along the Ho Chi Minh Trail, a network of pathways through neutral Laos and Cambodia (Map 35.5). Advanced American weapons and mass bombing, exceeding all the firepower used in World War II, caused extensive damage and countless casualties but failed to crush the Communists.

Then, in early 1968, Communist forces surprised the Americans with simultaneous attacks throughout South Vietnam during celebrations of the Lunar New Year, known in Vietnam as *Tet*. Militarily this **Tet Offensive** was a failure for North Vietnam, as U.S. forces soon regained all the ground taken in initial attacks. But the offensive undermined American morale. Stunned that the battered Communists could launch a major assault, and shocked by televised images of the violence, Americans concluded that victory was not in sight, as their leaders had claimed. In March, his credibility shaken,

President Johnson announced he would not seek reelection. Spring and summer 1968 were marked by antiwar protests and violence across the United States (Chapter 34). In November, Americans elected a new president, Richard Nixon, who promised an honorable end to the Vietnam War.

Nixon initiated **Vietnamization**, a process that transferred the fighting to South Vietnam's army, while gradually withdrawing U.S. troops and negotiating with the North. He also enlarged the conflict into a Second Indochina War, invading Cambodia in 1970 to destroy Communist bases and supply lines. In 1972, when negotiations stalled, he renewed massive bombing of North Vietnam. His efforts achieved their goal, an agreement with North Vietnam, signed in Paris in January 1973, suspending the conflict and providing for withdrawal of U.S. forces.

U.S. soldiers in Vietnam.

After U.S. withdrawal, North conquers South and reunifies Vietnam

But Nixon's tactics also left the region in chaos. In 1974, with the Americans gone, North Vietnam again began sending forces south, and in early 1975 it launched an all-out offensive. By April the Communists had conquered the South, uniting Vietnam under their rule. That same year Communist regimes took power in Laos and Cambodia, ending the Second Indochina War.

The Cambodian Catastrophe

But Southeast Asia's agony did not end. In 1975, Cambodia's new ruling Communist party, the **Khmer Rouge** (*k'MER ROOZH*), or "Red Khmer" (Khmer is Cambodia's main ethnic group), launched a radical mass campaign inspired by China's Great Proletarian Cultural Revolution. Led by Pol Pot, a Maoist fanatic intent on forging an agrarian Communist society, the Khmer Rouge sought to deurbanize Cambodia, seizing city dwellers at gunpoint and herding them to the countryside to work the fields. Urban professionals, including bankers, lawyers, doctors, teachers, and others who dared resist, were executed en masse, while thousands more died of overwork and starvation. In the genocidal next few years, based on widely varying estimates, from one to three million of Cambodia's seven million people may have perished.

Maoist Pol Pot leads genocidal antiurban campaign in Cambodia

Then Cambodia's catastrophe became more complex. Taking advantage of the chaos, Communist Vietnam in 1978 invaded Communist Cambodia, replacing Pol Pot's Khmer Rouge regime with a moderate Communist state called the People's Republic of Kampuchea (*KAHM-poo-CHĒ-uh*), the local name for Cambodia. But in 1979, alarmed by Vietnam's growing influence, Communist China invaded Communist Vietnam to punish it for invading Communist Cambodia.

Communist Vietnam ousts Communist Pol Pot from Cambodia

China's invasion was brief. Vietnam's army, with battle-tested troops and modern weapons supplied by Soviets or captured from Americans, rebuffed the Chinese forces. China soon withdrew, but its invasion heartened the Khmer Rouge and Cambodian nationalists, many of whom had fled to neighboring Thailand. These assorted rebels conducted civil war against Cambodia's Vietnam-backed regime throughout the 1980s. Displaying both the complexity and cynicism of Cold War politics, Communist Russia and Communist Vietnam supported the Cambodian regime, while their main foes—Communist China and capitalist America—backed the Cambodian rebels, including the murderous Khmer Rouge.

China tries to "punish" Vietnam as Cambodian turmoil continues

In the early 1990s, when the U.N. negotiated a truce and sent in peacekeepers, Cambodia finally regained some stability. Following national elections in 1993, it became a constitutional monarchy under King Norodom Sihanouk (*SĒ-uh-NOOK*), who had fled Cambodia before the 1970 U.S. invasion. In 1997, repudiated even by former supporters, Pol Pot was arrested and died the next year in custody. Cambodia's nightmare seemed to be over at last.

U.N. truce and elections finally stabilize Cambodia

Pro-Sukarno rally, Indonesia.

Sukarno leads Indonesia to independence from Dutch

View the **Image**
Indonesian Guerillas
on **myhistorylab.com**

View the **Image**
Indonesian Political Rallies
on **myhistorylab.com**

Sukarno first joins nonaligned nations, then sides with Soviets

Suharto ousts Sukarno and leads brutal pro-Western dictatorship

Muslim protests and financial crises finally force Suharto out

Indonesia Between East and West

Indonesia, the 3,000 mile–long island chain south of Indochina, also experienced both European imperialism and Japanese occupation. Before World War II, as the Dutch East Indies, it was exploited for its spices, coffee, oil, and rubber. After the war, led by a romantic nationalist named Sukarno, it became an independent nation, buffeted between East and West.

Sukarno, the "father of modern Indonesia," was a schoolteacher's son who completed a civil engineering degree before founding the Indonesian Nationalist Party in 1927. A gifted speaker whose views combined nationalism, Islam, and Marxism with Indonesian mysticism and magic, he sought to blend these incompatible ideals into an independence movement through the power of his personality. Imprisoned and later exiled by the Dutch, he returned in 1942 to act as an advisor to the occupying Japanese, urging them in vain to grant his people independence. When the war ended in 1945, he declared Indonesia independent. The Dutch sought to reassert control but gave up after four years of futile fighting. Indonesia became independent in 1949 (Map 35.6).

Sukarno and his colleague, Muhammad Yamin, formulated the **Panca Sila**, or Five Pillars, as the basis for Indonesia's development. Similar in some ways to Sun Yixian's *Three Principles of the People* (Chapter 32), Panca Sila tried to unify Indonesian peoples on a foundation of nationalism, internationalism, government by popular consent, social justice, and belief in one God. Panca Sila, however, could not transcend the differences among Indonesia's Muslims and Christians, rich and poor, and numerous ethnicities. Genuine national unity thus eluded Indonesia, as deep-seated poverty and religious tensions brought widespread suffering for decades.

In foreign affairs, like India's Nehru, Sukarno emerged as a leader of the nonaligned nations, rejecting alliance with either East or West. In 1955, at the Indonesian city of Bandung (*BAHN-doong*), he hosted a conference of 29 Asian and African nations—many of them newly independent—and urged them in a stirring speech to unite to advance their common interests. Eventually, however, attracted by Soviet aid, Sukarno led his nation into the Soviet camp, thereby enmeshing it in the Cold War and making himself a U.S. enemy. Alas, his new ally, the USSR, considered Indonesia relatively unimportant and invested few resources there.

Sukarno's policies thus led Indonesia into a dead end. Between 1965 and 1967, a military strongman named General Suharto turned the country around, launching a violent anti-Communist crusade that filled its rivers with headless corpses and killed more than three hundred thousand people. Ousting Sukarno in 1967, Suharto then ruled for three decades as a pro-Western and anti-Soviet dictator. The Western democracies overlooked his regime's corruption and repression.

By the 1990s, however, the Cold War was over, the USSR was gone, and the aging dictator was in trouble. With more than 200 million people—nearly 90 percent Muslim—Indonesia was the world's largest Muslim nation. But despite its rich resources and economic potential, most of its people lived in poverty and resented the vast wealth amassed by Suharto and his family. Concerned by the growing popularity of Islamist fundamentalism (Chapter 37), Suharto reached out to Muslims, making the pilgrimage to Mecca in 1990 and periodically visiting the tombs of Indonesian Muslim saints. But in return he expected Muslims to accept clear separation between religion and government, a distinction rejected by Islamist fundamentalists. In 1996 he repressed violent protests by students and Islamic leaders. Then an Asian financial crisis the next year undermined the Indonesian economy, and in 1998 a popular uprising forced Suharto to step down.

MAP 35.6   East and South Asia in the Early 21st Century

By the early 21st century, virtually all of Asia was free from foreign domination, and many of its nations had attained stability and prosperity. Note, however, that regional tensions persisted, and that millions of Asians remained poor. What factors fueled Asian prosperity? What factors help explain the persistence of poverty?

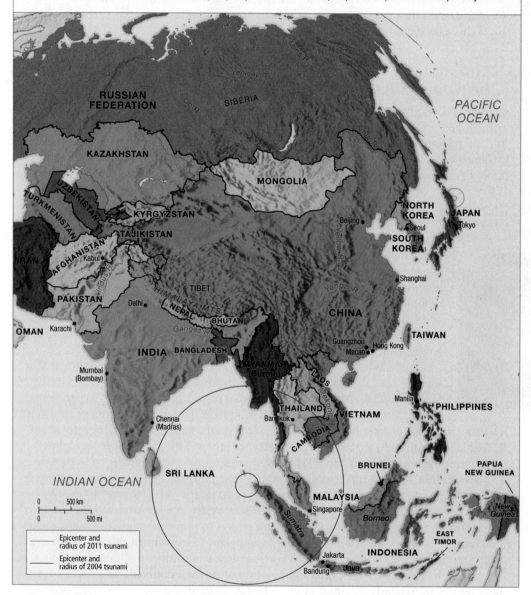

In 1999 a new government was elected, but ongoing unrest and corruption charges soon undermined its leader, who was replaced in 2001 by the famed Sukarno's daughter, Megawati Sukarnoputri. As president, she faced numerous problems, including a weak economy and an armed Islamist rebellion in the northwest. In 2002 a terrorist car bomb exploded at a nightclub on the Indonesian island of Bali, killing more than two hundred people. In 2003, resolving to stabilize her country, she launched an all-out military

Poverty, terrorism, and a deadly tsunami add to Indonesian instability attack on the Islamist rebels, but in September 2004, faced with widespread unemployment and charges of corruption, she was voted out of office.

Her successor, Susilo Bambang Yudhoyono (*yoo-dō-YŌ-nō*), often called "SBY," was greeted that December by an undersea earthquake that unleashed a colossal tsunami, wrecking coastal cities and killing at least two hundred thousand Indonesians. He nonetheless managed to improve the economy and crack down on corruption, leading to his easy reelection in 2009.

Changes in Asian Societies

Sweeping economic and social changes accompanied Asia's upheavals. Eager to escape foreign domination by acquiring wealth and power, Asian nations expanded their industry and technology, exploiting Cold War rivalries to get aid from the Soviets or the West. Millions of Asians moved from rural villages to industrial cities, bringing changes in family and gender roles and presenting new challenges for Asian societies.

Inoculation of Asian child in the 1950s.

Asian populations increase greatly despite efforts to curb growth

Asian cities grow rapidly as people seek urban jobs

Industry, Technology, Population, and Urbanization

In the decades after World War II, aware that industry, technology, and commerce had brought wealth and power to the West, Asian nations sought to expand in these areas. At first the Cold War aided their efforts: eager to support Asian friends, Americans provided Japan, Taiwan, and South Korea with economic assistance and access to Western markets, while Soviets aided India and initially Communist China. In time, however, Asians developed their own economic approaches, typically combining market capitalism with central government planning.

Japan led the way, creating by the 1970s an economic powerhouse that was the envy of Asia. By the 1980s Taiwan and South Korea had imitated Japan's success. After abandoning Mao's disastrous antiurban experiments, China, too, achieved momentous economic growth by blending central state control with open market incentives, while India used a similar combination to attain global leadership in electronics and computer technology. By the 21st century, global economic power, wielded by the West for several centuries, was shifting back to Asia.

Meanwhile, modern medicines and inoculations, increasingly available to ordinary Asians, helped accelerate Asian population growth. Death rates declined markedly, especially among children, while traditional Asian preference for large families initially kept birth rates high. Eventually government efforts to promote smaller families, such as China's rigorous "one child per family" campaign, reduced birth rates through contraception and abortion, combined with economic incentives for limiting family size. Despite such efforts, however, Asia's population more than doubled, from under 1.5 billion in 1950 to nearly 4 billion in 2010—roughly 60 percent of the world's people.

The attraction of large cities, which offered not just industrial jobs but also educational and cultural opportunities, combined with population growth to promote mass urbanization. Tens of millions of Asians moved from rural villages to large urban areas, despite the antiurban efforts of Mao Zedong and Pol Pot. Millions found jobs in industry and commerce, but since there were not enough jobs for all, millions of others joined a vast urban underclass of destitute people dwelling in sordid slums. Yet mass migrations to the cities continued, as percentages of Asians in urban areas tripled, from under 15 percent in 1945 to over 50 percent by 2010—by which time a dozen Asian cities had metropolitan populations exceeding ten million people.

Rural Asia also experienced great changes. Policies promoted by both capitalists and Communists gave land to small farmers, curtailing such practices as tenant farming and absentee landlordism. Fast-growing, high-yield "miracle rice," developed in the 1960s, together with synthetic fertilizers, vastly expanded Asian farm output, accelerating the Green Revolution. More and more clinics and schools enhanced village life, while new technologies, such as radios, televisions, and wireless phones, connected even small remote settlements with the outside world.

High-yield crops and new technologies begin to transform rural Asia

Changing Family and Gender Roles

Asia's upheavals also affected the traditional Asian family. The partition of India and Pakistan, wars in Korea and Vietnam, and violent mass campaigns in China and Cambodia tore apart millions of families, destroying their homes, dividing their loyalties, and causing mass dislocation. But urban growth played an even more disruptive and transformative role. For when rural Asian families moved to cities, they frequently did so in stages, with one spouse moving first to find employment, then often living there alone for a time and sending money back to the village. Since whole clans rarely moved to the city at once, large extended families, long dominant in villages, typically gave way to smaller nuclear families in cities. Government birth control programs, along with urban crowding, also led city couples to keep families small.

Urbanization undermines traditional Asian families

In cities, moreover, new institutions assumed many of the family's traditional roles. In cities, for example, education meant public schools teaching academic subjects (such as calculating, reading, and writing), rather than families passing on practical skills (such as farming, carpentry, spinning, and weaving) as in the traditional village. In cities, care for the sick and elderly was supplied by public clinics and government pension programs rather than by the family. In cities, social discipline was furnished by courts and police, who punished offenses (such as loitering or urinating in public) that were not crimes in the village, where heads of families resolved conflicts and punished offenders. In cities, recreation occurred at public settings such as taverns, teahouses, movies, concerts, and sporting events, while in villages it often meant visiting with one's extended family. In cities, worship took place at temples, or did not take place at all (especially in Communist countries where religion was discouraged), while in villages it typically occurred at family shrines. Urbanization thus diminished the family's role in many Asian people's lives.

Urban institutions, schools, and clinics take on traditional family roles

Urbanization also affected traditional gender roles. When men moved to the city to find jobs, their wives often stayed behind to run the household and thus grew accustomed to heading the family by the time they rejoined their husbands. When women moved to the city to find jobs, they acquired greater independence and gained a new status as family wage earners by sending money they earned back to the village. When families were reunited, men often tried to reassert their family authority, sometimes reacting to their reduced status by abusing their wives and children. But traditional patriarchal dominance nonetheless gradually waned.

In the meantime, Asian women acquired political and civil rights, along with greater reproductive and economic freedom. Political reforms in most Asian countries gave women the right to vote, along with legal rights and educational opportunities that in theory (though often not in practice) made them equal to men. Access to government-provided contraceptives and abortions also helped women control the timing of pregnancies and family size. Economic pressures to enhance family income, combined with exposure to Western media depicting women in professional roles, encouraged Asian women to seek jobs outside the home and even to pursue careers in such areas as business, medicine, and law.

Asian women gain legal rights and greater economic opportunities

Many Asian women still treated as subordinate by men

Asian women did not, however, gain full equality with men. In most Asian societies, women who worked outside the home, often with lower pay and less potential for advancement than men, were still expected to fulfill traditional roles in the household, and even in the workplace. In Japanese corporations, for example, women were often expected to serve tea to male executives, while female political leaders were rare in Japan, Korea, and Taiwan. Elsewhere in Asia, however, talented and ambitious women—such as Indira and Sonia Gandhi in India, Benazir Bhutto in Pakistan, Jiang Qing in China, and Megawati Sukarnoputri in Indonesia—played very prominent and highly visible roles.

In villages across Asia, patriarchal attitudes persisted. In many cases parents still arranged marriages, the bride's family still supplied a dowry, and wives were still seen as their husband's property. On occasion, as in times gone by, an Indian or Pakistani husband who was unhappy with his wife might abuse or even kill her so he could seek a new wife. By the early 21st century, however, such practices were increasingly rare.

Sometimes practices intended as progressive, when combined with traditional patriarchal attitudes, had unintended results. In China, for example, the "one child per family" program and ready access to abortion, combined with the age-old preference for male children and new technologies that can identify a child's sex before birth, led many families to abort girls or sell their newborn daughters on the black market. A gender imbalance thus developed among Chinese children, with boys outnumbering girls in some places by 10 percent or more. Illegal commercial networks sold many orphaned Chinese girls into domestic servitude or urban prostitution.

Indian women receiving military training.

Still, despite the resilience of some traditional attitudes and behaviors, the transformation of Asian societies was profound. By the early 21st century, instead of living in villages in patriarchal families and producing their own food and goods, most Asians lived in urban areas in small nuclear families and worked for wages with which they bought food and goods. Asia's upheavals and urbanization had brought mass trauma and distress, but Asians in the process had acquired new wealth, new technologies, new outlooks, and new ways of life.

CHAPTER
REVIEW

Putting It in Perspective

In the decades after World War II, global connections contributed to conflicts in Asia, as efforts to gain independence from the West and implement new ideals, combined with Cold War ideologies and tensions, produced dramatic and often violent upheavals. The bloody partitioning of India, Mao's catastrophic mass campaigns in China, disastrous wars in Korea and Indochina, deadly repressions and revolts in Indonesia, and Pol Pot's genocidal policies in Cambodia killed millions of people and shattered millions of lives. Rapid transformation from rural to urban societies created mass dislocation, disrupting and altering traditional family and gender roles.

Eventually, however, global connections helped Asian nations gain stability and prosperity. Japan and South Korea flourished, capitalizing on global commerce by blending market capitalism with central state planning. India used Soviet and Western aid, modern agricultural science, and technological know-how to reduce poverty and instability. China, after years of disastrous turmoil, achieved stability and economic growth by combining authoritarian governance with open market incentives and global trade. By the early 21st century, although regional hostilities continued to cloud its horizons, Asia's growing political and economic strength suggested that Asians had survived their upheavals and were moving toward global leadership.

Reviewing Key Material

KEY CONCEPTS

nonaligned nations, 838
Green Revolution, 838
Red Guards, 848
Gang of Four, 850
Vietminh, 851
Geneva Accords, 851

Viet Cong, 852
Tet Offensive, 852
Vietnamization, 853
Khmer Rouge, 853
Panca Sila, 854

KEY PEOPLE

Ho Chi Minh, 836, 851
Jawaharlal Nehru, 838
Indira Gandhi, 838
Rajiv Gandhi, 838
Sonia Gandhi, 839
Zulfikar Ali Bhutto, 840
Benazir Bhutto, 840
Pervez Musharraf, 840
Asif Ali Zardari, 840
Douglas MacArthur, 840
Jiang Jieshi (Chiang
    Kaishek), 842
Lin Biao, 844
Mao Zedong, 844
Kim Il-sung, 844
Kim Jong-il, 846
Park Chung-hee, 846

Kim Dae-jung, 846
Zhou Enlai, 846
Richard Nixon, 849
Jiang Qing, 850
Deng Xiaoping, 850
Jiang Zemin, 850
Vo Nguyen Giap, 851
Ngo Dinh Diem, 851
Pol Pot, 853
Norodom Sihanouk,
    853
Sukarno, 854
Suharto, 854
Megawati Sukarnoputri,
    855
Susilo Bambang
    Yudhoyono, 856

ASK YOURSELF

1. How was each major Asian nation affected by the Cold War? Why did it have such a devastating impact in Asia?
2. Why was British India divided into two nations when it gained independence in 1947? Why was there such ongoing hostility between India and Pakistan?
3. What factors aided Japan's economic miracle? How did each of the other Asian nations seek to imitate Japan's success?
4. What was Mao Zedong's vision for China, and how did he try to implement it? Why did his efforts fail, and why were they so disastrous?
5. How and why did anti-colonialism and the Cold War contribute to conflicts and upheavals in Southeast Asia? What were the results and impacts of these conflicts and upheavals?
6. How did technology, urbanization, and population growth impact traditional family and gender roles in Asia?

GOING FURTHER

Baxter, C. *Bangladesh: From a Nation to a State.* 1997.
Beeson, M., ed. *Contemporary Southeast Asia.* 2004.
Benson, Linda. *China Since 1949.* 2002.
Bhasin, K., et al., eds. *Against All Odds: Essays on Women, Religion and Development from India and Pakistan.* 1994.
Brass, P. *The New Cambridge History of India: The Politics of Independence.* 1990.
Brown, Judith. *Nehru: A Political Life.* 2003.
Cummings, B. *Korea's Place in the Sun.* 1997.
Dreyer, June T. *China's Political System.* 5th ed. 2005.
Ebrey, Patricia B., et al. *East Asia: A Cultural, Social, and Political History.* 2006.
Evans, R. *Deng Xiaoping and the Making of Modern China.* 1993.
Friend, T. *Indonesian Destinies.* 2003.
Gamer, R. E. *Understanding Contemporary China.* 2002.
Ganguly, S., ed. *South Asia.* 2006.
Guha, Ramachandra. *India After Gandhi.* 2007.
Halberstam, David. *The Coldest Winter: America and the Korean War.* 2007.
Harrison, S., et al. *India and Pakistan: The First 50 Years.* 1999.
Jones, O. B. *Pakistan: Eye of the Storm.* 2002.
Karnow, S. *Vietnam: A History.* 2nd ed. 1997.
Kingsbury, D. *Southeast Asia: A Political Profile.* 2nd ed. 2005.
Kingston, J. *Japan in Transformation, 1952–2000.* 2001.
Lee Feigon. *China Rising: The Meaning of Tiananmen.* 1990.
Mahbubani, K. *The New Asian Hemisphere: The Irresistible Shift of Global Power to the East.* 2008.
McCargo, D. *Contemporary Japan.* 2nd ed. 2004.
McLain, J. *Japan: A Modern History.* 2001.
Meisner, M. *Mao's China, and After.* 1986.
Meredith, R. *The Elephant and the Dragon: The Rise of India and China.* 2005.
Merrill, John. *Korea: The Peninsular Origins of the War.* 1989.
Neher, C. *Southeast Asia: Crossroads of the World.* 2nd ed. 2005.
Olson, J., and R. Roberts. *Where the Domino Fell: America and Vietnam, 1945–1995.* 4th ed. 2004.
Osborne, M. *Southeast Asia: An Introductory History.* 9th ed. 2004.
Reischauer, E., and M. Jansen. *The Japanese Today.* 2nd ed. 2004.

Schirokauer, C., and D. Clark. *Modern East Asia*. 2004.

Schoppa, R. K. *Revolution and Its Past: Identities and Change in Modern Chinese History*. 2nd ed. 2006.

Spence, J. *Mao Zedong*. 1999.

Spence, J. *The Search for Modern China*. 1990.

Stueck, W., ed. *The Korean War in World History*. 2004.

Tao Jie et al., eds. *Holding Up Half the Sky: Chinese Women Past, Present, and Future*. 2004.

Tarling, N. *Southeast Asia: A Modern History*. 2002.

Terrill, R. *The New Chinese Empire*. 2003.

Tinker, H. *South Asia: A Short History*. 1990.

Vatikiotis, M. *Indonesian Politics Under Suharto*. 1993.

Vickers, A. *A History of Modern Indonesia*. 2005.

Wasserstrom, J., ed. *Twentieth Century China*. 2002.

Key Dates and Developments

1945–1952	U.S. occupation of Japan		1972	Nixon's visit to China
1946–1949	Chinese Civil War and Communist victory		1973	U.S. withdrawal from Vietnam
1946–1954	First Indochina War		1975–1978	Cambodian genocide
1947	Independence and division of India and Pakistan		1978–1997	Deng Xiaoping's economic reforms in China
1949	Independence of Indonesia		1984	Assassination of Indira Gandhi in India
1950–1953	Korean War		1989	Tiananmen Square Massacre in China
1958–1960	Great Leap Forward in China		1998	Testing of nuclear weapons by India and Pakistan
1960–1963	Split between China and USSR		2000	Meeting of North and South Korean leaders
1964–1975	Vietnam War/Second Indochina War		2004	Tsunami devastates Indonesia and much of southern Asia
1966–1969	Great Proletarian Cultural Revolution in China		2005	North Korea claims to have developed nuclear weapons
1969	Border wars between China and USSR		2007	Assassination of Benazir Bhutto in Pakistan
1971	Independence of Bangladesh from Pakistan			

PEARSON myhistorylab™ Connections

Reinforce what you learned in this chapter by studying the many documents, images, maps, review tools, and videos available at www.myhistorylab.com.

Read and Review

✓● **Study** and **Review** Chapter 35

📖● **Read** the **Document**

Jinnah, the "Father" of Pakistan (1947), p. 838

Gandhi Speaks Against the Partition of India (pre-1947), p. 838

Jawaharlal Nehru, from *The Autobiography of Jawarharlal Nehru*, p. 838

🔍● **View** the **Map**

Map Discovery: Civil War in China, ca. 1947, p. 842

🔍● **View** the **Image**

Mahatma Gandhi, p. 837

Indonesian Guerillas, p. 854

Indonesian Political Rallies, p. 854

((●● **Listen** to the **Audio**

Communist China 1, p. 842

Communist China 2, p. 844

Communist China 3, p. 848

Communist China 4, p. 850

Research and Explore

👁● **Watch** the **Video**

Video Lectures: Gandhi in India, p. 838

🔍● **View** the **Map**

Interactive Map: The Emergence of Modern China, 1919 to the Present, p. 842

((●● **Listen** to the **Chapter Audio** for Chapter 35 on **myhistorylab.com**

36 Reform and Revolution in Latin America, 1914–Present

((•— Listen to the **Chapter Audio** for Chapter 36 on **myhistorylab.com**

- What factors affected Latin America's relations with the rest of the world in the 20th century?

- Why did Argentina, Brazil, and Chile vacillate between dictatorship and democracy after 1945?

- In what ways are modern Latin American nations affected by debt, population issues, and poverty?

- In what ways have Latin American gender roles and religious preferences changed since 1945?

Juan and Evita Perón

Juan and Evita Perón ride through Buenos Aires in June 1951. Evita is wearing her trademark mink coat to ward off the chill of the Argentinian winter. The Peróns were Latin America's ultimate power couple, the most skillful politicians Argentina had ever seen (page 872).

Salvador Allende (*eye-YEHN-dā*), president of Chile, entered his office at the Moneda Palace in Santiago at 6 AM Tuesday, September 11, 1973. That was an unusually early arrival for a man who customarily handled paperwork until late in the evening, but this was an unusual day. A military conspiracy was attempting to overthrow his freely elected Marxist government, and Allende wanted to organize resistance as rapidly as possible. By late morning, however, planes were bombing the palace, tanks were clearing the streets of the government's defenders, and the conspirators were offering Allende safe passage out of the country. The president chose instead to remain at his post, and shortly after 2 PM, as infantry began to storm the palace, Salvador Allende committed suicide, using a pistol given him by Cuba's president Fidel Castro.

Latin America

Allende's death was only the beginning of the Chilean tragedy. The military regime that replaced him turned Santiago's soccer stadium into a detention, torture, and execution center in the weeks following September 11. Opponents of the regime disappeared by the thousands. Political parties were abolished, the constitution was suspended, and Chilean democracy was extinguished. An authoritarian dictatorship clamped its iron fist around the throat of a nation that, at the outset of the 20th century, had been widely considered a model of representative government. The explanation of these events is found not solely in Chile's domestic history but in the global situation to which Latin America was connected in the 20th century.

Latin America and the World Since 1914

The principal nations of Latin America entered the 20th century in varying stages of political and economic development. For each of them, the century's first four decades proved turbulent. World War II and the Cold War that followed it made isolationism unworkable throughout the Western Hemisphere. Quickly, every major nation of Latin America became part of a wider and more complex global system.

In the process, Latin American concerns were often subordinated to superpower rivalries. The United States supported brutal military dictatorships in Argentina, Brazil, and Chile in the 1960s and 1970s, largely out of fear that those countries would otherwise become Communist. The Soviet Union maintained close ties with Cuba, a Communist regime after 1959, as a means of encouraging Communist development in other Latin American states.

As the Cold War waned and eventually ended, so did many oppressive Latin American regimes that had been supported by either the United States or the Soviet Union. Argentina in 1983, Brazil in 1985, and Chile in 1990 all returned to democratic rule. But the fundamental problems of modernization, poverty, and inequality that had been ignored during the Cold War remained unsolved and largely unaddressed. In the final years of the 20th century, they reemerged to present young democracies with daunting difficulties, calling into question the long-term stability of Latin America.

Read the **Document**

Francisco García Calderón, Excerpt from Latin America: Its Rise and Progress

on **myhistorylab.com**

Connections: Latin America in the Global Economy

When Latin America won independence from Spain and Portugal in the 1820s, the new nations found it difficult to establish links to the world economy. Mexico emerged from the independence period economically devastated, while South American countries found that their remoteness from Europe reduced opportunities for transatlantic trade once the colonial connection was gone. Landowners and manufacturers responded by producing crops and goods for localities and regions rather than for foreign markets.

European industrialization stimulates Latin American economies

By 1900, however, the situation had changed dramatically. European industrialization rapidly increased demands for the resources and food that Latin America could provide. Coffee and rubber from Brazil, tin from Bolivia, copper and nitrates from Chile, sugar from Cuba, wheat and beef from Argentina, and wool from Argentina and Uruguay were shipped to Europe and the United States. In return, Latin Americans purchased large quantities of European-made clothing, tools, and machines. This developing commercial relationship stimulated foreign investment in Latin America, particularly in railways, roads, bridges, and mines. Foreign control of important sectors of the economy became a sensitive political issue in Mexico, Chile, Bolivia, Peru, and other nations in the opening years of the 20th century.

Despite this concern, Latin America's integration into a global import–export economy led to rapid growth and prosperity. Brazilian and Argentine elites grew tremendously wealthy, and their investments in commercial enterprises attracted European immigrants to fill labor shortages. Immigration stimulated urbanization and the development of a working class committed to unionization. These immigrants remained excluded from political power because they could not vote until they became citizens, and citizenship, considered not a right but a privilege, was granted to very few. Political elites gained the support of the increasingly prosperous middle classes by granting them access to the political system. Then both upper and middle classes worked together to keep the working classes relatively powerless.

A coffee bar in Buenos Aires in 1950.

Latin America suffers during the Great Depression

The Great Depression upset this comfortable collaboration. Global demand for Latin American commodities and foodstuffs declined drastically, ending decades of growth and undermining confidence in political leaders who failed to control the damage (Map 36.1). Middle-class citizens broke with political elites and supported military takeovers, attempted in eight Latin American nations between 1929 and 1933. Military and civilian governments alike tried to limit the impact of the Depression by promoting economic diversification through industrialization. If Latin American nations could produce more of their own industrial goods, they would be less affected by global economic fluctuations. New industries would also provide additional manufacturing jobs for urban working classes.

Populist leaders build urban coalitions in diversified economies

Countries with small domestic markets and economies built around the production of one or two commodities found industrialization difficult. These included the tin-centered economy of Bolivia, the coffee- and banana-based economies of Central America, and the oil-dominated economy of Venezuela. More diversified economies in nations with larger populations were more successful. Argentina, Brazil, and Mexico were able to manufacture their own products to replace imports, while Chile applied industrial technologies to improve output in its copper and nitrate mines. As a result of the growing number and importance of these manufacturing jobs, the working classes became

MAP 36.1   Commodity Production in South America, 1900

As the 20th century began, South America's productivity made it a valuable trading partner with Europe, North America, and Asia. Notice the concentrations of commodities: rubber in the Amazon basin of Brazil, coffee in southern Brazil, cattle and sheep in Argentina and Uruguay. What factors account for such concentrations?

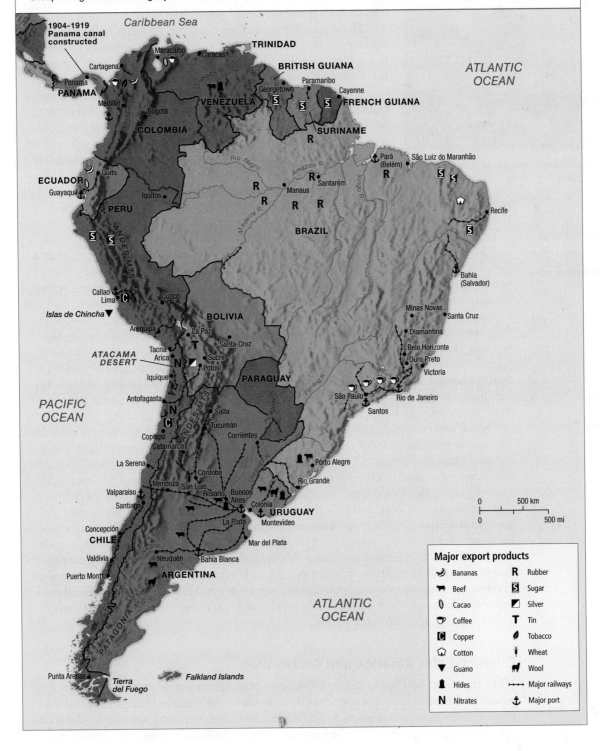

Major export products

⚘ Bananas	R Rubber
🦃 Beef	S Sugar
◊ Cacao	⬎ Silver
☕ Coffee	T Tin
C Copper	⬕ Tobacco
⌂ Cotton	⬈ Wheat
▼ Guano	🦙 Wool
🛋 Hides	⊢⊣⊢⊣ Major railways
N Nitrates	⚓ Major port

Loading wheat onto a freight ship at La Guirara harbor, Venezuela.

🔍 **View** the **Image**

Unloading Coffee in Brazil

on **myhistorylab.com**

Massive debt incapacitates Latin American economies

increasingly strong and assertive, forming labor unions and offering a new power base for populist politicians. Juan Perón in Argentina, Getúlio Vargas in Brazil, Arturo Alessandri in Chile, and Lázaro Cárdenas in Mexico all appealed to workers and created urban-based coalitions that competed for power with traditional agricultural and landed elites.

These populist leaders were unable, however, to build solid economies. By the 1960s Latin America was no longer completely dependent on fully industrialized nations, but it relied on them for some commodities and could be adversely affected by global changes over which it had no control. Machine tools and large capital equipment still had to be imported, and if global market prices of exports like copper, coffee, beef, and grain declined, so would Latin America's ability to pay for those imports. Increasing exports would only depress world prices and further reduce the region's ability to pay. When such developments occurred, industrial workers suffered greatly, and their unions responded to deteriorating economic conditions with strikes, demonstrations, and in Argentina and Uruguay, urban terrorism.

As public order came apart, military regimes took control in Brazil (1964), Chile (1973), and Argentina (1976). These developments were nothing new. Ever since Latin America won its independence, its military leaders had claimed and exercised the right to overthrow incompetent or corrupt civil governments. But these new regimes, unlike previous ones, did not quickly return power to civilians. Instead, they abolished political parties and civil rights, imprisoned and tortured their political opponents, and based their continued control on their ability to restore economic prosperity. Excluding the working classes from political and economic influence, the military governments built partnerships with multinational corporations, refinanced their debts, and stimulated their economies by borrowing enormous sums abroad. Between 1970 and 1980, Latin America's foreign debt soared from $27 billion to $231 billion, with interest payments alone rising from $2 billion to $18 billion.

For a time refinancing and borrowing worked, and news of the Brazilian and Chilean "economic miracles" encouraged foreign banks to lend them even more money. But during the global economic downturn of 1980–1983, the debt-ridden nations found themselves caught between rising interest payments and sharply reduced export earnings. International lenders such as the World Bank and the International Monetary Fund offered help in refinancing massive debt, but only if the debtor nations reformed their economies, cut government expenditures, and welcomed additional foreign trade and global investment. Latin America accepted these conditions, but enormous sums flowed out of the region to repay the debt to the industrialized world, leading to a decade of declining economic output. Discredited military dictators retired and handed debt problems over to civilian governments willing to accept political accountability and leave office once their terms expired. Though the debt problem remained unsolved, Latin America's connections to global financial markets were rebuilt.

Conflict: Latin America and Global War

When the Great War broke out in 1914, few Latin Americans thought their region would be affected. They assumed that the crisis between Austria-Hungary and Serbia was a European issue irrelevant to the Western Hemisphere. But soon two battles took place nearby: in autumn 1914 the German Pacific Squadron defeated the British in a naval battle off Coronel, Chile, and then, on December 8, that squadron was destroyed by more British warships at the Battle of the Falkland Islands off the Argentine coast. More significantly, Britain's naval blockade of Germany, and Germany's retaliation by U-boat warfare, made Atlantic shipping risky, especially for nations like Chile and Argentina, traditional exporters to many European nations.

But the Great War did not seriously affect Latin America until the United States became a combatant in April 1917. After that, Brazil actively participated on the Allied side and earned a seat at the Paris Peace Conference in 1919. Chile's copper and nitrates found a willing buyer as the United States began expanding a small army into a huge force destined for battle in Europe. Chilean prosperity was intense but brief: the end of the war also ended sizable United States orders for Chilean resources. Most other Latin American nations were relieved as the return to peacetime conditions in the Atlantic reestablished their access to European markets. In sum, the Great War left Latin America on the sidelines, avoiding the trauma and death experienced in Europe and, to a lesser extent, in the Middle East and Africa.

Two decades after the Armistice, the outbreak of World War II placed Latin America in a very different situation. During the 1930s, Germany and Italy demonstrated an interest in the Western Hemisphere. German money financed the Nacista Party in Chile, an imitation of the German National Socialist Party. Germany also underwrote nationalistic German organizations in cities with large German populations, such as São Paulo, Brazil, and Buenos Aires, Argentina, and, in the United States, New York, St. Louis, Cincinnati, and Milwaukee. Italy provided small sums of money and plenty of advice to the fascistic Integralista Party in Brazil. These activities had limited effects, but Nazi and fascist ideologies clearly threatened the Western Hemisphere.

European issues affect Latin America

Germany's aggression against Austria and Czechoslovakia in 1938 led the hemisphere's foreign ministers, meeting in Lima, Peru, to sign a declaration of hemispheric unity against subversion from within or invasion from outside. The outbreak of war in September 1939 led to a more extensive declaration, creating a neutrality zone extending 300 miles off the coasts of North and South America and providing for inter-American economic coordination. After France, Holland, and Denmark were conquered by Germany in 1940, their colonies in the West Indies and South America became potential bases for German attacks or sabotage against the Panama Canal. The United States was authorized by all hemispheric nations to establish a protectorate over those colonies.

Japan's attack on Pearl Harbor brought the United States into the war, and most Latin American nations cooperated closely with their northern neighbor. Mexico sent a squadron of fighter pilots to fly in the Philippines in 1944, and 250,000 Mexicans enlisted in the U.S. armed forces. Tens of thousands of **braceros** (*brah-SAIR-ōz*), or immigrant workers, entered the United States to work in factories in place of U.S. citizens called to active duty. Panama worked closely with the United States to protect the Panama Canal. Chile resumed its Great War role as a valued supplier of minerals. But the most significant Latin American roles were played by two longtime rivals, Brazil and Argentina.

Mexican workers help the U.S. economy in wartime

Brazil made several crucial contributions to the Allied war effort. Its government leased to the United States a large tract of land in Natal, where Brazil juts eastward into the South Atlantic, only 1,900 miles from West Africa. There the United States constructed a huge air base that by 1944 was the busiest in the world. Transatlantic air travel was impossible in World War II because of limited fuel capacities, so U.S. troops and cargo for the invasion of Europe were shuttled from air bases in the United States to Panama, then to Natal, then to West Africa, and then to England. In return for leasing rights in Natal, the United States gave Brazil a complete steel plant, transplanted immediately after the war from western Pennsylvania to Volta Redonda in Brazil's southeast. Brazil then built South America's largest steel industry around it. Brazil also supplied the Allies with rubber, a vital raw material, after Japan took control of most of the world's rubber by occupying Southeast Asia's sprawling plantations.

Brazil plays an active role in World War II

In addition to these material contributions, Brazil played an active combat role in the war. When Germany declared war on the United States in December 1941, Washington had made no meaningful preparations to defend commercial shipping along the country's eastern seaboard. During the first five months of 1942, German U-boats went unchallenged as they sank U.S. ships. Brazil then sent its own submarines to patrol the seaboard and the Caribbean, freeing U.S. submarines for action against Japan. Brazilians also sent a 25,000-soldier infantry division into combat in Italy in 1944.

Argentina's policies irritate the United States

In contrast, Argentina's army overthrew its civilian government in 1943 to prevent a declaration of war against Germany. Most Argentine officers had been posted to Germany for military training in the 1920s and 1930s, and they were convinced that the German Army was invincible. Although it became difficult to maintain that belief in 1943, Argentina remained neutral until April 1945, when it declared war on Germany and Japan in order to qualify for membership in the newly established United Nations Organization. After the war ended, Argentina permitted tens of thousands of German bureaucrats, soldiers, and war criminals to enter the country under assumed names to escape Allied military courts. These policies earned Argentina the hostility of the U.S. government for the next decade, while its archrival Brazil prospered economically and was seriously considered for a permanent seat on the United Nations Security Council.

U.S. president Theodore Roosevelt running a steam shovel during construction of the Panama Canal, 1906.

Connections and Conflict: Latin America and the United States

Late in his presidency, Porfirio Díaz of Mexico lamented: "Poor Mexico! So far from God. So close to the United States." Latin America's geographic proximity to the United States has been a source of connections and conflicts for two centuries. The **Monroe Doctrine** of 1823 committed the United States to defend the newly created Latin American states against any European efforts at recolonization. For the next fifty years, the United States was deeply involved in its own westward expansion (or manifest destiny) and its bloody Civil War. Thereafter, the United States began constructing commercial links with its southern neighbors, spearheaded by entrepreneurs like Minor Cooper Keith, who built railways across Central America and helped create the United Fruit Company, and W. R. Grace and Company, which underwrote telegraph networks and financed the Brazilian rubber industry.

Then in 1895 revolution broke out in Cuba, one of Spain's few remaining Western Hemispheric colonies. The United States expressed outrage at Spain's brutal suppression of Cuban revolutionaries and was also tempted by the prospect of seizing some of Spain's Caribbean possessions as a prelude to building a canal across Central America. Two months after an explosion of unclear origin destroyed its battleship *Maine* in Havana harbor in February 1898, the United States declared war on Spain. By August 1898 the war was over, leaving the victorious United States in possession of Guam, the Philippines, and Puerto Rico. Cuba became independent in principle, although the Platt Amendment, passed by the U.S. Senate in 1901, gave Washington unprecedented rights of intervention there.

Building on the Platt Amendment, U.S. president Theodore Roosevelt extended the right of intervention to the entire Caribbean basin. His 1904 **Roosevelt Corollary** to the

Monroe Doctrine asserted the right to intervene in the internal affairs of nations when Washington found evidence of "chronic wrongdoing," including an inability to pay debts, keep order, or dispense justice. Between 1901 and 1928, the United States intervened militarily in Mexico, Central America, and the Caribbean more than fifty times. This aggressive behavior, called **gunboat diplomacy**, infuriated Latin Americans and helped bring to power military dictators who promised to maintain order and protect the investments of United States citizens and companies.

In the late 1920s, this policy began to change. Reuben Clark, legal counsel to the U.S. Department of State, argued in a 1928 memorandum that gunboat diplomacy and the Roosevelt Corollary violated the intent and spirit of the Monroe Doctrine by destabilizing weaker states and making foreign intervention more rather than less likely. Five years later, Theodore Roosevelt's distant cousin Franklin became president of the United States and committed that country to "the policy of the good neighbor" with respect to Latin America. In one of his folksy "fireside chat" radio addresses, Franklin Roosevelt observed that while a good neighbor does not remain indifferent to dangers threatening the house next door, neither does he break the door down whenever his neighbor does something he does not like. Roosevelt's **Good Neighbor Policy** ushered in a new era of U.S. policy toward Latin America, in which the United States claimed it would respect the laws of its neighbors, refrain from military or political influence in their affairs, and restrict itself to economic investment and diplomatic persuasion. Interestingly, however, United States intervention in Latin America actually increased during Roosevelt's presidency. The forms of engagement were more subtle and respectful, and connections were preferred to conflicts, but those connections remained active and strong.

Latin American support for the United States during World War II seemed to solidify the Good Neighbor Policy. But the end of World War II did not end global conflict, as the Cold War developed between capitalist and Communist states. At first Latin America played a minor role in this confrontation. The principal capitalist nation was the United States, a country so powerful that no state in the Western Hemisphere was willing to oppose it openly. In Argentina, President Juan Perón spoke vaguely of a "Third Way" between capitalism and Communism but never attempted to implement his ideas. Other nations of Latin America supported the United States through the Organization of American States, a hemispheric association dominated by Washington.

Then in 1958, Cuban guerrillas led by Fidel Castro mounted a serious challenge to that island's dictator, Fulgencio Batista (*full-HEHN-see-yō bah-TEE-stah*). The United States, viewing Castro as an honest, idealistic young hero, gave him some support by embargoing arms shipments to Batista. But after Castro came to power in January 1959, U.S. president Dwight Eisenhower discovered that Castro was far more radical than he had suspected. Castro quickly imposed his own dictatorship, shooting thousands of Batista's supporters and nationalizing industries and U.S.-owned corporations.

Workers at a banana plantation owned by the United Fruit Company, Guatemala.

Gunboat diplomacy gives way to the Good Neighbor Policy

Read the **Document**

Juan Perón, Excerpt from The Voice of Perón

on **myhistorylab.com**

Read the **Document**

Fidel Castro, "History Will Absolve Me," 1953

on **myhistorylab.com**

Cuban revolutionary Camillo Cienfuegos and others in front of a statue of Cuban revolutionary hero José Martí, February 1959.

The United States responded vigorously to Castro's leftist policies. It trained a paramilitary force of Cuban exiles to invade the island and overthrow Castro, but that force was disastrously defeated in an April 1961 landing at the Bay of Pigs in southern Cuba. The invaders were captured, the U.S. role was exposed, and a triumphant Castro drew closer to the Soviet Union, proclaiming himself a Communist.

View the Image

Soviet Deputy Premier in Cuba

on **myhistorylab.com**

The Cuban Missile Crisis brings the world to the brink of war

Soviet premier Nikita Khrushchev called Cuba an "unsinkable aircraft carrier in the Caribbean" and supplied the island with oil and machinery, but he feared a second U.S. invasion. Addressing this and other concerns, including the U.S. superiority in nuclear weapons and the continued Western presence in Berlin, Khrushchev in 1962 placed medium-range ballistic missiles in Cuba. When U.S. spy flights revealed their presence, President John F. Kennedy placed a naval quarantine line around Cuba and demanded their removal. The Cuban Missile Crisis lasted 13 days and brought the world to the edge of nuclear war, but it ended peacefully when Khrushchev removed the missiles in return for Kennedy's public pledge not to invade Cuba and private pledge to withdraw obsolete U.S. missiles from Turkey.

Read the Document

John F. Kennedy and Cuba (1961)

on **myhistorylab.com**

The Cuban Missile Crisis affected the Cold War profoundly (Map 36.2). Kennedy and Khrushchev, shaken by their brush with catastrophe, installed direct electronic communication between the White House and the Kremlin and signed a limited nuclear test ban treaty in 1963. Later that year Kennedy was murdered by an assassin linked to a pro-Castro organization, and in 1964 Khrushchev was removed by Soviet leaders

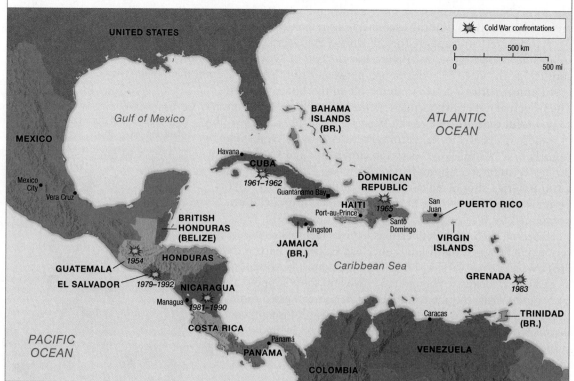

MAP 36.2 Cold War Confrontations in Latin America, 1954–1992

The Cold War struggle between capitalism and Communism was waged in several regions of the world at the same time. Note the number of confrontations in the small geographic area of Central America and the Caribbean Sea. Why did these Latin American nations play such a prominent role in the Cold War?

exasperated by his adventurism in placing the missiles in Cuba in the first place. Castro remained in control of Cuba into the 21st century, protected by the U.S. realization that it could, after all, survive in the same hemisphere with a Communist state.

But Cold War issues continued to affect relations between Latin America and the United States. In 1965 the Johnson administration landed Marines in the Dominican Republic to suppress a reformist revolution that Washington wrongly believed to be Communist. Between 1970 and 1973, the Nixon administration waged economic warfare against the freely elected Marxist government of Salvador Allende in Chile, destabilizing it and giving the Chilean armed forces a reason for overthrowing it, as described in this chapter's opening. And in the 1980s, the Reagan administration confronted a grassroots leftist governing coalition in Nicaragua, the **Sandinista Front for National Liberation,** which overthrew dictator Anastasio Somoza in 1979 and established close ties with Cuba and the Soviet Union. The United States tried unsuccessfully to arm counterrevolutionary forces and isolate Nicaragua within the hemisphere. Ironically, the Sandinista government was eventually removed in 1990, not by subversion but by losing a free election and quietly withdrawing into political opposition.

The end of the Cold War in 1990 and the collapse of the Soviet Union the following year removed the Communist–capitalist confrontation from the troubled relationship between Latin America and the United States. In this more relaxed international atmosphere, economic and cultural connections that had remained strong but submerged during the Cold War suddenly resurfaced. U.S. and global investment in Brazil, Chile, and Mexico flourished, enhanced by the establishment of the **North American Free Trade Area (NAFTA)** linking Canada, Mexico, and the United States in 1993. Washington supported other efforts to lower trade barriers across Central and South America. Immigration into the United States from Latin American countries increased greatly, and people of Hispanic descent became the largest U.S. minority population group in 2005. In the process, U.S. cuisine, music, and entertainment became Latinized to an extent inconceivable only twenty years earlier.

These developments laid the foundation for a more productive and mutually respectful relationship between the United States and Latin America. The regional and global conflicts of the 20th century gave way to the potentially beneficial connections of the 21st. For the first time, interhemispheric relations were largely determined not by those states' responses to events set in motion by external forces but by their own reactions to each other.

◉ **Watch** the **Video**
The Cuban Missile Crisis
on **myhistorylab.com**

U.S. attitudes toward Latin America change when the Cold War ends

Democracy and Dictatorship in Latin America

During the 20th century, Latin American nations were faced with the same choice between dictatorship and democracy that confronted Europe, Asia, and Africa. Argentina, Brazil, and Chile experienced different types of dictatorships before democratizing near the end of the century. In Mexico, political and social revolution between 1910 and 1920 changed the nation's governing structures and replaced one-man rule with one-party rule.

Argentina: The Failure of Political Leadership

Argentina's 19th-century political system (Map 36.3) was dominated by an elite of wealthy merchants, large estate owners, and military officers. Reformers created a political movement, the Unión Cívica Radical (**UCR,** or Radical Civic Union), which rebelled several times between 1890 and 1910 in an effort to crack this elite's power. Finally, in 1916, a change in Argentina's election laws made possible a reasonably honest election, which was won by the UCR candidate, Hipólito Yrigoyen (*hih-PŌ-lē-tō ear-ih-G-yen*).

The UCR fails to improve the condition of Argentine workers

Yrigoyen was an effective candidate but a poor president. His UCR promoted working-class wage increases and improvements in working conditions. But in 1919, as wages stagnated while food prices rose as a result of increased demand from war-ravaged Europe, Argentina was swept by strikes. Yrigoyen's government broke the strikes, shooting hundreds of demonstrators in the capital city of Buenos Aires and alienating its working-class supporters. This action permanently weakened the UCR, and a coalition of conservatives and military leaders overthrew the government in 1930. This coalition ruled Argentina for the next 13 years, reversing progress toward democracy. Then the Argentine army took over the government in 1943, and two years later Colonel Juan Domingo Perón (*peh-RŌN*) emerged as the nation's leader.

PERÓN'S APPEAL TO ARGENTINES. Juan Perón was a modern-day *caudillo*, ruling through a combination of charm, magnetism, and cunning. He understood that the UCR had recognized the growing political leverage of the Argentine middle and working classes and that Yrigoyen had alienated the working class through strikebreaking and indifference. Perón, resolving not to make the same mistake, built a political power base within the working class.

Perón's affection for working people was both genuine and calculated. He showered them with benefits: minimum-wage and maximum-hours legislation, paid vacations, the "13th month" (a Christmas bonus of one month's pay), and, most important, the security of knowing that their welfare was foremost in his mind. While addressing his beloved **descamisados** (*dez-cah-mē-SAH-dōz*, or "shirtless people," Argentina's manual laborers), Perón would take off his own shirt and tie and stand before them bare-chested, flashing his magnificent smile and assuring them of his affection for them. They repaid him with their loyalty and their votes, providing him with the margin of victory in the elections of 1946 and 1951. Perón constructed a strong base of support that lasted for decades after he was driven out of office in 1955.

Perón was ably assisted by his wife Evita (*AY-VĒ-tah*), an exceptionally shrewd politician known for her fur coats and platinum-colored hair (see page 862). A mediocre film actress and radio "weather girl," María Eva Duarte

MAP 36.3   Argentina

Argentina is the second largest nation in South America and is five times the size of France. Observe that the country extends for 2,000 miles from north to south. What impact would this have on Argentina's climate?

DOCUMENT 36.1 Eva Perón Discusses Why She Joined Juan D. Perón

The people's enemies were and remain Perón's enemies.

I have seen them approach him with every kind of malice and lie.

I want to denounce them definitively.

Because they will be the eternal enemies of Perón and of the people, here and every place in the world where the flag of justice and liberty is raised. We have defeated them, but they belong to a race that will never die definitively.

Perón's enemies . . . I have seen them up close and personal.

I never remained in the rearguard of his battles.

I was in the front line of combat, fighting the short days and the long nights of my zeal, infinite like the thirst of my heart. And I carried out two tasks—I don't know which was more worthy of a small life like mine, but my life in the end—one, to fight for the rights of my people, and the other, to watch Perón's back.

In this double duty, immense for me, armed with nothing but my ardent heart, I met the enemies of Perón and my people.

They are the same!

Yes! I never saw anyone from our race—the race of the people—fighting against Perón.

But I did see the others. They cannot be near the people or the men whom the people elect to lead them.

And they definitely cannot be the leaders of the people.

The leaders of the people must be fanatics for the people.

If not, they grow dizzy at the top—and they do not return!

SOURCE: *Evita: In My Own Words* – English translation Copyright © 1996 by Laura Dail. Reprinted by permission of The New Press.

---

met Colonel Perón in 1943 and married him two years later (see "Eva Perón Discusses Why She Joined Juan D. Perón"). More radical than he in her political thinking, perhaps because of her own impoverished childhood, Evita encouraged lower-class resentment for the wealthy, while her magnificent wardrobe inspired the poor to think that if a destitute girl like her could become rich, one day they might do the same. This blend of anger and hope made her the idol of millions of Argentines. When she died of cancer in 1952 at age 32, two million people attended her funeral. And at a time when only 20 million people lived in Argentina, a petition with 6 million signatures was presented to Pope Pius XII, asking for her canonization as a Catholic saint.

Juan Perón builds a working-class political base

Evita Perón becomes Latin America's most influential female leader

When Perón fell from power in 1955, the causes were of his own making: gross mismanagement of agricultural policy and squandering Argentina's huge postwar credit balances. In addition, in a bitter quarrel with the Catholic Church over its refusal to make Evita a saint, he decided to penalize it by legalizing divorce. The military leaders who sent Perón into exile in Spain thought they were rid of a typical Latin American dictator, despite his two victories in free elections and his undeniable personal popularity.

Perón dominates Argentine politics even after his overthrow

They were mistaken. The succession of military and civilian governments that followed Perón proved even less capable of handling Argentina's problems. Meanwhile, the exiled former president urged his followers to cast blank ballots in Argentine elections to demonstrate support for him. The totals were high enough to embarrass the government: in one case, the winner actually ran second to "blank." Perón's support *grew* while he was exiled, as younger people who could not remember his mistakes fell in love with his legend. "Peronism without Perón" haunted Argentine politics as the destabilization caused by blank ballots led to military dictatorships, which in turn were fought bitterly by urban terrorist groups like the **Montoneros** (*mawn-tawn-AIR-ōz*).

Urban terrorism became a disturbingly common feature of Latin American political life in the late 1960s. Argentina's Montoneros, Uruguay's **Tupamaros** (*too-pah-MAH-rōz*),

Urban terrorism plagues Argentina and Uruguay

and less effective bands in other South American states robbed banks, dynamited power plants, and kidnapped and murdered government officials. These groups stood far to the political left, considering traditional Communist parties to be tools of the establishment. The Montoneros hated the police, the military, executives of large companies, and U.S. and European diplomats, all of whom they characterized as oppressors. When several Montoneros kidnapped and killed an Argentine general in 1970, the army realized it had to come to terms with Perón. Only he seemed to have the personal prestige to stabilize the country, and they expected his return would split the Montoneros, some of whom considered him an oppressor, while others fondly remembered his kindness to the working class.

Jorge Luís Borges in his Buenos Aires apartment.

ARGENTINE ARTISTRY: JORGE LUÍS BORGES. As social and political difficulties wracked Argentina, the nation's most famous literary figure entered the final decades of his exceptionally creative life. Jorge Luís Borges (*HOAR-hā loo-EES BOAR-hāz*, 1899–1986), born in Buenos Aires, was of mixed Argentine and English ancestry and spoke English as his first language. Educated in Geneva, Switzerland, he moved back to Buenos Aires in 1921 and quickly became an influential literary figure. From 1937–1946, he worked as a cataloguer at a branch of the Buenos Aires Municipal Library, a job that bored him but that gave him ample opportunity to hide in the stacks and read. Like Einstein in the patent office in Bern, Switzerland, his mundane work gave him time to think and write.

In 1946 Borges was fired by Perón because of his political leanings. During the Perón years, he wrote many of the short stories that earned him an international reputation as a master of that craft. When Perón was overthrown, Borges became director of the National Library of Argentina; with nine hundred thousand books at his disposal, he promptly went blind from an eye condition inherited from his father's side of the family. He continued to write, however, and had won virtually every significant literary award in the world, except for the Nobel Prize for Literature, by the time of his death in 1986.

Borges had his opinions about Argentina's political turbulence, and those opinions got him into trouble with Perón, but they seldom appear in his poetry or fiction. Most of his stories embrace universal themes: the search for meaning in life, the relationship between time and space (again reminiscent of Einstein), and the concept of infinity. Borges's fiction suggests that there is no such thing as material substance; the sensible world consists exclusively of ideas, which themselves exist only as long as they are perceived within people's minds. The human search for meaning in an infinite universe is futile. Since material things do not exist, time is not restricted by them, and there are multiple strands of time coexisting at once, some intersecting and others paralleling each other.

All of this might seem overly philosophical, but Borges's short stories, few of which are more than six pages long, are both fascinating and haunting. In *The Aleph*, a man finds in a cellar a small, bright sphere in which all the places in the world, seen from every conceivable angle, coexist at once. In *The Book of Sand*, a peddler of Bibles sells a man a book that has neither beginning nor end, and no page of which, once examined, ever appears again. In *The Other*, Borges himself, seated on a bench by the Charles River in Cambridge, Massachusetts, in 1969, discovers to his horror that the man seated next to him is also Borges, seated on a bench by the Rhône River in Geneva sometime between 1914 and 1921. This master of short fiction lived in Argentina during times of upheaval but in many ways stood apart from his society, writing vividly of abstract concepts that his words made concrete.

ARGENTINA AFTER PERÓN. Borges was not the only Argentine dismayed when, in 1973, after months of negotiations, the 78-year-old Perón returned triumphantly from exile to become president again. But his death the next year left the presidency to his fourth wife, Isabel, who had run as his vice president in 1973. Mystified by the duties of the presidency, she began consulting astrologers. In 1976, as inflation rose to 4,640 percent per year, she was removed by the military. The new military dictatorship waged a **"dirty war"** against Peronists, Montoneros, and Communists, imprisoning people without trial, torturing them to death, and disposing of the bodies in unmarked graves. More than 25,000 people disappeared this way between 1976 and 1978.

The Argentine military dictatorship wages war against leftists

Every Thursday morning between 1977 and 1983, the **Mothers of the Plaza de Mayo** (*MĪ-yō*) marched around that square in front of the Casa Rosada, the presidential residence in Buenos Aires, to protest the disappearance of their husbands and children. At first the regime ignored them and the economy turned prosperous. But in 1982 the military leadership broke off negotiations with Great Britain over the future of the Falkland Islands (which Argentines call the Malvinas), claimed by both countries since 1833. Argentine soldiers invaded the islands on April Fool's Day, 1982, quickly finding that the joke was on them. Rather than let the rocky, windswept islands go, British prime minister Margaret Thatcher launched a massive military expedition to retake them. The British won the Falklands War, Thatcher was triumphantly reelected, and the Argentine military dictatorship collapsed.

Borges protested the "dirty war" and ridiculed the Falklands conflict, calling it "two bald men fighting over a comb." He welcomed the restoration of civilian government in 1983 as Raúl Alfonsín (*ahl-fahn-SĒN*) of the UCR was elected president. Generals who had conducted the "dirty war" were put on trial and convicted, but lower-ranking officers were exempted in 1987 to avoid the threat of a military revolt. Meanwhile, the trauma of those whose relatives "disappeared" continued to haunt Argentine society. Yet Perón's political successors won office in their own right and proved to be ordinary politicians, neither magical nor charismatic.

Argentina's most vexing problem after 1990 was neither the military nor the Peronistas but the economy. Burdened with a huge foreign debt, a commercial system that failed to modernize after World War II, and a legacy of bitterness between management and labor, Alfonsín was unable to control triple-digit inflation and a shrinking gross domestic product (GDP). In 1991 Argentina, Brazil, Paraguay, and Uruguay established **MERCOSUR**, the "Common Market of the South," in an effort to imitate the success of the European Community. But in 1999 Brazil devalued its currency, raising the cost of Argentine products in Brazil and creating in Argentina a massive trade deficit. The following year the Argentine currency collapsed. Argentines were forbidden to take money out of the country, banks closed for indefinite periods, and one of the world's potentially richest nations resorted to barter for ordinary transactions. Modest stability returned late in 2002, but Argentina's underlying economic problems remained, calling into question not only the nation's financial health, but also the long-term survival of its democracy.

Brazil's currency devaluation wrecks the Argentine economy

Brazil: Development and Inequality

Brazil emerged from the Great War as South America's most powerful and prosperous nation (Map 36.4), but this prosperity depended on high world market prices for rubber and coffee. In the early 1920s, competition from Southeast Asia cut world rubber prices by 95 percent and bankrupted many Brazilian rubber planters. Then, in 1929, staggering political and economic mismanagement caused coffee prices to collapse. The next year, politically progressive military officers joined forces with politicians resentful of Brazil's powerful coffee-growing states, São Paulo, Minas Gerais, Rio de Janeiro, and Rio Grande do Sul, to overthrow the Brazilian Republic in the Revolution of 1930. Now an unimposing provincial governor from southern Brazil, Getúlio (*jeh-TOO-lē-yō*) Vargas, began a 24-year reign as that nation's most capable 20th-century leader.

Pressures on Brazilian coffee and rubber lead to revolution

| MAP **36.4** | Brazil |

Brazil is the largest nation in South America and the fifth largest nation in the world. Notice that although most of the country is inland, most of the principal cities are near the seacoast. What factors account for this distribution of population?

GETÚLIO VARGAS AND MODERNIZATION.

Brazil's presidents had long been weak, as real power rested with governors and strongmen of the country's most important states. Vargas surprised everyone by moving swiftly to remake Brazil. He removed the governors of every state except one, replacing them with federal "interventors" reporting directly to him. This move provoked an armed rebellion in the state of São Paulo, which the army suppressed after four months' intense fighting. By defeating the Paulista Revolt of 1932, Vargas discredited advocates of state power and strengthened the central government. He used his opportunity to press for extensive bridge and road projects and to grant women the vote in 1932, endorsing the demands of the Brazilian Federation of Feminine Progress and its suffragist founder, the botanist Bertha Lutz.

Brazil was then drawn into the global upheavals of the 1930s by its large Italian and German immigrant communities. The Integralistas, a fascist organization led by Plínio Salgado, a well-to-do young politician who altered his appearance to resemble Adolf Hitler's, fought in the streets with the Communist-dominated National Liberation Alliance. Vargas used fears of a radical takeover to move against both extremes and suspend constitutional guarantees in 1937. He replaced democratic government with a military-backed dictatorship called the *Estado Nôvo* (*ess-TAH-dō Nō-vō*), or New State.

With Congress exiled and democratic processes discarded, Vargas could act as he pleased. His new state included elements of fascism, but Vargas was a pragmatist indifferent to ideology. He saw the world heading for war and seized the opportunity to position Brazil advantageously on the side of the United States.

Vargas uses his dictatorial authority to remake Brazil

Using the *Estado Nôvo*'s centralized executive powers, Vargas aggressively pursued economic development. Labor and management were placed under state control, appointments to civil service positions were based on merit, and the federal government created a number of state-owned manufacturing enterprises. Most of the groundwork for Brazil's remarkable economic expansion of the late 1950s was laid under the Estado Nôvo. But even a smooth political operator like Vargas could not conceal the fact that Brazilians fighting for democracy in Europe were governed by dictatorship at home. In October 1945 the military returned from the war, removed Vargas from office, and held free elections.

Rio de Janeiro in the 1940s.

MODERNITY AND ITS STRESSES, 1954–1964. Vargas's legacy was both personal and substantive. An engaging, warm-hearted man who cared deeply for Brazil's land and people, he was also a clever, manipulative politician. He had recognized the need to modernize Brazil by developing its transportation network, improving its harbors, and encouraging the growth of its local industries. In 1955 one of his protégés, Juscelino Kubitschek (*hoo-seh-LĒ-nō KOO-bih-check*), won the presidency with the slogan "Fifty Years of Progress in Five," a commitment to build on the foundations Vargas had laid. Kubitschek's administration built roads, bridges, and hydroelectric plants, erected immense public-housing complexes, and granted extensive subsidies to developing industries such as steel and automobiles. In the process, however, inflation spiraled out of control, and by 1960 Brazilians worked harder than ever yet enjoyed *less* purchasing power. Brazil's constitution prohibited its presidents from seeking immediate reelection, and although Kubitschek remained personally popular, he was replaced in 1960 by a popular young candidate, Jânio Quadros (*HAH-nē-ō KWAH-drōss*).

Kubitschek's program modernizes Brazil at the cost of massive inflation

Quadros, the energetic reforming mayor of São Paulo, won the election by appealing to Vargas's political opponents. But in Brazil presidential and vice-presidential races are separate, and the vice president elected in 1960, João Goulart (*ZHWOW goo-LAHRT*), was a Vargas supporter and, in the eyes of many, a dangerous leftist. When Congress refused to enact Quadros's huge budget and the impulsive president resigned, the Brazilian military considered deposing Goulart. This standoff was broken by a compromise, but Goulart proved less successful at running the economy than he was at plundering it through graft, corruption, and cronyism. By April 1964 the army overthrew him and replaced him with a military government. For modernized Brazil, this action seemed to belong to an earlier age, and when it was not followed by the long-established practice of returning control to civilians, Brazilians were shocked.

MILITARY RULE, 1964–1985. The 21-year dictatorship that followed was notorious for its brutal violation of human rights. The regime abolished civil and political rights while systematically torturing and killing its opponents. But an economic boom between 1967 and 1974 helped the new government greatly, promoting foreign investment in the northeast and the Amazon valley and making vast sums available for highways and industrial development. Brazil's economy grew at an average rate of 10 percent over that seven-year period. By 1974, manufactured goods exceeded coffee as the nation's most valuable export. Purchasing power rose for nearly all classes of Brazilians during those years, and prosperity encouraged many to overlook the military oppression.

The Brazilian military installs a two-decade dictatorship

Brazil's experience inspired imitation, as both Chile (in 1973) and Argentina (in 1976) were taken over by military dictatorships that revoked human rights and stimulated economic growth. But Brazil's economy began to slow down in 1975, when a killing frost—highly unusual for Brazil—devastated the coffee crop and sent world coffee prices soaring. As competitors such as Nigeria and Colombia took advantage of the situation, Brazil lost a significant share of the world coffee market. The global recession of 1974–1975, brought on by an Arab oil embargo (Chapter 37), also depressed the prices of Brazilian exports. At the same time, the country's huge foreign debt was burdened by rising interest rates. The military regime, having borrowed heavily abroad to finance its economic reforms, was now unable to pay the installments. Inflation reached 100 percent by 1980, hurting the middle and working classes and the poor, and strikes swept through Brazilian factories.

Military rule creates an economic boom

BRAZILIAN ARTISTRY: PELÉ. Before, during, and after the two decades of military rule, the aspect of everyday life that most united Brazilians was their national sport: soccer. The game was introduced to Brazil in 1894 by Charles Miller, a Brazilian teenager of English descent. Only whites could play in organized leagues until 1923, but by the 1930s the

The Brazil side that won the 1958 World Cup, with Garrincha (first from left) and Pelé (third from left) in the front row.

sport was fully integrated. It quickly became a national obsession, punctuated by Brazilian victories in the World Cup tournaments of 1958, 1962, 1970, 1994, and 2002.

The appeal of soccer was grounded in several factors. There was no other organized sport in Brazil to compete with it. It could be played on any level stretch of ground, without expensive apparatus: all that was needed was a ball and a couple of orange crates to mark the goals. It rewarded improvisation and individual skill, and the rhythms of soccer reminded many Brazilians of their most popular dance, the samba. By 1950, when Brazil hosted the World Cup tournament, Rio de Janeiro boasted the world's largest soccer stadium, seating 175,000 people, with standing room for 42,000 more.

Brazilian soccer stars were adored like movie stars in Hollywood, and many of them either adopted "stage names" or went by a single name. Leônidas, the "Black Diamond," invented the bicycle kick in the 1930s; the maneuver involves performing a backward half-somersault while kicking the ball in the opposite direction, over your head or shoulder. The fabled Mané Garrincha, whose legs were deformed by vitamin deficiencies and malnutrition, capitalized on his disabilities to dribble the ball through and around baffled defenders; he was a mainstay of the World Cup championship teams of 1958 and 1962. But the most famous soccer artist of the 20th century was Edson Arantes do Nascimento, whose friends called him Pelé. Born in 1941, he played on all three Brazilian World Cup championship teams between 1958 and 1970.

Pelé had every skill required not only for success but also for stardom. Joseph Page says it best: "He had it all: speed, mobility, a sense of oneness with the ball, uncanny vision, a fearsome shot off either foot, and, the crowning touch, an audacious, instinctive creativity." Pelé was both an amazingly productive goal-scorer and a marvelous passer who made all his teammates look spectacular. Films of his games show a man who dominated the field as though the sport had been invented for his personal fulfillment. Beyond this, his sunny disposition and expansive personality made him the ideal ambassador for soccer, a star who loved people and would talk with anyone. An artist with a soccer ball and a captivating person, Pelé and his exceptional teammates gave Brazilians ample reason to feel proud during the difficult decade of the 1960s.

Economic pressures force the military to return power to civilians

RETURN TO DEMOCRACY . . . AGAIN. By the late 1970s, economic problems encouraged Brazilians to question the government on other grounds. Its human rights policy alienated the powerful Catholic Church, which denounced the government through the National Council of Brazilian Bishops and supported striking workers. Even former supporters of the military dictatorship began calling for a return to civilian rule, and the regime had little choice but to liberalize. Gradually it eased restrictions on personal liberties, and in 1985 Brazil held its first free presidential election since 1960.

Civilian rule was welcomed throughout the country, but the two-decade military dictatorship had traumatized everyone. The people no longer viewed the army as an impartial guarantor of good government, though a younger group of generals tried to reassure civilians that the military would no longer intervene in politics. Yet the new civilian leaders proved no more capable of handling the economy than their military predecessors. Inflation exceeded 200 percent in both 1985 and 1990, wiping out the economic gains of 1967–1974.

◄●├ Read the Document

Brazil's Constitution of 1988

on **myhistorylab.com**

In 2000, of Latin American nations, only Argentina's economic situation was worse. Then, in 2002 the Brazilian presidency was won by Luís Inacio da Silva (*ē-NAH-sē-ō dah SEAL-vah*), who called himself Lula. A former auto mechanic, he was the first president in Brazilian history to come from a nonprivileged background, and his career as a labor organizer and leftist politician led wealthy Brazilians to view him as a dangerous radical. But once in office, Lula and his economic team rescued Brazil from the brink of financial default, revised the public pension system, and made significant progress in reforming the nation's antiquated, inequitable tax structure. His practical policies raised the possibility that Brazil might begin to close the gap between rich and poor and reach its economic potential.

Chile: Socialism, Militarism, and Democracy

For Chile, the early decades of the 20th century were disruptive. The country's institutional framework had come apart in the Revolution of 1891 (Chapter 28), and politicians in Chile's capital of Santiago had been unable to reassemble it. The country was troubled by wildly fluctuating copper and nitrate prices after World War I. Reformers such as Arturo Alessandri tried to modernize but were periodically replaced by military regimes that proved no more capable of stabilizing the nation.

Chilean miners mine for copper.

The Great Depression devastated Chile. Exports of copper and nitrates, as well as their prices on the world market, declined steeply. The military regime, unable to cope with the social chaos caused by the Depression, called Alessandri back to office in 1932. He drastically reduced government spending, and the gradual global economic recovery in the mid-1930s helped stabilize Chile's economy. But the nation's rigid class structure, dominated by ancient families of Basque origin, kept the majority of its citizens on the edge of poverty. World War II temporarily eased social tensions by increasing demand for Chile's minerals, but the end of the war reduced that demand and plunged the "shoestring republic," one of the planet's most geographically isolated nations, into the Cold War.

The Great Depression cripples Chile

CHILE AND THE COLD WAR. At first Chile seemed an unlikely place for Cold War confrontation. Despite the country's deep class divisions, which seemed ripe for Marxist analysis, neither Moscow nor Washington considered the country particularly important until a Marxist physician named Salvador Allende began running for president every six years, from 1952 through 1970.

Allende preached a message of social equality and redistribution of wealth that caught the imaginations of many lower-class Chileans. After Fidel Castro's revolution in Cuba, the United States came to view an Allende victory as a potential propaganda disaster for capitalism. Such an event would be the first instance of a Marxist candidate winning a truly free election and would stamp Communism as the "wave of the future" in Latin America. Chile therefore took on a significance out of all proportion to its actual status in international affairs. In 1964 the United States poured millions of dollars into the campaign of Allende's opponent, Eduardo Frei (*FRĪ*). Frei won the election, but his moderate reform programs did not achieve the "Revolution in Liberty" he had promised. The 1970 elections were widely viewed as a showdown between capitalism and Marxism.

Once again the United States spent heavily to influence the outcome, but this time, in a three-way race, Allende won the presidency by a narrow margin. He promised that at the end of his six-year term he would leave office willingly and turn power over to his legal successor. Yet Communist governments did not permit free elections, and although Allende was a Socialist, much of his support came from Communists. The Chilean military, recalling its unsuccessful efforts to govern the country in the 1920s and 1930s, initially supported Allende as the rightful president, preventing would-be revolutionaries from taking action.

ALLENDE'S MARXIST EXPERIMENT. The United States, however, was determined to remove Allende from office. The Nixon administration cut off Chile's sources of credit and pressured foreign lenders to call in their debts. At the same time, Allende miscalculated drastically. He authorized huge wage increases for Chilean workers, hoping that a sharp increase in the demand for manufactured goods would stimulate industrial production. All it stimulated was runaway inflation, which rose to 566 percent annually by 1973. In rural areas, peasants seized lands from their owners and ignored Allende's demands that they return them. By mid-1973 Chile was plagued by a series of strikes, the most serious of which were two work stoppages by truckers, indispensable movers of goods and services in that oddly shaped land. The military had backed Allende for nearly three years despite strong U.S. pressure, but it finally decided to remove him after the second truckers' strike.

Allende's election leads to U.S. destabilization efforts

On September 11, 1973, Chilean air force planes bombed the Moneda Palace, and as tanks shelled the building and infantry broke in, Allende committed suicide. More than two thousand people died in the bloodiest military takeover in South American history. Power passed to a four-man *junta* composed of chiefs of the Chilean armed services. The dominant member, General Augusto Pinochet ($\bar{o}$-*GOOSE-t$\bar{o}$ p$\bar{e}$-n$\bar{o}$-SHAY* or *p$\bar{e}$-n$\bar{o}$-SHET*), had supported Allende until his final month in office. Pinochet, following the model of the Brazilian military dictatorship, refused to return power to civilian officials and ruled Chile for 17 years.

CHILEAN ARTISTRY: PABLO NERUDA. Watching these events in horror was Pablo Neruda, Chile's finest poet and the 1971 winner of the Nobel Prize for Literature. Born in Santiago in 1904, Neruda began writing poetry at the age of 9. Three years later he met the Chilean poet Gabriela Mistral, herself a Nobel Prize winner, who encouraged his ambitions and urged him to read British and American poets. Neruda soon discovered the writings of the American Walt Whitman, who became the major influence on his work.

After completing his education, Neruda joined the Chilean foreign service in 1927 and was posted to several South and East Asian and Eastern European countries, where he became, as he later recalled, "a citizen of the world." By the 1930s he was a dedicated Communist, serving in Spain as a Chilean diplomat during the Spanish Civil War. Returning to Chile in 1938, he left the foreign service and became a professional writer and poet, as well as an active Communist politician.

Pinochet installs a brutal military dictatorship

Neruda remained a Communist until Nikita Khruschev's Secret Speech in 1956 (Chapter 34) disillusioned him and forced him to critically examine his earlier adherence to Marxism. But he never lost his sympathy for the condition of the working classes in Chile and elsewhere, and he used his 1971 Nobel acceptance speech to call attention to their plight. Only Borges matched him in international fame among Latin American writers, and the two men were friends for many years, despite their disagreements about many current issues. Ill with heart disease for years, Neruda died suddenly on September 23, 1973, twelve days after the overthrow of Allende, whom he had supported vigorously.

NOT WANTED

GENERAL AUGUSTO PINOCHET

because of his crimes against humanity!

PROTEST VISIT OF CHILE'S HITLER TO U.S.
Wed., Sept. 7, 5:00pm
Lan-chile 6 W. 51 ST. at 5ᵗʰ AVE.

Anti-Pinochet poster, 1977.

PINOCHET'S BRUTAL DICTATORSHIP. In a series of violent outbreaks during the first five months of the military dictatorship, Neruda's home was looted and vandalized after his death. This was only one way in which Pinochet's government attacked its opponents. Suspects were beaten, tortured, and held without bail or notification to families, and in many cases they simply disappeared. Some were buried in mass graves in remote areas; others were thrown alive out of airplanes over the Pacific, after having their bellies slit open so the bodies would not float. The regime, acting on its belief that authoritarian government was superior to popular sovereignty, set out to destroy Chilean democracy, declaring all political parties illegal, dissolving Congress, and suspending the constitution.

Pinochet turned Chile's economy over to economists from the University of Chicago, and in the late 1970s Chile experienced impressive prosperity. Social programs were either slashed or abolished, and the lower classes were placed on what amounted to an austerity program. Inflation declined to 32 percent in 1978 and 10 percent in 1982. Chile's economy grew at an average rate of 7 percent from 1976 through 1981, although purchasing power declined and the gap between rich and poor widened dramatically.

In 1980 Pinochet wrote a new constitution extending his presidential term to 1990. But a recession in the early 1980s dampened public enthusiasm for his regime, and the Latin American financial crisis of 1982, brought on by Mexico's decision to default on its foreign debt, hit the Chilean economy hard. Unemployment soon reached 30 percent of the work force, and the regime was forced to confront urban demonstrations on the 11th of each month, beginning on September 11, 1983, the tenth anniversary of the takeover.

As the economy slowly recovered, international pressure on the regime mounted. Pope John Paul II, for example, visited Santiago in 1986 and refused to appear in public with Pinochet. The Pope, who advocated democracy in Poland and other Soviet bloc nations, could not appear to endorse the destroyer of Chilean democracy. The United States continued to support the dictatorship because of Pinochet's anti-Communist policies, but most European states urged Pinochet to step down.

In 1988, apparently convinced of his own popularity, Pinochet held a special election: a "yes" vote would retain him in office until 1997, while a "no" vote would call for a return to civilian rule. Opposition forces created an alliance called the **Concertación** (*kahn-sair-tah-sē-ŌN*), which orchestrated television advertisements complete with rock music proclaiming "The Moral Supremacy of the No." The alliance also rented a large network of computers to monitor the election for vote fraud. By a 55–43 percent margin, "no" defeated "yes," and after some cautious bargaining, Pinochet accepted the verdict. His democratically elected successors were committed to restoring democracy, working for social justice, and promptly investigating human rights abuses that had occurred during the military dictatorship. By 2010, Chile's democratic institutions had been reinvigorated, and the nation's economy was the most stable in South America.

Mexico: The Legacy of the Revolution

Mexico, dominated by dictators for most of the 19th century, changed dramatically early in the 20th (Map 36.5). The dictator Porfirio Díaz had worked hard from 1876 to

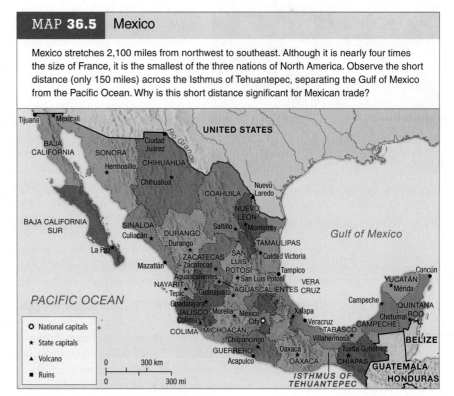

MAP 36.5 | Mexico

Mexico stretches 2,100 miles from northwest to southeast. Although it is nearly four times the size of France, it is the smallest of the three nations of North America. Observe the short distance (only 150 miles) across the Isthmus of Tehuantepec, separating the Gulf of Mexico from the Pacific Ocean. Why is this short distance significant for Mexican trade?

1910 to modernize the nation, attracting foreign investment, building a large railway network, and working closely with scientists and technicians to develop an industrial base. But social and political repression remained, with most Mexican peasants working as a landless class and voting rights limited to a very small number of property-owning men. Many educated Mexicans believed that economic modernization could not succeed without social and political reform. Díaz was driven out in a violent revolution in 1911, and the leader of the rebels, Francisco Madero, became president of Mexico.

THE REVOLUTION OF 1910–1920. In 1911 it appeared that the Mexican Revolution was over, but it lasted nine more years. Madero, focusing on political democracy, underestimated the severity of Mexico's social and economic problems. Rival leaders Emiliano Zapata and Pancho Villa (*VĒ-yah*) took up arms against him on behalf of vast numbers of impoverished Mexicans. In 1913, elements in the Mexican army that had previously supported the Díaz dictatorship took advantage of these divisions to overthrow and murder Madero. Mexico then endured seven years of turbulence, civil war, and U.S. intervention before the revolution finally ended in 1920.

Mexico embarks on a social revolution

The Mexican Revolution developed into a more radical social movement than observers had expected in 1910. The Constitution of 1917 provided a means for far-reaching land redistribution to the peasants. It also placed severe restrictions on the Catholic Church (whose leadership, like that of the military, had supported Díaz) and granted unprecedented rights to organized labor. If implemented completely, it would revolutionize the ownership of property and the exercise of power in Mexico. But it was so radical that even its partial implementation brought on recurring cycles of rebellion, civil war, and political assassination, with displaced elites fighting radical reformers for control of the country.

Dream of a Sunday Afternoon in the Alameda Central by Diego Rivera (1947). Frida Kahlo is to the left of the figure of death.

In the midst of this chaos, the government commissioned some of Mexico's most prominent artists to paint educational murals on the walls of public buildings. The purpose was to display great events in Mexican history to the three out of four adults who, in 1920, could not read, but the consequence was to create an artistic school known as Mexican muralism. Its chief practitioners—José Clemente Orozco, David Alfaro Siqueiros, and Diego Rivera—quickly became famous throughout the world for their strikingly innovative use of vivid colors and dramatic techniques. Rivera's wife, Frida Kahlo, while not herself a muralist, also became a powerful nationalistic artist in her own right. Together their work publicized the sufferings and achievements of Mexican historical figures as well as populist themes.

Rivera's highly realistic and colorful murals conveyed a clear social message—that it was time to return the Amerind to the mainstream of Mexican society. Rivera and Kahlo, as well as Siqueiros, were Communists, and their leftist politics and social activism typified the radicalism of many who experienced the Mexican Revolution. It was that sort of radicalism that those who wished to institutionalize the Revolution hoped to channel into stabilizing activities.

The PRI brings stability without genuine democracy

INSTITUTIONALIZATION: THE PRI. The development of the Institutional Revolutionary Party, or **PRI**, ended social and political turmoil. Claiming to embody the true spirit of the Mexican Revolution, it was so successful in winning elections that it was nicknamed the "Factory of Presidents." The PRI's corporate structure guaranteed representation for peasants, workers, middle class, and military, thus tying it closely to the principal elements of Mexican society. With widespread support, the PRI found it easy to elect candidates, but it also resorted to vote fraud in those few instances when popularity was not enough. From 1929 to 2000, its dominance gave Mexico one of Latin America's most politically stable governments.

This political stability, however, concealed serious social and economic inequalities. Even though the Constitution of 1917 had been designed to alleviate poverty, by 1929 most Mexican peasants still had no hope of owning enough land to feed their families. During the presidency of Lázaro Cárdenas (1934–1940), this situation was partially corrected. Cárdenas nationalized foreign oil companies and transferred farmland from large landowners to collective farms, similar in some respects to those in Soviet Russia. He became the most popular president in Mexican history, a revolutionary icon whose faded photograph still hangs on the walls of dwellings throughout Mexico.

POLITICAL AND ECONOMIC STRAINS. The Cárdenas presidency marked the most radical phase of the Mexican Revolution. When World War II began and Mexico sided firmly with the United States, radicalism and even egalitarianism were suppressed. In the immediate postwar years, the PRI restrained domestic opposition and increased its power through corruption and favoritism. When Fidel Castro seized power in nearby Cuba and attempted to export Communism to other Latin American countries, Mexico reacted sharply, fearing both Communist action and U.S. reaction. Mexican apprehension grew even stronger in the 1980s, when leftist rebellions in Nicaragua and El Salvador sent refugees fleeing into Mexico, threatening to destabilize a nation for which political stability, won with such difficulty, had become an end in itself.

Mexican relations with the United States remained close. In 1963 the Kennedy administration agreed to return a disputed border region to Mexico. Thirty years later, the creation of the North American Free Trade Area appeared highly beneficial to the Mexican economy, which had grown consistently between 1958 and 1973 but had been depressed since the mid-1980s by low crude oil prices. A U.S. loan of $20 billion (repaid with interest two years later) lent support to Mexico's economy in the mid-1990s, and NAFTA, which reduced tariffs between the United States, Mexico, and Canada, promised to stimulate economic growth for all its participants.

Mexico maintains good relations with the United States

These developments might have worked to the PRI's advantage, but the party was damaged by three scandalous events. First, President Gustavo Díaz Ordaz ordered the army and police to shoot hundreds of student demonstrators in Mexico City just before the 1968 Olympic Games. The students had been protesting the authoritarian nature of Mexico's allegedly democratic government, and this "Tlatelolco Massacre" proved that they were right. The slaughter undermined the PRI's reputation and credibility. Second, revelations that Carlos Salinas (*sah-LĒ-nahss*), president from 1988 to 1994, had embezzled hundreds of millions of dollars from the federal treasury forced him to flee the country following the end of his term. The scandal spotlighted PRI corruption and cost the party much of the legitimacy it had earned through more than six decades of reasonably competent rule. Third, the PRI candidate for president claimed to have won the 1994 election despite the widespread belief that Cuahtémoc (*kwah-TĀ-mock*) Cárdenas, son of Lázaro, had actually won, and that the PRI had stolen the election through massive vote fraud. By the late 1990s, the PRI was under serious challenge.

Scandals bring down the PRI

For the first time since the 1920s, other parties presented competitive alternatives to the PRI, and in 2000 one of them, the Partido del Acción Nacional (PAN, or National Action Party), elected its presidential candidate, Vicente Fox, in the most stunning Mexican political upheaval in eighty years. Mexico then embarked on a transition from one-party government to multiparty democracy.

The PRI loses a presidential election

Fox had a difficult time in office. The PRI remained in control of Congress, blocking most of his initiatives. Extensive illegal immigration to the United States troubled relations

View the **Map**

Atlas Map: Latin America, 2004

on **myhistorylab.com**

between the two neighbors. Even NAFTA, which had been implemented with such high hopes, fell victim to globalization of the world economy. Although many jobs from the United States relocated to Mexico because of its cheap labor, many more relocated from Mexico to China, where labor was even less expensive. Fox was succeeded as president in 2006 by Felipe Calderón of PAN, but this second successive non-PRI president faced growing economic difficulties.

Six Regional Transitions

By the early 21st century, the principal nations of Latin America had begun to emerge from long, difficult struggles with their authoritarian heritage. Argentina, Brazil, Chile, and Mexico had developed democratic institutions and had committed their societies to making those institutions work. The region seemed more politically stable than at any other time since the era of independence. Yet it still faced critical social and economic transitions, six of which are considered here.

Gender Roles

For centuries, Latin American women were largely confined to the home and the care of children, placing them outside the public sphere. The Spanish and Portuguese conquests had brought the Iberian concept of **machismo,** the praise of masculine virility and power, into Amerind societies already dominated by men. Iberian-American women were expected to be models of spiritual and moral superiority and purity, models that do not allow active participation in the sometimes corrupt aspects of public life.

Women such as Evita Perón broke with this model in some ways, but not in others. Evita exercised immense influence in Argentina between 1945 and 1952, but that influence derived largely from her ability to depict herself as "the mother of the people," thereby retaining traditional feminine attributes while projecting her energies into the public sphere. When she fell ill with uterine cancer, her physician was too embarrassed to disclose to her the true severity of her illness, because it was a female disorder—and Evita, observing the same convention, never asked about her condition until it was too late.

Evita Perón's example reveals one dimension of the challenge facing Latin American women. In the 20th century, they gained access to higher education and pursued careers in various professions, including medicine and law. But while they began to play public roles in areas such as human rights, education, and economic security, they did not address issues such as workplace equality and reproductive rights. Many Latin American women remain uncomfortable with those and similar issues, in part because action in such matters requires a level of political activism that might compromise the spiritual and moral purity associated with womanhood.

A Peruvian couple, late 19th century.

Latin American women face systemic challenges

Inequality

Latin American societies were highly stratified, with tremendous inequalities of wealth between upper and lower classes. In the 16th century, Iberian social structures were imposed upon Amerind societies that were themselves hierarchical. The Spanish and Portuguese kings simply replaced the Aztec and Inca emperors, and Iberian conquistadors replaced Amerind nobles. After independence, Iberian-descended owners of large landed estates and prosperous merchants and bankers formed a new aristocracy based on

Amerinds from Tierra del Fuego, Chile.

wealth. They restricted their ranks by limiting other groups' access to higher education and legally barring them from land ownership.

These inequalities continue to trouble Latin America in the 21st century. Although Mexico and Argentina allow access to higher education based on merit, Brazil, the region's largest and potentially most prosperous country, views higher education as solely for privileged elites. Fewer than 1 percent of adult Brazilians have college or university degrees, a figure that demonstrates how difficult it is for lower-class Brazilians to attain upward social mobility.

((•—[Listen to the **Audio**

Latin America

on **myhistorylab.com**

Debt

To reduce debt, Latin American nations struggle to increase economic productivity, but the two aims often work against each other. Argentina, Brazil, and Mexico, in particular, are burdened with huge indebtedness to foreign lenders, most of it occurring recently. As the new civilian governments took charge of their nations' economies, they took responsibility for existing debts but also increased them. In the 1990s, Latin American nations finally began to achieve some prosperity, as massive foreign investment reduced inflation and produced solid economic growth. Yet the region remains highly vulnerable to fluctuations in global demand for its exports, as well as to sharp swings in world financial markets: Mexico's financial system crashed in 1994, and Argentina's in 2000.

During this economic turmoil, international agencies such as the International Monetary Fund and the World Bank lent large sums to Latin American countries to help them cover interest payments on existing debt. This new money came with conditions: recipients were required to open their economies to foreign investment, reduce inflation, and minimize government's role in economic life. The last of these promoted democratization by encouraging military leaders, most of them wedded to governmental control of the economy, to turn their powers over to civilians. But it also increased the size of the debt it was helping to service. Without significant increases in economic productivity, Latin American debt will continue to weigh heavily on the region.

Debt continues to hamper Latin American economies

Demographic pressures hinder Latin America's development

Population

The prospects for sustainable economic growth and meaningful social change in Latin America are profoundly affected by population growth. Demand for resources, availability of jobs, and provision of adequate social services are all population dependent. In the 1960s it was frequently stated that Latin America's "population explosion" would doom the region to perpetual poverty if drastic measures were not taken to control the size of families. In 1970 the average number of children per Latin American family was six. Three decades later, access to contraception and improvements in education for women had helped reduce the number of children per family in nations such as Mexico and Brazil to 2.5.

Yet because children and youth constitute such a large proportion of Latin American populations, in coming years millions will be ready for the workplace but unable to find employment. This situation will have a negative impact on Latin American productivity and ability to pay interest on debts. It will also promote emigration. Progress has been made in controlling population growth, but decades of sustained effort will be required to stabilize that growth at economically beneficial levels.

The skyline of São Paulo, Brazil's largest city.

Poverty

The four transitions already discussed must be successfully completed if Latin America is to emerge from the cycle of poverty that has plagued it for centuries. Poor people cannot afford to educate women, cannot struggle effectively against inequality and for social justice, and cannot contribute to their nations' efforts to reduce indebtedness. Nor can the poor be counted on to reduce population growth, since many of them see large numbers of children as insurance for old age, not as obstacles to economic advancement. As long as Latin American elites, who control the productive capacities of their nations, fail to grasp the importance of distributing wealth and purchasing power more equitably, their societies will remain impoverished and weak. Poverty, in turn, will negate the best efforts of democratic governments to modernize those societies and improve living standards.

Religion

As Latin America entered the 21st century, its religious allegiance was changing significantly for the first time in nearly five hundred years. The Iberian conquest installed Catholicism as the only religion permissible under colonial rule. Iberian Catholicism, rich in tradition and ritual, proved attractive to Amerinds, whose own religious practices were often highly ritualized. Until the 1960s, no other religion enjoyed a significant following in Latin America.

Latin American Catholicism begins to lose some of its influence

Then reforms in the Roman Catholic Church diminished its appeal to Latin Americans. The Second Vatican Council, held from 1962 to 1965, brought together Church officials and theologians from around the world to try to modernize Catholicism in response to total war, the Holocaust, the emergence of Marxism, and other upheavals of the 20th century. The Council's changes in the Catholic Mass, designed to simplify the worship service and increase popular participation through the use of local languages, troubled many Latin Americans who cherished the complex rituals they had known since childhood. Some turned to evangelical Protestant Christianity, which since the early 1970s has been growing rapidly in Latin America, in part because it provides the ceremony and mystery that many Latin American Catholics expect in their religious services.

In addition to simplifying the Mass, Catholicism addressed the appeal of Marxists like Cuba's Castro and Chile's Allende by advocating improvement in the conditions endured by the poor. Latin American bishops and cardinals were expected to take the side of the poor against the wealthy elites, and to stand firmly for social and economic justice. Theologians from Mexico and Brazil developed a concept of **liberation theology**, which held that Jesus of Nazareth had preached not only a message of love but also a message of opposition to unjust government. Liberation theologians urged cooperation between Catholics and Marxists against Latin American upper classes that kept the poor impoverished. That message was sometimes dangerous to deliver, as evidenced by the assassination of Roman Catholic bishop Oscar Romero of El Salvador by a right-wing death squad in 1980.

Despite such risks, liberation theology flourished from 1968 through 1979, but after that a new Catholic leader, Pope John Paul II (1979–2005), restrained its practitioners. The new pope, who supported anti-Marxist liberation throughout Eastern Europe, was not unmoved by

Mayan ceremony on the steps of a Catholic church, Mexico.

cries for justice. But he believed that the Catholic faith and Marxism, which denies that anything spiritual can exist, could never be reconciled, and that cooperation between the two was shortsighted and dangerous. Catholicism's abandonment of liberation theology nonetheless disappointed many Latin American Catholics. Efforts by Catholics and evangelical Protestants to develop a theology that addresses Latin American realities testify to religious transitions ongoing in the region.

Putting It in Perspective

Latin American countries passed through many dramatic changes during the 20th century. Each of the region's main nations—Argentina, Brazil, Chile, and Mexico—endured either violent revolutions or brutal military dictatorships. Each entertained fresh hopes for the consolidation of democracy as the century ended. Cuba played a surprisingly significant role during the Cold War because of Fidel Castro's Communist revolution, but its ability to destabilize the region waned with the end of that conflict and the Soviet Union's collapse. By the early 21st century, Latin America seemed politically stable, poised to

fulfill its sizable potential and improve living standards for its hundreds of millions of people.

Latin American societies remained profoundly traditional, however, burdened with inequitable social hierarchies and deeply held convictions about the subordinate role of women and the irrelevance of higher education for both men and women. Important progress had been made in limiting the pace of population growth, an achievement that required the alteration of long-standing religious beliefs and social conventions, but economic and social inequalities remain as challenges to prosperity.

Reviewing Key Material

KEY CONCEPTS

braceros, 867
Monroe Doctrine, 868
Roosevelt Corollary, 868
gunboat diplomacy, 869
Good Neighbor Policy, 869
Sandinista Front for
    National Liberation, 871
North American Free
    Trade Area (NAFTA),
    871
UCR, 871
descamisados, 872

Montoneros, 873
Tupamaros, 873
"dirty war," 875
Mothers of the Plaza de
    Mayo, 875
MERCOSUR, 875
Estado Nôvo, 876
Concertación, 881
PRI, 882
machismo, 884
liberation theology,
    886

KEY PEOPLE

Salvador Allende, 863,
    879
Theodore Roosevelt, 868
Franklin Roosevelt, 869
Fidel Castro, 869
Hipólito Yrigoyen, 871
Juan Perón, 872

Evita Perón, 872
Getúlio Vargas, 875
Arturo Alessandri, 879
Augusto Pinochet, 880
Porfirio Díaz, 881
Lázaro Cárdenas, 883
Oscar Romero, 886

ASK YOURSELF

1. In what ways were Juan Perón's presidencies beneficial to Argentina, and in what ways were they harmful? What circumstances undermined Argentine stability after Perón was gone?
2. How did the Cold War, and the Castro regime in Cuba, affect Latin American stability? Why did Salvador Allende's government appear so disturbing to the United States?
3. Why did military regimes in Argentina, Brazil, and Chile eventually relinquish power to civilians?
4. How did the Institutional Revolutionary Party stabilize Mexican politics?

GOING FURTHER

Andrews, George. *Afro-Latin America, 1800–2000*. 2004.
Constable, Pamela, and Arturo Valenzuela. *A Nation of Enemies: Chile Under Pinochet*. 1991.
Hahner, June. *Emancipating the Female Sex: The Struggle for Women's Rights in Brazil, 1850–1940*. 1990.
Harding, Rachel. *A Refuge in Thunder: Candomblé*. 2000.

Kaufman, Edy. *Crisis in Allende's Chile: New Perspectives.* 1988.

Knight, Alan. *The Mexican Revolution.* 1986.

Loveman, Brian. *Chile: The Legacy of Hispanic Capitalism.* 1999.

Meyer, Michael, and William Sherman. *The Course of Mexican History.* 6th ed. 1999.

Pablos, Julia. *Women in Mexico: A Past Unveiled.* 1999.

Pérez, Louis, Jr. *Cuba: Between Reform and Revolution.* 1995.

Rock, David. *Argentina, 1516–1987.* 1987.

Skidmore, Thomas. *Brazil: Five Centuries of Change.* 1999.

Skidmore, Thomas. *The Politics of Military Rule in Brazil, 1964–1985.* 1988.

Szulc, Tad. *Fidel: A Critical Portrait.* 1986.

Taylor, Diana. *Disappearing Acts: Spectacles of Gender and Nationalism in Argentina's "Dirty War."* 1997.

Thomas, Hugh. *Cuba: The Pursuit of Freedom.* 1971.

Turits, Richard. *Foundations of Despotism: Peasants, the Trujillo Regime, and Modernity in Dominican History.* 2003.

Womack, John, Jr. *Zapata and the Mexican Revolution.* 1968.

Woodward, Ralph. *Central America: A Nation Divided.* 1999.

Key Dates and Developments

Argentina

1916	Yrigoyen (UCR) elected president
1930	Military coup overthrows President Yrigoyen
1943	Military coup overthrows President Castillo
1946–1955	First presidency of Juan D. Perón
1952	Death of Evita Perón
1973–1974	Second presidency of Juan D. Perón
1976–1983	Military dictatorship and "dirty war"
1982	Argentina defeated by Britain in Falklands War
1983	Raúl Alfonsín elected president
2000	Argentine currency collapses

Brazil

1919	Brazil participates in Paris Peace Conference
1921	World rubber prices collapse
1929	World coffee prices collapse
1930	Revolution brings Getúlio Vargas to power
1930–1945	First presidency of Getúlio Vargas
1937	Creation of the *Estado Nôvo*
1942	Brazil declares war on Germany
1946	Volta Redonda steel plant opens
1950–1954	Second presidency of Getúlio Vargas
1958, 1962, 1970, 1994, 2002	Brazil wins Soccer World Cup
1964–1985	Military dictatorship

1967–1974	Brazilian "Economic Miracle"
1975	Freeze destroys Brazilian coffee crop
1985	Democracy returns
2002	Luís Inacio de Silva ("Lula") elected president

Chile

1920–1924	First presidency of Arturo Alessandri
1932–1938	Second presidency of Arturo Alessandri
1964–1970	Presidency of Eduardo Frei; United States begins to intervene in Chilean politics
1970–1973	Presidency of Salvador Allende
1973	Overthrow and suicide of Allende
1973–1990	Augusto Pinochet's military dictatorship
1988	Referendum rejects Pinochet's rule
1998–2000	Pinochet arrested in Britain
2000	Socialist Ricardo Lagos elected president

Mexico

1910–1920	The Mexican Revolution
1928	Creation of the "Official Party" (PRI in 1945)
1934–1940	Presidency of Lázaro Cárdenas
1963	U.S. returns El Chamizal to Mexico
1968	Tlatelolco Massacre
1993	Creation of NAFTA
2000	Vicente Fox elected as first non-PRI president since 1924

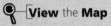 myhistörylab Connections

Reinforce what you learned in this chapter by studying the many documents, images, maps, review tools, and videos available at www.myhistorylab.com.

Read and Review

✓● Study and Review Chapter 36

📖● Read the Document

Francisco García Calderón, Excerpt from *Latin America: Its Rise and Progress,* p. 863

Juan Perón, Excerpt from *The Voice of Perón*, p. 869

Fidel Castro, "History Will Absolve Me," 1953, p. 869

John F. Kennedy and Cuba (1961), p. 870

Brazil's Constitution of 1988, p. 878

🔍● View the Image

Unloading Coffee in Brazil, p. 866

Soviet Deputy Premier in Cuba, p. 870

((●● Listen to the Audio

Latin America, p. 885

👁● Watch the Video

The Cuban Missile Crisis, p. 871

Research and Explore

🔍● View the Map

Atlas Map: Latin America, 2004, p. 884

((●● Listen to the Chapter Audio for Chapter 36 on **myhistorylab.com**

37

Postcolonial Challenges in Africa and the Middle East, 1939–Present

((•—[Listen to the **Chapter Audio** for Chapter 37 on **myhistorylab.com**

- How did World War II lead to the decolonization of Africa?

- What factors account for the differing ways in which African nations gained their freedom?

- What challenges did the newly independent African nations face?

- What factors connected Arab nationalism and the Palestinian question?

- In what ways have Islamic nations reacted to the challenges of modernity?

Signing of the Camp David Accords

U.S. president Jimmy Carter looks on approvingly as Egyptian president Anwar al-Sadat (at left) and Israeli prime minister Menachem Begin (at right) sign the Camp David Peace Accords in Washington, March 26, 1979. The peace treaty between Egypt and Israel split the anti-Israeli coalition in the Middle East and marked the beginning of a new era in that region (page 909).

On a sweltering late summer afternoon in September 1961, a small plane crashed in the newly independent nation of Congo. It was carrying United Nations Secretary-General Dag Hammarskjöld (DAHG HAH-mur-shuld) to a meeting with the prime minister of a province attempting to secede from Congo. Hammarskjöld, who died in the crash, was working to negotiate a peaceful settlement of the year-old Congo Crisis. Although he died a hero to the Western world, many black Africans viewed him as a paternalistic white European who was seeking to maintain European influence in the newly emerging nations of Africa.

Forty years later, on a cool, late summer morning in September 2001, the United Nations Secretary-General led a hushed General Assembly in a moment of silence for nearly three thousand people killed the previous week by planes crashed deliberately in a terrorist attack on the United States. Unlike Dag Hammarskjöld, this Secretary-General was not characterized as a paternalistic white European. He was Kofi Annan (KŌ-fē AHN-ahn), a black African from Ghana, a nation independent for only four years at the time of Hammarskjöld's crash.

During those 40 years, the nations of Africa and the Middle East changed dramatically. Although they broke colonial ties with the West, they continued to struggle with resentments and problems developed under colonial rule and in the following decades. The emergence of independent nations in Africa and Southwest Asia, and their efforts to meet the challenges of modernization, could now be seen as watershed developments, filled with meaning for the entire world.

The Context of African Decolonization

In 1910, the possibility that Africans might once again administer their own affairs appeared remote. The global wars of 1914–1918 and 1939–1945 changed that, giving Africans hope that they might be able to break free from their colonial ties to European nations.

The Impact of World War II

Italy's 1935 invasion of Ethiopia, a country whose two millennia of independence had made it a symbol of African resistance to outside rule, combined with Nazi Germany's fanatical racism to convince most Africans to oppose fascism during World War II. African volunteers fought for France and Britain, and when African soldiers led by British officers liberated Ethiopia from Italy in 1941, all Africa rejoiced. Africans even came to hope that their contributions to an eventual Allied victory might help end colonial rule throughout the continent.

Africa's support for the Allied cause was significant. Britain recruited sizable numbers of volunteers in its colonies through village chiefs, while French general Charles de Gaulle's Free French movement (Chapter 33) drafted more than a hundred thousand men in French West Africa alone. Even more crucial to the Allied effort was Africa's resource base, particularly after Japan took resource-rich Southeast Asia in 1941–1942. Africa provided the Allies with large quantities of cotton, palm oil, tin,

((•─ **Listen** to the **Audio**
Decolonization 1
on **myhistorylab.com**

Africa participates actively
in World War II

Workers load cocoa onto a United Africa Company ship at Apapa Wharf, Nigeria, in 1940.

rubber, coffee, tea, and cocoa. These contributions, which assisted both Allied armies and Allied populations at home, placed Britain and France in Africa's debt.

The contributions, however, were not completely beneficial for Africans. Many African soldiers died in combat or returned home maimed, while European exporters paid African producers low fixed prices for their products, which were then sold in Europe at inflated wartime rates. As manufactured goods from Europe were sold in Africa at equally inflated prices, the war left the average African producer materially worse off than before. To Africans in 1945, colonialism offered few benefits.

Africa did gain some long-term advantages from the war. The Allies built airports and improved harbor facilities throughout West Africa, turning Freetown (Sierra Leone) into a vital Atlantic port and developing Accra (Gold Coast) as a staging area for the movement of troops to North Africa. In South Africa, the local manufacture of clothing, tools, and machinery was stimulated by wartime reductions in European imports, and by the end of the war manufacturing replaced mining as the principal element in the country's economic base. Although these industries were owned by whites, they provided a framework of modernization that could be used by independent nations if and when colonialism ended.

Africa derives advantages from World War II

The war also furnished Africans who fought it with perspective and increased self-respect. Notions of white racial superiority vanished as Europeans destroyed themselves and devastated Europe. African soldiers who witnessed the liberation of German death camps saw for themselves the terrifying consequences of belief in a master race. Never again would African military veterans willingly accept white colonial domination.

European attitudes also changed as a result of the war. Charles de Gaulle, for example, knew that France's colonies had given him a base of support without which his Free French movement would have collapsed. He convened a conference of delegates from throughout French Africa at Brazzaville in the French Congo in 1944. There he listened to African aspirations for autonomy within the empire, and explicitly guaranteed major economic, social, and political reforms for African peoples under French rule. As provisional president of France from 1944 to 1946, he fulfilled those commitments. At the same time, the British government, its financial resources depleted by the war, began withdrawing from South Asia and laid plans for movement toward self-government for Britain's African colonies.

European Preparations for Colonial Autonomy

Decolonization in Asia in the first decade after the war did not guarantee that it would follow quickly in Africa. Nationalist movements in Asia dated back to at least 1900, and independence there was earned only after long, grinding struggles. In contrast, most of sub-Saharan Africa's colonial territories lacked nationalist movements in 1945 (Map 37.1). Nonetheless, Britain and France knew from the Asian example that nationalism was a dagger pointed at the heart of colonialism. Colonial officials hoped that the appeal of nationalism could be reduced by granting local autonomy to African colonies while retaining final control in London and Paris.

((•—[**Listen** to the **Audio**
Africa/Zulus 2
on **myhistorylab.com**

Britain and France revise their policies toward Africa

Immediately after the war, in an effort to reshape its empire, Britain developed a complex colonial policy. Its sense of urgency was heightened by the **Fifth Pan-African Congress**, held in Manchester, England, in late summer of 1945. At that gathering,

MAP **37.1**	Africa in 1945

At the end of World War II, the map of Africa had changed very little from what it had looked like in 1919. Notice that most of the continent remained under European colonial rule. Only four independent nations existed: Egypt (partially occupied by British troops), Ethiopia, Liberia, and the Union of South Africa. How would the sweep of decolonization across the continent alter the map of Africa?

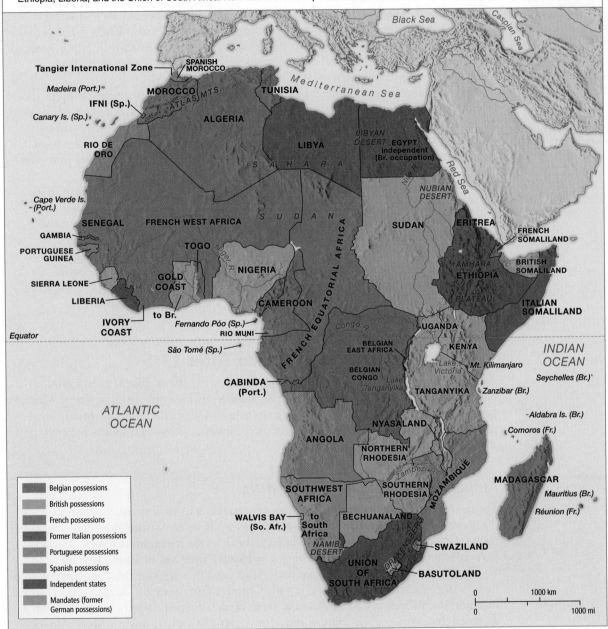

nationalist leaders such as Jomo Kenyatta of Kenya, Léopold Senghor of Senegal, and Kwame Nkrumah (*KWAH-mā un-KROO-mah*) of Gold Coast announced their intention of creating independence movements. Hoping to prevent this, Britain launched a serious effort to modernize its colonies economically and socially. Although only 4 percent of African teenagers were attending secondary schools in 1960, the British

Kwame Nkrumah, Ghanaian independence leader and first president of the country.

Belgium and Portugal prohibit political activity in their African colonies

established colonial universities and improved roads and port facilities. They restructured local government on a democratic basis, forcing nationalist politicians to compete for public support against local chiefs, who could be more easily controlled by the British. In 1948, the white racist National Party won a startling electoral victory in South Africa and implemented its ruthless **apartheid** system of institutionalized racial discrimination. These events frightened London: British settlers in East and Central Africa might be inspired to treat their African majorities similarly, which in turn would increase the appeal of Marxist nationalist movements among Africans. London granted those settlers considerable local autonomy in an effort to prevent South African influence from spreading northward.

Like Britain, France initiated a broad program of economic stimulation in its African colonies, hoping to prevent the development of nationalist movements like the Vietminh in Indochina (Chapter 35). African representation in the French National Assembly was increased, and a new "French Union" was designed to promote joint consideration of policies and programs for the entire empire. Unlike Britain, however, France did not envision local autonomy.

Even Belgium planned for more aggressive economic and social development in its colonies, Ruanda-Urundi and the Belgian Congo. But Brussels continued its traditional policy of obstructing the formation of an African elite, discouraging African access to European universities. Both Belgium and Portugal also prohibited all local political activity, either by Africans or white settlers, expecting to prevent the development of nationalism by simply outlawing politics entirely. Portuguese repression, implemented more rigorously than its Belgian counterpart, held off the independence of its African empire until 1975, more than a decade longer than any of the more flexible European democracies.

The Transformation of Africa After 1945

Africa changed dramatically in the fifty years following World War II as struggles for independence and freedom transformed the continent. Throughout these years, African nationalists hoped that the end of European rule and white domination would bring prosperity and dignity. Independent existence, however, proved far more challenging than they had anticipated.

African Nationalism and the Cold War

The tendency of European and American governments to view decolonization in the context of the Cold War complicated their responses to African independence movements. France, having been defeated in Indochina by the Vietminh (Chapter 35), was particularly concerned about Communist influence. Since Sékou Touré, Kwame Nkrumah, and several other African nationalist leaders were Marxists, and since revolutionary organizations such as Algeria's FLN received weapons and supplies from Soviet bloc nations, including Czechoslovakia, most French prime ministers before de Gaulle assumed that Moscow was controlling African nationalist movements. Many American, Belgian, British, and Portuguese officials held the same assumption.

This conclusion was partly true. The Soviet Union was committed to the destruction of European colonialism in Africa and Asia and routinely offered independence movements verbal support, especially at the United Nations. Moscow also provided weapons and supplies to nationalist movements. But to be a Marxist, particularly in a colonial setting, was significantly different from being a Communist and accepting direction from the Soviet Union.

Read the Document

African National Congress Against Imperialism (1927), Josiah Gumede

on **myhistorylab.com**

Many African nationalists viewed Marxism as an attractive alternative to capitalism. Instead of the apparent chaos of a capitalist marketplace, Marxism offered the stability of an economy controlled by the government. Instead of competition, Marxism offered cooperation, which was highly regarded in traditional African societies. Instead of inequality of wealth, Marxism held that wealth should be distributed "to each according to his needs." These aspects of Marxism were appealing, and they did not require acceptance of Communism. Indeed, becoming Communist seemed to many nationalists to be exchanging one set of European masters for another.

A Marxist poster exhorting Africans and other colonial peoples to rise up against Western powers.

African nationalist leaders often complicated the situation further by accepting aid from both Soviets and Americans during the Cold War. Nkrumah of Ghana, Julius Nyerere of Tanzania, Kenneth Kaunda of Zambia, and Jomo Kenyatta of Kenya were skilled at using superpower competition to their advantage, as was the Egyptian nationalist leader Gamal Abdel Nasser. Both Moscow and Washington lobbied for the support of newly independent nations in the United Nations General Assembly, too easily assuming that governments not openly supportive were aligned with the other side. Once the Cold War ended, it was easier to understand the reality of the situation. African nationalist leaders had been acting in what they believed to be the interests of their own new nations, not in the interests of ideologies like Communism and capitalism, and not in the interests of white, non-African nations like the United States and the Soviet Union.

African nationalist leaders play Washington off against Moscow in the Cold War

North Africa

The Second World War brought German, Italian, British, and American troops to North Africa, throwing that region into turmoil and destabilizing the French and Italian colonial possessions of Morocco, Algeria, Tunisia, and Libya. When Italy lost the war, it also lost Libya (Map 37.2). Morocco and Tunisia were French protectorates, enjoying some degree of local autonomy under native rulers. Meanwhile, the French war in Indochina distracted colonial officials and nationalists alike until 1954, when Algeria took the lead in the struggle for independence in North Africa.

Algeria was technically not a colony, but three departments of France, much as Hawaii is part of the United States. Ninety percent of its residents were Arab or Berber Muslims, but 10 percent were Europeans, many of them descendants of French settlers from the 1830s. On the day World War II ended in Europe, May 8, 1945, a victory parade in the Algerian town of Sétif was disrupted by fights between Algerian nationalists and French soldiers. Eighty-eight French and more than a thousand Algerians died. Combat veterans such as Ahmed Ben Bella and Belkacem Krim responded by forming a secret nationalist organization, the *Front de Libération National*, or FLN. France's defeat in Indochina by the Vietminh gave the FLN confidence to launch the All Saints' Day Rising on November 1, 1954, a coordinated revolt in 45 Algerian cities signaling the beginning of Algeria's struggle for independence.

Algeria liberates itself through armed struggle

That struggle quickly earned the name "the dirty war." The FLN, which never numbered more than twenty thousand, was unable to oppose French army units in conventional warfare, so it used terrorist tactics, planting bombs in schools, post offices, and restaurants, often near windows so that survivors would be blinded by flying glass. The French responded with systematic torture of suspects, a strategy that caused increasing numbers of Algerians to support independence. Each side massacred innocent people connected with the other. By 1958 France had 750,000 soldiers stationed in Algeria, but

MAP 37.2 Decolonization in Africa and Asia, 1941–1985

In 1945, only four African states were independent (Map 37.1). Note that by 1985, nearly the entire continent was self-governing. Most African nations gained independence during the period 1957–1965, a time characterized by British prime minister Harold Macmillan as one in which "winds of change" gusted across Europe's colonial possessions. Comparing Africa with the Middle East and Asia, what does this map tell you about patterns of decolonization?

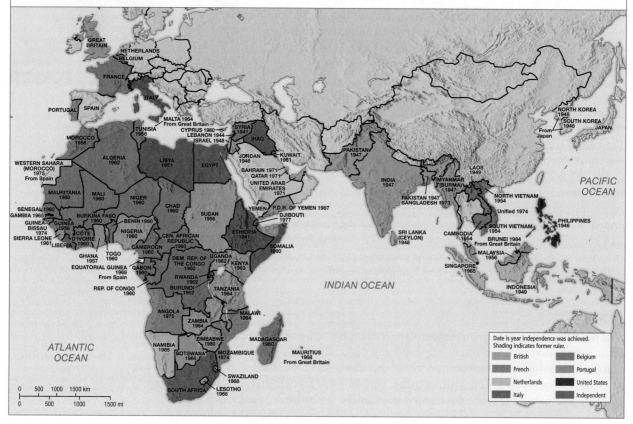

they could not discover and disarm every underground FLN operative. The great majority of Algerian Muslims resisted the French at every turn, sabotaging their military bases, cutting the throats of their sentries at night, and concealing and protecting FLN fighters during French military sweeps and searches.

On May 13, 1958, when the French National Assembly created a cabinet committed to negotiating with the FLN, the French army in Algeria seized control from civilian authorities and threatened to invade France itself unless a government was formed that would keep Algeria French. Blackmailed by its own military, the Assembly turned to France's only hero of World War II, Charles de Gaulle. Invested with emergency powers for six months, de Gaulle pushed through a new French constitution providing for a strong presidency, ran successfully for that office, and used his position to address not only the Algerian war but also the future of the French Empire itself.

De Gaulle's policy toward Algeria astonished nearly everyone. By mid-1959 Algerian Muslim resistance had convinced him that they would never accept continued French rule, and he was not

Members of a women's section of the FLN at a rally supporting Algerian independence.

willing to station a million-man army there to guarantee it. The only alternative was to negotiate Algerian independence, and when de Gaulle's attitude became known, the army revolted in 1960 and 1961, attempting to remove the president and cancel the negotiations. Both times de Gaulle put down the revolt, persuading most French people to support his plan for disengagement while ordering rank-and-file soldiers to arrest or shoot their officers in defense of the government's authority. De Gaulle survived an organized campaign of assassination attempts and successfully removed France from Algeria in 1962.

The rest of North Africa was already free. France, overextended in Algeria, had freed Morocco and Tunisia in 1956, while Egypt, technically independent since 1922, became fully so when British troops evacuated the Suez Canal Zone in 1955. Only Spanish Morocco, also known as Western Sahara, remained as a last vestige of European imperialism north of the Sahara.

The new nations adopted differing styles of governance. Morocco remained a monarchy, as did Libya until 1969. In that year King Idris was overthrown in a conspiracy led by Colonel Muammar al-Qaddafi (*kuh-DAH-fē*), who ruled as a military dictator into the 21st century. The father of Tunisian independence, Habib Bourguiba (boor-GĒ-buh), ruled Tunisia as "president for life" until driven out in 1987; his replacement was no more democratic. The Egyptian revolution of 1952 that overthrew King Farouk brought the army to power under Gamal Abdel Nasser (1952–1970), Anwar al-Sadat (1970–1981), and Hosni Mubarak (1981-2011). In Algeria, the FLN ruled alone until 1988, when an opposition movement of Islamist fundamentalists weakened it to the point that the military was forced to step in, an action that provoked widespread atrocities as fundamentalists then fought the military. North Africa's difficulties since independence have been primarily political; the region has by and large achieved economic stability and has escaped the health crises and extensive poverty common in sub-Saharan Africa.

> **Read** the **Document**
> *Frantz Fanon, from The Wretched of the Earth*
> on **myhistorylab.com**

Issues of governance arise in North Africa

Sub-Saharan Africa

South of the Sahara, hopes for new beginnings flourished in the late 1950s. The success of independence movements in North Africa inspired Africans farther south to press harder for self-determination. Between 1957 and 1965, one former colony after another gained its freedom. In the following decades, however, the hopes that accompanied independence dimmed. Climatic changes caused severe droughts south of the Sahara, and as the desert expanded southward, millions were displaced and malnourished. In the 1980s, an incurable disease called AIDS (acquired immune deficiency syndrome) infected tens of millions of Africans, mostly south of the Sahara. By 1995, nations such as Uganda, Botswana, and Zimbabwe were experiencing population reductions, as life expectancy for men fell into the upper 30s. Africans south of the Sahara had overcome colonialism, but not poverty and disease.

Britain liberates its African colonies

BRITAIN'S RETREAT FROM EMPIRE. Britain's African empire slipped away more slowly than France's. Beginning in 1947, London gradually surrendered control over the Gold Coast. There the dynamic nationalist leader Kwame Nkrumah became secretary of the United Gold Coast Convention, modeled to some extent on the successful Indian National Congress. Nkrumah led a series of strikes against British rule in the late 1940s, for which he spent several years in prison, eventually becoming prime minister when the Gold Coast became independent Ghana in 1957. By that time, failure in the 1956 Suez Crisis (discussed later in this chapter) had convinced London that it could not retain all its far-flung possessions.

A pro-independence demonstration in Ghana.

The West African colony of Nigeria gained freedom in 1960, while Sierra Leone and The Gambia followed in 1961.

Read the **Document**

Kwame Nkrumah on African Unity (1960s)

on **myhistorylab.com**

In British East Africa, four colonies (Kenya, Uganda, Tanganyika, and Zanzibar) followed separate paths to become three independent nations. Nationalists led by Julius Nyerere (*nē-eh-RĀ-rā*) formed the Tanganyikan African Nationalist Union (TANU) in 1954, using Nkrumah's Gold Coast Convention as a model. Nyerere brought different African peoples together through use of the Swahili language, for centuries the language of East African trade. Tanganyika gained independence in 1961, merging in 1964 with the offshore island sultanate of Zanzibar to create Tanzania. In neighboring Uganda, the Uganda People's Congress led a political alliance that gained freedom for the colony in 1962.

Kenya's independence movement was the last to succeed in British East Africa. Oppression of Africans by white settlers in the lush Kenyan highlands provoked a rural uprising there in 1952, led by an organization called Mau Mau (*MAOW MAOW*). This organization sought sweeping redistribution of white-owned lands to Kenyans rather than political independence, and most Kenyan nationalists disapproved of its violent tactics. Mau Mau burned white settlers' crops and farmhouses, and British troops fought back, killing more than ten thousand rebels in 13 years and imprisoning nationalist leaders in the mistaken belief that Mau Mau was a top-down political movement rather than a grassroots uprising. By 1955 Mau Mau was defeated, but London turned against the settlers whose oppression had caused the uprising. Nationalist leader Jomo Kenyatta, released from prison in 1961, led his party to victory in parliamentary elections, and Kenya became independent in 1963.

Julius Nyerere, first president of Tanzania.

In British Central Africa, two hundred thousand white settlers in Southern Rhodesia imposed apartheid-style segregationist laws modeled on those of South Africa. In 1953 London permitted settlers to create the Federation of Rhodesia and Nyasaland, which settlers hoped would become a state like South Africa, with enough economic power to suppress nationalist movements by force. More extreme racist legislation followed, while nationalists organized strikes and demonstrations that quickly turned violent.

Read the **Document**

Jomo Kenyatta, from Facing Mt. Kenya: The Tribal Life of the Gikuyu

on **myhistorylab.com**

British prime minister Macmillan speaks of a "wind of change"

In 1960 British prime minister Harold Macmillan, in a speech in Cape Town, South Africa, referred to the "wind of change" that was sweeping across Africa. The wind, of course, was African nationalism, and Britain was forced to acknowledge it. In 1964, Northern Rhodesia, led by Kenneth Kaunda, won its independence as Zambia, and Nyasaland, led by Sir Hastings Banda, became independent Malawi. But white settlers in Southern Rhodesia, trying to prevent a similar development in that region, declared independence from Britain in 1965 as a white-supremacist state. Supported by South Africa, but condemned by Britain and most of the rest of the world, Rhodesia held out against several separate African nationalist movements until 1980. Then a peace settlement brought a black-majority government to power in the renamed state of Zimbabwe.

Suspected Mau Mau sympathizers under guard in Kenya, late 1952.

FAILURE OF THE FRENCH COMMUNITY. The Algerian war and de Gaulle's election as president called into question the future of the French Empire in Africa. France's new constitution, adopted in 1958, guaranteed all French colonies the right to self-determination, which might consist of independence or continued affiliation with France in the newly created "French Community." De Gaulle

hoped that, given a choice between total independence and continued ties with France, the colonies would choose the latter. Initially
all did so except Guinea, whose nationalist leader, the militant
Marxist trade unionist Sékou Touré (*SĀ-koo too-RĀ*), campaigned
vigorously against the Community, convincing 95 percent of voters
to cast ballots against it.

De Gaulle responded to Touré's victory angrily, granting
Guinea immediate independence and withdrawing all French
economic aid and equipment. Filing cabinets were shipped back
to France, telephones torn from walls, and light bulbs removed
from their sockets. All Guineans who had worked for the French
government, as soldiers or civil servants, were fired at once and
denied pensions. De Gaulle may have expected that these actions
would force Guinea to come back to the French Community, but
Touré turned to the Soviets and Nkrumah's Ghana for help, and
the new nation became a symbol of African defiance of
colonialism. Meanwhile its economy, always fragile, collapsed.

A literacy class in Cameroon, c. 1960.

The French then hoped that Guinea's example would discourage other nationalist
movements, but it did just the reverse. As Touré gained folk hero status, and British

The French Community
fails

West Africa moved rapidly toward independence, the French Community was
obviously failing. Between 1958 and 1960, all of France's African colonies except
Djibouti (*jih-BOO-tē*) voted for independence. Disappointed, de Gaulle nevertheless
reacted realistically, no doubt with the trauma of Algeria's fight for independence in
mind. Agreements with the new states guaranteed continued French economic domination, a relationship later described as **neocolonialism**. For the rest of the century,
France exercised extensive influence over its former empire, sending in the military to
defend its commercial interests when political instability threatened.

CHAOS IN BELGIUM'S EMPIRE. In Central Africa, Belgium owned three colonies: the
Congo, Rwanda, and Urundi. The Congo, most notably, was rich in diamonds and
other precious minerals. In 1959, mild pressure from the new Congolese National
Movement, headed by an educated labor union leader named Patrice Lumumba,
brought an offer of independence from the Belgian government, which was frightened
by the prospect of Algerian-style war. But Belgium had done little to prepare the
Congolese to rule themselves; there were only 16 university-educated Congolese in the
entire colony. No sooner had independence been celebrated on July 1, 1960, than the
new country fell apart.

Lumumba, who became prime minister, governed energetically but had no political organization or associates whose talents matched his own. Moreover, the tribal

Belgium's sudden
withdrawal throws the
Congo into chaos

nature of Congolese society proved a hindrance to national
rule. Tribes in the Congo were much more important than
political movements, and each tribe distrusted the others.
Lumumba's tribal power base was in the countryside, but he
had to rule from the capital city, Leopoldville, where his
backers were outnumbered by supporters of the president,
Joseph Kasavubu. Both rivals were astonished when the
resource-rich province of Katanga seceded from Congo
less than a week after independence was declared. The
Congolese army promptly mutinied; its soldiers, divided by
tribal loyalties of their own and trained by their Belgian
officers to consider nationalists like Lumumba and Kasavubu

Patrice Lumumba with Dag Hammarskjöld.

barbarians, now refused to obey the new leaders. Soldiers imprisoned their officers and began molesting black and white citizens alike. In response, Belgium intervened militarily to protect Belgian nationals. It also supported Katanga's secession, hoping this would further weaken Lumumba's position and justify the return of Belgian control.

Lumumba and Kasavubu, surrounded by chaos, sought U.N. intervention against Belgium but then discovered that Secretary-General Dag Hammarskjöld, a Swede, insisted on negotiating with Katanga as though it were independent. The Congolese leaders suspected a European plot to recolonize Congo, and on July 14, 1960, they appealed to the Soviets to intervene. Although the two men acted jointly, the United States, which had been suspicious of Lumumba's leftist sympathies, concluded that he was a Communist holding Kasavubu hostage. When U.N. troops arrived in Leopoldville the next day, they moved quickly to block the Soviet Union and the Marxist government of Guinea from any influence in the Congo.

Had the U.N. entered Katanga and expelled Belgian forces, the secession would have collapsed. Instead, Katangese secession ruined prospects for a truly independent Congo and took the lives of both Lumumba and Hammarskjöld. Lumumba and Kasavubu fired each other (although neither had the authority to do so), and in the resulting turmoil, Lumumba ended up in the hands of Katangese soldiers, who murdered him in January 1961. As recounted at the opening of this chapter, Hammarskjöld, flying between Leopoldville and Katanga in a tireless effort to bring about a settlement, was killed that September in a plane crash.

Finally, at the end of 1962, the United Nations disarmed Belgian forces in Katanga and ended the secession. By that time Colonel Mobutu Sese Seko (*muh-BOO-too SĀ-sā SĀ-kō*) had emerged as a military strongman backed by the United States, which hoped to use him to control Congo's mineral resources. In November 1965 he overthrew the Congolese government and embarked on a 32-year military dictatorship of the unfortunate country, which he renamed Zaire.

Ethnic rivalries cause genocide in Rwanda

The other two Belgian colonies gained independence in 1962 under the names Rwanda and Burundi. The Hutu and Tutsi peoples, dominant in Rwanda and Burundi, respectively, had been wary of each other since German and Belgian colonial officials had designated the Tutsi as the (allegedly) more advanced of the two ethnic groups and had favored them over the Hutu. In 1994, a plane carrying the president of Rwanda was shot down by missiles fired from a Rwandan military base. This proved to be the signal for a deliberately orchestrated genocide, in which Hutu paramilitary formations, backed by some Rwandan army units, massacred more than five hundred thousand Tutsi. U.N. peacekeeping forces were pulled out, and since characterizing the conflict as genocide would have required intervention under international law and the United Nations Charter, that word was avoided in all official reports. The only outside forces remaining were two hundred soldiers from Ghana who had been sent to Rwanda as monitors for upcoming elections; they remained at their posts and saved thousands who would otherwise have been slaughtered.

The Rwandan catastrophe spilled over into neighboring Zaire, where Mobutu's dictatorship was crumbling as he neared death from cancer. Rwandan government forces, in pursuit of fleeing Hutu militias, crossed the border into eastern Zaire and linked up with movements resisting Mobutu. In 1997 Mobutu fled into exile, and resistance forces proclaimed the Democratic Republic of Congo. But Congo's enormous mineral wealth attracted military intervention against the new government from Angola, Rwanda, Uganda, and Zimbabwe, and eastern Congo exploded into a multinational conflict that by 2010 had killed more than four million people in the bloodiest conflict since World War II. Various attempts were made to end the fighting, but none have proved workable.

PORTUGAL'S UNIQUE DECOLONIZATION. The Portuguese Empire in Africa resisted the impulse toward independence for some time. Portugal was a poor country by European standards, and its government considered its African colonies vital to the Portuguese economy. There would therefore be no peaceful road to independence.

In 1961 the colonies of Angola, Mozambique, and Portuguese Guinea erupted in violent demonstrations against colonial rule. Antônio Salazar's fascist government (1932–1968) dispatched most of the Portuguese army to its colonies in an unsuccessful effort to suppress the fighting. As hostilities continued throughout the 1960s, Portuguese forces were gradually horrified by their own brutalities against people fighting for the sort of freedom Portuguese themselves would have cherished. By April 1974 the discontent of Portuguese soldiers had convinced several members of the military high command that Portugal could not win these wars. During one of its periodic reports to the government in Lisbon concerning the progress of the fighting, the high command overthrew that government and granted independence to the Portuguese Empire, effective in April 1975. Civil wars broke out in Angola and Mozambique, with Marxists taking power in both countries and retaining control until after the Soviet Union's collapse in 1991.

The Portuguese army supports decolonization

From Apartheid to Freedom in South Africa

The struggle against colonialism took place throughout the continent, but for decades the attention of Africans and non-Africans alike was fixed on South Africa, an autonomous British dominion until it declared full independence in 1961. South Africa had fought against Germany and Japan in World War II under a coalition government headed by General Jan Christiaan Smuts, but his defeat by Daniel Malan's National Party in 1948 ushered in a new and disturbing era. Malan campaigned on a platform of apartheid, or strict racial segregation, under which white South Africans systematically discriminated against black South Africans (who made up the majority of the population) and people of mixed racial background (whom white South Africans called "Coloreds"). Sexual relations between whites and either blacks or Coloreds were absolutely prohibited under the Immorality Act. Blacks and Coloreds were denied the right to vote, were limited to menial occupations, and mostly lived in poverty. Police brutality against these oppressed groups was systematized and encouraged by the government and its supporters.

The National Party introduces apartheid in South Africa

Read the Document

Nelson Mandela, from Freedom, Justice and Dignity for All South Africa: Statements and Articles by Mr. Nelson Mandela

on **myhistorylab.com**

Staggered by the regime's ruthlessness, blacks fought back through strikes and protests organized by the **African National Congress.** The ANC formed an alliance with the outlawed South African Communist Party, and the government promptly suppressed both organizations. ANC leaders such as Nelson Mandela and his law partner Oliver Tambo were removed from society, Mandela to a life prison term and Tambo to exile. Another resistance leader, Steve Biko, one of the founders of the Black Consciousness Movement, died in 1977 from brain injuries he received while in police custody.

Antigovernment riots and police atrocities called the world's attention to this Nazi-style governance, as did *Cry, the Beloved Country*, a devastating fictional indictment of apartheid written in 1948 by a white South African politician, Alan Paton. White resistance to apartheid also came from the speeches of Helen Suzman, a member of parliament. The U.N. repeatedly censured

Police beating antiapartheid demonstrators in Durban, South Africa, 1959.

South Africa, its athletes were banned from the Olympic Games, and it was increasingly isolated and condemned.

Eventually apartheid collapsed from a combination of internal and external pressures. By the late 1980s, internal opposition from blacks, Coloreds, and moderate whites increased, while international economic sanctions gravely weakened the country's economy. In 1989, Prime Minister F. W. de Klerk opened negotiations with the ANC, releasing Mandela in 1990 and working with him to end apartheid in 1993. With all South Africans finally allowed to vote, Mandela was elected president in 1994, and South Africa began a long-overdue transition to multiracial democracy.

A significant stage in that transition was official recognition that the apartheid system had provoked violence and crime on all sides. Central to this recognition was the creation of an innovative Truth and Reconciliation Commission, which held public hearings and granted amnesty to anyone willing to confess his or her crimes. This made the atrocities of the past a matter of public record, which the government considered an indispensable condition for multiracial cooperation. The amnesties proved controversial, because they permitted torturers and murderers to escape punishment, but for many the public testimony allowed healing to begin. In the early 21st century, South Africa looked to a difficult future, but with a degree of national unity not thought possible in 1990.

Nelson Mandela.

"THE STRUGGLE IS MY LIFE"
NELSON MANDELA
GAOLED 5th AUGUST 1962
SENTENCED TO LIFE IMPRISONMENT
12th JUNE 1964 FOR HIS ACTIONS
AGAINST APARTHEID

Watch the Video
Africa as an Urban, Not Rural, Place
on **myhistorylab.com**

Challenges Facing Independent Africa

Throughout Africa and across the globe, the destruction of European colonialism stimulated excitement and hope, particularly among the young. Within Africa, young nationalists and idealists set to work building independent states. From the United States, young people came to Africa as part of the Peace Corps, a volunteer program created by President John F. Kennedy that builds infrastructure and improves education in developing nations. For a few years, the future of Africa seemed bright.

But nearly a century of colonial rule had molded African realities in ways agreeable to Europeans but often obstructive to Africans. The Cold War, with its superpower competition for the allegiance of newly formed countries, brought foreign pressures to nations like the Congo. Many African leaders proved poorly trained, corrupt, overwhelmed by the magnitude of the task facing them, or a combination of all three.

Politics: Democracy or Dictatorship?

Before the Europeans arrived, African societies were organized along tribal lines. Clan lineage and collective tribal decision making were determining factors in setting policy, and kings or emperors, despite their exalted titles, usually ruled by consultation. In contrast, European colonial governments were top-down dictatorships administered from cities thousands of miles away. Dismissing captive peoples as inferior, they ruled through a blend of paternalism, patronage, and brutality. By 1945, most living Africans were unfamiliar with preimperial governing structures. Colonial despotism was the only form of government they had ever known.

The problems of the new nations were compounded because their boundaries had been drawn by European imperialists and were completely unsuited to African realities. Cutting across village, clan, and tribal communities, the lines looked neat and crisp on maps of Africa but left local populations bewildered and divided. When independence arrived, peoples speaking different languages, practicing different customs, worshiping

European imperialism holds back the growth of African democracy different gods, and observing different traditional structures of social organization were expected to unify and to participate in European-style, multiparty democracies.

Independence movements committed to popular sovereignty and parliamentary governance struggled with these African realities. Trying to reconstruct ethnic and tribal communities, politicians formed parties based more on those communities than on political or economic policies. This structure made parliamentary compromise difficult and allowed authoritarian leaders to assert that multiple parties destroyed national unity instead of promoting it. From this argument, it was a short step to one-party dictatorship, and this step was taken by Kwame Nkrumah in Ghana, Sir Hastings Banda in Malawi, Sékou Touré in Guinea, and Emperor Bokassa I in the Central African Republic. Other rulers, like Jomo Kenyatta in Kenya, Kenneth Kaunda in Zambia, and Julius Nyerere in Tanzania, endorsed democratic ideals and permitted some criticism of the government but ruled for decades as authoritarian leaders.

The opening of parliament in newly independent Ghana, 1957.

Pluralistic politics gradually emerged in several nations in the 1990s, but only after the death or removal of the leaders listed above. In other countries, the fall of one dictator simply led to the rise of another. Political difficulties proved a long-lasting legacy of imperial rule.

Economic Underdevelopment

European economic exploitation of Africa was as destructive as political domination. Imperialists plundered the continent of mineral wealth and agricultural commodities. They forced African farmers to turn their land over to the production of valuable crops for export. As cultivation of basic foodstuffs was neglected, a continent that had always been able to feed itself turned into a net importer of food. Development of local industries was not permitted; Europe's interest lay in exploiting its colonies, not in modernizing them.

Independent African nations, led by elites often educated in Europe or North America, eagerly set out to industrialize. They hoped a North Atlantic model of modernization would enable Africans to replace European manufactured goods with locally made products, ending the export of African wealth to developed countries. For a number of reasons, this did not happen.

African economies are unprepared for independence

First, independent African societies contained too few educated people to industrialize on their own. Britain, France, Italy, Belgium, and Portugal had educated young Africans not for the challenges of independence but for the service of colonialism. The small number of trained Africans that European schools produced could not modernize their countries without massive expert assistance from the developed world.

Second, European technology and equipment were indispensable to African industrialization, and Europeans made them available at outrageous prices, payable not in African currencies (worthless in Europe) but in African minerals and commodities. This arrangement perpetuated the old colonial trading patterns and European economic control.

Third, African roads, railways, and telegraph and telephone lines were designed not for independent states but for colonies. Rail lines and roads ran from interior farming communities or mining districts directly to seaports, from which African wealth could be efficiently shipped to Europe or North America. Seldom did roads link one inland community with another. Electronic communications were equally European oriented: a resident of Nairobi, Kenya, could place a telephone call to London relatively easily, but to call Mogadishu in the neighboring country of Somalia required routing to London, then

African infrastructure was designed for Europe's convenience

to Rome (since Somalia had been an Italian colony), and from there to Mogadishu. Again the old colonial infrastructure perpetuated neocolonialism and hindered the development of relations between independent African nations.

One-product economies make African development difficult

Bagging cotton for export in Sudan, 1960s.

Fourth, many new nations were burdened with economies dominated by one crop or one mineral. Zambia's copper, Ghana's cacao, Gabon's timber, and Sierra Leone's diamonds absorbed so much of the productive capacity, financial investment, and human talent of those countries that economic diversification seemed both impractical and undesirable. It was easier and more profitable to continue supplying those products to the developed world than it would be to convert to a balanced economy, which, even if it could be achieved, might actually leave the country less prosperous than before.

These and other factors impeded the growth of healthy economies and tempted African leaders with the prospect of riches. Those who continued neo-colonialism and assisted the developed world in exploiting African agricultural and mineral wealth were handsomely rewarded for their services. Corrupt, manipulative dictators kept their populations in poverty while placing their illegal gains in Swiss bank accounts and living in luxury in the midst of squalor. Only in the 1990s did many African countries begin to develop the foundations of modern economies.

Social Challenges: Poverty, Ignorance, Disease

Underlying the economic difficulties of the newly liberated nations was a fundamental, sobering reality: Africa, a continent rich in cultures and traditions, was impoverished in areas indispensable to modernization. Its crops and minerals were subject to global market shortages and surpluses that Africans could not control. Deposits of coal, the cheapest fuel available for early-stage industrialization, were conspicuously absent from most African nations, and those few countries with significant oil reserves, like Algeria, Libya, and

A satellite photograph of a dust storm over Morocco in 2003.

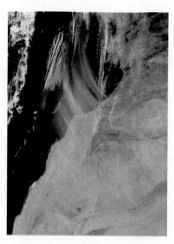

Nigeria, discovered after independence that those fields were still the property of multinational oil companies. Much of Africa's mineral wealth had already been taken away by Europeans, and as the Sahara Desert crept farther south following post-1950 changes in rainfall patterns, even a renewable resource like food became increasingly scarce. Africa's poverty, whatever its causes, was an undeniable fact, one with which all its newly liberated nations would have to cope.

Dealing with poverty was made especially difficult by the low educational levels of most Africans. A few elite Africans had been educated in Europe and the United States, but the vast majority had not, and a significant minority had never been educated at all. Most students attending African schools did so only long enough to learn how to read, write, and do basic arithmetic. These problems stemmed in part from imperial powers' indifference to the education of ordinary Africans and in part from the overwhelmingly rural character of most African societies, which made formal education less useful than backbreaking daily labor. The inadequate education of most Africans placed the already troubled new nations at an even more serious disadvantage.

Serious social problems confront African nations

As the decades turned over and the generation that had won independence aged and died, educational deficiencies were to some degree remedied, while poverty often deepened. Then a massive continental health crisis devastated many of Africa's weakest societies: the global spread of HIV/AIDS, a condition first identified in the Belgian Congo in 1959 that destroys the immune system and leaves the body open to lethal infections. It is most deadly in impoverished countries with poor health care systems, and it has devastated Malawi, Uganda, Zimbabwe, and South Africa. By 2007 between 25 and 30 percent of adults in eastern, southern, and Central Africa were HIV positive, and average life expectancy had fallen by four to ten years. Because most of its victims are young adults, HIV/AIDS kills or weakens the most economically productive sector of the population and leaves many young children orphaned. The burden it places on African health care systems is catastrophic.

All of these challenges are formidable obstacles for African nations hoping to modernize. Only insofar as Africa makes political and economic progress will it be able to create a stable framework for addressing poverty, ignorance, and disease.

The Transformation of the Middle East

The Second World War transformed the regions in which it was fought and the people who contributed to the war effort. For the Middle East, the war's most dramatic consequence was the creation of Israel, an entirely new state whose presence focused Arab hostilities in the region and elevated regional conflicts to global significance.

The State of Israel and the Palestinian Conflict

In the 19th century, European Jews were divided over their prospects in modern national states dominated by Christians. Some hoped to assimilate by becoming secularized and adopting nationalism as a sort of substitute religion. Others, the **Zionists**, followed journalist Theodor Herzl's belief that Jews would always be outsiders in Christian Europe; only a state of their own would afford them genuine security. After witnessing the anti-Semitic hatred heaped upon Captain Dreyfus (Chapter 27), Herzl concluded that escape from Europe was the only rational strategy for Jews. His Zionist movement unsuccessfully sought territory for a Jewish homeland in remote locations such as Uganda and Wyoming, but Palestine, the ancestral home of the Jewish people, became the movement's preferred objective.

Zionism's problem was that Palestine, part of the Ottoman Empire until 1918 and a British mandate after that, was populated by a Jewish minority and an Arab majority. Jewish nationalism was therefore bound to oppose Arab nationalism in the Middle East, and since Britain considered Arab friendship vital to the preservation of its connection to India and its exploitation of Persian Gulf oil, prospects for creation of a Jewish state seemed unlikely.

The **Balfour Declaration**, issued in 1917 by British foreign secretary Arthur Balfour to gain Jewish support for the Allied side in World War I, placed Britain on record in support of a Jewish homeland in Palestine, provided the rights of existing Arab residents were not infringed. That clause negated the entire document. Local Arab communities resisted Jewish immigration, and during World War II many Arabs quietly sympathized with Nazi war aims. If Germany won the war, Arabs understood, it would take Palestine from the defeated British and expel the Jews. But Germany lost, and knowledge of the Nazi extermination of millions of European Jews heightened Zionism's appeal to Jews and swung American public opinion in favor of the creation of a Jewish state in Palestine. In 1945 the World Zionist Congress demanded that Palestine be opened to one million Jews, while U.S. president Harry Truman asked Britain to admit one hundred thousand displaced Jews from war-torn Europe into Palestine. Several Arab states responded with warnings that they would use military force to oppose the creation of a Jewish state in Palestine.

Britain vainly sought a peaceful solution even as Jewish terrorist groups like the Irgun (*ear-GOON*) destabilized Palestine with bombings and murders in an effort to force the British out. In 1947 the United Nations recommended ending the mandate by partitioning Palestine into two states, one Palestinian and one

View the **Map**

Interactive Map: The Emergence of the Modern Middle East

on **myhistorylab.com**

View the **Map**

Interactive Map: The Formation of Modern Israel

on **myhistorylab.com**

Zionism seeks a homeland for the Jewish people

Young women members of the Irgun receiving military training in the 1940s.

MAP **37.3** The Arab-Israeli Conflict, 1947–2007

The proclamation of the State of Israel on May 14, 1948, was immediately followed by Israel's War of Independence against several Arab nations. Other Arab-Israeli wars followed in 1956, 1967, and 1973. Observe that the United Nations Partition Plan of November 1947 (see enclosure) established two states in the British mandate of Palestine, one Jewish and one Arab, as well as an international zone surrounding Jerusalem. But this plan was invalidated by the War of Independence, and Israel's borders were further modified by its occupation of the Sinai Peninsula, Gaza, the West Bank, and the Golan Heights in 1967. The continuing Israeli-Palestinian conflict focuses on the establishment of the type of Palestinian state originally conceptualized in the Partition Plan of 1947. How do the territories occupied by Israel in 1967 continue to affect Arab-Israeli relations?

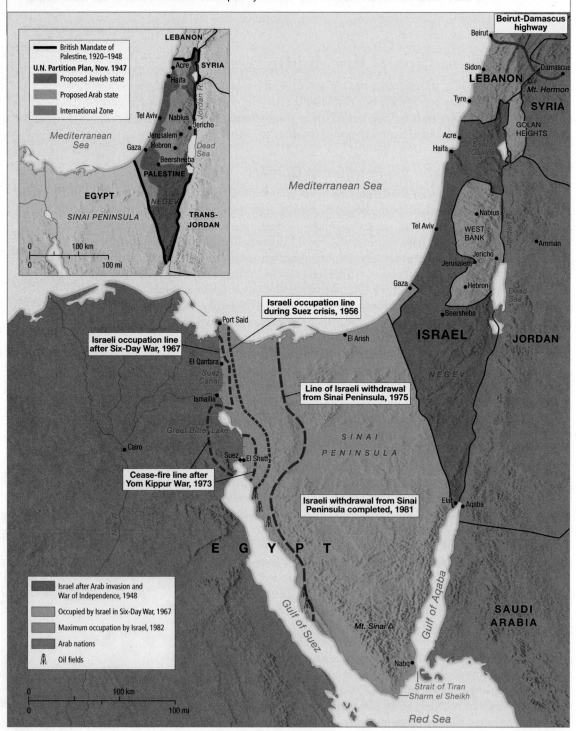

Jewish (Map 37.3). Arab leaders rejected this solution, demanding that all Palestine be constituted as one state led by Arabs. More than seven hundred thousand Palestinian Muslims and Christians fled the country as the State of Israel was proclaimed on May 14, 1948. The new nation guaranteed Jews throughout the world a safe haven from future persecution. It was immediately attacked by seven Arab states, led by Egypt.

The Arab-Israeli War of 1948–1949 transformed the Middle East. Israeli forces outnumbered those of their enemies, and since Israeli independence was immediately recognized by both the U.S. and USSR, Israel could purchase modern weapons from both America and Communist-dominated Czechoslovakia. Israeli victory in 1949 left the Arab states with humiliated armies and governments that had lost credibility with their own people. Arab monarchies in Syria (1949), Egypt (1952), and Iraq (1958) were overthrown by military conspiracies dedicated to secularization, modernization, and eventual victory over Israel. Meanwhile, more than half a million Palestinians suffered in impoverished refugee camps in Jordan, deprived of clean water, decent shelter, and hope for the future.

The failure of Israel, the Arab states, and the U.N. to solve this refugee problem created the **Palestinian Question**. In 1949 the U.N. estimated that 726,000 refugees were living in makeshift camps. Unlike displaced persons in Europe and India after 1945, these people were neither resettled in foreign lands nor returned to their own. By 2010, many of those born in the camps immediately after the 1948–1949 war had become grandparents, presiding over extended families whose members knew no other life. In 1949 one of the refugees assassinated King Abdullah of Jordan, widely considered the most moderate and realistic of the Arab leaders. The teeming camps became breeding grounds of hatred for all such moderates, as well as for Israel and its allies, especially the United States.

The War of 1948–1949 creates the Palestinian Question

Arab Nationalism and the Arab-Israeli Wars

Egypt, the most powerful Arab state, led the anti-Israeli coalition, and its 1952 revolution against King Farouk posed a serious threat to the Jewish state. A military dictatorship, installed under the leadership of Colonel Gamal Abdel Nasser, aimed for a more modern, secular regime that could avenge the humiliation of 1948–1949 and destroy Israel. Nasser was hailed as a champion of Arab nationalism, but he was much more than that. He was a charismatic, messianic figure who aspired to nothing less than the unification of all Arabs under his leadership.

This pan-Arabism would be difficult to achieve because the states in which Arabs lived had long engaged in internal tribal, regional, and religious conflict. With the exception of Israel, all Middle Eastern and North African states that became independent after 1945 were Arab, but most of their populations were neither exclusively Arab in ethnicity nor exclusively Sunni Muslim in religion. Lebanon was torn by civil strife in 1958, in 1975–1976, and throughout the 1980s. Yemen was divided into two states for two decades after 1962, with North Yemen backed by Saudi Arabia and South Yemen supported by Egypt and the Soviet Union. After gaining independence in 1956, the Sudan's northern region, Islamic and Arabic speaking, struggled against its non-Islamic, non-Arabic southern region. After fighting its brutal war for liberation from France in 1954–1962, Algeria endured severe civil strife between its secularist military government and a cohesive, well-financed Islamist fundamentalist movement.

Despite these obstacles, Nasser worked toward unification. His pan-Arabism led him to smuggle arms to Algeria's anti-French rebels and to establish close ties with the Soviet Union, which increasingly backed Arab nationalism to gain influence in the Middle East. In 1956, troubled by Nasser's policies, the United States cut off funding for the Aswan High Dam, an Egyptian power project designed to control the yearly flooding of the Nile.

Nasser attempts to unite the Arab world

View the **Image**

Construction of the Aswan Dam, Egypt

on **myhistorylab.com**

The Suez Crisis makes Nasser a hero

Nasser responded by seizing the Suez Canal from the British, a daring move that delighted Arab nationalists (see "Speech by President Gamal Abdel Nasser of Egypt, September 15, 1956"). International attention quickly focused on the region when in November 1956 an Israeli attack on Egypt across the Sinai Peninsula was accompanied by a joint Anglo-French effort to retake the Canal. But neither Britain nor France had consulted the United States, and President Dwight Eisenhower opposed their military action, fearing that the real winners in a prolonged struggle would be the Soviets and their Arab nationalist allies. Interestingly, the USSR also opposed the Anglo-French action, fearing precisely the opposite: a swift Egyptian defeat. Britain and France, having alienated both superpowers, were forced to agree to a cease-fire and eventual withdrawal. The Suez Crisis made Nasser an Arab hero while convincing Britain that it would be unable to hold its African empire in the long term. It also emboldened the Israelis, whose armored forces had performed brilliantly against their Egyptian counterparts.

For the next decade, Nasser pursued his dream of Arab unity. In 1958 Syria's Arab nationalist government joined with Egypt to create the United Arab Republic (UAR), marking the high point of pan-Arabism. That July, however, the king of Iraq was assassinated in a military coup, and the United States was frightened into sending marines to Lebanon to stop what appeared to be Nasser's plan to unite the entire region. But the marines were greeted on Lebanon's beaches by startled sunbathers and soft-drink vendors; no Nasserites could be located. Iraq, like Saudi Arabia, realized that joining the UAR meant sharing its oil revenues with Egypt and petroleum-poor Syria; it stood aside, and in 1961 a military coup in Damascus ended Syria's partnership with Egypt. Disappointed, Nasser turned inward, intent on building socialism at home.

Arab unity appeared dead, but Nasser's Egypt remained indispensable to Arab efforts against Israel. Egypt's defeats in 1948–1949 and 1956 only strengthened Nasser's resolve to modernize his armed forces in order to stand a chance of defeating Israel. The problem was that after the events of 1956 cut Nasser off from Western aid, this modernization

---

DOCUMENT 37.1 Speech by President Gamal Abdel Nasser of Egypt, September 15, 1956

In these decisive days in the history of mankind, these days in which truth struggles to have itself recognized in international chaos where powers of evil domination and imperialism have prevailed, Egypt stands firmly to preserve her sovereignty . . . Egypt nationalized the Egyptian Suez Canal Company. When Egypt granted the concession to de Lesseps [in the 1860s] it was stated in the concession between the Egyptian Government and the Egyptian Company that the Company of the Suez Canal is an Egyptian company subject to Egyptian authority. Egypt nationalized this Egyptian company and declared freedom of navigation will be preserved.

But the imperialists became angry. Britain and France said Egypt grabbed the Suez Canal as if it were part of France or Britain. The British Foreign Secretary forgot that only two years ago he signed an agreement stating the Suez Canal is an integral part of Egypt. Egypt declared she was ready to negotiate. But

as soon as negotiations began, threats and intimidations started . . .

We believe in international law. But we will never submit. We shall show the world how a small country can stand in the face of great powers threatening with armed might. Egypt might be a small power, but she is great inasmuch as she has faith in her power and convictions . . .

We shall defend our freedom and independence to the last drop of our blood. This is the staunch feeling of every Egyptian. The whole Arab nation will stand by us in our common fight against aggression and domination. Free peoples, too, people who are really free will stand by us and support us against the forces of tyranny . . .

SOURCE: *The Suez Canal Problem, 26 July–22 September 1956*, U.S. Department of State Publication No. 6392 (Washington, 1956), 345–351.

depended on military assistance from the Soviet Union, whose equipment was inferior to Israel's. Egyptian military leaders failed to assess the weapons situation realistically and advised Nasser poorly.

In 1963, Israel's decision to draw water from the Jordan River (Map 37.3) revitalized Nasser's cause. At Arab summits he hosted in January and September 1964, participants established the **Palestine Liberation Organization (PLO)**, a coalition of more than thirty anti-Israeli organizations dedicated to Israel's destruction and its replacement by a secular Palestinian state. Now the Palestinian Question was attached to Egypt's foreign policy. In 1966 a radical wing of Syria's Ba'ath Party took power in Damascus and pressed Egypt for war with Israel. Nasser, whose armed forces still lacked adequate offensive weaponry, decided to ally with Syria in hopes of restraining its new radical regime. But he miscalculated drastically.

Border clashes between Syria and Israel triggered a crisis in the spring of 1967. Fearing an Israeli attack on Egypt, Nasser blockaded Israeli shipping at the mouth of the Gulf of Aqaba. Israel responded on June 5 with a devastating predawn air strike, destroying Egypt's air force on the ground. It followed up with a shattering armored offensive that took the Sinai Peninsula, East Jerusalem, the West Bank of the Jordan River, and Syria's Golan Heights.

Gamal Abdel Nasser.

In the short run, that brief, dramatic campaign, which came to be called the Six-Day War of June 1967, closed the Suez Canal for eight years and ended Nasser's goal of Arab leadership. Secular military dictatorships like his had come to power promising to defeat Israel; when they failed to do so, they lost their legitimacy in the view of Muslim traditionalists. In the long run, the lands occupied by Israel during the war became a crucial obstacle to regular relations between Israel and its Arab neighbors. Sinai was returned to Egypt in 1981–1982, but by then Israelis had begun building settlements in Palestinian areas of the occupied West Bank, seeming to signal Israel's intent to control those lands indefinitely.

The Six-Day War changes the Middle East

Following Nasser's sudden death in 1970, his successor, Anwar al-Sadat, expelled Soviet advisors and joined Syria in a surprise attack on Israel on October 6, 1973, the Jewish holy day of Yom Kippur and the tenth of Ramadan, Islam's holiest month. This Yom Kippur/Ramadan War ended in Arab defeat, but only after massive U.S. aid made up for initial Israeli setbacks. Arab oil-exporting nations embargoed oil shipments to nations supporting Israel, more than doubling the price of gasoline and plunging Europe, America, and Japan into severe recessions. Sadat's initial victories won him great respect in Egypt and gave him the leverage to break the cycle of warfare in the Middle East.

In 1977, convinced that continued tension with Israel would permanently impoverish Egypt, Sadat opened peace talks with the Jewish state. After the conclusion of peace in 1979 (see page 890), Egypt eventually regained the Sinai. But this peace also cracked the anti-Israeli coalition, leading to Egypt's expulsion from the League of Arab States and to Sadat's 1981 assassination by Islamist fundamentalists. His successor, Hosni Mubarak, nonetheless maintained Egypt's peace with Israel.

Egypt and Israel make peace

The Development of Islamist Fundamentalism

Egypt's startling decision to make and maintain peace with Israel astounded the Islamic world. The foundation of Israel and the inability of Islamic countries to destroy it produced anguished soul-searching among Muslims. Once again, Islamic regimes confronted the reality and consequences of Western technological supremacy. As Ira Lapidus demonstrates in his superb work, *A History of Islamic Societies*, Islamic responses were developed in the centuries-old context of Islamic connections and conflicts with the West.

NINETEENTH-CENTURY ISLAMIC RESPONSES. In the 19th century, **Islamic modernism** developed in reaction to the challenges posed by technologically advanced European societies. Many educated Muslims appreciated Western achievements and political values. These elites wanted to reshape Islam along European social and political lines, forming secular nationalist states to replace multinational states like the Ottoman Empire.

Islamic modernism and reformism seek to change the nature of Islamic states

Islamic modernism held that if Muslims wished to compete militarily with European powers, they would have to centralize power in national states, establish Western-style education, industrialize their economies, and employ European military techniques and technologies. The Young Turks, during the last decade of the Ottoman Empire, were the first such modernist group to exercise power, preparing the way for Kemal Atäturk's later creation of a secular Turkish state.

Children in Mauritania learn to read Arabic by studying the Qu'ran using prayer boards.

Islamic reformism was a different response, developed by Sufi brotherhoods, tribal and religious leaders, and many farmers and merchants. They advocated a revitalization of Islam itself, both religiously and socially. Reformist scholars argued for the purification of Islamic beliefs and rituals in the light of proper understanding of the Qur'an and Shari`ah. They contended that corrupt forms of Islam should be abolished, by force if necessary. Non-Muslim practices and peoples should not be tolerated. True Muslims must emphasize theological purity, moral rightness, and unwavering commitment to the creation of a righteous Islamic society throughout the world. Wahhabism (Chapter 22) was a reformist movement that eventually succeeded in creating a new nation, Saudi Arabia.

Modernism and reformism were not mutually exclusive. One could preach a return to the principles of early Islam while simultaneously recommending educational and technological modernization. Reformism in colonial areas could be transformed into resistance to foreign rule. But in the 1970s, Muslims found neither modernism nor reformism adequate to deal with existing realities. In this context, they developed a third response: **Islamic revival**.

ISLAMIC REVIVAL SINCE THE 1970S. After the Yom Kippur/Ramadan War of 1973 and Egypt's subsequent decision to make peace with Israel, Islamic revival spread rapidly throughout the Muslim world. In a religious context, Islamic revival was similar to Islamic reformism, embracing various movements designed to emphasize personal religious devotion and purify Islamic practice. But in a cultural context, Islamic revival went further, denouncing Western values such as materialism, individualism, moral relativism, religious tolerance, sexual permissiveness, greater freedom for women, drug culture, and rock music. Islamic revival movements believe that these values and practices undermine Muslim family life and religious authority.

Islamic revival challenges Western values

Attacking Western values and stressing Islamic fundamentals, including the Qur'an and sayings of the Prophet, these movements are often described together in the West as **Islamist fundamentalism.** But in practice they vary widely. Some are tolerant, others intolerant; some are democratic, others authoritarian; some are peaceful, others revolutionary; some are open to dialogue with the West, others are not. Islamist fundamentalist movements view moderate Muslim regimes as corrupt, excessively cooperative with the West, and insufficiently devoted to the purification of Islamic religious practice. Such

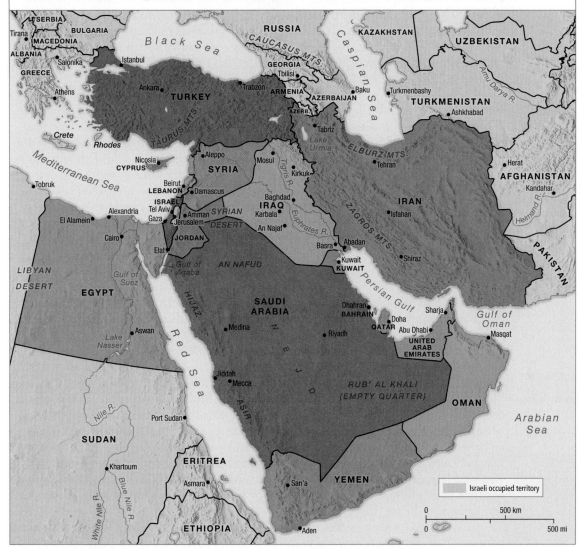

MAP 37.4 The Middle East Since 1945

The independence of the United Arab Emirates in 1971 ended European colonial rule in the Middle East. Notice the central geographic position of Iraq, mirroring the central position of Mesopotamia in ancient times. Since 1948 the region has been plagued by frequent wars: the various Arab-Israeli wars (Map 37.3), the Iran–Iraq War of 1980–1988, the Persian Gulf War of 1991, and the American invasions of Afghanistan in 2001 and Iraq in 2003. What accounts for the continuing turmoil in this region?

movements seek to remove moderate regimes from power, and thus are dedicated to political as well as religious change. But some of these groups are devoted to peaceful, evolutionary political change, while others are *jihadist* (Chapter 11), using violence as the principal tool for creating change.

ISLAMIC REVOLUTION IN IRAN. In 1979, the removal of the secular, modernizing Shah of Iran by traditionalists backing a conservative Shi'ite cleric, the Ayatollah Ruhollah Khomeini (*eye-ah-TŌ-lah roo-HŌ-lah hō-MĀ-nē*), brought Islamist fundamentalists to power. The Shah, a Sunni Muslim ruling a largely Shi'ite country, was widely criticized for modernization's impact on traditional Iranian society. Drug use, alcohol consumption,

Watch the **Video**
The 1979 Islamic Revolution in Iran: A Turning Point for the Middle East and the World
on **myhistorylab.com**

Iran's Islamic Revolution challenges traditional Muslim regimes and Western styles of dress and conduct deeply offended many Shi'ites. But the Shah had also been protected by the United States, and his removal was accelerated by three foreign policy concerns: American support for Israel, the failure of secular regimes like his to destroy the Jewish state, and the frustration caused in the Muslim world by Egypt's peace with Israel. Ayatollah Khomeini proclaimed an Islamic Republic, in which religious leaders would exercise all executive, legislative, and judicial authority. Iran's opposition to the role played by the United States in the Middle East put it on a collision course with Washington, and a crisis erupted in 1979 when Iranian militants broke into the U.S. Embassy in Tehran and captured 52 embassy personnel whom it claimed were spies. This violation of diplomatic immunity caused a crisis lasting until the hostages were released in 1981 and poisoned U.S.-Iranian relations for decades thereafter.

View the Image
Ayatollah Khomeini
on **myhistorylab.com**

Read the Document
Islam and the State in the Middle East: Ayatollah Khomeini's Vision of Islamic Government (Mid–20th Century)
on **myhistorylab.com**

ANTI-ISRAELI AND ANTI-WESTERN TERRORISM. We begin this section with a direct disclaimer. Terrorism is a highly sensitive subject in the modern world, and there are those who maintain that to attempt to understand the motives of terrorists, or the factors that make terrorism seem attractive to certain people, is to defend or approve of terrorism. This attitude is misguided. To understand an action or a condition is not the same as approving of it. To decide not to attempt to understand an action or a condition, because to do so may be controversial, is an act of willful ignorance. This section contains observations about the nature of terrorism and the conditions that help to nourish it. Those observations are provided in the hope that readers will understand terrorism, not that they will approve of it.

Although peace with Egypt brought Israel unprecedented military security, it also encouraged groups that fought Israel through terrorism, since Arab states could no longer hope for success through conventional military means. Terrorist attacks stem not from power but from the lack of it. States or organizations that lack the military, economic, or diplomatic resources to fight powers they consider oppressors sometimes turn to terrorism as a means of striking back. The Irgun, a Jewish organization, had resorted to terrorism after World War II in an effort to drive the British out of Palestine. Terrorism is therefore not a philosophy, an ideology, or a form of government: it is a tactic used by the weak against the strong.

Israel's overwhelming military superiority in the Middle East, together with Egypt's departure from the anti-Israeli coalition, led some to turn to terrorism. Groups such as Islamic Jihad, Hezbollah (*HEZ-buh-lah*), and Hamas (*hah-MAHS*) carried out attacks on Israeli forces in Lebanon, parts of which were occupied by Israel in 1982 in an effort to expel Palestinian organizations that had taken refuge there under Syrian protection. One year later, suicide bombers killed 241 U.S. Marines and 58 French soldiers sent to Lebanon in an effort to pacify that country by separating Israeli forces from Palestinians and Syrians.

Terrorist groups such as these justified their actions by pointing to Israel's prolonged occupation of the territories taken in the 1967 war, in violation of a United Nations Security Council resolution. Frustrations on both sides led to abusive behavior and provocations. Islamic states such as Iran and Syria openly supported terrorist activities, while moderates in the Palestinian-Arab community were overcome by those preaching hatred. As terrorist groups flourished, those endorsing peaceful paths to change were marginalized.

Terrorism takes root in the Middle East

Terrorist attacks were intended to force Israel to withdraw from the occupied West Bank territories and make concessions to the Palestinians, but the growth of terrorism had no noticeable effect on Israeli policy. In 1988, Palestinian groups shifted their focus to attacking Israeli soldiers and civilians in the occupied territories. This *Intifada* (*in-ti-FAH-dah*), or "shaking off," was designed both to damage Israel's occupying forces and to call world attention to injustices against Palestinians. It caused significant physical and psychological trauma in Israel but did not bring about an Israeli withdrawal. In the 1990s, events in the Persian Gulf temporarily sidetracked the *Intifada*, but it later returned at the same time that a global wave of terrorist attacks occurred.

Persian Gulf Wars and Global Terrorism

Islamist fundamentalism defined as enemies not only non-Islamic states but also all secularized Arab states, including Iraq, ruled since 1972 by Saddam Hussein, a military dictator whose socialistic Ba'ath Party had taken power in a 1968 coup. Believing that Iran had been weakened militarily by its break with America, Saddam in 1980 attempted to seize an Iranian waterway linking his country to the Persian Gulf. The ensuing Iran–Iraq War dragged on for eight years, killing nearly two million soldiers and civilians and severely straining both countries' economies. It ended in 1988 with modest territorial gains for Iraq.

Two years later, Saddam tried to make up for the war's economic losses by seizing the oil-rich nation of Kuwait, claimed for decades by Iraq as its nine-teenth province. But his ambitions were thwarted by the United States, which organized a 32-nation U.N. coalition, supported by Saudi Arabia and other Arab nations fearing Iraqi expansionism. In early 1991, in the **Persian Gulf War**, the coalition expelled Iraq from Kuwait. Its success greatly heightened U.S. leverage in the Middle East. That leverage, coupled with Israeli restraint in the face of Iraqi efforts to draw Israel into the war and split the coalition, shattered the longstanding Arab refusal to recognize Israel's right to exist. Saudi Arabia, which for decades had poured money into the anti-Israeli cause, now stated that Israel had earned the right to be treated as a good neighbor and cut off funding for the PLO, which had backed Iraq in the Persian Gulf War.

Left without financial backing, in 1993 PLO leader Yasir Arafat signed a peace agreement with Israeli prime minster Yitzhak Rabin (*rah-BĒN*). Under its terms, Israel accepted the necessity of creating a Palestinian state, and the PLO recognized Israel as a legitimate nation. Peace between Israel and Jordan followed in 1994, and it appeared that the troubled Middle East might be on the verge of a solution to the vexing Palestinian Question.

Then violence again shattered the possibility of peace. An Israeli extremist, outraged at these developments, assassinated Rabin at a peace rally in 1995. The next year, terrorist groups found a safe haven in Afghanistan, where the Taliban came to power. This ultrafun-damentalist movement subjected its citizens to the full rigors of seventh-century Islamic law, characterized by mutilation and execution for offenses that elsewhere were punished by imprisonment or fines. Under Taliban rule, women were banned from employment and denied an education. Throughout the 1990s, militant fundamentalists organized and trained in Afghanistan for actions throughout the Middle East. Terrorists orchestrated attacks on Israelis, worked to undermine the Egyptian government, murdered thousands in Algeria, carried out assaults on U.S. embassies and ships, and solidified Iran's Islamic Republic.

In 2000, negotiations in America over Palestinian statehood came close to reaching an agreement but ultimately failed. A tragic sequence of events followed. The *Intifada* was renewed on the West Bank, while in Israel a new hard-line government opposed further concessions to the Palestinians. Then, on September 11, 2001, came a dramatic attack on the United States. Members of a terrorist network called Al Qaeda (*AHL Kĺ-dah*) hijacked four commercial airliners and deliberately crashed them into both towers of the World Trade Center in New York City (collapsing both buildings), the Pentagon in Washington, and an open field in Pennsylvania (the last crash resulting from a struggle

Iraq's seizure of Kuwait leads to regional conflict

Oil wells burning during the Persian Gulf War.

 **Watch** the **Video**
President Bush on the Gulf War

on **myhistorylab.com**

View the **Image**
Rabin and Arafat Shake Hands at the White House, 1993

on **myhistorylab.com**

Al Qaeda attacks the United States

between passengers and hijackers). Aghast at its vulnerability and the deaths of almost three thousand Americans, the United States attacked Afghanistan and removed its Taliban government, which had furnished bases to Al Qaeda.

Two years later, a coalition of forces led by the United States invaded Iraq and destroyed the Ba'athist regime. Washington's stated objective was to establish a democratic government in Iraq, thereby removing it as a possible base for terrorist attacks. Since Iraq apparently was not involved in the 2001 attacks on America, however, the Iraq War of 2003 proved highly controversial, and it increased hatred of America throughout the Islamic world. Countries seen as supporters of the American-led invasion, including Spain, Indonesia, Britain, and Saudi Arabia, were themselves attacked by terrorists.

The destruction of Ba'athist Iraq, moreover, left Iran as the Persian Gulf's main power, dramatically altering the balance of forces in Islamic Southwest Asia. In 2005, as Iraq under U.S. occupation struggled to form a democracy acceptable to its Shi'ite, Sunni Arab, and Kurdish populations, Iranian voters elected as president Mahmoud Ahmadinejad (*ahk-mah-DĒ-nih-jahd*). The new president was an Islamist fundamentalist whose desire to develop a uranium-enrichment program far more sophisticated than that required to produce nuclear fuel for peaceful purposes led many to conclude that he hoped to build nuclear weapons and destroy Israel.

Demonstrations and protests in 2011 oust dictatorships in Tunisia and Egypt

For nearly a decade after the September 11 attacks, Western societies debated whether or not Islam was compatible with democracy, and many scholars questioned the desire of Muslims for democratic government. Then in January 2011, street demonstrations in Tunis rapidly toppled the one-party state that had governed Tunisia since independence in 1956. Suddenly the flame of revolution ignited much of the Middle East, as protests and revolts broke out in Algeria, Libya, Bahrain, Jordan, Syria, Yemen, and most significantly, Egypt. Weeks of protest in Cairo culminated in the overthrow of the three-decade dictatorship of Hosni Mubarak in February 2011. Simultaneously, violent revolution in Libya endangered the 32-year rule of Muammar Qaddafi.

No one could predict the future course of revolt in the Middle East, just as no one could predict whether or not the emerging governments in Tunisia and Egypt would be either democratic or stable. But the long debate over whether or not ordinary Muslims wanted responsible government seemed to have been resolved.

CHAPTER
REVIEW

Putting It in Perspective

In the early 21st century, the problems of Africa and the Middle East seemed overwhelming. Some of Africa's problems had natural causes, such as severe droughts that pushed the Sahara farther south and the catastrophic AIDS epidemic that reduced populations in sub-Saharan Africa. Others, however, were legacies of colonialism, which left most African nations without the industrial resources required for modernization and unfamiliar with the functioning of modern democratic societies. Although many of these new nations were dangerously unstable, the former colonial powers of Europe often washed their hands of Africa after

independence, reducing aid to minimal levels. Rapid population growth meant that most families lived in poverty and frustrated efforts to improve literacy rates and public health. These enormous problems undermined the hopes Africans once held for the benefits of decolonization and independence.

The Middle East faced a different set of challenges. Terrorist attacks against Israel, the United States, and other lands perceived as their supporters marked the resurgence of an Islamist fundamentalism that was amplified by anti-Western resentments and failure to resolve the Palestinian Question. In the face of this resurgence, Islamic societies had to choose: Would they continue efforts to modernize, secularize, and democratize, even if such changes proved incompatible with their traditional values and cultures? Or would they pursue the antimodernist and antimaterialistic philosophies that were still powerfully attractive to many Muslims? Would they find a way to coexist in peace with Israel? Or would they persist in efforts to destroy the Jewish state? On the answers to such questions rest the future stability and prosperity of the Middle East.

Reviewing Key Material

KEY CONCEPTS

decolonization, 892
Fifth Pan-African Congress, 892
apartheid, 894
neocolonialism, 899
African National Congress (ANC), 901
Zionists, 905
Balfour Declaration, 905
Palestinian Question, 907

Palestine Liberation Organization (PLO), 909
Islamic modernism, 910
Islamic reformism, 910
Islamic revival, 910
Islamist fundamentalism, 910
Intifada, 912
Persian Gulf War, 913

KEY PEOPLE

Dag Hammarskjöld, 891, 900
Kofi Annan, 891
Charles de Gaulle, 891
Jomo Kenyatta, 893
Léopold Senghor, 893
Kwame Nkrumah, 893
Julius Nyerere, 898
Sékou Touré, 899
Patrice Lumumba, 899

Mobutu Sese Seko, 900
Nelson Mandela, 901
Theodor Herzl, 905
Gamal Abdel Nasser, 907
Anwar al-Sadat, 909
Ayatollah Ruhollah Khomeini, 911
Saddam Hussein, 913
Yasir Arafat, 913
Yitzhak Rabin, 913

ASK YOURSELF

1. How and why did World War II lead to the decolonization of Africa?
2. How and why did Britain and France differ in their attitudes toward African nationalism?
3. How were Arab nationalism and the Palestinian Question connected?
4. How does Islamist fundamentalism affect the conflict between modernity and tradition in the Islamic world?

GOING FURTHER

Ansprenger, F. *The Dissolution of the Colonial Empires.* 1989.
Berman, Bruce, and John Lonsdale. *Unhappy Valley: Conflict in Kenya and Africa.* 1992.
Commins, David. *The Wahhabi Mission and Saudi Arabia.* 2006.
Cook, David. *Understanding Jihad.* 2005.
Cooper, Fred. *Africa Since 1940.* 2000.
Davidson, B. *The Black Man's Burden: Africa and the Curse of the Nation-State.* 1992.
Dekmejian, R. H. *Islam in Revolution: Fundamentalism in the Arab World.* 1995.
Dubow, S. *Racial Segregation and the Origins of Apartheid in South Africa.* 1989.
El Khazen, M. *The Breakdown of the State in Lebanon, 1967–1976.* 2000.
Esposito, J. L., ed. *The Iranian Revolution: Its Global Impact.* 1990.
French, Howard. *A Continent for the Taking.* 2004.
Goodman, David. *Fault Lines: Journeys into the New South Africa.* 1999.
Hargreaves, J. D. *Decolonization in Africa.* 1988.
Keddie, N. R. *Modern Iran: Roots and Results of Revolution.* 2006.
Keddie, N. R. *Women in Muslim Societies: The Long Path of Change.* 2004.
Long, D. E. *The Kingdom of Saudi Arabia.* 1997.
Louis, W. R., and R. Owen. *Suez 1956: The Crisis and Its Consequences.* 1989.
Mamdani, Mahmood. *When Victims Become Killers: Colonialism, Nativism, and the Genocide in Rwanda.* 2001.
Mandela, Nelson. *Long Walk to Freedom.* 1994.
Musallam, A. M. *The Iraqi Invasion of Kuwait.* 1996.
Roy, Olivier. *Globalized Islam: The Search for a New Ummah.* 2004.
Shillington, Kevin. *History of Africa.* 1995.
Smith, C. *Palestine and the Arab-Israeli Conflict.* 2004.
Throup, D. W. *Economic and Social Origins of Mau Mau.* 1987.

Key Dates and Developments

African Independence

1935	Italy invades Ethiopia
1941	Liberation of Ethiopia
1944	Brazzaville Conference
1945	Fifth Pan-African Conference
1948	National Party wins South African elections
1951	Independence: Libya
1956	Independence: Morocco, Tunisia, the Sudan Suez Crisis
1957	Independence: Ghana
1958	Independence: Guinea All-African People's Conference in Ghana
1960	Independence: Senegal, Mauritania, Mali, Upper Volta, Ivory Coast, Chad, Central African Republic, Gabon, Togo, Dahomey, Cameroon, Congo, Nigeria, Somalia Congo Crisis
1961	Murder of Lumumba; death of Hammarskjöld Independence: Tanganyika
1962	Independence: Algeria, Uganda, Rwanda, Burundi
1963	Independence: Kenya Nelson Mandela imprisoned in South Africa
1964	Independence: Zambia, Malawi Creation of Tanzania
1965–1980	White supremacist government in Southern Rhodesia
1966	Independence: Botswana, Lesotho
1968	Independence: Swaziland
1974	Revolution in Portugal
1975	Independence: Guinea-Bissau, Angola, Mozambique
1977	Independence: Djibouti
1980	Independence: Zimbabwe
1990	Independence: Namibia
1993	Release of Nelson Mandela
1994	Free elections in South Africa

The Middle East Since 1945

1946	Independence of Transjordan
1948	Foundation of the State of Israel
1948–1949	First Arab-Israeli War
1949	Revolution in Syria
1952	Revolution in Egypt (Nasser)
1956	Suez Crisis
1958	United Arab Republic (Egypt and Syria) Revolution in Iraq
1964	Formation of the Palestine Liberation Organization
1967	Six-Day War
1968	Ba'athist Revolution in Iraq
1970	Death of Nasser
1973	Yom Kippur/Ramadan War
1979	Peace between Egypt and Israel Islamic Republic proclaimed in Iran
1980–1988	Iran–Iraq War
1981	Assassination of Sadat
1982	Israel invades Lebanon
1988	First Palestinian *Intifada*
1990	Iraq invades Kuwait
1991	Persian Gulf War
1993	Oslo Accords: PLO recognizes Israel
1994	Peace between Jordan and Israel
1995	Assassination of Rabin
2000	Second Palestinian *Intifada*
2001	September 11 terrorist attacks against U.S. United States invades Afghanistan
2003	United States invades Iraq
2011	Demonstrations and revolts sweep the Middle East

PEARSON
myhistͦrylab Connections

Reinforce what you learned in this chapter by studying the many documents,
images, maps, review tools, and videos available at www.myhistorylab.com.

Read and Review

✓●─[Study and **Review** Chapter 37

📖●─[Read the **Document**

African National Congress Against Imperialism (1927),
Josiah Gumede, p. 894

Frantz Fanon, from *The Wretched of the Earth*, p. 897

Kwame Nkrumah on African Unity (1960s), p. 898

Jomo Kenyatta, from *Facing Mt. Kenya: The Tribal Life of
the Gikuyu*, p. 898

Nelson Mandela, from *Freedom, Justice and Dignity
for All South Africa: Statements and Articles by
Mr. Nelson Mandela*, p. 901

Islam and the State in the Middle East: Ayatollah
Khomeini's Vision of Islamic Government (Mid–20th
Century), p. 912

🔍─[View the **Map**

Interactive Map: The Emergence of the Modern Middle
East, p. 905

Interactive Map: The Formation of Modern Israel, p. 905

🔍─[View the **Image**

Construction of the Aswan Dam, Egypt, p. 908

Ayatollah Khomeini, p. 912

Rabin and Arafat Shake Hands at the White House,
1993, p. 913

((●─[Listen to the **Audio**

Decolonization 1, p. 891

Africa/Zulus 2, p. 892

👁─[Watch the **Video**

President Bush on the Gulf War, p. 913

Research and Explore

👁─[Watch the **Video**

Africa as an Urban, Not Rural, Place, p. 902

👁─[Watch the **Video**

The 1979 Islamic Revolution in Iran: A Turning Point for
the Middle East and the World, p. 911

Glossary

African diaspora "Dispersed" or transplanted Africans and their descendants.

African National Congress An organization founded in South Africa in 1912 by educated African professionals to combat white racial repression.

Afrikaners Descendants of Dutch and other European immigrants who settled in southernmost Africa near the Cape of Good Hope after 1652; also called Boers.

Anschluss Union of Austria with Germany, carried out by Hitler in 1938.

Anticolonialism Resistance to colonial rule.

Apartheid A system of institutionalized racial discrimination established in South Africa in 1948.

Appeasement A policy of giving in to a potential aggressor in order to maintain peace.

Armistice A temporary cessation of hostilities between warring powers.

Assembly line A process by which products are manufactured in continuous flow through a series of stations that each perform a separate function.

Ausgleich An 1867 compromise that granted Hungarians autonomy by dividing the Austrian Empire into self-governing Austrian and Hungarian sections, thereby transforming it into the Dual Monarchy of Austria-Hungary.

Baby Boom A huge surge of births in the United States in the two decades following the end of World War II.

Balance of power A situation in which key nations offset each other's strengths, so that none is strong enough to impose its will on the others.

Balfour Declaration Issued in 1917, this statement placed Britain on record in support of a Jewish homeland in Palestine.

Bastille A large prison and arsenal in eastern Paris whose capture in 1789 by supporters of the National Assembly frightened King Louis XVI into capitulating to the French Revolution.

Bill of Rights A written document specifying the rights that King William III and Queen Mary of England were required to endorse in 1689 as conditions of their rule.

Blank check Issued in July 1914, a guarantee that Germany would support any action Austria might take against Serbia in the aftermath of the assassination of Austrian Archduke Franz Ferdinand.

Blitzkrieg "Lightning war," an innovative German tactic based on radio coordination between armored units and dive-bombers; instrumental in Germany's defeat of Poland in 1939.

Bloody Sunday A day in January 1905 on which a massive, peaceful workers' demonstration was fired on by imperial Russian troops, killing several hundred.

Bolsheviks Literally, "those in the majority" in the Russian Social Democratic Party after 1903; led by Lenin, they seized power in the October Revolution of 1917 and later became the Soviet Communist Party.

Bosnian Crisis of 1908–1909 A serious international crisis that tied Austria closer to Germany and provoked an immense eight-year military buildup in Russia.

Boston Tea Party A protest in 1773 by Britain's colonists in Boston against a tax levied on tea.

Boyar class An aristocracy that played a significant role throughout much of Russian history.

Braceros Mexican immigrant workers who began entering the United States in 1942 to work in factories replacing U.S. workers drafted during World War II.

Brezhnev Doctrine The assertion in 1968, following the Warsaw Pact's invasion of Czechoslovakia, that the Soviet Union had the right to intervene in other communist countries to protect the global interests of socialism, as defined by Soviet leaders.

Bridewealth   In Africa, a payment from the groom to the parents of the bride to compensate them for the loss of their daughter and assure them that he would treat her well.

Calico   Indian cotton cloth that came from Calicut on India's Malabar Coast.

Capitalism   An economic system based on competition among private enterprises.

Cash crops   Commodities that when harvested could be sold for money to purchase food and other necessities.

Cassava   A large hardy root plant from the American tropics, native to Brazil and used as a food staple in Africa; also called manioc.

Caudillos   Latin American leaders who ruled as strong personalities and often failed to develop stable and enduring political and economic institutions.

Charter companies   Trading associations protected by royal monopoly.

Civil rights movement   A nationwide campaign for racial equality in the United States in the twentieth century.

Cohong   Merchant guild of Guangzhou (Canton); a group of Chinese firms authorized by the imperial government to conduct commerce with foreigners.

Collective farms   In Soviet Russia, multifamily farms supposedly owned by their members but actually run by the state.

Collective liability   A Russian practice whereby all members of a community were jointly responsible for taxes and other obligations, and were considered liable for the actions of everyone in the community.

Committee of Public Safety   A group of officials given broad powers in 1793–1794 to protect France from foreign and domestic enemies.

Common market   The European Economic Community, a coalition of nations agreeing to reduce tariffs on each other's goods to expedite commercial growth.

Communists   Revolutionary socialists who promoted violent overthrow of the existing political and social order.

Concertación   A Chilean democratic alliance that successfully defeated General Augusto Pinochet's referendum on continuation of military rule in 1988.

Congress system   An ongoing mechanism devised by Prince Metternich to enable Europe's major powers to hold periodic meetings to preserve order.

Conservatives   People who sought to retain the structures and ways of the past.

Containment of communism   A United States Cold War policy based on George Kennan's assertion that communism, if contained geographically and prevented from expanding, would eventually collapse.

Continental System   Napoleon's insistence that all European countries dominated by France boycott British goods.

Coolie trade   The hiring or kidnapping of poor Chinese workers to serve as cheap labor in places such as Cuba, Peru, or California.

Cossacks   A diverse assortment of frontier adventurers dwelling in the steppe lands north of the Black and Caspian Seas.

Cottage industry   A system under which peasants would make products in their own cottages and sell them to merchant capitalists.

Council of the Indies   A board established by King Carlos I of Spain in 1524 to supervise every aspect of governance in Spanish America.

Criollos   White people of European ancestry born in Spanish America.

Cuban missile crisis   A grave confrontation between the United States and the Soviet Union over the presence of Soviet nuclear missiles in Cuba.

Cubism   An artistic style using geometric shapes to produce bold images.

Daimyo   Hereditary regional warlords who dominated segments of Japan.

D-Day   June 6, 1944, the day on which the Allies invaded France to begin to liberate Western Europe from German occupation.

Decolonization   A process whereby colonized peoples in Asia and Africa gained independence from Western imperial domination, often through nationalistic "liberation movements."

Deism   A rational religion that viewed God not as a divinity deeply involved in human affairs, but as a master mechanic or "great watchmaker," who created the universe as a vast machine, established the laws by which it operated, and then mostly left it alone.

Descamisados "Shirtless ones," Argentina's manual laborers who formed the base of support for President Juan D. Perón.

Détente A relaxation of international tensions.

Dictators In the twentieth century, leaders who wielded total control, dominated weak elected institutions, and used the army and police to stifle dissent.

Diplomatic Revolution of 1890–1907 The process whereby Bismarck's diplomacy was reversed and Germany was encircled by France, Russia, and Britain.

Dirty war The Argentine military government's repression, torture, and murder of Peronists, Montoneros, and Communists from 1976 to 1978; also used to describe the French-Algerian War of 1954–1962.

Dominion government A compromise whereby large British colonies such as Canada and Australia were granted self-government while technically remaining dominions of the British Empire.

Domostroi "Household Order," a manual advising Russians on running their families.

Duma A Russian council or parliament.

Dutch learning Western techniques of shipbuilding, weaponry, art, sciences, music, and medicine, transmitted to Japan by the Dutch.

Economic nationalism The creation of tariff walls and trade barriers to protect a country's industries and products from international competition.

The elect In Calvinist Christianity, people chosen beforehand by God for salvation.

Eleven Years' Tyranny The period between 1629 and 1640 when King Charles I ruled England without calling Parliament.

Enclosures The practice by English landowners of fencing or hedging off large tracts of land to pasture their sheep or to implement new farming methods.

Enlightenment A European intellectual movement, inspired by boundless faith in human reason, that sought by using reason to achieve progress in all areas of human endeavor.

Enterprise of the Indies Columbus's detailed plan for a westward maritime expedition to discover a shorter route from Europe to East Asia.

Estado Nôvo "New State," a military-backed dictatorship established by Getúlio Vargas in Brazil in 1937.

Estates General A nationwide assembly of representatives from the three estates of French society.

Fascism An ideology that promoted belligerent nationalism and repressive dictatorship, subjecting individual rights to the goals of the nation and its leader.

Fifth Pan-African Congress A meeting in Manchester, England, in 1945 in which several African nationalists announced their intention to create independence movements.

Floating world Japanese urban amusement areas offering men escape from austerity in indulgent nightlife.

Fronde A rebellion of French nobles between 1648 and 1653 attempting to reverse the trend toward royal absolutism.

Fulani A pastoral West African people who became enchanted with Sufism and founded the Sokoto Caliphate in 1809.

Gang of Four A group of Chinese radicals who sought to seize power after Mao's death in 1976 in order to renew the Cultural Revolution.

Gauchos Cowboys of the Argentine backlands.

Geneva Accords A multinational agreement reached in 1954 to end French colonial rule in Indochina.

Genocide The deliberate and systematic destruction of an entire race or ethnic group.

Global warming A sustained increase in average global temperatures, accompanied by fears of impending environmental disaster and debates about how humans impact their environment and how they should respond.

Glorious Revolution A cooperative effort by the English Parliament and an invasion force from the Netherlands to overthrow King James II in 1688.

Good Neighbor policy United States President Franklin Roosevelt's 1933 commitment that the United States would respect the laws of its Latin

American neighbors and refrain from military or political involvement in their affairs.

Great purges   Stalin's systematic effort to eliminate his opponents in 1936–1938.

Great Trek   A mass migration of Afrikaners northeast from Cape Colony into South Africa's interior, beginning in the 1830s.

Green revolution   A global agricultural movement that used synthetic fertilizers and scientifically-developed high-yield crops to enhance farm output.

Guillotine   A scaffold devised to release a heavy blade that instantly beheaded its victims.

Gunboat diplomacy   Aggressive behavior by the United States toward Latin American nations.

Haiku   Concise 17-syllable Japanese poems organized in three successive lines of five, seven, and five syllables.

Hiroshima   The Japanese city that was the first to be destroyed by atomic bombing in 1945.

Holy fools   Radical religious ascetics in Muscovy who renounced all worldly goods, wore few clothes, and uttered cryptic phrases that many Russians considered prophetic.

ICBM   Intercontinental Ballistics Missile, an unmanned rocket that can be launched from one continent to hit targets on another continent.

Icons   Stylized wooden paintings depicting Christian holy persons, venerated as sources of grace and often displayed in Orthodox churches.

Ideologies   Comprehensive systems of thought intended to explain and transform society in accordance with certain political, social, and cultural ideals.

Imperialism   The use of military force (or the threat of such use) to establish European colonies in Africa, India, and Southeast Asia, and to open up countries such as China to Western commercial exploitation.

Impressionism   An artistic style that sought to depict subjective impressions made on the painter by scenes from nature and modern urban life.

Indulgence   In the Christian Church, a remission of the punishment due for sins that were sacramentally forgiven; designed to reduce or eliminate suffering in purgatory.

Industrialization   A momentous shift from a rural agrarian economy to an urban manufacturing economy.

Inflation   A situation in which money declines in value and the prices of goods and services rise.

Intifada   "Shaking off," an uprising designed to damage Israeli occupation forces and to call world attention to injustices perpetrated against Palestinians.

Irish Home Rule   A quest to gain domestic autonomy for Ireland.

Islamic modernism   A nineteenth century reaction to the challenges posed by technologically advanced European societies; modernists wanted to reshape Islam along European social and political lines.

Islamic reformism   A nineteenth century reaction to the challenges posed by technologically advanced European societies; reformists wanted to revitalize Islam by purifying it religiously and socially.

Islamic revival   A 1970s reaction to the continued existence of the State of Israel; revivalists denounced materialistic Western values as subversive of Muslim family life and religious authority.

Islamist fundamentalism   A generic term for movements dedicated to political as well as religious change that view moderate Muslim regimes as excessively cooperative with the West.

Jim Crow laws   Post-Reconstruction laws that sanctioned racial discrimination in the southern United States.

Jingoism   Belligerent popular nationalism based on warlike pride in a country's colonial conquests.

Jujitsu   A Japanese form of hand-to-hand combat using holds, blows, and throws to disable an opponent.

Junkers   East Prussian noble families who furnished officers for the Prussian army.

Junta   Provisional governments appointed in Spanish America to rule on behalf of the imprisoned King Carlos IV; later used as a generic term for provisional military governments throughout the region.

Kabuki   A form of Japanese drama in which elaborately made-up and costumed men performed both male and female roles using elaborate and seductive gestures.

Khmer Rouge "Red Khmer," the Cambodian Communist Party that took power in 1975 and slaughtered nearly two million people.

Khoisan Unique languages, distinguished by clicking sounds, spoken by the indigenous inhabitants of southern Africa.

Kremlin A fortified area in central Moscow housing churches, palaces, and government headquarters.

Laissez faire A French term meaning "let them do as they choose," asserting that governments should not intervene in economic affairs.

La Reforma The Mexican revolutionary movement that overthrew Santa Anna in 1854 and then attempted to implement democratic reforms and a liberal constitution.

League of Nations An international organization (1919–1945) designed to maintain peace by cooperation among its members.

League of Nations Mandates Lands entrusted to specified nations, mostly Britain and France, allegedly to help prepare the people for self-rule.

Lebensraum The Nazi concept that "living space" for the German Master Race must be conquered from Poland and Russia.

Liberalism An ideology based on liberty, calling for constitutional governments with restricted powers, elected legislatures, and safeguards protecting people's rights.

Liberation theology A Catholic theological concept holding that Jesus of Nazareth preached not only a message of love, but also a message of opposition to unjust government; developed by theologians from Mexico and Brazil.

Limited monarchy An English alternative to royal absolutism in which nobles and the middle classes worked together to restrict the authority of the ruler.

Long March The 6,000-mile retreat of the Chinese Communists from southern to northwestern China, enabling them to escape destruction by Nationalist forces and to rebuild their movement.

Loyalists Colonists in British North America who opposed the revolt against their mother country.

Luddites English workers between 1811 and 1816 bent on breaking machines they blamed for taking their jobs.

Luftwaffe The name for the German Air Force between 1935 and 1945.

Machismo The Iberian concept of the exaltation of masculine virility and power.

MAD Mutual Assured Destruction, a policy of nuclear deterrence based on the assumption that since nuclear war would destroy both sides, neither side would be foolish enough to start one.

Mahdists Disciples of Muhammad Ahmed, a Sudanese mystic who claimed to be al-Mahdi, "the divinely-inspired one," and who fought the British to establish a radical anti-Western Islamic regime in the 1880s.

Mahgrib The Muslim term for North Africa, meaning "the West," since it was the western part of the Islamic world.

Malabar coast India's southwestern seaboard, home to several Portuguese, Dutch, and British commercial centers in the sixteenth and seventeenth centuries.

Mandarins A Portuguese rendition of a Southeast Asian term for government ministers, used to refer to a Chinese scholar-bureaucrat class recruited through extremely rigorous civil service examinations.

Manifest Destiny The belief by many people in the United States that their country had a god-given right to expand and control the entire continent of North America.

Maratha A Hindu nationalist movement founded to resist Mughal rule in India.

March of the Women A march in 1789 by six thousand hungry French women that forced King Louis XVI to move from Versailles to Paris.

Maroons Runaway slaves who established independent wilderness communities in the Americas, where they maintained many African customs.

Marshall Plan A United States economic aid program, also called the European Recovery Program, designed to preclude communist expansion by strengthening Europe economically after World War II.

Master race The Nazi assertion that Germans are descended from ancient Aryans and are destined to dominate "subhuman" or inferior races.

Matrilineal Pertaining to a society in which children trace their heritage and ancestral descent through their mother's family line.

Matrilocal Pertaining to an arrangement in which married couples customarily live in or near the home territory of the wife's family or clan.

May Fourth protests A series of anti-Western demonstrations that spread quickly across China in 1919, laying the groundwork for nationalist revolution.

Mercantilism A policy designed to create a condition in which a country's trading exports exceeded its imports in value.

Mercosur The "Common Market of the South," established by Argentina, Brazil, Paraguay, and Uruguay in 1991.

Mestizos People of mixed descent in Iberian America.

Metropolitan The head bishop of the Russian Orthodox Church.

Middle East A modern term used to refer to West Asia and Egypt.

Middle Passage The name given to the voyage westward across the Atlantic from West Africa during which slaves bound for the Americas suffered terrible hardships.

Militarism An exaltation of the armed forces, coupled with the assertion that military might is central to a nation's character.

Monroe Doctrine Issued by United States President James Monroe in 1823, it committed the United States to defend the newly created Latin American states against any European efforts at recolonization.

Montoneros An Argentine urban terrorist group in the 1960s and 1970s.

Mothers of the Plaza de Mayo Women who marched in front of Argentina's executive mansion each Thursday between 1977 and 1983 to protest the disappearance of their husbands and children.

Napoleonic Code Napoleon's codification of French laws that guaranteed all male citizens equality before the law.

National self-determination The right of each nationality to freely decide its own political status.

National Socialist German Workers Party A fascist, anti-Semitic, racist mass movement whose supporters were often called Nazis.

Nationalism An intense devotion to one's own cultural-linguistic group and to its embodiment in a unified, independent state.

Nationalization The takeover of private properties or enterprises by the national state.

Nativism Domestic opposition to immigration from Asia and southern and eastern Europe into the United States.

NATO North Atlantic Treaty Organization, an alliance concluded in 1949 and designed to protect Western Europe against Soviet expansion.

Nawabs Local Indian princes whom the British called "nabobs."

Nazis Nickname for supporters of the National Socialist German Workers Party, a fascist, anti-Semitic, racist mass movement led by Adolf Hitler.

Nazi-Soviet Pact Non-aggression pact between Germany and the Soviet Union in 1939 whereby Germany granted the USSR part of Poland and several other territorial adjustments in return for grain, oil, and timber; also called the Molotov-Ribbentrop Pact.

Neocolonialism Continued economic domination of former colonies by the power that had ruled them before they gained political independence.

Ninety-five Theses A set of propositions challenging the Christian Church's power to forgive sins and grant indulgences; issued by Martin Luther in 1517.

Nonaligned nations A group of countries in the 1950s that refused to side with either the United States or the Soviet Union.

North American Free Trade Area Known as NAFTA, an economic agreement linking Canada, the United States, and Mexico in 1993.

North German Confederation The unification of all states in North Germany following Prussia's victory over Austria in 1866.

Nuclear families Families made up only of parents and their children.

Old believers Those who rejected Patriarch Nikon's changes in Russian Orthodox practices and openly defied church and state leaders in the seventeenth century.

Open Door policy Proclaimed by the United States in 1899, calling for free and equal trade with China and for the preservation of China's territorial integrity.

Opium An addictive narcotic drug made from a certain kind of poppy.

Pale of Jewish Settlement A broad band of lands along Russia's western borders where Jews were allowed to reside, although they were increasingly subjected to assorted legal limitations and abuses.

Palestine Liberation Organization "PLO," founded in 1964; a coalition of more than thirty anti-Israeli organizations dedicated to Israel's replacement by a secular Palestinian state.

Palestinian question A refugee problem created by the displacement of Palestinians during the Israeli War for Independence of 1948–1949 and never settled thereafter.

Panca Sila "Five Pillars" proposed by Ahmed Sukarno and Muhammad Yamin as the basis for the development of independent Indonesia.

Paris Commune A revolutionary government that governed Paris from March to May 1871, opposing the national government of France.

Peninsulares White residents of Spanish America who had been born in Spain.

People of color A term applied in Saint-Domingue to former slaves and persons of mixed racial heritage who were legally free but were treated by whites as socially inferior.

Persian Gulf War A 1991 conflict in which a 32-nation coalition expelled Iraq from Kuwait and shattered the long-standing Arab refusal to recognize Israel's right to exist.

Petrograd Soviet A council of deputies elected by workers and soldiers in the capital of Russia in 1917; it struggled for power against the Provisional Government.

Philosophes Eminent French thinkers who dominated the Enlightenment in the eighteenth century.

Physiocrats The leading economic thinkers of the Enlightenment who were convinced that increased production and trade would enhance national wealth.

Poder moderador "Moderative power" under the Brazilian Empire, giving the emperor authority to reconcile disputes between branches of government and prevent radical swings of the electorate in any extreme direction.

Polygyny The practice by which a man took more than one wife.

Porfiriato A period of political repression and rapid economic development in Mexico during the dictatorship of Porfirio Díaz.

Porteños "Port dwellers" in Buenos Aires, Argentina, who considered themselves superior to illiterate gauchos.

Predestination The belief that God long ago decided everyone's eternal fate.

PRI The Institutional Revolutionary Party, claiming to embody the true spirit of the Mexican Revolution of 1910.

Prime Minister The British system, initiated in 1721, in which the same person exercises both legislative and executive authority by serving as leader of both Parliament and the royal government.

Proletariat A large class of landless laborers who moved to cities and entered the industrial work force.

Protectorate A country controlled by an outside power claiming to provide security.

Provisional government A temporary cabinet composed largely of Duma leaders after the tsar of Russia was overthrown in 1917.

Purgatory In Christian belief, a place of suffering that purified the soul so it could enter heaven.

Puritanical Referring to people who uphold an austere moral code and simple religious practices.

Puritans Calvinist Christians who considered Anglicanism too much like Roman Catholicism and developed their own simplified church in England.

Quinine An alkaloid substance derived from the bark of cinchona trees and used to prevent and treat malaria.

Race A concept that divides human beings into categories based on external characteristics, especially skin color.

Racism The belief that race was the main determinant of human traits and abilities, with some races seen as superior to others.

Rape of Nanjing The Japanese Army's massacre and abuse of hundreds of thousands of Chinese in Nanjing in December 1937.

Recaptives People from various West African cultures who had been freed from slave trading vessels and were then resettled in Sierra Leone.

Reconstruction Efforts by the Northern United States to reintegrate the South into the Union following the Civil War.

Red Guards   Radical paramilitary units striving to restore Maoist revolutionary fervor by attacking all vestiges of capitalist elitism in China.

Reign of Terror   The actions of French revolutionary tribunals in condemning and executing hundreds of thousands of people believed to be opposed to the French Revolution.

Relativism   The view that truth and morality vary from one person, group, or situation to another.

Relativity   Einstein's assertion that measurements of time, space, and motion vary with the movements and perceptions of observers.

Reparations   Payments by a country defeated in war to compensate for war damages.

Repeating rifles   Weapons that can quickly be reloaded and refired by inserting cartridges into the breech.

Residencia   A thorough audit of a Spanish colonial official's conduct during his term of office.

Revolution   The overthrow or renunciation of one government or ruler and the substitution of another by those being governed.

Romanticism   A rejection of the rationalism of the Enlightenment, emphasizing emotion, passion, exuberance, heroism, and the beauty of nature.

Roosevelt Corollary   United States President Theodore Roosevelt's 1904 amplification of the Monroe Doctrine, asserting a U.S. right to intimidate or overthrow Latin American governments that did not behave acceptably.

Royal absolutism   A system of governance in which the ruler's authority is said to come directly from God, and in which no earthly institution may override that authority.

Sacraments   In the Christian Church, sacred rites believed to bestow the graces needed for salvation.

Salon   Regular gatherings during the Enlightenment where eminent thinkers and writers mingled with political and social leaders.

Sandinista Front for National Liberation   A leftist coalition that overthrew Nicaraguan dictator Anastasio Somoza in 1979 and established close ties with Cuba and the Soviet Union.

Sans-culottes   The urban working poor during the French Revolution, who wore ordinary trousers instead of the culottes, or knee-breeches, worn by the nobles.

Sati   A practice in India whereby a widow cremated herself on her dead husband's funeral pyre.

Satyagraha   "Truth force," Gandhi's nonviolent way to combat oppression by refusing to cooperate with oppressors.

Scramble for concessions   The period from 1896–1899 during which European nations pressed China for special privileges, called concessions, that would allow them to exploit key regions of China.

SDI   Strategic Defense Initiative, or "Star Wars," an elaborate space-based missile defense system on which United States President Ronald Reagan authorized research and development in the 1980s.

Sepoys   Indian soldiers trained and commanded by the British.

Service state   Tsar Peter I's reform of Russian government, requiring all nobles to serve in either the military or the bureaucracy.

Shanghai massacre   Jiang Jieshi's slaughter of Chinese Communists in Shanghai in 1927.

Sharecroppers   Americans who farmed lands supplied by a landowner, to whom they then were required to pay half their harvest.

Slavery   An institution in which some people owned other human beings and subjected them to involuntary service.

Socialism   An ideology based on equality, calling for redistribution of income, improved working conditions, and the political empowerment of workers.

Socialism in One Country   Stalin's program that focused on strengthening the USSR while requiring communists everywhere to postpone world revolution and support the Soviet state.

Soviet   Russian word for "council," referring to elected bodies of workers' delegates in 1905 and 1917; later used to refer to the regime that ruled Russia from 1917 until 1991.

Soviet Bloc   A post-World War II coalition of Soviet-dominated "satellite" regimes in Poland, Romania, Bulgaria, Hungary, East Germany, and Czechoslovakia.

Stateless societies   Independent African villages and federations of villages ruled by local patriarchs and chiefs.

Summit conference   A face-to-face meeting of the world's most powerful leaders.

Surrealism   Art that sought to challenge perceptions or to portray Freud's unconscious world of drives, fantasies, and dreams.

Table of Ranks   Tsar Peter I's fourteen-level organizational ladder, requiring state officials and military officers to work their way up through a series of promotions based on performance rather than heredity or prestige.

Taiping Rebellion   A vast uprising in China between 1850 and 1864, fueled by anti-Manchu hostility and Western religious ideas.

Tanzimat   "Reorganization," a sweeping set of reforms enacted from 1839 to 1876 and designed to modernize and Westernize the Ottoman Empire.

Tennis Court Oath   A pledge taken in 1789 by representatives in France's National Assembly not to disperse until France obtained a written constitution.

Tet Offensive   A surprise attack on South Vietnamese and United States forces launched by the Viet Cong in 1968 and coinciding with Tet, the Vietnamese Lunar New Year.

Thagi   The work of professional bandits or "thugs" who attacked and strangled travelers in India as part of a religious ritual.

Trans-Siberian Railway   A 5,800-mile railroad stretching across Russia from west to east.

Treaty of Tordesillas   A 1494 agreement between the Portuguese and Spanish designed to divide the world between them.

Trench warfare   A brutalizing, degrading form of combat in which soldiers lived and died fighting in ditches eight feet deep; caused by the stalemate on the Western Front during the Great War.

Triple Alliance   The alliance of Austria-Hungary, Germany, and Italy (1882–1914).

Triple Entente   The alliance of Britain, France, and Russia (1907–1914).

Triple Intervention   The combination of Russia, France, and Germany that pressured Japan to renounce the Liaodong peninsula in Manchuria in 1895.

Truman Doctrine   U.S. President Harry Truman's 1947 proclamation that the United States must "support free peoples who are resisting attempted subjugation by armed minorities or by outside pressures."

Tsar   A Russian version of the title "caesar" used by Roman and Byzantine emperors, first used in Russia by Grand Prince Ivan III.

Tupamaros   An Uruguayan urban terrorist group in the 1960s and 1970s.

Turtle ships   Innovative Korean ships whose decks were protected with iron plating.

Twelfth Imam   Also called the "Hidden Imam"; a messianic Muslim leader who vanished in the ninth century C.E.; Shi'ites believe he will return to create a religious kingdom and usher in a period of prosperity and peace enduring until the Last Judgment.

U-boats   German term for "Under-the-Sea-Boats," or submarines.

UCR   Radical Civic Union, an Argentine reform movement that became the nation's largest political party in the early twentieth century.

United Nations   An international peace-keeping body designed to replace the defunct League of Nations in 1945.

Universal male suffrage   Voting rights for all men.

Urdu   An Indian language written with the Persian alphabet and employing many Persian terms.

U-2 Affair   The crash of an American spy plane in the USSR on May 1, 1960 that became an international incident and was used to cancel a summit conference in Paris.

Vaccination   The process of immunizing people against disease by injecting them with a weak dose of the disease so that they can build immunity to it.

Viceroy   "Vice-king," an official responsible for the execution of the monarch's orders in a large subdivision of the empire or realm.

Viet Cong   "Vietnamese Communists," a nickname given to the paramilitary guerrilla units of the National Liberation Front of South Vietnam.

Vietminh   The Vietnamese Independence Brotherhood League, a coalition of nationalists formed in 1941 and led by the Indochinese Communist Party in a struggle to liberate Vietnam from French colonial rule.

Vietnamization   A process by which the United States transferred responsibility for fighting the Vietnam War to the army of South Vietnam.

Wahhabism   The austere, deeply puritanical brand of Islam practiced in Saudi Arabia since the 1740s.

Warsaw Pact   A Soviet-led alliance of East European communist states designed to counterbalance NATO.

Westernization   The adoption by non-Western nations of Western-style industries, technologies, institutions, and ideologies.

Women's suffrage   Voting rights for all women.

Young Turks   Young reformist rebels who collaborated with dissident Ottoman army officers in 1908 to force the sultan to restore the constitution and parliament.

Zaibatsu   Large Japanese conglomerates that each owned a diverse array of industries, businesses, banks, and resources.

Zemski sobor   A specially convened "Assembly of the Land" made up of delegates from Muscovy's various classes.

Zemstvo   An assembly elected in each Russian county and province after 1864 and charged with caring for local needs such as roads, schools, medicine, and emergency food supplies.

Zimmermann Note   An effort by a German diplomat to bribe Mexico into an alliance against the United States in 1917; intercepted and decoded by the British, it outraged public opinion in the neutral United States.

Zionists   Followers of Theodor Herzl's conviction that Jews would always be outsiders in Christian Europe and that they should therefore seek the establishment of a Jewish state.

Credits

Cover (left), Se-Quo-Yah, Library of Congress; (background), Japanese view American steamship in harbor - 19th c., Library of Congress; (right), Empress Wu, The British Library/Photolibrary.

Intro **p. xlvi,** Guignet, Jean Adrien (1816–1854), Erich Lessing/Art Resource, NY; **p. xlvii,** Hong Kong, China: Hong Kong office workers walk beneath a vast array of commercial advertising signs, 02 November 2000, in the city's trendy watering-hole of Lan Kwai Fong. For the seventh consecutive year, Hong Kong has retained its ranking as the freest economy in the world, according to a global survey of 161 countries compiled by Washington think-tank, the Heritage Foundation, and the Wall Street Journal., FREDERIC J. BROWN/AFP/Getty Images.

Chapter 19 **p. 417,** Portugals claims to the New World, Library of Congress; **p. 421,** The discovery of the New World. This woodcut is from a series created (c. 1493) to publicize Columbus's discoveries. Columbus was never shaken in his belief that he had reached the outer rim of the orient. This exotic look of the boat and the eastern costumes of the men who are exchanging items with the naked natives may have been intended to support this claim, Library of Congress; **p. 423,** Portolan atlas of 9 charts and a world map, Library of Congress; **p. 427,** Portugal, Algarve, Western Region, Caravela Santa Bernarda, replica of 500-year-old Portuguese caravela on rough waters of Atlantic Ocean between Lagos and Arma√ß√£, summer, Paul Bernhardt/Dorling Kindersley; **p. 431,** Plaza de Armas, Cuzco Peru, Library of Congress; **p. 432,** D'Espanol y Mulata produce Morisca, Breamore House, Hampshire, England; **p. 434,** Map of the northeast coast of North America, 1607, drawn by Samuel de Champlain, Library of Congress; **p. 436,** Library of Congress; **p. 437,** Women preparing manioc, Library of Congress.

Chapter 20 **p. 441,** Martin Luther (1483–1546). German religious reformer, Luther defends himself before Holy Roman Emperor Charles V at the Diet in Worms, 17–18 April 1521. Line engraving, 19th century, The Granger Collection, NYC; **p. 444,** Johann Tetzel, Library of Congress; **p. 445,** Copy of Schadow's Martin Luther, Dorota and Mariusz Jarymowicz/Dorling Kindersley; **p. 447,** Anne Boleyn (1507–1536), second wife of Henry VIII. Executed for adultery, Library of Congress; **p. 448,** Portrait John Calvin, protestant reformer, Library of Congress; **p. 451,** Greer and Mills Allegory Jesuits, Library of Congress; **p. 453,** Fleet of English ships at sea lighting warning beacons, Brian Delft/Dorling Kindersley; **p. 457,** This Jesuit missionary, wearing his distinctive Catholic vestments, is baptizing an Indian in New France. French Jesuits proved to be more tolerant than most European missionaries in allowing Indian converts to retain at least some of their own customs, Library of Congress; **p. 458,** Witches being hanged in public, Three women hang by the neck from a scaffold while animals frolic around a fat figure sitting on a stool nearby. Woodcut, Dorling Kindersley; **p. 460,** Albrecht Duerer, "Peasants at Market", Library of Congress.

Chapter 21 **p. 465,** Eastern Asia, China, Beijing, Forbidden City, Gate of Supreme Harmony, statue of imperial bronze lion, Chen Chao/Dorling Kindersley; **p. 469,** (top) Toyotomi Hideyoshi, Library of Congress; **p. 469,** (bottom) Japan, Honshu, Himeji Castle, Demetrio Carrasco/Dorling Kindersley; **p. 471,** (top) Title page of *Atlas and Nomenclature of the Human Body* introductory chapter to *A New Book of Anatomy* 18th c. Japanese book, National Library of Medicine; **p. 471,** (bottom) Route from Edo to Nagasaki. This scroll map depicts an aerial view of one of the most famous roads in old Japan - the Takaido Highway- as it looked from 1660 to 1736. Edo yori Nagasaki made yadotsuke, funamichi meisho jyuseki, ca. 1660–1736. Watercolor, Library of Congress; **p. 472,** Japan Honshu Tokyo, Jon Burbank/Eye Ubiquitous/Alamy; **p. 473,** The forbidden city, Dorling Kindersley; **p. 476,** A Chinese blue and white porcelain vase Ming Dynasty, Judith Miller/Sloan's/Dorling Kindersley; **p. 482,** Eastern Asia, China, Beijing, Forbidden City, Hall of Moral Cultivation, Qianlong, Chen Chao/Dorling Kindersley; **p. 484,** Gunang Zhou, Library of Congress.

Chapter 22 **p. 489,** View on the Water Castle, situated at the mouth of the river, and on the Batavian roadstead. Drawn by Johan Rach 1764 (top 1045), Atlas van Stolk, Museum het Schielandhuis, Rotterdam; **p. 494,** Portuguese ports in the Indian Ocean, Library of Congress; **p. 496,** A VOC Dutch East India Company artifact Ayutthaya, Dorling Kindersley; **p. 498,** Sunehri Masjid: The "Golden Mosque", with three gilt domes, was built in 1722. On 22 March 1739, Nadir Shah stood on its roof to watch the massacre of Delhi's citizens, Ram Rahman/Dorling Kindersley; **p. 502,** Chronicles of Java, Library of Congress; **p. 504,** Islamic Floral Bookbinding, Library of Congress; **p. 506,** The largest room in Harem this hall was used for entertainments Against one wall stands a large throne form which the sultan would view the proceedings Topkapi Palace Topkapi Sarayi Istanbul, Dorling Kindersley; **p. 507,** Medina, Library of Congress.

worth the paper they were printed on, Library of Congress; **p. 761,** Synagogue being burned during Kristallnacht November 9 10 1938, Library of Congress; **p. 764,** (top) Marcus Garvey, half-length portrait, facing left, in uniform, Library of Congress; **p. 764,** (bottom) Ataturk, Kemal (until 1934 Kemal Pascha) Turkish politician Saloniki 1881(?), Istanbul 10.11.1938. Ataturk promotes Latin script on a visit to the provinces. Photo, c.1929, Akg-images/Newscom; **p. 766,** Prince Faisel with Lawrence of Arabia, National Archives and Records Administration; **p. 767,** Mohandas Gandhi, full-length portrait, seated on platform, beside spinning wheel, group of men seated and standing behind him, Library of Congress; **p. 771,** Yearning for Military Heroes Japanese Patriotic Society Members Dressed as Samurai approx 1925, National Archives and Records Administration.

Chapter 33   p. 776, Pearl Harbor Attack 7 December 1941, Motor launch rescues a man from the water alongside the burning USS West Virginia BB 48 USS Tennessee BB 43 is inboard, National Archives and Records Administration; **p. 778,** 18, Julio 1936–1937: A civilian with a gun, a ghost of a soldier behind him, Library of Congress; **p. 781,** Munich Conference 1938, National Archives and Records Administration; **p. 782,** (top) World War II, National Archives and Records Administration; **p. 782,** (bottom) Adolf Hitler joyous after receiving news that Marshal Petain had asked for an armistice Photo taken at Hitler's headquarters at Bruly de Pesche Belgium, National Archives and Records Administration; **p. 784,** Result of the London Blitz by German bombers, Trinity Mirror/Mirrorpix/Alamy; **p. 786,** Chinese Condemned for collaboration with Japanese, Library of Congress; **p. 789,** Erwin Rommel the Desert Fox, National Archives and Records Administration; **p. 792,** Woman factory worker, Library of Congress; **p. 793,** Hungarian Jewish women elected for work march toward the camp after disinfection and head shaving Auschwitz Birkenau Poland, Library of Congress; **p. 795,** Five starving men in German concentration camp at time of liberation by U. S. Army, Library of Congress; **p. 796,** American troops hit invasion beach, Library of Congress; **p. 800,** (top) U.S. Marine receives communion from a catholic chaplain atop Mount Suribachi an enemy strongpoint on southern Iwo Jima, National Archives and Records Administration; **p. 800,** (bottom) WWII A view of the atomic bomb damage to Hiroshima Japan taken from the Chamber of Commerce Building The bridge shown in this picture crosses the Matoyasu River The building on the extreme right is the Agricultural Exposition Hall the buildings on the left are the remains of the Shima Hospital 6 October 1945, National Archives and Records Administration.

Chapter 34   p. 806, The Baker Day explosion of the fifth atomic bomb at Bikini as recorded by an automatic camera from a nearby island, National Archives and Records Administration; **p. 808,** Crimean Conference Here in the courtyard of Livadia Palace Yalta Crimea are British Prime Minister Winston Churchill U. S. President Franklin D Roosevelt and Marshal Joseph Stalin during a recess of the Big Three Conference in February 1945, Standing behind Pres Roosevelt is Admiral William D. Leahy, Behind the Prime Minister are Admiral Sir Andrew Cunningham and Air Marshal Portal At far left are Secretary of State Edward St, U. S. Army Photo; **p. 812,** Fresh milk flown to isolated sectors of Berlin, Library of Congress; **p. 815,** Model of a Soviet A1 space rocket, Dorling Kindersley; **p. 819,** Political cartoon by Guernsey Le Pelley depicting John F. Kennedy and Nikita Krushchev during the Cuban missile crisis I've Changed My Mind Let's Argue on the Bench, Library of Congress; **p. 821,** Aerial view of Levittown Long Island New York during the 1950s, National Archives and Records Administration; **p. 822,** (top) Rosa Parks, three-quarter length portrait, seated toward front of bus, facing right, Montgomery, Alabama, The Library of Congress; **p. 822,** (bottom) Negro drinking at "Colored" water cooler in streetcar terminal, Oklahoma City, Oklahoma, The Library of Congress; **p. 823,** (top) Photograph of a Female Demonstrator Offering a Flower to a Military Police Officer, 10/21/1967, National Archives and Records Administration; **p. 823,** (bottom) Khrushchev visits Albanian factory, Library of Congress; **p. 825,** Stop the arms race: for detente and peaceful coexistence: 25 years - Stockholm Appeal, Library of Congress; **p. 828,** Gorbachev beholds a shattered hammer and sickle, Library of Congress.

Chapter 35   p. 835, Tourists walking on the street in a town, Dotonbori, Osaka, Japan, SuperStock/Alamy; **p. 838,** Slum Dwellers of India, Samrat35/Dreamstime.com; **p. 841,** High school students in science class working on projects. 01 Jul 1959, John Dominis/Time Life Pictures/Getty Images; **p. 843,** 1948 Chinese communist troops study artillery, Library of Congress; **p. 844,** Chinese guerrillas near border 1949, Library of Congress; **p. 846,** (top) A South Korean youngster carries a sack of rice on her head after receiving it from the newly established government in Seoul during the week of May 21, Library of Congress; **p. 846,** (middle) South Gate (Namdaemun). Seoul, South Korea age footstock/SuperStock; **p. 846,** (bottom) Court of death for Chinese farmer, Library of Congress; **p. 848,** (top) China, Shanghai, copies of Mao's Little Red Book for sale at street market, Chen Chao/Dorling Kindersley; **p. 848,** (bottom) Nixon at the Great Wall, National Archives and Records Administration; **p. 850,** China, Shanghai, Yu Gardens (Yu Yuan), Huxingting Teahouse, visitors on crowded zig-zag bridge over lake leading to structure dating built in 1784, with modern skyline rising above in background, elevated view, Colin Sinclair/Dorling Kindersley; **p. 853,** Troops of the 173rd Airborne Brigade press toward Viet Cong positions at tree line after being heliborne into battle positions by UH 1Ds, Note new kind of canteen bag on back of soldier in foreground, U. S. Army Photo; **p. 854,** Crowd hears Sukarno, Library of Congress; **p. 856,** Fear of the unknown, French Indochina, Library of Congress; **p. 858,** Young Indian women, dressed in colorful saris, get military training on campus of Darrang College, Library of Congress.

Chapter 36   p. 862, Bettmann/CORBIS; **p. 864,** Mucho de cafe, Library of Congress; **p. 866,** ca. 1955: A consignment of wheat being loaded on to a freight ship at La Guirara harbour, Venezuela, Jack Manning/Three Lions/Getty Images; **p. 868,** Theodore Roosevelt running an American steam shovel at Culebra Cut Panama Canal 1906, Library of Congress; **p. 869,** (top) Working on a banana plantation, Two men harvest bananas at a United Fruit Company plantation, Tiquisate, Guatemala, 1945, Frank Scherschel/Time & Life Pictures/Getty Images; **p. 869,** (bottom) Cuba in throes of new revolution, Library of Congress; **p. 874,** Argentina's writer Jorge Luis Borges talks in his Buenos Aires apartment on Nov. 20, 1981, AP Photo/Eduardo Di Baia; **p. 876,** Brazil Sandos Rio De Janiero traffic 1944, Library of Congress; **p. 878,** Black and white photograph of the World Cup 1958 Brazil side including Garrincha Didi Pele who was 17 at the time Vava and Zagalo the left winger who scored the fourth goal in the final Also 1950s famous Real Madrid team, Dorling

Kindersley; **p. 879**, June 1950: Men mining small amounts of copper, Eliot Elisofon/Time & Life Pictures/Getty Images; **p. 880**, Not wanted in the United States or anywhere else on earth: General Augusto Pinochet, because of his crimes against humanity, Library of Congress; **p. 882**, Rivera, Diego (1886–1957) ©ARS, NY, Dream of a Sunday Afternoon in the Alameda Park, detail, 1947–1948. Fresco, Schalkwijk/Art Resource, NY; **p. 884**, (top) Peruvian soldier and wife, Library of Congress; **p. 884**, (bottom) Alakaluf Fuegians, dressed in guanaco skins, Chile, 1895, The Print Collector/Alamy; **p. 885**, South America, Brazil, Sao Paulo City, high-rise buildings in ultra modern city dominating skyline, with old colonial Cathedral Metropolotana on Praca da Se below, Alex Robinson/Dorling Kindersley; **p. 886**, Mayan Ceremony on step of Church, Library of Congress.

Chapter 37 **p. 890**, The Signing of the Camp David Accords President Carter looks on as Israeli Prime Minister Menachem Begin to Carter's left and Egyptian President Anwar Sadat to Carter's right sign the historic pact, March 26, 1979, at a formal ceremony held on the North Lawn of the White House, National Archives and Records Administration; **p. 892**, Cocoa is loaded onto a United Africa Company ship at Apapa Wharf, Nigeria on June 14, 1940, AP Photo; **p. 894**, Kwame Nkrumah below right President of Ghana at the UN Julius K Nyerere Nationalist leader of Tanganyika below right, Library of Congress; **p. 895**, Resolutely support the people of Asia, Africa and Latin America in their struggle against imperialism, www.maopost.com; **p. 896**, Algerian Rally, 27th June 1962: Members of a women's section of the Algerian nationalist movement the FLN (National Army of Liberation), at a rally supporting independence, Agence France Presse/Hulton Archive/Getty Images; **p. 897**, Ghanian Independence Protesters, Library of Congress; **p. 898**, (top) Nyerere, Library of Congress; **p. 898**, (bottom) Suspected Mau Mau prisoners are guarded by members of the Fifth Battalion King's African Rifles in the Nyeri district of Kenya, Nov. 13, 1952, AP Photo; **p. 899**, (top) Pedagogy/Learning to write. Evening classes for the illiterate in Cameroon (Africa): Woman with a baby on her arm, writing on a blackboard (French Grammar), akg-images/Paul Almasy/Newscom; **p. 899**, (bottom) Dag Hammarskjold; Patrice Lumumba Prime Min. of the Congo Patrice Lumumba (C) and Dag Hammarskjold at a UN Security Council discussion about the RB-47 incident, Bob Gomel/Time & Life Pictures/Getty Images; **p. 901**, Debris Litters Field of Protest Sticks and shoes are strewn about Cato Manor slum area in Durban South Africa June 18 as police disperse demonstrating African women. A group of women raided a beer hall to protest police action against their home brewing activities. The beer hall was set on fire. Three persons were killed and 15 injured as a result of the fighting that followed, AP Photo; **p. 902**, England, London, bronze bust of Nelson Mandela, Philip Enticknap/Dorling Kindersley; **p. 903**, The British Governor announcing independence to the parliament in Ghana. 1957, Sueddeutsche Zeitung Photo/The Image Works; **p. 904**, (top) Workers in Sudan bag a large pile of cotton ca. 1963, Paul Almasy/CORBIS; **p. 904**, (bottom) Dust Storm over Morocco. A number of thick plumes of Saharan Desert dust light brown pixels were blowing from Morocco toward the northwest over the Canary Islands off Africa's northwest coast. This true color image was acquired by the Moderate Resolution Imaging Spectroradiometer MODIS aboard NASAs Aqua satellite on March 12 2003, NASA Earth Observing System; **p. 905**, Irgun youths train, Library of Congress; **p. 909**, Cairo, Eqypt - January 1: Picture dated from the 1950s in Cairo of Egyptian president Gamal Abdel Nasser (1918–1970). Army officer, Nasser became dissatisfied with the corruption of the Farouk regime and was involved in the military coup of 1952. He assumed the premiership in 1954 and then presidential powers, deposing his fellow officer, General Mohammed Neguib. Officially elected president in 1956, he nationalized the Suez Canal, AFP/Getty Images; **p. 910**, Children learn to read Arabic by studying the Koran with prayerboards; Atar, Mauritania. 01 Aug 1966, David Boyer/National Geographic/Getty Images; **p. 913**, Operation Desert Storm Damaged Iraqi tank and oil fires, U.S. Army Photo.

Index